LOVELESS

BLACKWATER FALLS

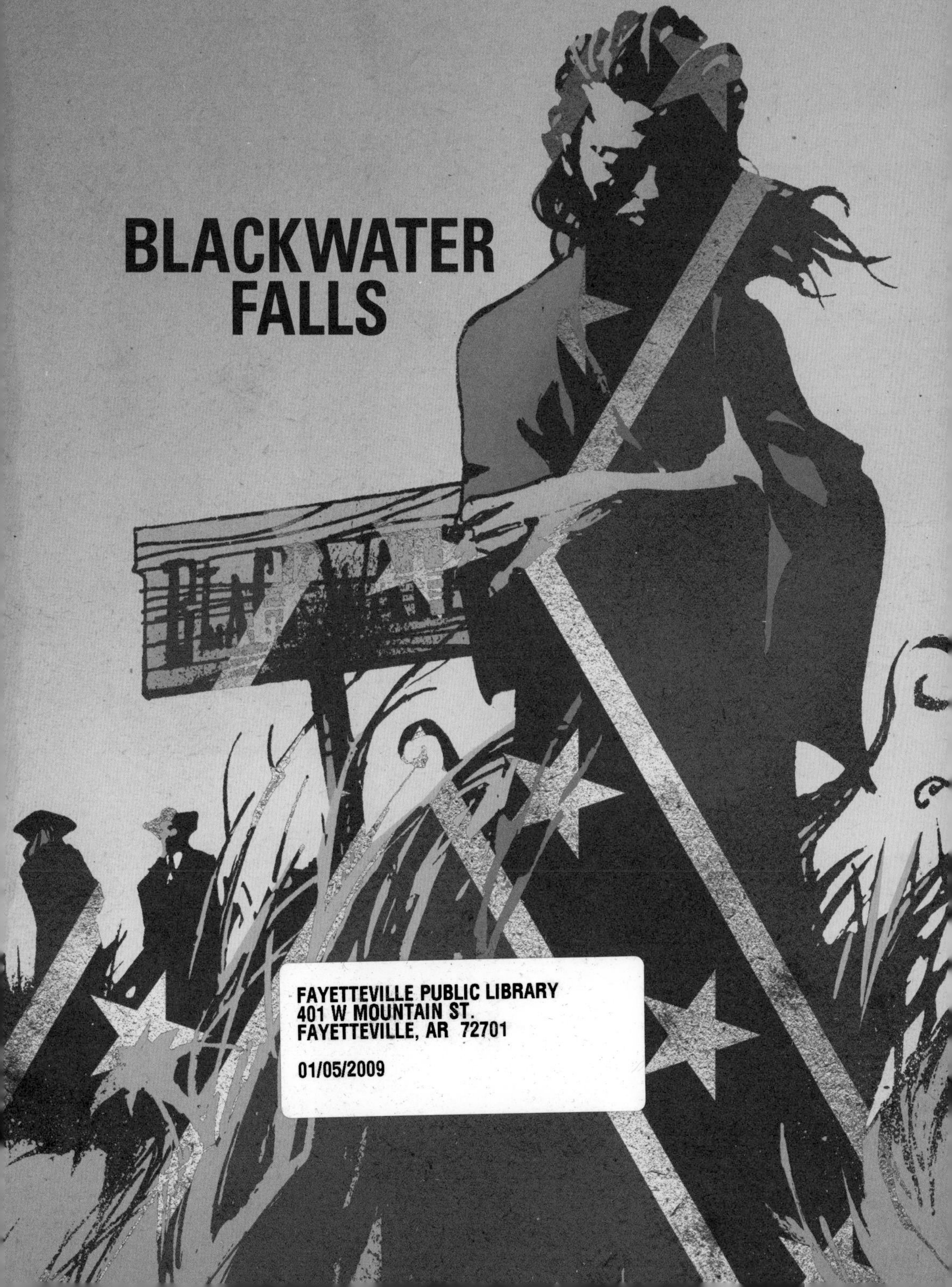

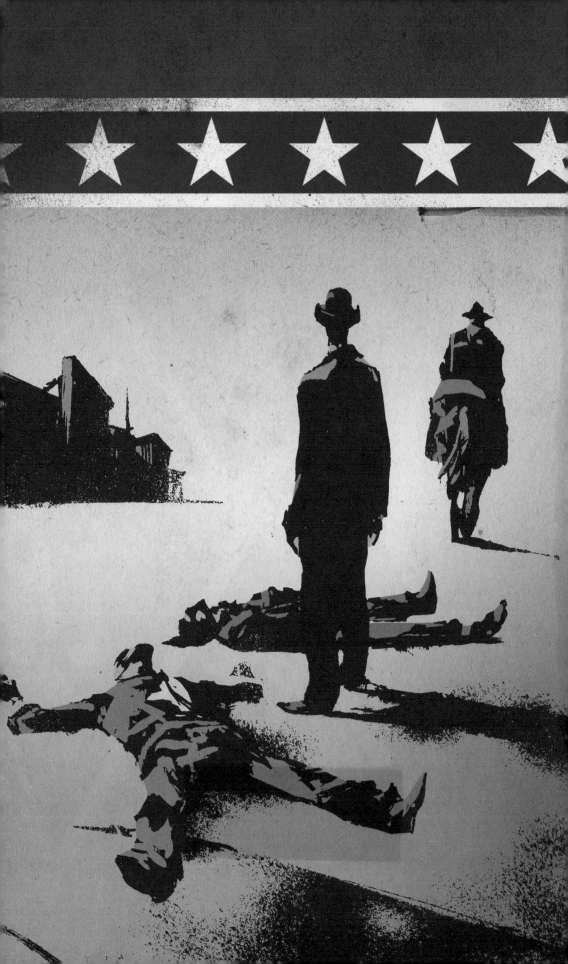

LoVELesS

BLACKWATER FALLS

BRIAN AZZARELLO
writer

DANIJEL ZEZELJ
artist

Another Day   *Morning Seeds*   *Black and Blue*
Deep Rivers   *Top of Thunder*   *Memory Served*

WERTHER DELL'EDERA
artist
Blackwater Falls Chapters 1-6

Patricia Mulvihill and **Lee Loughridge** *colorists*
Clem Robins *letterer*

Original series covers by
MARCELO FRUSIN
Loveless created by
BRIAN AZZARELLO and **MARCELO FRUSIN**

Cover illustration by Marcelo Frusin
Publication design by Brainchild Studios/NYC.

LOVELESS: BLACKWATER FALLS
Published by DC Comics. Cover, text and
compilation Copyright © 2008 DC Comics.
All Rights Reserved.

Originally published in single magazine form
as LOVELESS 13-24. Copyright © 2007, 2008
Brian Azzarello and Marcelo Frusin. All Rights
Reserved. All characters, their distinctive
likenesses and related elements featured
in this publication are trademarks of Brian
Azzarello and Marcelo Frusin. VERTIGO is
a trademark of DC Comics, The stories,
characters and incidents featured in this
publication are entirely fictional. DC Comics
does not read or accept unsolicited
submissions of ideas, stories or artwork.

DC Comics, 1700 Broadway, New York, NY 10019
A Warner Bros. Entertainment Company.
Printed in Canada. First Printing.
ISBN: 978-1-4012-1495-1

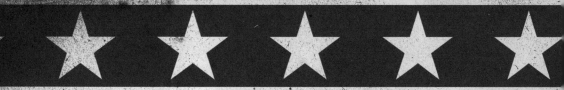

Who's Who

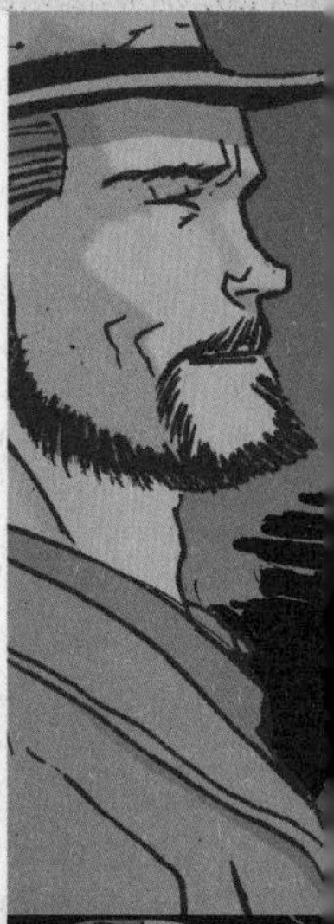

WES CUTTER

BLACKWATER'S LEAST FAVORITE SON. Captured and imprisoned by Union troops and presumed dead by his friends and family during the Civil War, he returned to discover that the town had turned against him—a living reminder of their defeat. Playing each of the town's factions against the other in a lethal game of chess, he found himself appointed sheriff by the carpetbaggers who call the shots…until the townsfolk hired an assassin to end his term permanently.

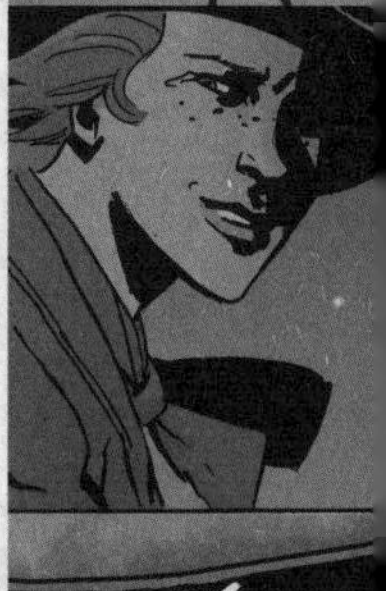

RUTH CUTTER *A.K.A. "JAMES WRIGHT"*

WES'S WIFE IS THE SECRET SCOURGE of the wilderness around Blackwater. She's cut her hair, taken a young man's name and waged a shadowy one-woman war against her and Wes's enemies—haunted all the while by the memories of how she suffered at the hands of Yankee troops while he was gone. It was Ruth who found Wes after Blackwater's hired gun shot him, and Ruth who shot back…

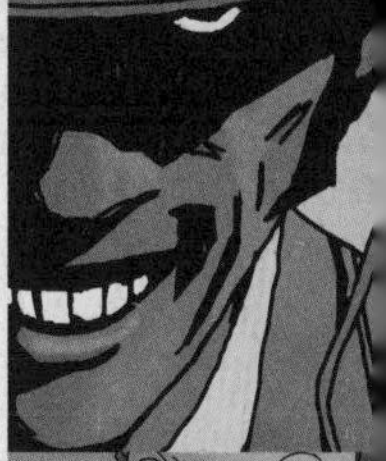

ATTICUS MANN

MAYBE THE MOST DANGEROUS PERSON IN BLACKWATER who doesn't go by the name Cutter. Freed slave, former Union soldier, present-day bounty hunter, Mann harbors undying hatred for the Confederates who made his life hell, and bears little love for the arrogant Yankees either—even though he was as one of their number when he secretly took part in the assault on Ruth years ago.

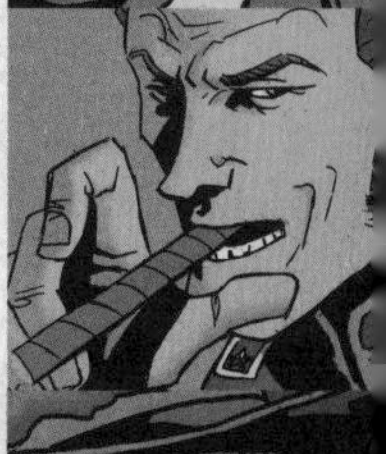

COLONEL SILAS REDD

THE UNION COMMANDER charged with keeping the peace in Blackwater. After forging an uneasy truce with Wes, he led an assault on the diehard Rebel guerrillas who had murdered his troops and lynched freed slaves, only to get shot in the leg for his trouble.

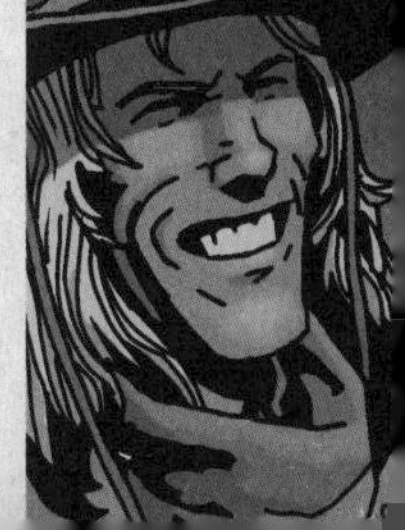

BOYD JOHNSON

A TRUE BASTARD SON OF THE SOUTH, Johnson led the lynch mob that took down Colonel Redd, firing the shot himself and narrowly escaping the raid despite the best efforts of his nemesis, Atticus Mann. A former comrade-in-arms of Wes Cutter's, he's the most wanted man in Blackwater.

JEREMIAH TROTTER

THIS CARPETBAGGER IS AN OFFICIAL WITH THE LAWSON COMPANY, the outfit appointed by the Federal Government to oversee the Reconstruction of Blackwater. Desperate for peace—if only because it drives up profits—it's his job to keep the Union troops from razing the town.

ABRAM RIVERS

THE CLOSEST THING BLACKWATER HAS TO AN OLD WISE MAN, this one-armed businessman just wants outsiders to mind their own business. If that means hiring a hit man to take out Sheriff Wes Cutter, so be it.

PUNCH

THE KILLER ABRAM AND HIS INNER CIRCLE hired to do their dirty work. After drawing Cutter out with a rampage made to look like the handiwork of Bloody Bill, Wes and Boyd's crazed former commander, he made his move. Unfortunately for him, Ruth Cutter was there to make the next one.

SERGEANT FOLEY

AN IRISH IMMIGRANT, THIS UNION THUG knows that Catholics have it almost as bad as blacks in Blackwater from both the Yankees and the Rebels. Fine by him—he hates them all back.

CAPTAIN LORD

DURING THE WAR, THIS SADISTIC SOLDIER was in charge of the occupation of Blackwater. It was he who oversaw the "punishment" of Ruth Cutter, an act that has left Ruth with deep psychological wounds.

JONNY CUTTER

WES'S BROTHER AND ONE-TIME RIVAL FOR RUTH'S AFFECTIONS, Jonny stayed in Blackwater while Wes headed for the front. His seeming cowardice cloaked a gunrunning operation for the Rebel guerrillas, but once it was uncovered he ran off, telling Ruth only that her husband was dead. Reports of Wes's demise, as it turned out, had been greatly exaggerated...

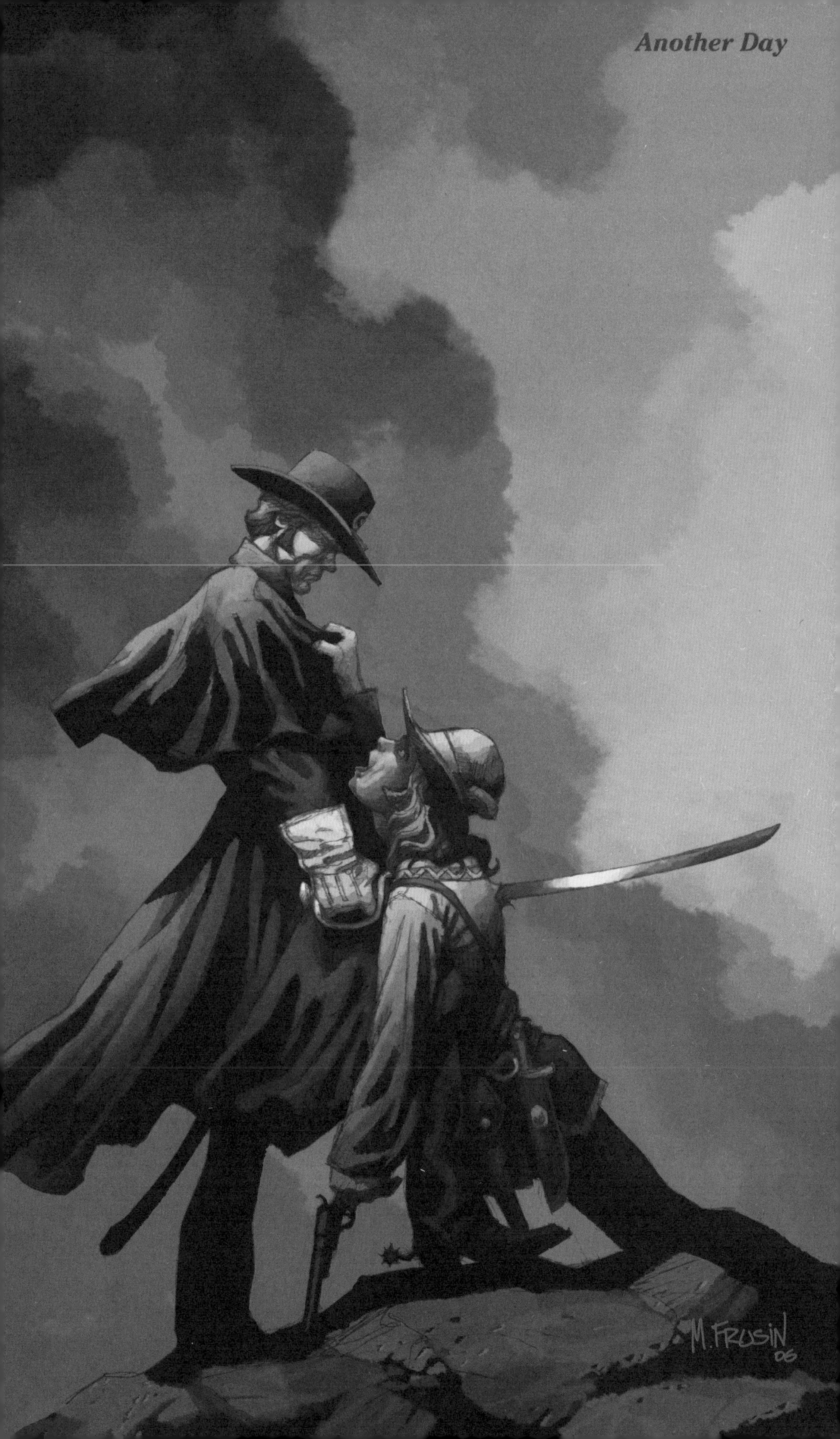
M. FRUSIN
06

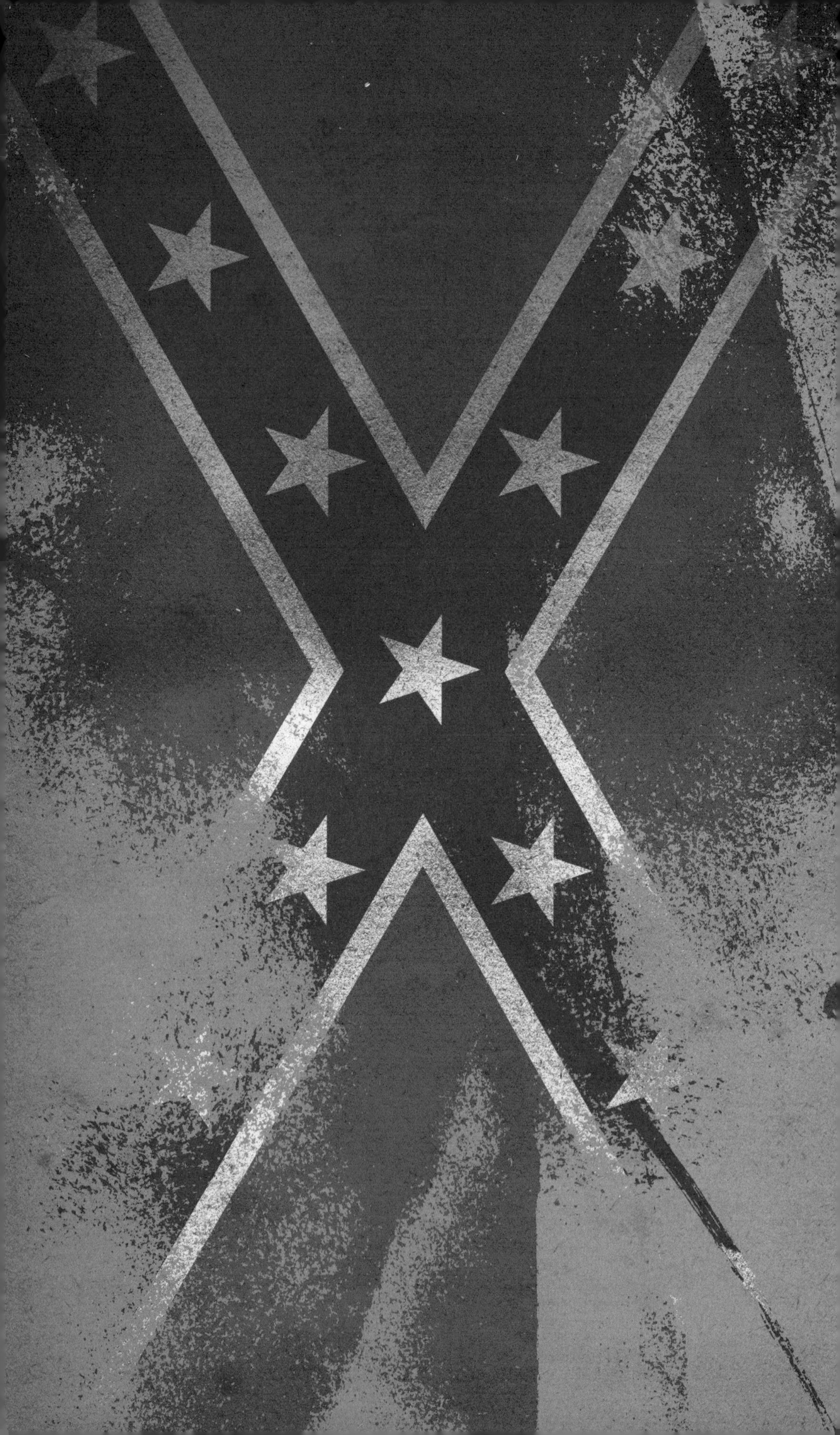

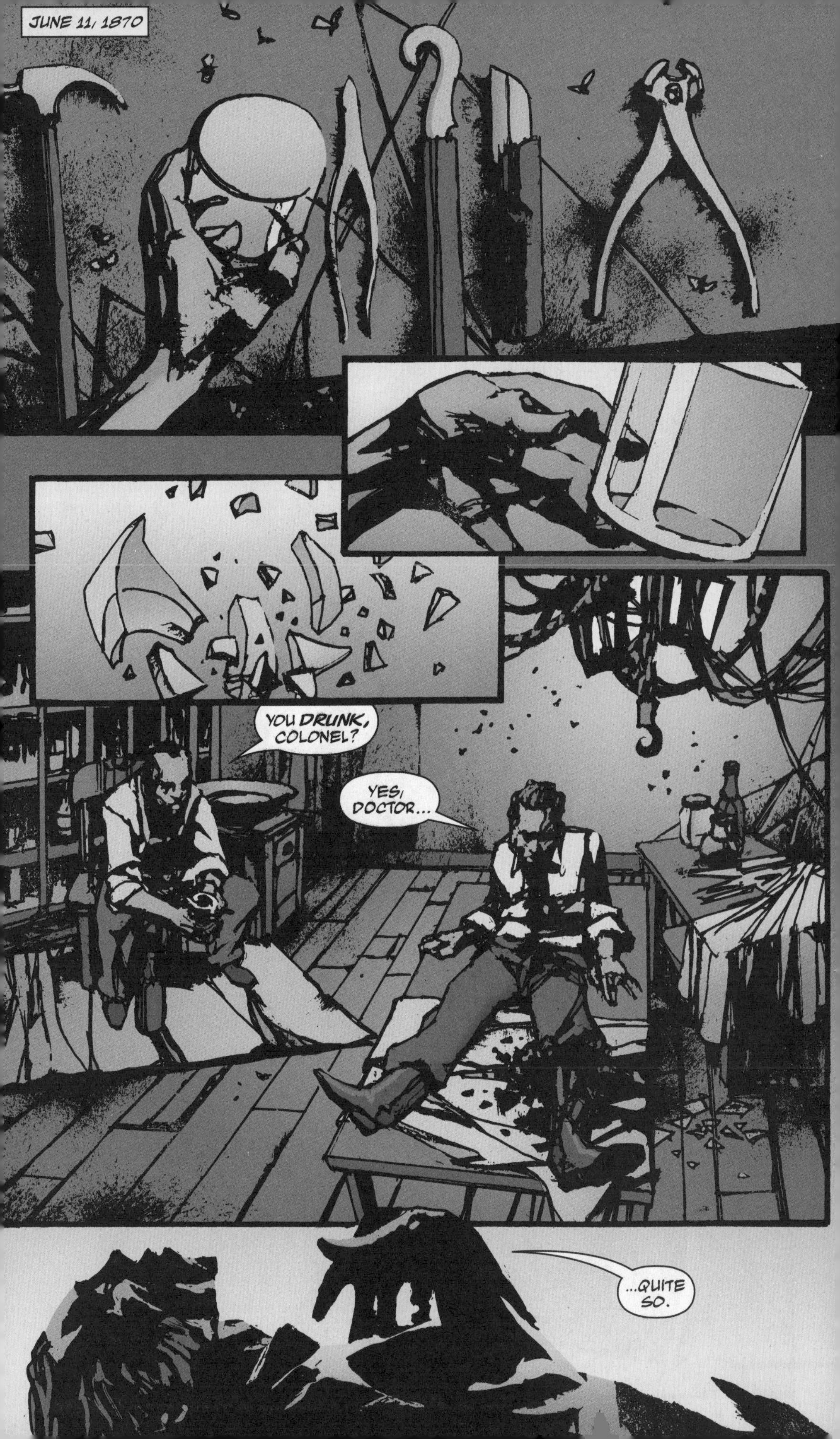
JUNE 11, 1870
YOU DRUNK, COLONEL?
YES, DOCTOR...
...QUITE SO.

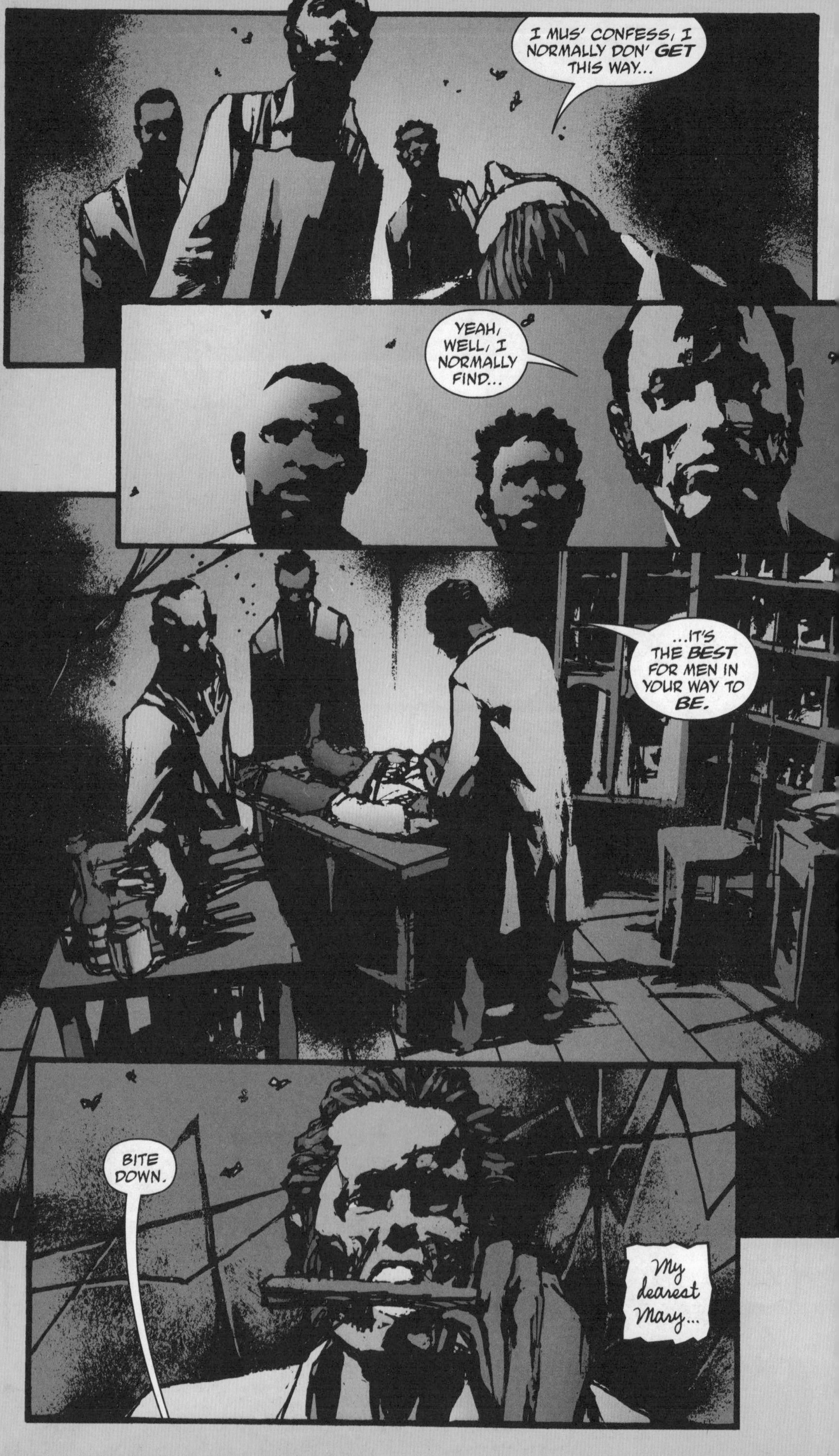
I MUS' CONFESS, I NORMALLY DON' GET THIS WAY...
YEAH, WELL, I NORMALLY FIND...
...IT'S THE BEST FOR MEN IN YOUR WAY TO BE.
BITE DOWN.
My dearest Mary...

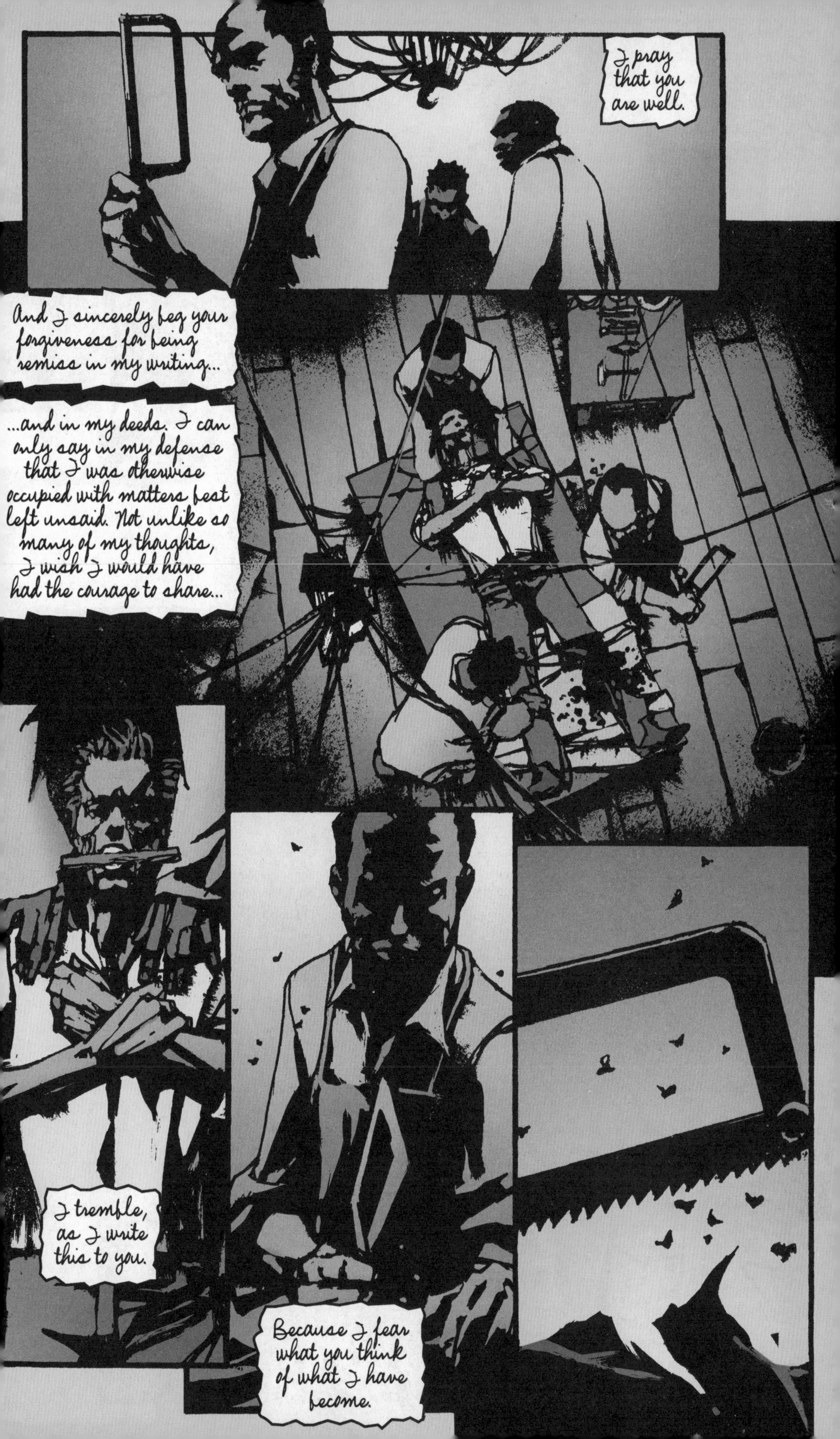
I pray that you are well.
And I sincerely beg your forgiveness for being remiss in my writing...
...and in my deeds. I can only say in my defense that I was otherwise occupied with matters best left unsaid. Not unlike so many of my thoughts, I wish I would have had the courage to share...
I tremble, as I write this to you.
Because I fear what you think of what I have become.

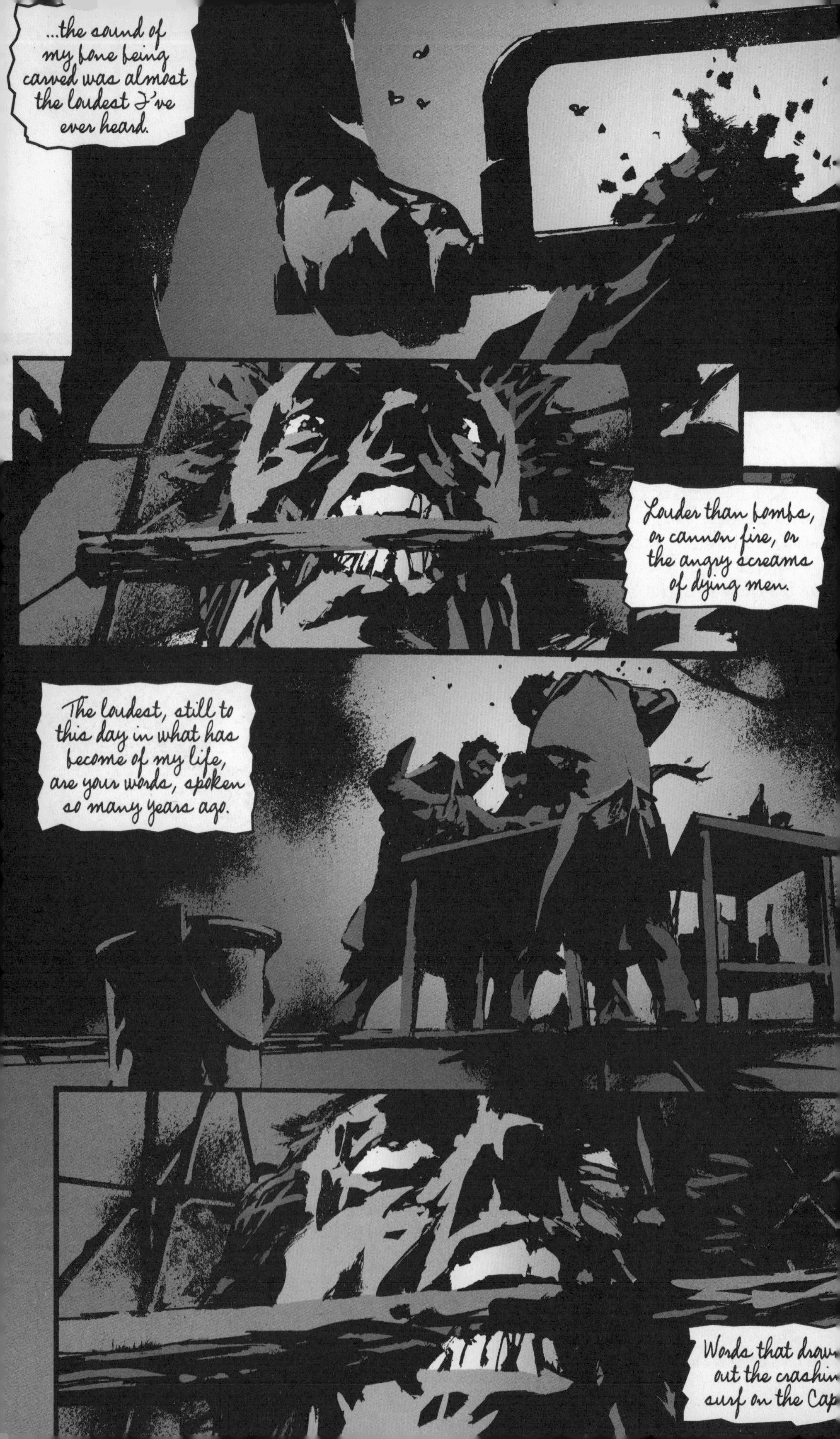
...the sound of my bone being carved was almost the loudest I've ever heard.
Louder than bombs, or cannon fire, or the angry screams of dying men.
The loudest, still to this day in what has become of my life, are your words, spoken so many years ago.
Words that drow
out the crashin
surf on the Cap

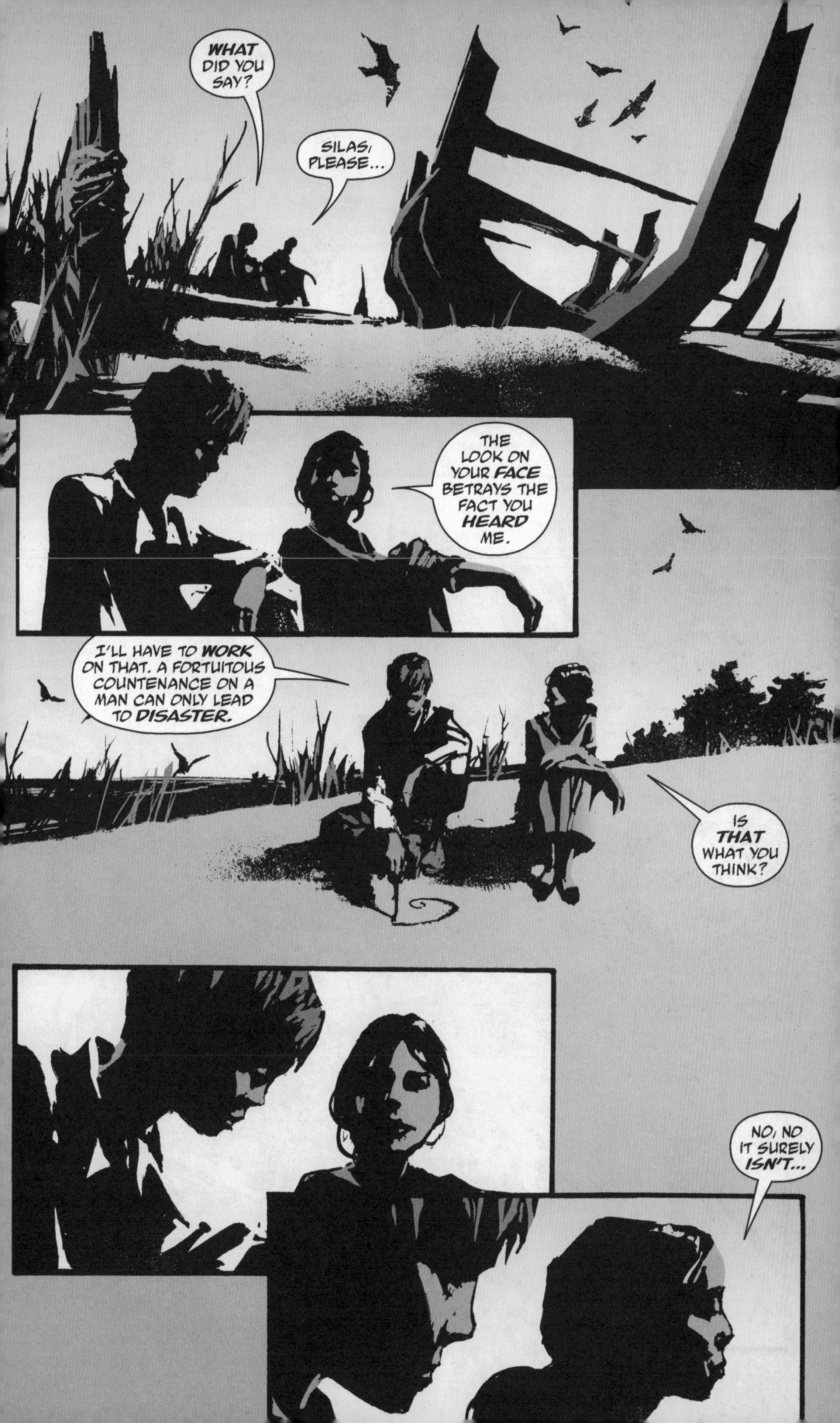
WHAT DID YOU SAY?
SILAS, PLEASE...
THE LOOK ON YOUR FACE BETRAYS THE FACT YOU HEARD ME.
I'LL HAVE TO WORK ON THAT. A FORTUITOUS COUNTENANCE ON A MAN CAN ONLY LEAD TO DISASTER.
IS THAT WHAT YOU THINK?
NO, NO IT SURELY ISN'T...

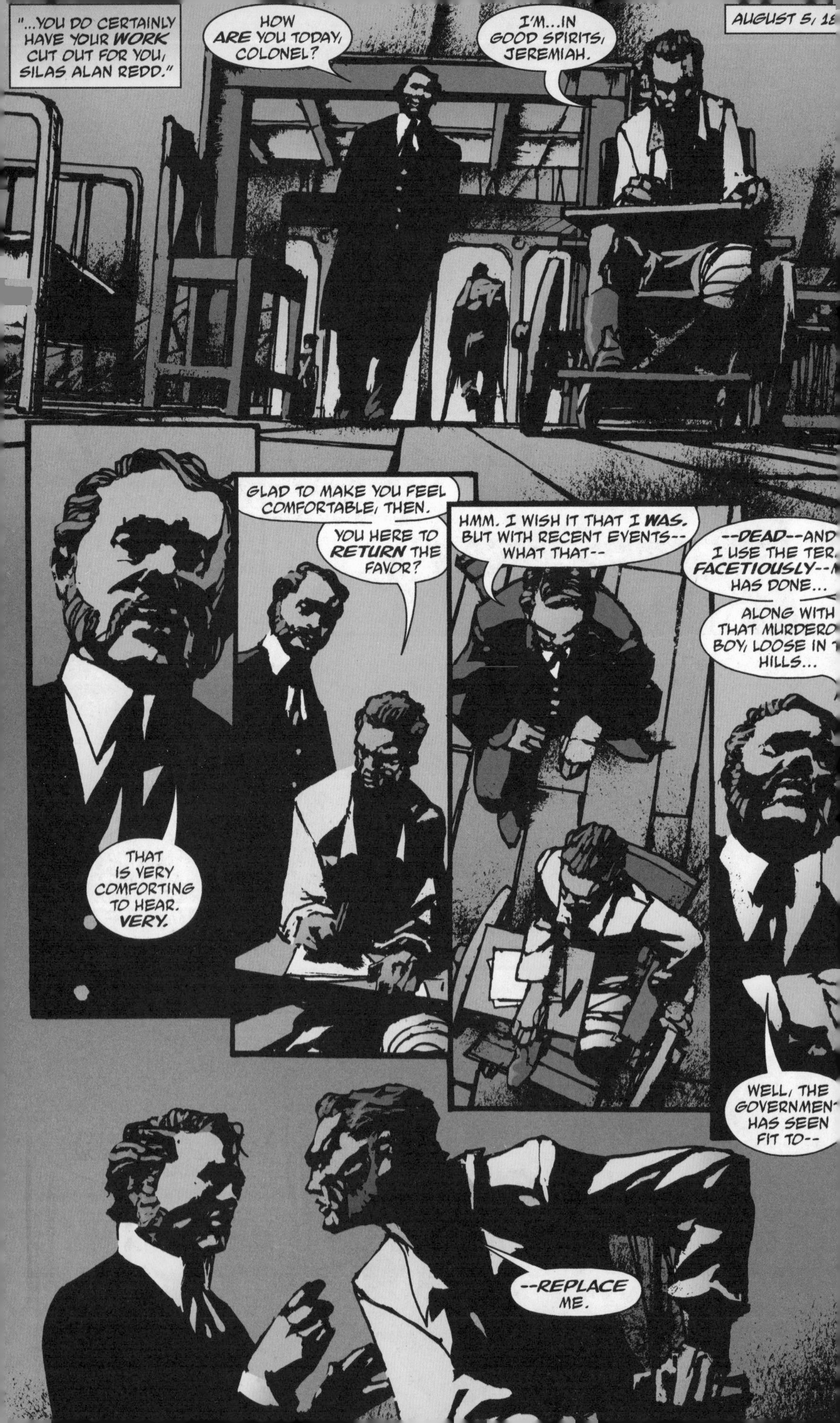
"...YOU DO CERTAINLY HAVE YOUR WORK CUT OUT FOR YOU, SILAS ALAN REDD."
HOW ARE YOU TODAY, COLONEL?
I'M...IN GOOD SPIRITS, JEREMIAH.
AUGUST 5, 18
THAT IS VERY COMFORTING TO HEAR. VERY.
GLAD TO MAKE YOU FEEL COMFORTABLE, THEN.
YOU HERE TO RETURN THE FAVOR?
HMM. I WISH IT THAT I WAS. BUT WITH RECENT EVENTS-- WHAT THAT--
--DEAD--AND I USE THE TER FACETIOUSLY-- HAS DONE...
ALONG WITH THAT MURDERO BOY, LOOSE IN HILLS...
WELL, THE GOVERNMEN HAS SEEN FIT TO--
--REPLACE ME.

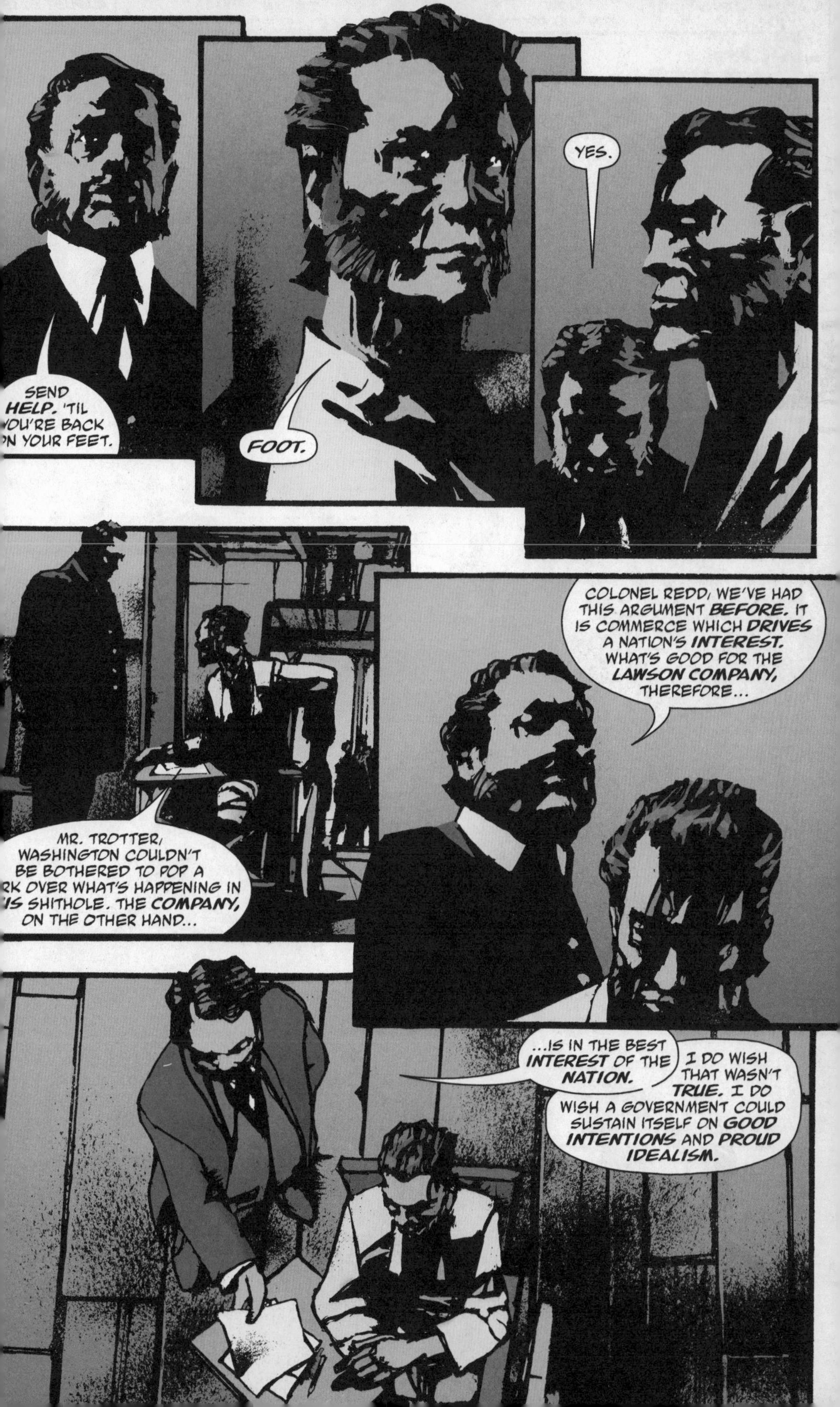
SEND HELP. 'TIL YOU'RE BACK ON YOUR FEET.
FOOT.
YES.
MR. TROTTER, WASHINGTON COULDN'T BE BOTHERED TO POP A RK OVER WHAT'S HAPPENING IN IS SHITHOLE. THE COMPANY, ON THE OTHER HAND...
COLONEL REDD, WE'VE HAD THIS ARGUMENT BEFORE. IT IS COMMERCE WHICH DRIVES A NATION'S INTEREST. WHAT'S GOOD FOR THE LAWSON COMPANY, THEREFORE...
...IS IN THE BEST INTEREST OF THE NATION.
I DO WISH THAT WASN'T TRUE. I DO WISH A GOVERNMENT COULD SUSTAIN ITSELF ON GOOD INTENTIONS AND PROUD IDEALISM.

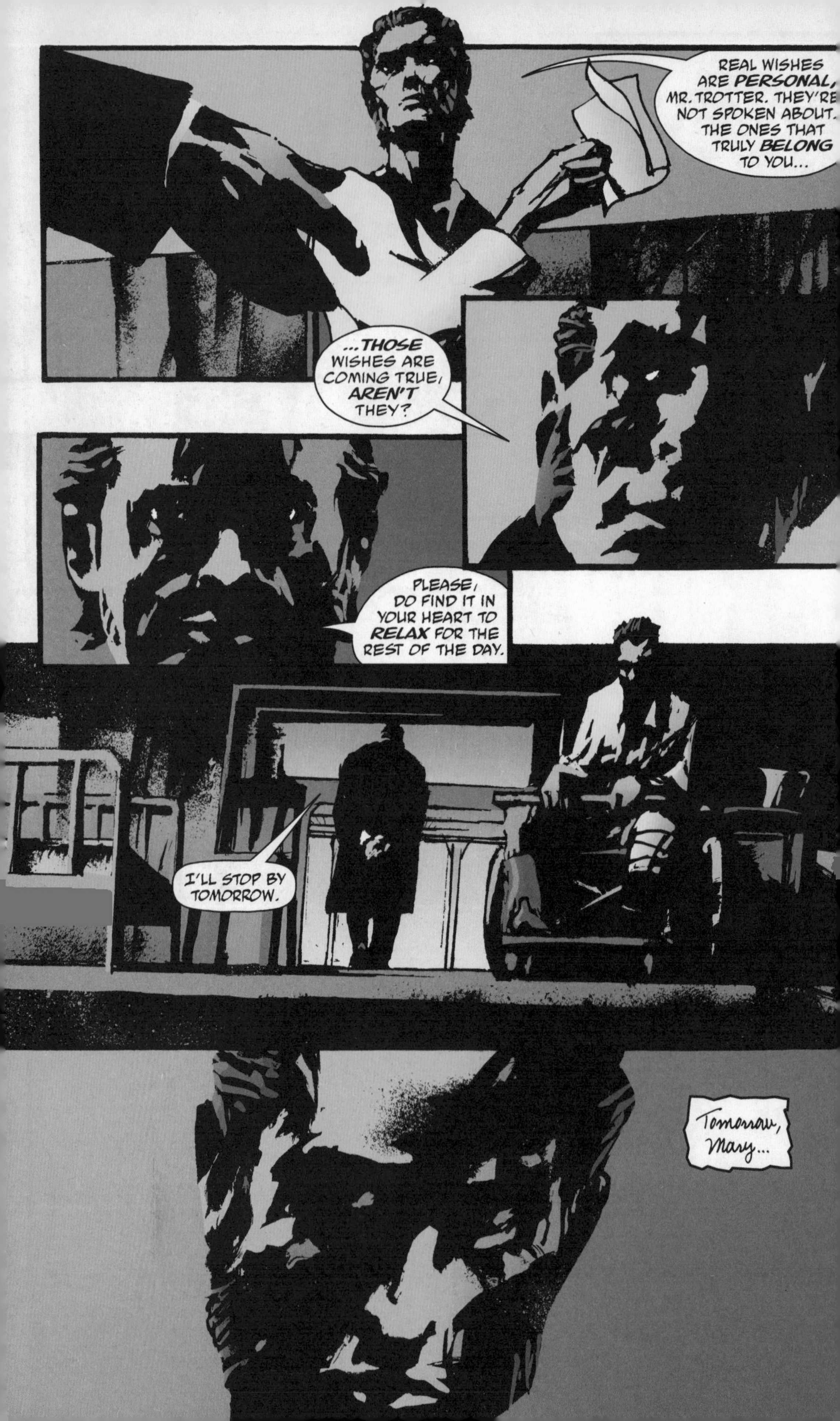
REAL WISHES ARE PERSONAL, MR. TROTTER. THEY'RE NOT SPOKEN ABOUT. THE ONES THAT TRULY BELONG TO YOU...
...THOSE WISHES ARE COMING TRUE, AREN'T THEY?
PLEASE, DO FIND IT IN YOUR HEART TO RELAX FOR THE REST OF THE DAY.
I'LL STOP BY TOMORROW.
Tomorrow, Mary...

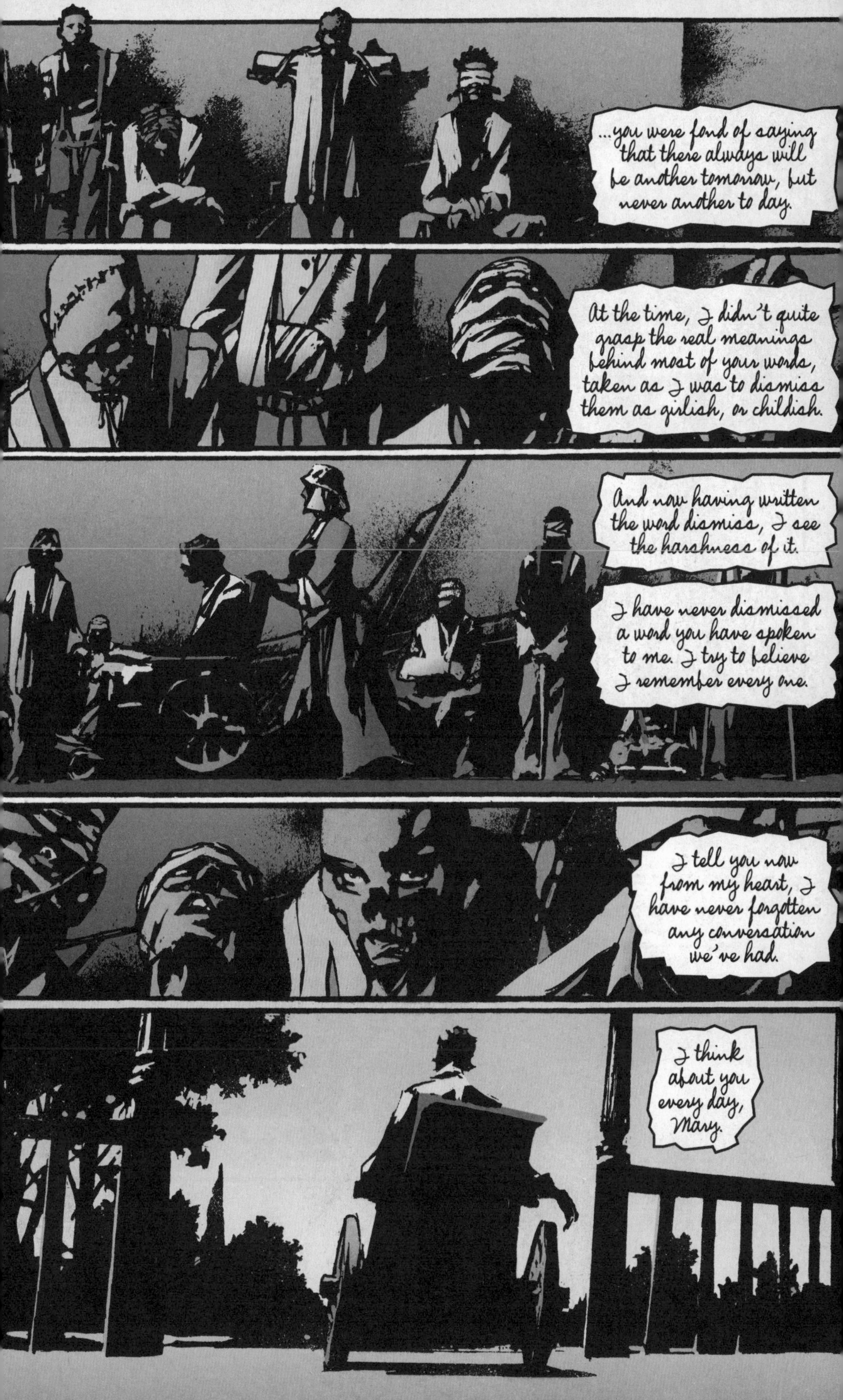
...you were fond of saying that there always will be another tomorrow, but never another to day.
At the time, I didn't quite grasp the real meanings behind most of your words, taken as I was to dismiss them as girlish, or childish.
And now having written the word dismiss, I see the harshness of it.
I have never dismissed a word you have spoken to me. I try to believe I remember every one.
I tell you now from my heart, I have never forgotten any conversation we've had.
I think about you every day, Mary.

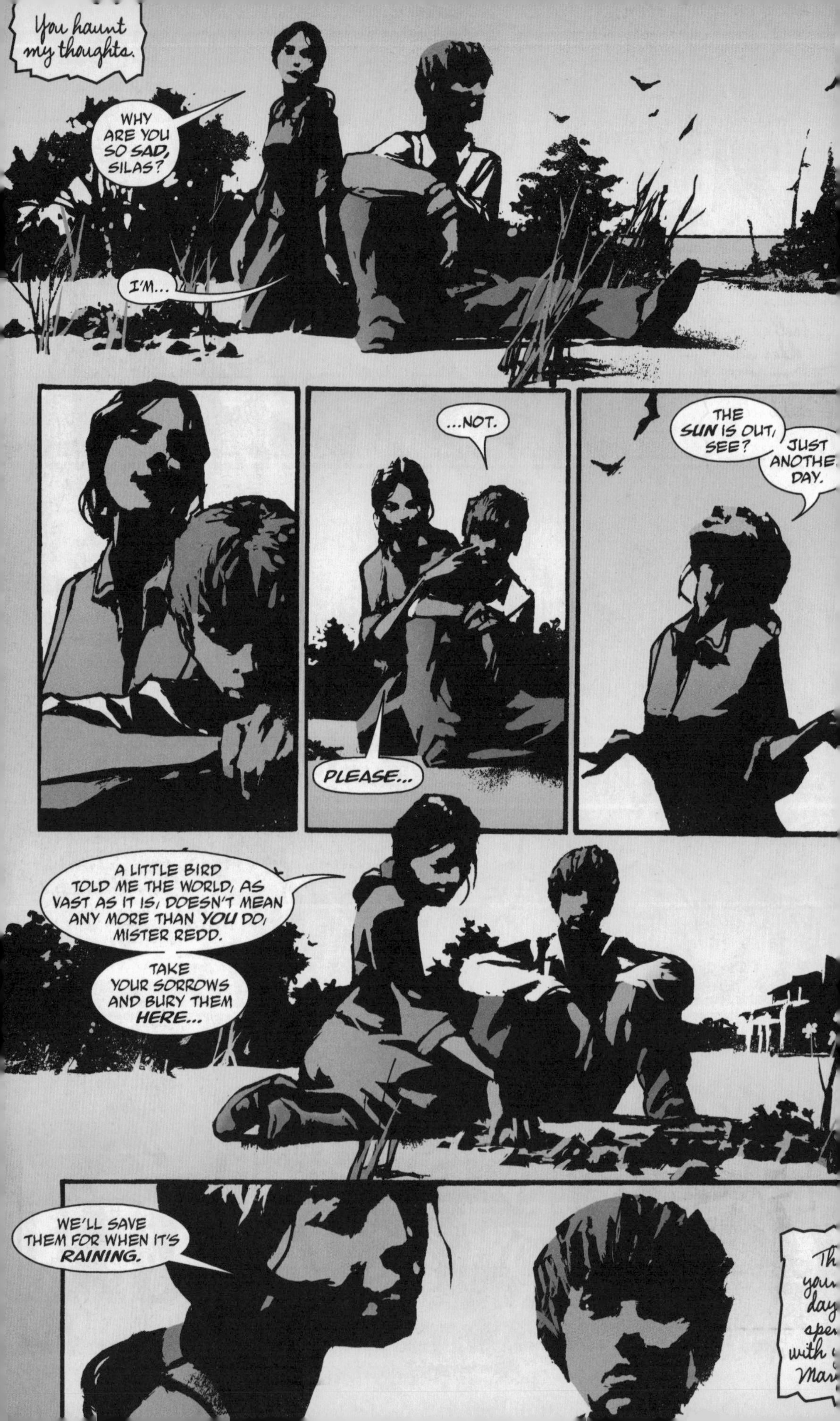
You haunt my thoughts.
WHY ARE YOU SO SAD, SILAS?
I'M...
...NOT.
PLEASE...
THE SUN IS OUT, SEE?
JUST ANOTHE DAY.
A LITTLE BIRD TOLD ME THE WORLD, AS VAST AS IT IS, DOESN'T MEAN ANY MORE THAN YOU DO, MISTER REDD.
TAKE YOUR SORROWS AND BURY THEM HERE...
WE'LL SAVE THEM FOR WHEN IT'S RAINING.

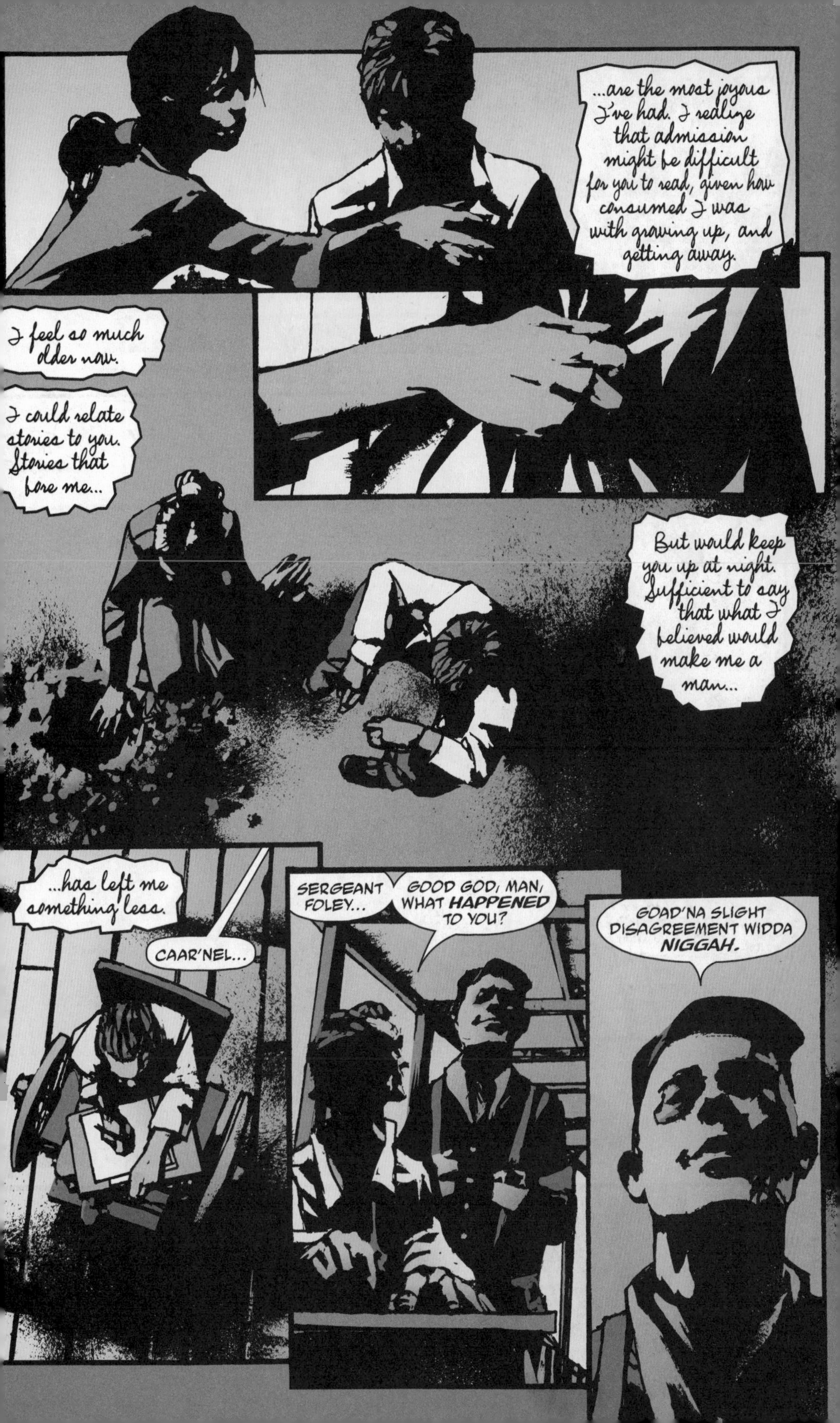
...are the most joyous I've had. I realize that admission might be difficult for you to read, given how consumed I was with growing up, and getting away.
I feel so much older now.
I could relate stories to you. Stories that bore me...
But would keep you up at night. Sufficient to say that what I believed would make me a man...
...has left me something less.
CAAR'NEL...
SERGEANT FOLEY...
GOOD GOD, MAN, WHAT HAPPENED TO YOU?
GOAD'NA SLIGHT DISAGREEMENT WIDDA NIGGAH.

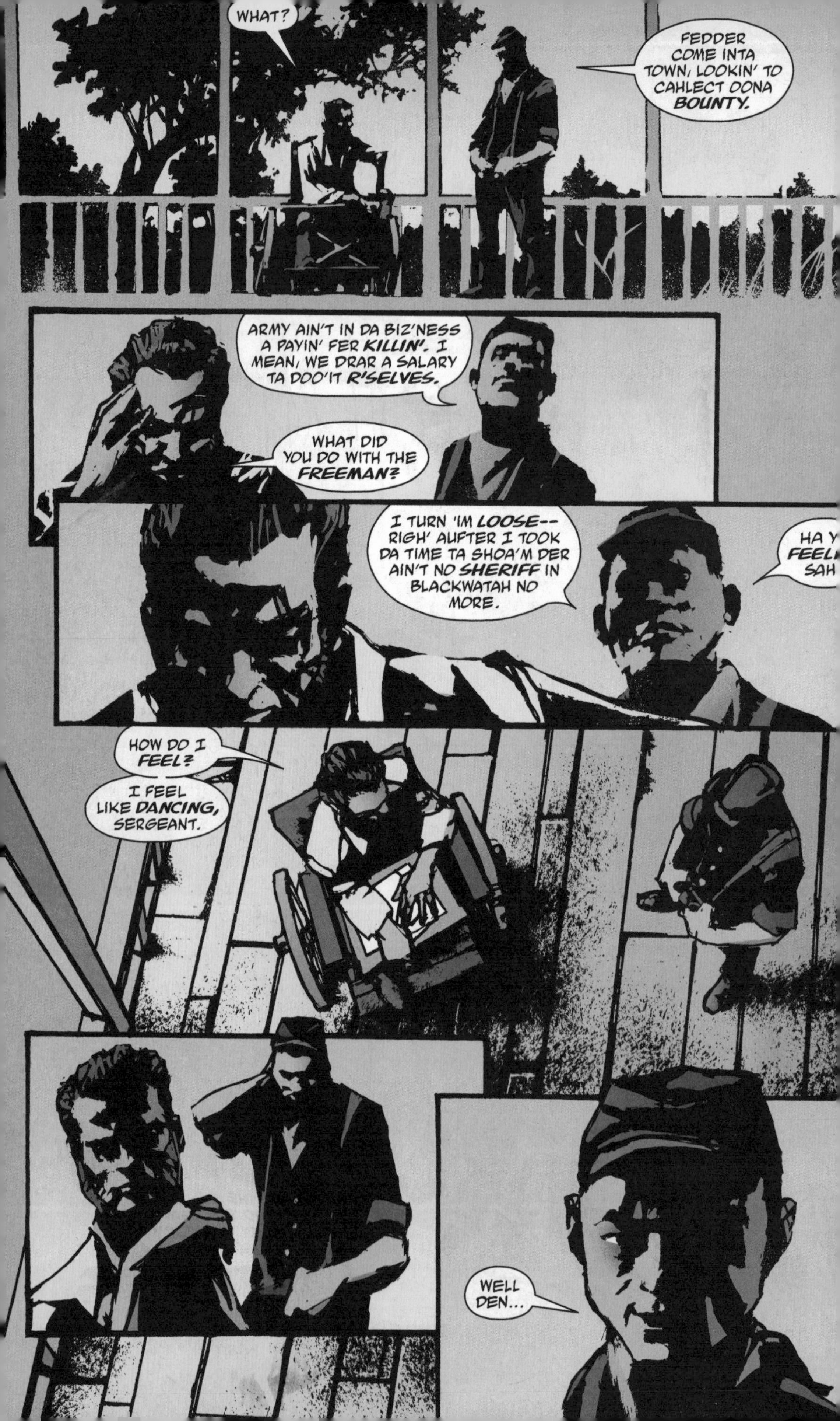
WHAT?
FEDDER COME INTA TOWN, LOOKIN' TO CAHLECT OONA BOUNTY.
ARMY AIN'T IN DA BIZ'NESS A PAYIN' FER KILLIN'. I MEAN, WE DRAR A SALARY TA DOO'IT R'SELVES.
WHAT DID YOU DO WITH THE FREEMAN?
I TURN 'IM LOOSE-- RIGH' AUFTER I TOOK DA TIME TA SHOA'M DER AIN'T NO SHERIFF IN BLACKWATAH NO MORE.
HOW DO I FEEL?
I FEEL LIKE DANCING, SERGEANT.
WELL DEN...

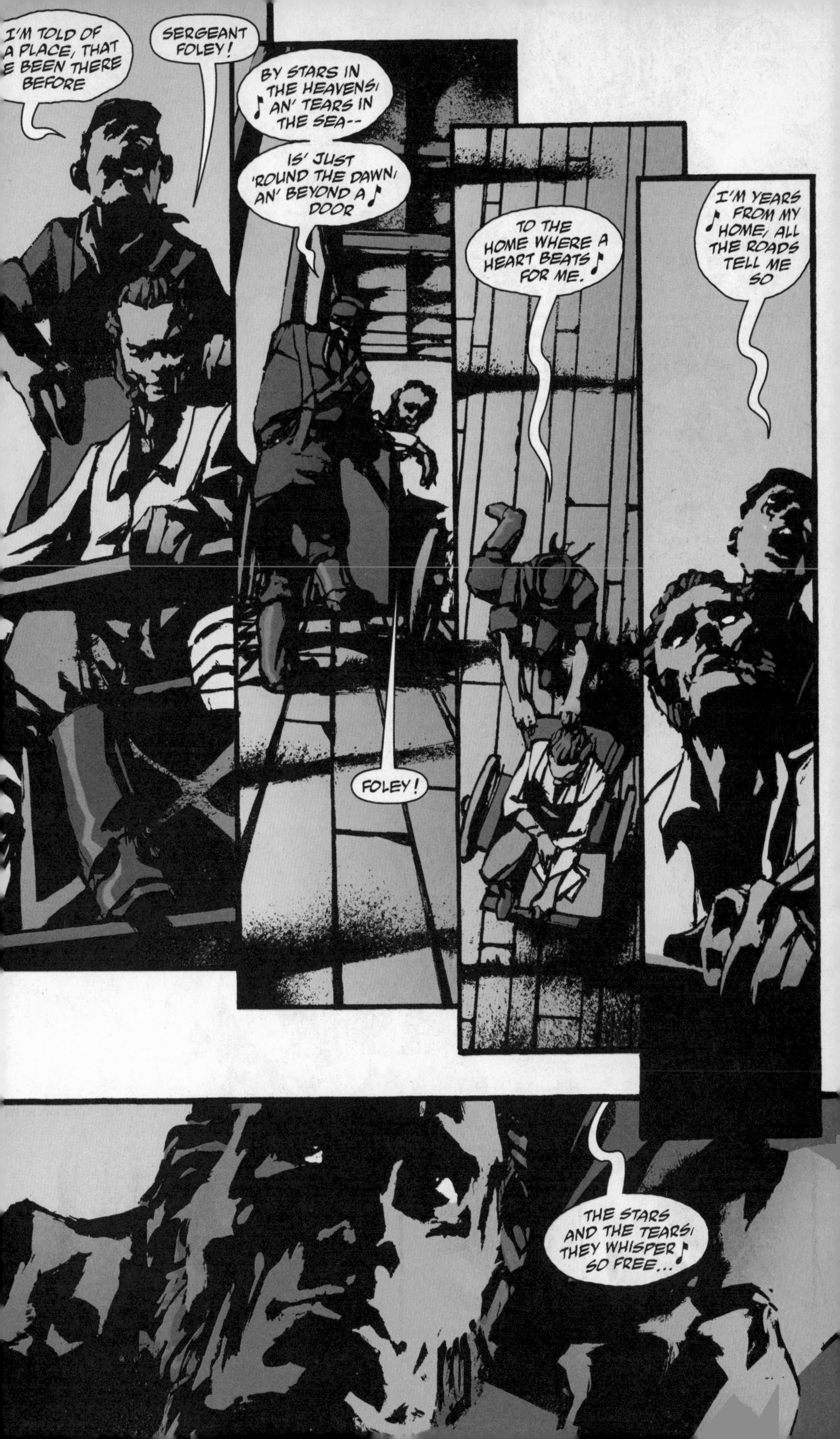
I'M TOLD OF A PLACE, THAT E BEEN THERE BEFORE
SERGEANT FOLEY!
BY STARS IN THE HEAVENS, AN' TEARS IN THE SEA--
IS' JUST 'ROUND THE DAWN, AN' BEYOND A DOOR
FOLEY!
TO THE HOME WHERE A HEART BEATS FOR ME.
I'M YEARS FROM MY HOME, ALL THE ROADS TELL ME SO
THE STARS AND THE TEARS, THEY WHISPER SO FREE...

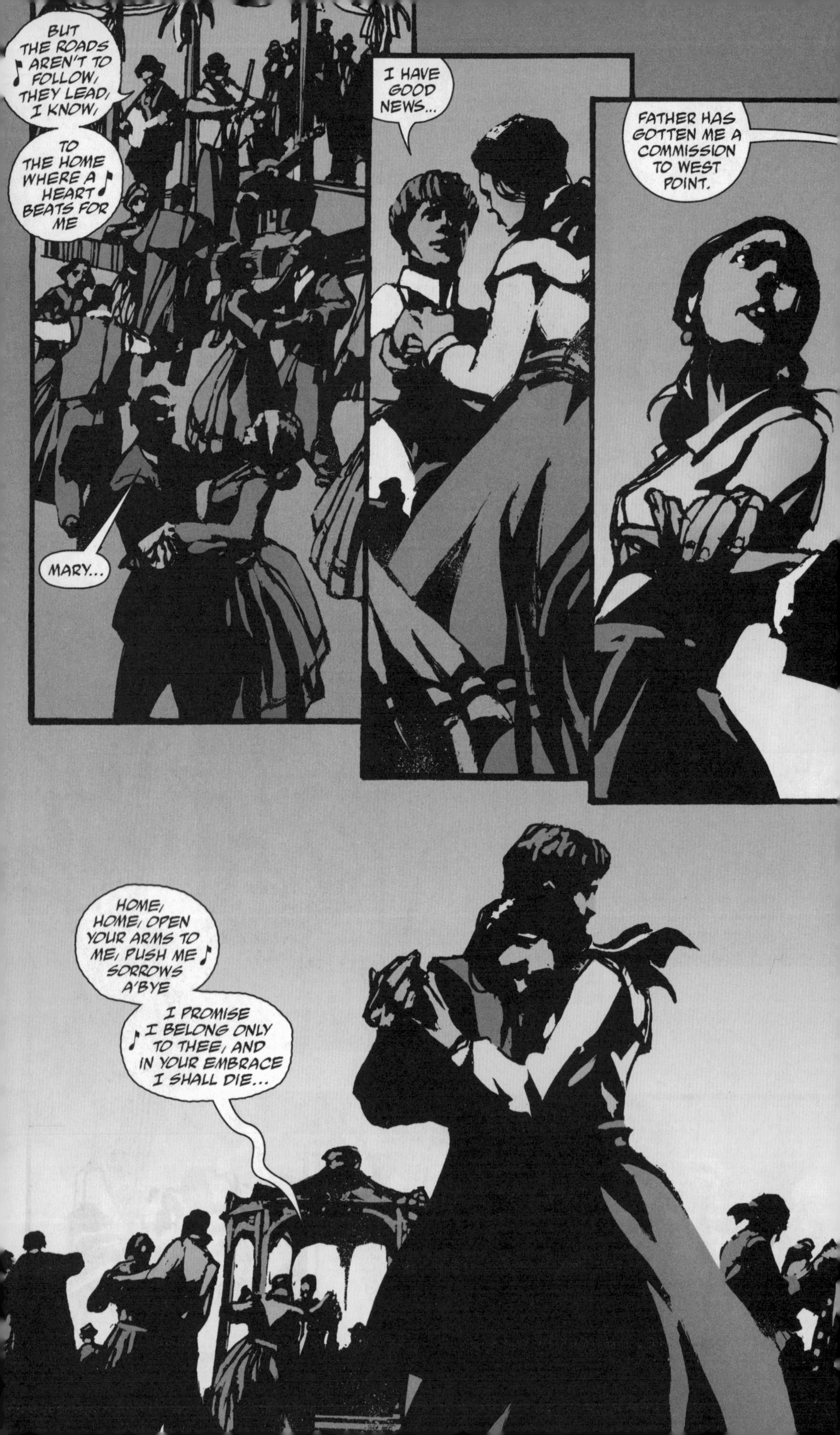

BUT THE ROADS AREN'T TO FOLLOW, THEY LEAD, I KNOW,
TO THE HOME WHERE A HEART BEATS FOR ME
MARY...
I HAVE GOOD NEWS...
FATHER HAS GOTTEN ME A COMMISSION TO WEST POINT.
HOME, HOME, OPEN YOUR ARMS TO ME, PUSH ME SORROWS A'BYE
I PROMISE I BELONG ONLY TO THEE, AND IN YOUR EMBRACE I SHALL DIE...

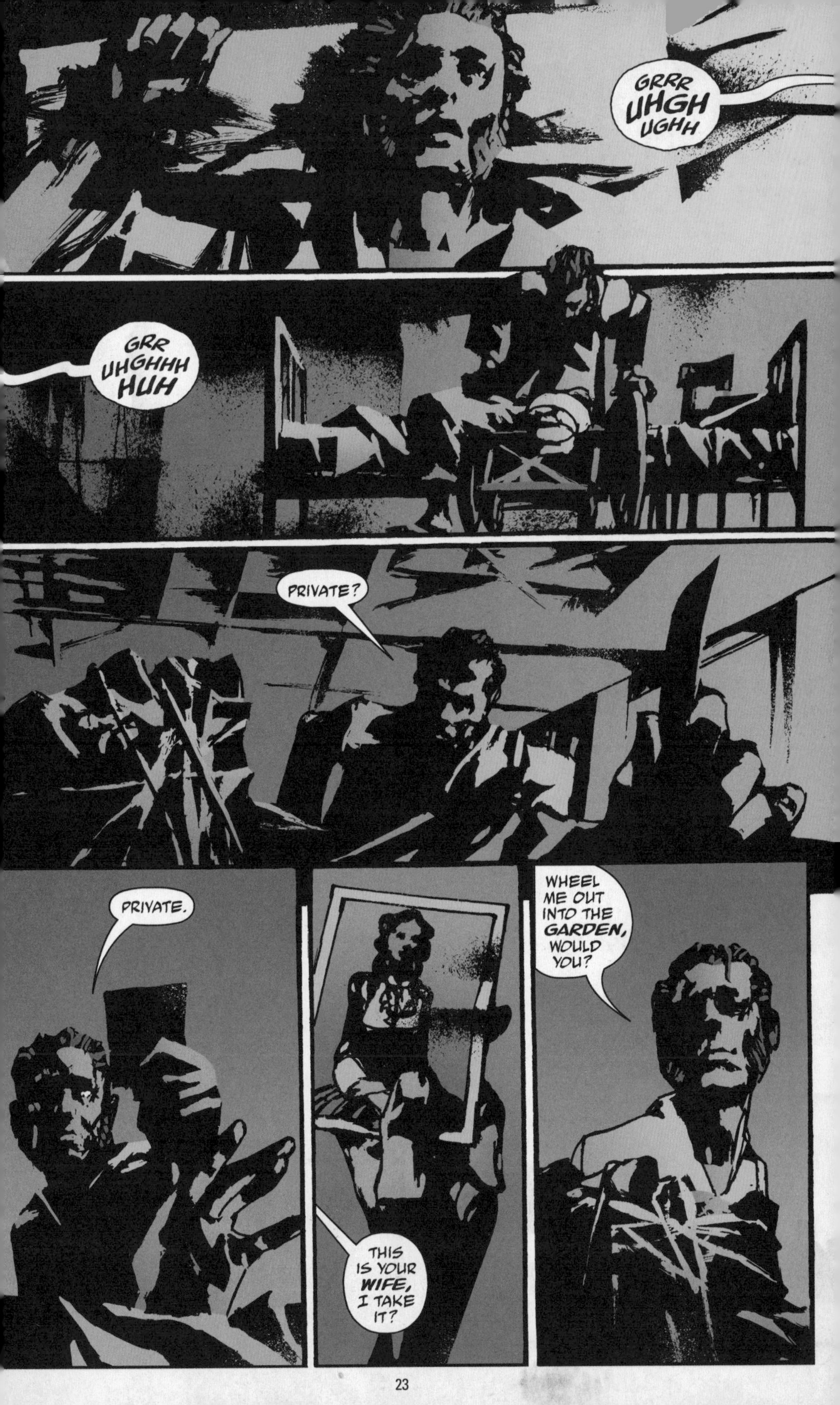

GRRR UHGH UGHH
GRR UHGHHH HUH
PRIVATE?
PRIVATE.
THIS IS YOUR WIFE, I TAKE IT?
WHEEL ME OUT INTO THE GARDEN, WOULD YOU?

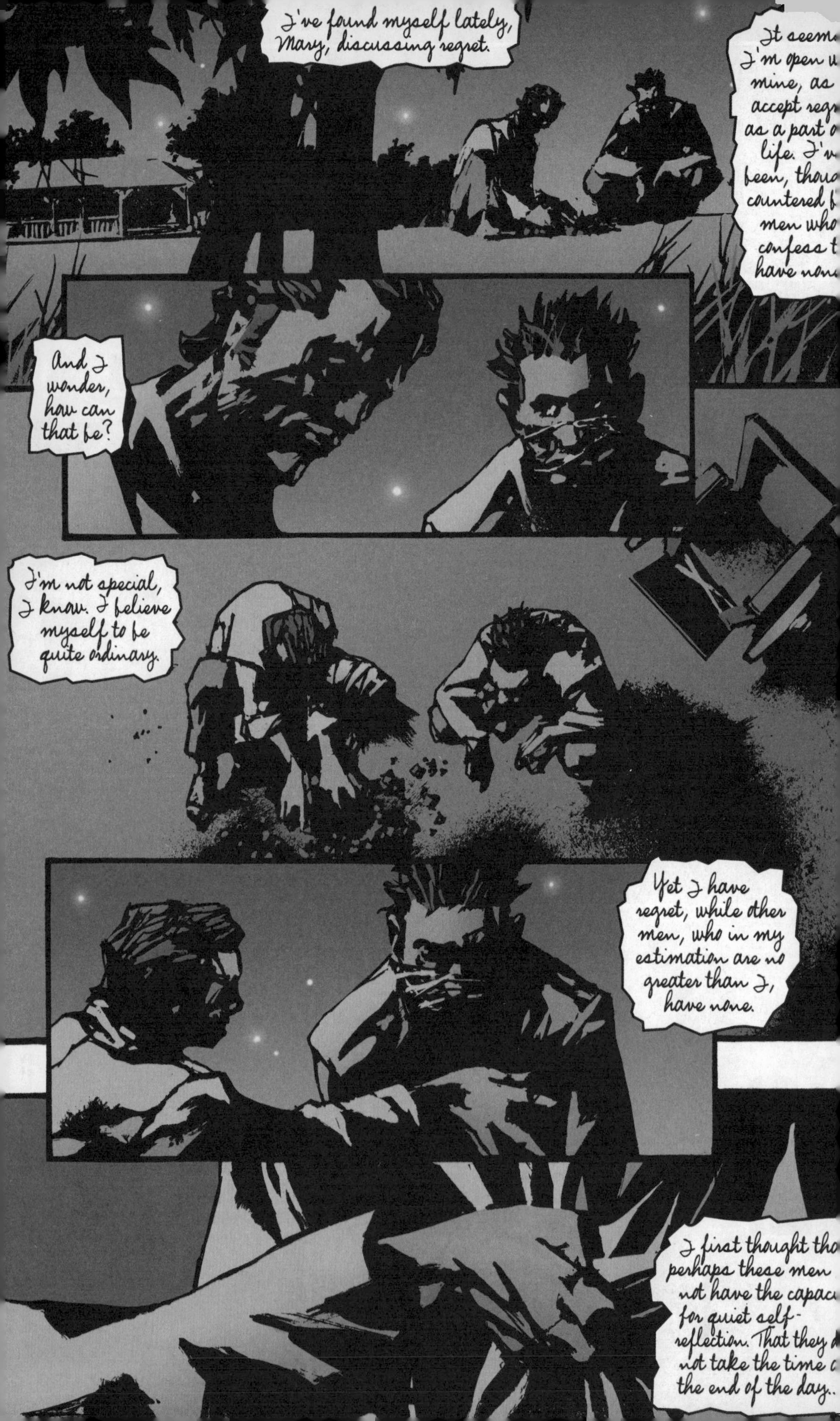
I've found myself lately, Mary, discussing regret.
It seem I'm open u mine, as accept reg as a part o life. I'v been, thou countered b men who confess t have none
And I wonder, how can that be?
I'm not special, I know. I believe myself to be quite ordinary.
Yet I have regret, while other men, who in my estimation are no greater than I, have none.
I first thought tha perhaps these men not have the capac for quiet self-reflection. That they d not take the time a the end of the day...

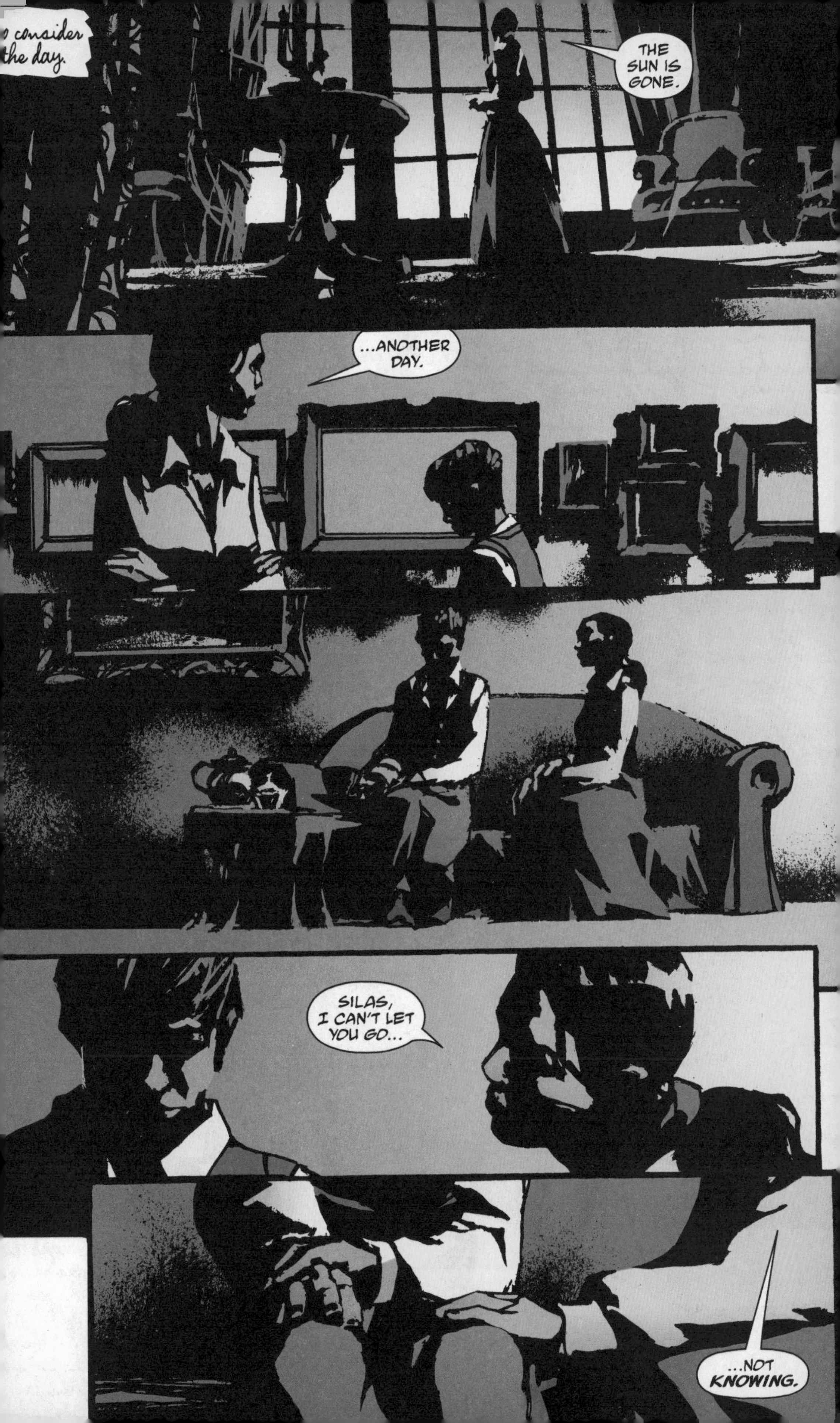
...o consider the day.
THE SUN IS GONE.
...ANOTHER DAY.
SILAS, I CAN'T LET YOU GO...
...NOT KNOWING.

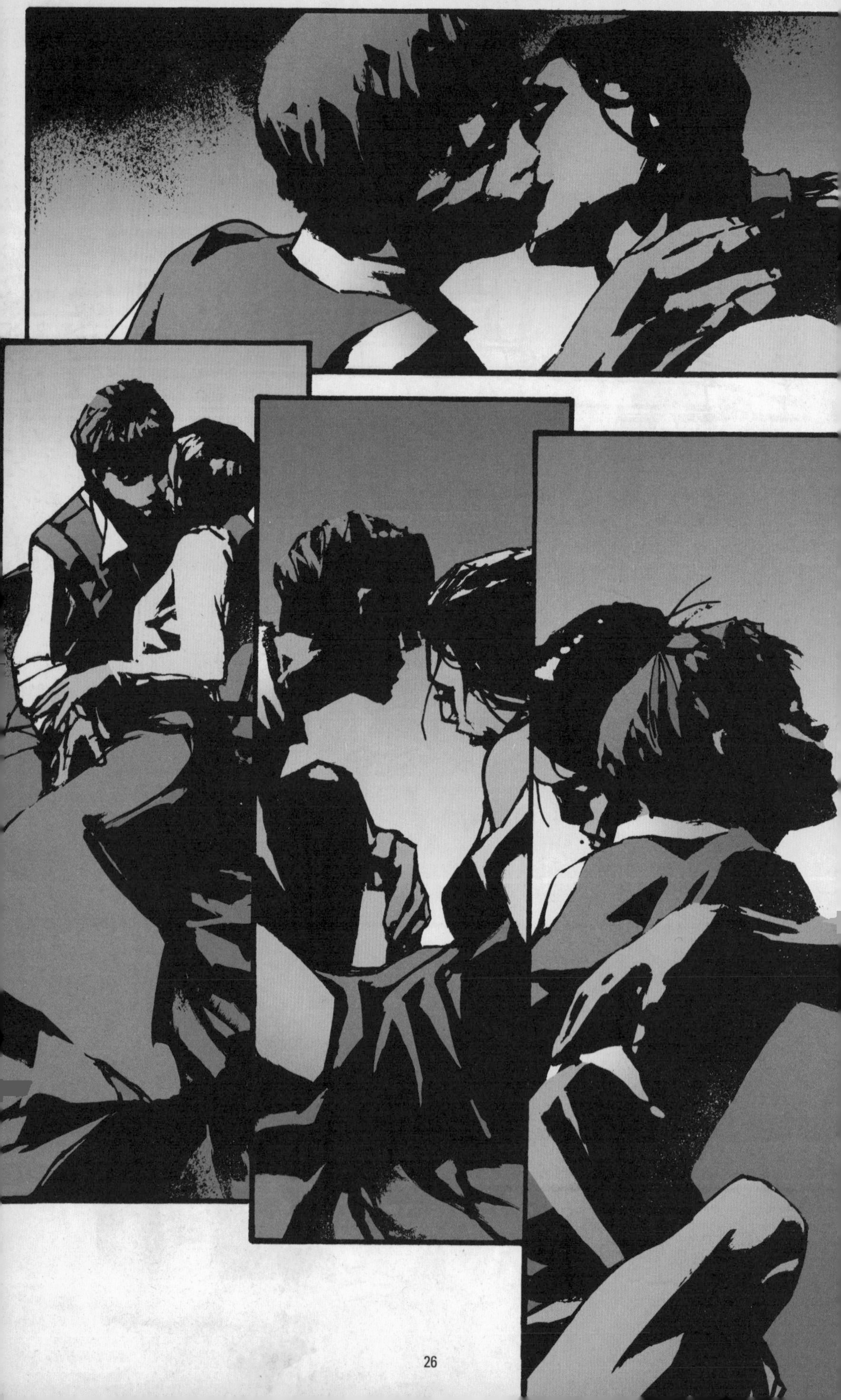

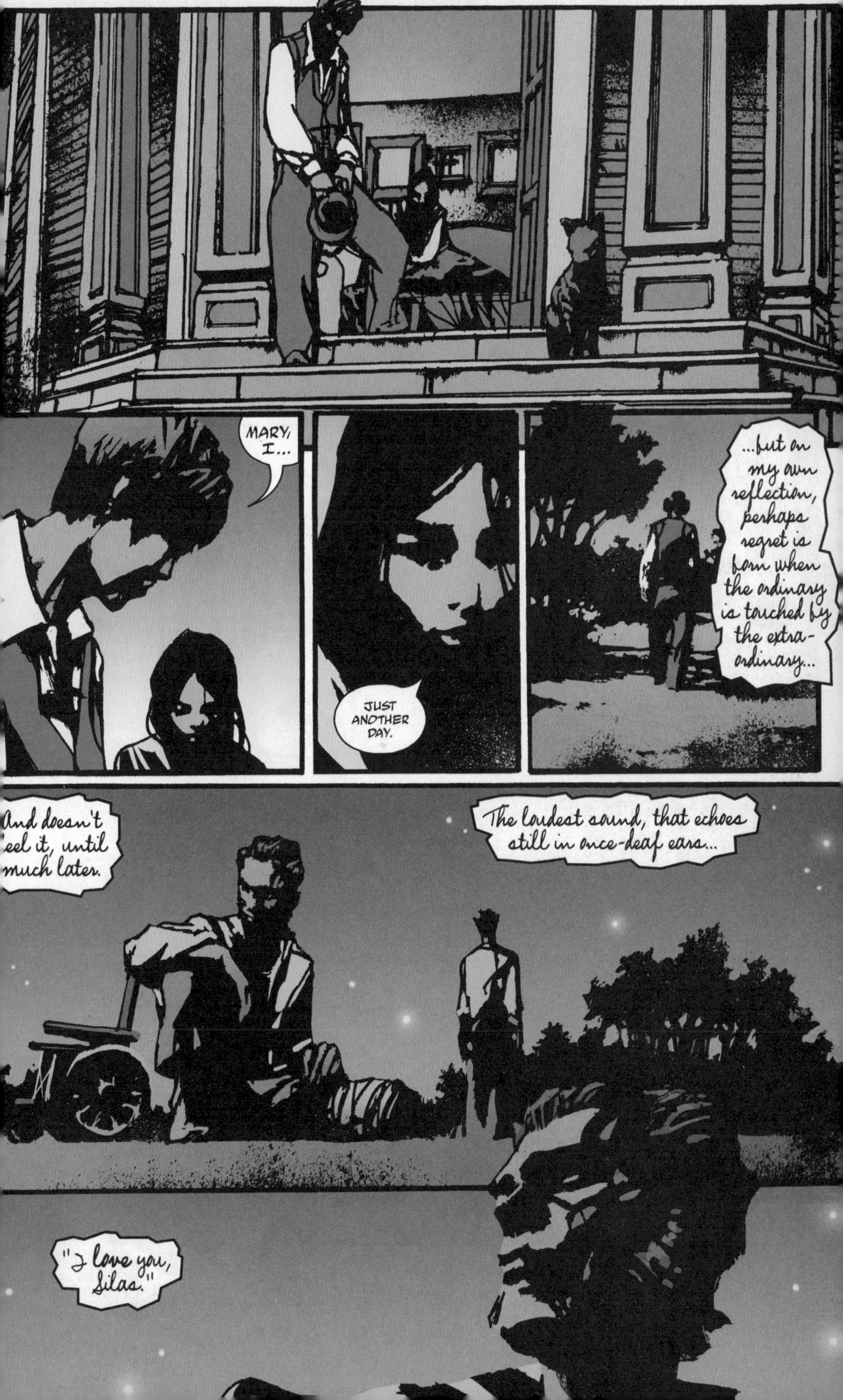
MARY, I...
JUST ANOTHER DAY.
...but on my own reflection, perhaps regret is born when the ordinary is touched by the extra-ordinary...
And doesn't eel it, until much later.
The loudest sound, that echoes still in once-deaf ears...
"I love you, Silas."

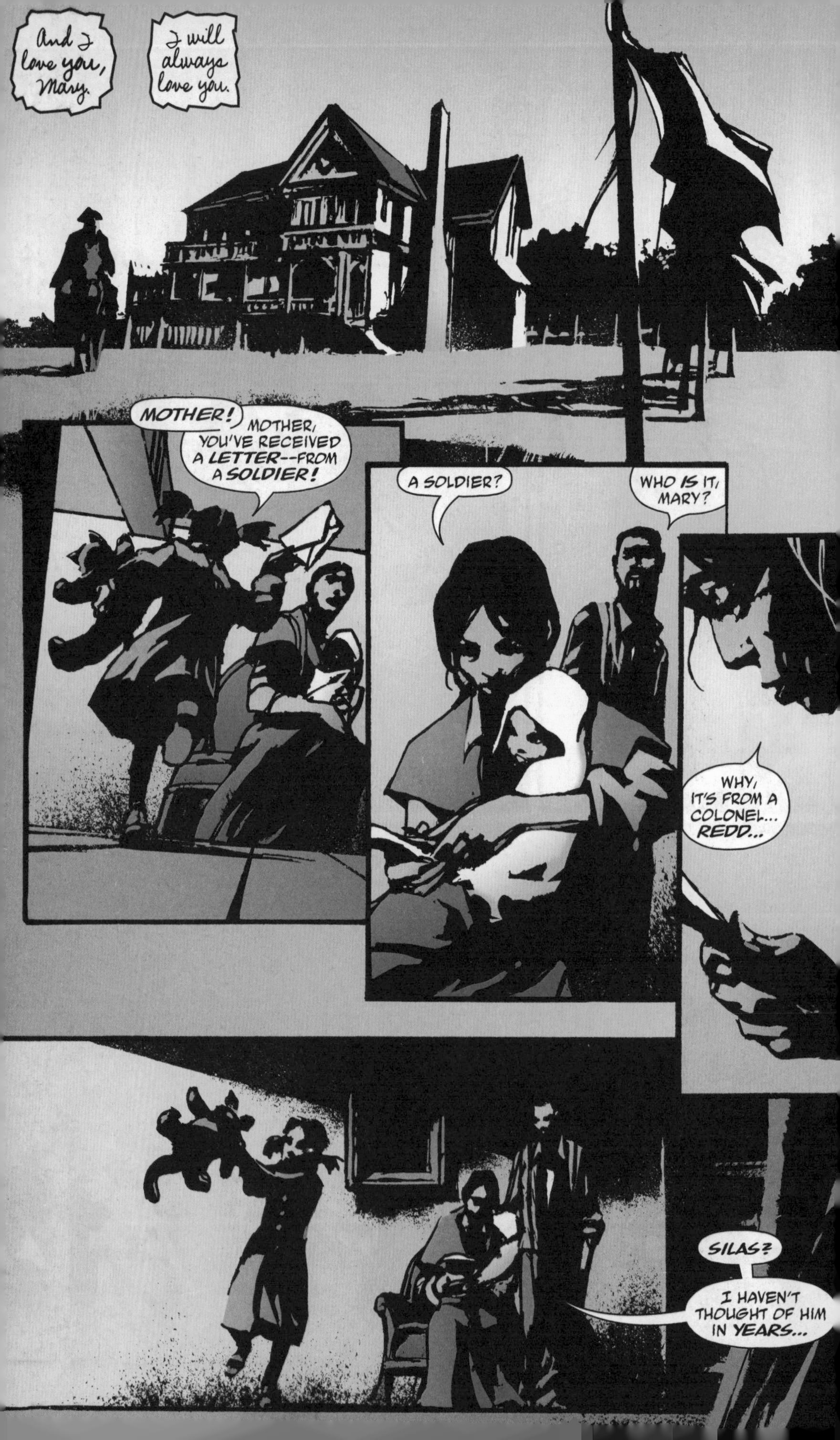
And I love you, Mary.
I will always love you.
MOTHER!
MOTHER, YOU'VE RECEIVED A LETTER--FROM A SOLDIER!
A SOLDIER?
WHO IS IT, MARY?
WHY, IT'S FROM A COLONEL... REDD...
SILAS?
I HAVEN'T THOUGHT OF HIM IN YEARS...

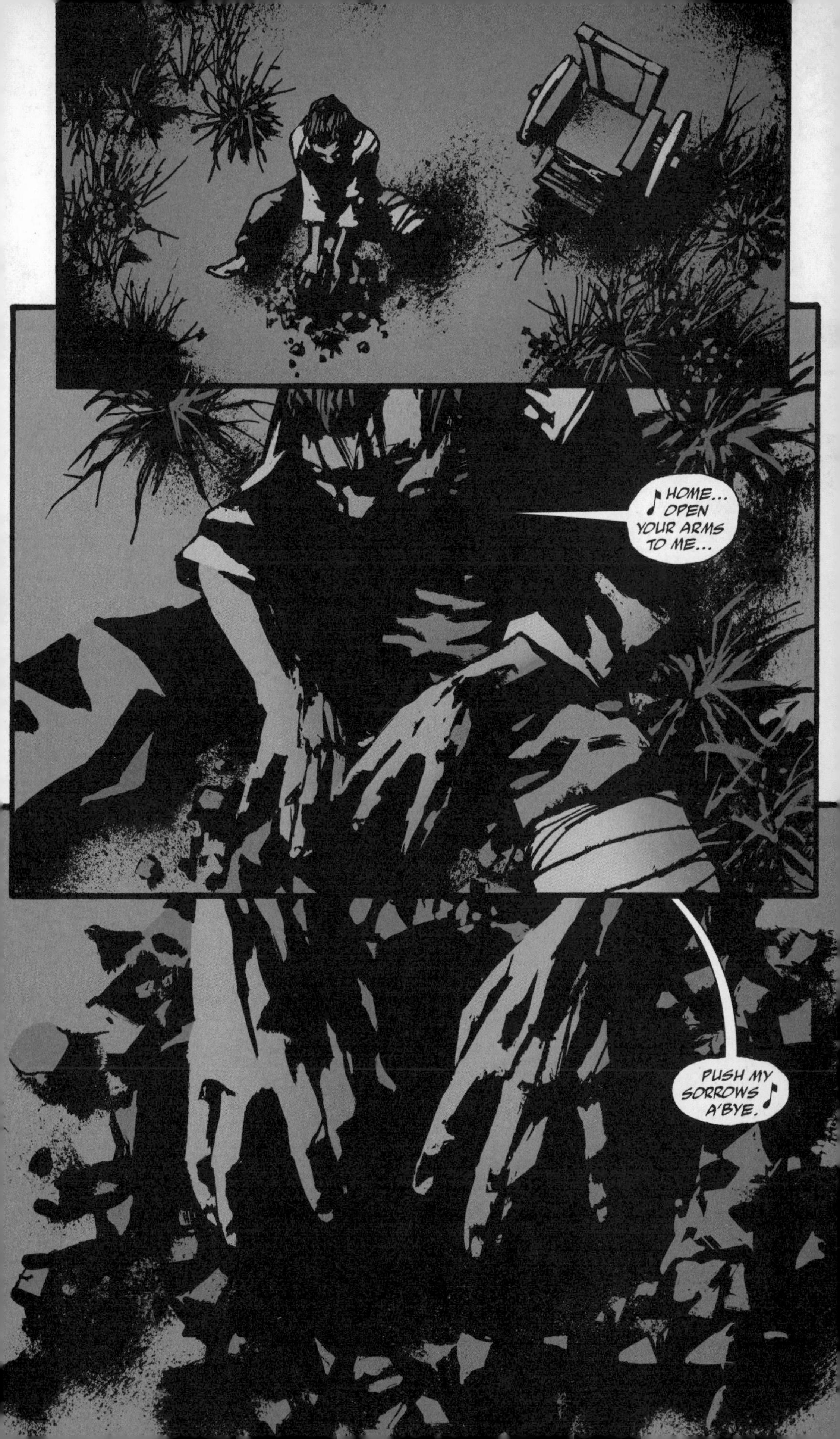
♪ HOME... OPEN YOUR ARMS TO ME...
PUSH MY SORROWS A'BYE. ♪

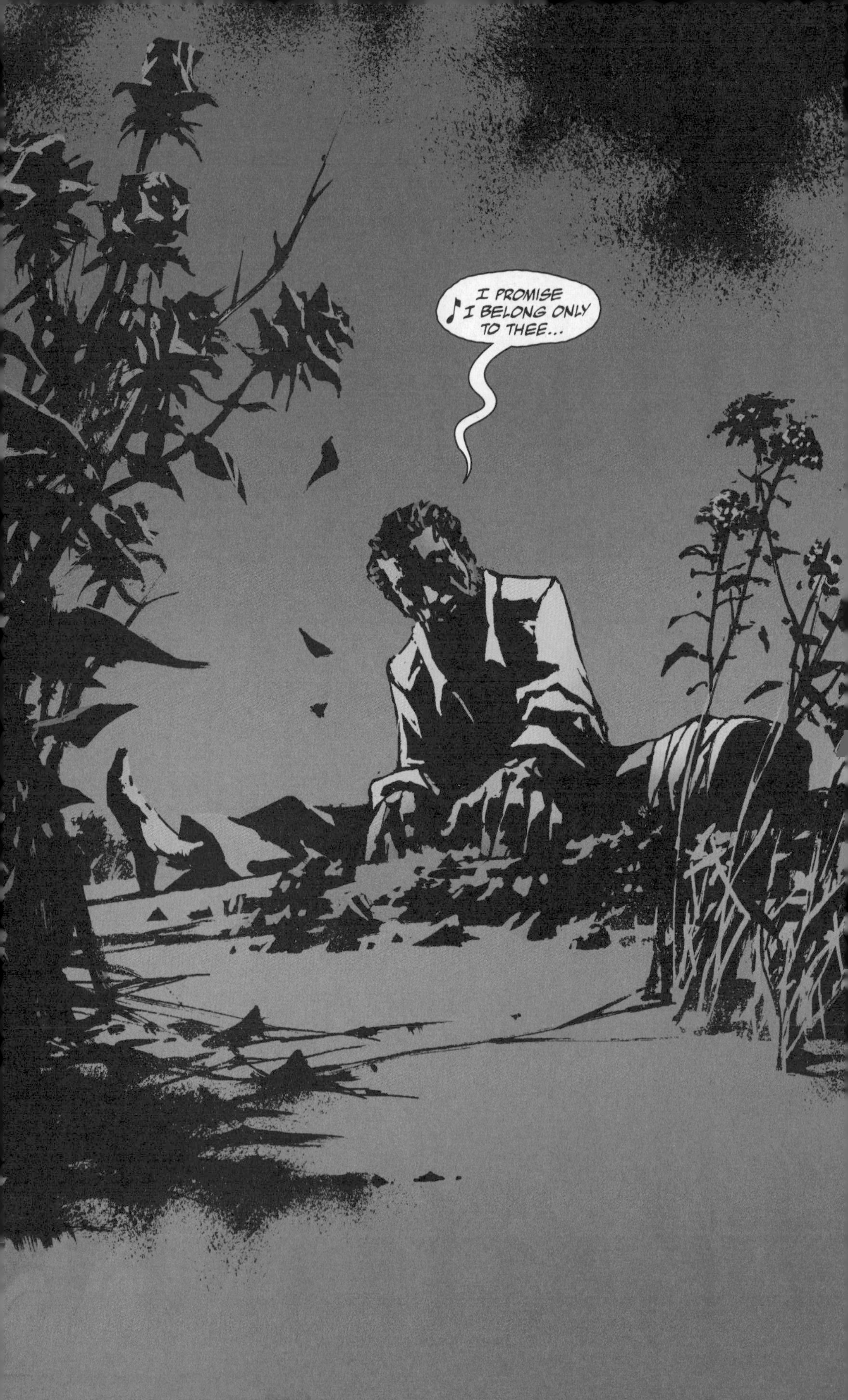
♪ I PROMISE I BELONG ONLY TO THEE...

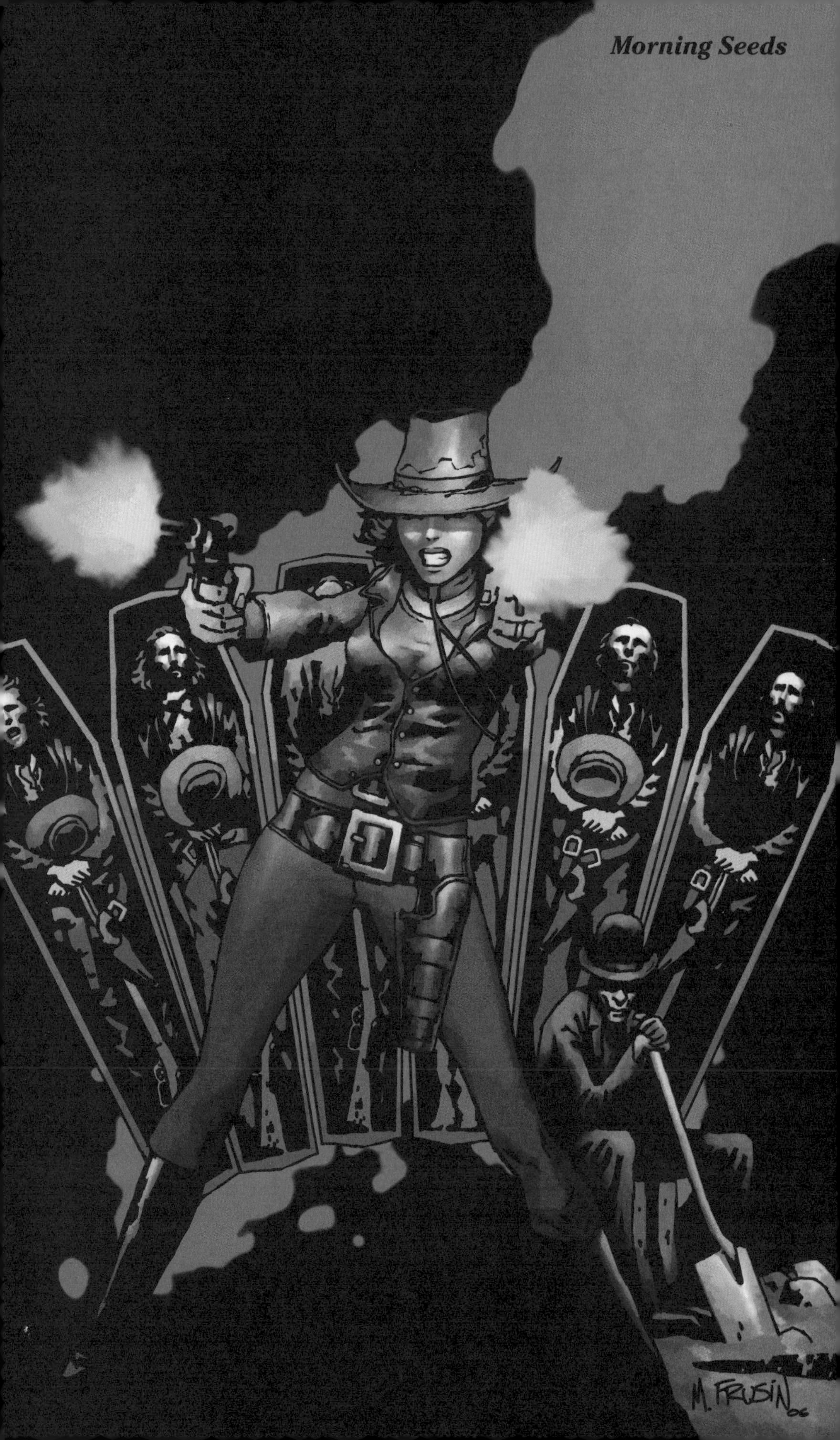
M. FRUSIN 06

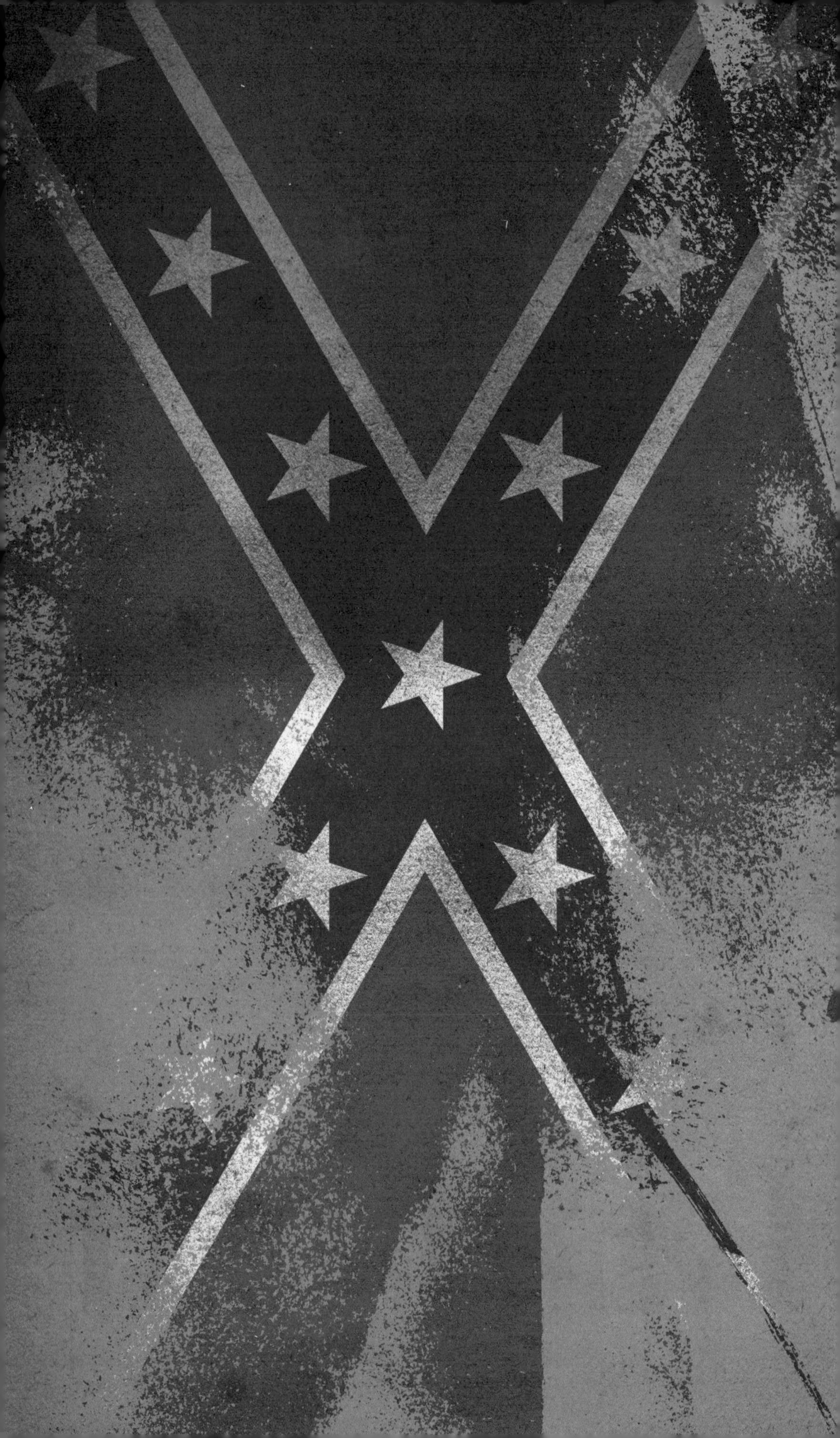

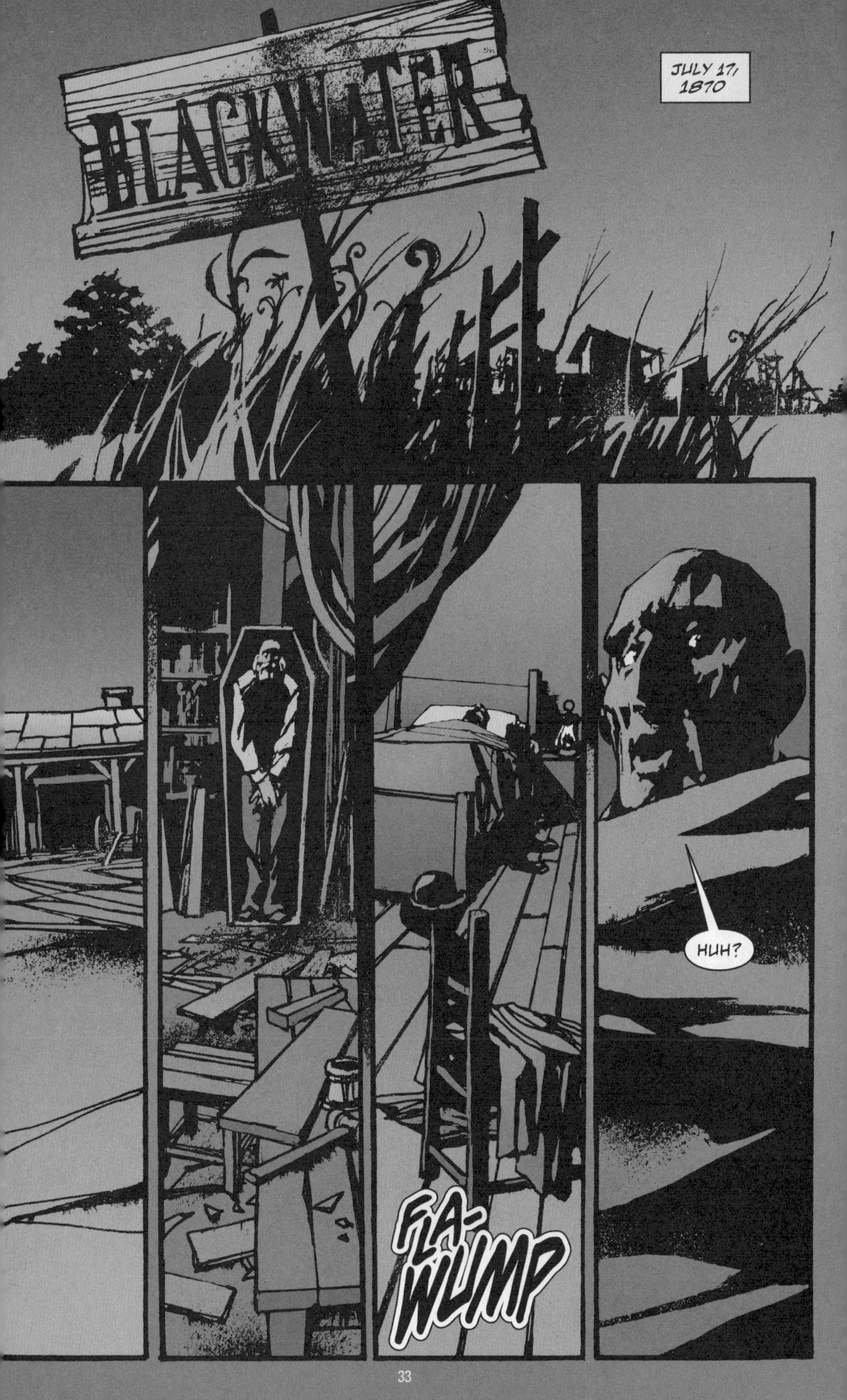
BLACKWATER
JULY 17, 1870
HUH?
FLA-WUMP

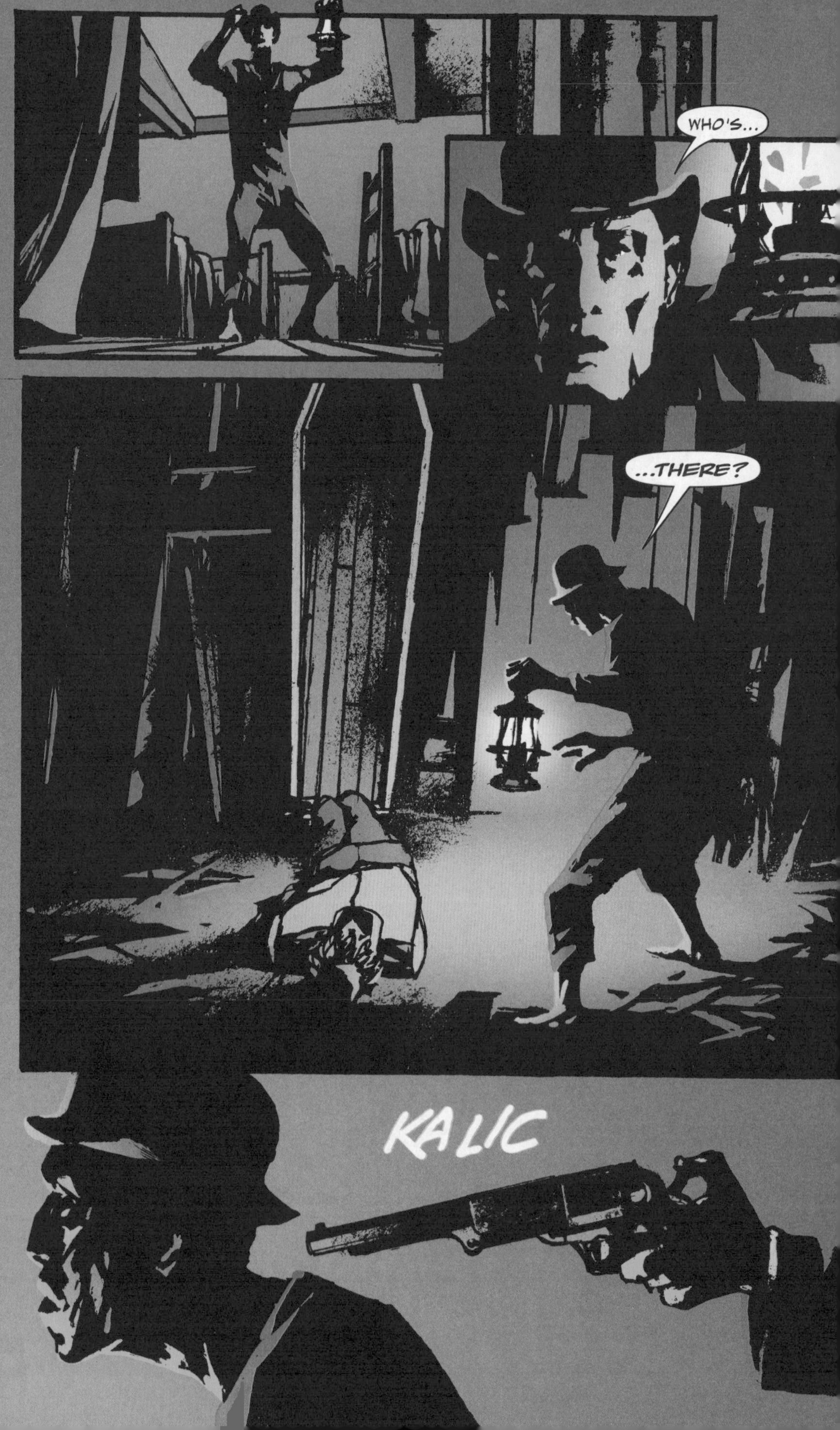
WHO'S...
...THERE?
KALIC

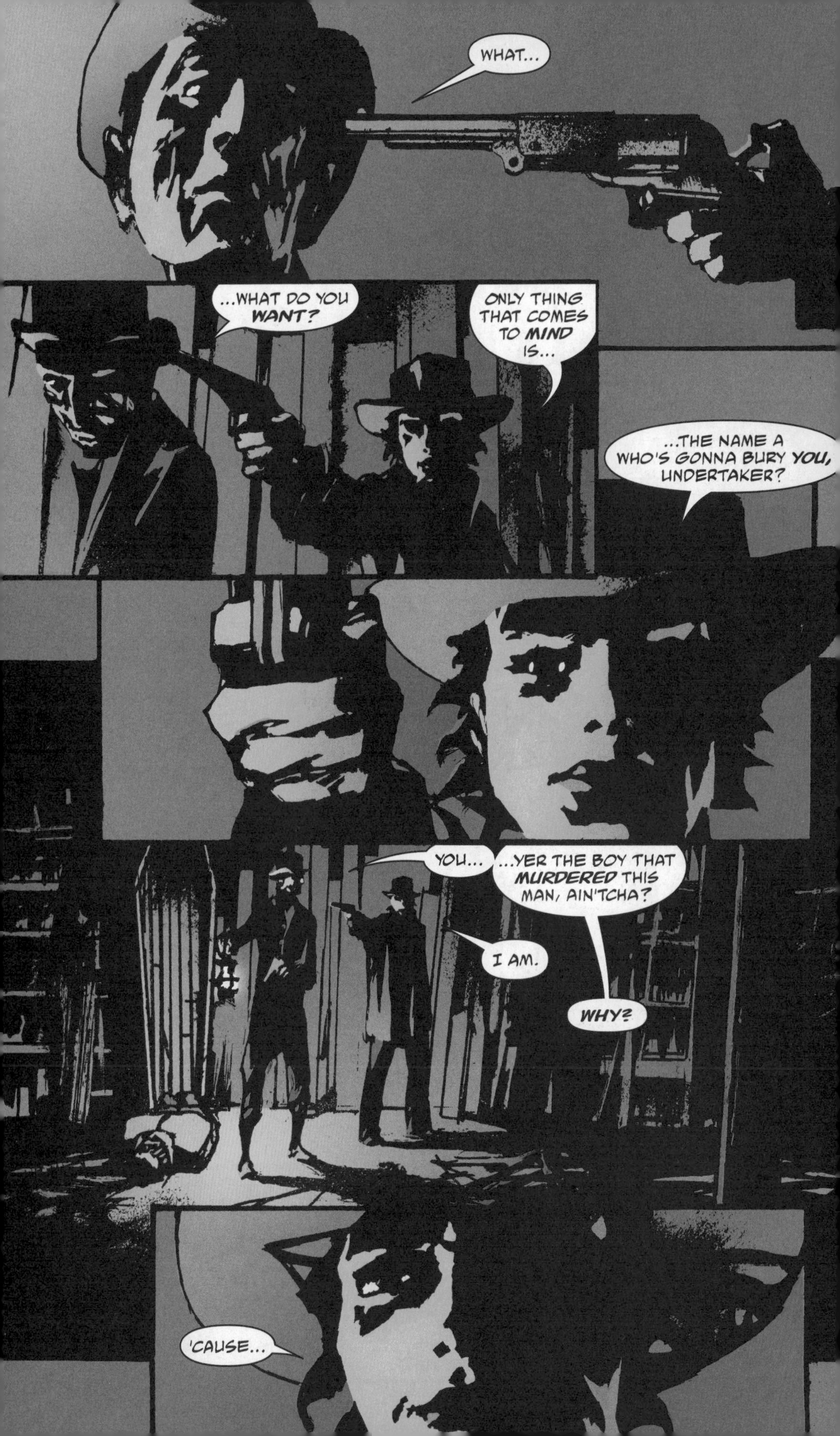
WHAT...
...WHAT DO YOU WANT?
ONLY THING THAT COMES TO MIND IS...
...THE NAME A WHO'S GONNA BURY YOU, UNDERTAKER?
YOU...
...YER THE BOY THAT MURDERED THIS MAN, AIN'TCHA?
I AM.
WHY?
'CAUSE...

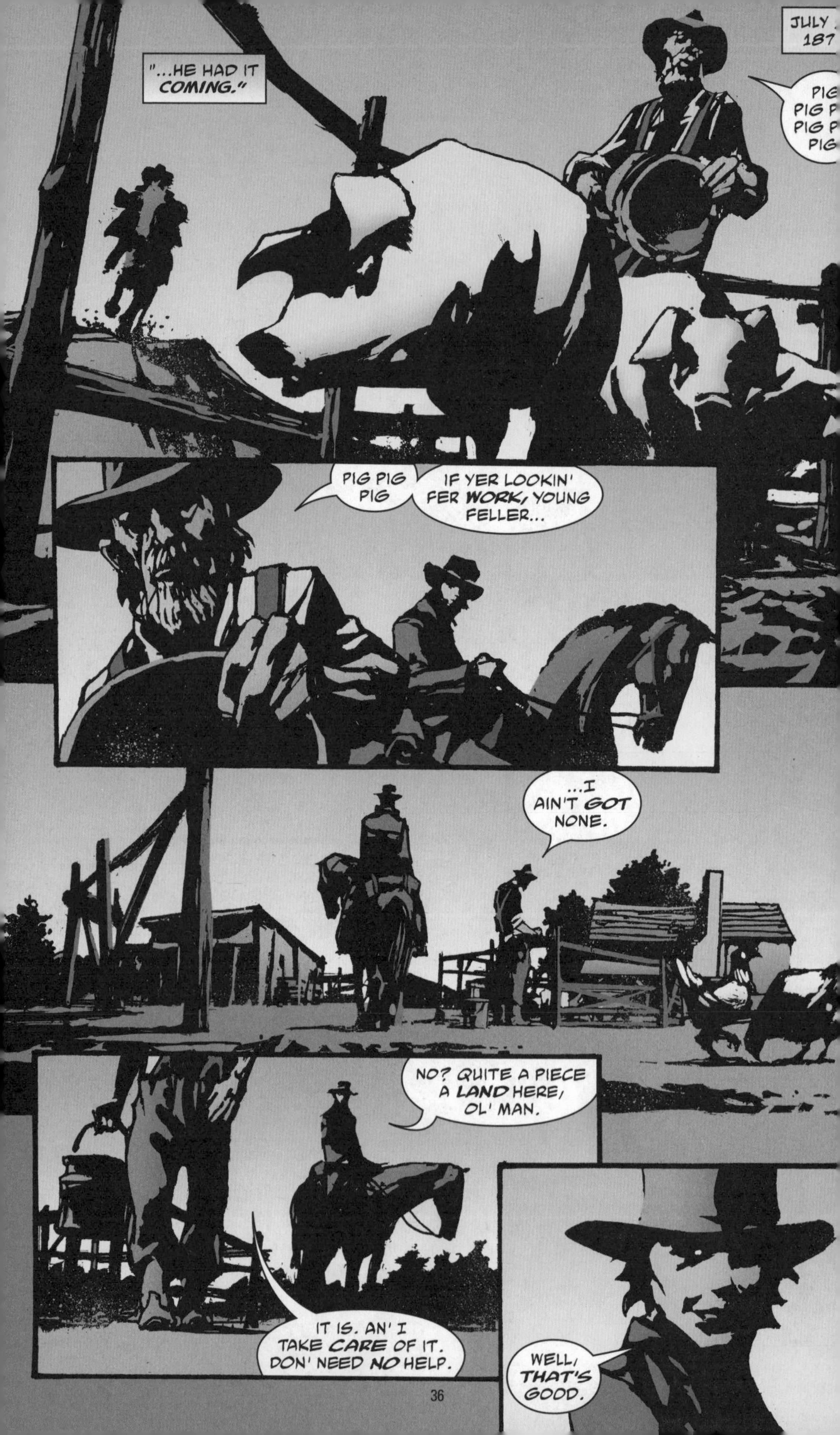

"...HE HAD IT COMING."
JULY 187
PIG PIG P PIG P PIG
PIG PIG PIG
IF YER LOOKIN' FER WORK, YOUNG FELLER...
...I AIN'T GOT NONE.
NO? QUITE A PIECE A LAND HERE, OL' MAN.
IT IS. AN' I TAKE CARE OF IT. DON' NEED NO HELP.
WELL, THAT'S GOOD.

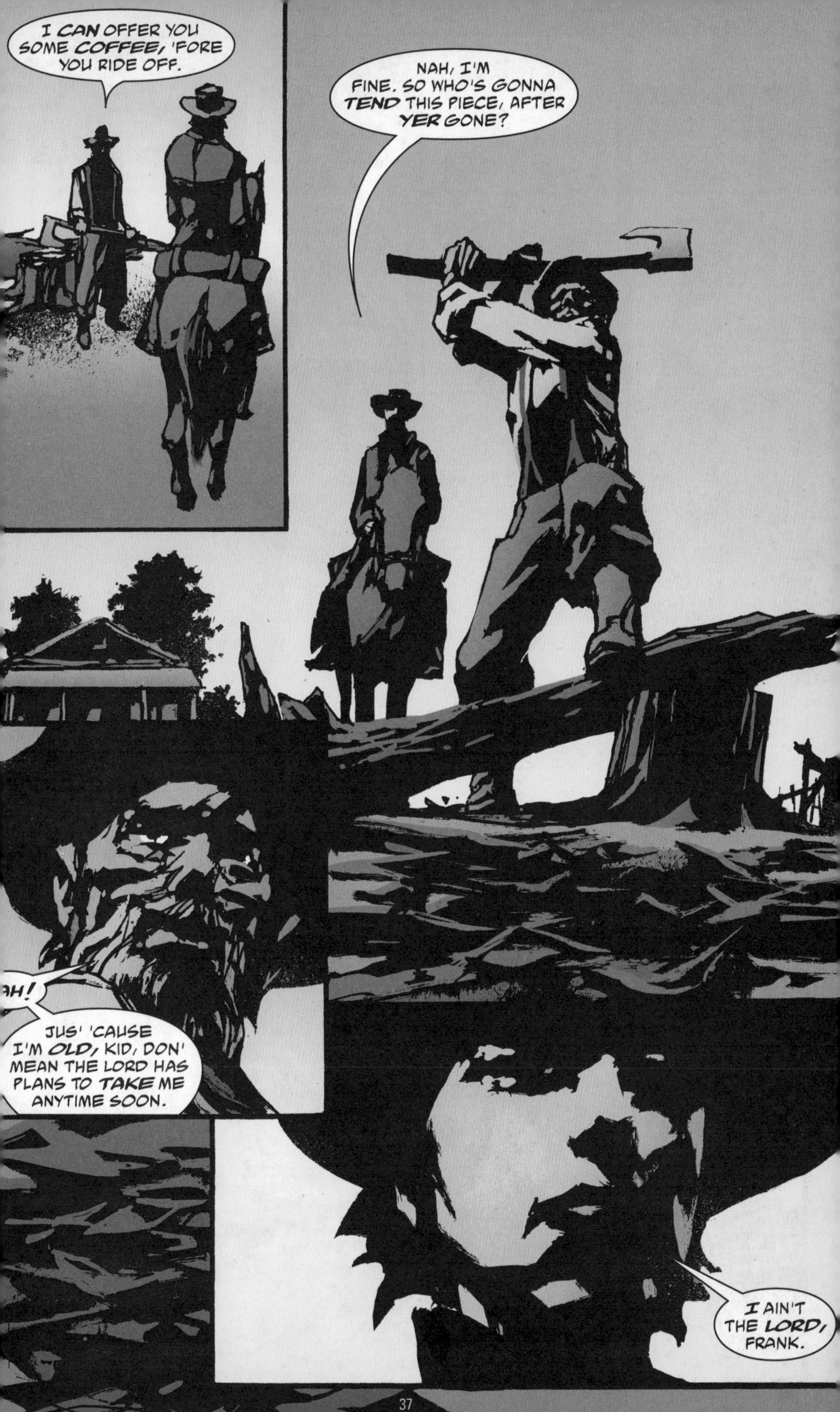
I CAN OFFER YOU SOME COFFEE, 'FORE YOU RIDE OFF.
NAH, I'M FINE. SO WHO'S GONNA TEND THIS PIECE, AFTER YER GONE?
AH!
JUS' 'CAUSE I'M OLD, KID, DON' MEAN THE LORD HAS PLANS TO TAKE ME ANYTIME SOON.
I AIN'T THE LORD, FRANK.

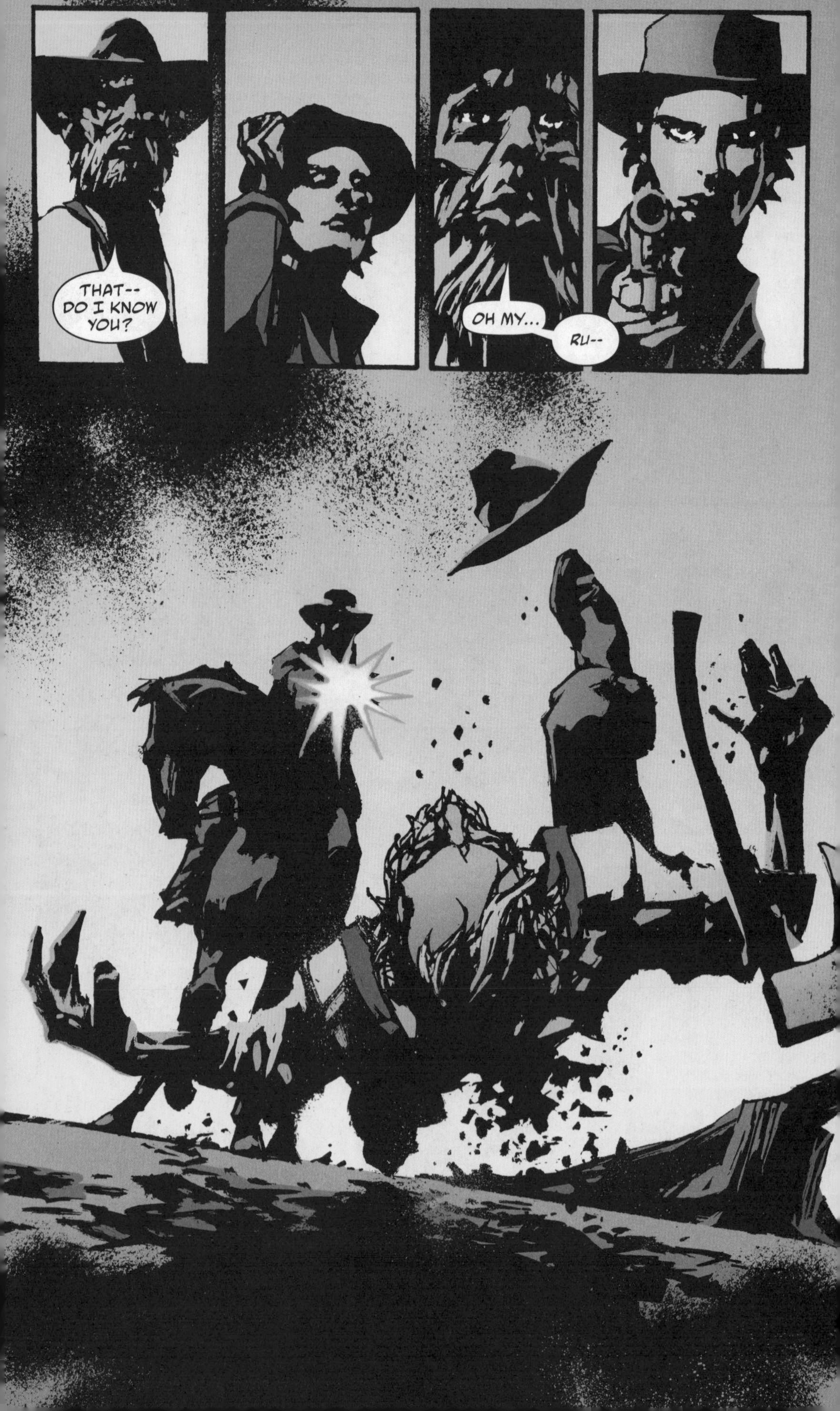
THAT-- DO I KNOW YOU?
OH MY...
RU--

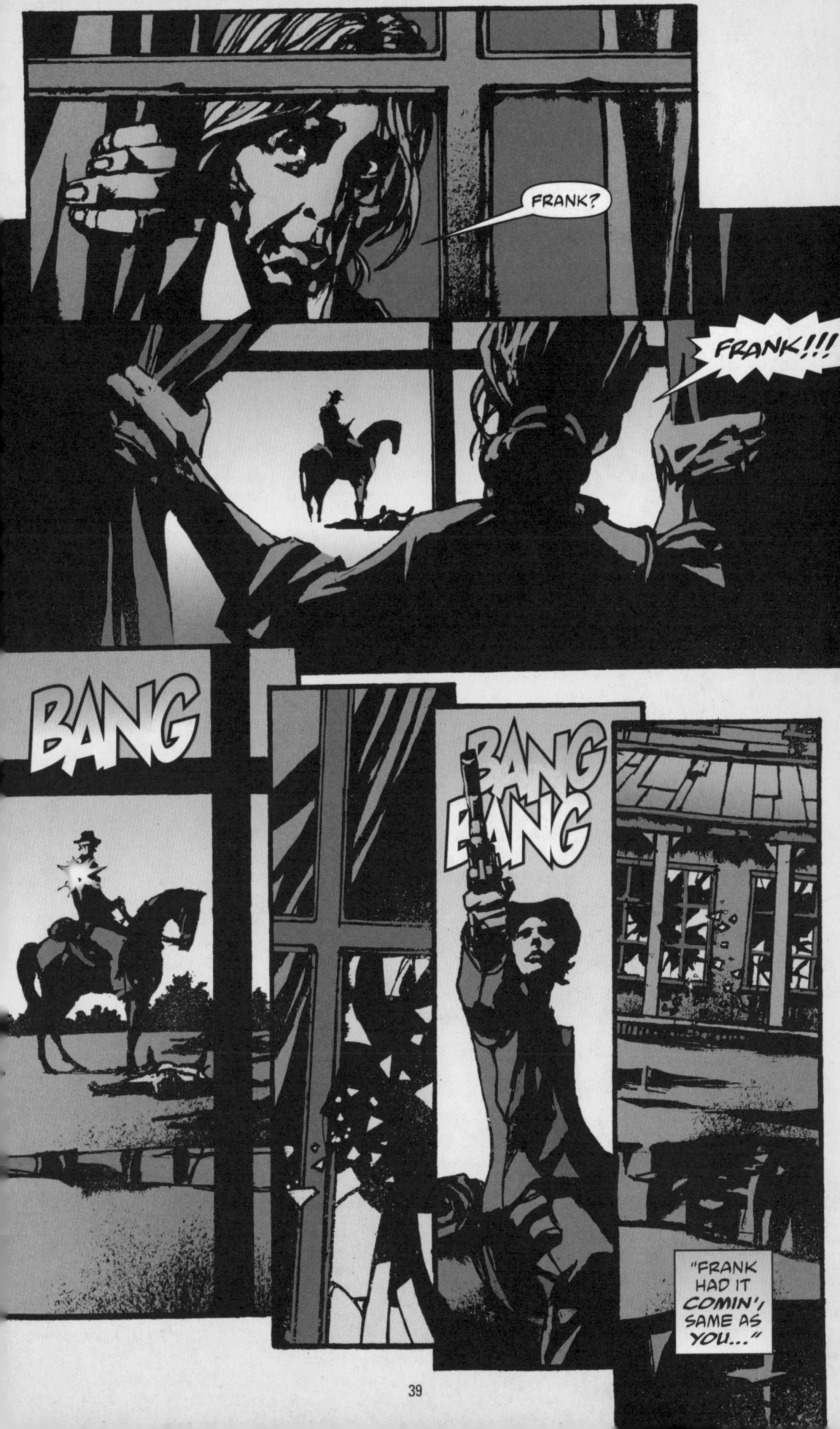
FRANK?
FRANK!!!
BANG
BANG
BANG
"FRANK HAD IT COMIN', SAME AS YOU..."

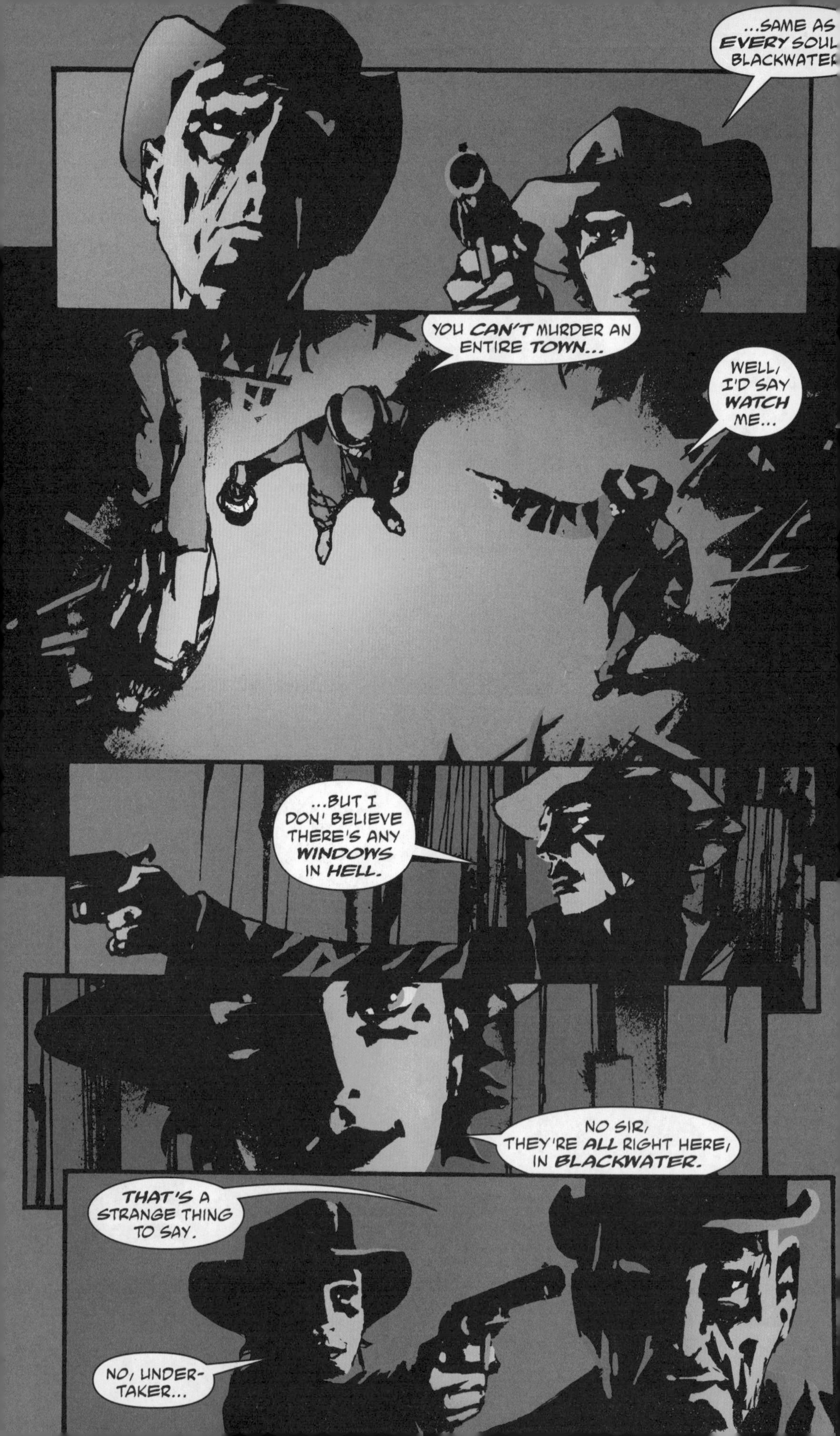
...SAME AS EVERY SOUL BLACKWATER
YOU CAN'T MURDER AN ENTIRE TOWN...
WELL, I'D SAY WATCH ME...
...BUT I DON' BELIEVE THERE'S ANY WINDOWS IN HELL.
NO SIR, THEY'RE ALL RIGHT HERE, IN BLACKWATER.
THAT'S A STRANGE THING TO SAY.
NO, UNDER-TAKER...

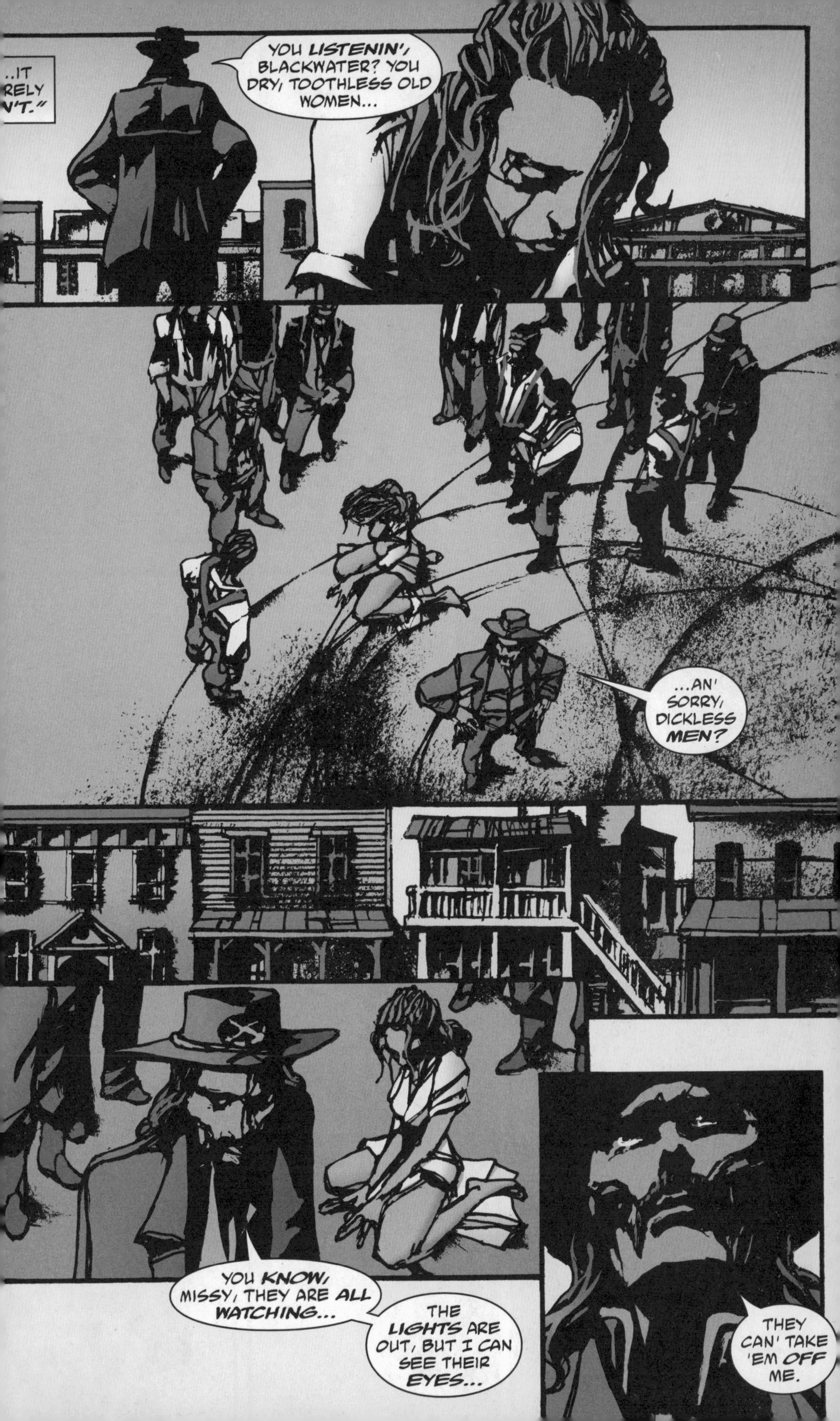
..IT
RELY
N'T."
YOU LISTENIN', BLACKWATER? YOU DRY, TOOTHLESS OLD WOMEN...
...AN' SORRY, DICKLESS MEN?
YOU KNOW, MISSY, THEY ARE ALL WATCHING...
THE LIGHTS ARE OUT, BUT I CAN SEE THEIR EYES...
THEY CAN' TAKE 'EM OFF ME.

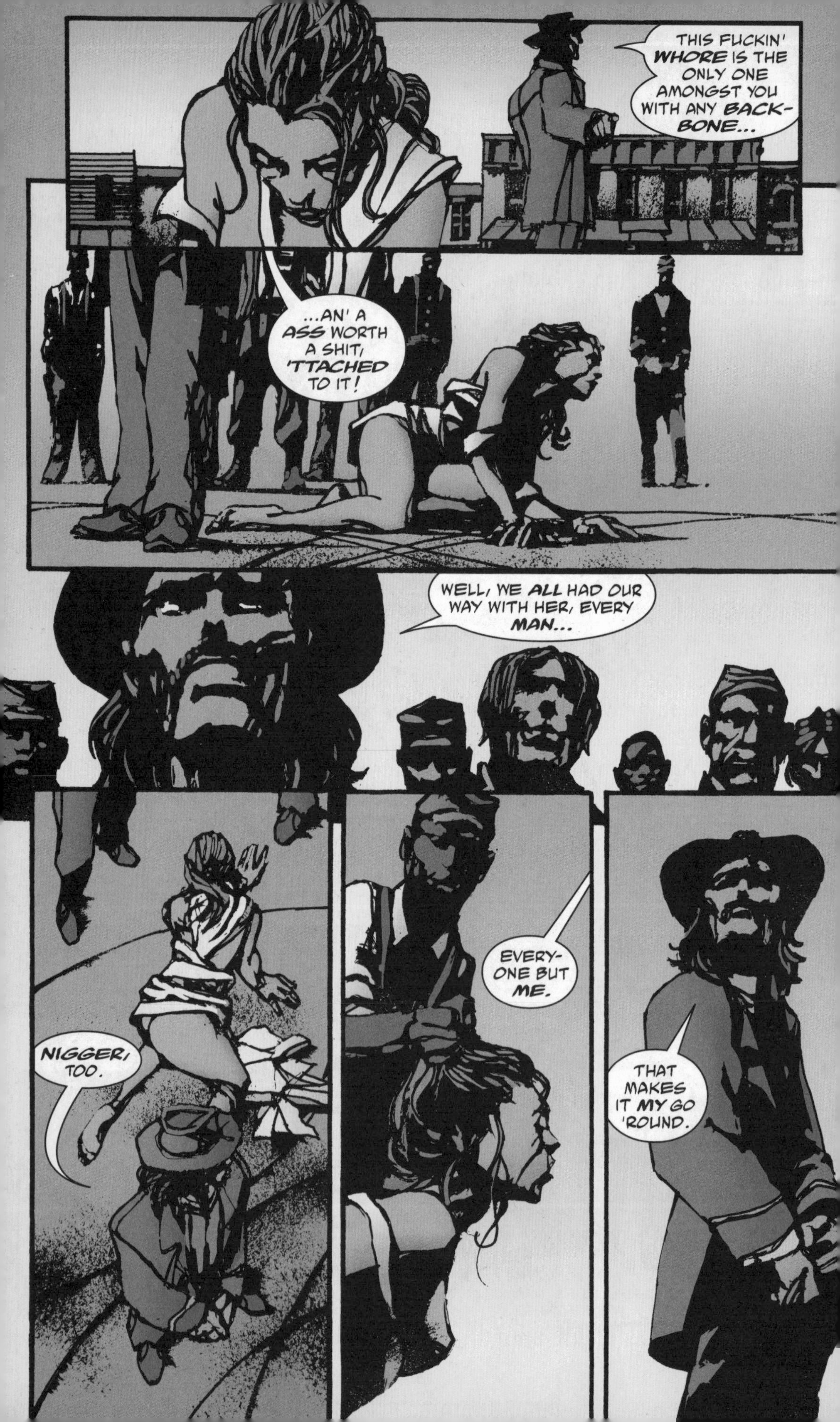
THIS FUCKIN' WHORE IS THE ONLY ONE AMONGST YOU WITH ANY BACK-BONE...
...AN' A ASS WORTH A SHIT, 'TTACHED TO IT!
WELL, WE ALL HAD OUR WAY WITH HER, EVERY MAN...
NIGGER, TOO.
EVERY-ONE BUT ME.
THAT MAKES IT MY GO 'ROUND.

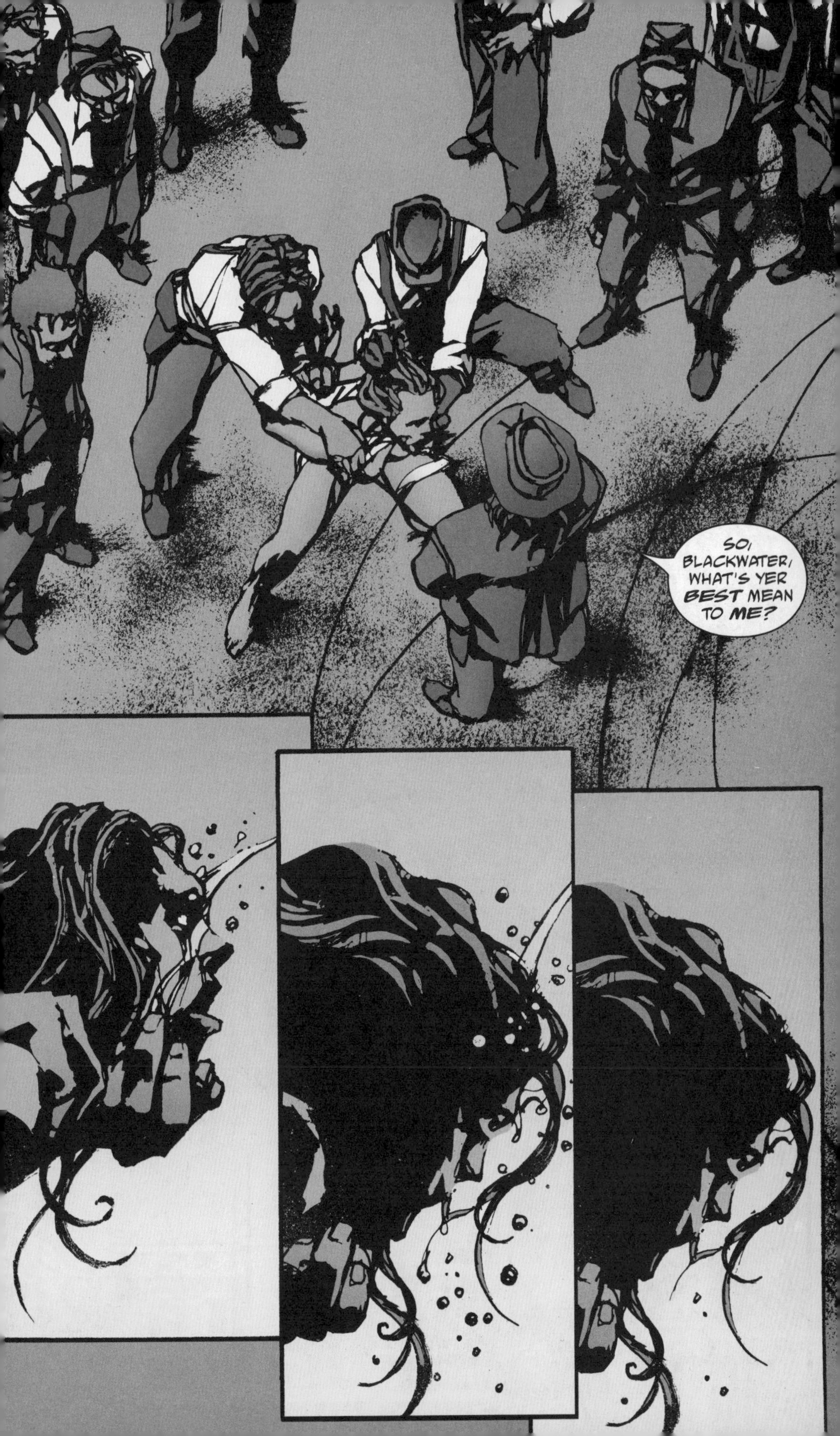
SO, BLACKWATER, WHAT'S YER BEST MEAN TO ME?

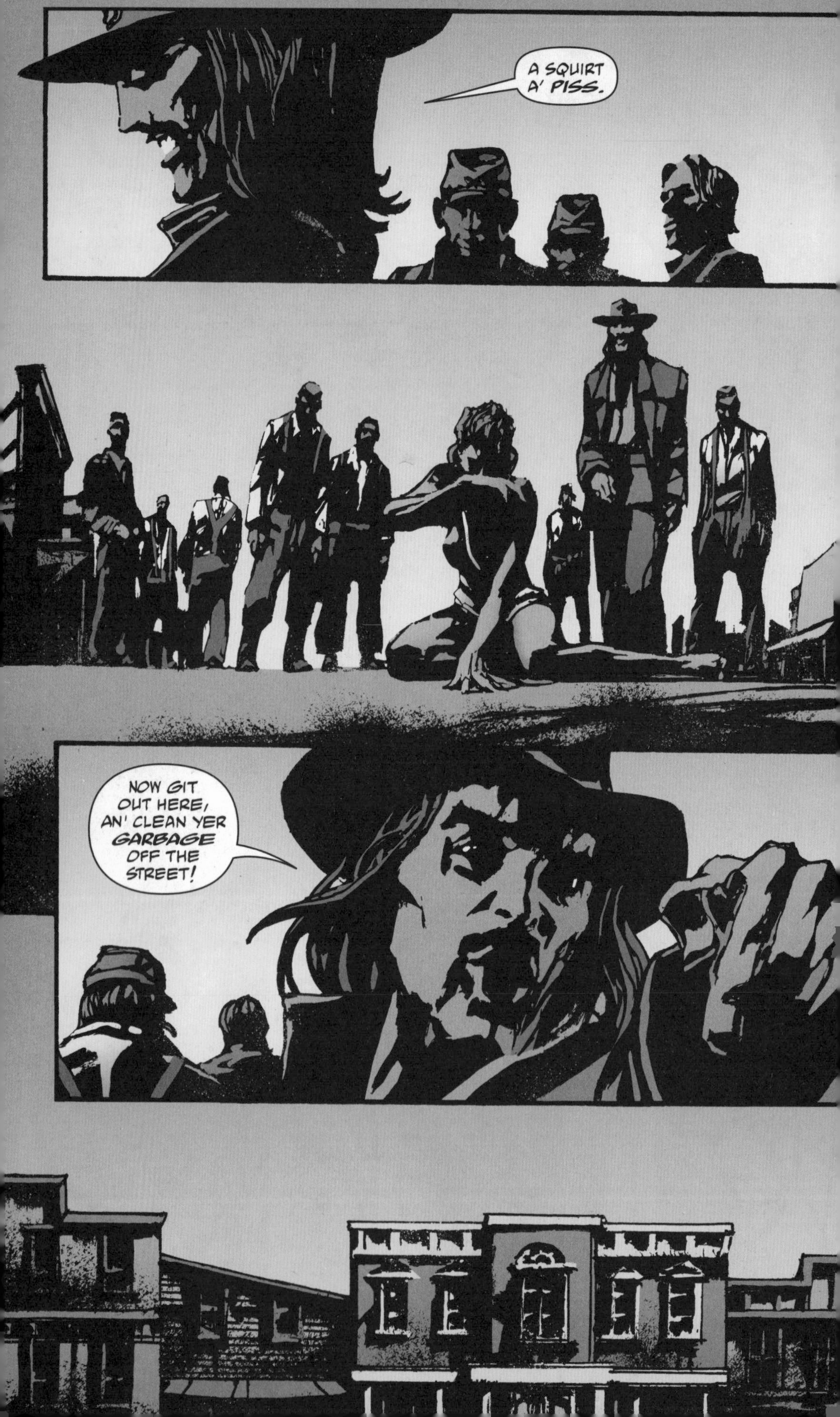
A SQUIRT A' PISS.
NOW GIT OUT HERE, AN' CLEAN YER GARBAGE OFF THE STREET!

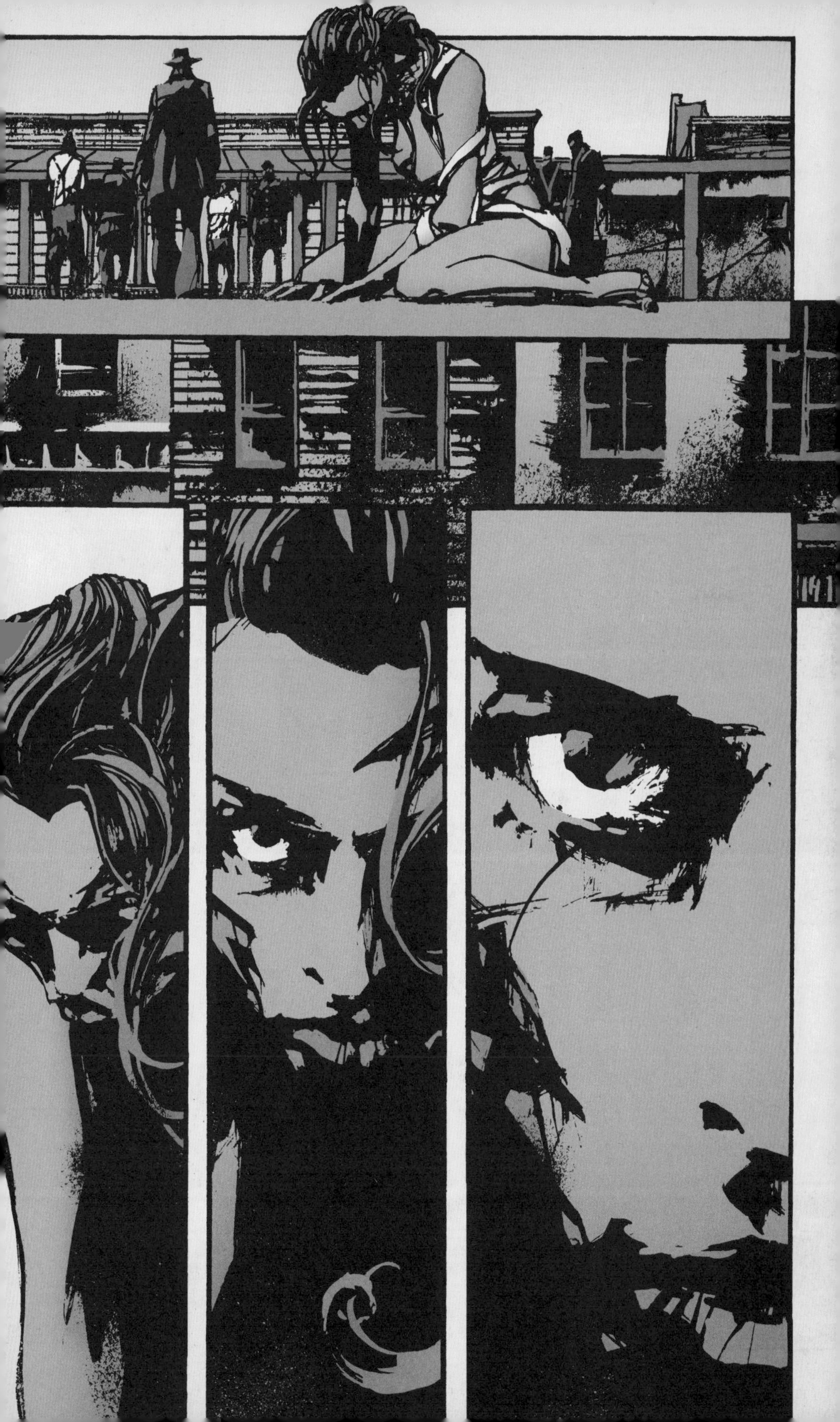

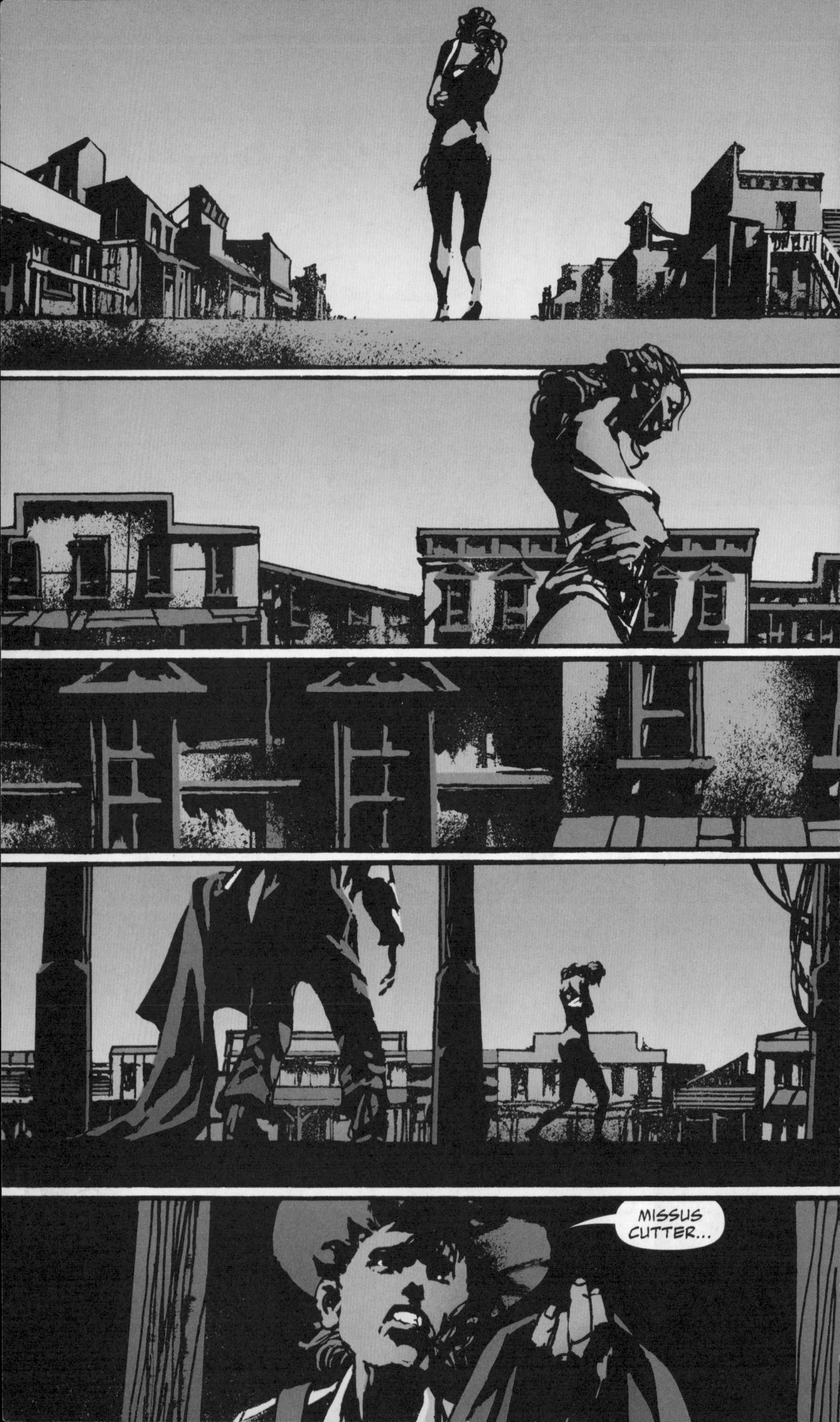
MISSUS CUTTER...

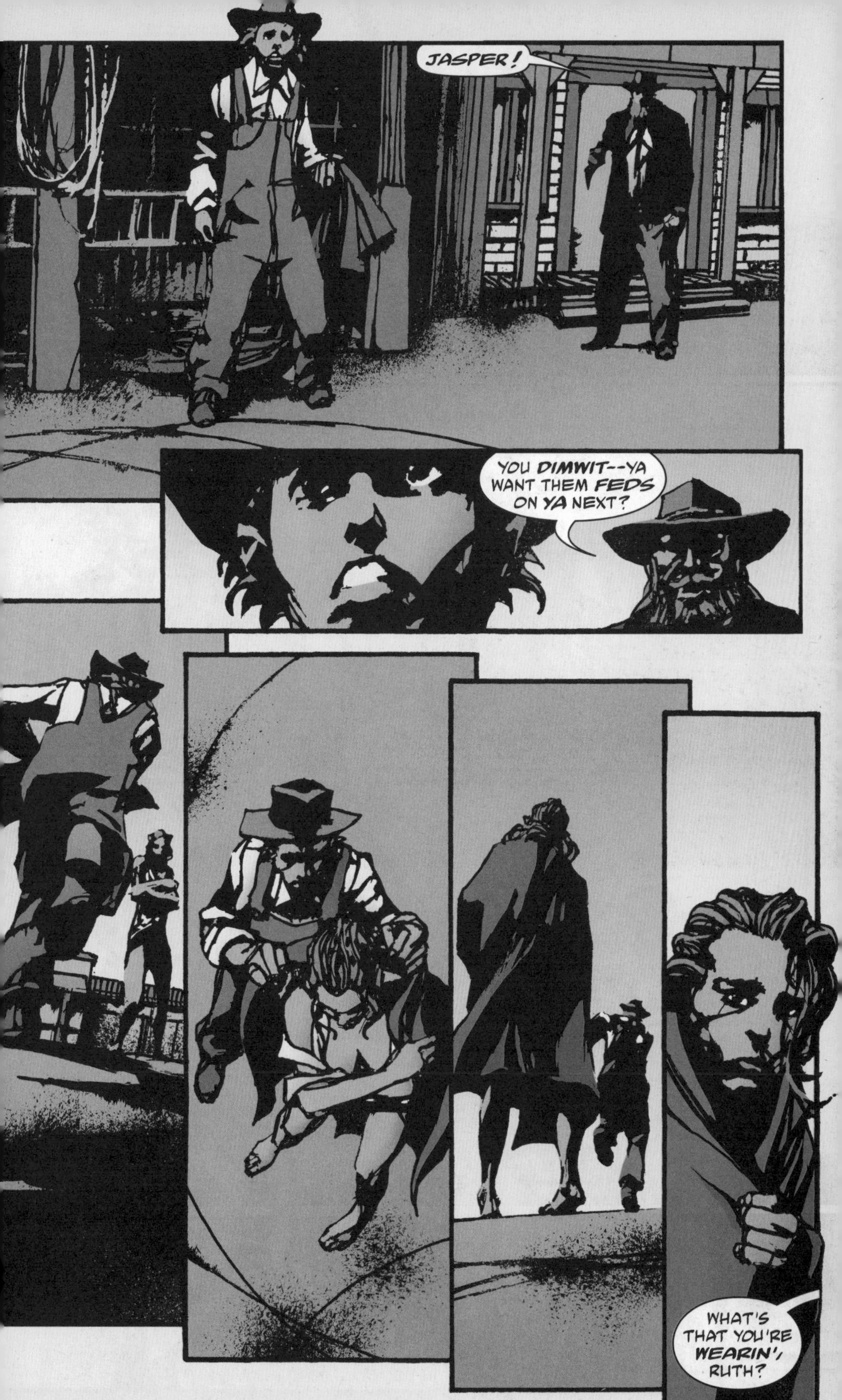
JASPER!
YOU DIMWIT--YA WANT THEM FEDS ON YA NEXT?
WHAT'S THAT YOU'RE WEARIN', RUTH?

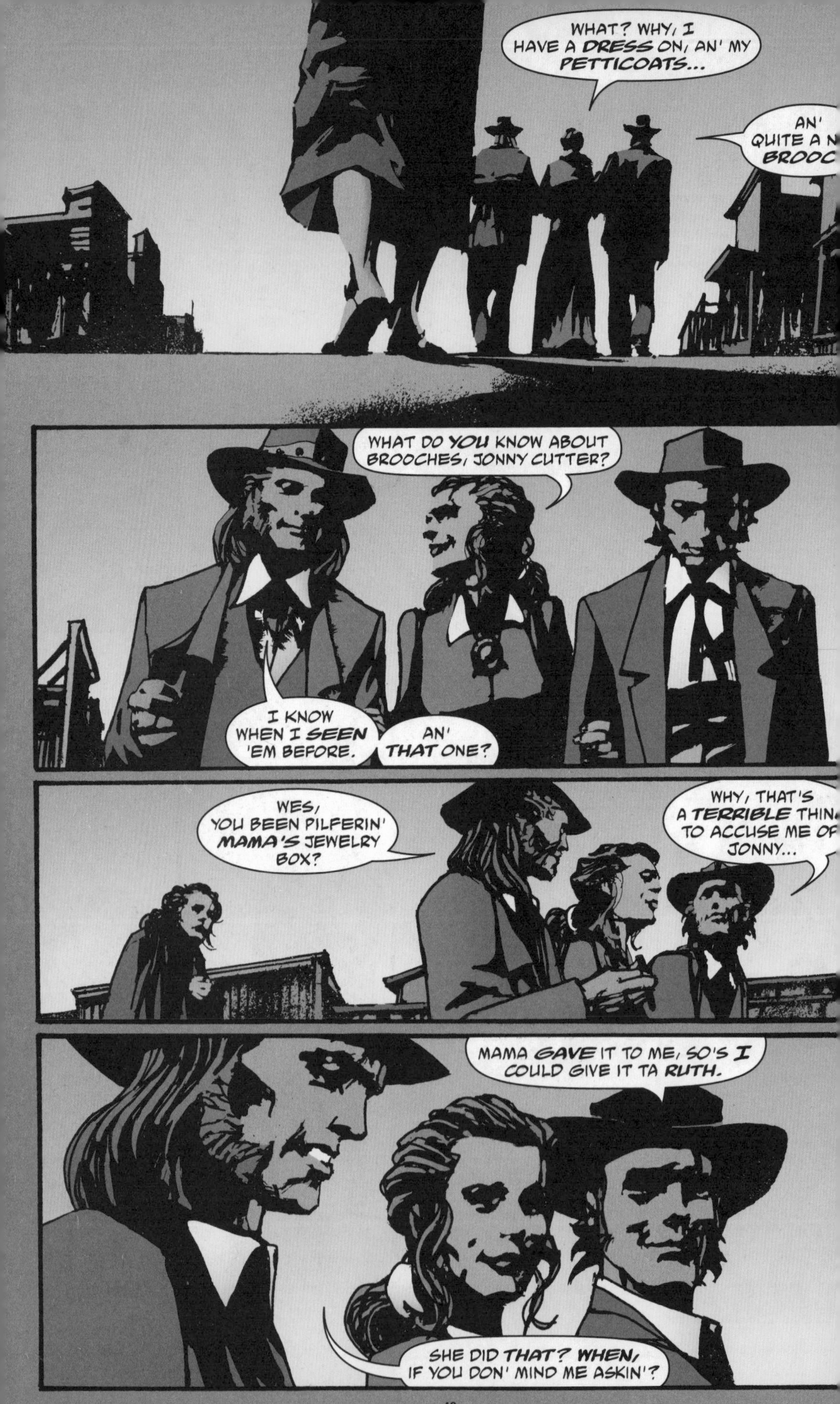

WHAT? WHY, I HAVE A DRESS ON, AN' MY PETTICOATS...
AN' QUITE A N BROOC
WHAT DO YOU KNOW ABOUT BROOCHES, JONNY CUTTER?
I KNOW WHEN I SEEN 'EM BEFORE.
AN' THAT ONE?
WES, YOU BEEN PILFERIN' MAMA'S JEWELRY BOX?
WHY, THAT'S A TERRIBLE THIN TO ACCUSE ME OF JONNY...
MAMA GAVE IT TO ME, SO'S I COULD GIVE IT TA RUTH.
SHE DID THAT? WHEN, IF YOU DON' MIND ME ASKIN'?

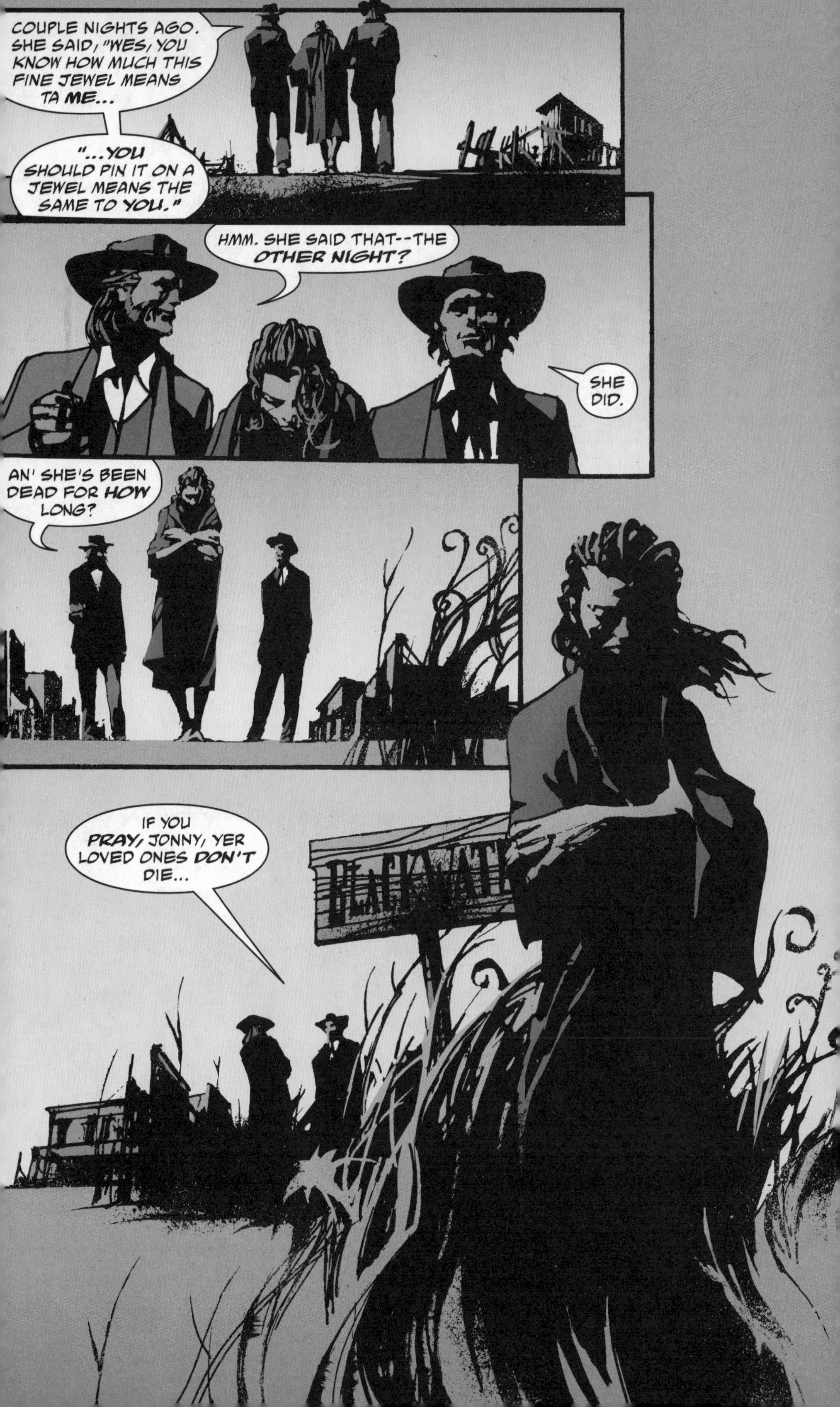
COUPLE NIGHTS AGO. SHE SAID, "WES, YOU KNOW HOW MUCH THIS FINE JEWEL MEANS TA ME...
"...YOU SHOULD PIN IT ON A JEWEL MEANS THE SAME TO YOU."
HMM. SHE SAID THAT--THE OTHER NIGHT?
SHE DID.
AN' SHE'S BEEN DEAD FOR HOW LONG?
IF YOU PRAY, JONNY, YER LOVED ONES DON'T DIE...

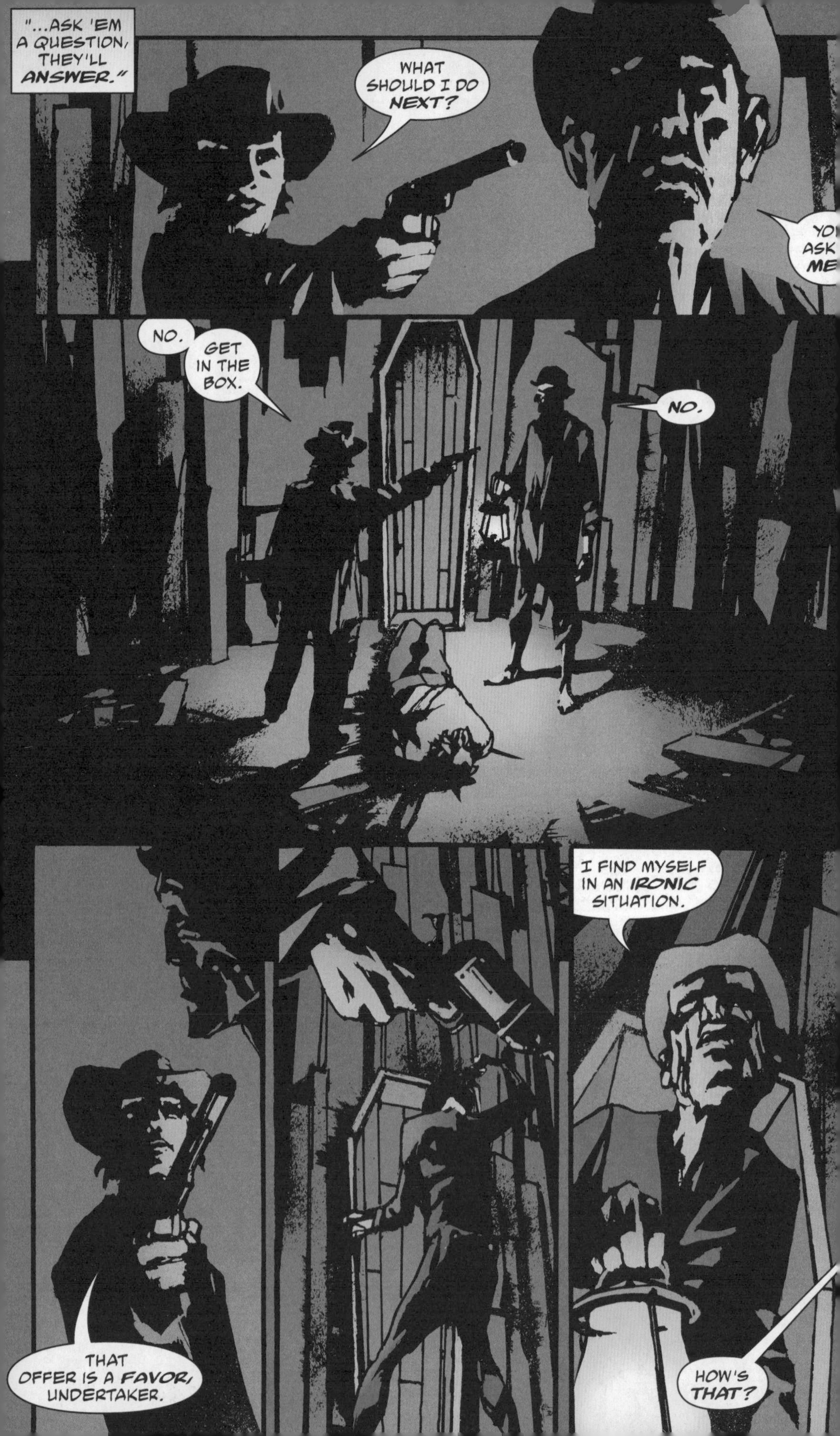
"...ASK 'EM A QUESTION, THEY'LL ANSWER."
WHAT SHOULD I DO NEXT?
YO ASK ME
NO.
GET IN THE BOX.
NO.
THAT OFFER IS A FAVOR, UNDERTAKER.
I FIND MYSELF IN AN IRONIC SITUATION.
HOW'S THAT?

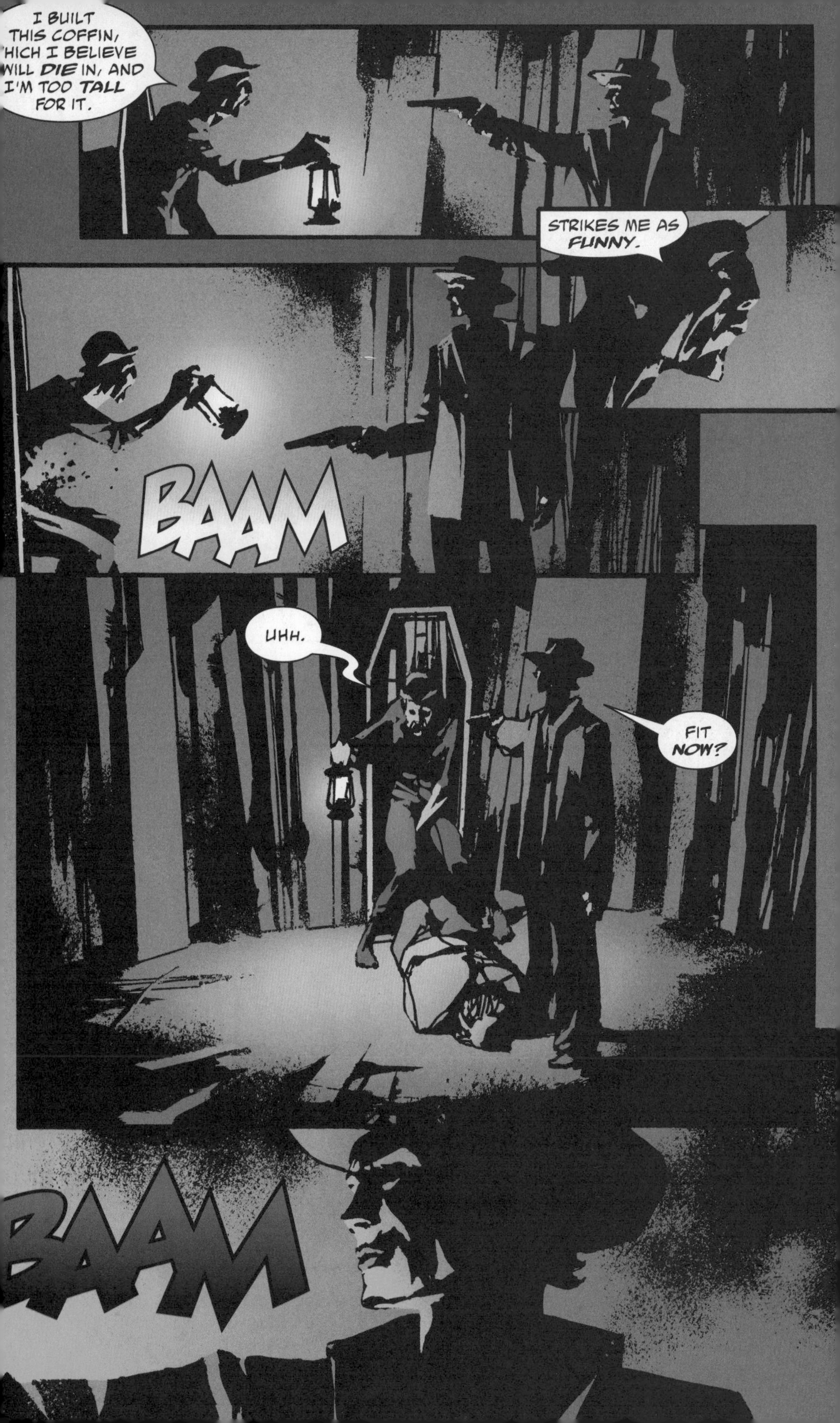
I BUILT THIS COFFIN, HICH I BELIEVE WILL DIE IN, AND I'M TOO TALL FOR IT.
STRIKES ME AS FUNNY.
BAAM
UHH.
FIT NOW?
BAAM

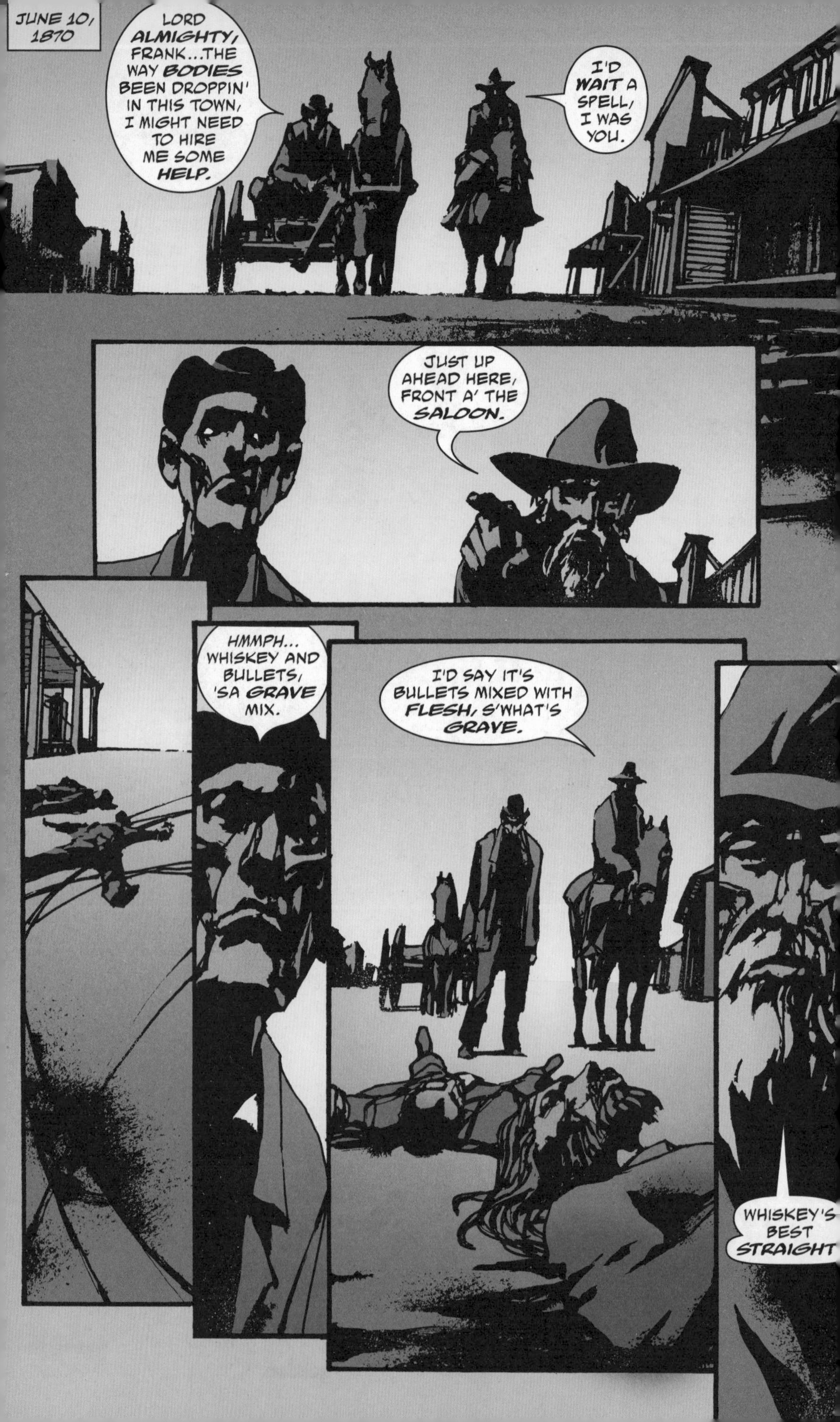
JUNE 10, 1870
LORD ALMIGHTY, FRANK...THE WAY BODIES BEEN DROPPIN' IN THIS TOWN, I MIGHT NEED TO HIRE ME SOME HELP.
I'D WAIT A SPELL, I WAS YOU.
JUST UP AHEAD HERE, FRONT A' THE SALOON.
HMMPH... WHISKEY AND BULLETS, 'SA GRAVE MIX.
I'D SAY IT'S BULLETS MIXED WITH FLESH, S'WHAT'S GRAVE.
WHISKEY'S BEST STRAIGHT

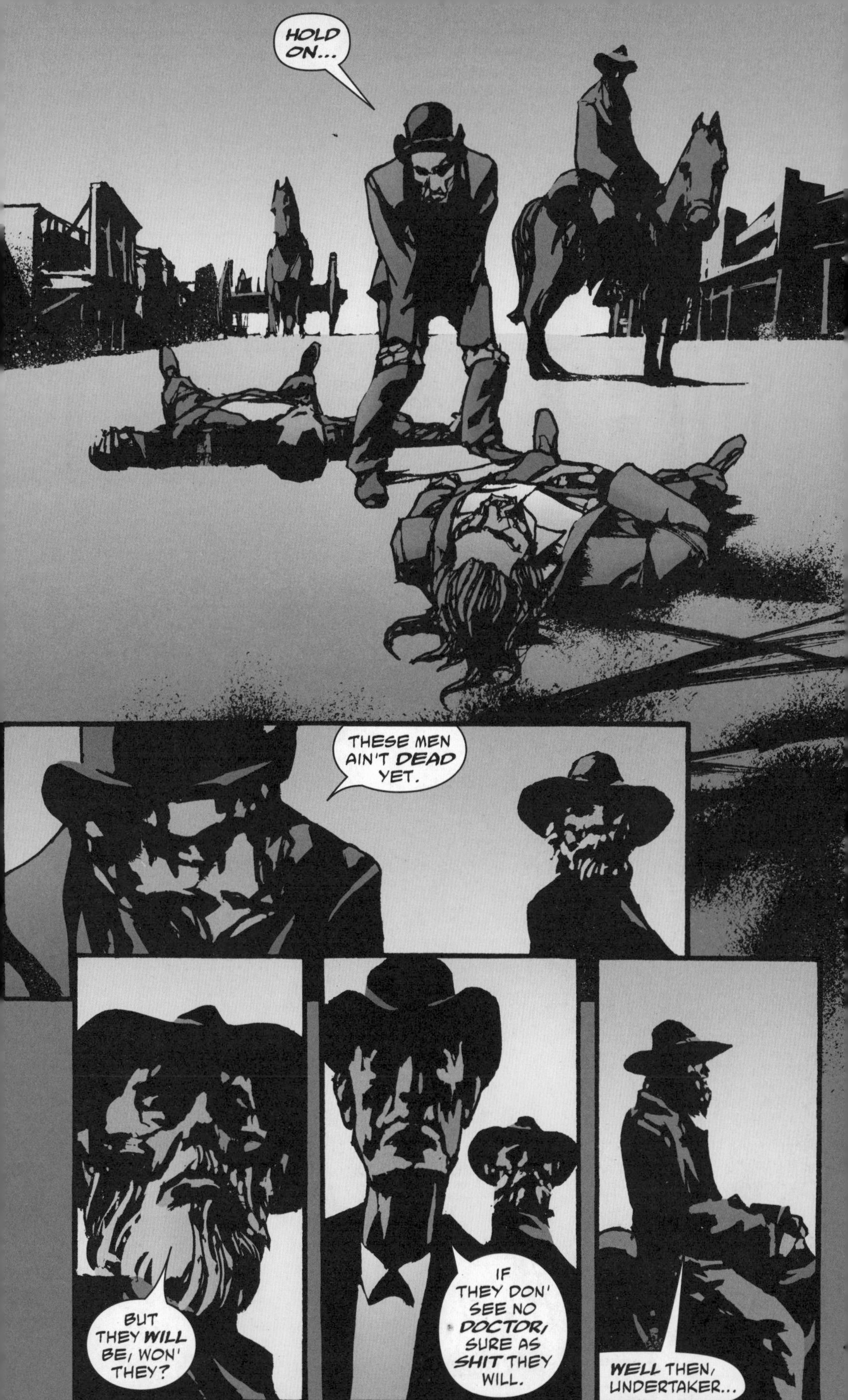
HOLD ON...
THESE MEN AIN'T DEAD YET.
BUT THEY WILL BE, WON' THEY?
IF THEY DON' SEE NO DOCTOR, SURE AS SHIT THEY WILL.
WELL THEN, UNDERTAKER...

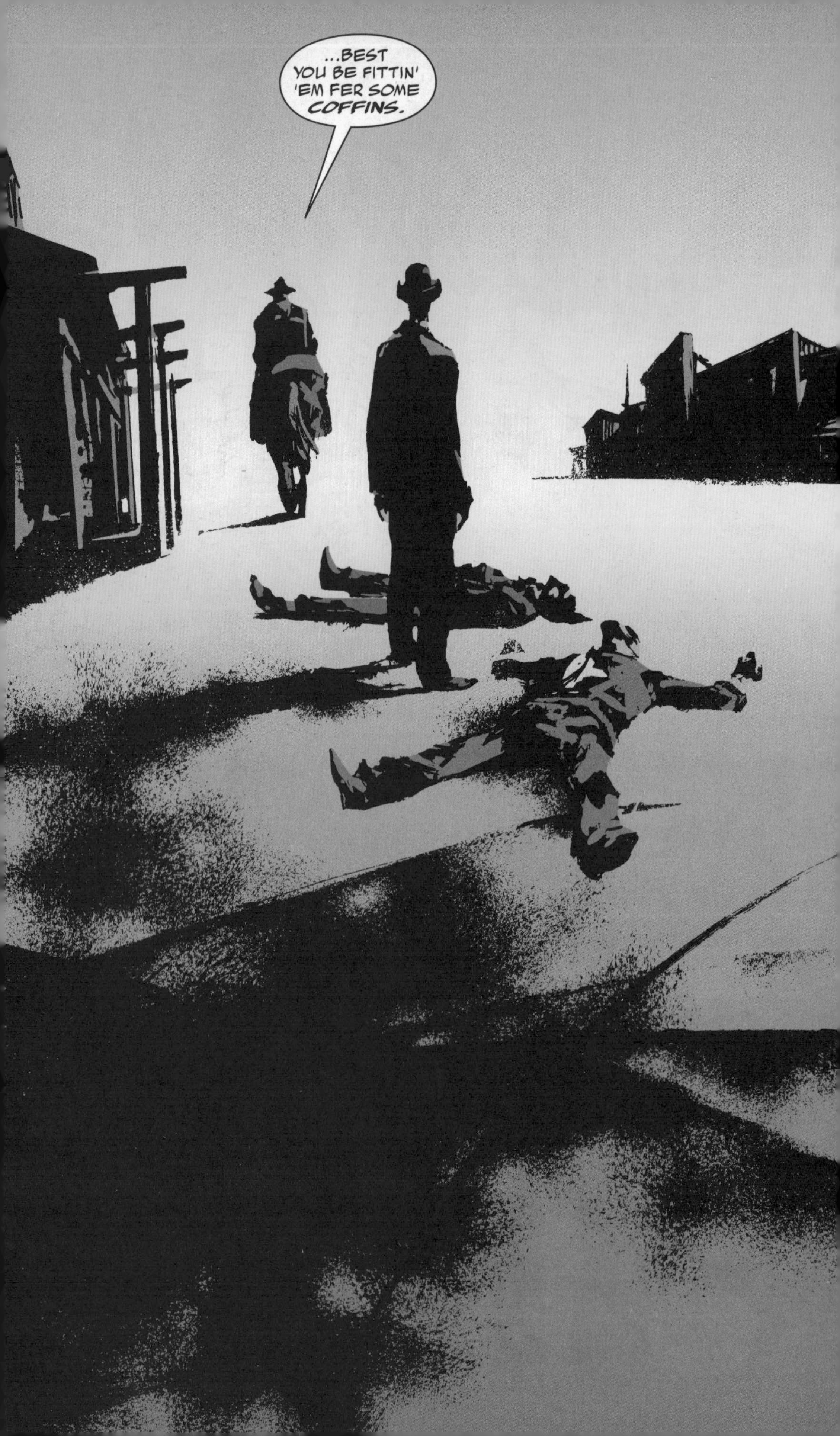
...BEST YOU BE FITTIN' 'EM FER SOME COFFINS.

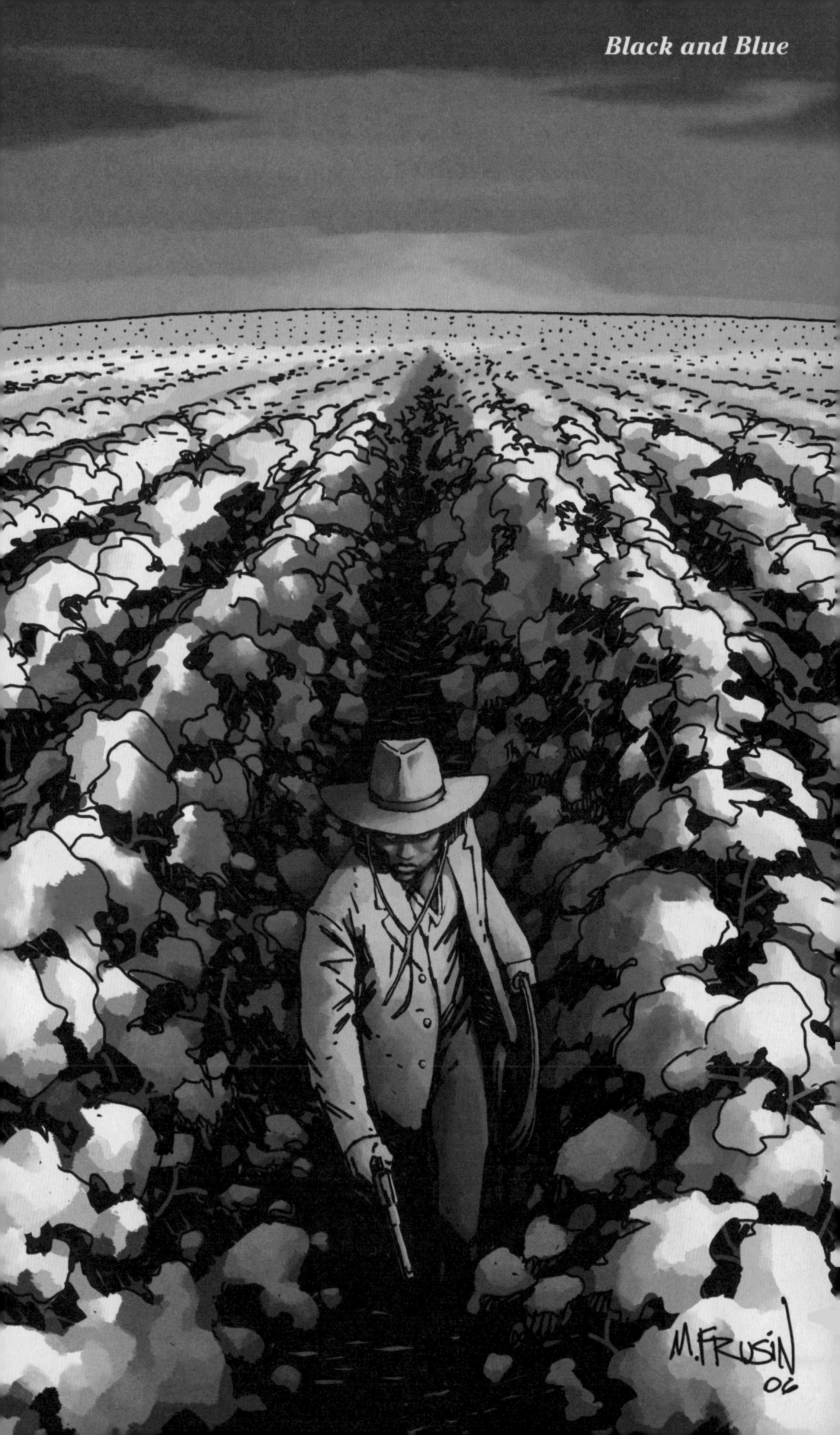
M.FRUSIN
06

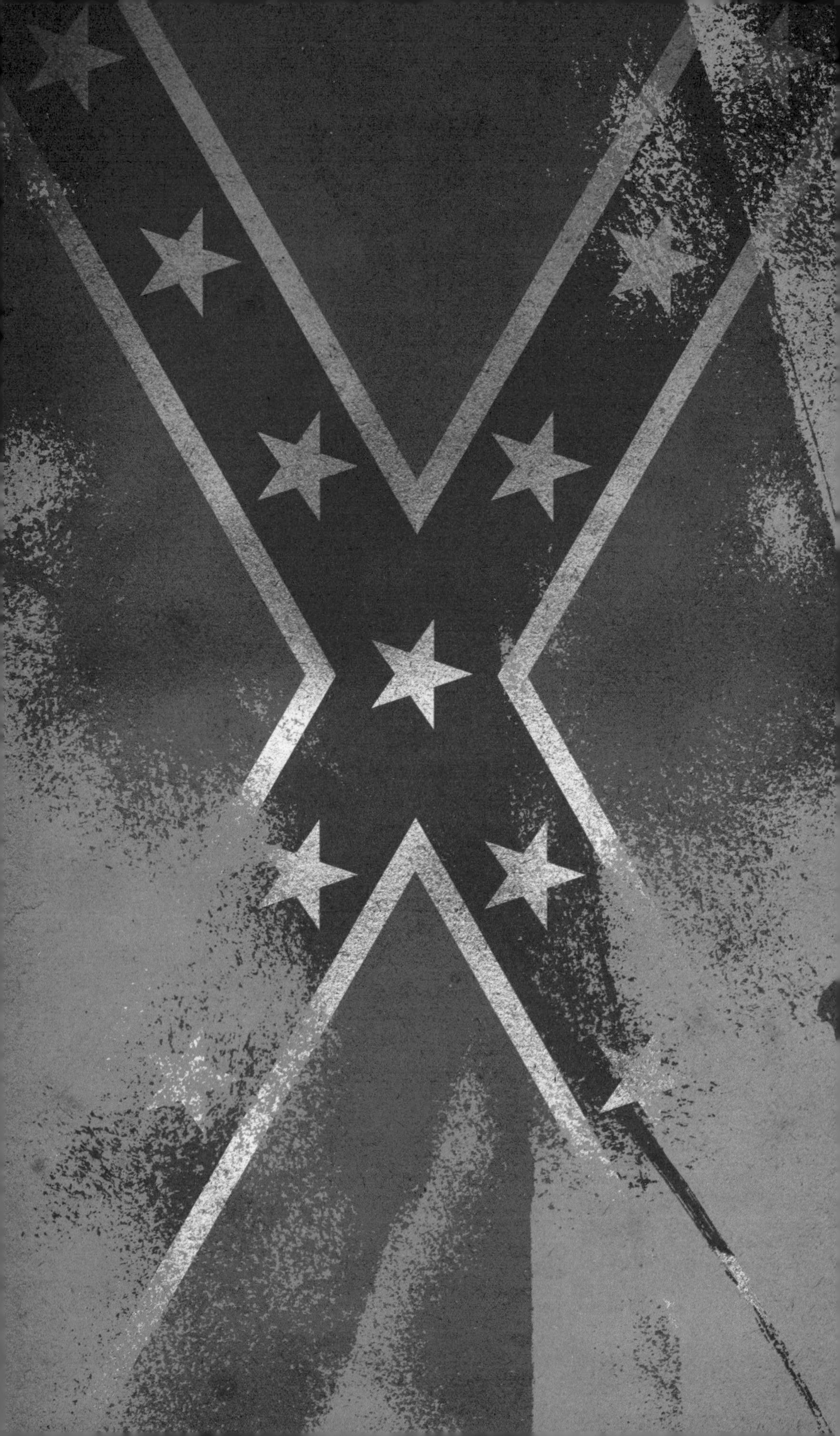

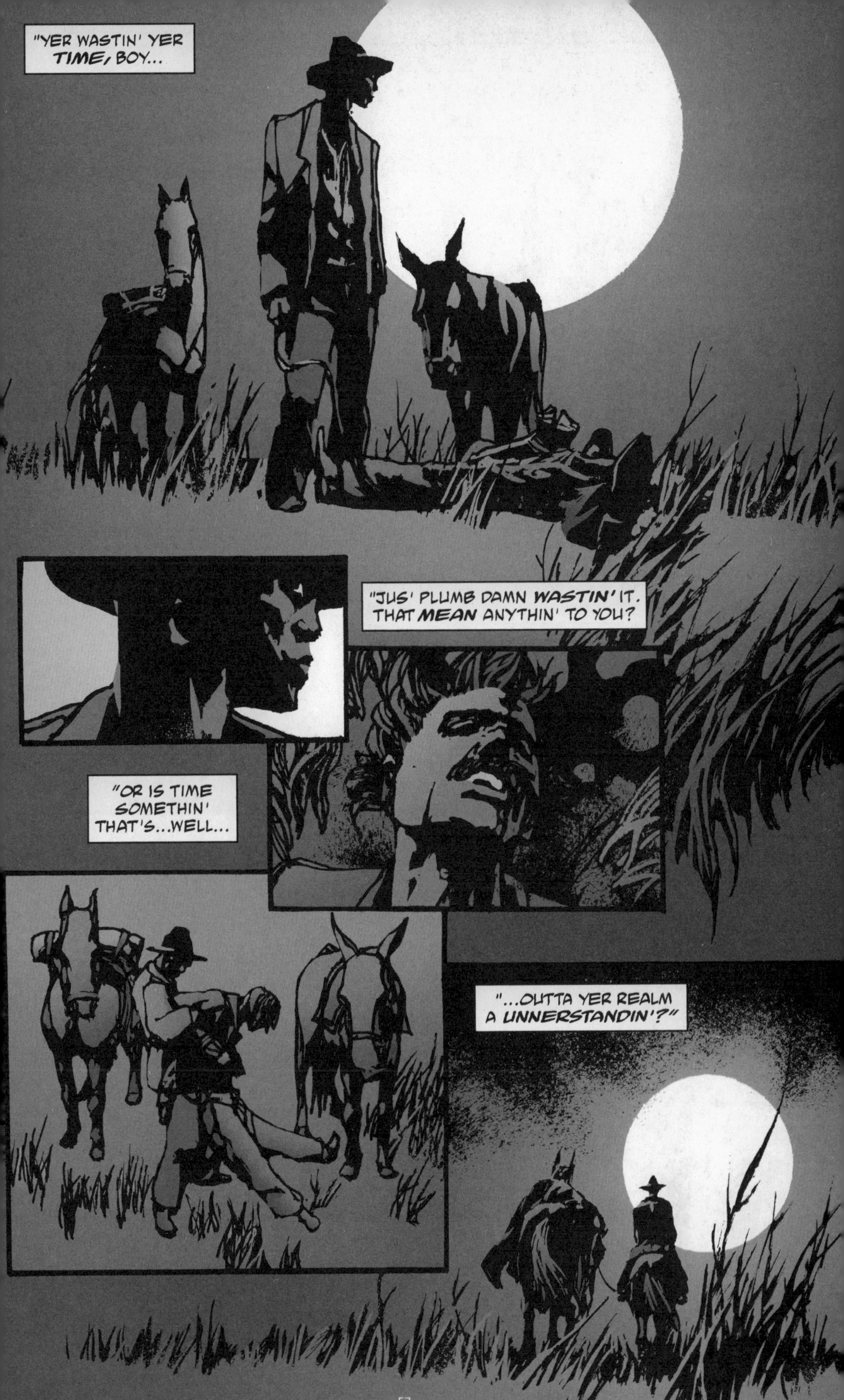
"YER WASTIN' YER TIME, BOY...
"JUS' PLUMB DAMN WASTIN' IT. THAT MEAN ANYTHIN' TO YOU?
"OR IS TIME SOMETHIN' THAT'S...WELL...
"...OUTTA YER REALM A UNNERSTANDIN'?"

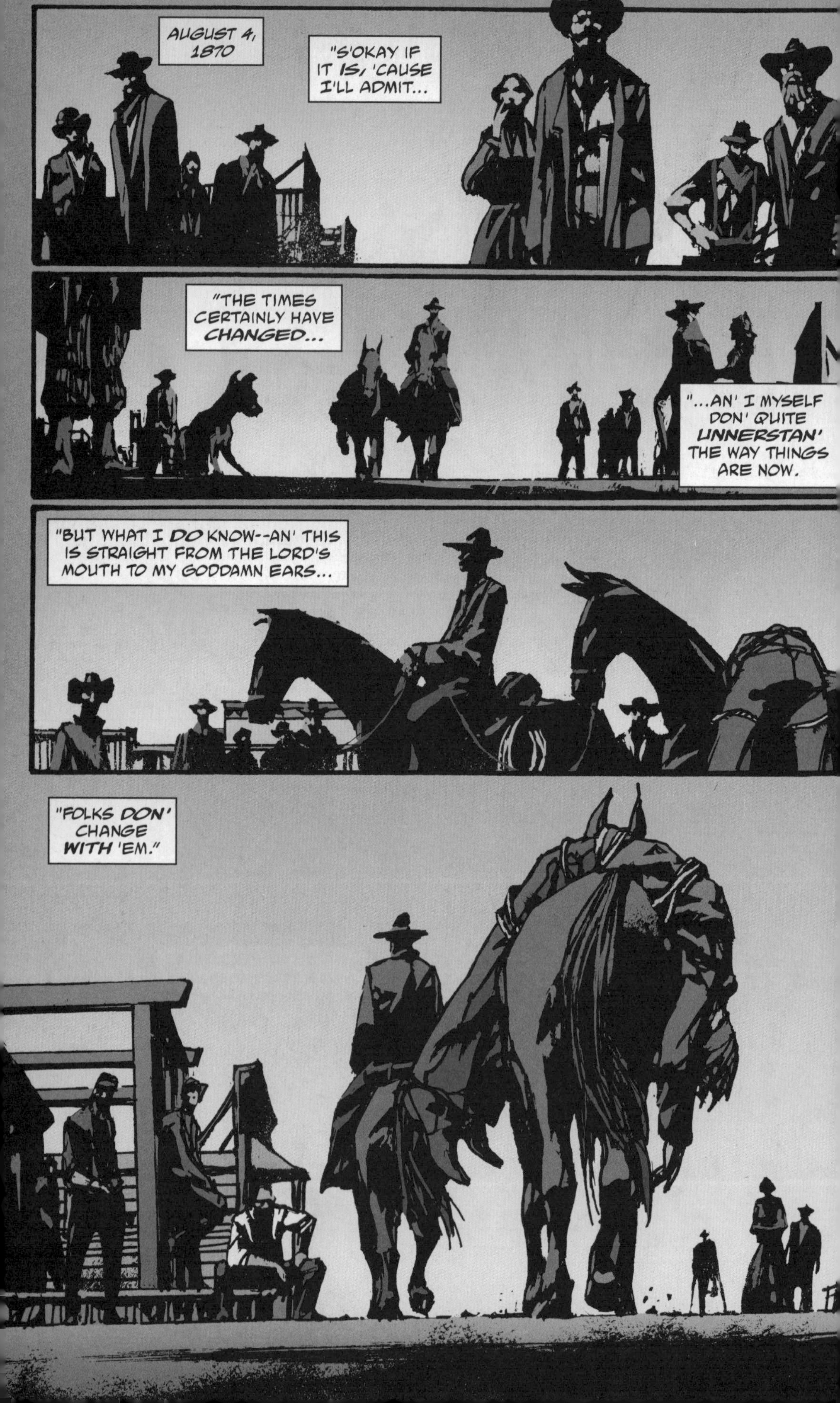
AUGUST 4, 1870
"S'OKAY IF IT IS, 'CAUSE I'LL ADMIT...
"THE TIMES CERTAINLY HAVE CHANGED...
"...AN' I MYSELF DON' QUITE UNNERSTAN' THE WAY THINGS ARE NOW.
"BUT WHAT I DO KNOW--AN' THIS IS STRAIGHT FROM THE LORD'S MOUTH TO MY GODDAMN EARS...
"FOLKS DON' CHANGE WITH 'EM."

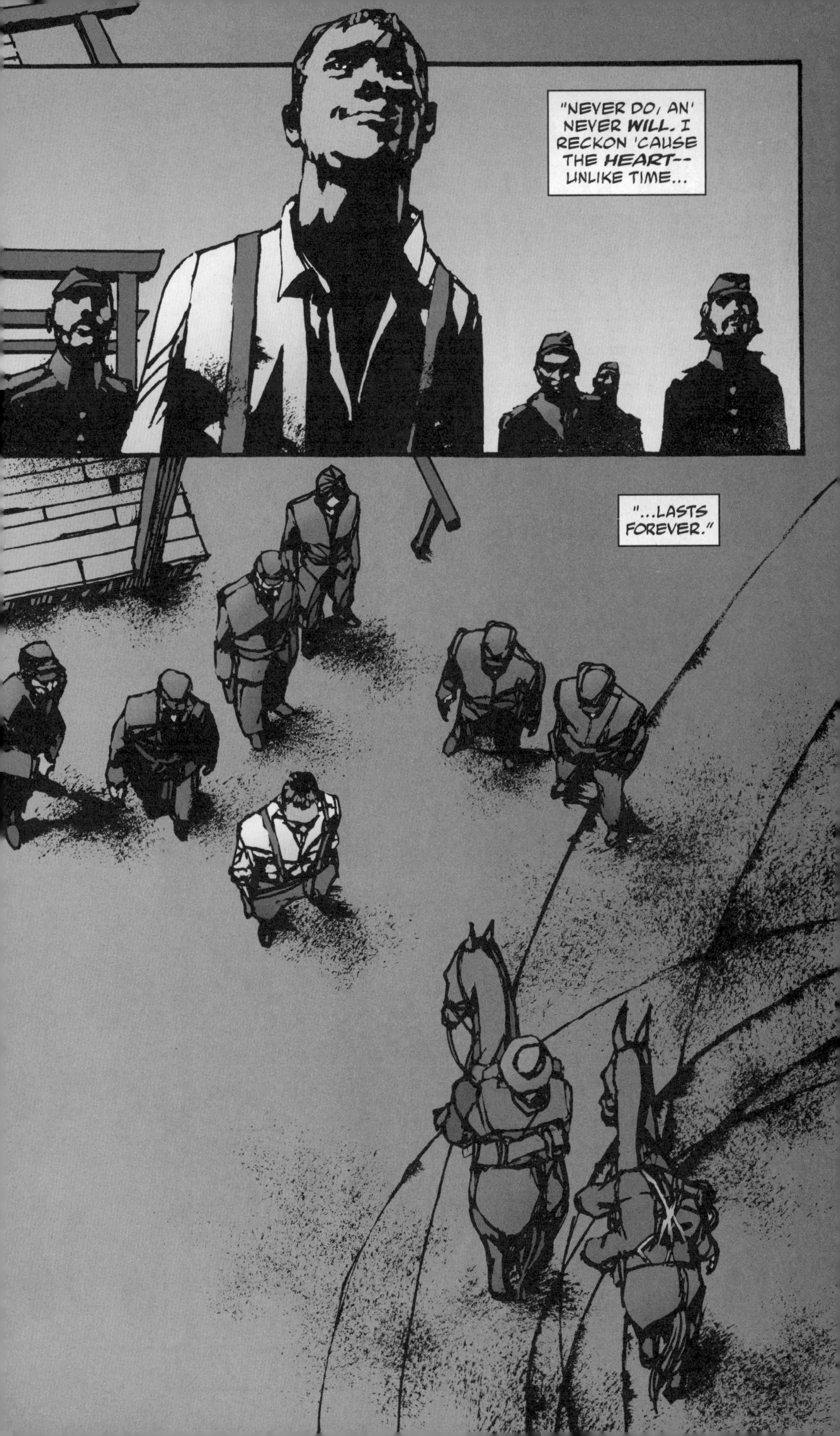
"NEVER DO, AN' NEVER **WILL**. I RECKON 'CAUSE THE **HEART**-- UNLIKE TIME...
"...LASTS FOREVER."

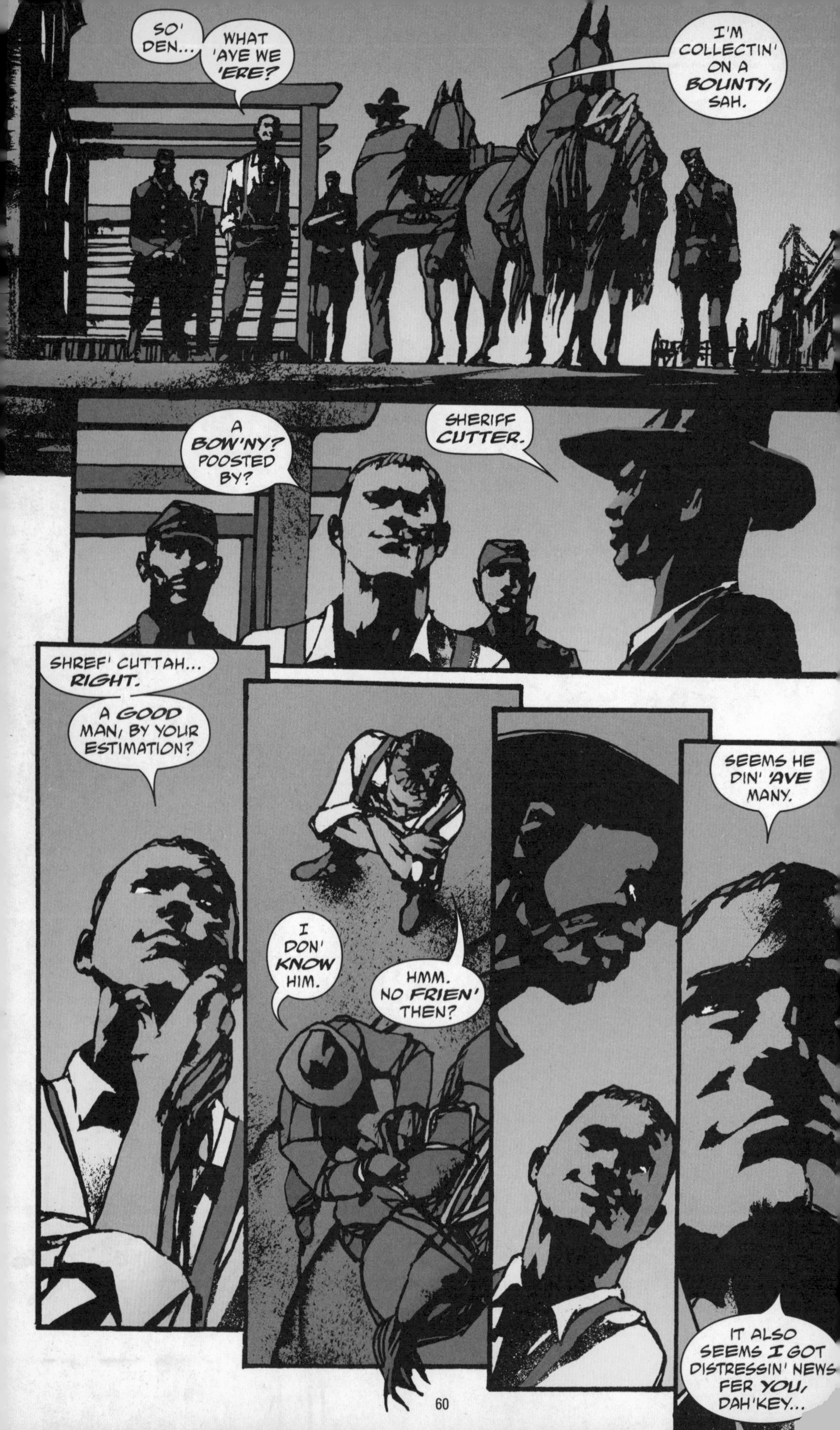
SO' DEN...
WHAT 'AYE WE 'ERE?
I'M COLLECTIN' ON A BOUNTY, SAH.
A BOW'NY? POOSTED BY?
SHERIFF CUTTER.
SHREF' CUTTAH... RIGHT.
A GOOD MAN, BY YOUR ESTIMATION?
I DON' KNOW HIM.
HMM. NO FRIEN' THEN?
SEEMS HE DIN' 'AVE MANY.
IT ALSO SEEMS I GOT DISTRESSIN' NEWS FER YOU, DAH'KEY...

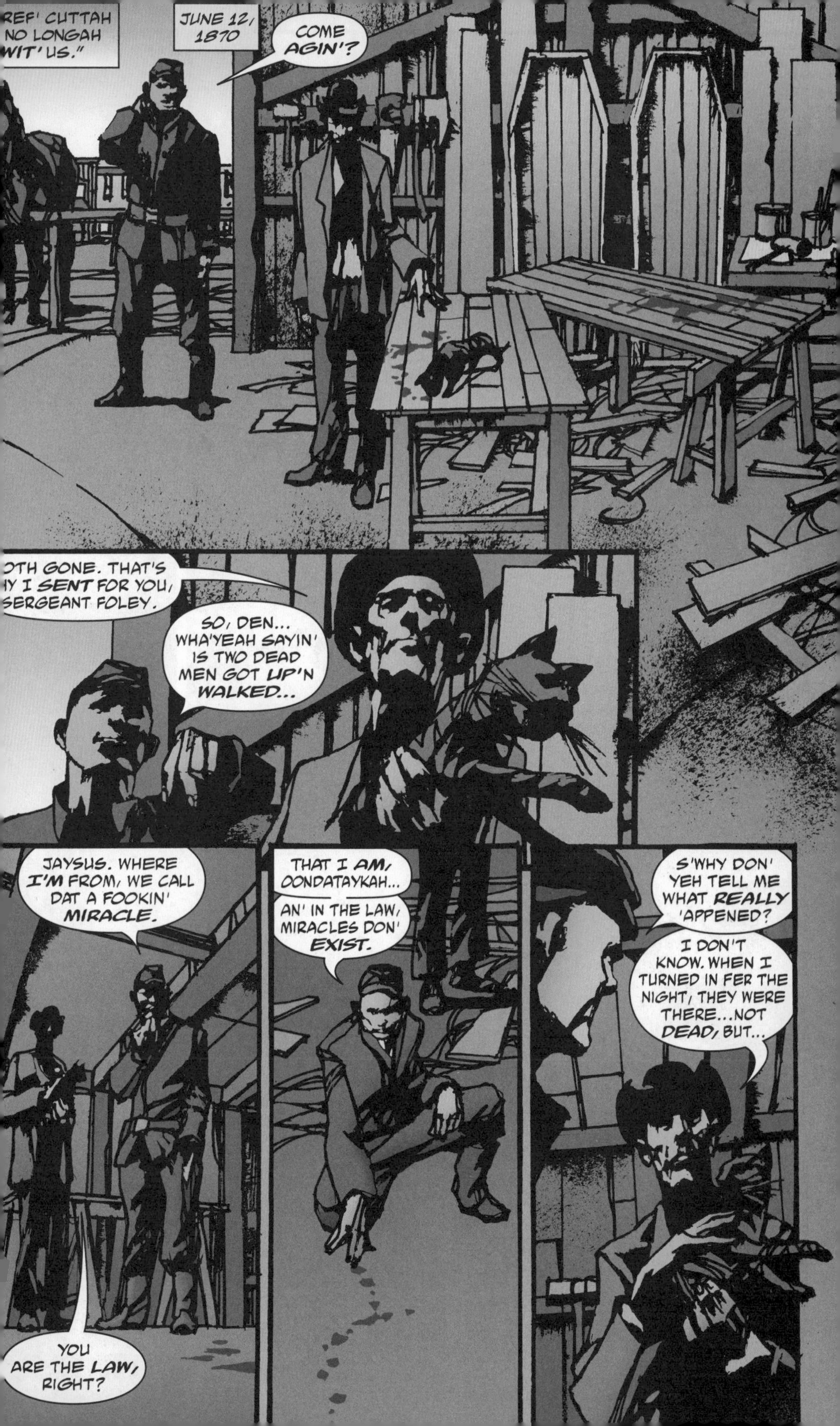
REF' CUTTAH NO LONGAH WIT' US."
JUNE 12, 1870
COME AGIN'?
OTH GONE. THAT'S Y I SENT FOR YOU, SERGEANT FOLEY.
SO, DEN... WHA'YEAH SAYIN' IS TWO DEAD MEN GOT UP'N WALKED...
JAYSUS. WHERE I'M FROM, WE CALL DAT A FOOKIN' MIRACLE.
YOU ARE THE LAW, RIGHT?
THAT I AM, OONDATAYKAH...
AN' IN THE LAW, MIRACLES DON' EXIST.
S'WHY DON' YEH TELL ME WHAT REALLY 'APPENED?
I DON'T KNOW. WHEN I TURNED IN FER THE NIGHT, THEY WERE THERE...NOT DEAD, BUT...

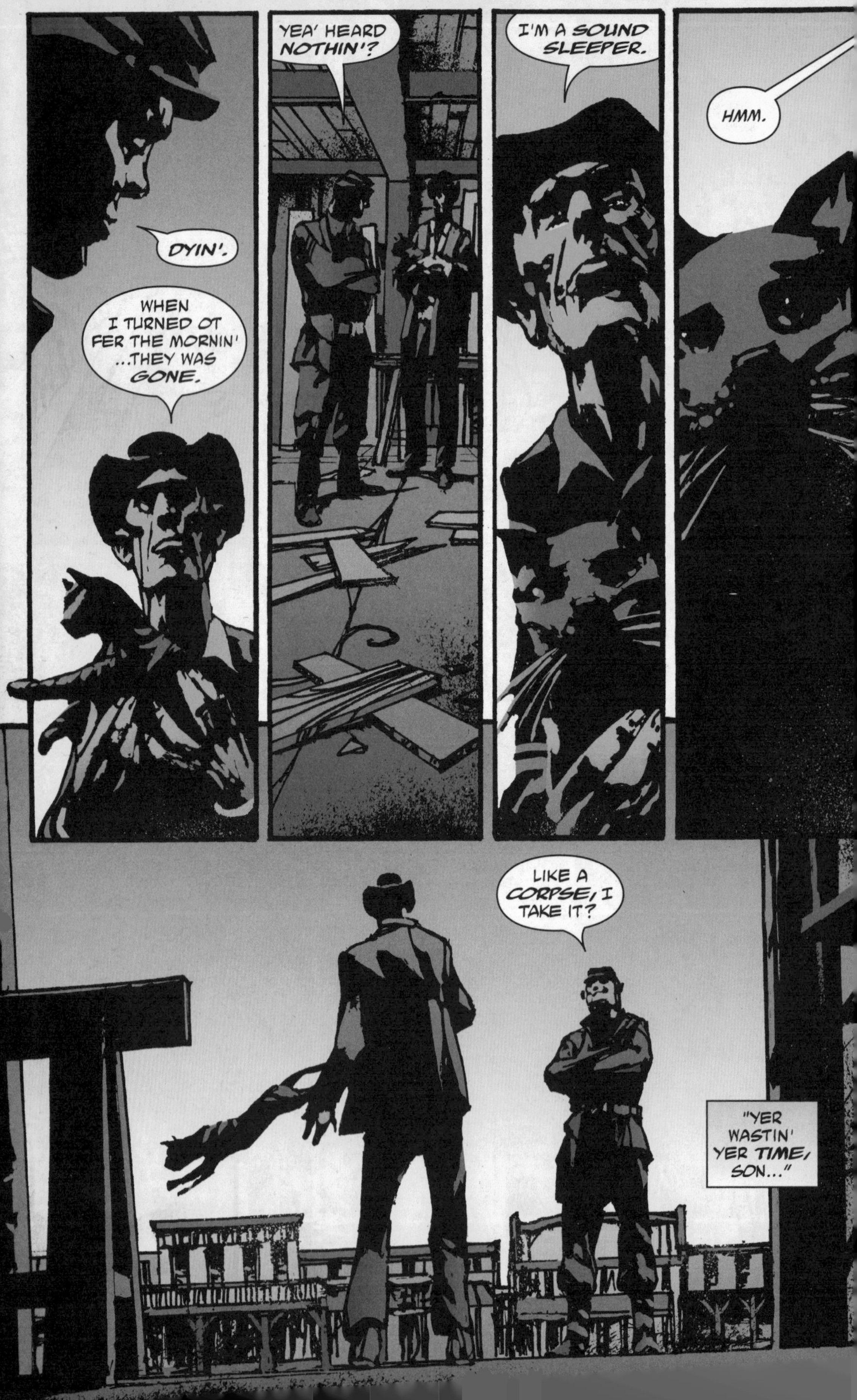
DYIN'.
WHEN I TURNED OT FER THE MORNIN' ...THEY WAS GONE.
YEA' HEARD NOTHIN'?
I'M A SOUND SLEEPER.
HMM.
LIKE A CORPSE, I TAKE IT?
"YER WASTIN' YER TIME, SON..."

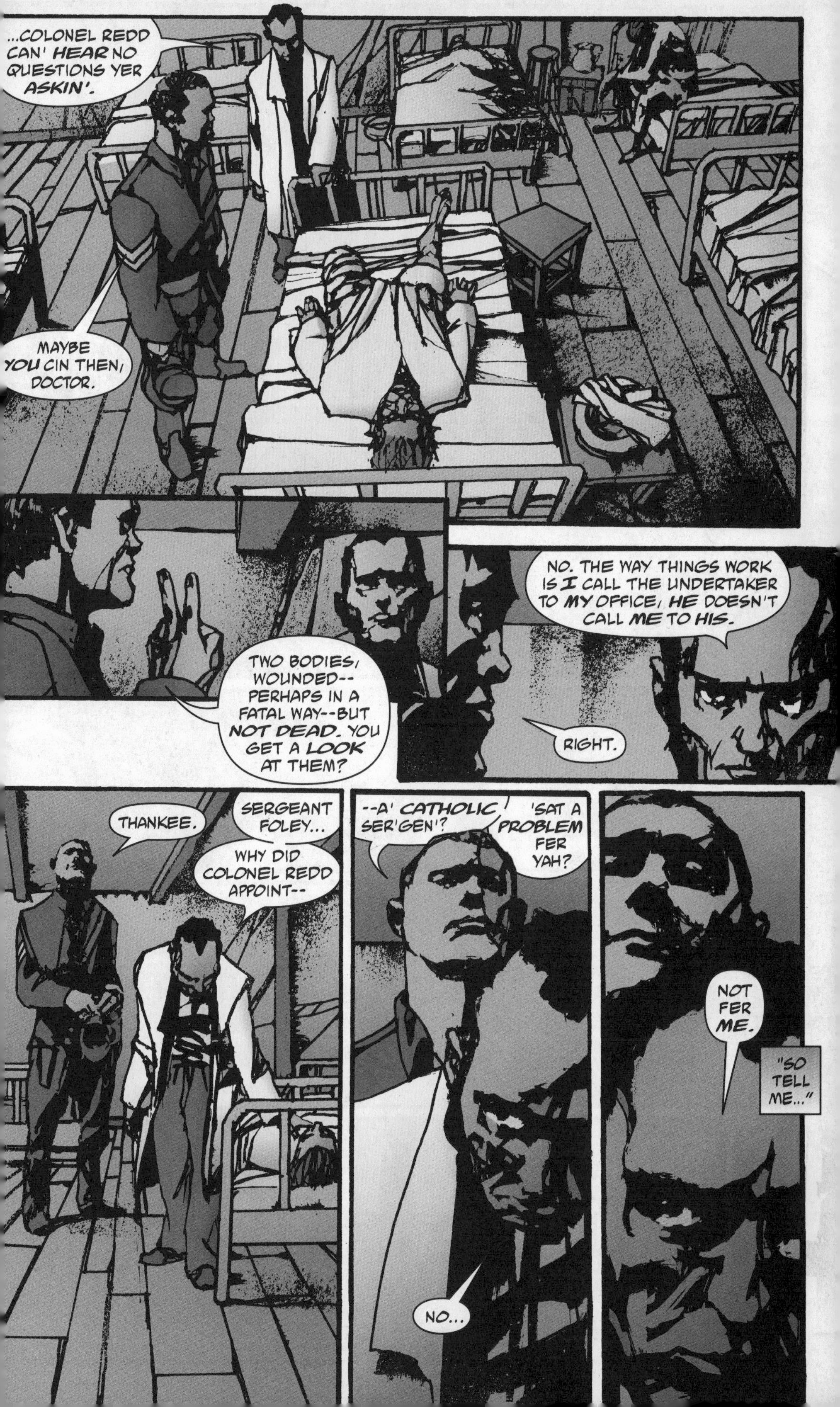
...COLONEL REDD CAN' HEAR NO QUESTIONS YER ASKIN'.
MAYBE YOU CIN THEN, DOCTOR.
TWO BODIES, WOUNDED--PERHAPS IN A FATAL WAY--BUT NOT DEAD. YOU GET A LOOK AT THEM?
NO. THE WAY THINGS WORK IS I CALL THE UNDERTAKER TO MY OFFICE, HE DOESN'T CALL ME TO HIS.
RIGHT.
THANKEE.
SERGEANT FOLEY...
WHY DID COLONEL REDD APPOINT--
--A' CATHOLIC SER'GEN'?
'SAT A PROBLEM FER YAH?
NO...
NOT FER ME.
"SO TELL ME..."

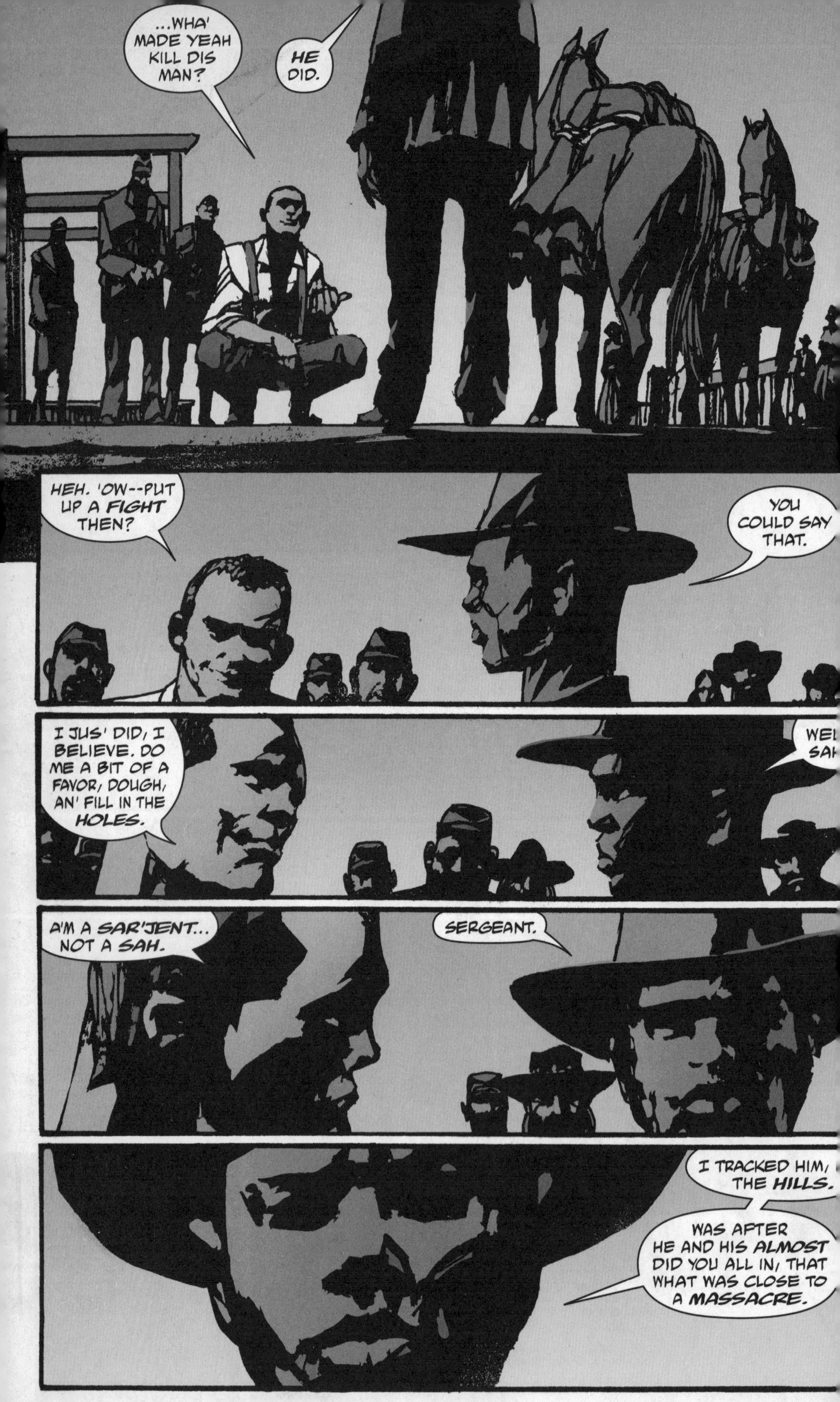
...WHA' MADE YEAH KILL DIS MAN?
HE DID.
HEH. 'OW--PUT UP A FIGHT THEN?
YOU COULD SAY THAT.
I JUS' DID, I BELIEVE. DO ME A BIT OF A FAVOR, DOUGH, AN' FILL IN THE HOLES.
A'M A SAR'JENT... NOT A SAH.
SERGEANT.
I TRACKED HIM, THE HILLS.
WAS AFTER HE AND HIS ALMOST DID YOU ALL IN, THAT WHAT WAS CLOSE TO A MASSACRE.

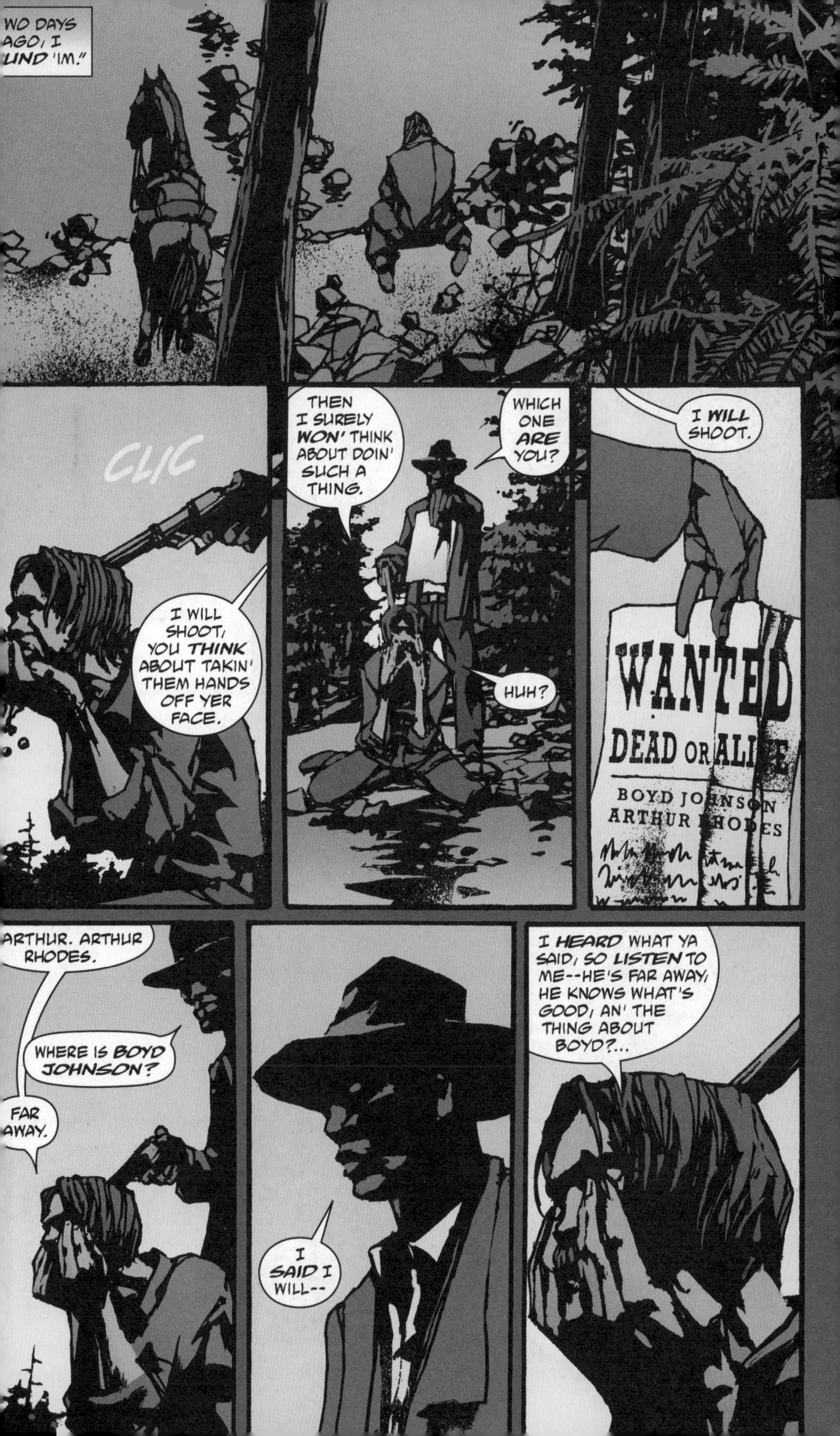

WO DAYS AGO, I UND 'IM."
CLIC
I WILL SHOOT, YOU THINK ABOUT TAKIN' THEM HANDS OFF YER FACE.
THEN I SURELY WON' THINK ABOUT DOIN' SUCH A THING.
WHICH ONE ARE YOU?
HUH?
I WILL SHOOT.
WANTED
DEAD OR ALI
BOYD JOHNSON
ARTHUR RHODES
ARTHUR. ARTHUR RHODES.
WHERE IS BOYD JOHNSON?
FAR AWAY.
I SAID I WILL--
I HEARD WHAT YA SAID, SO LISTEN TO ME--HE'S FAR AWAY, HE KNOWS WHAT'S GOOD, AN' THE THING ABOUT BOYD?...

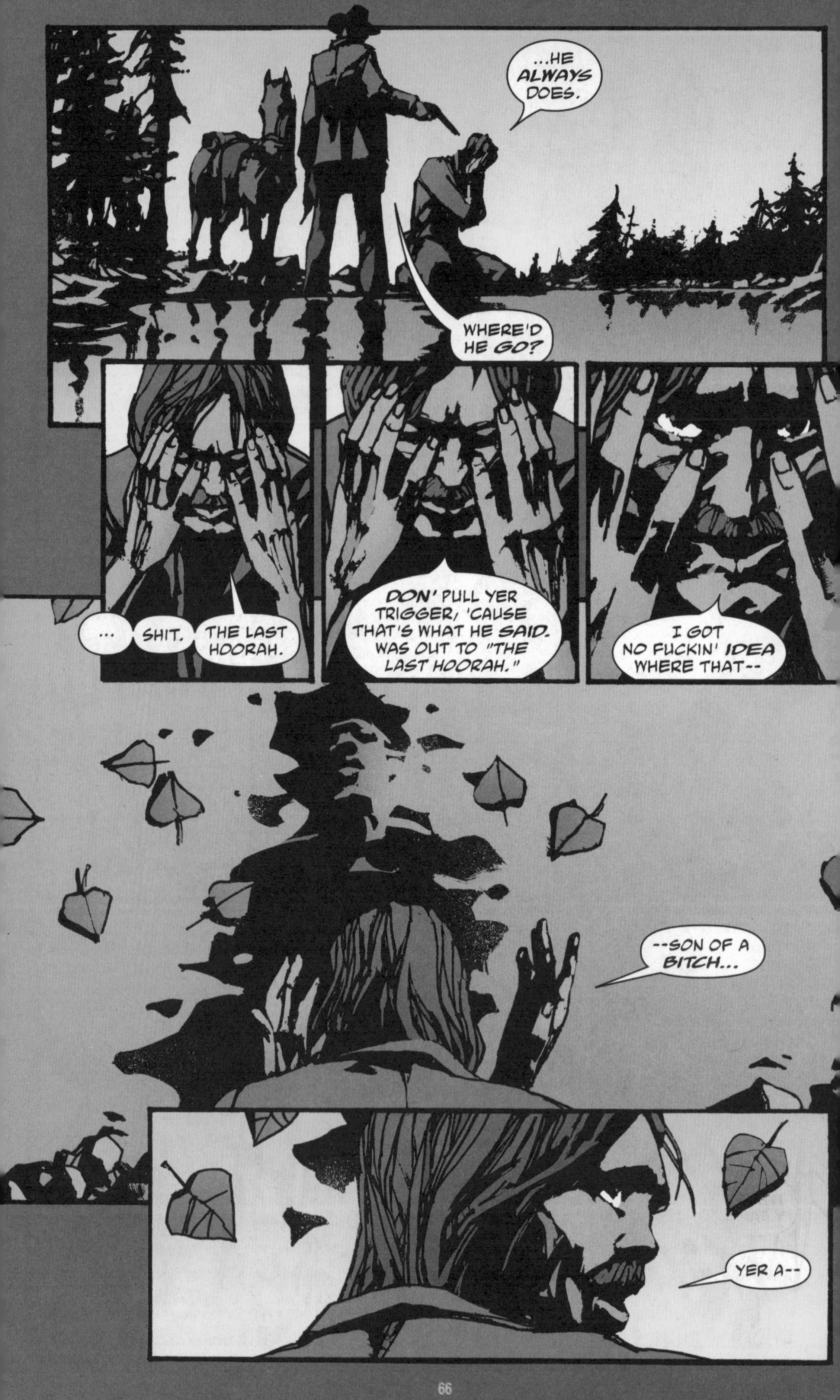
...HE ALWAYS DOES.
WHERE'D HE GO?
...
SHIT.
THE LAST HOORAH.
DON' PULL YER TRIGGER, 'CAUSE THAT'S WHAT HE SAID. WAS OUT TO "THE LAST HOORAH."
I GOT NO FUCKIN' IDEA WHERE THAT--
--SON OF A BITCH...
YER A--

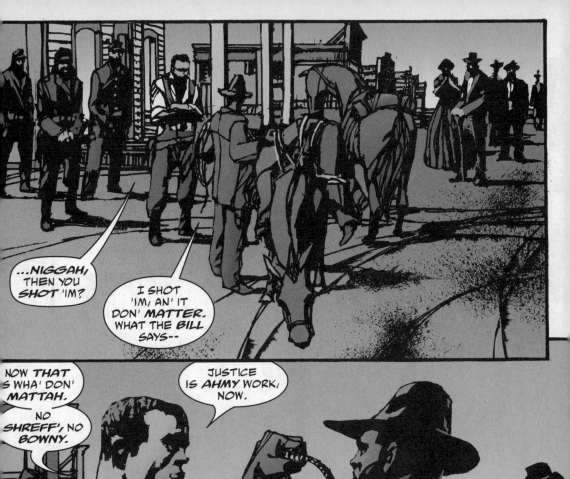

...NIGGAH, THEN YOU SHOT 'IM?

I SHOT 'IM, AN' IT DON' MATTER. WHAT THE BILL SAYS--

NOW THAT S WHA' DON' MATTAH. NO SHREFF', NO BOWNY.

JUSTICE IS AHMY WORK, NOW.

I WAS IN THE ARMY ONCE.

WERE YEAH?

'TIL I SHOT A WHITE BOY WAS PROTECTIN' A CRIMINAL.

A DAH'KEY SHOOTIN' A WHITE BOY, NOW DAT'S CRIMINAL...

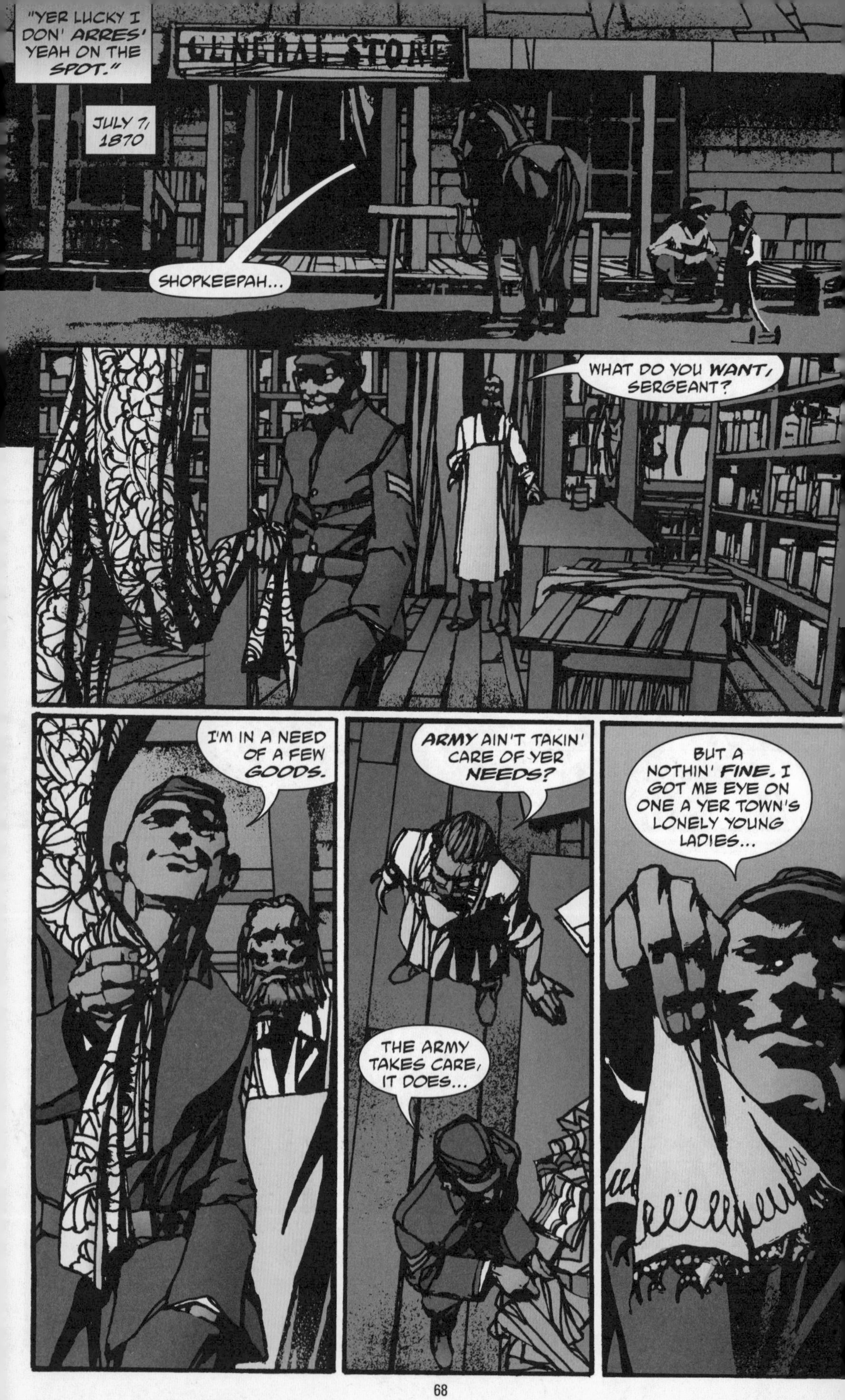
"YER LUCKY I DON' ARRES' YEAH ON THE SPOT."
GENERAL STORE
JULY 7, 1870
SHOPKEEPAH...
WHAT DO YOU WANT, SERGEANT?
I'M IN A NEED OF A FEW GOODS.
ARMY AIN'T TAKIN' CARE OF YER NEEDS?
THE ARMY TAKES CARE, IT DOES...
BUT A NOTHIN' FINE. I GOT ME EYE ON ONE A YER TOWN'S LONELY YOUNG LADIES...

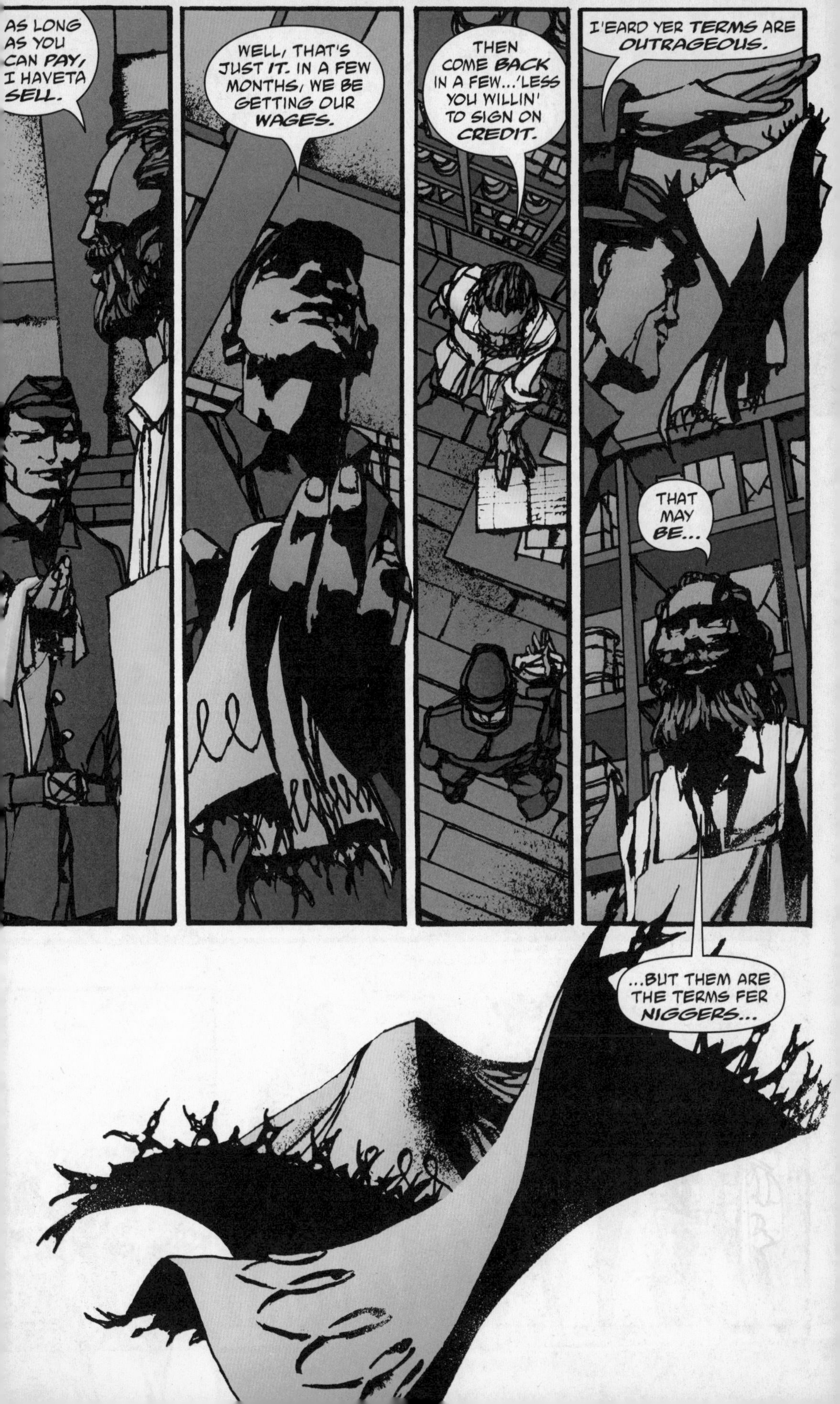
AS LONG AS YOU CAN PAY, I HAVETA SELL.
WELL, THAT'S JUST IT. IN A FEW MONTHS, WE BE GETTING OUR WAGES.
THEN COME BACK IN A FEW...'LESS YOU WILLIN' TO SIGN ON CREDIT.
I'EARD YER TERMS ARE OUTRAGEOUS.
THAT MAY BE...
...BUT THEM ARE THE TERMS FER NIGGERS...

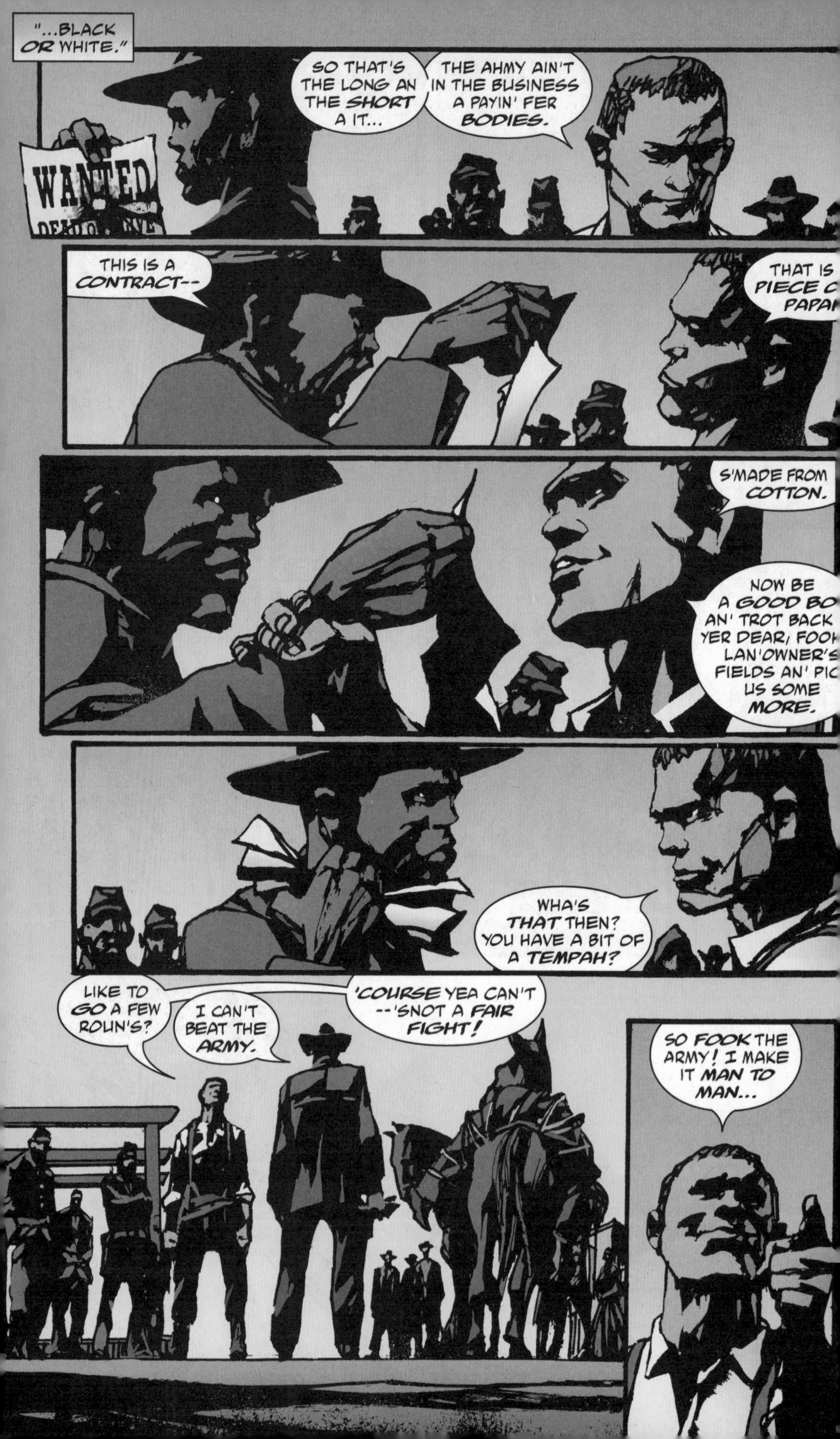
"...BLACK OR WHITE."
SO THAT'S THE LONG AN THE SHORT A IT...
THE AHMY AIN'T IN THE BUSINESS A PAYIN' FER BODIES.
WANTED
THIS IS A CONTRACT--
THAT IS PIECE C PAPAI
S'MADE FROM COTTON.
NOW BE A GOOD BO AN' TROT BACK YER DEAR, FOOK LAN'OWNER'S FIELDS AN' PIC US SOME MORE.
WHA'S THAT THEN? YOU HAVE A BIT OF A TEMPAH?
LIKE TO GO A FEW ROUN'S?
I CAN'T BEAT THE ARMY.
'COURSE YEA CAN'T --'SNOT A FAIR FIGHT!
SO FOOK THE ARMY! I MAKE IT MAN TO MAN...

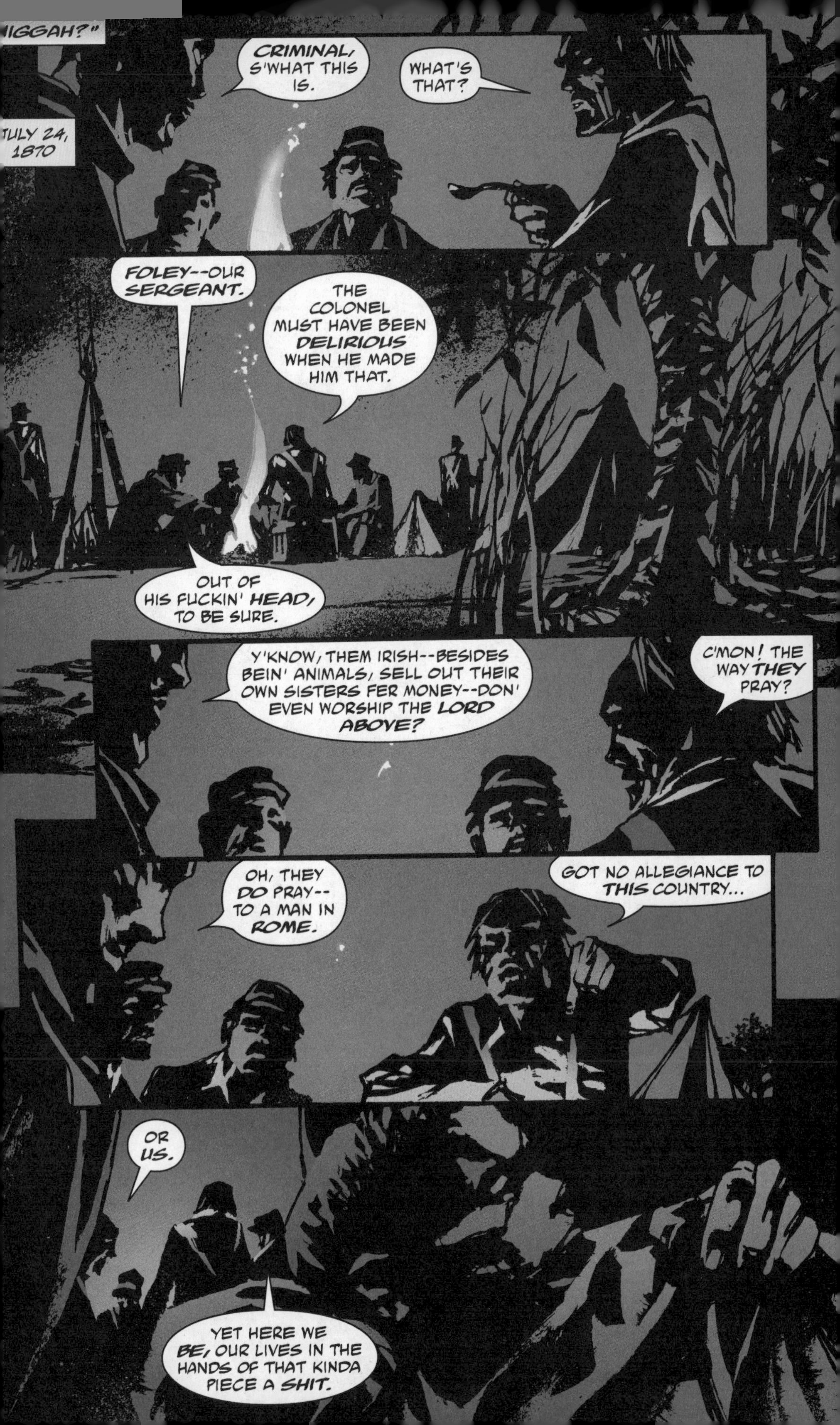
IGGAH?"
CRIMINAL, S'WHAT THIS IS.
WHAT'S THAT?
JULY 24, 1870
FOLEY--OUR SERGEANT.
THE COLONEL MUST HAVE BEEN DELIRIOUS WHEN HE MADE HIM THAT.
OUT OF HIS FUCKIN' HEAD, TO BE SURE.
Y'KNOW, THEM IRISH--BESIDES BEIN' ANIMALS, SELL OUT THEIR OWN SISTERS FER MONEY--DON' EVEN WORSHIP THE LORD ABOVE?
C'MON! THE WAY THEY PRAY?
OH, THEY DO PRAY-- TO A MAN IN ROME.
GOT NO ALLEGIANCE TO THIS COUNTRY...
OR US.
YET HERE WE BE, OUR LIVES IN THE HANDS OF THAT KINDA PIECE A SHIT.

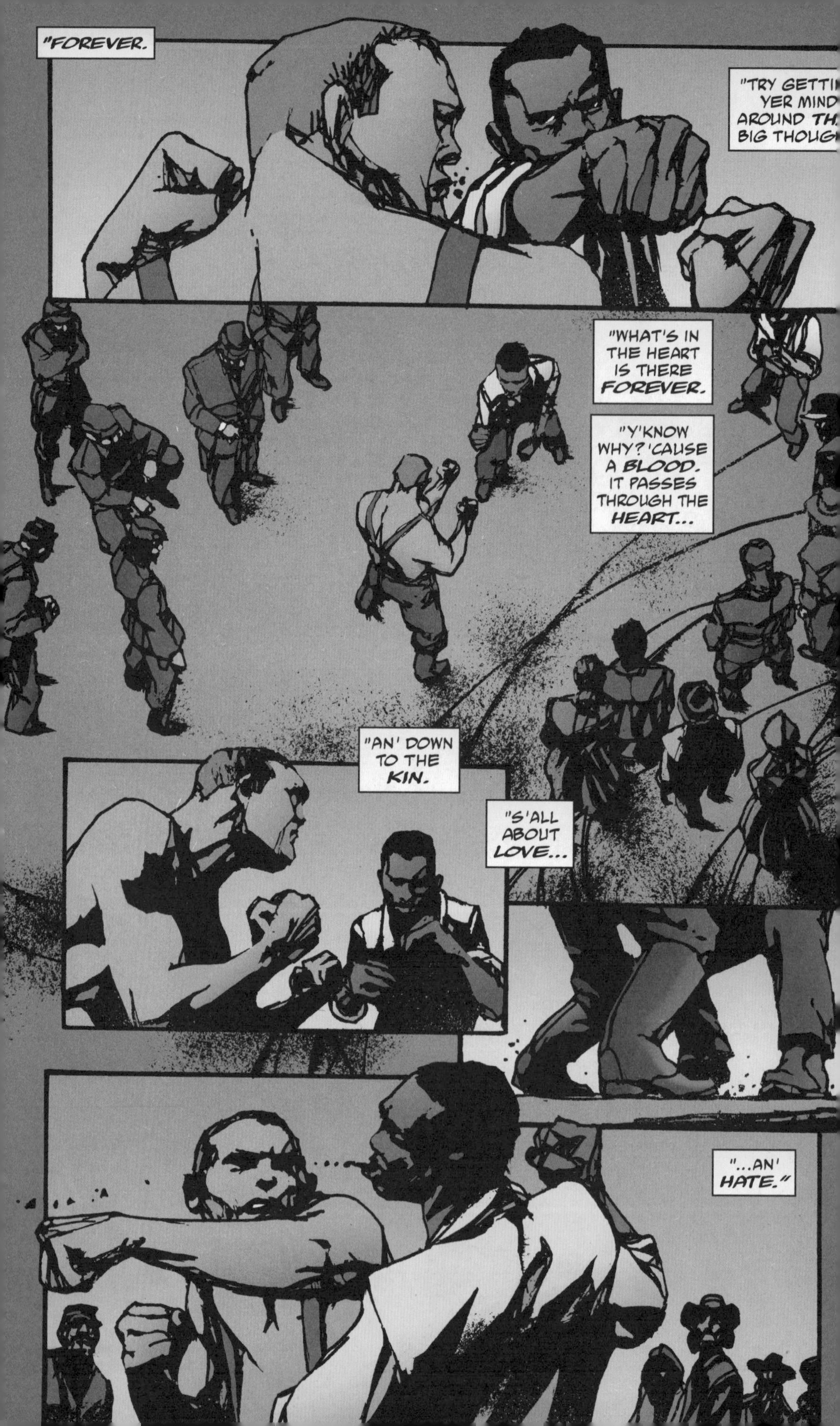
"FOREVER.
"TRY GETTI YER MIND AROUND TH BIG THOUG
"WHAT'S IN THE HEART IS THERE FOREVER.
"Y'KNOW WHY? 'CAUSE A BLOOD. IT PASSES THROUGH THE HEART...
"AN' DOWN TO THE KIN.
"S'ALL ABOUT LOVE...
"...AN' HATE."

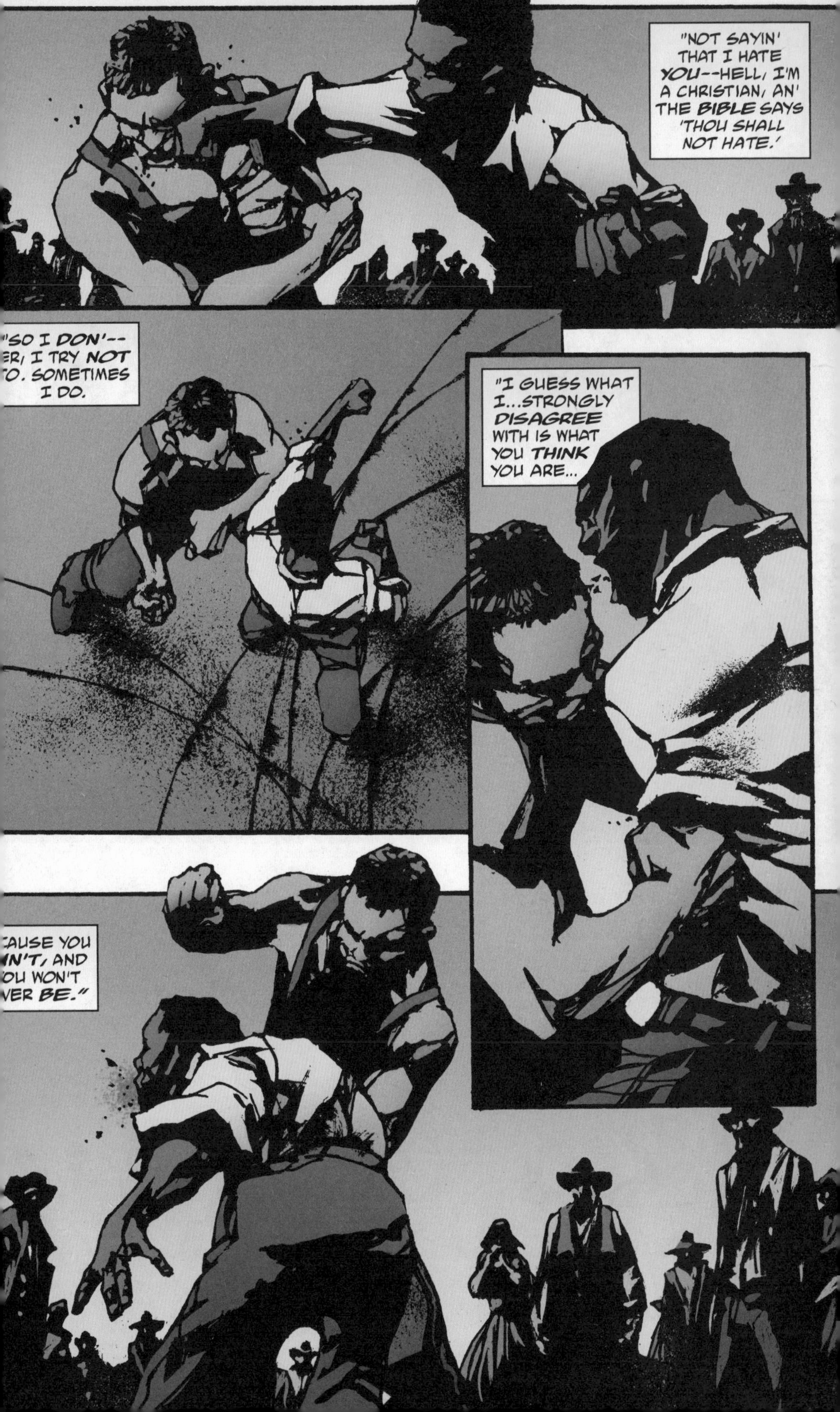
"NOT SAYIN' THAT I HATE YOU--HELL, I'M A CHRISTIAN, AN' THE BIBLE SAYS 'THOU SHALL NOT HATE.'
"SO I DON'-- ER, I TRY NOT TO. SOMETIMES I DO.
"I GUESS WHAT I...STRONGLY DISAGREE WITH IS WHAT YOU THINK YOU ARE...
CAUSE YOU N'T, AND OU WON'T VER BE."

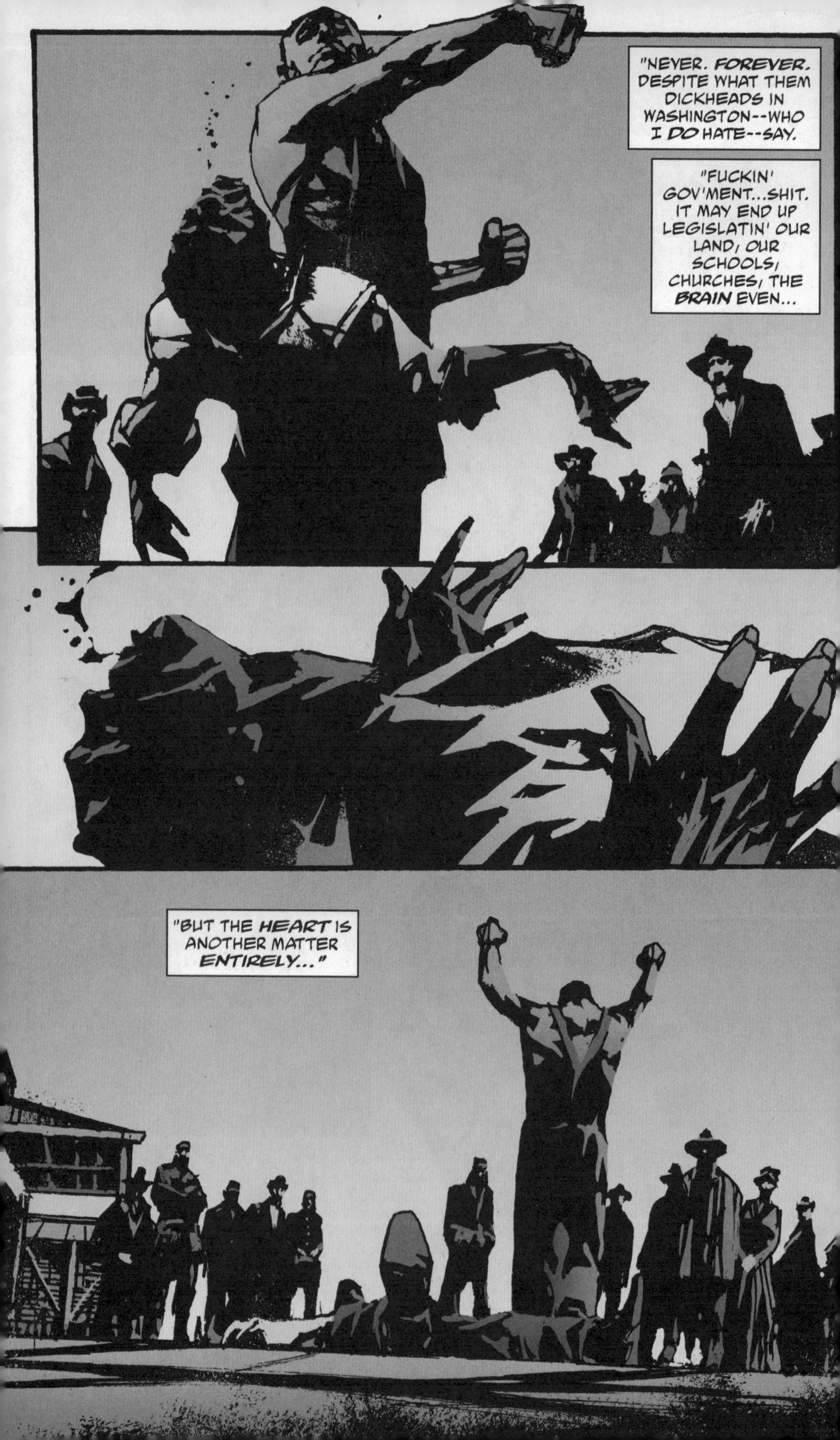
"NEVER. FOREVER. DESPITE WHAT THEM DICKHEADS IN WASHINGTON--WHO I DO HATE--SAY.
"FUCKIN' GOV'MENT...SHIT. IT MAY END UP LEGISLATIN' OUR LAND, OUR SCHOOLS, CHURCHES, THE BRAIN EVEN...
"BUT THE HEART IS ANOTHER MATTER ENTIRELY..."

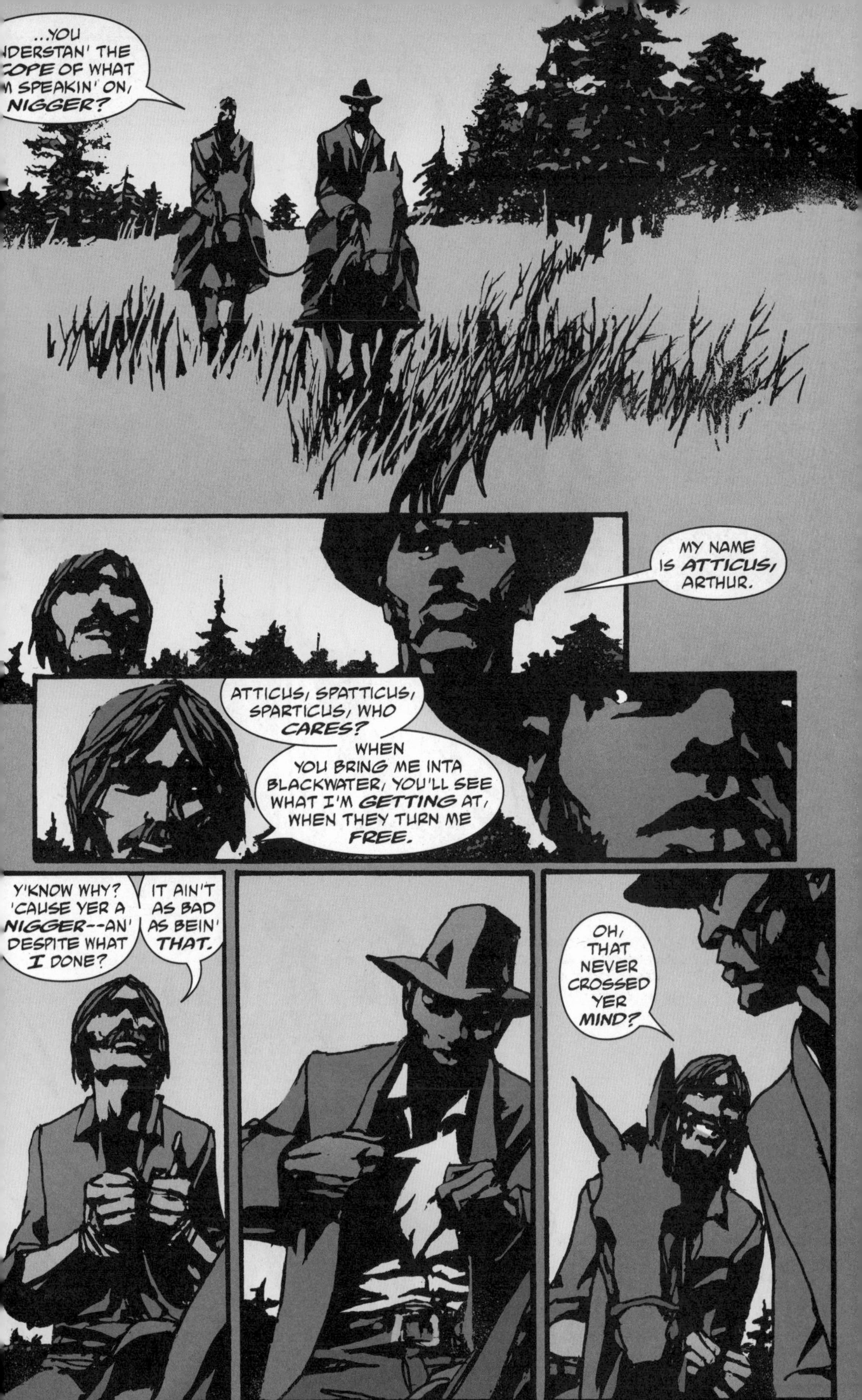

...YOU NDERSTAN' THE COPE OF WHAT M SPEAKIN' ON, NIGGER?
MY NAME IS ATTICUS, ARTHUR.
ATTICUS, SPATTICUS, SPARTICUS, WHO CARES?
WHEN YOU BRING ME INTA BLACKWATER, YOU'LL SEE WHAT I'M GETTING AT, WHEN THEY TURN ME FREE.
Y'KNOW WHY? 'CAUSE YER A NIGGER--AN' DESPITE WHAT I DONE?
IT AIN'T AS BAD AS BEIN' THAT.
OH, THAT NEVER CROSSED YER MIND?

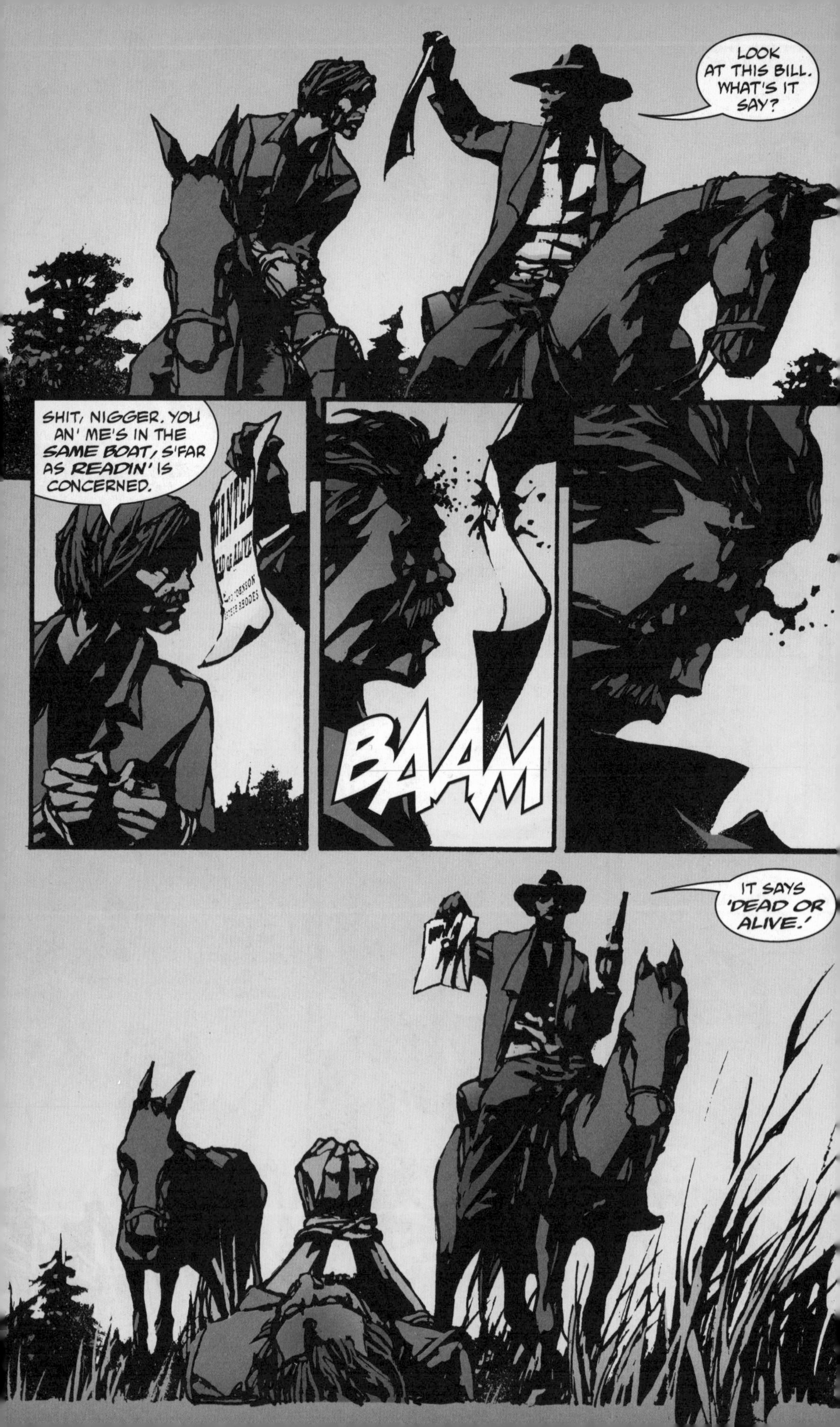

LOOK AT THIS BILL. WHAT'S IT SAY?
SHIT, NIGGER. YOU AN' ME'S IN THE *SAME BOAT*, S'FAR AS *READIN'* IS CONCERNED.
BAAM
IT SAYS *'DEAD OR ALIVE.'*

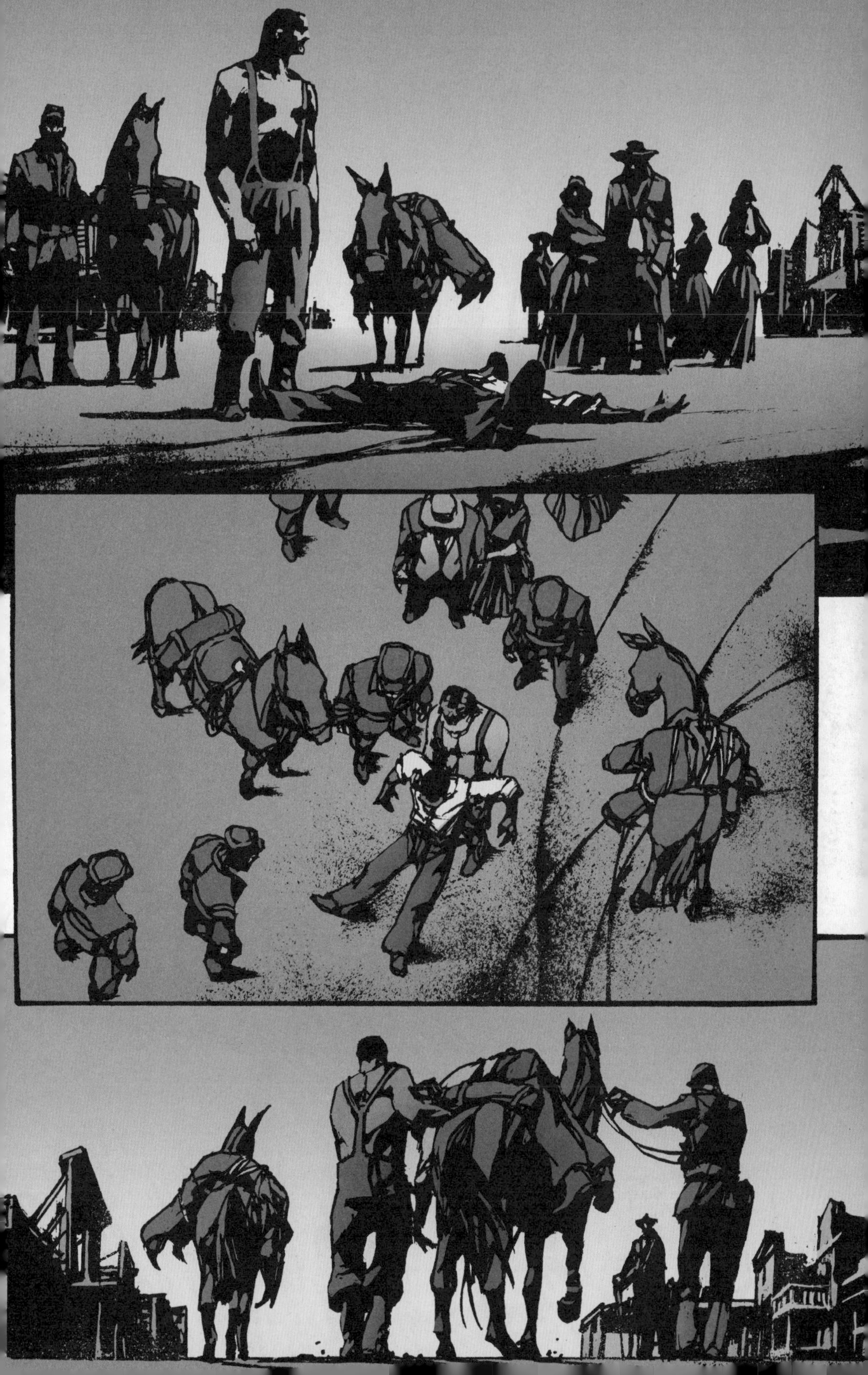

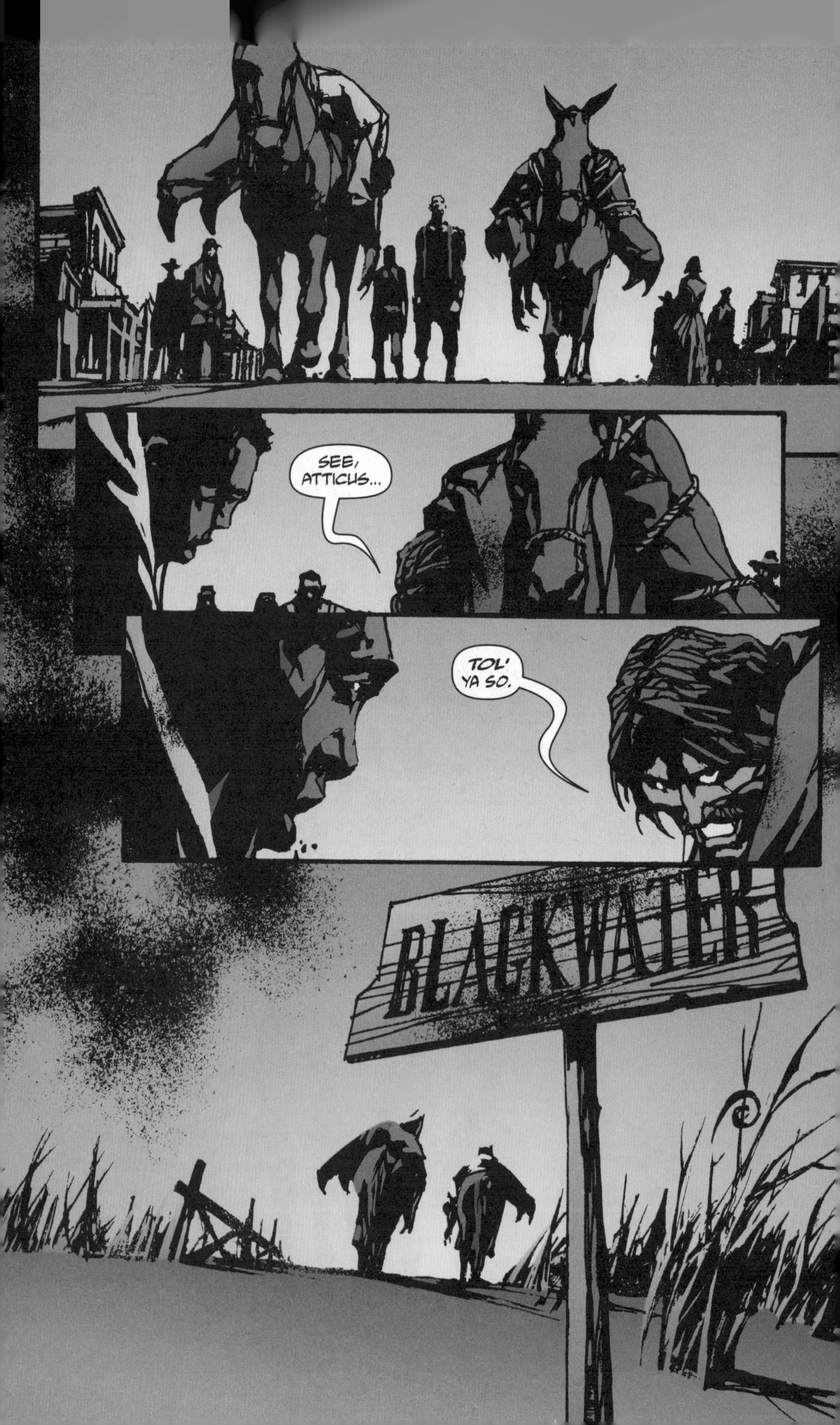
SEE, ATTICUS...
TOL' YA SO.
BLACKWATER

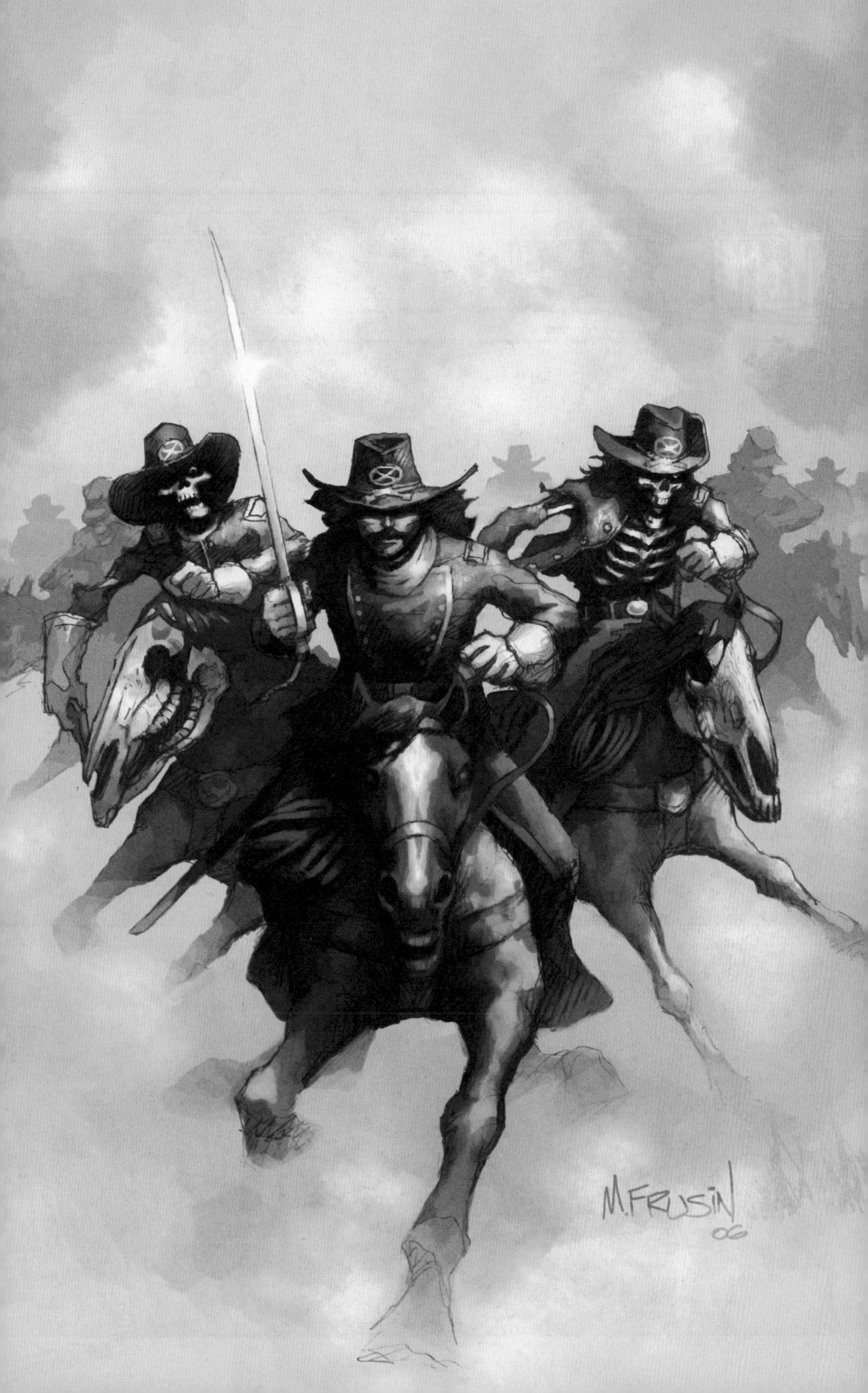
M.FRUSIN
06

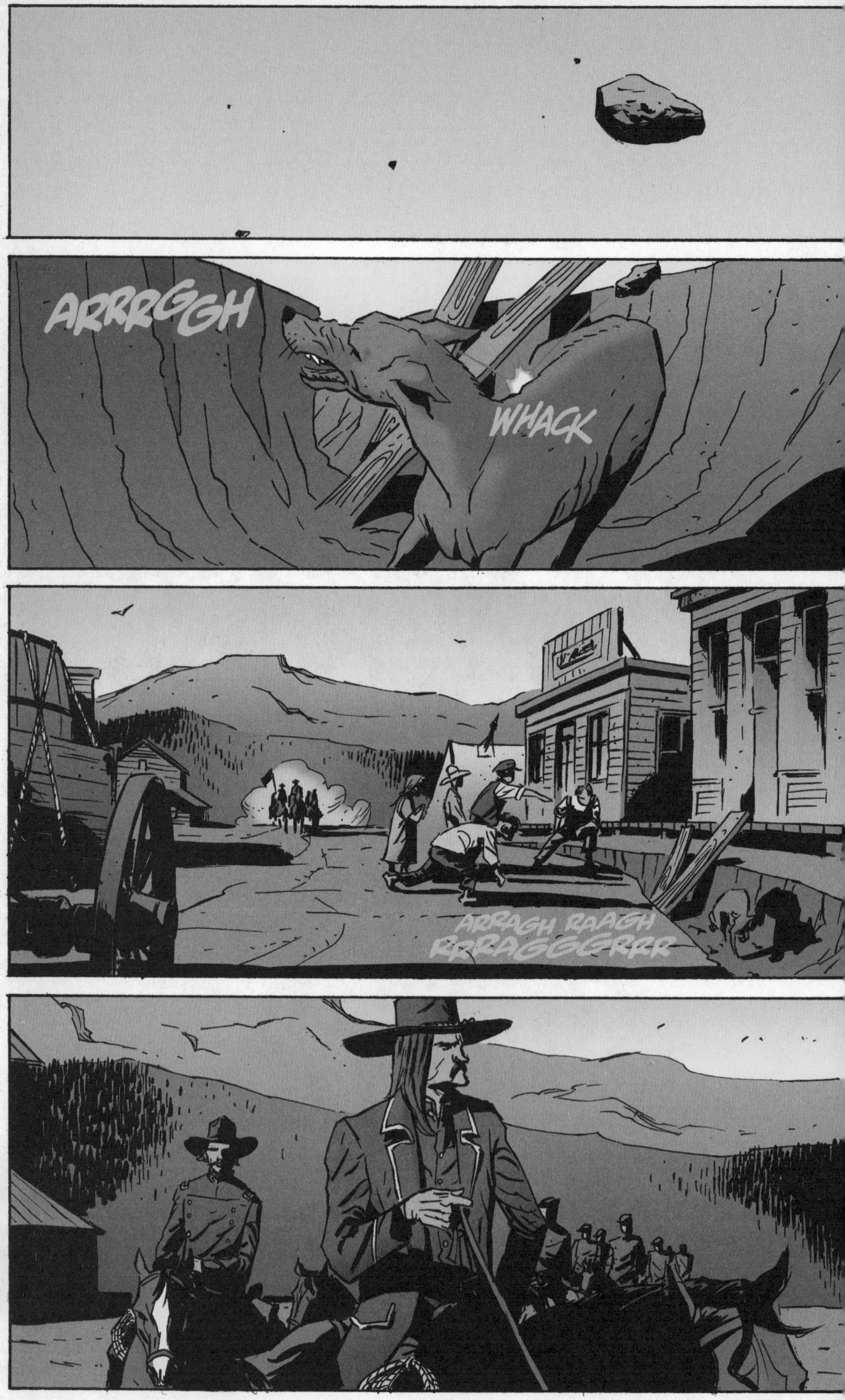
ARRRGGH
WHACK
ARRAGH RAAGH
RRRAGGGRRR

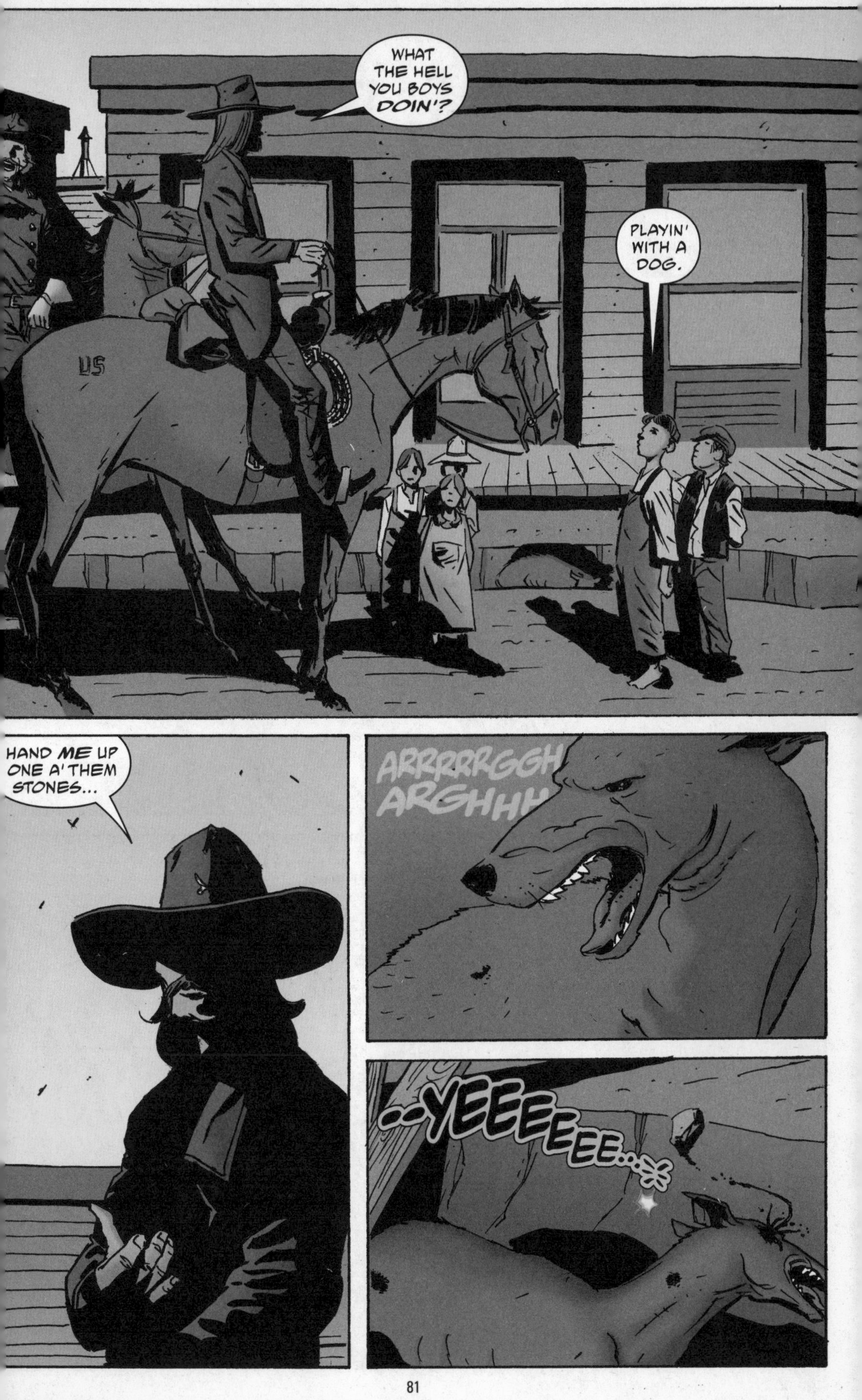
WHAT THE HELL YOU BOYS DOIN'?
PLAYIN' WITH A DOG.
HAND ME UP ONE A' THEM STONES...
ARRRRRGGH ARGHHH
--YEEEEEEE...

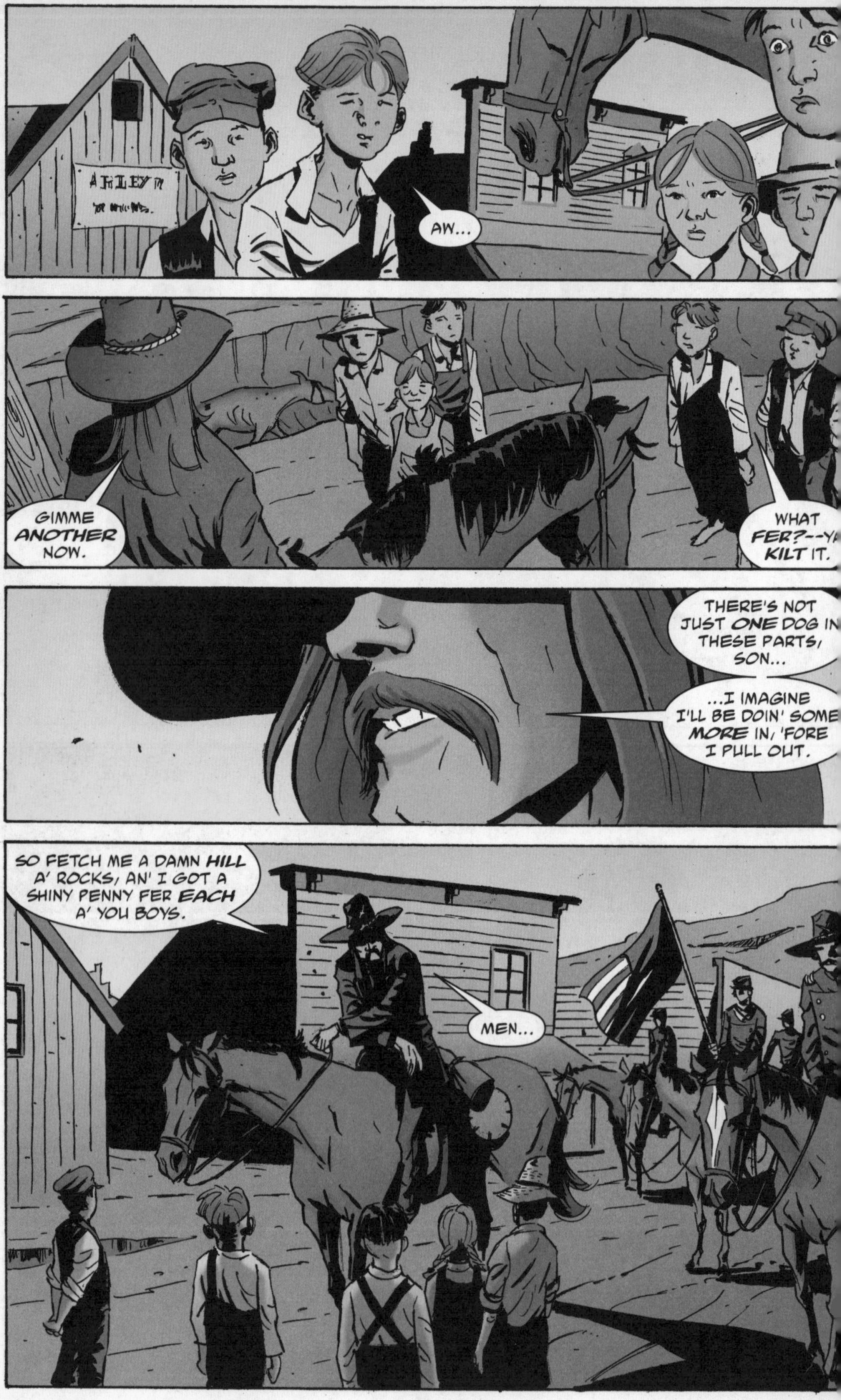
AW...
GIMME ANOTHER NOW.
WHAT FER?--Y KILT IT.
THERE'S NOT JUST ONE DOG IN THESE PARTS, SON...
...I IMAGINE I'LL BE DOIN' SOME MORE IN, 'FORE I PULL OUT.
SO FETCH ME A DAMN HILL A' ROCKS, AN' I GOT A SHINY PENNY FER EACH A' YOU BOYS.
MEN...

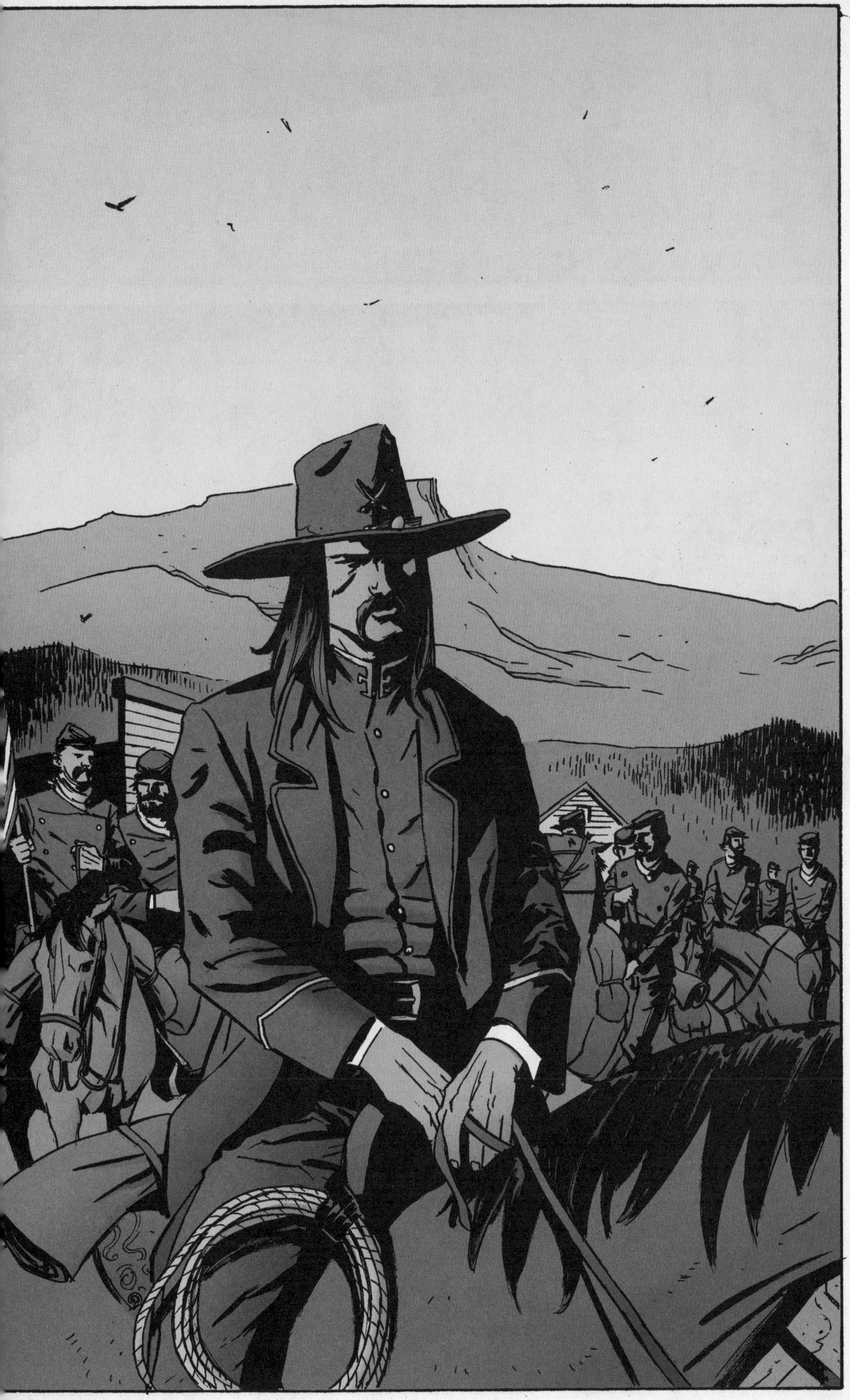

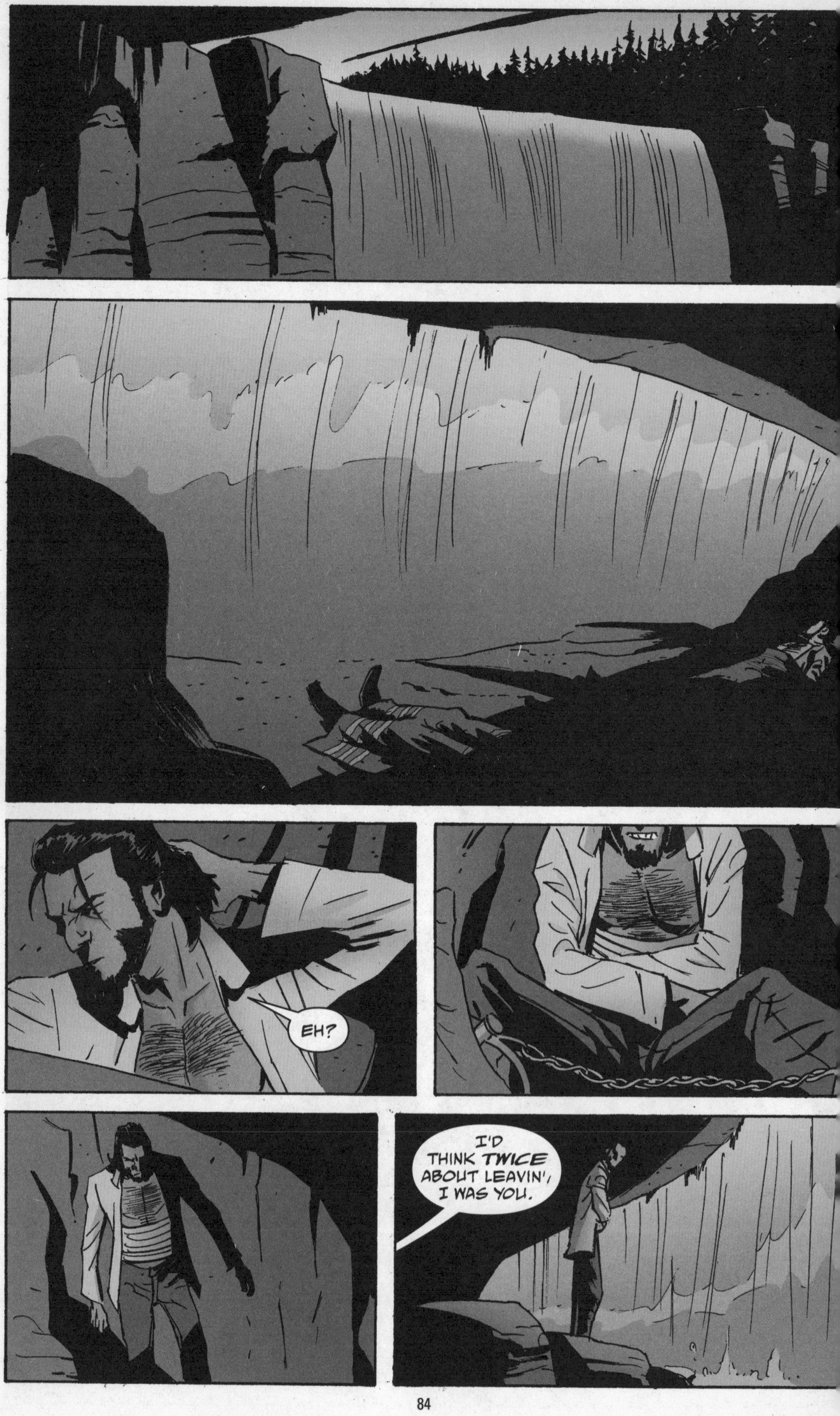
EH?
I'D THINK TWICE ABOUT LEAVIN', I WAS YOU.

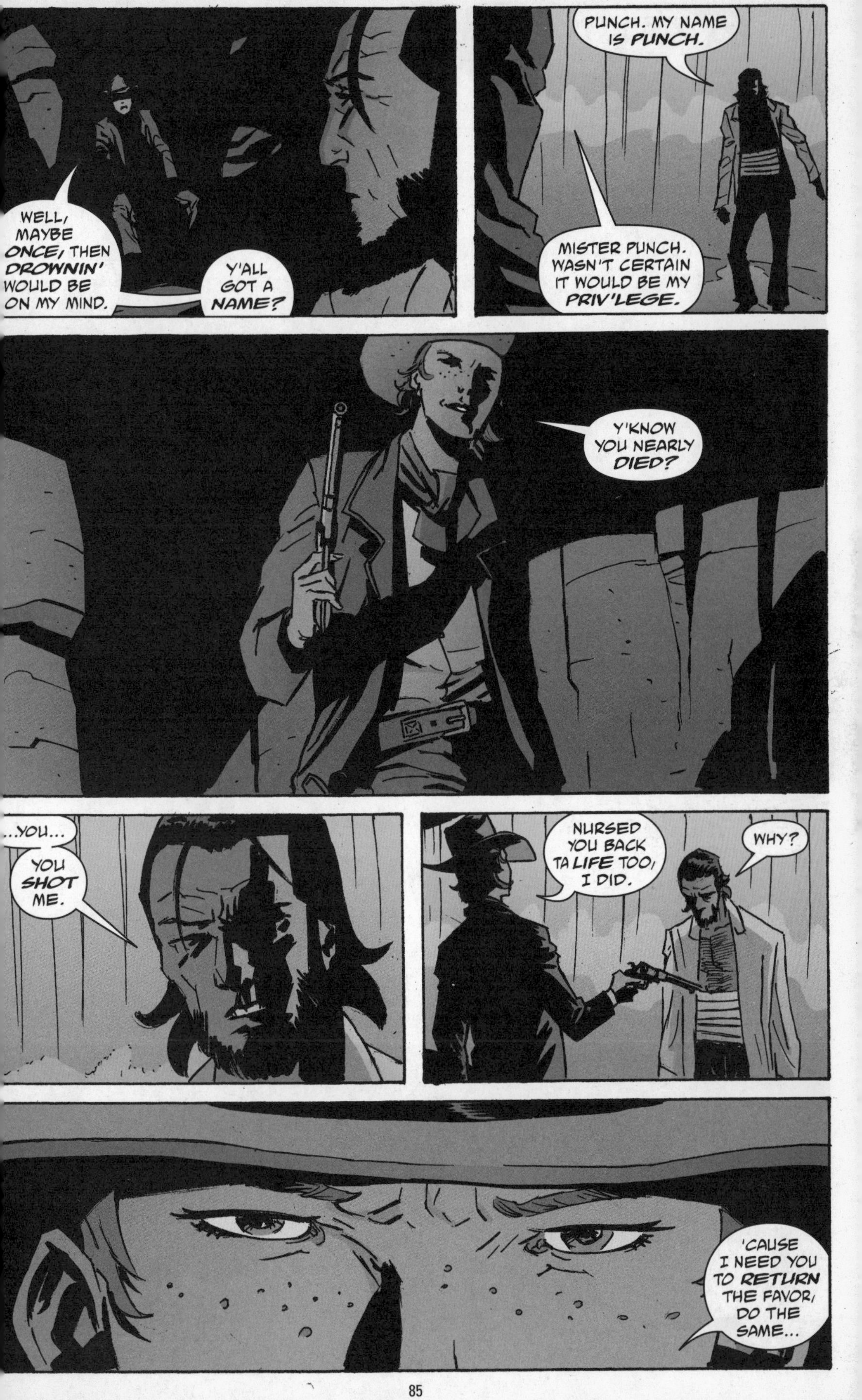
WELL, MAYBE ONCE, THEN DROWNIN' WOULD BE ON MY MIND.
Y'ALL GOT A NAME?
PUNCH. MY NAME IS PUNCH.
MISTER PUNCH. WASN'T CERTAIN IT WOULD BE MY PRIV'LEGE.
Y'KNOW YOU NEARLY DIED?
...YOU...
YOU SHOT ME.
NURSED YOU BACK TA LIFE TOO, I DID.
WHY?
'CAUSE I NEED YOU TO RETURN THE FAVOR, DO THE SAME...

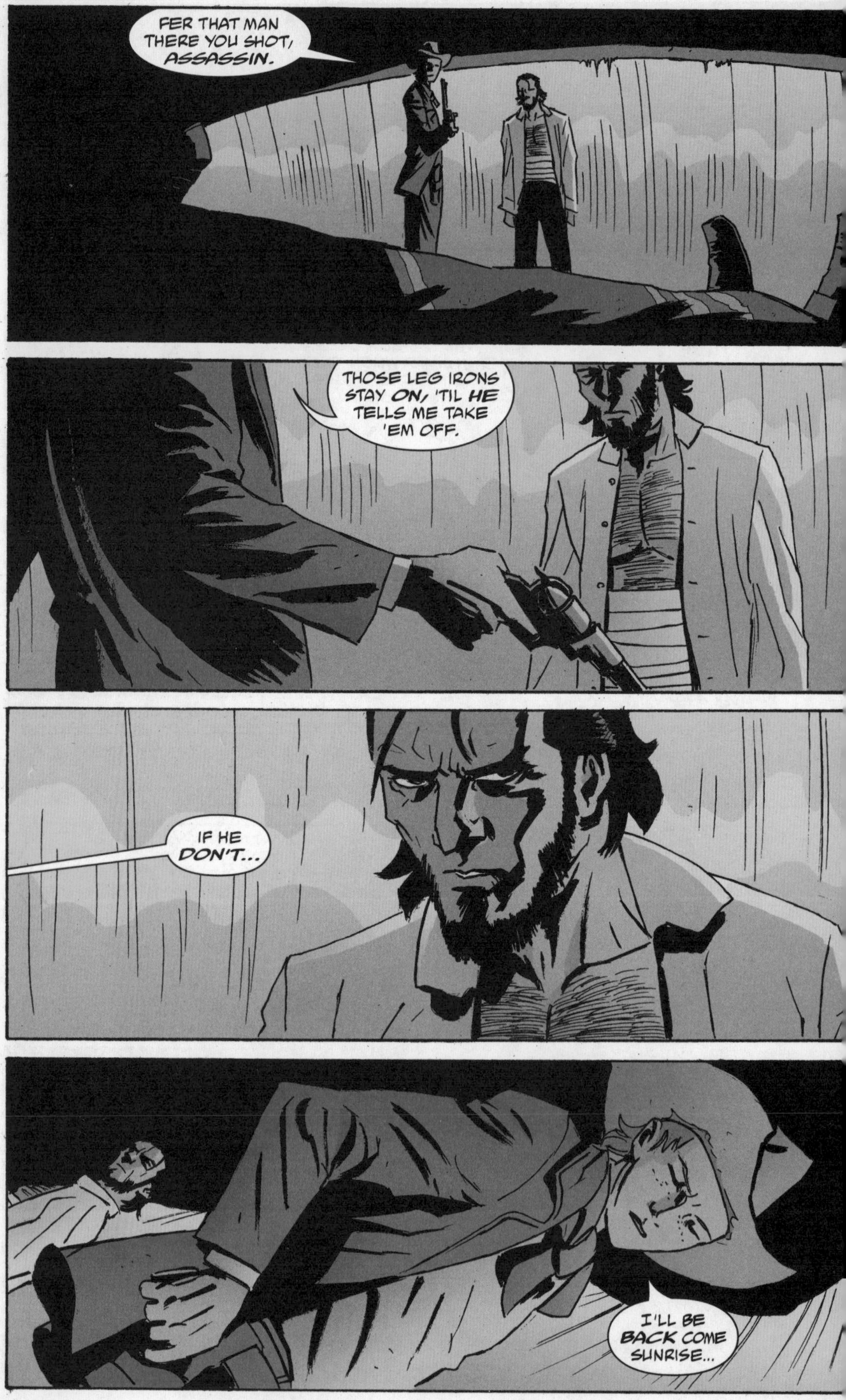
FER THAT MAN THERE YOU SHOT, ASSASSIN.
THOSE LEG IRONS STAY ON, 'TIL HE TELLS ME TAKE 'EM OFF.
IF HE DON'T...
I'LL BE BACK COME SUNRISE...

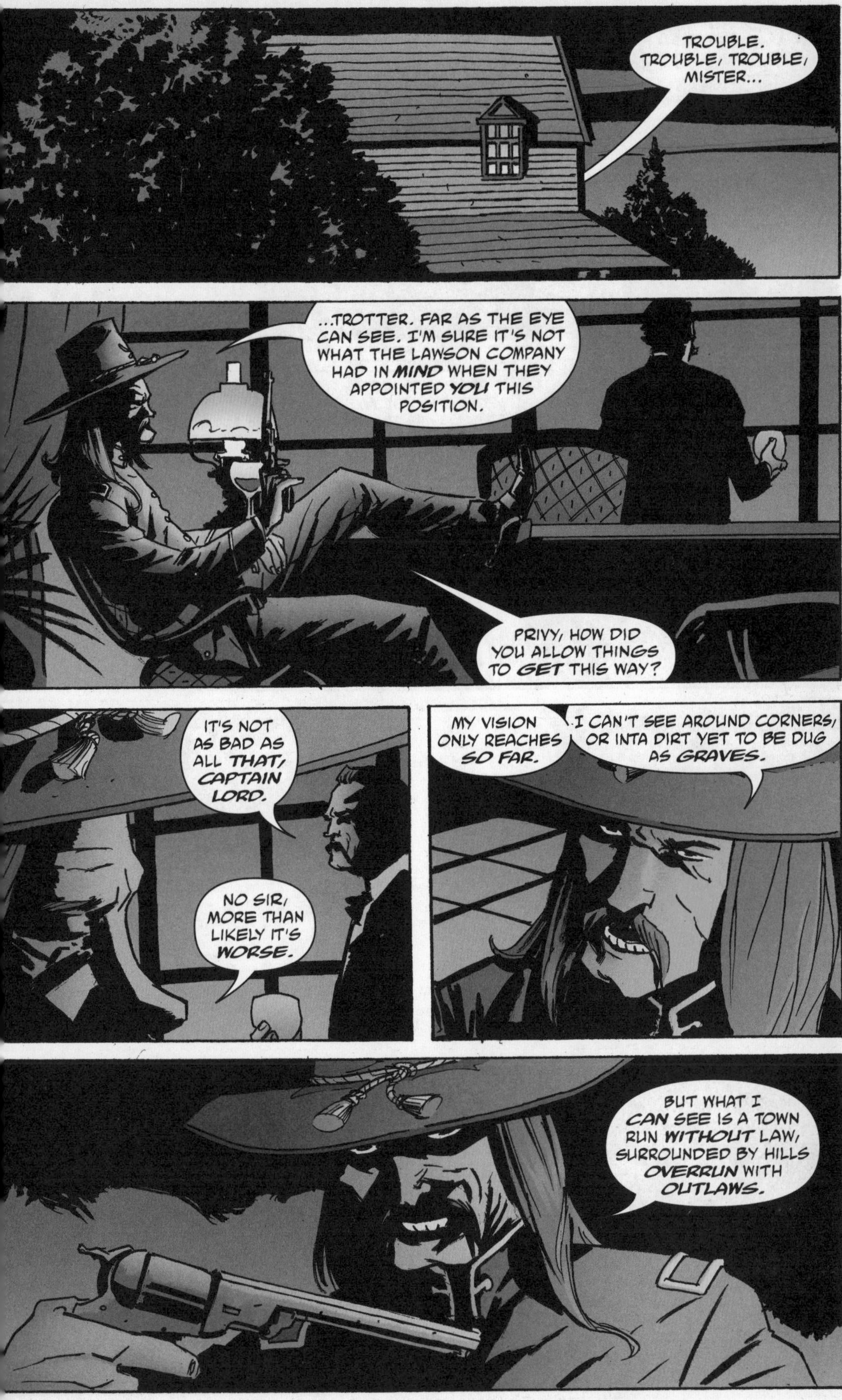
TROUBLE. TROUBLE, TROUBLE, MISTER...
...TROTTER. FAR AS THE EYE CAN SEE. I'M SURE IT'S NOT WHAT THE LAWSON COMPANY HAD IN MIND WHEN THEY APPOINTED YOU THIS POSITION.
PRIVY, HOW DID YOU ALLOW THINGS TO GET THIS WAY?
IT'S NOT AS BAD AS ALL THAT, CAPTAIN LORD.
NO SIR, MORE THAN LIKELY IT'S WORSE.
MY VISION ONLY REACHES SO FAR.
I CAN'T SEE AROUND CORNERS, OR INTA DIRT YET TO BE DUG AS GRAVES.
BUT WHAT I CAN SEE IS A TOWN RUN WITHOUT LAW, SURROUNDED BY HILLS OVERRUN WITH OUTLAWS.

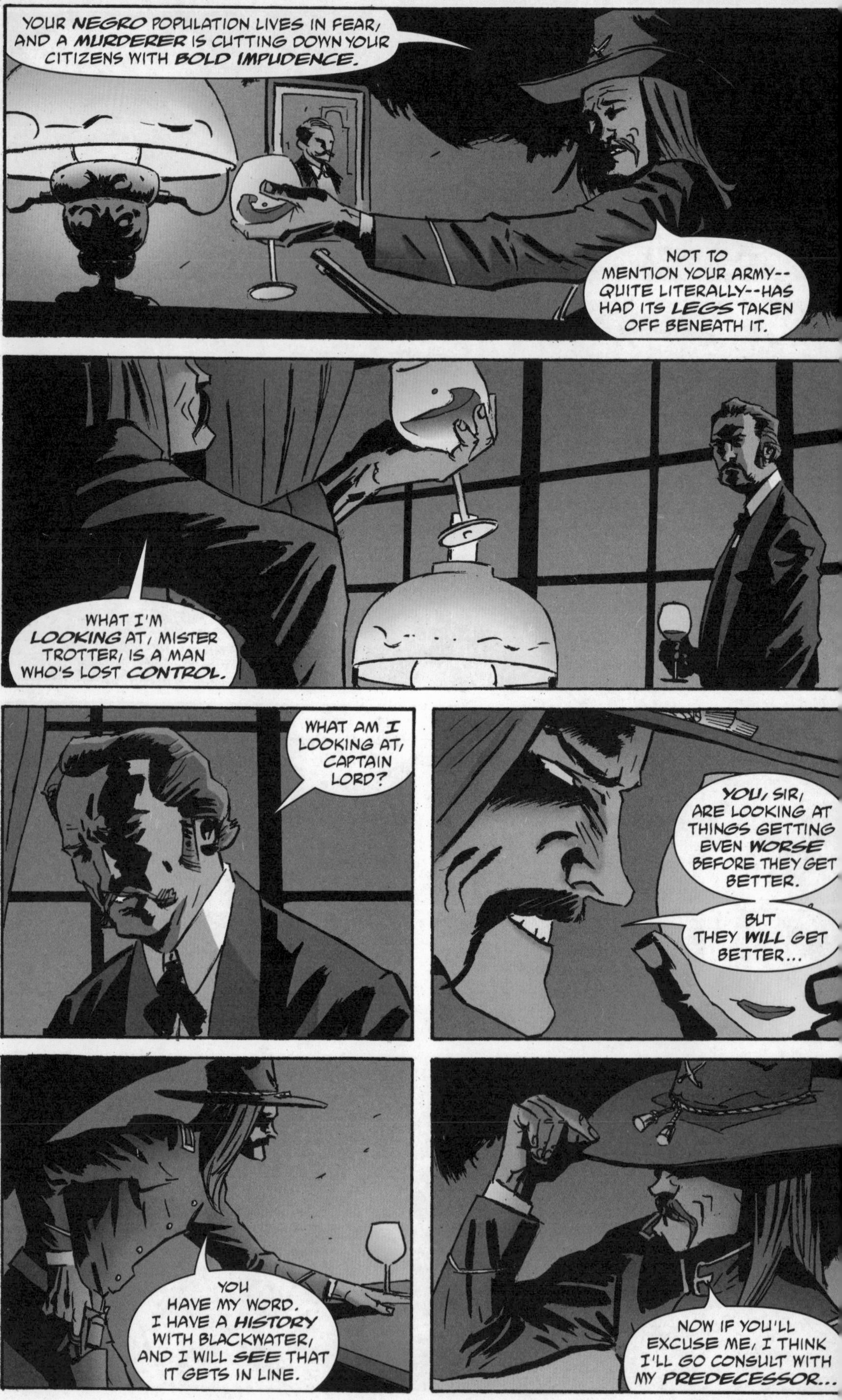
YOUR NEGRO POPULATION LIVES IN FEAR, AND A MURDERER IS CUTTING DOWN YOUR CITIZENS WITH BOLD IMPUDENCE.
NOT TO MENTION YOUR ARMY--QUITE LITERALLY--HAS HAD ITS LEGS TAKEN OFF BENEATH IT.
WHAT I'M LOOKING AT, MISTER TROTTER, IS A MAN WHO'S LOST CONTROL.
WHAT AM I LOOKING AT, CAPTAIN LORD?
YOU, SIR, ARE LOOKING AT THINGS GETTING EVEN WORSE BEFORE THEY GET BETTER.
BUT THEY WILL GET BETTER...
YOU HAVE MY WORD. I HAVE A HISTORY WITH BLACKWATER, AND I WILL SEE THAT IT GETS IN LINE.
NOW IF YOU'LL EXCUSE ME, I THINK I'LL GO CONSULT WITH MY PREDECESSOR...

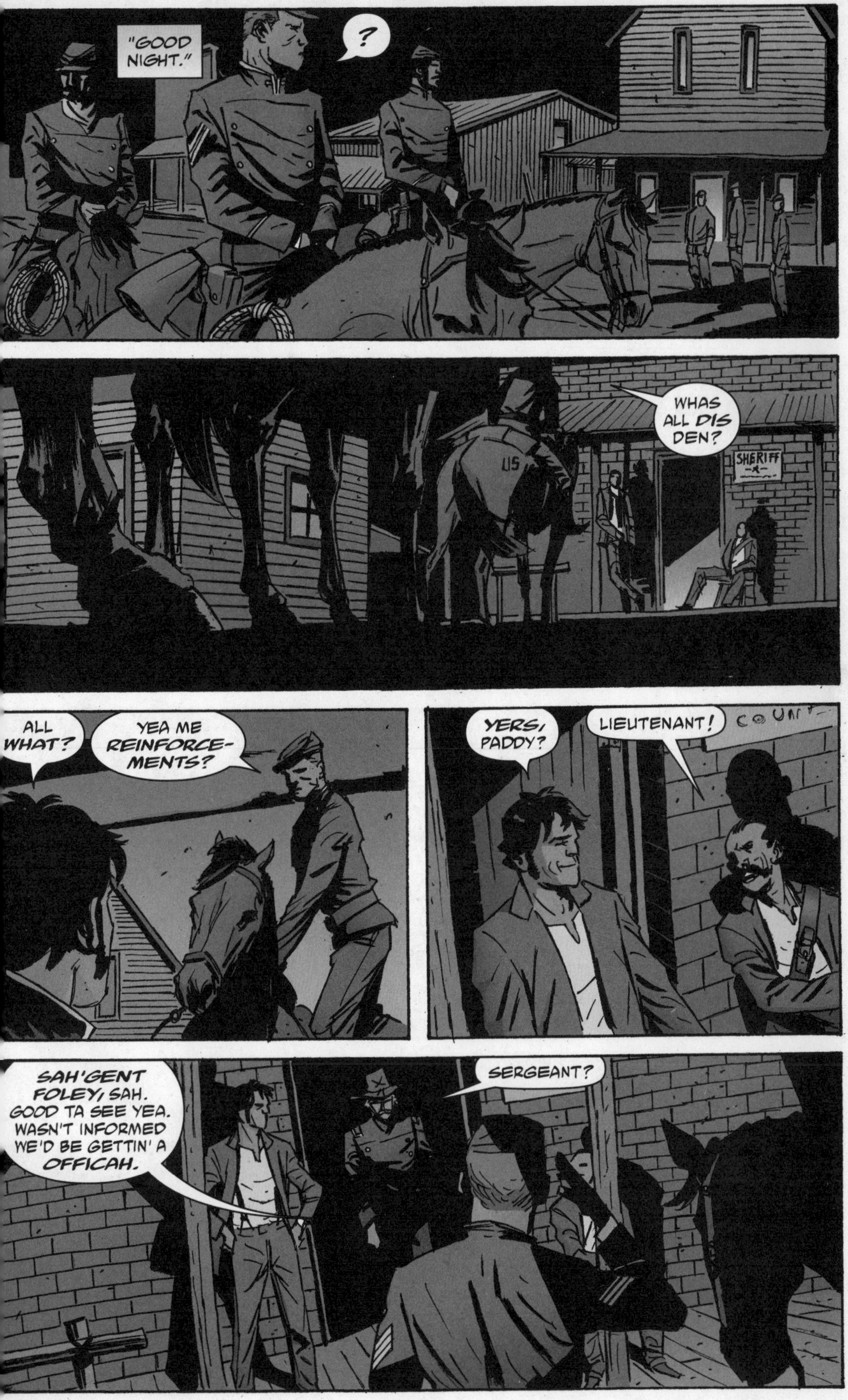
"GOOD NIGHT."
?
WHAS ALL DIS DEN?
SHERIFF
ALL WHAT?
YEA ME REINFORCE-MENTS?
YERS, PADDY?
LIEUTENANT!
SAH'GENT FOLEY, SAH. GOOD TA SEE YEA. WASN'T INFORMED WE'D BE GETTIN' A OFFICAH.
SERGEANT?

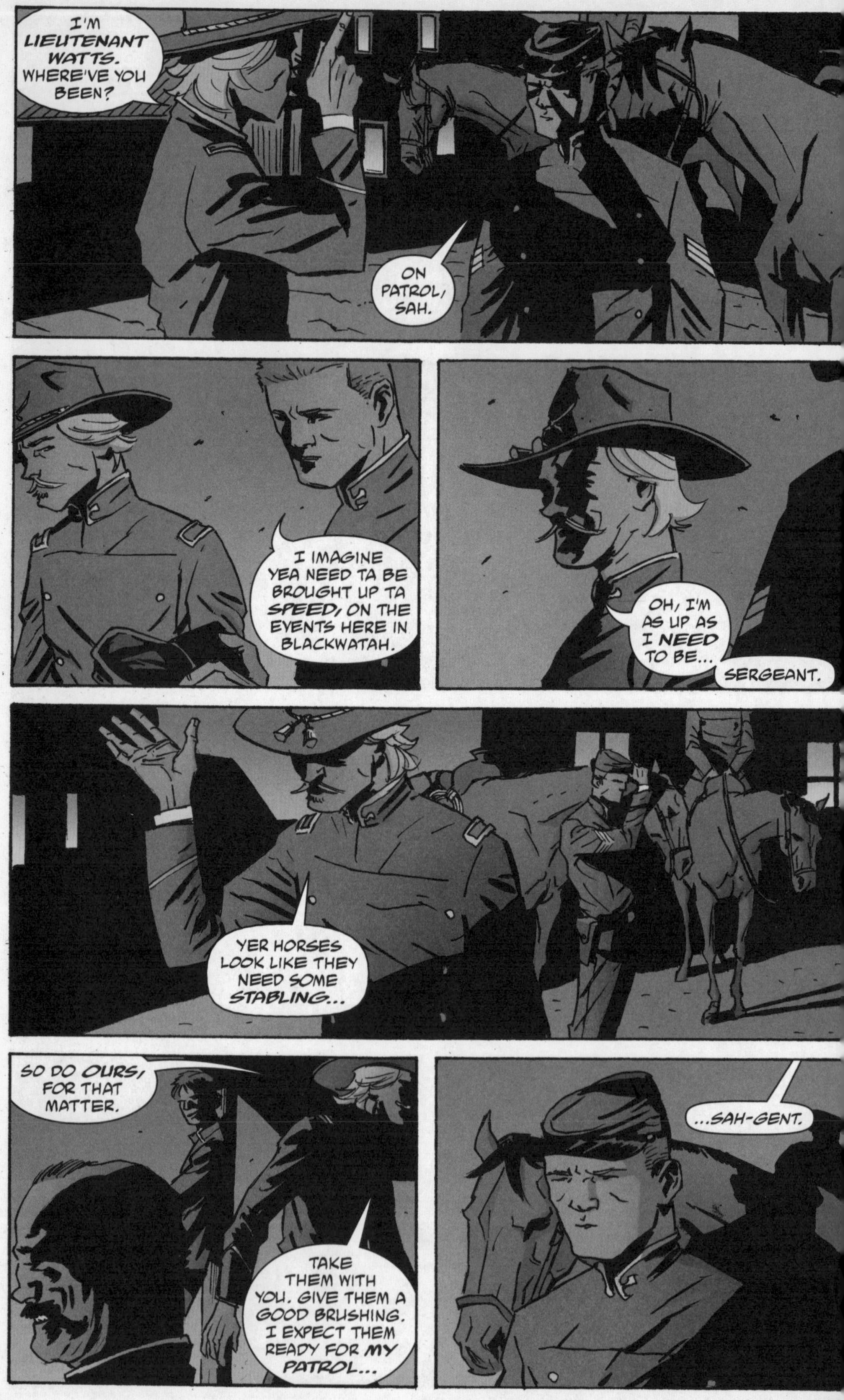
I'M LIEUTENANT WATTS. WHERE'VE YOU BEEN?
ON PATROL, SAH.
I IMAGINE YEA NEED TA BE BROUGHT UP TA SPEED, ON THE EVENTS HERE IN BLACKWATAH.
OH, I'M AS UP AS I NEED TO BE...
SERGEANT.
YER HORSES LOOK LIKE THEY NEED SOME STABLING...
SO DO OURS, FOR THAT MATTER.
TAKE THEM WITH YOU. GIVE THEM A GOOD BRUSHING. I EXPECT THEM READY FOR MY PATROL...
...SAH-GENT.

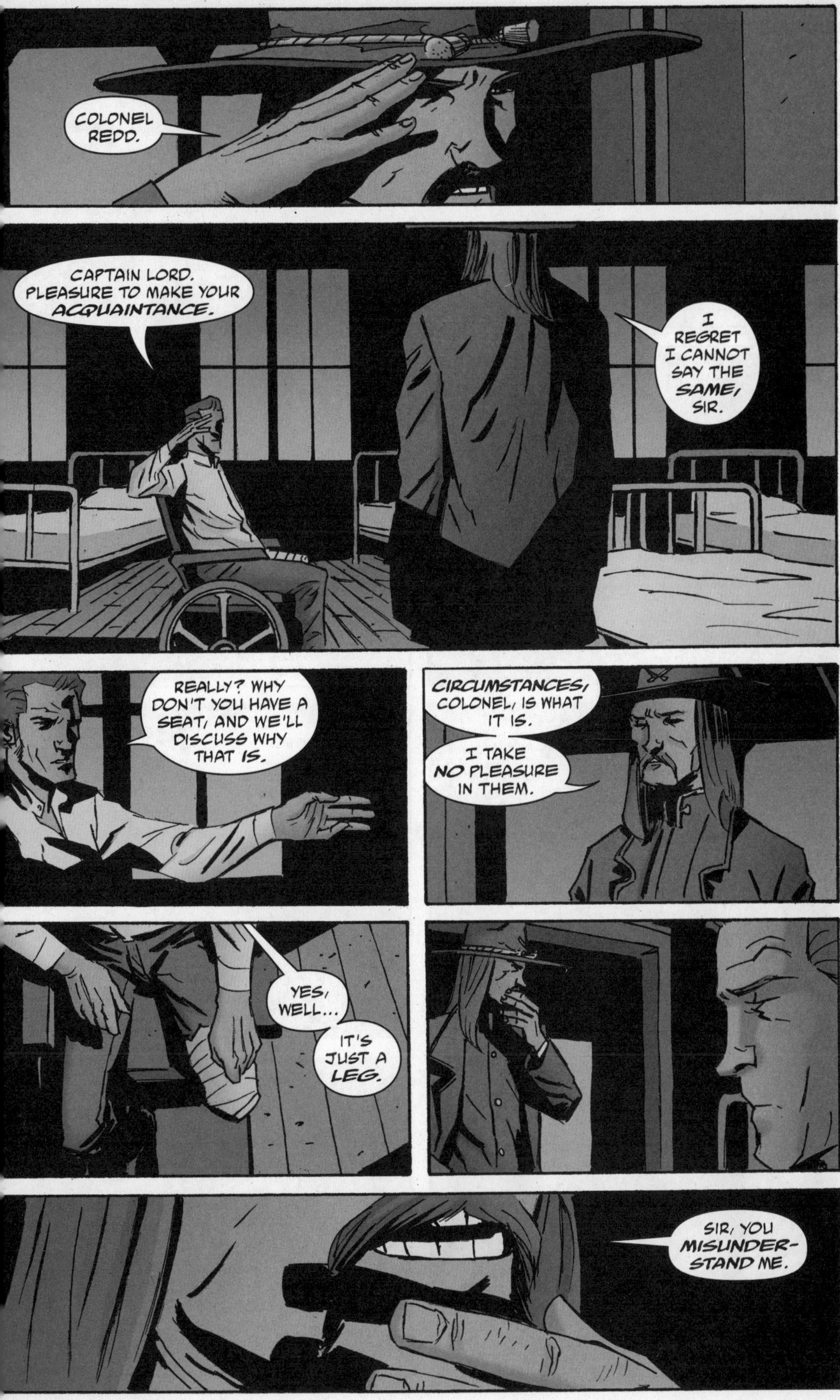
COLONEL REDD.
CAPTAIN LORD. PLEASURE TO MAKE YOUR ACQUAINTANCE.
I REGRET I CANNOT SAY THE SAME, SIR.
REALLY? WHY DON'T YOU HAVE A SEAT, AND WE'LL DISCUSS WHY THAT IS.
CIRCUMSTANCES, COLONEL, IS WHAT IT IS.
I TAKE NO PLEASURE IN THEM.
YES, WELL...
IT'S JUST A LEG.
SIR, YOU MISUNDER-STAND ME.

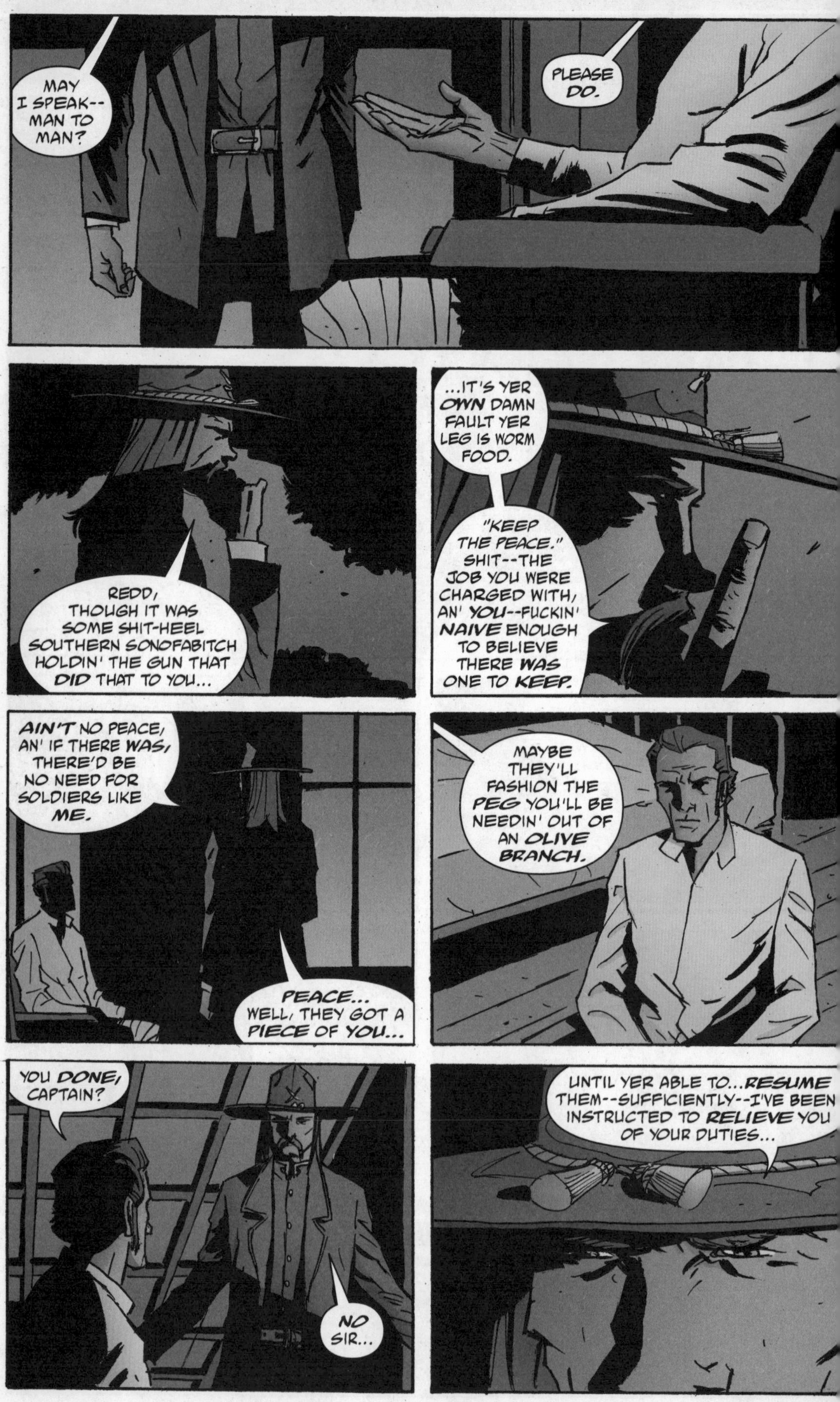
MAY I SPEAK--MAN TO MAN?
PLEASE DO.
REDD, THOUGH IT WAS SOME SHIT-HEEL SOUTHERN SONOFABITCH HOLDIN' THE GUN THAT DID THAT TO YOU...
...IT'S YER OWN DAMN FAULT YER LEG IS WORM FOOD.
"KEEP THE PEACE." SHIT--THE JOB YOU WERE CHARGED WITH, AN' YOU--FUCKIN' NAIVE ENOUGH TO BELIEVE THERE WAS ONE TO KEEP.
AIN'T NO PEACE, AN' IF THERE WAS, THERE'D BE NO NEED FOR SOLDIERS LIKE ME.
PEACE... WELL, THEY GOT A PIECE OF YOU...
MAYBE THEY'LL FASHION THE PEG YOU'LL BE NEEDIN' OUT OF AN OLIVE BRANCH.
YOU DONE, CAPTAIN?
NO SIR...
UNTIL YER ABLE TO...RESUME THEM--SUFFICIENTLY--I'VE BEEN INSTRUCTED TO RELIEVE YOU OF YOUR DUTIES...

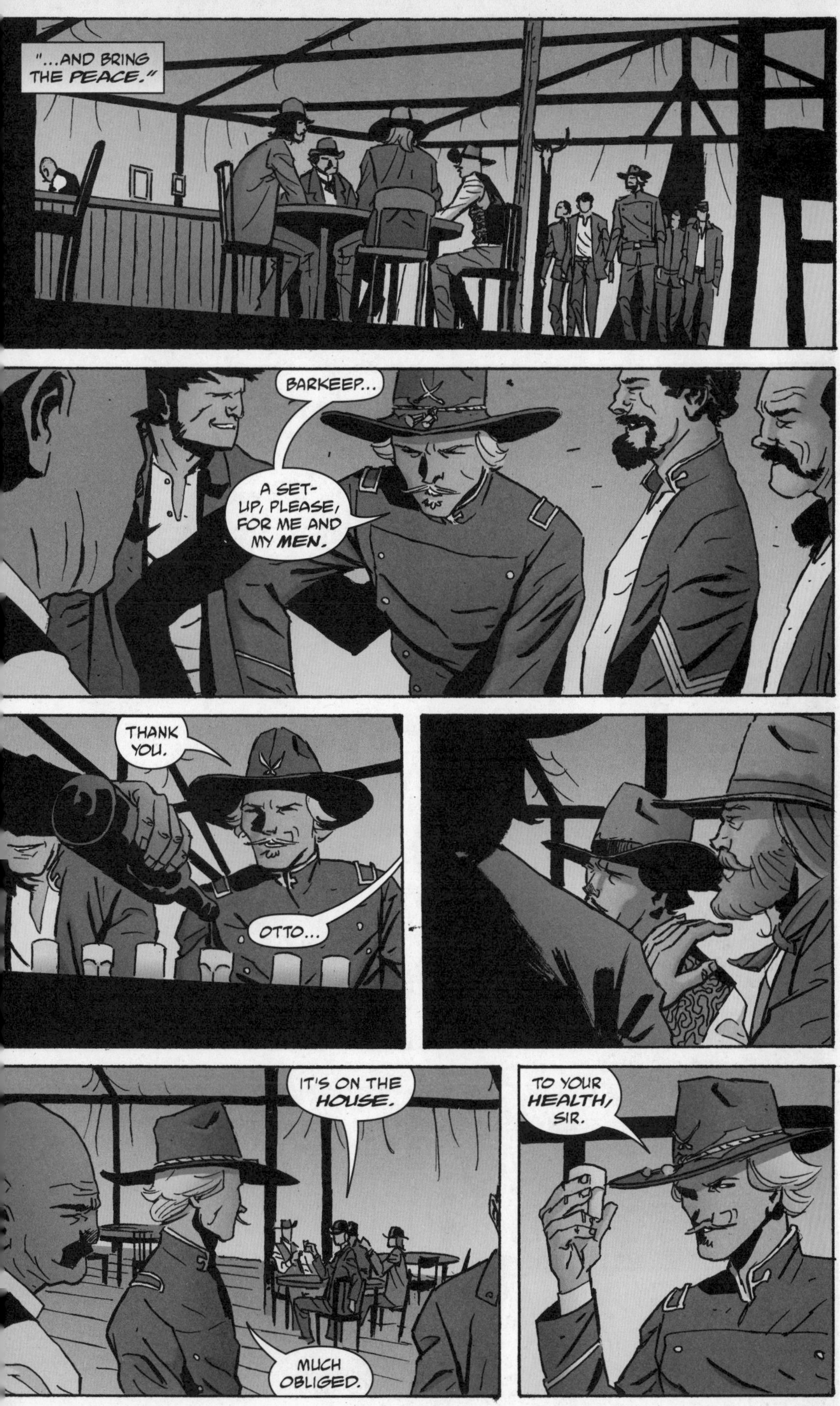
"...AND BRING THE PEACE."
BARKEEP...
A SET-UP, PLEASE, FOR ME AND MY MEN.
THANK YOU.
OTTO...
IT'S ON THE HOUSE.
MUCH OBLIGED.
TO YOUR HEALTH, SIR.

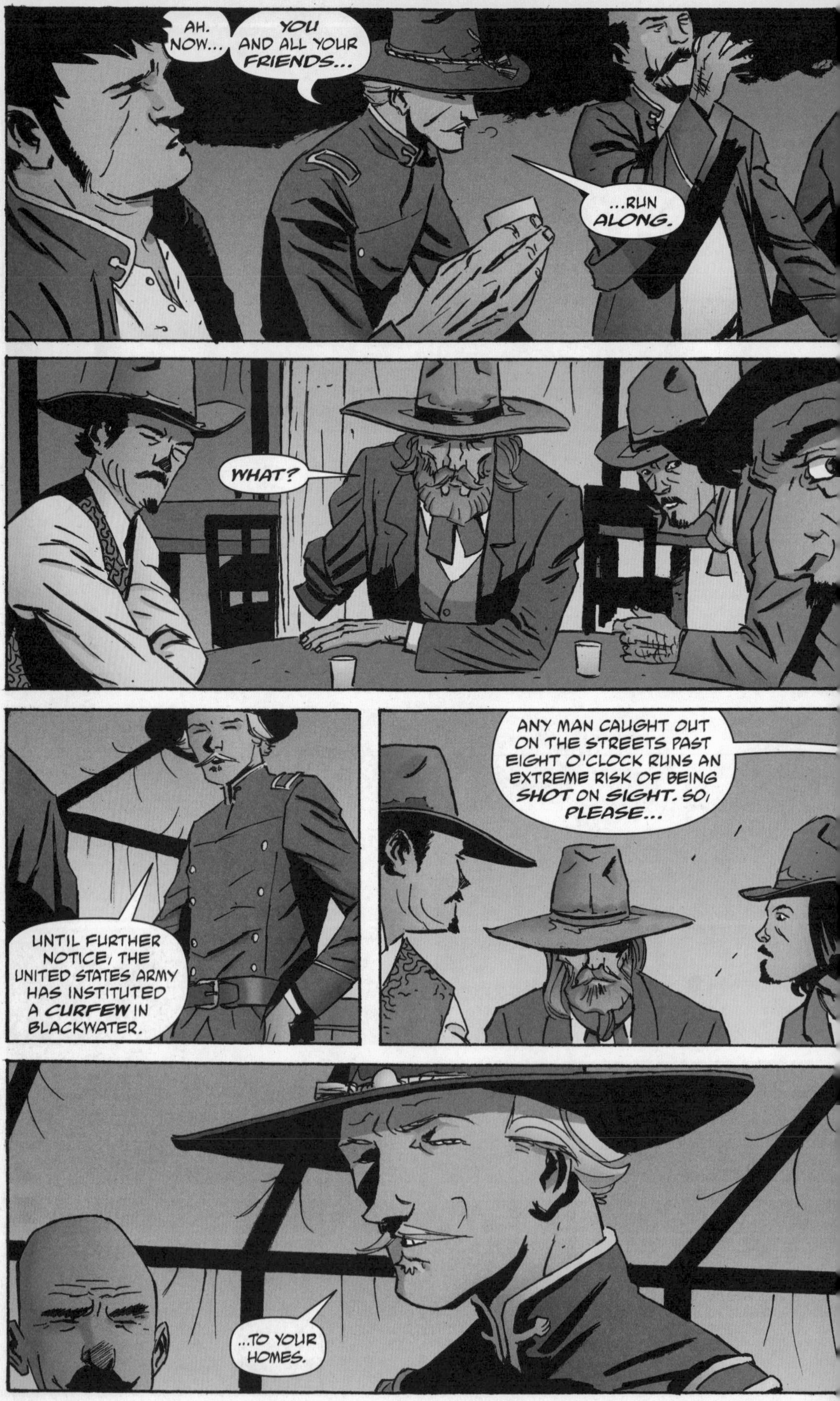
AH. NOW...
YOU AND ALL YOUR FRIENDS...
...RUN ALONG.
WHAT?
UNTIL FURTHER NOTICE, THE UNITED STATES ARMY HAS INSTITUTED A CURFEW IN BLACKWATER.
ANY MAN CAUGHT OUT ON THE STREETS PAST EIGHT O'CLOCK RUNS AN EXTREME RISK OF BEING SHOT ON SIGHT. SO, PLEASE...
...TO YOUR HOMES.

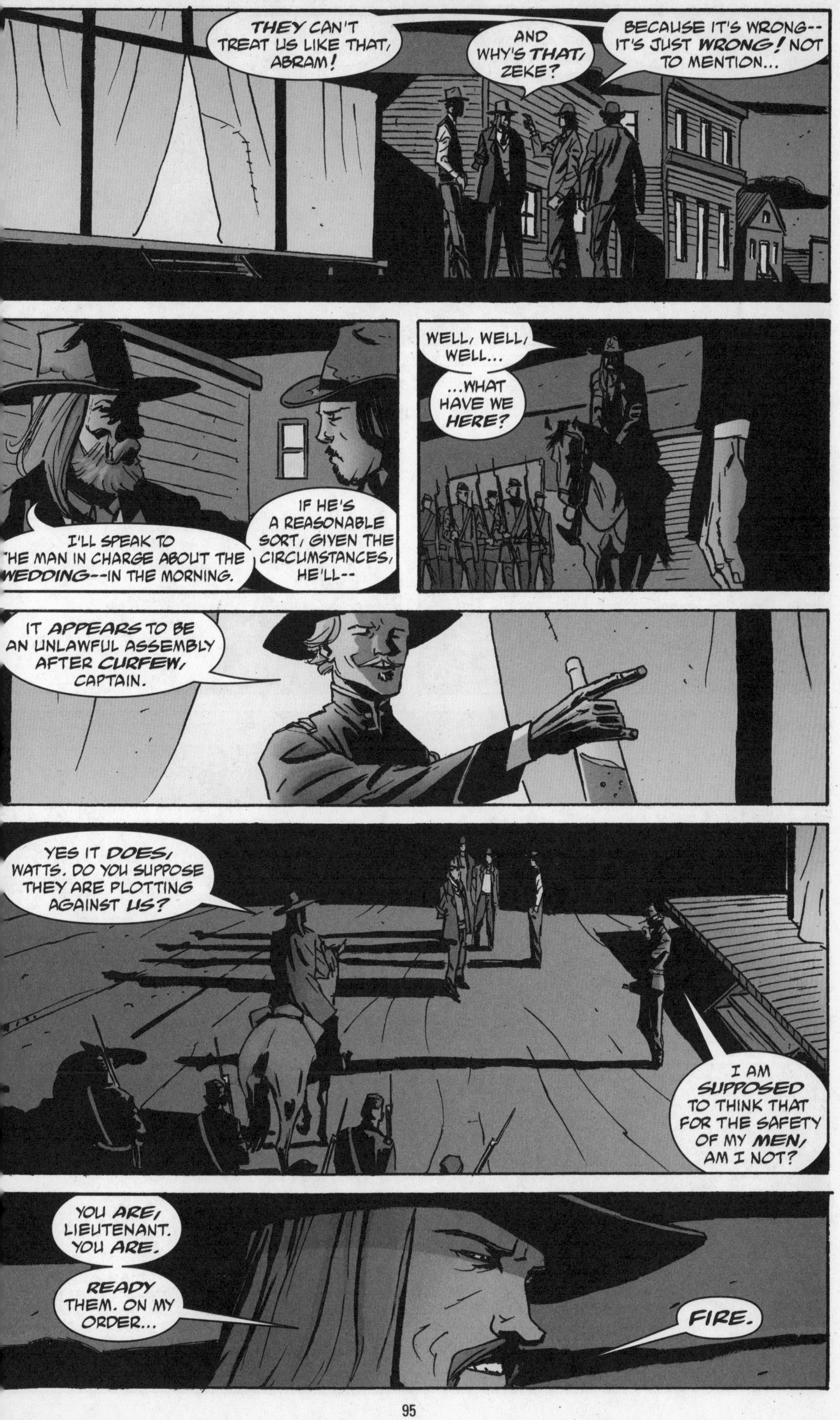
THEY CAN'T TREAT US LIKE THAT, ABRAM!
AND WHY'S THAT, ZEKE?
BECAUSE IT'S WRONG-- IT'S JUST WRONG! NOT TO MENTION...
I'LL SPEAK TO THE MAN IN CHARGE ABOUT THE WEDDING--IN THE MORNING.
IF HE'S A REASONABLE SORT, GIVEN THE CIRCUMSTANCES, HE'LL--
WELL, WELL, WELL...
...WHAT HAVE WE HERE?
IT APPEARS TO BE AN UNLAWFUL ASSEMBLY AFTER CURFEW, CAPTAIN.
YES IT DOES, WATTS. DO YOU SUPPOSE THEY ARE PLOTTING AGAINST US?
I AM SUPPOSED TO THINK THAT FOR THE SAFETY OF MY MEN, AM I NOT?
YOU ARE, LIEUTENANT. YOU ARE.
READY THEM. ON MY ORDER...
FIRE.

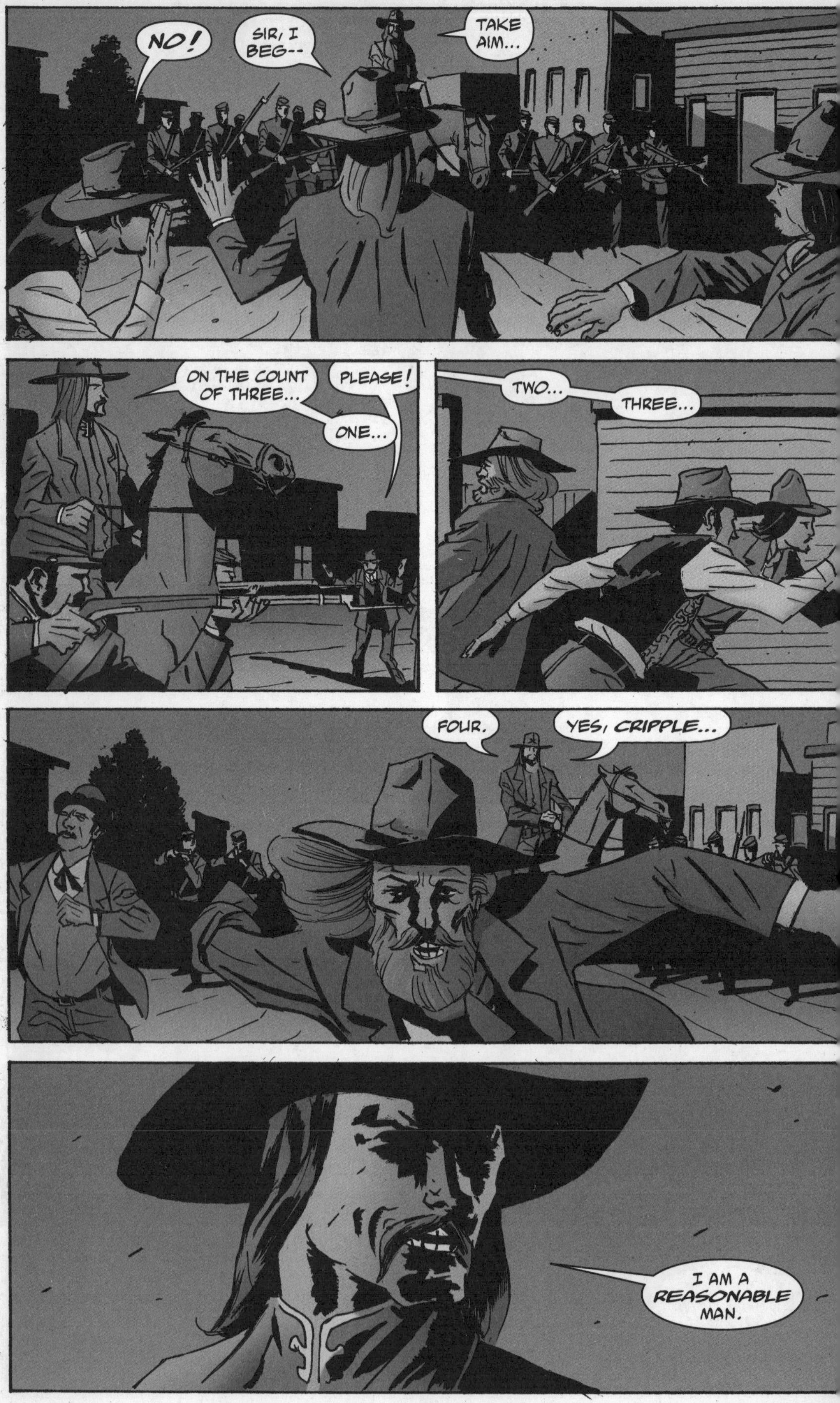
NO!
SIR, I BEG--
TAKE AIM...
ON THE COUNT OF THREE...
ONE...
PLEASE!
TWO...
THREE...
FOUR.
YES, CRIPPLE...
I AM A REASONABLE MAN.

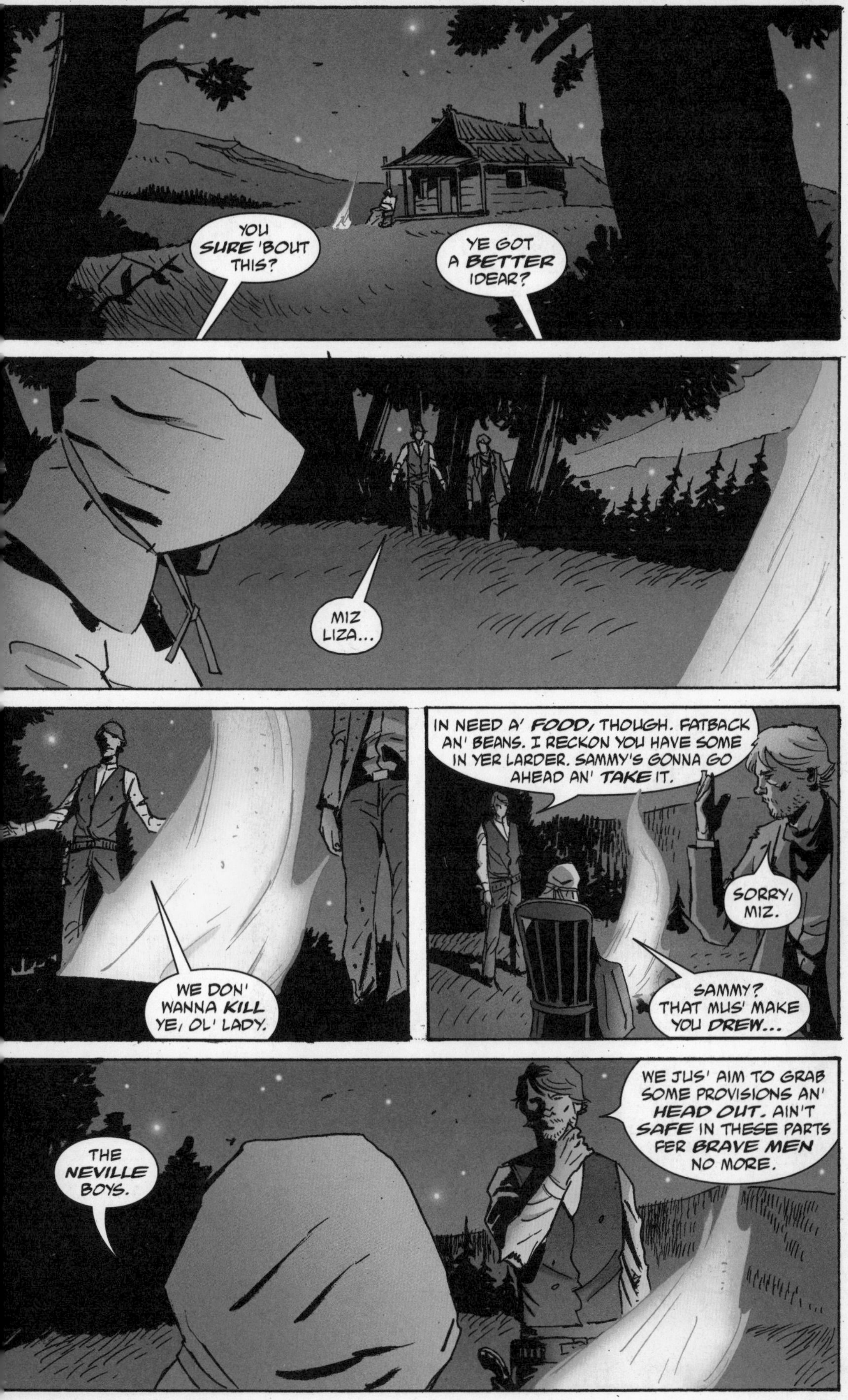

YOU SURE 'BOUT THIS?
YE GOT A BETTER IDEAR?
MIZ LIZA...
WE DON' WANNA KILL YE, OL' LADY.
IN NEED A' FOOD, THOUGH. FATBACK AN' BEANS. I RECKON YOU HAVE SOME IN YER LARDER. SAMMY'S GONNA GO AHEAD AN' TAKE IT.
SORRY, MIZ.
SAMMY? THAT MUS' MAKE YOU DREW...
THE NEVILLE BOYS.
WE JUS' AIM TO GRAB SOME PROVISIONS AN' HEAD OUT. AIN'T SAFE IN THESE PARTS FER BRAVE MEN NO MORE.

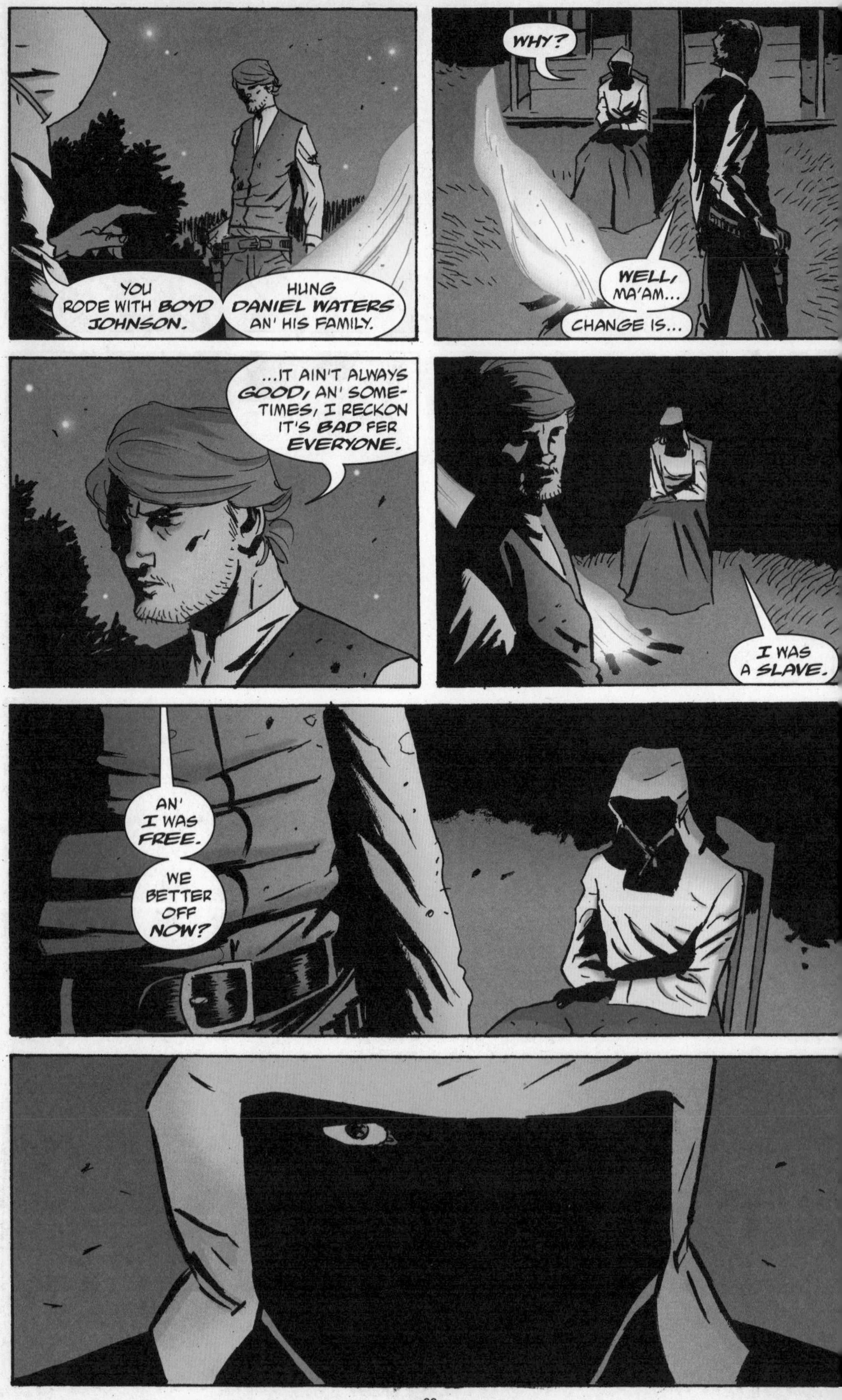
YOU RODE WITH BOYD JOHNSON.
HUNG DANIEL WATERS AN' HIS FAMILY.
WHY?
WELL, MA'AM...
CHANGE IS...
...IT AIN'T ALWAYS GOOD, AN' SOMETIMES, I RECKON IT'S BAD FER EVERYONE.
I WAS A SLAVE.
AN' I WAS FREE.
WE BETTER OFF NOW?

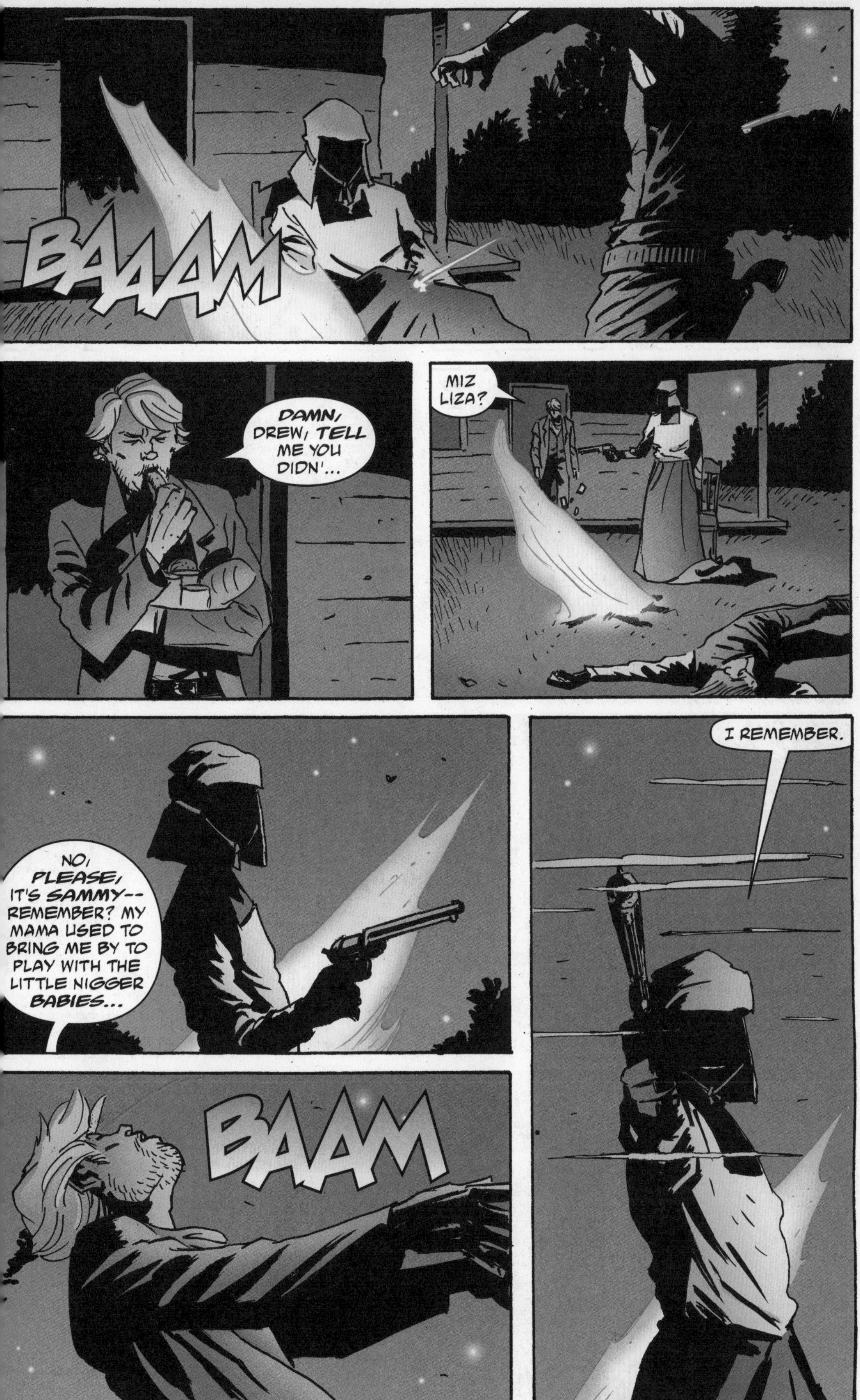
BAAAM
DAMN, DREW, TELL ME YOU DIDN'...
MIZ LIZA?
NO, PLEASE, IT'S SAMMY-- REMEMBER? MY MAMA USED TO BRING ME BY TO PLAY WITH THE LITTLE NIGGER BABIES...
I REMEMBER.
BAAM

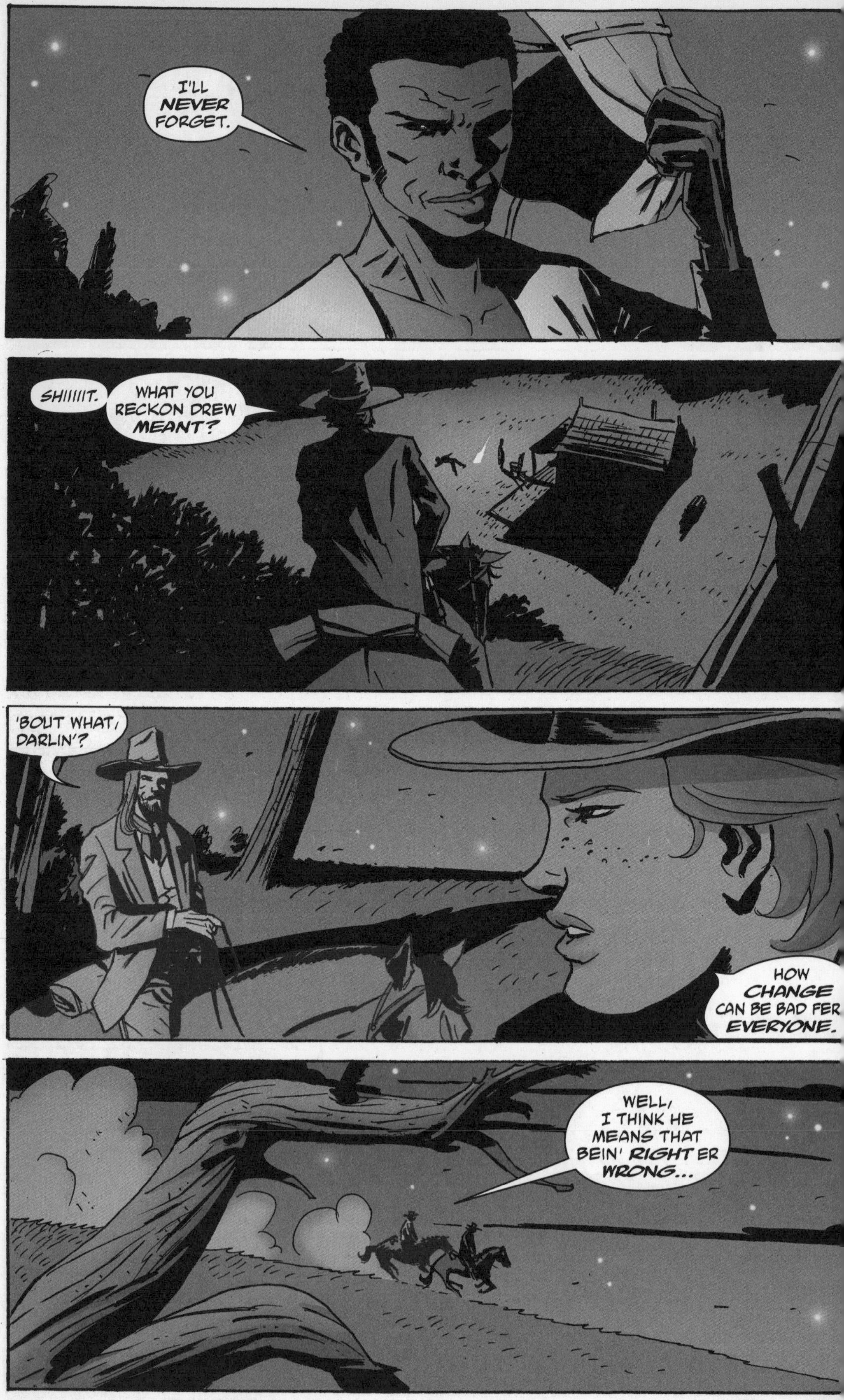
I'LL NEVER FORGET.
SHIIIIIT.
WHAT YOU RECKON DREW MEANT?
'BOUT WHAT, DARLIN'?
HOW CHANGE CAN BE BAD FER EVERYONE.
WELL, I THINK HE MEANS THAT BEIN' RIGHT ER WRONG...

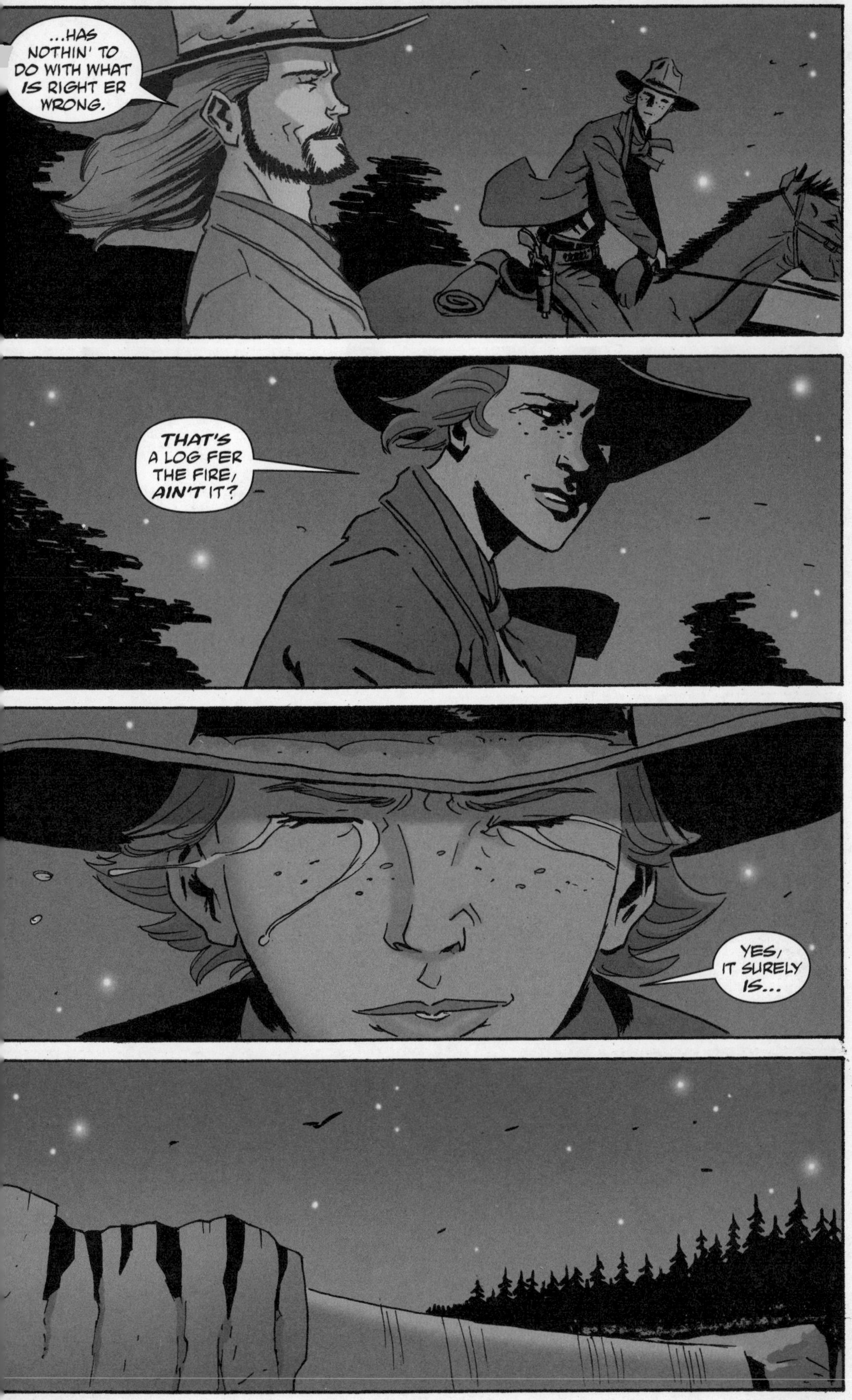
...HAS NOTHIN' TO DO WITH WHAT IS RIGHT ER WRONG.
THAT'S A LOG FER THE FIRE, AIN'T IT?
YES, IT SURELY IS...

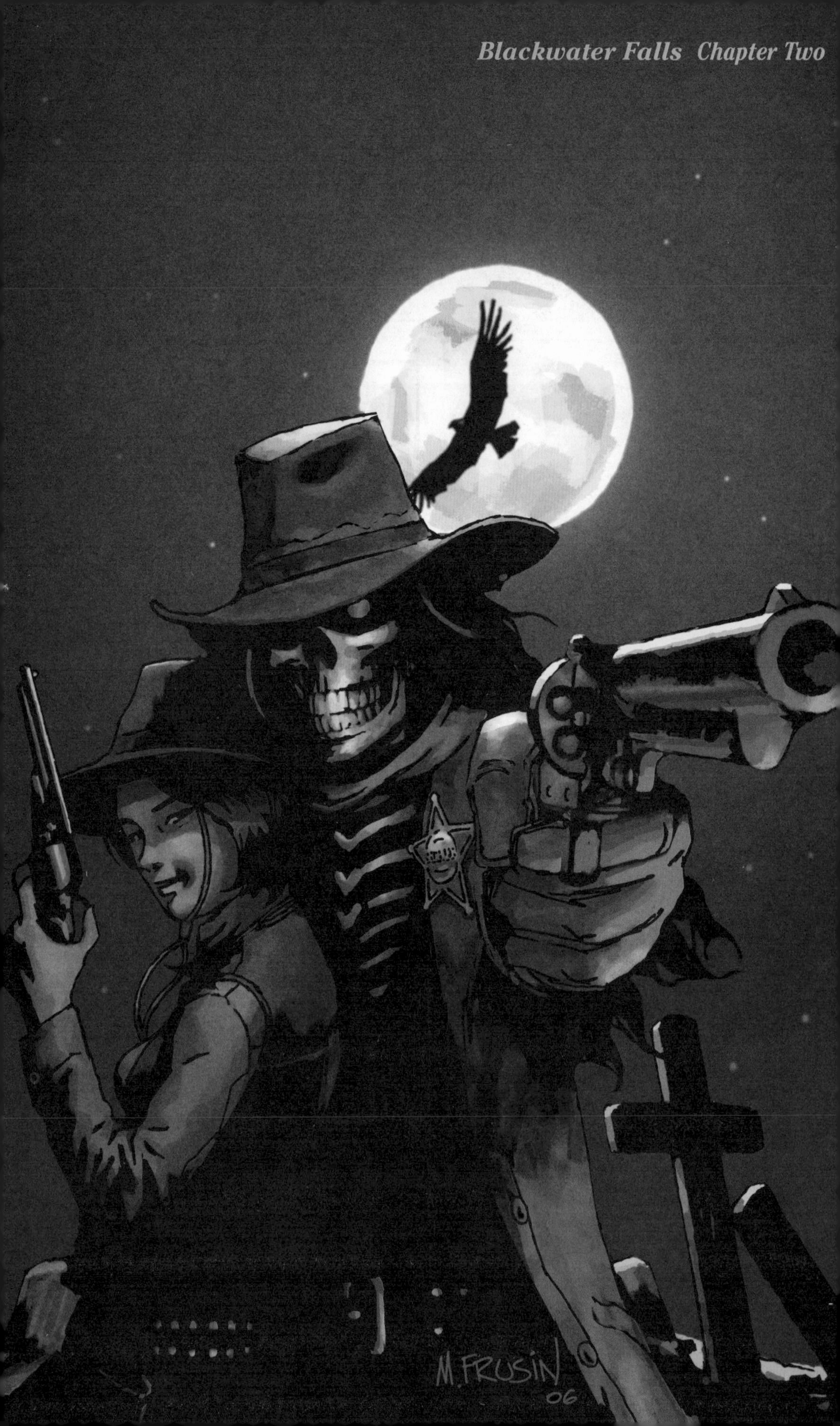
Blackwater Falls Chapter Two
M. FRUSIN
06

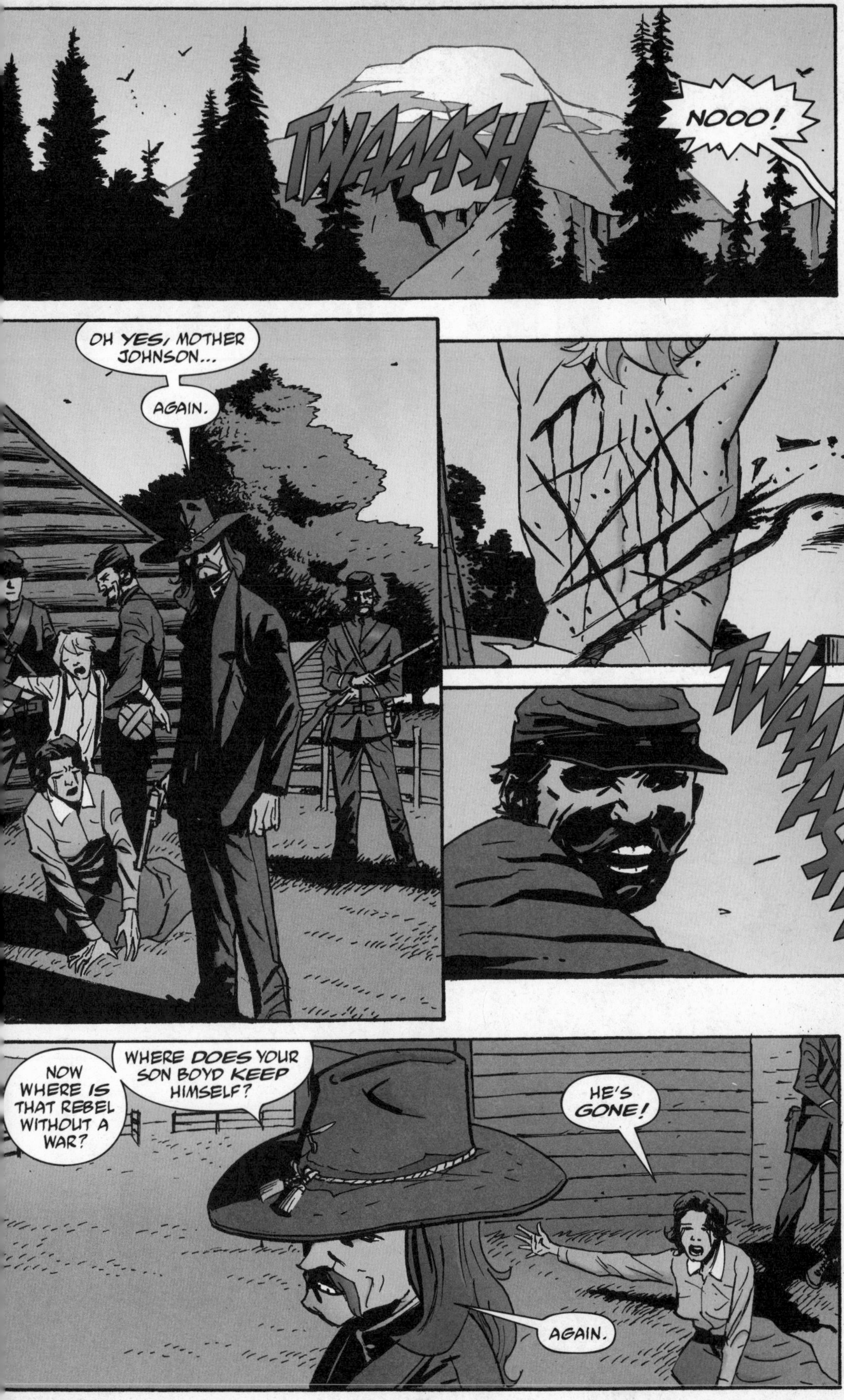
TWAAASH
NOOO!
OH YES, MOTHER JOHNSON...
AGAIN.
TWAAASH
NOW WHERE IS THAT REBEL WITHOUT A WAR?
WHERE DOES YOUR SON BOYD KEEP HIMSELF?
HE'S GONE!
AGAIN.

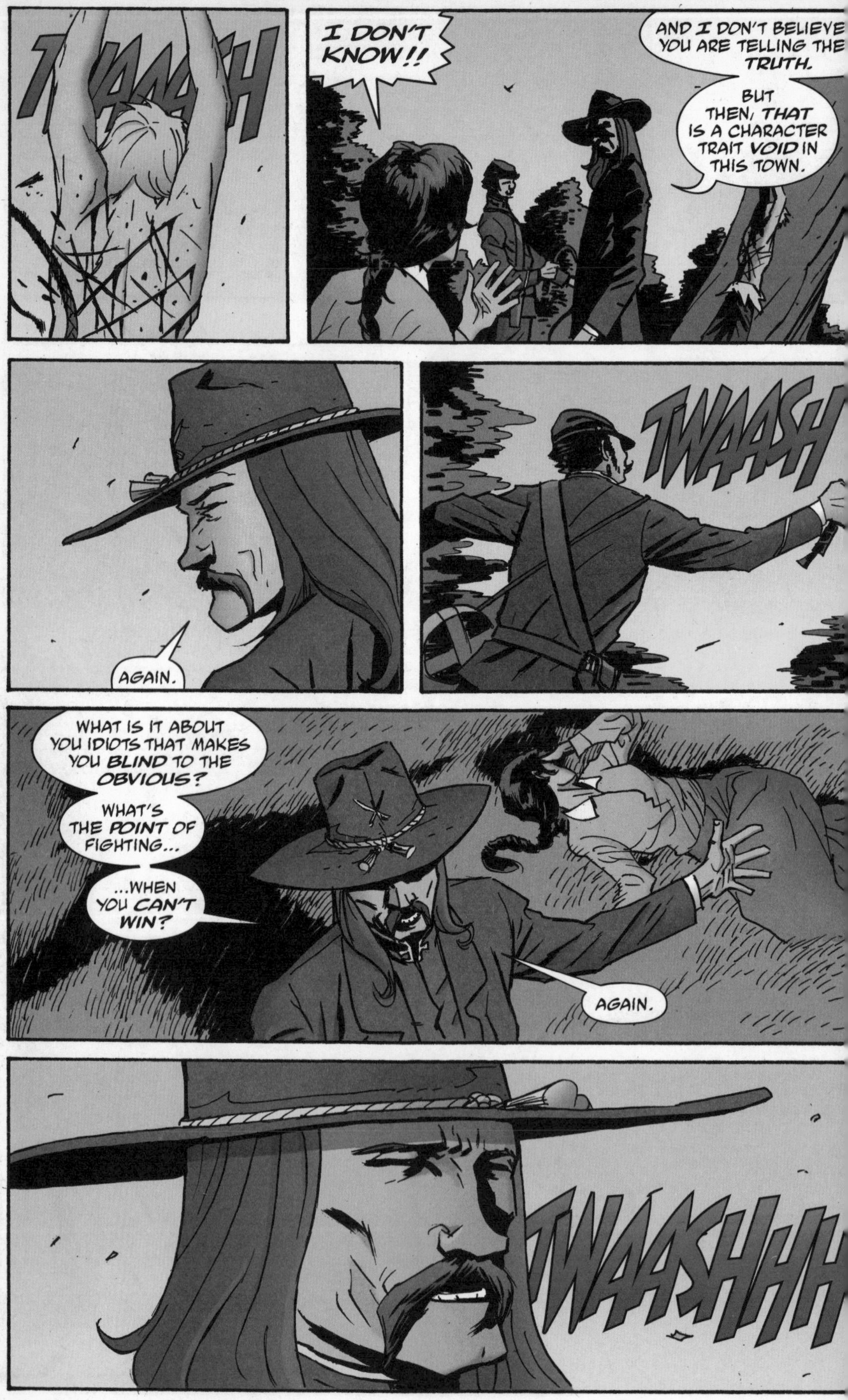
TWAAASH
I DON'T KNOW!!
AND I DON'T BELIEVE YOU ARE TELLING THE TRUTH.
BUT THEN, THAT IS A CHARACTER TRAIT VOID IN THIS TOWN.
AGAIN.
TWAASH
WHAT IS IT ABOUT YOU IDIOTS THAT MAKES YOU BLIND TO THE OBVIOUS?
WHAT'S THE POINT OF FIGHTING...
...WHEN YOU CAN'T WIN?
AGAIN.
TWAASHHH

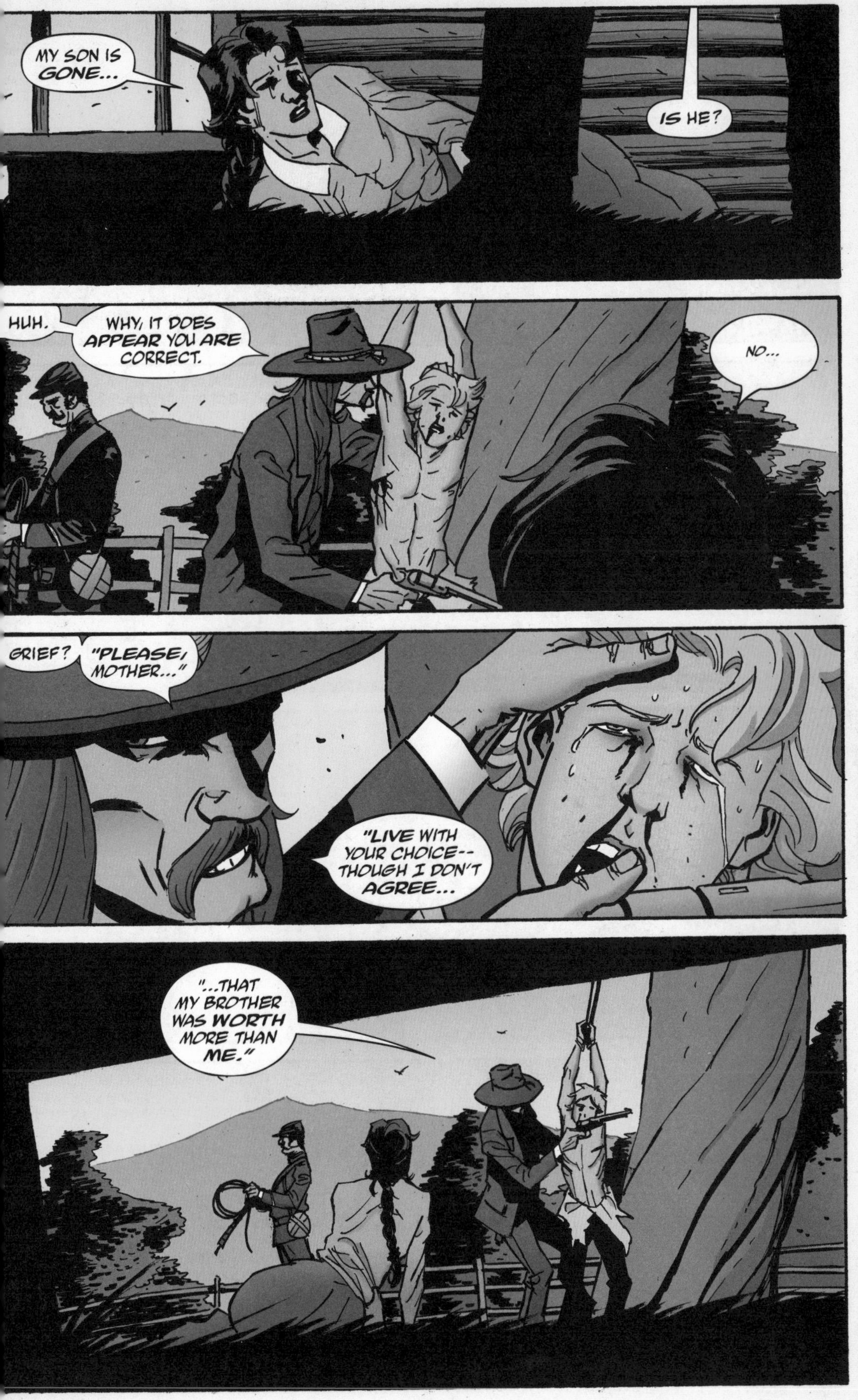
MY SON IS GONE...
IS HE?
HUH.
WHY, IT DOES APPEAR YOU ARE CORRECT.
NO...
GRIEF?
"PLEASE, MOTHER..."
"LIVE WITH YOUR CHOICE-- THOUGH I DON'T AGREE...
"...THAT MY BROTHER WAS WORTH MORE THAN ME."

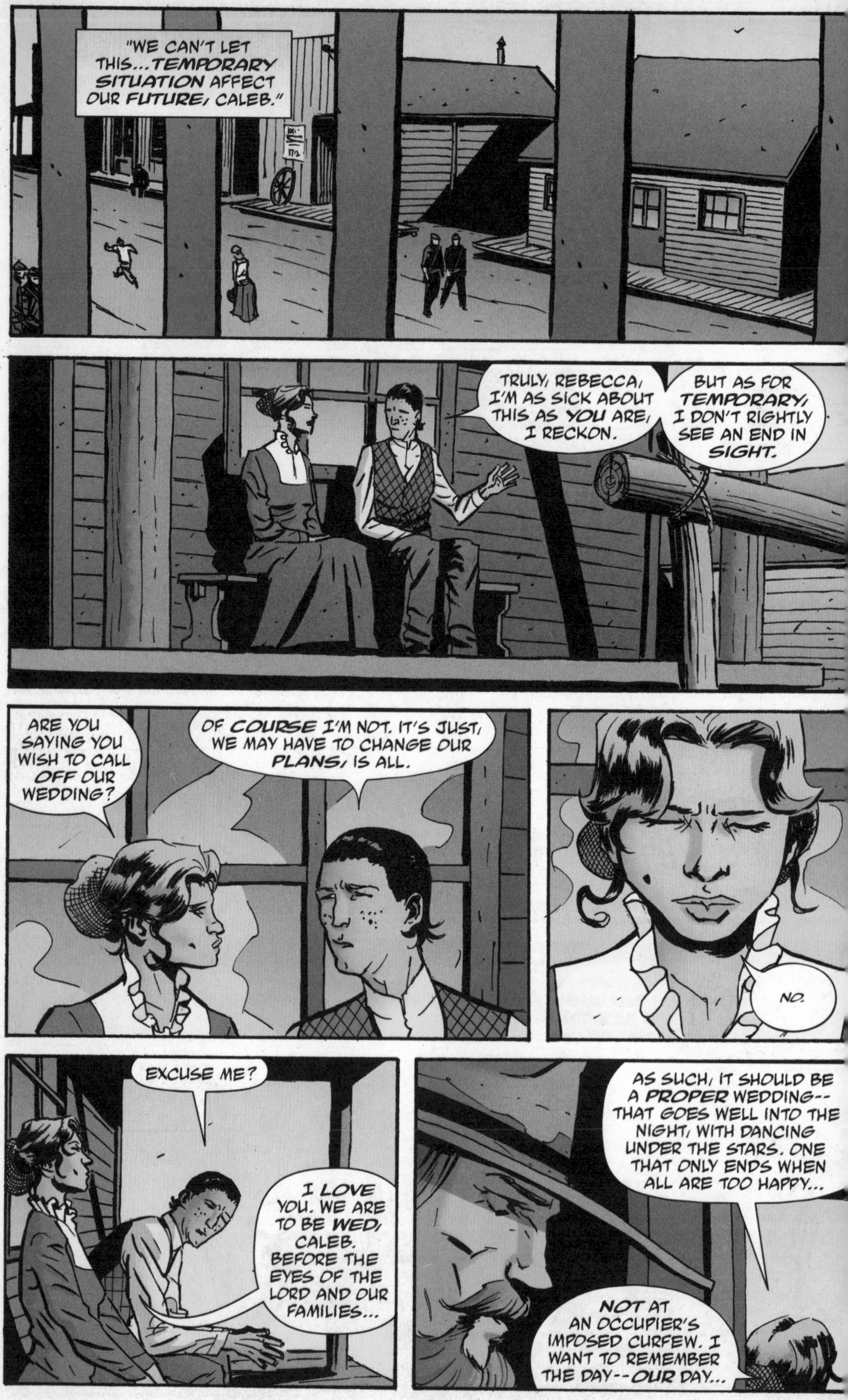
"WE CAN'T LET THIS... TEMPORARY SITUATION AFFECT OUR FUTURE, CALEB."
TRULY, REBECCA, I'M AS SICK ABOUT THIS AS YOU ARE, I RECKON.
BUT AS FOR TEMPORARY, I DON'T RIGHTLY SEE AN END IN SIGHT.
ARE YOU SAYING YOU WISH TO CALL OFF OUR WEDDING?
OF COURSE I'M NOT. IT'S JUST, WE MAY HAVE TO CHANGE OUR PLANS, IS ALL.
NO.
EXCUSE ME?
I LOVE YOU. WE ARE TO BE WED, CALEB. BEFORE THE EYES OF THE LORD AND OUR FAMILIES...
AS SUCH, IT SHOULD BE A PROPER WEDDING-- THAT GOES WELL INTO THE NIGHT, WITH DANCING UNDER THE STARS. ONE THAT ONLY ENDS WHEN ALL ARE TOO HAPPY...
NOT AT AN OCCUPIER'S IMPOSED CURFEW. I WANT TO REMEMBER THE DAY--OUR DAY...

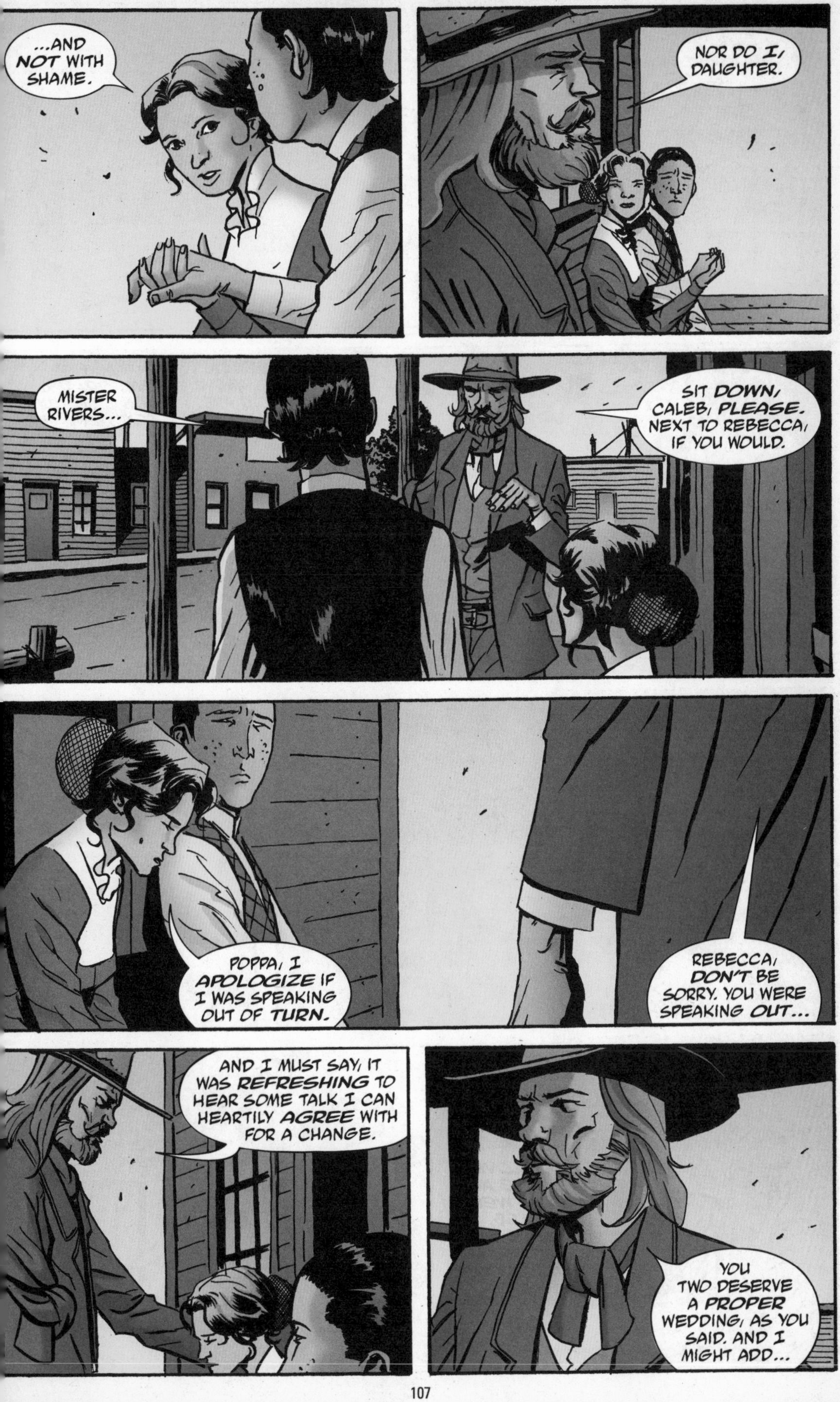

...AND NOT WITH SHAME.
NOR DO I, DAUGHTER.
MISTER RIVERS...
SIT DOWN, CALEB, PLEASE. NEXT TO REBECCA, IF YOU WOULD.
POPPA, I APOLOGIZE IF I WAS SPEAKING OUT OF TURN.
REBECCA, DON'T BE SORRY. YOU WERE SPEAKING OUT...
AND I MUST SAY, IT WAS REFRESHING TO HEAR SOME TALK I CAN HEARTILY AGREE WITH FOR A CHANGE.
YOU TWO DESERVE A PROPER WEDDING, AS YOU SAID. AND I MIGHT ADD...

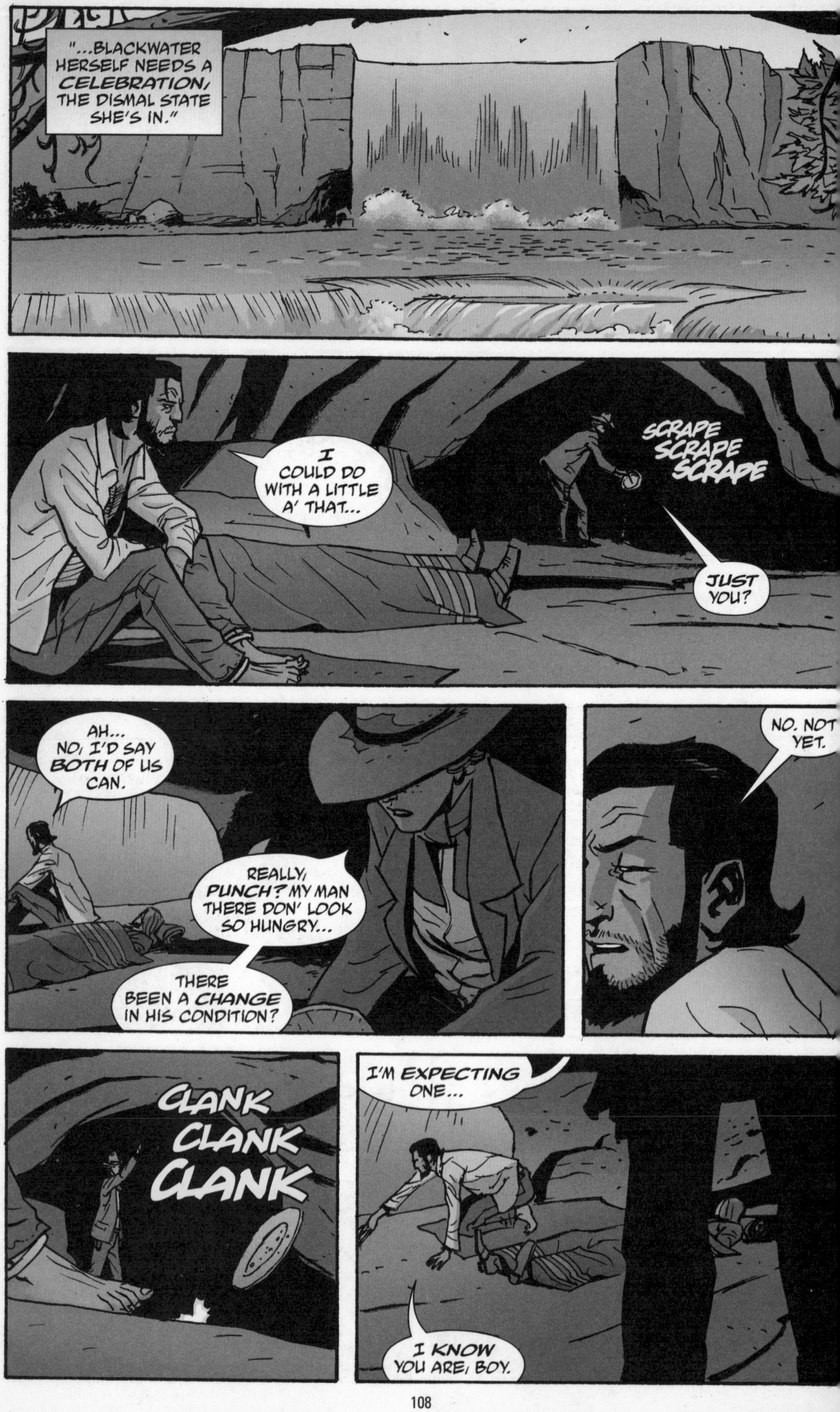
"...BLACKWATER HERSELF NEEDS A CELEBRATION, THE DISMAL STATE SHE'S IN."
I COULD DO WITH A LITTLE A' THAT...
SCRAPE SCRAPE SCRAPE
JUST YOU?
AH... NO, I'D SAY BOTH OF US CAN.
REALLY, PUNCH? MY MAN THERE DON' LOOK SO HUNGRY...
THERE BEEN A CHANGE IN HIS CONDITION?
NO. NOT YET.
CLANK CLANK CLANK
I'M EXPECTING ONE...
I KNOW YOU ARE, BOY.

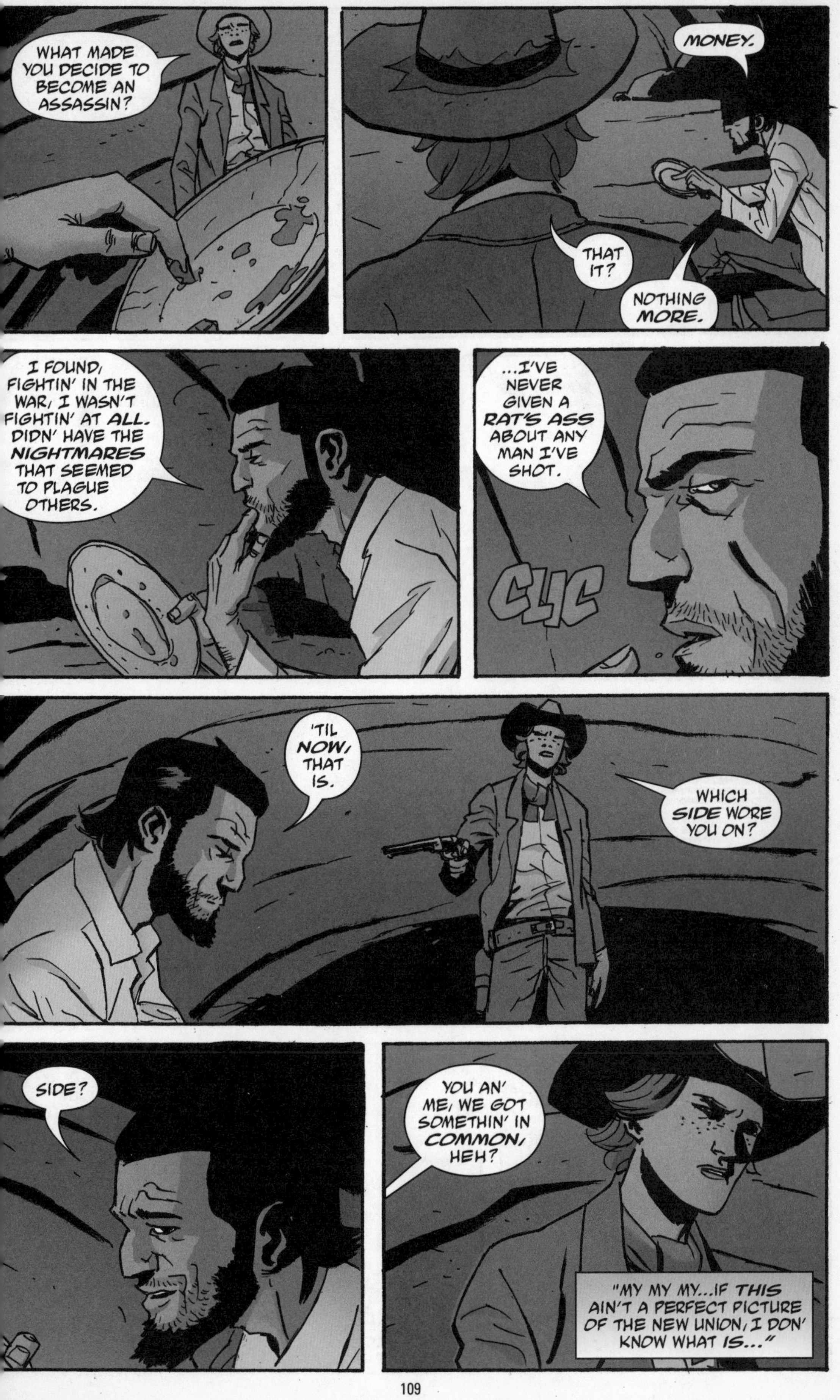
WHAT MADE YOU DECIDE TO BECOME AN ASSASSIN?
MONEY.
THAT IT?
NOTHING MORE.
I FOUND, FIGHTIN' IN THE WAR, I WASN'T FIGHTIN' AT ALL. DIDN' HAVE THE NIGHTMARES THAT SEEMED TO PLAGUE OTHERS.
...I'VE NEVER GIVEN A RAT'S ASS ABOUT ANY MAN I'VE SHOT.
CLIC
'TIL NOW, THAT IS.
WHICH SIDE WORE YOU ON?
SIDE?
YOU AN' ME, WE GOT SOMETHIN' IN COMMON, HEH?
"MY MY MY...IF THIS AIN'T A PERFECT PICTURE OF THE NEW UNION, I DON' KNOW WHAT IS..."

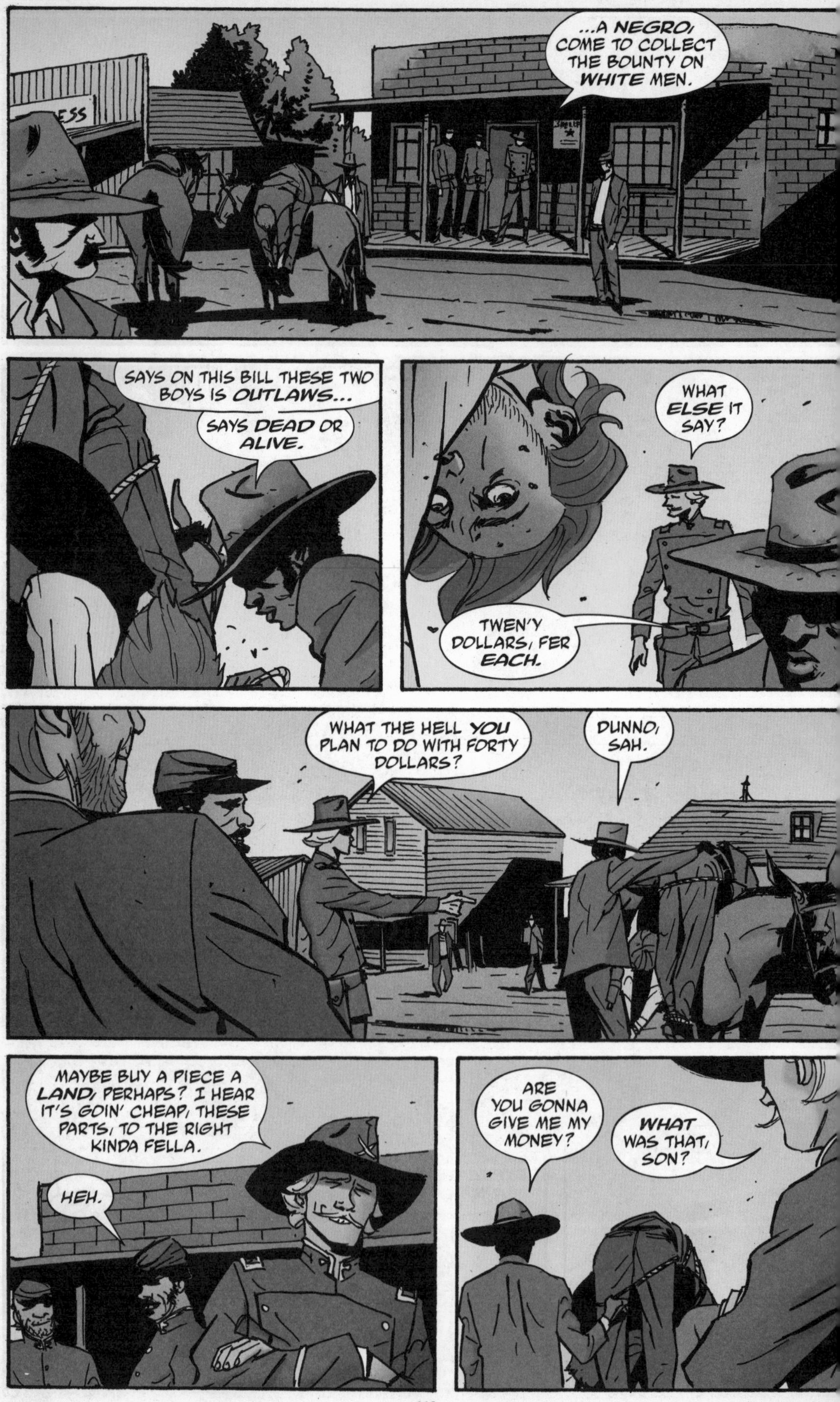
...A NEGRO, COME TO COLLECT THE BOUNTY ON WHITE MEN.
SAYS ON THIS BILL THESE TWO BOYS IS OUTLAWS...
SAYS DEAD OR ALIVE.
WHAT ELSE IT SAY?
TWEN'Y DOLLARS, FER EACH.
WHAT THE HELL YOU PLAN TO DO WITH FORTY DOLLARS?
DUNNO, SAH.
MAYBE BUY A PIECE A LAND, PERHAPS? I HEAR IT'S GOIN' CHEAP, THESE PARTS, TO THE RIGHT KINDA FELLA.
HEH.
ARE YOU GONNA GIVE ME MY MONEY?
WHAT WAS THAT, SON?

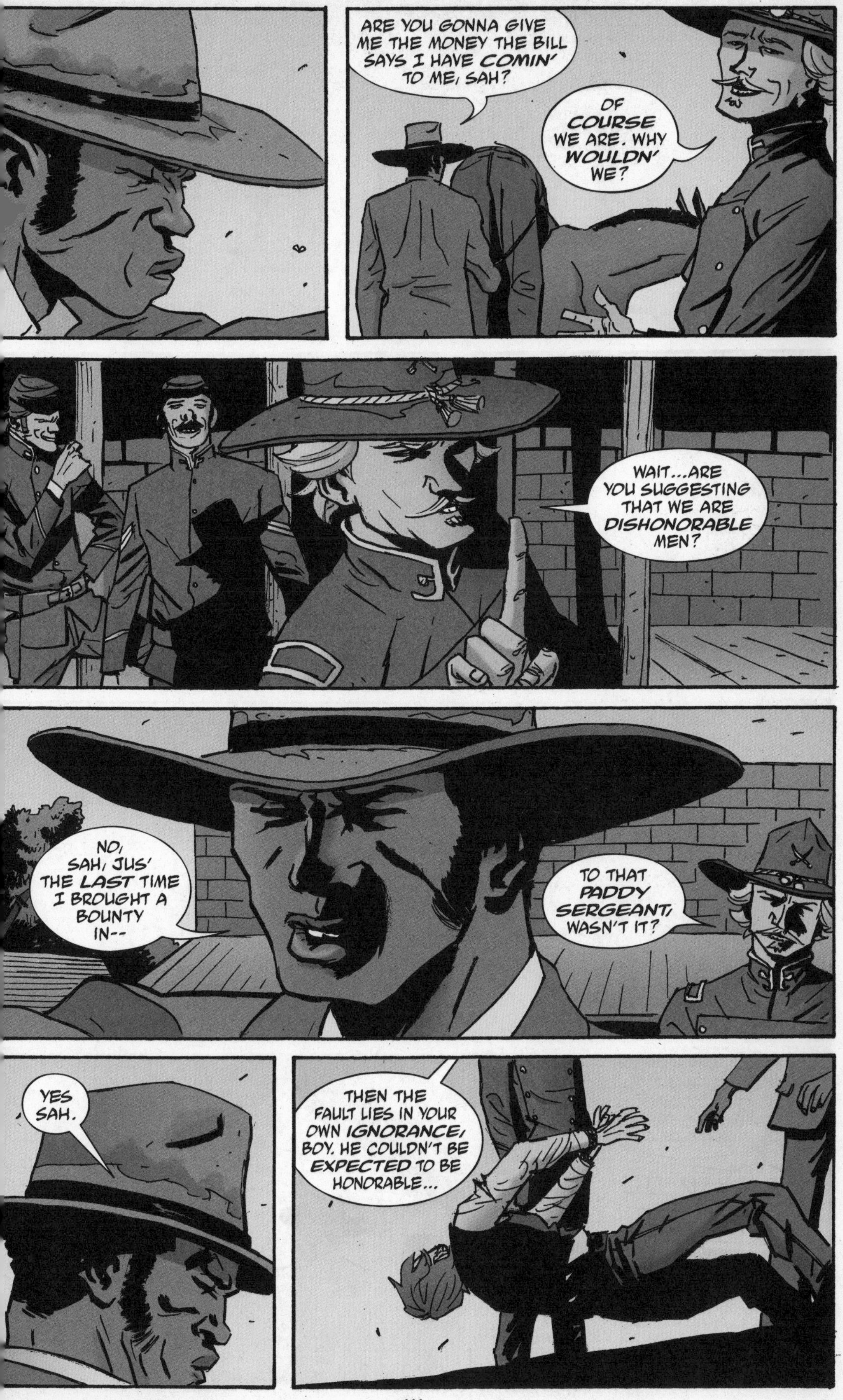
ARE YOU GONNA GIVE ME THE MONEY THE BILL SAYS I HAVE COMIN' TO ME, SAH?
OF COURSE WE ARE. WHY WOULDN' WE?
WAIT...ARE YOU SUGGESTING THAT WE ARE DISHONORABLE MEN?
NO, SAH, JUS' THE LAST TIME I BROUGHT A BOUNTY IN--
TO THAT PADDY SERGEANT, WASN'T IT?
YES SAH.
THEN THE FAULT LIES IN YOUR OWN IGNORANCE, BOY. HE COULDN'T BE EXPECTED TO BE HONORABLE...

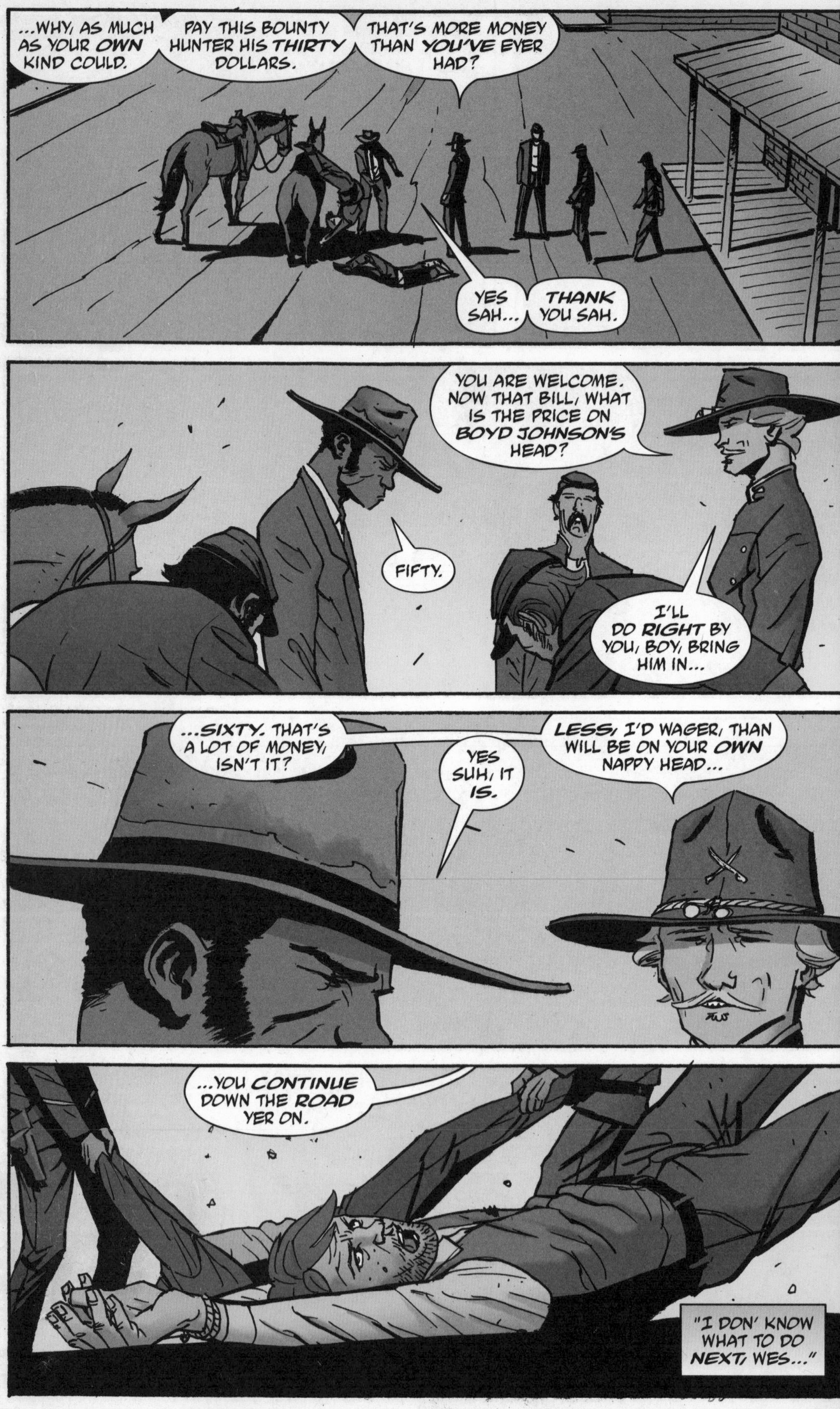

...WHY, AS MUCH AS YOUR OWN KIND COULD.
PAY THIS BOUNTY HUNTER HIS THIRTY DOLLARS.
THAT'S MORE MONEY THAN YOU'VE EVER HAD?
YES SAH...
THANK YOU SAH.
YOU ARE WELCOME. NOW THAT BILL, WHAT IS THE PRICE ON BOYD JOHNSON'S HEAD?
FIFTY.
I'LL DO RIGHT BY YOU, BOY, BRING HIM IN...
...SIXTY. THAT'S A LOT OF MONEY, ISN'T IT?
YES SUH, IT IS.
LESS, I'D WAGER, THAN WILL BE ON YOUR OWN NAPPY HEAD...
...YOU CONTINUE DOWN THE ROAD YER ON.
"I DON' KNOW WHAT TO DO NEXT, WES..."

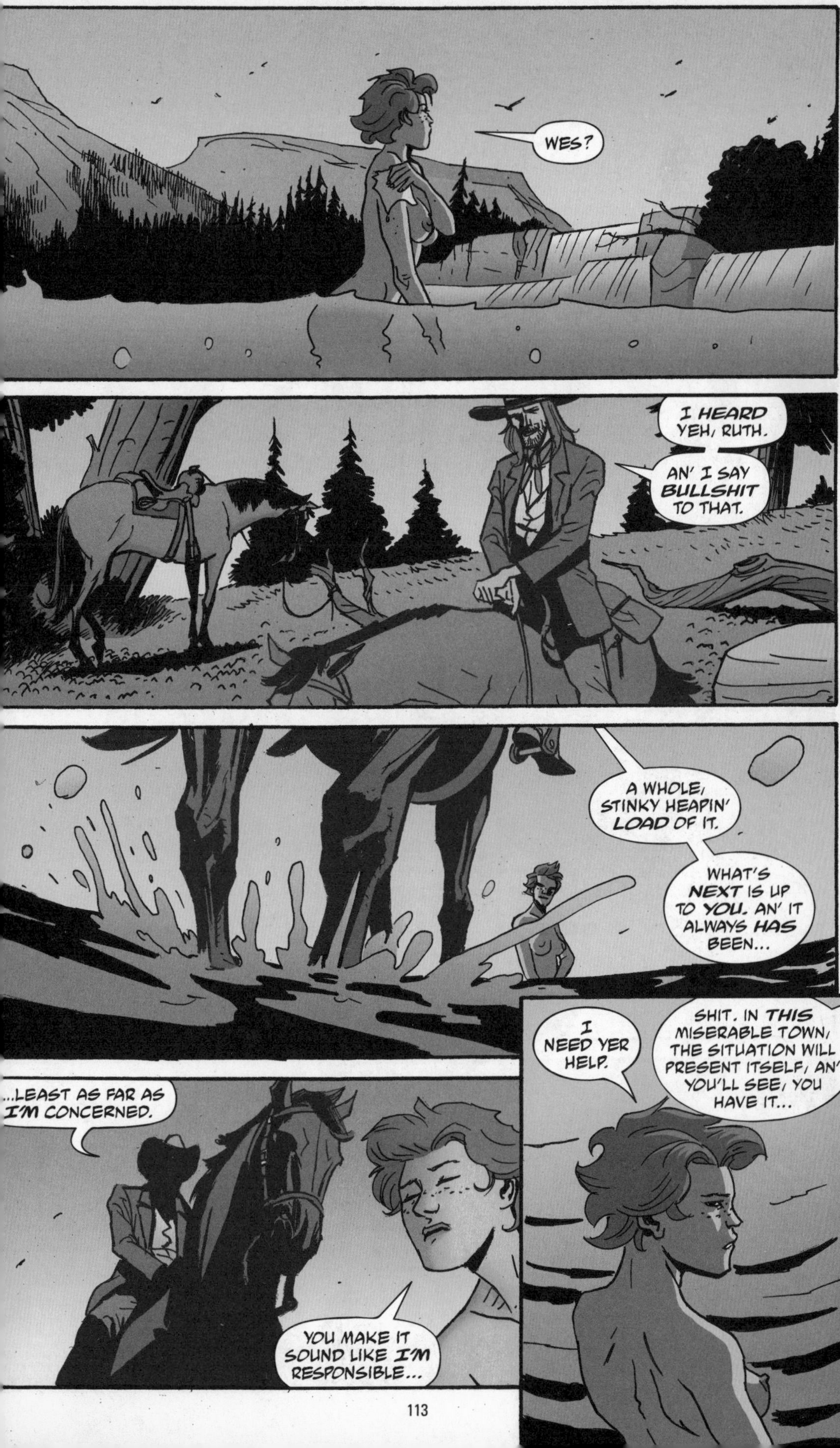

WES?
I HEARD YEH, RUTH.
AN' I SAY BULLSHIT TO THAT.
A WHOLE, STINKY HEAPIN' LOAD OF IT.
WHAT'S NEXT IS UP TO YOU. AN' IT ALWAYS HAS BEEN...
...LEAST AS FAR AS I'M CONCERNED.
YOU MAKE IT SOUND LIKE I'M RESPONSIBLE...
I NEED YER HELP.
SHIT. IN THIS MISERABLE TOWN, THE SITUATION WILL PRESENT ITSELF, AN' YOU'LL SEE, YOU HAVE IT...

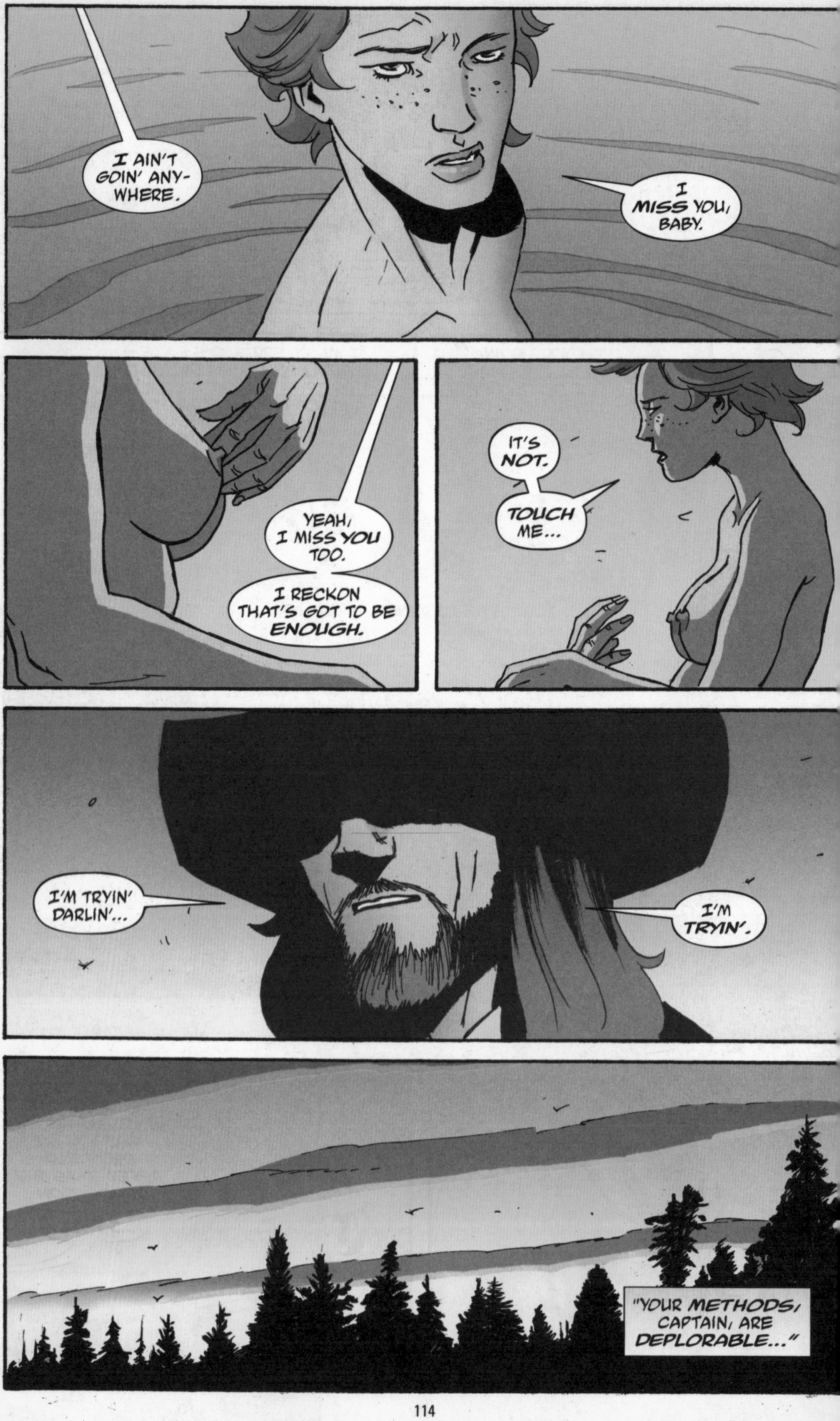
I AIN'T GOIN' ANYWHERE.
I MISS YOU, BABY.
YEAH, I MISS YOU TOO.
I RECKON THAT'S GOT TO BE ENOUGH.
IT'S NOT.
TOUCH ME...
I'M TRYIN' DARLIN'...
I'M TRYIN'.
"YOUR METHODS, CAPTAIN, ARE DEPLORABLE..."

...I REFUSE TO ALLOW YOU TO OPERATE IN SUCH A MANNER.

TERRORIZING THE POPULATION OF BLACKWATER--WHAT IS THE POINT, SIR?

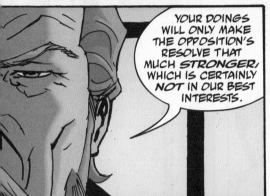

YOUR DOINGS WILL ONLY MAKE THE OPPOSITION'S RESOLVE THAT MUCH STRONGER, WHICH IS CERTAINLY NOT IN OUR BEST INTERESTS.

I MEAN, FOR GOD'S SAKE-- EVERY MAN, WOMAN OR CHILD IN THIS TOWN IS NOT A CRIMINAL AND CANNOT BE TREATED AS SUCH--DO YOU UNDERSTAND ME?

ALLOW? MR. TROTTER, IT IS NOT IN YOUR JURISDICTION TO GRANT ME ALLOWANCE.

AND IF I HAVE TO KILL A CHILD TO EXPOSE THOSE WHO YOU SO GENTEELLY REFER TO AS THE OPPOSITION...

...I WILL.

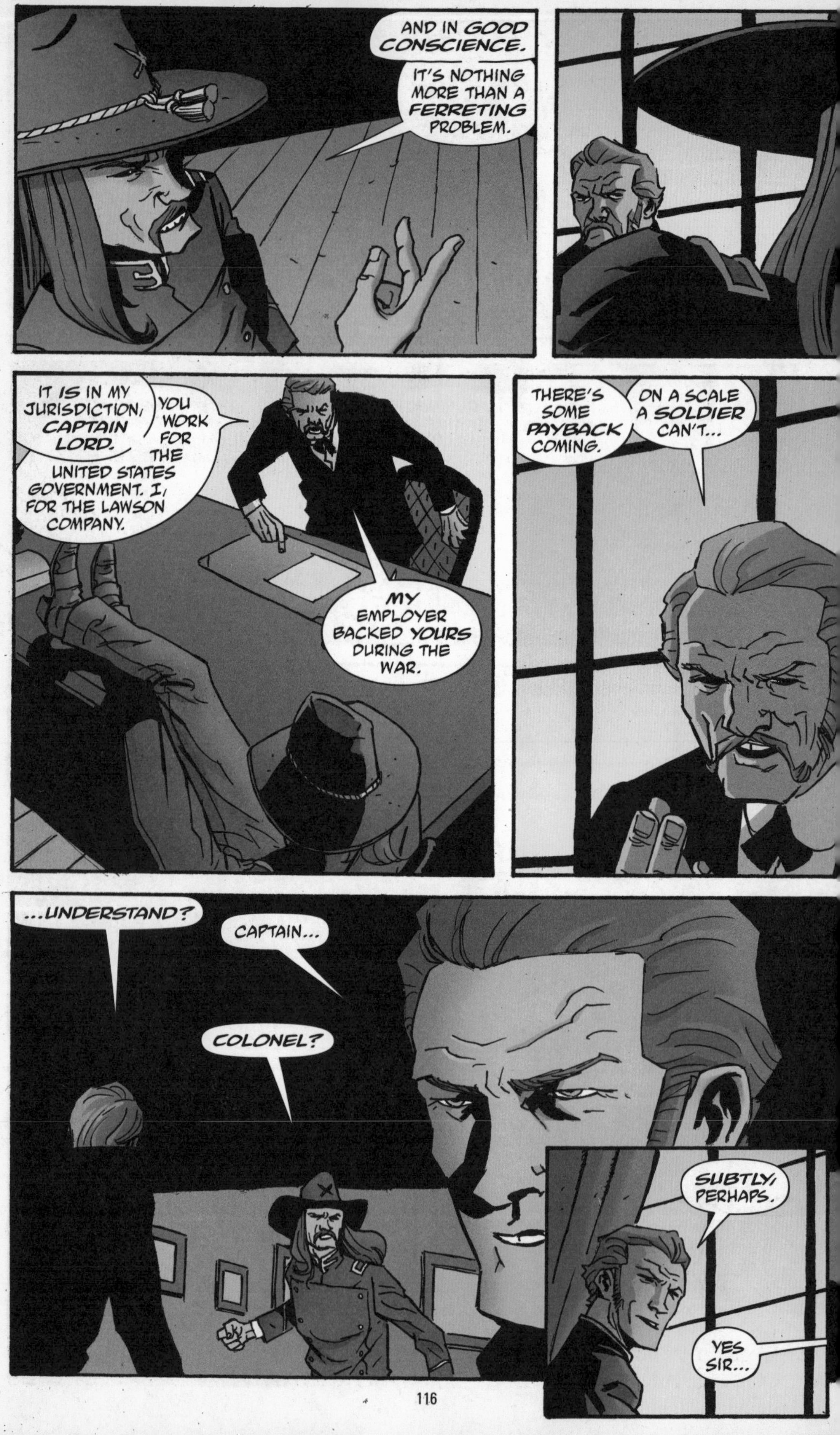
AND IN GOOD CONSCIENCE.
IT'S NOTHING MORE THAN A FERRETING PROBLEM.
IT IS IN MY JURISDICTION, CAPTAIN LORD.
YOU WORK FOR THE UNITED STATES GOVERNMENT. I, FOR THE LAWSON COMPANY.
MY EMPLOYER BACKED YOURS DURING THE WAR.
THERE'S SOME PAYBACK COMING.
ON A SCALE A SOLDIER CAN'T...
...UNDERSTAND?
CAPTAIN...
COLONEL?
SUBTLY, PERHAPS.
YES SIR...

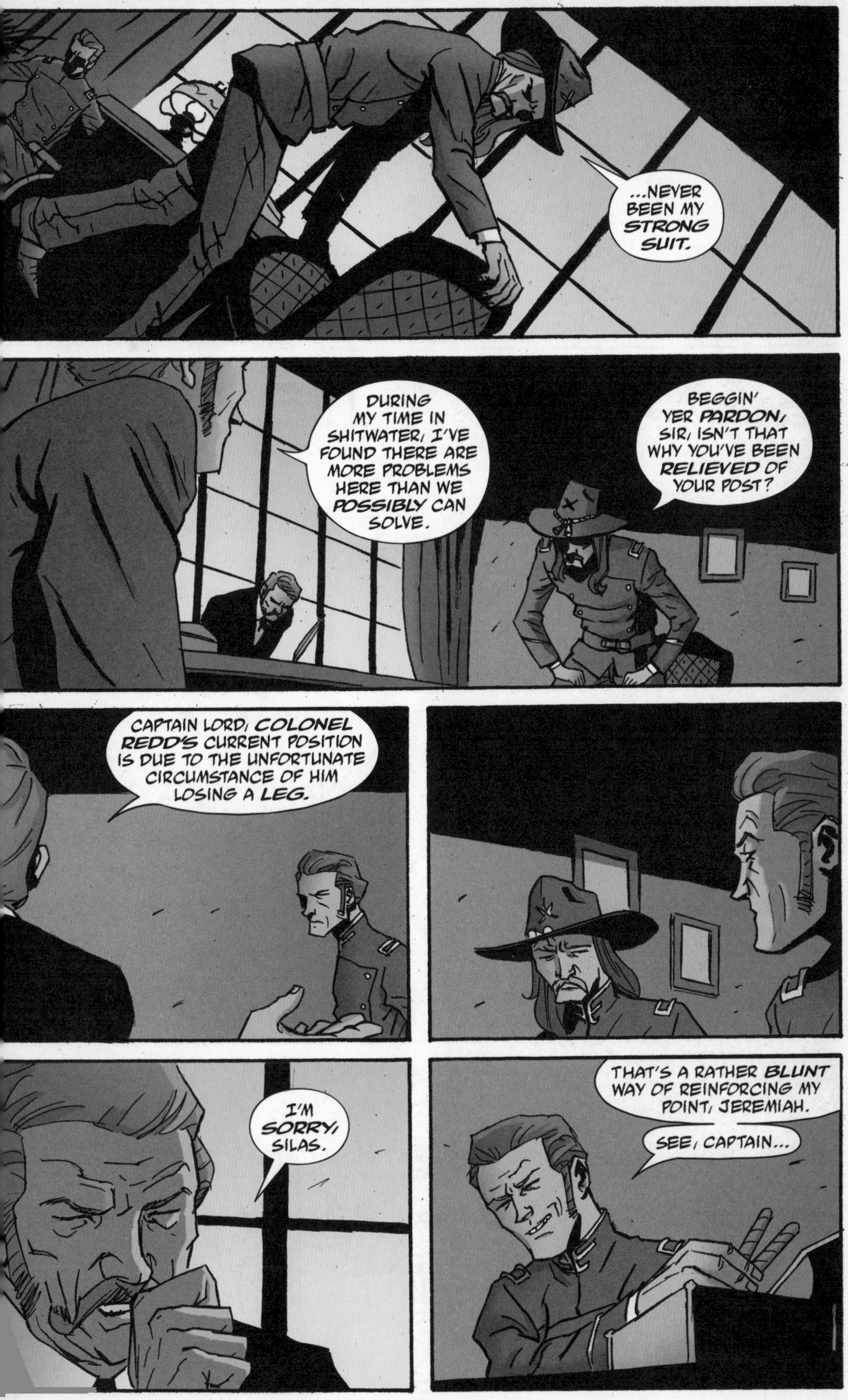
...NEVER BEEN MY STRONG SUIT.
DURING MY TIME IN SHITWATER, I'VE FOUND THERE ARE MORE PROBLEMS HERE THAN WE POSSIBLY CAN SOLVE.
BEGGIN' YER PARDON, SIR, ISN'T THAT WHY YOU'VE BEEN RELIEVED OF YOUR POST?
CAPTAIN LORD, COLONEL REDD'S CURRENT POSITION IS DUE TO THE UNFORTUNATE CIRCUMSTANCE OF HIM LOSING A LEG.
I'M SORRY, SILAS.
THAT'S A RATHER BLUNT WAY OF REINFORCING MY POINT, JEREMIAH.
SEE, CAPTAIN...

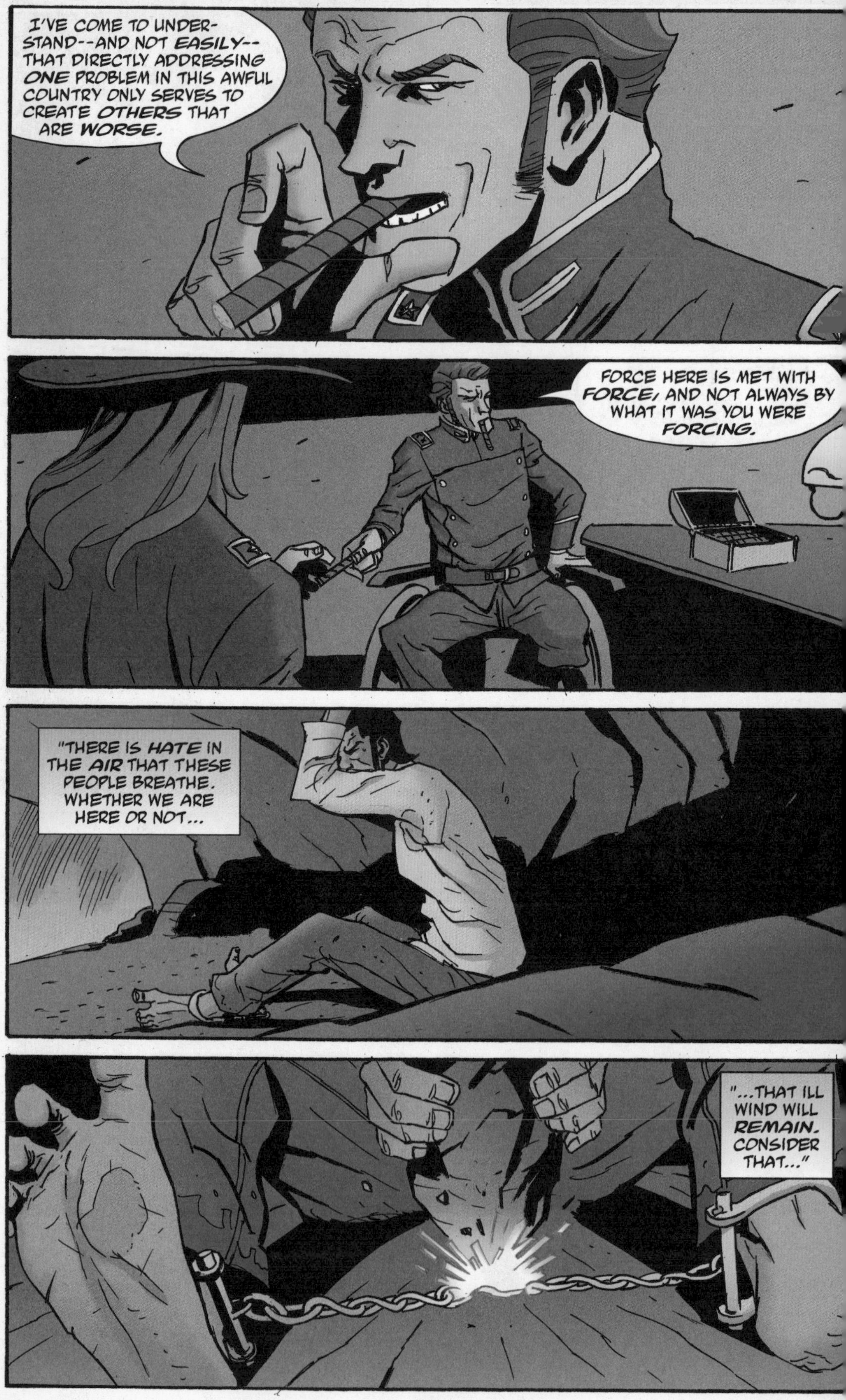
I'VE COME TO UNDER-STAND--AND NOT EASILY--THAT DIRECTLY ADDRESSING ONE PROBLEM IN THIS AWFUL COUNTRY ONLY SERVES TO CREATE OTHERS THAT ARE WORSE.
FORCE HERE IS MET WITH FORCE, AND NOT ALWAYS BY WHAT IT WAS YOU WERE FORCING.
"THERE IS HATE IN THE AIR THAT THESE PEOPLE BREATHE. WHETHER WE ARE HERE OR NOT...
"...THAT ILL WIND WILL REMAIN. CONSIDER THAT..."

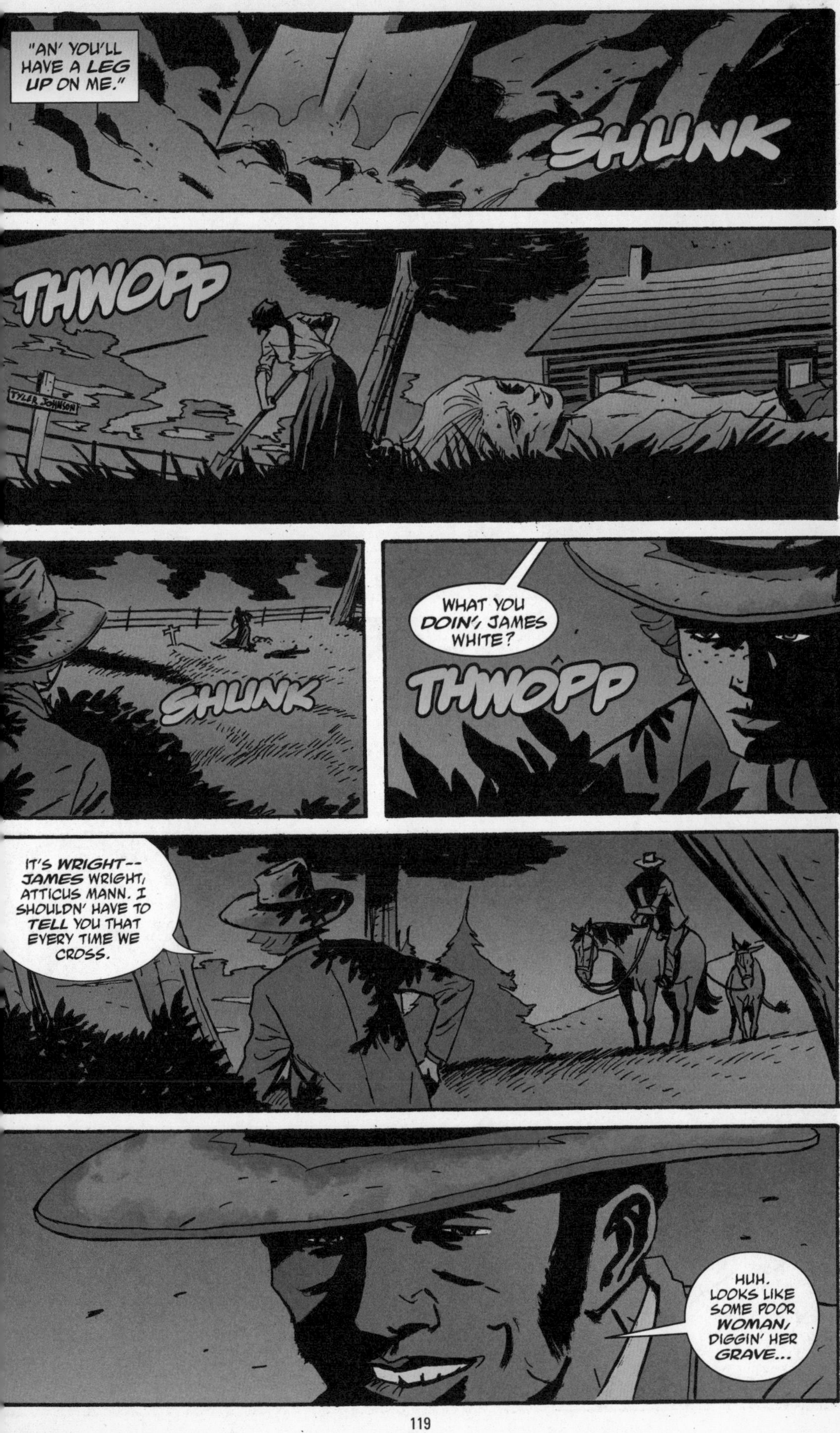
"AN' YOU'LL HAVE A LEG UP ON ME."
SHUNK
THWOPP
TYLER JOHNSON
SHUNK
WHAT YOU DOIN', JAMES WHITE?
THWOPP
IT'S WRIGHT-- JAMES WRIGHT, ATTICUS MANN. I SHOULDN' HAVE TO TELL YOU THAT EVERY TIME WE CROSS.
HUH. LOOKS LIKE SOME POOR WOMAN, DIGGIN' HER GRAVE...

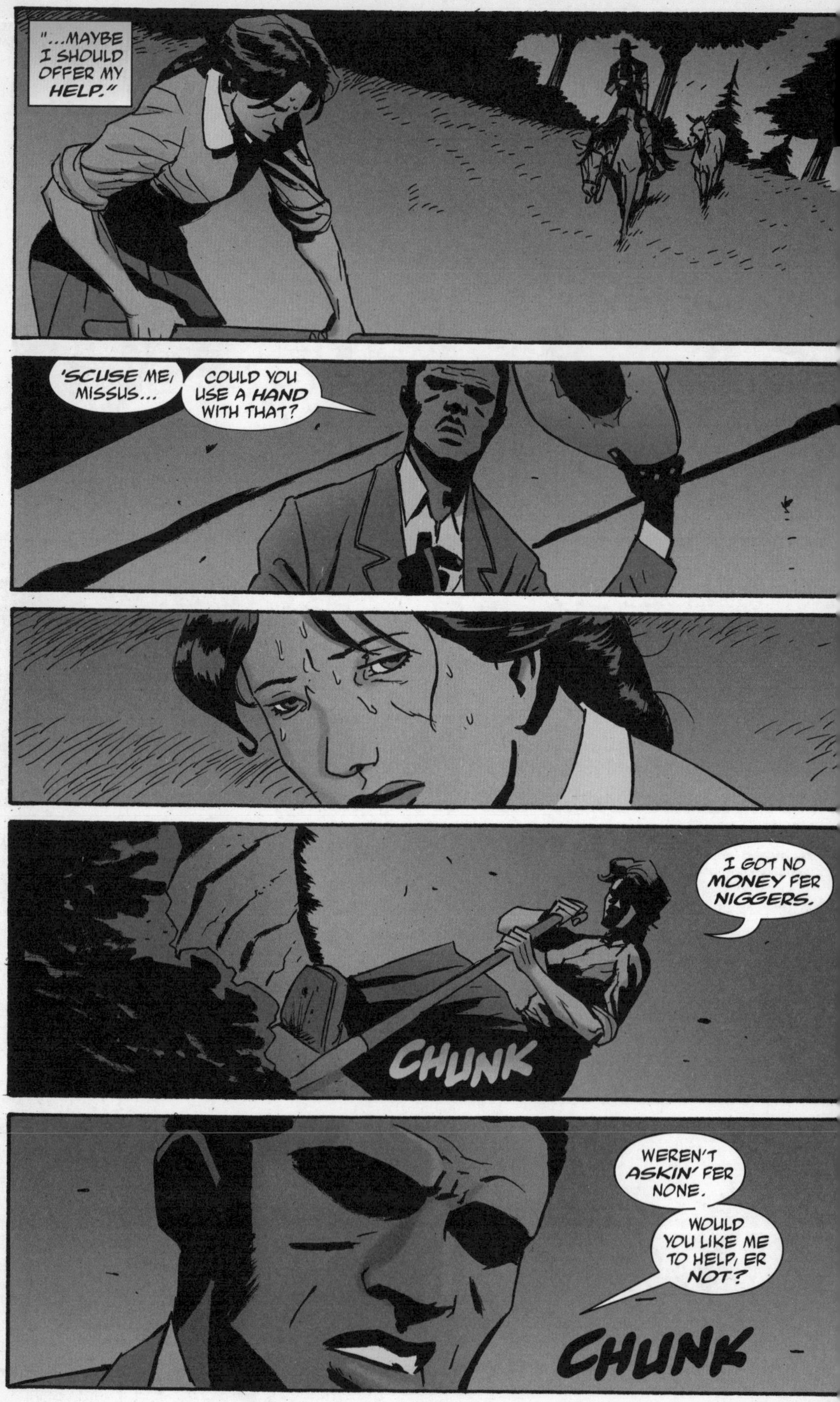
"...MAYBE I SHOULD OFFER MY HELP."
'SCUSE ME, MISSUS...
COULD YOU USE A HAND WITH THAT?
I GOT NO MONEY FER NIGGERS.
CHUNK
WEREN'T ASKIN' FER NONE.
WOULD YOU LIKE ME TO HELP, ER NOT?
CHUNK

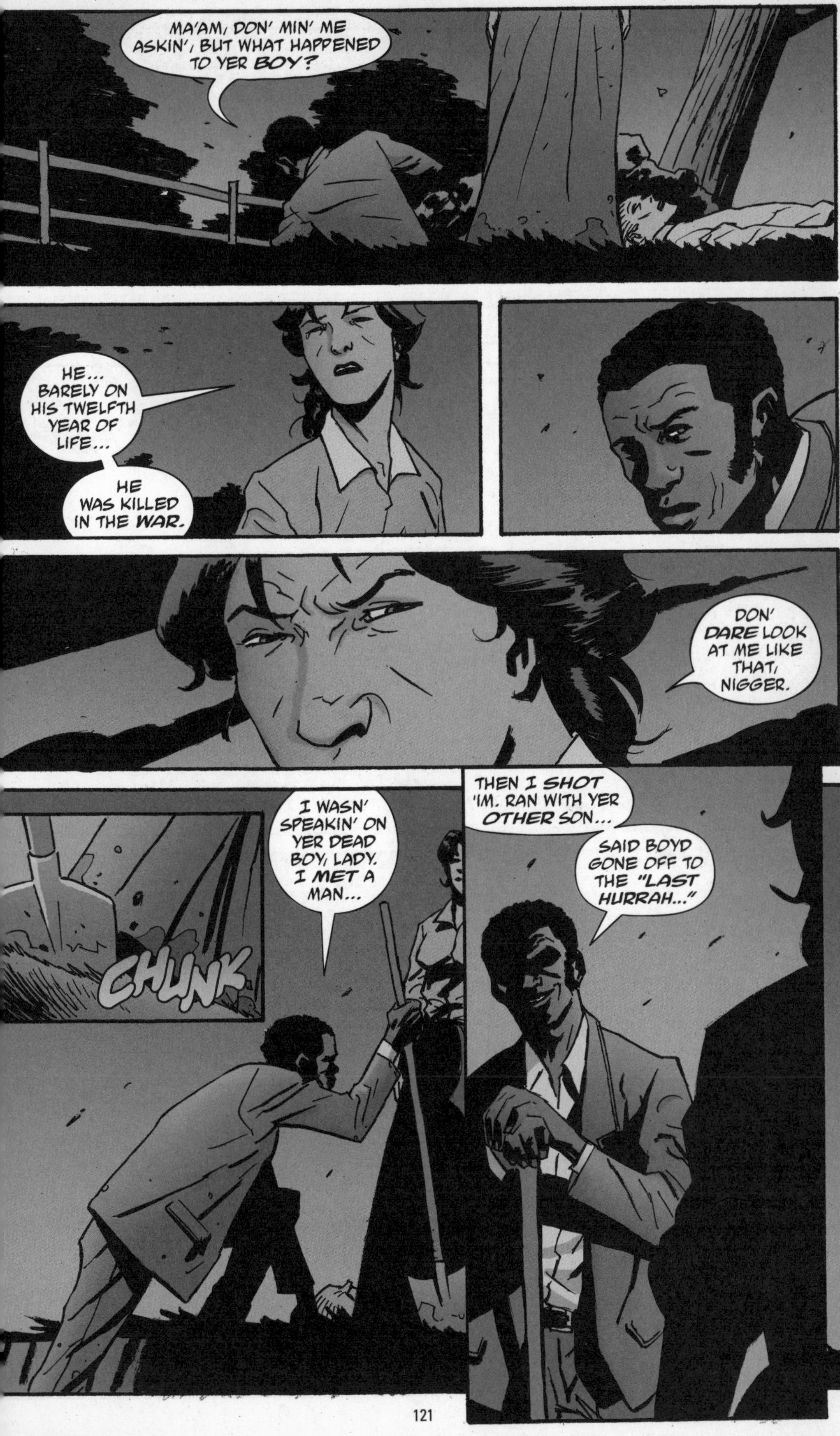
MA'AM, DON' MIN' ME ASKIN', BUT WHAT HAPPENED TO YER BOY?
HE... BARELY ON HIS TWELFTH YEAR OF LIFE...
HE WAS KILLED IN THE WAR.
DON' DARE LOOK AT ME LIKE THAT, NIGGER.
CHUNK
I WASN' SPEAKIN' ON YER DEAD BOY, LADY. I MET A MAN...
THEN I SHOT 'IM. RAN WITH YER OTHER SON...
SAID BOYD GONE OFF TO THE "LAST HURRAH..."

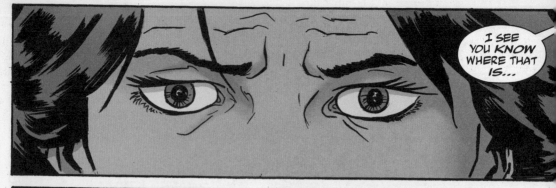

I SEE YOU *KNOW* WHERE THAT IS...

YOU'D DO RIGHT TO *TELL* ME.

S-PTOO

CHUNK

AAAHH!

SHIT, ATTICUS...

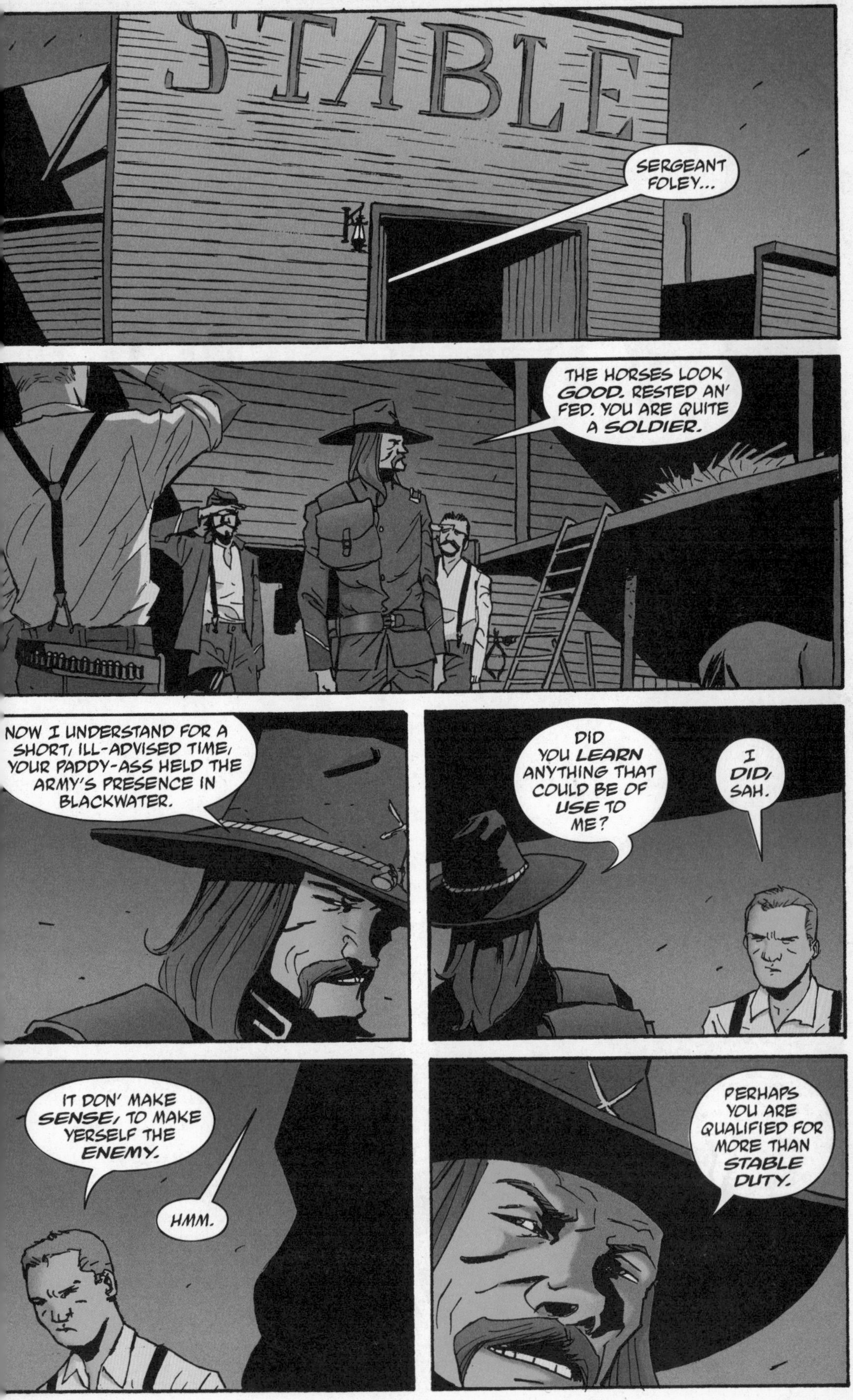
STABLE
SERGEANT FOLEY...
THE HORSES LOOK GOOD. RESTED AN' FED. YOU ARE QUITE A SOLDIER.
NOW I UNDERSTAND FOR A SHORT, ILL-ADVISED TIME, YOUR PADDY-ASS HELD THE ARMY'S PRESENCE IN BLACKWATER.
DID YOU LEARN ANYTHING THAT COULD BE OF USE TO ME?
I DID, SAH.
IT DON' MAKE SENSE, TO MAKE YERSELF THE ENEMY.
HMM.
PERHAPS YOU ARE QUALIFIED FOR MORE THAN STABLE DUTY.

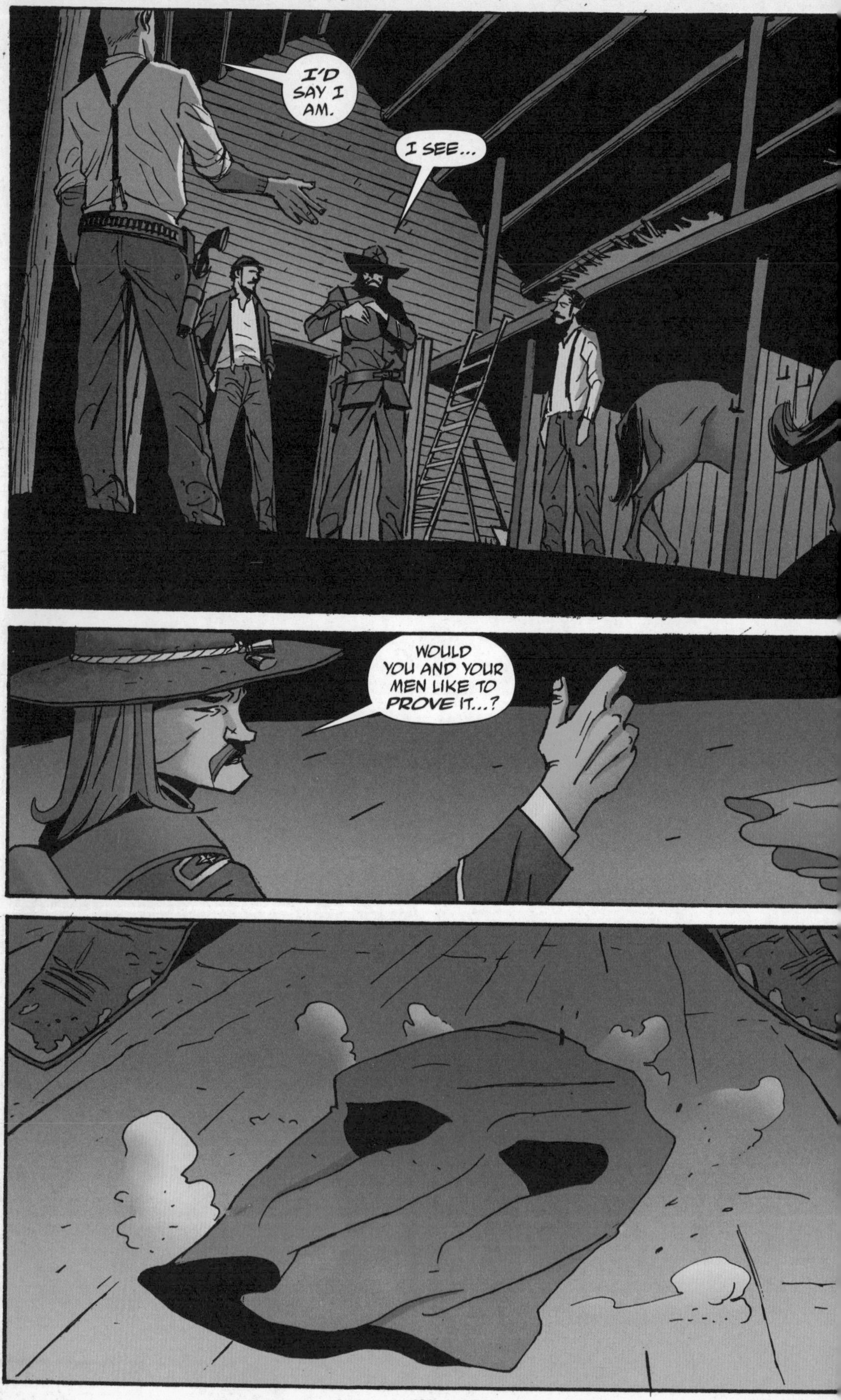
I'D SAY I AM.
I SEE...
WOULD YOU AND YOUR MEN LIKE TO PROVE IT...?

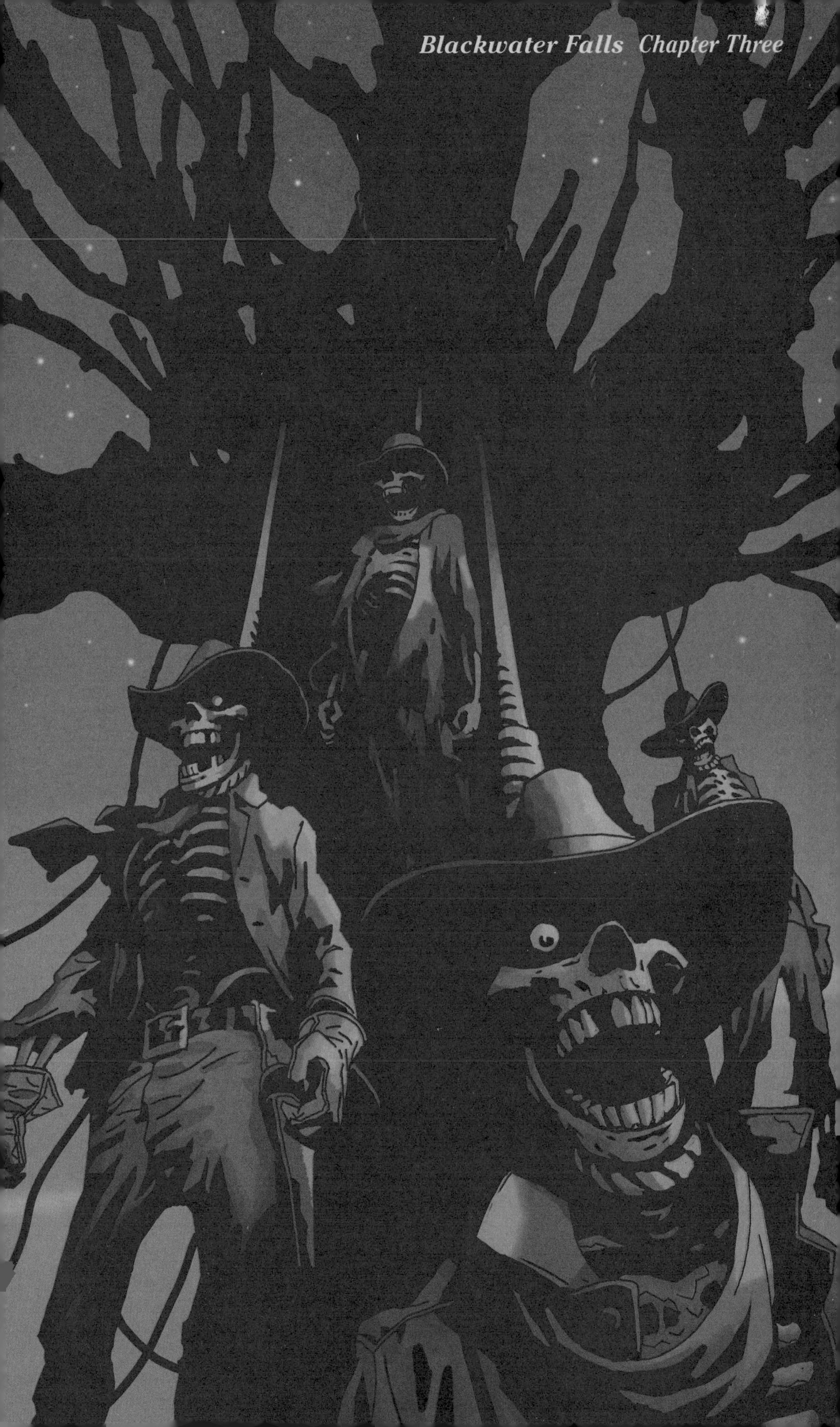
Blackwater Falls Chapter Three

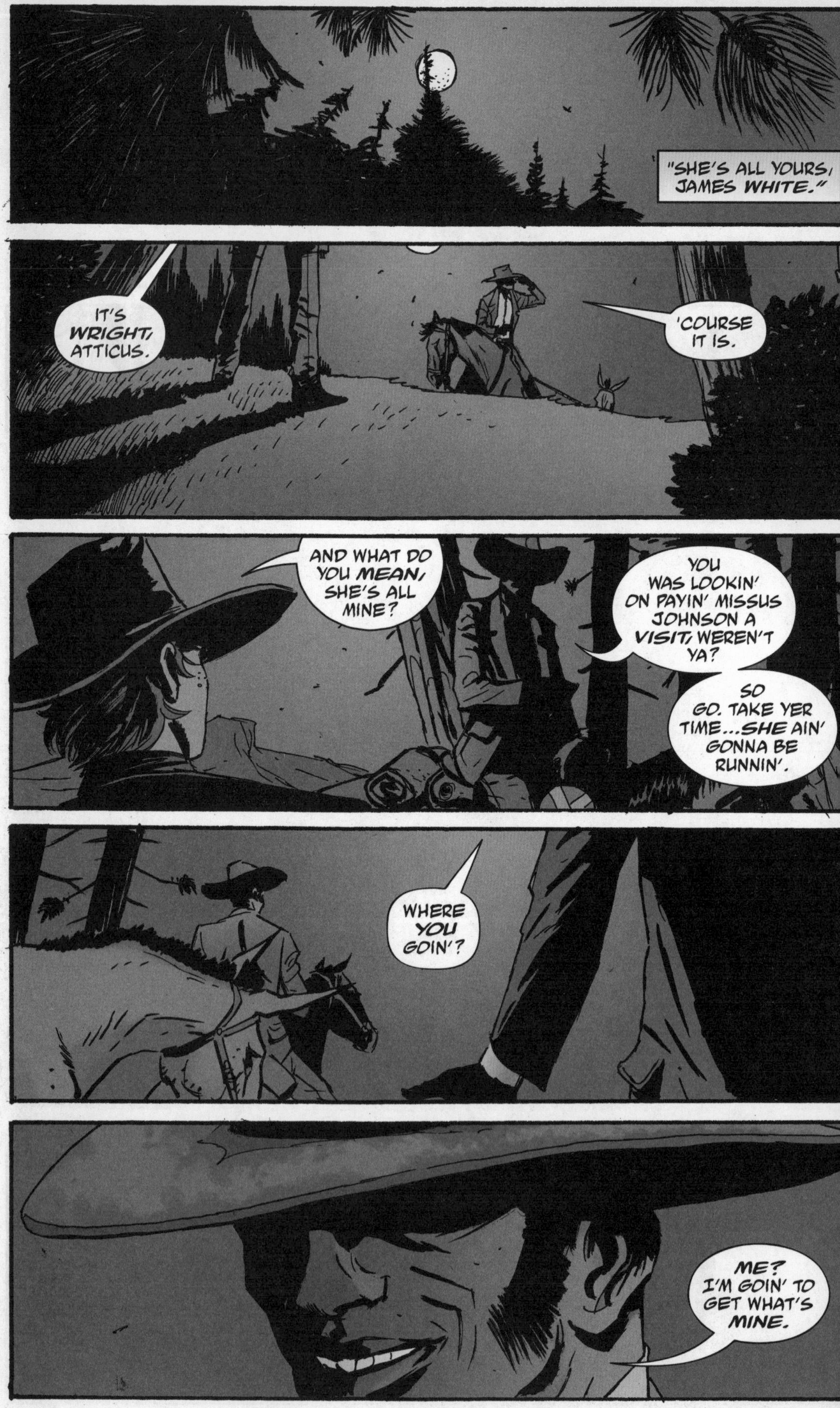
"SHE'S ALL YOURS, JAMES WHITE."
IT'S WRIGHT, ATTICUS.
'COURSE IT IS.
AND WHAT DO YOU MEAN, SHE'S ALL MINE?
YOU WAS LOOKIN' ON PAYIN' MISSUS JOHNSON A VISIT, WEREN'T YA?
SO GO. TAKE YER TIME...SHE AIN' GONNA BE RUNNIN'.
WHERE YOU GOIN'?
ME? I'M GOIN' TO GET WHAT'S MINE.

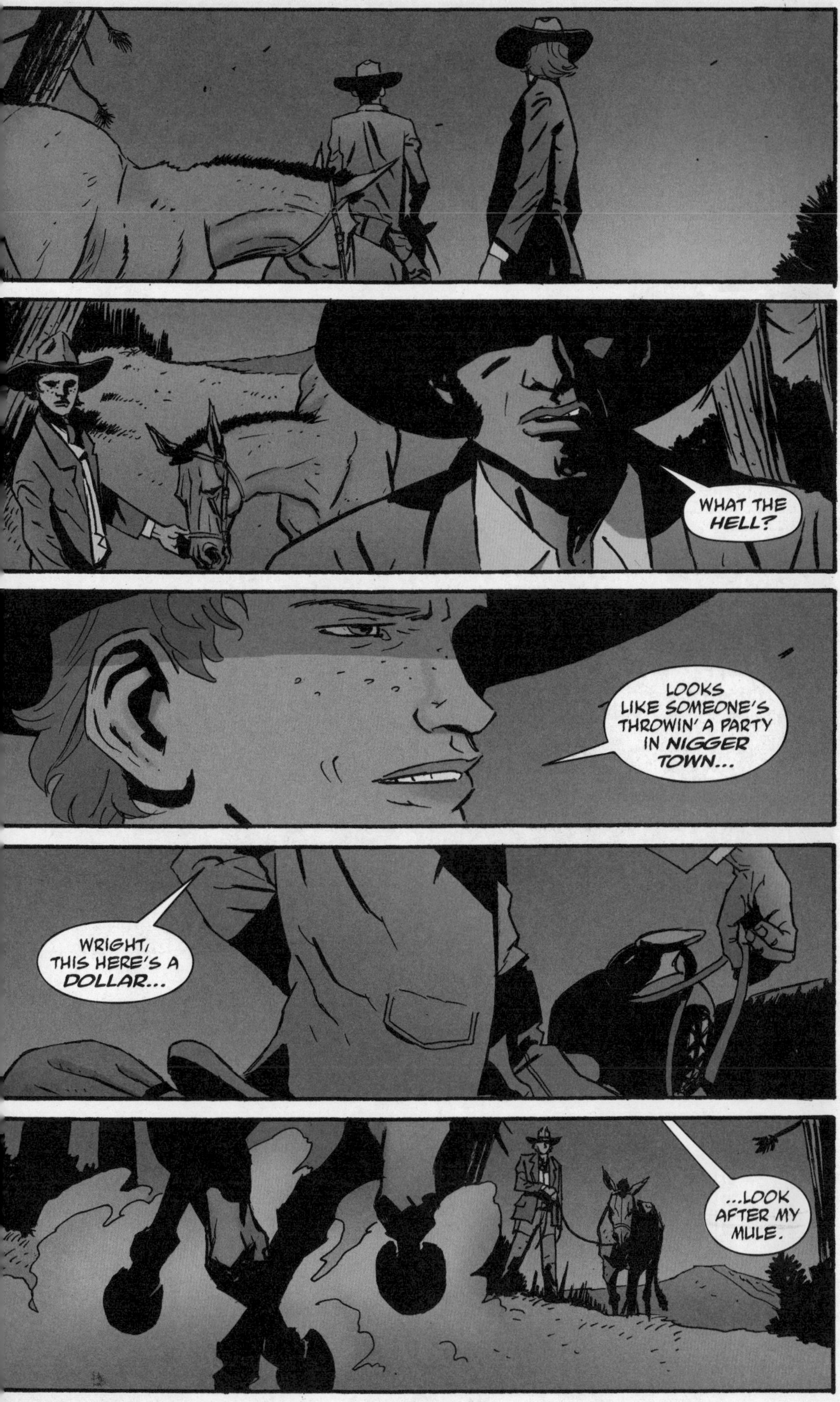
WHAT THE HELL?
LOOKS LIKE SOMEONE'S THROWIN' A PARTY IN NIGGER TOWN...
WRIGHT, THIS HERE'S A DOLLAR...
...LOOK AFTER MY MULE.

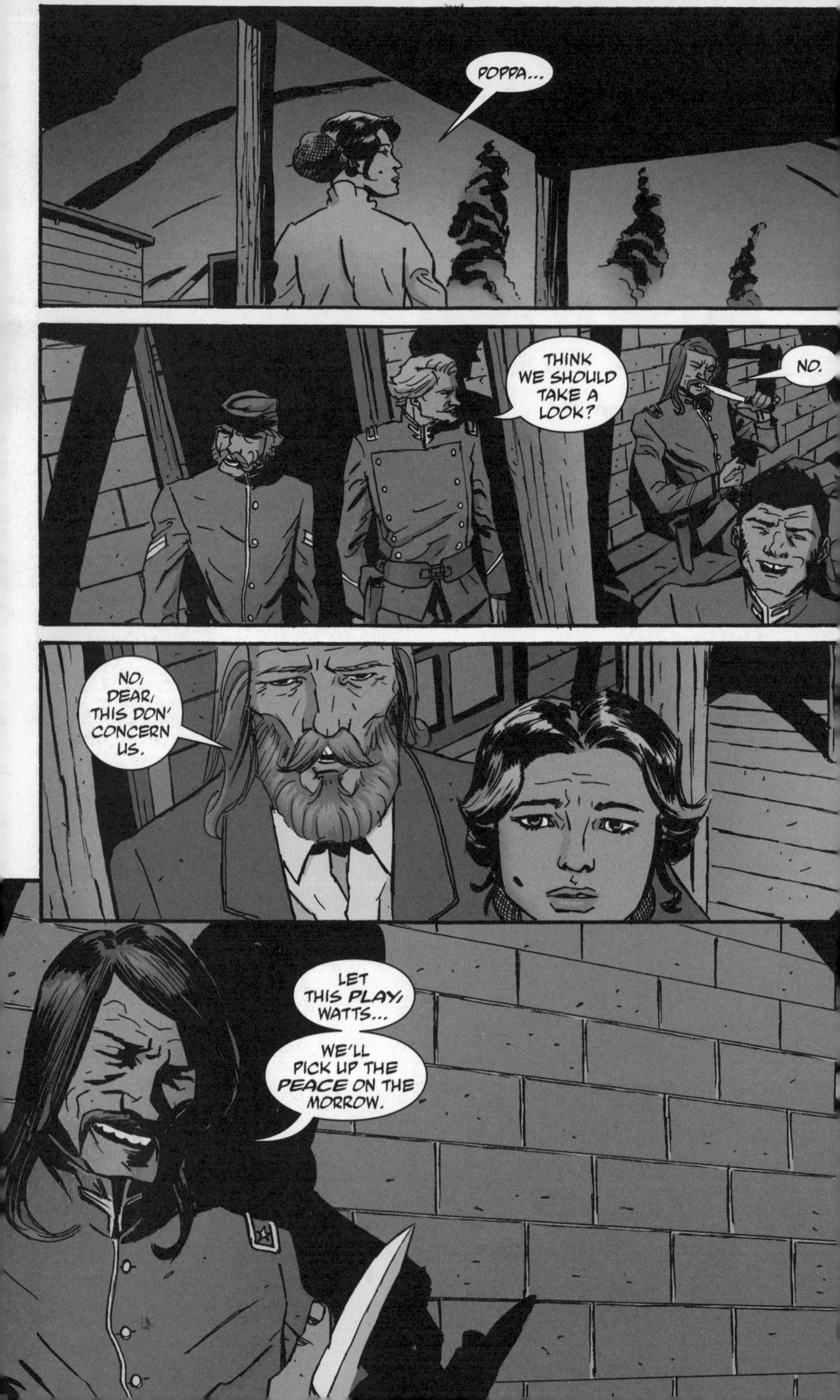
POPPA...
THINK WE SHOULD TAKE A LOOK?
NO.
NO, DEAR, THIS DON' CONCERN US.
LET THIS PLAY, WATTS...
WE'LL PICK UP THE PEACE ON THE MORROW.

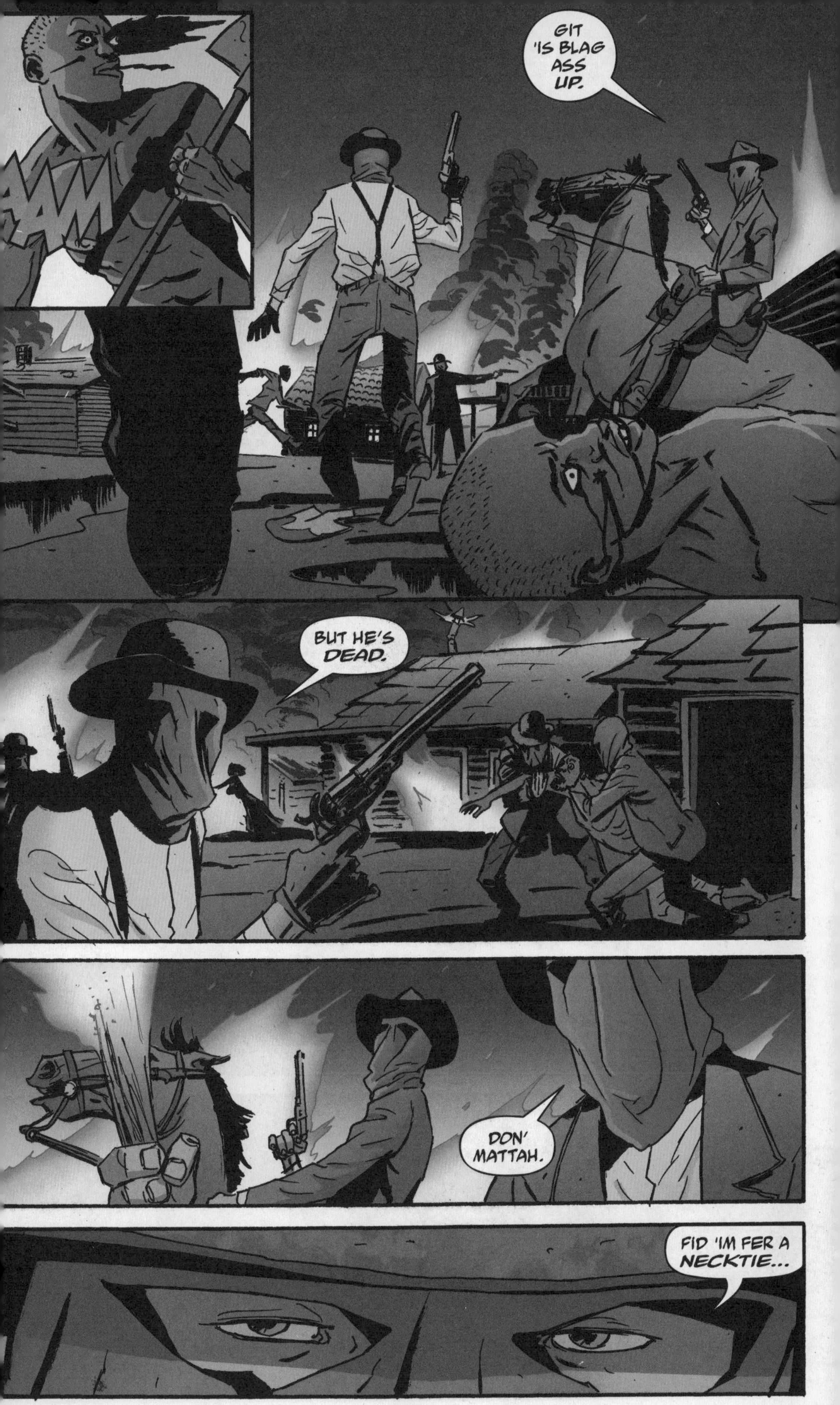
GIT 'IS BLAG ASS UP.
BUT HE'S DEAD.
DON' MATTAH.
FID 'IM FER A NECKTIE...

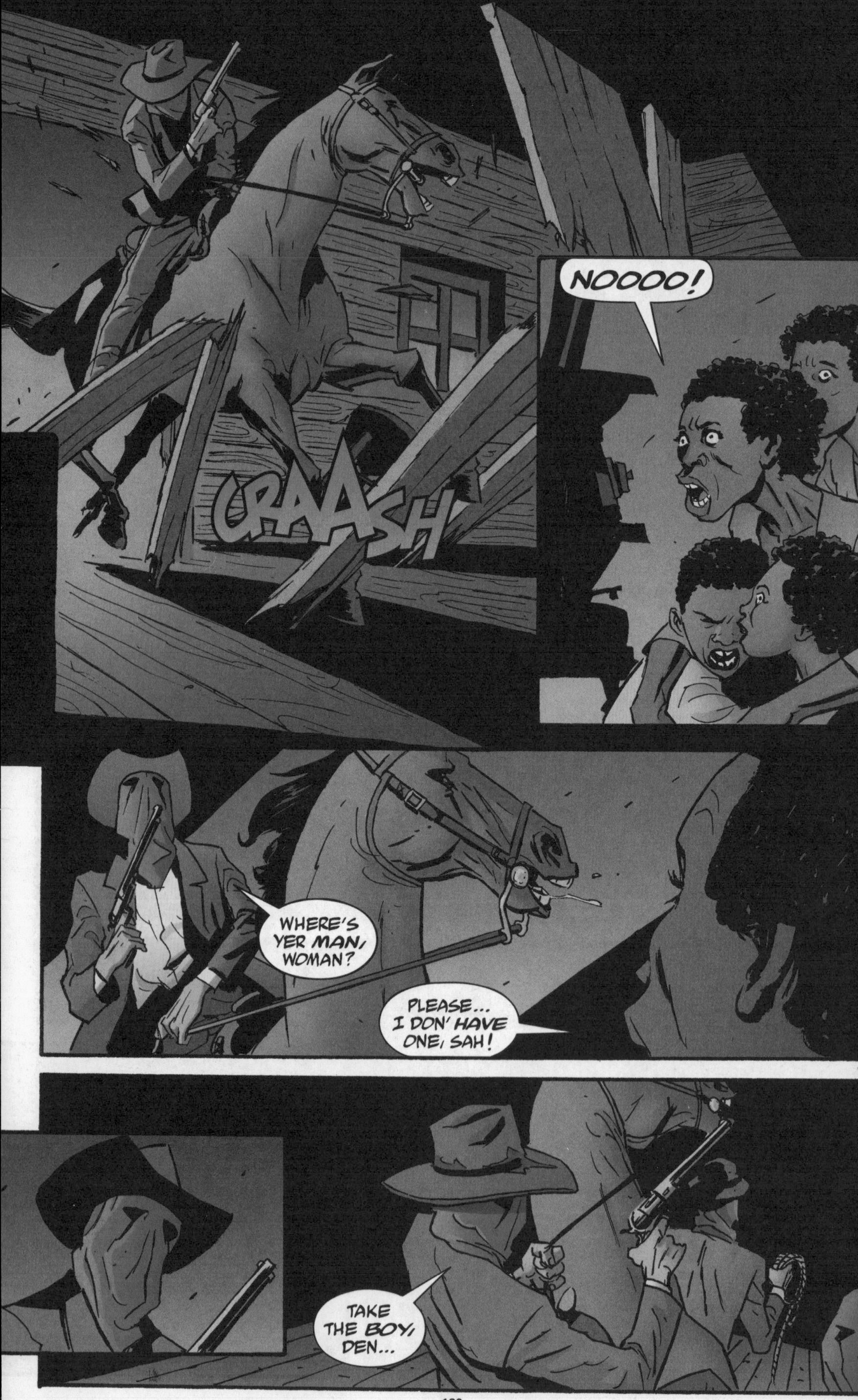
CRAAASH
NOOOO!
WHERE'S YER MAN, WOMAN?
PLEASE... I DON' HAVE ONE, SAH!
TAKE THE BOY, DEN...

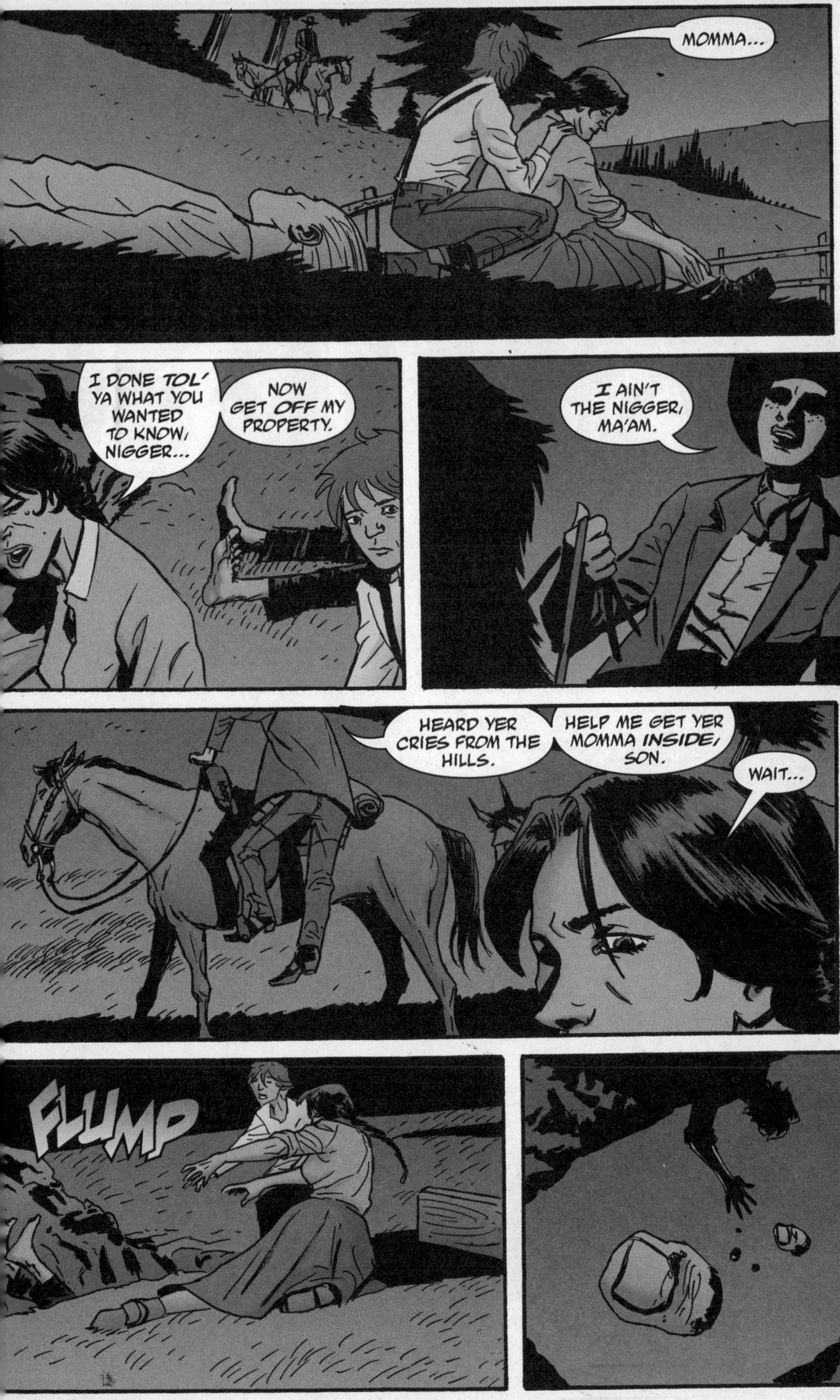
MOMMA...
I DONE TOL' YA WHAT YOU WANTED TO KNOW, NIGGER...
NOW GET OFF MY PROPERTY.
I AIN'T THE NIGGER, MA'AM.
HEARD YER CRIES FROM THE HILLS.
HELP ME GET YER MOMMA INSIDE, SON.
WAIT...
FLUMP

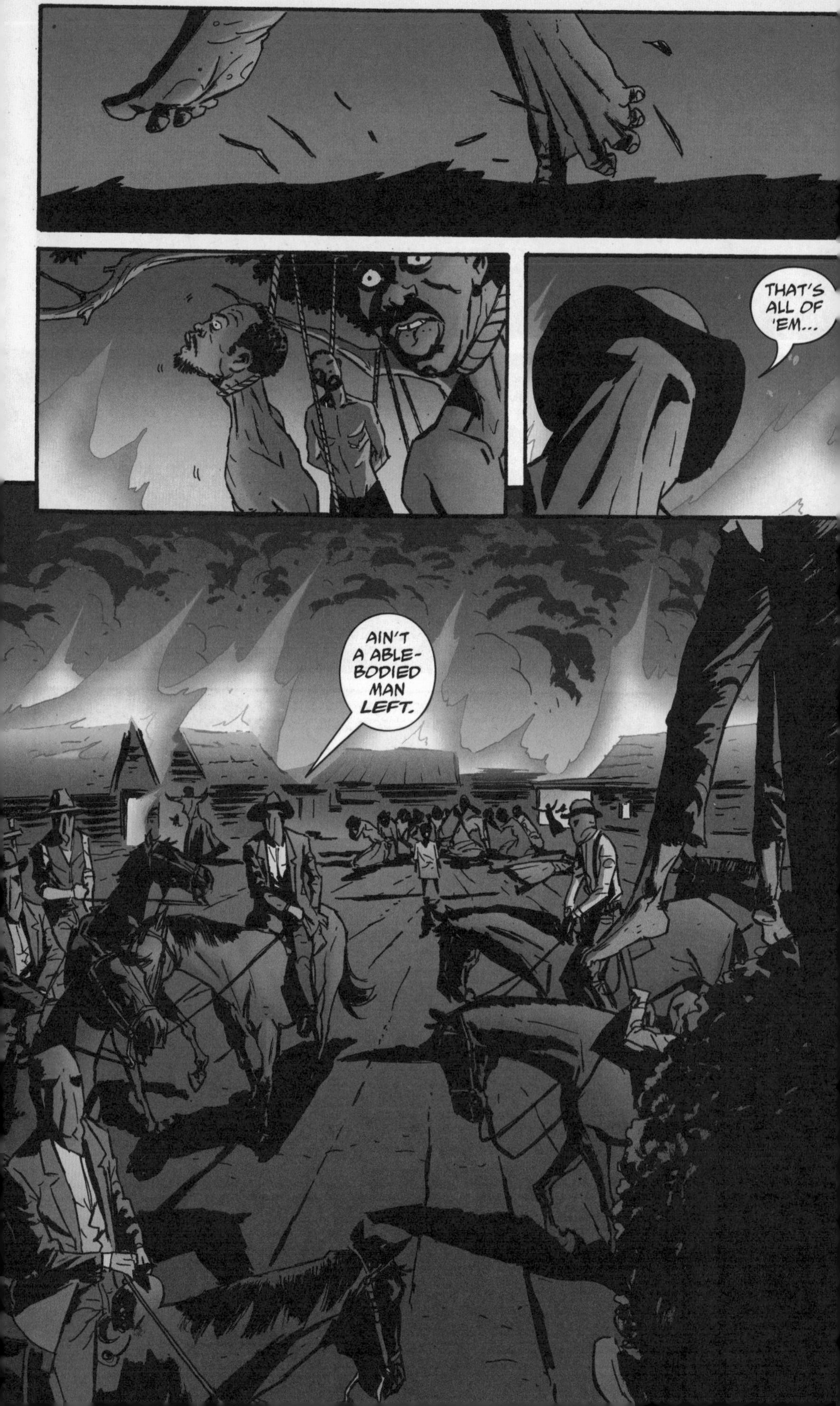
THAT'S ALL OF 'EM...
AIN'T A ABLE-BODIED MAN LEFT.

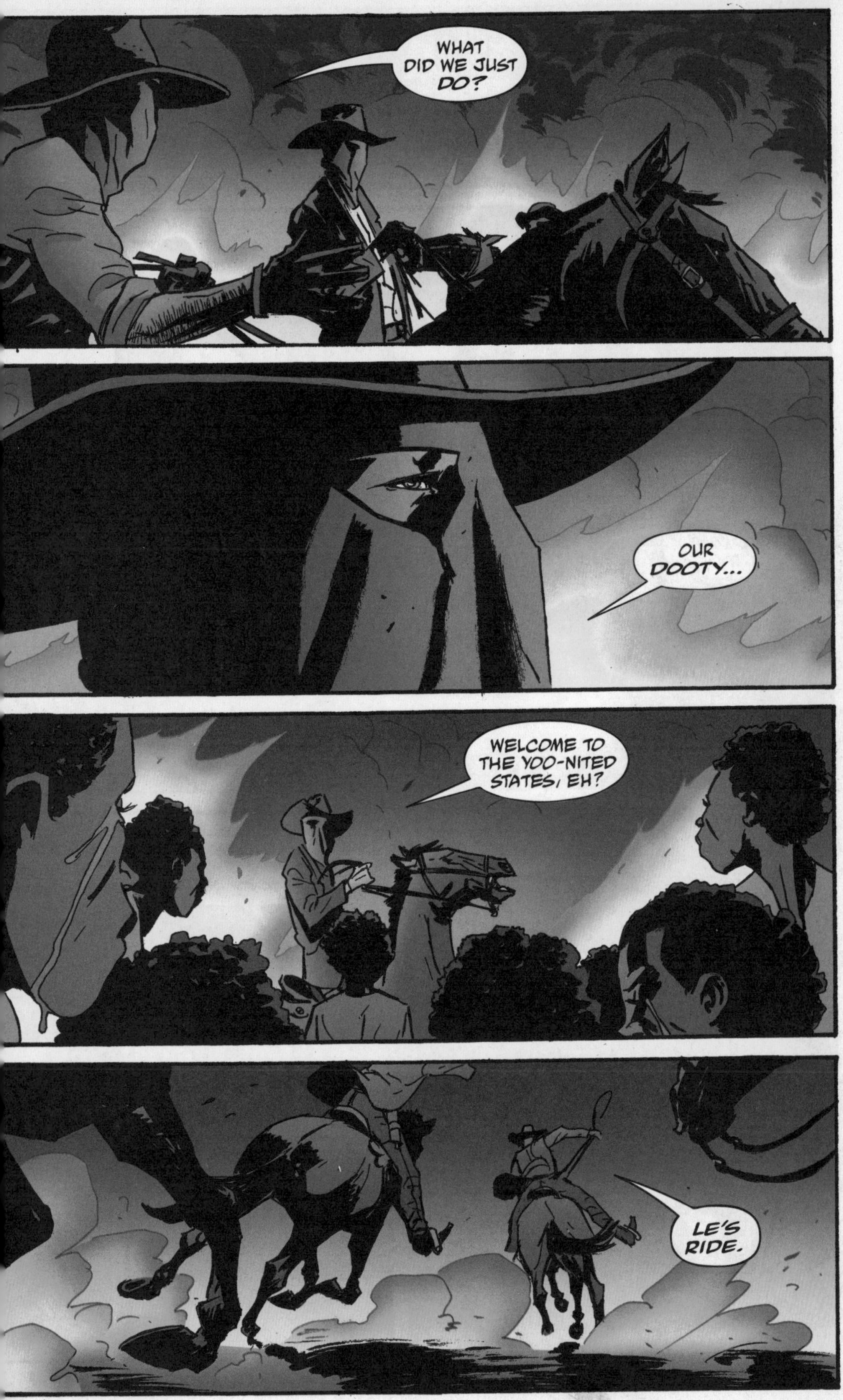
WHAT DID WE JUST DO?
OUR DOOTY...
WELCOME TO THE YOO-NITED STATES, EH?
LE'S RIDE.

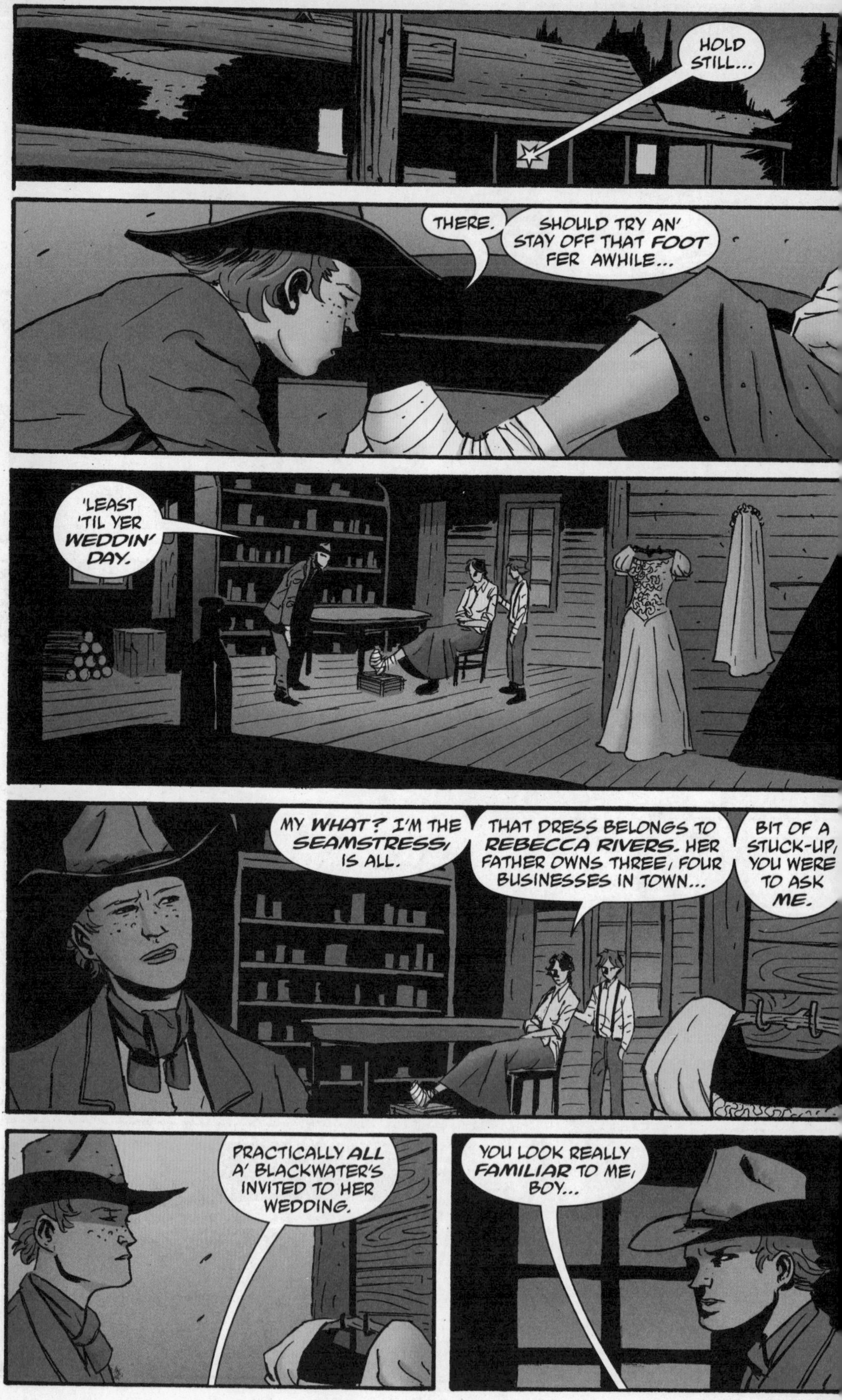
HOLD STILL...
THERE.
SHOULD TRY AN' STAY OFF THAT FOOT FER AWHILE...
'LEAST 'TIL YER WEDDIN' DAY.
MY WHAT? I'M THE SEAMSTRESS, IS ALL.
THAT DRESS BELONGS TO REBECCA RIVERS. HER FATHER OWNS THREE, FOUR BUSINESSES IN TOWN...
BIT OF A STUCK-UP, YOU WERE TO ASK ME.
PRACTICALLY ALL A' BLACKWATER'S INVITED TO HER WEDDING.
YOU LOOK REALLY FAMILIAR TO ME, BOY...

YOU *KNOW* MY SON?

JUS' ET.

NOT HIM...*BOYD.* BOYD JOHNSON. Y'*KNOW* 'IM?

NO, MA'AM.

Y'*HEARD* OF HIM...

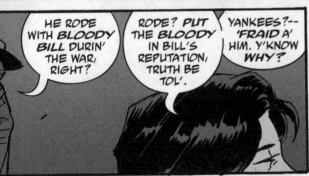

HE RODE WITH *BLOODY BILL* DURIN' THE WAR, RIGHT?

RODE? PUT THE *BLOODY* IN BILL'S REPUTATION, TRUTH BE TOL'.

YANKEES?-- 'FRAID A' HIM. Y'KNOW *WHY?*

AIN'T A SOUL--'CEPT FER NIGGERS, WHICH AIN'T *GOT NONE*-- DON' LIVE AN' DIE BY MY SON'S EXPLOITS.

HE'S A *HERO.*

THE BLACK PIECE A' SHIT TOOK MY TOES WENT AFTER HIM. GOOD. I HOPE HE *FINDS* 'IM.

MY SON WILL *BURN* THE FOOL *DOWN.*

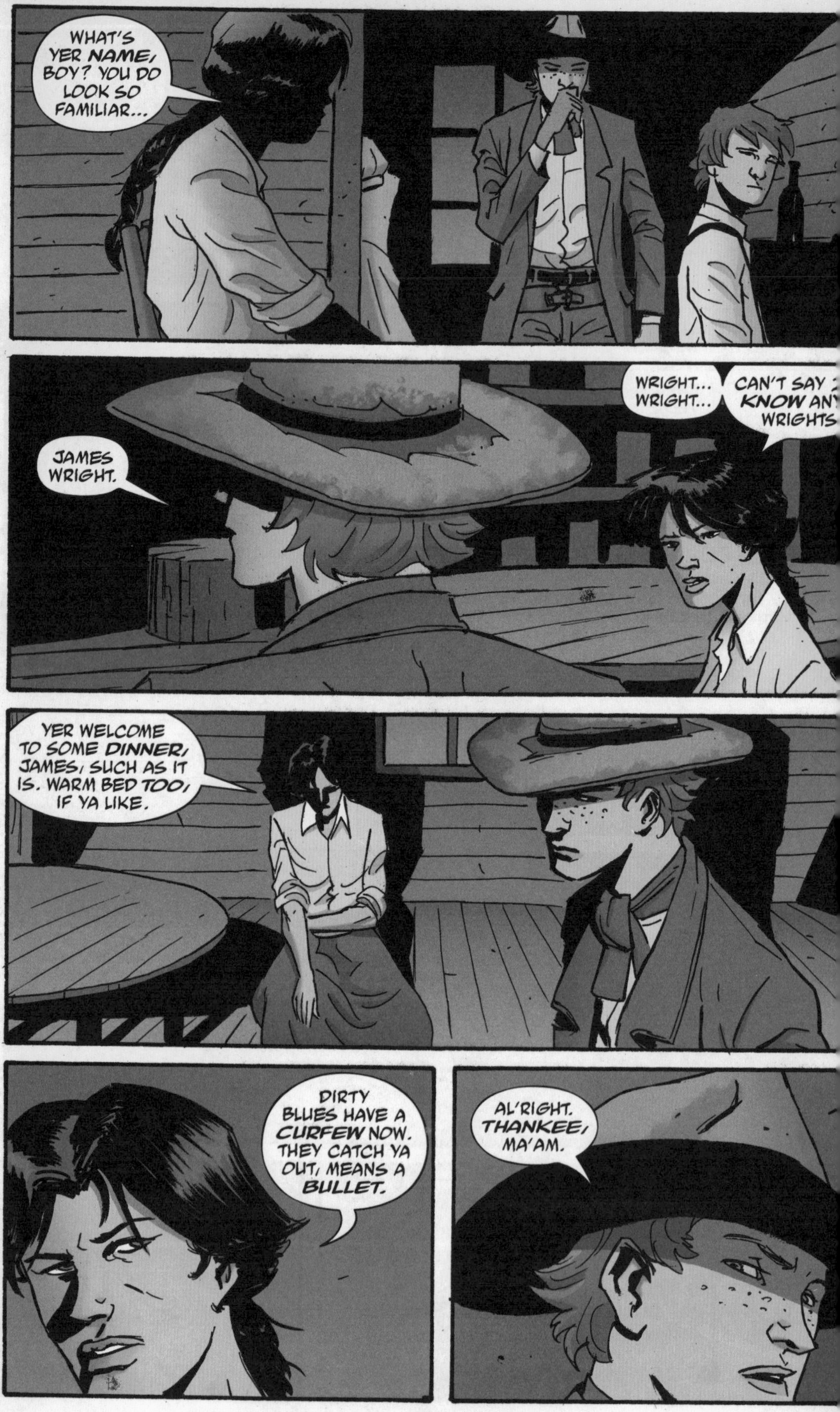
WHAT'S YER NAME, BOY? YOU DO LOOK SO FAMILIAR...
JAMES WRIGHT.
WRIGHT... WRIGHT...
CAN'T SAY I KNOW ANY WRIGHTS.
YER WELCOME TO SOME DINNER, JAMES, SUCH AS IT IS. WARM BED TOO, IF YA LIKE.
DIRTY BLUES HAVE A CURFEW NOW. THEY CATCH YA OUT, MEANS A BULLET.
AL'RIGHT. THANKEE, MA'AM.

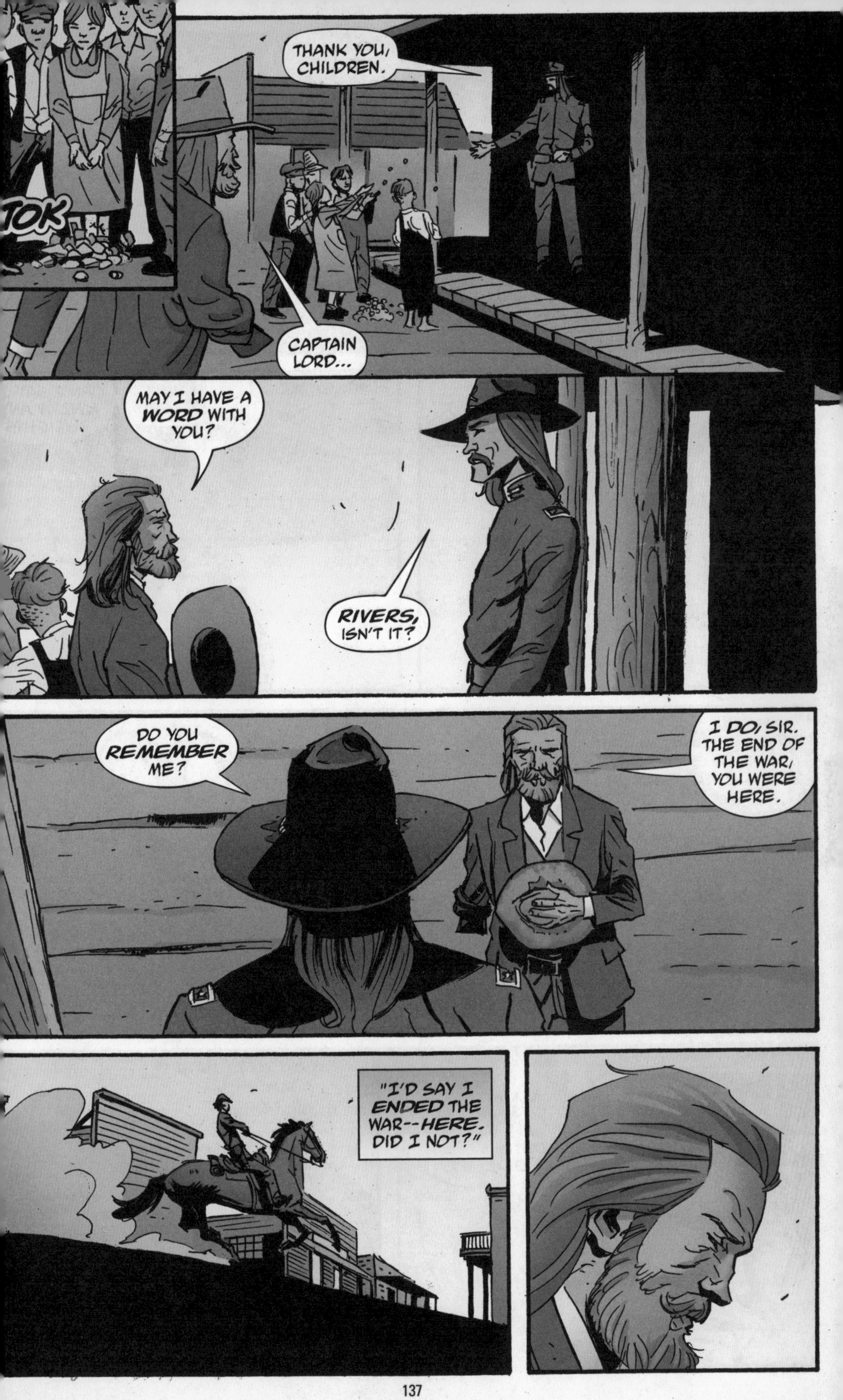
TOK
THANK YOU, CHILDREN.
CAPTAIN LORD...
MAY I HAVE A WORD WITH YOU?
RIVERS, ISN'T IT?
DO YOU REMEMBER ME?
I DO, SIR. THE END OF THE WAR, YOU WERE HERE.
"I'D SAY I ENDED THE WAR--HERE. DID I NOT?"

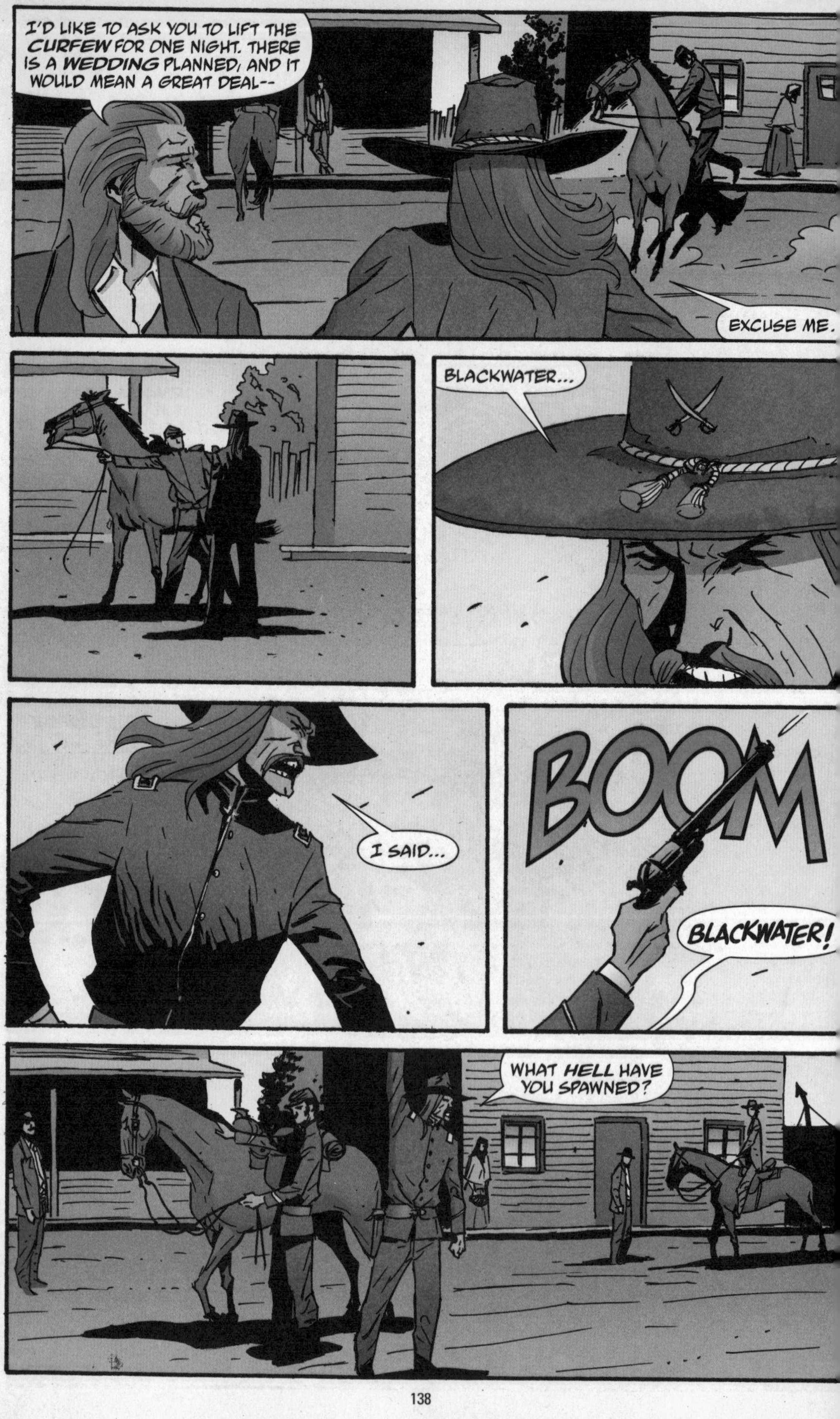
I'D LIKE TO ASK YOU TO LIFT THE CURFEW FOR ONE NIGHT. THERE IS A WEDDING PLANNED, AND IT WOULD MEAN A GREAT DEAL--
EXCUSE ME.
BLACKWATER...
I SAID...
BOOM
BLACKWATER!
WHAT HELL HAVE YOU SPAWNED?

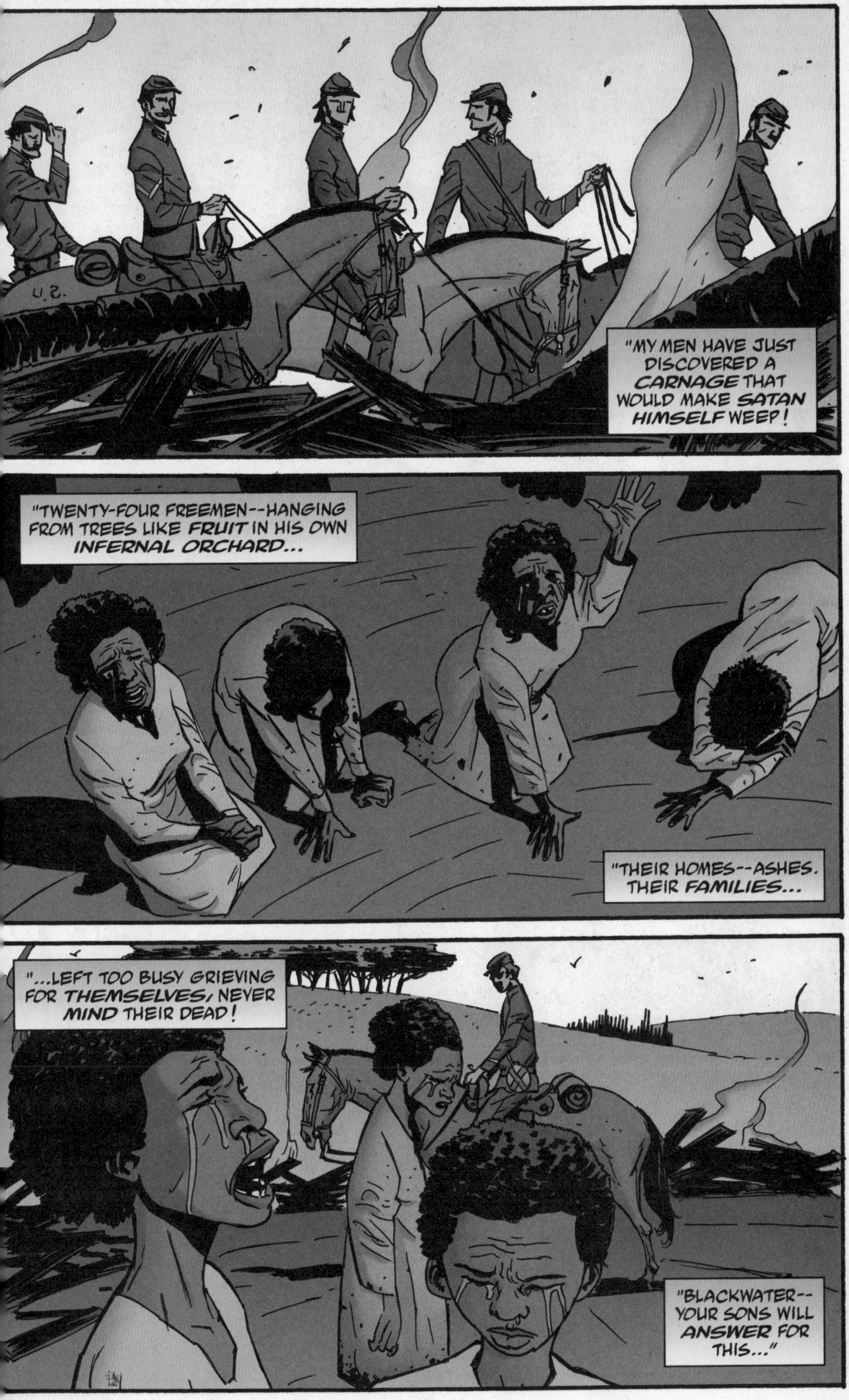
"MY MEN HAVE JUST DISCOVERED A CARNAGE THAT WOULD MAKE SATAN HIMSELF WEEP!
"TWENTY-FOUR FREEMEN--HANGING FROM TREES LIKE FRUIT IN HIS OWN INFERNAL ORCHARD...
"THEIR HOMES--ASHES. THEIR FAMILIES...
"...LEFT TOO BUSY GRIEVING FOR THEMSELVES, NEVER MIND THEIR DEAD!
"BLACKWATER--YOUR SONS WILL ANSWER FOR THIS..."

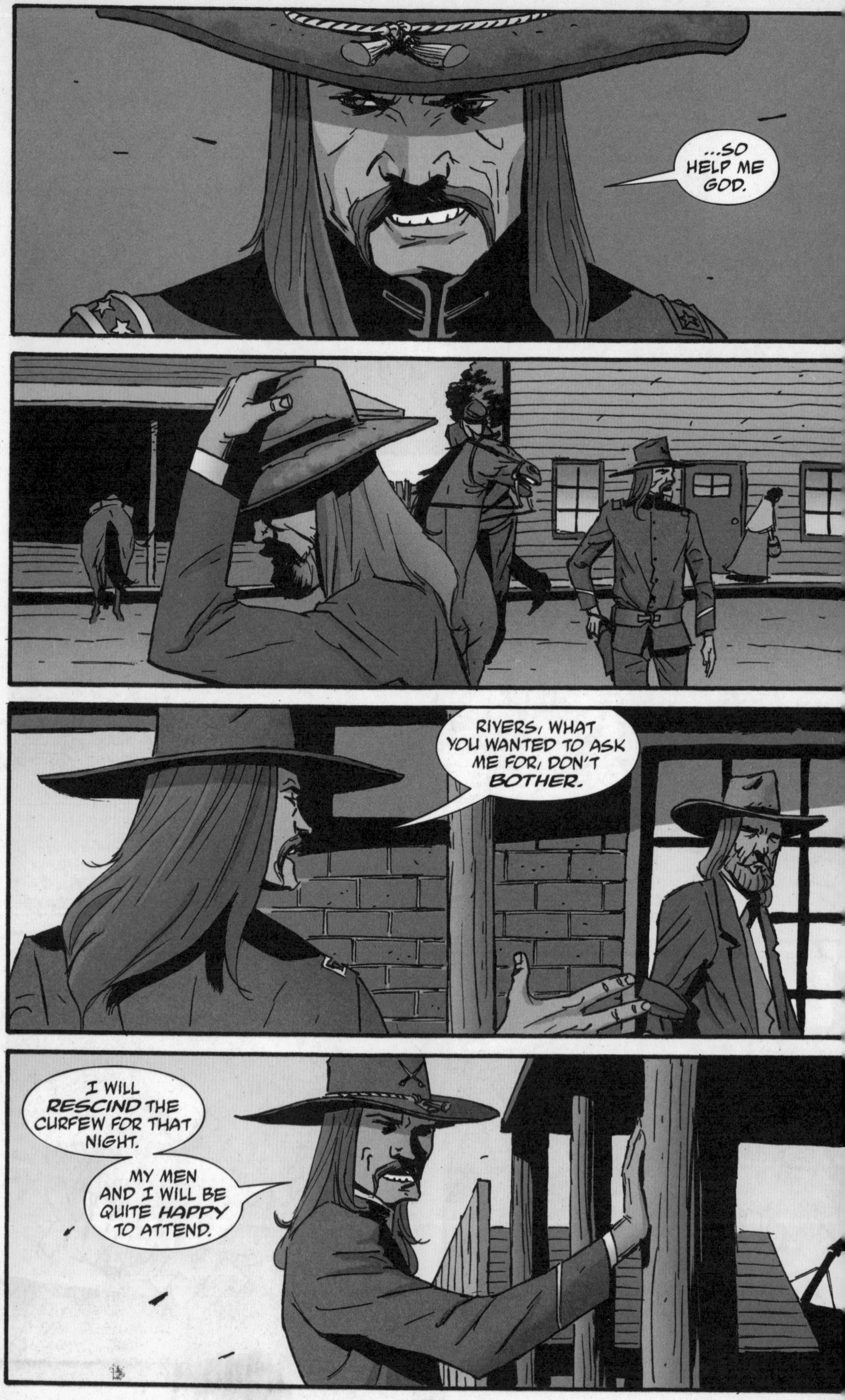
...SO HELP ME GOD.
RIVERS, WHAT YOU WANTED TO ASK ME FOR, DON'T *BOTHER*.
I WILL *RESCIND* THE CURFEW FOR THAT NIGHT.
MY MEN AND I WILL BE QUITE *HAPPY* TO ATTEND.

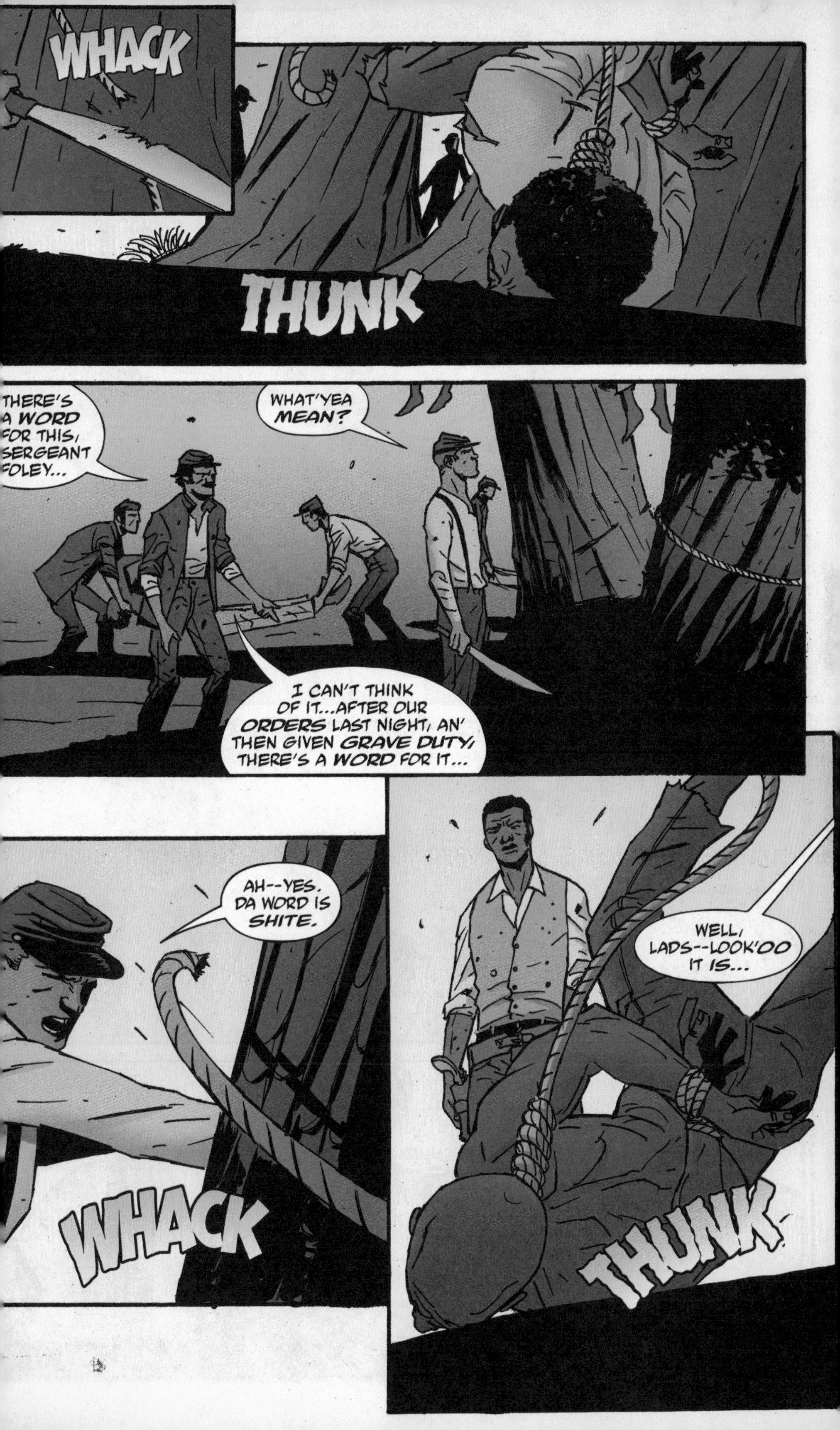
WHACK
THUNK
THERE'S A WORD FOR THIS, SERGEANT FOLEY...
WHAT'YEA MEAN?
I CAN'T THINK OF IT...AFTER OUR ORDERS LAST NIGHT, AN' THEN GIVEN GRAVE DUTY, THERE'S A WORD FOR IT...
AH--YES. DA WORD IS SHITE.
WHACK
WELL, LADS--LOOK'OO IT IS...
THUNK

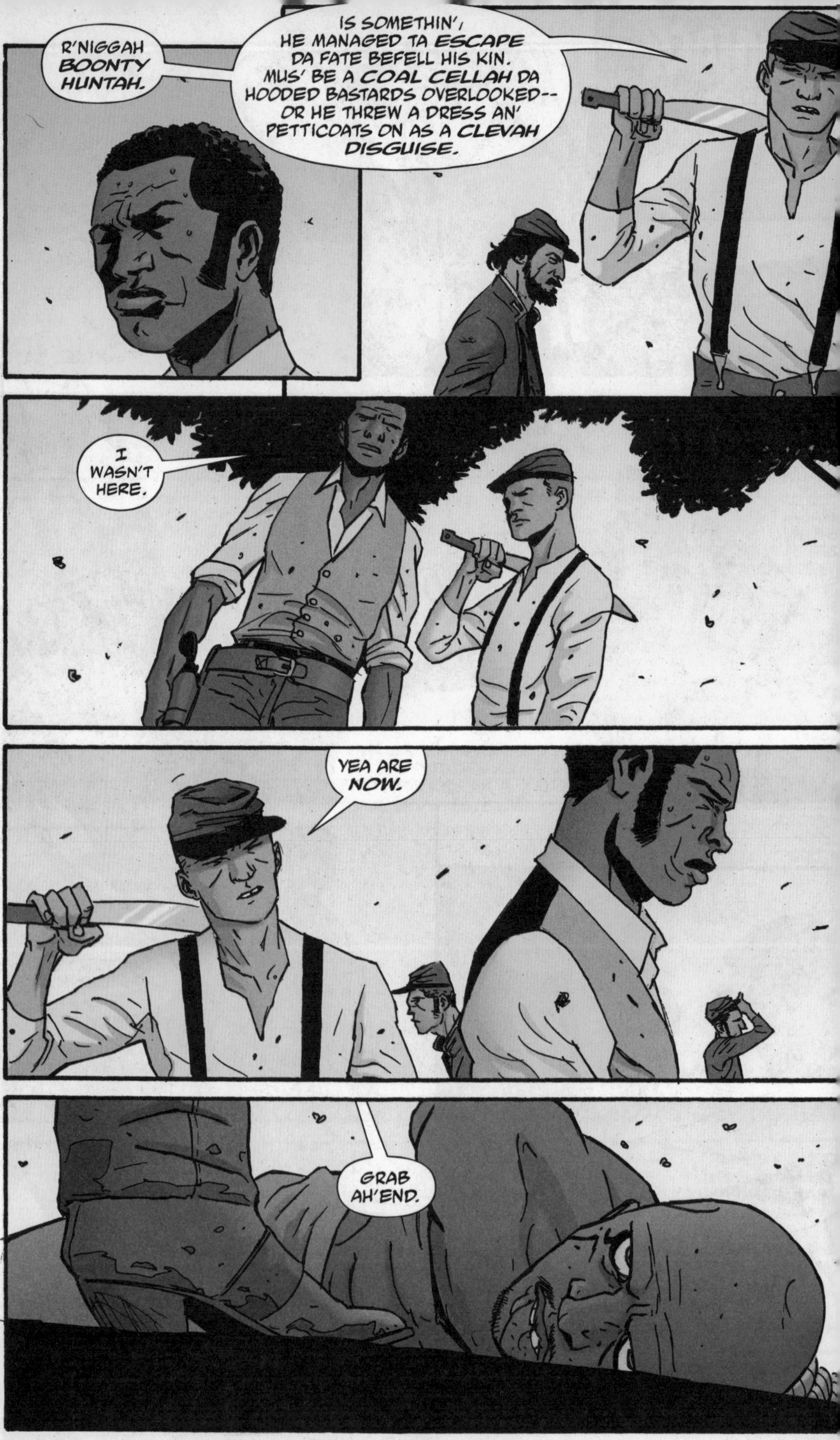
R'NIGGAH BOONTY HUNTAH.
IS SOMETHIN', HE MANAGED TA ESCAPE DA FATE BEFELL HIS KIN. MUS' BE A COAL CELLAH DA HOODED BASTARDS OVERLOOKED-- OR HE THREW A DRESS AN' PETTICOATS ON AS A CLEVAH DISGUISE.
I WASN'T HERE.
YEA ARE NOW.
GRAB AH'END.

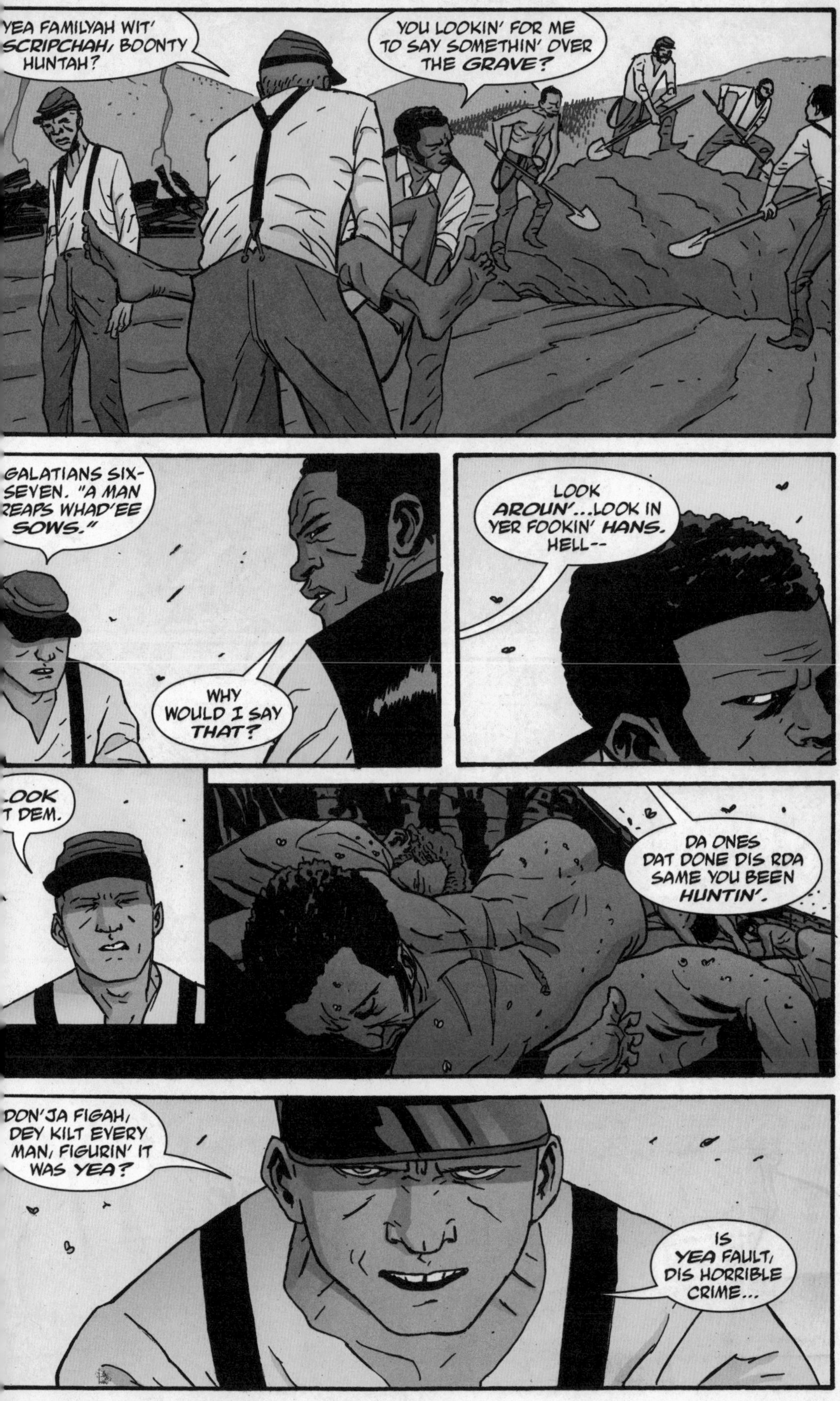

YEA FAMILYAH WIT' SCRIPCHAH, BOONTY HUNTAH?
YOU LOOKIN' FOR ME TO SAY SOMETHIN' OVER THE GRAVE?
GALATIANS SIX-SEVEN. "A MAN REAPS WHAD'EE SOWS."
WHY WOULD I SAY THAT?
LOOK AROUN'...LOOK IN YER FOOKIN' HANS. HELL--
LOOK T DEM.
DA ONES DAT DONE DIS RDA SAME YOU BEEN HUNTIN'.
DON'JA FIGAH, DEY KILT EVERY MAN, FIGURIN' IT WAS YEA?
IS YEA FAULT, DIS HORRIBLE CRIME...

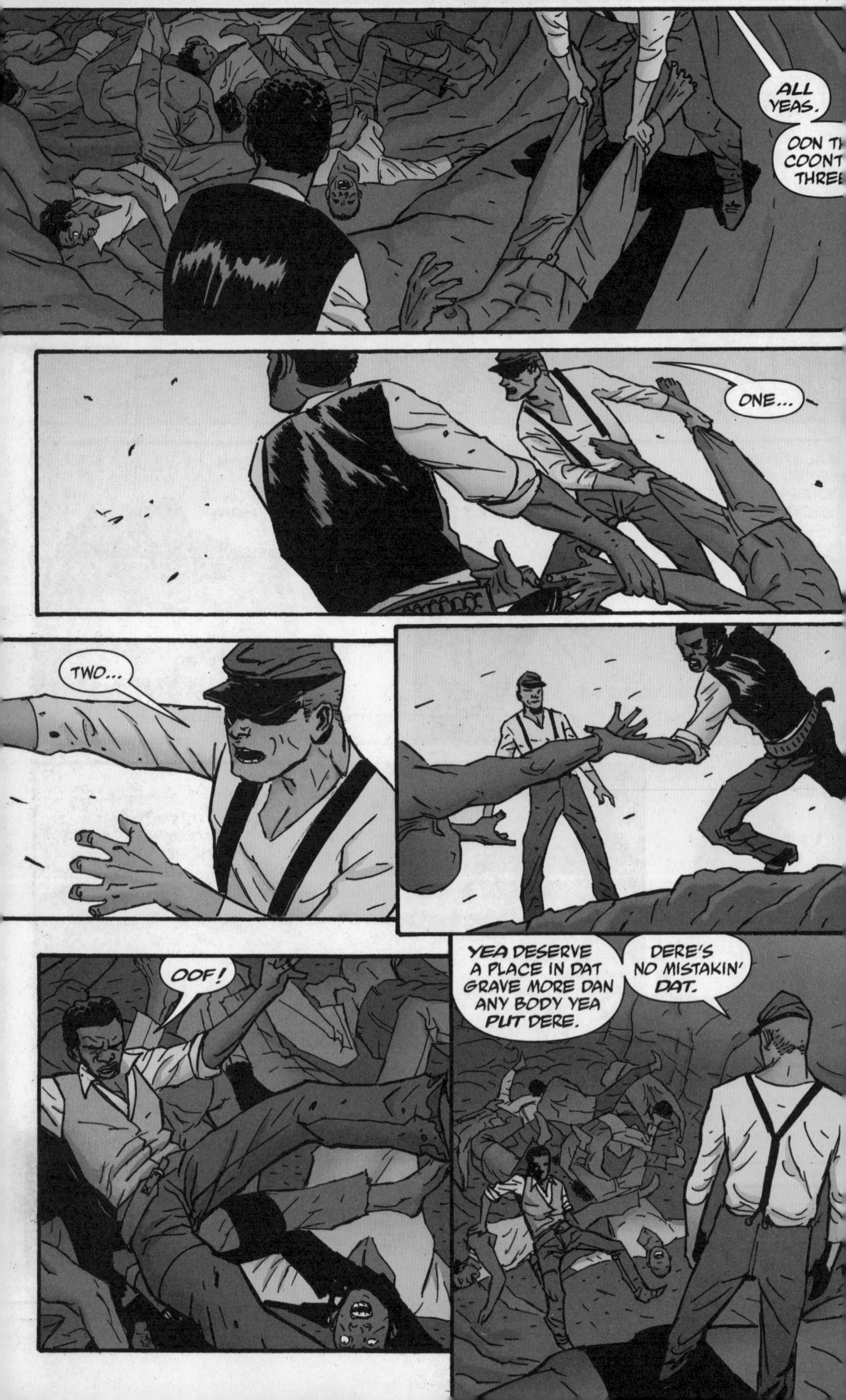
ALL YEAS.
OON TH COONT THREE
ONE...
TWO...
OOF!
YEA DESERVE A PLACE IN DAT GRAVE MORE DAN ANY BODY YEA PUT DERE.
DERE'S NO MISTAKIN' DAT.

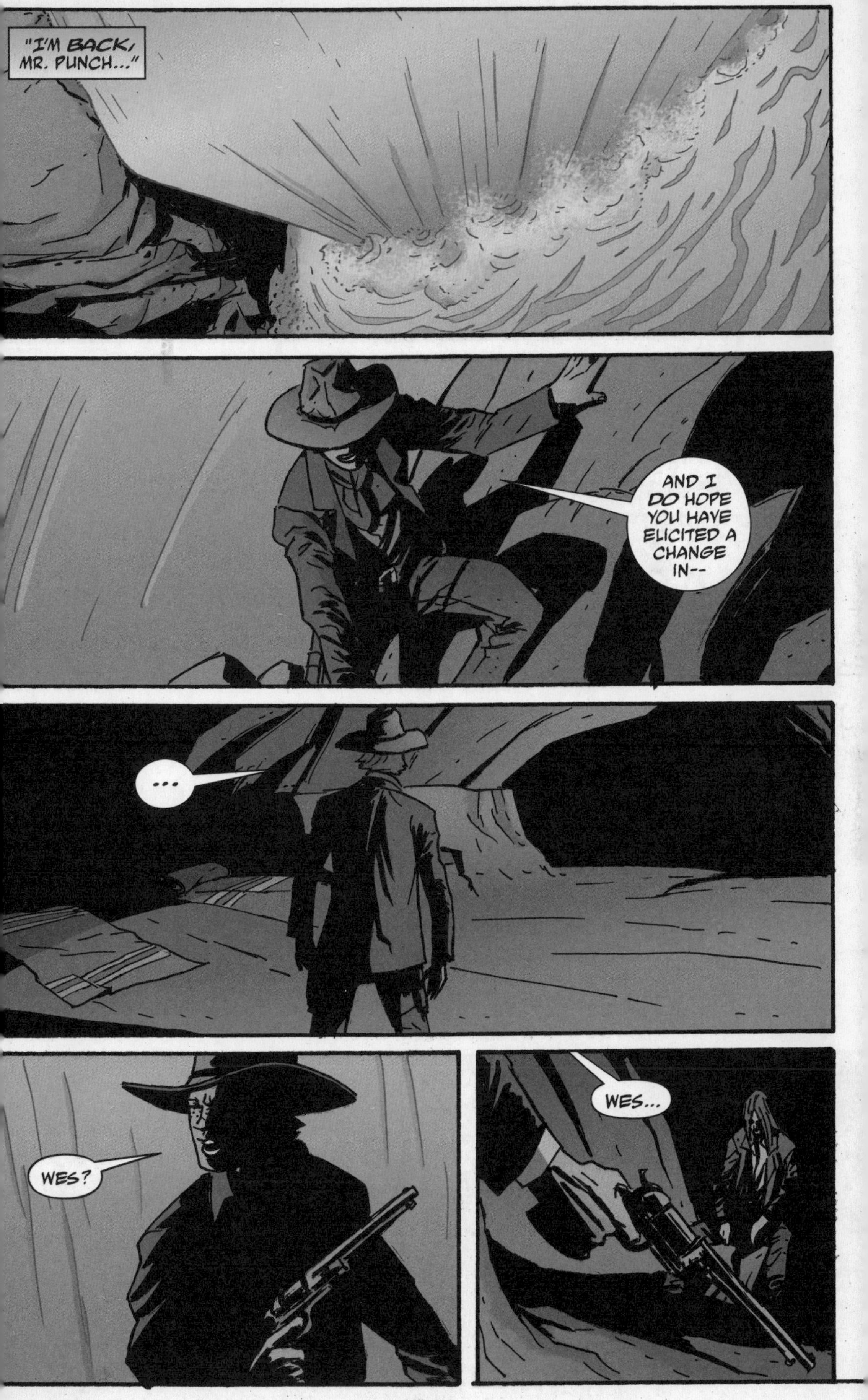
"I'M BACK, MR. PUNCH..."
AND I DO HOPE YOU HAVE ELICITED A CHANGE IN--
...
WES?
WES...

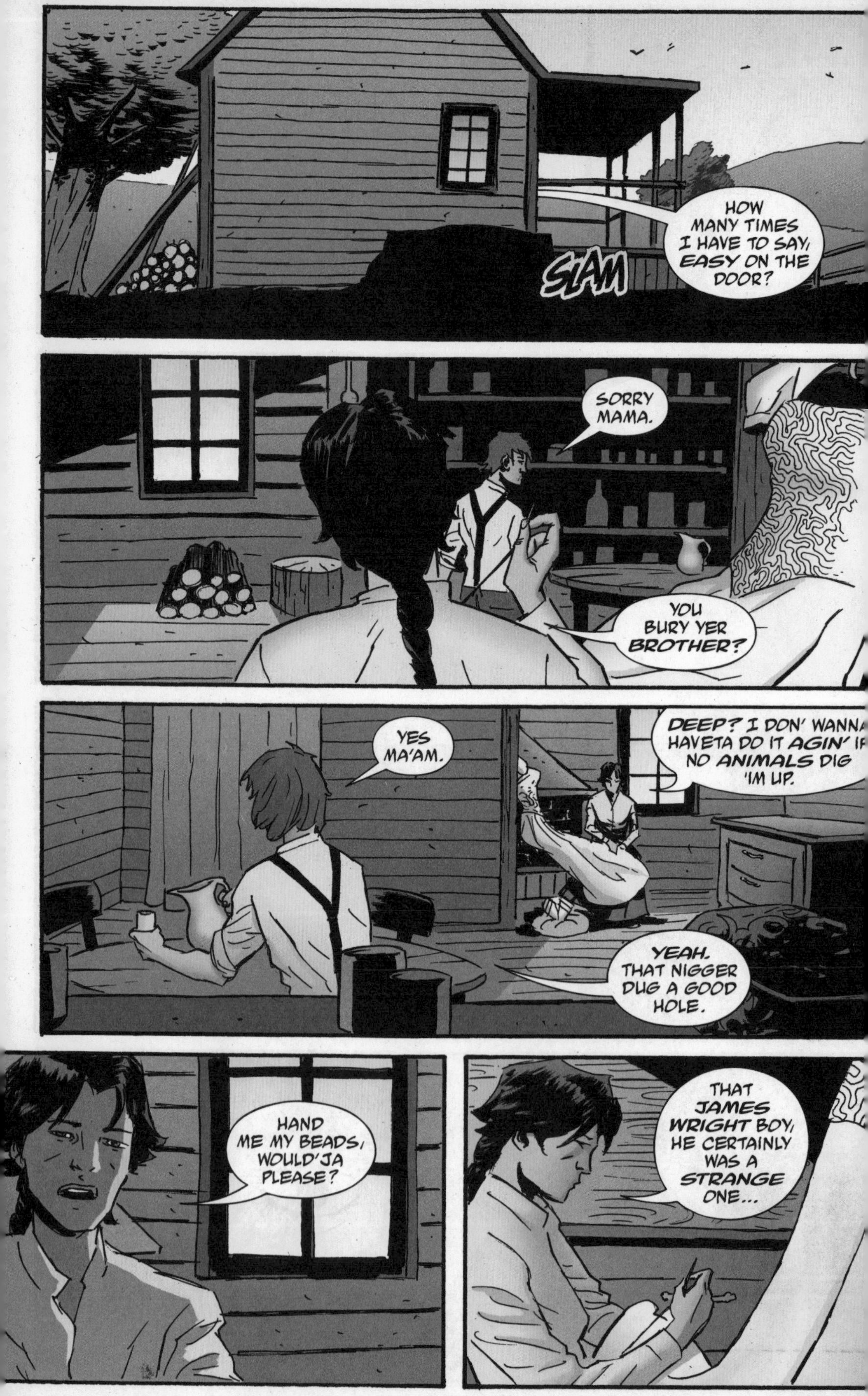
SLAM
HOW MANY TIMES I HAVE TO SAY, EASY ON THE DOOR?
SORRY MAMA.
YOU BURY YER BROTHER?
YES MA'AM.
DEEP? I DON' WANNA HAVETA DO IT AGIN' IF NO ANIMALS DIG 'IM UP.
YEAH. THAT NIGGER DUG A GOOD HOLE.
HAND ME MY BEADS, WOULD'JA PLEASE?
THAT JAMES WRIGHT BOY, HE CERTAINLY WAS A STRANGE ONE...

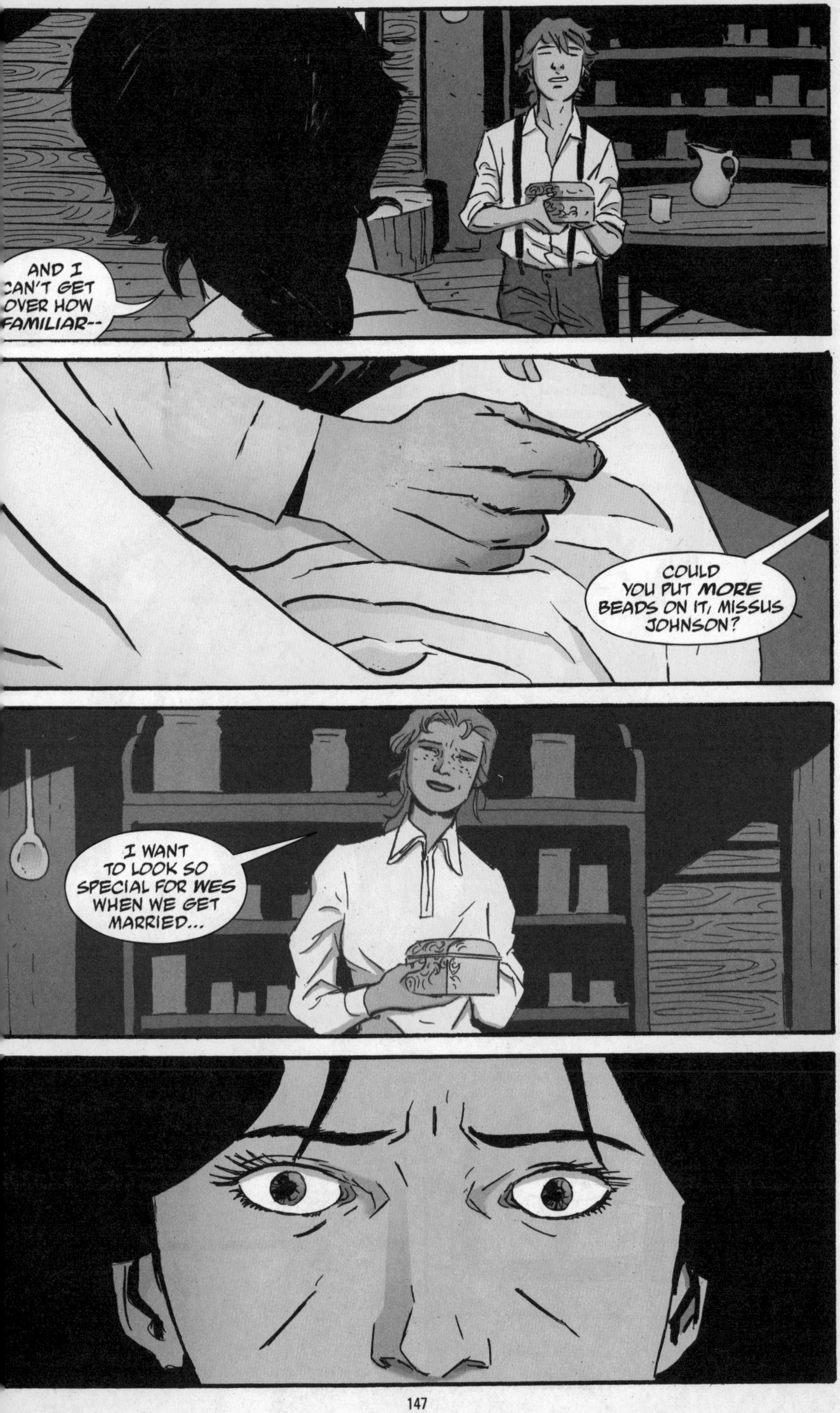
AND I CAN'T GET OVER HOW FAMILIAR--
COULD YOU PUT MORE BEADS ON IT, MISSUS JOHNSON?
I WANT TO LOOK SO SPECIAL FOR WES WHEN WE GET MARRIED...

Blackwater Falls Chapter Four

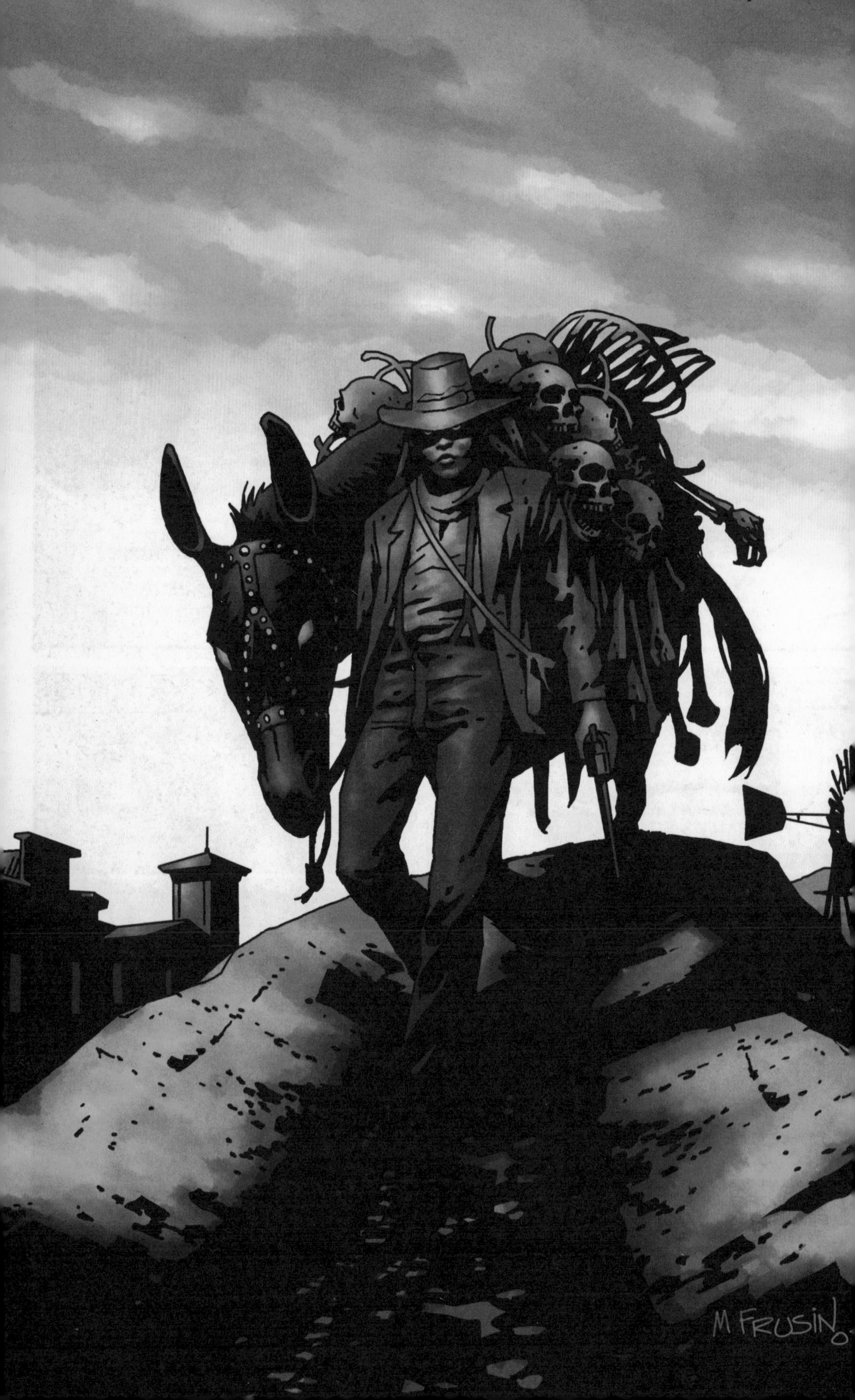
M FRUSIN

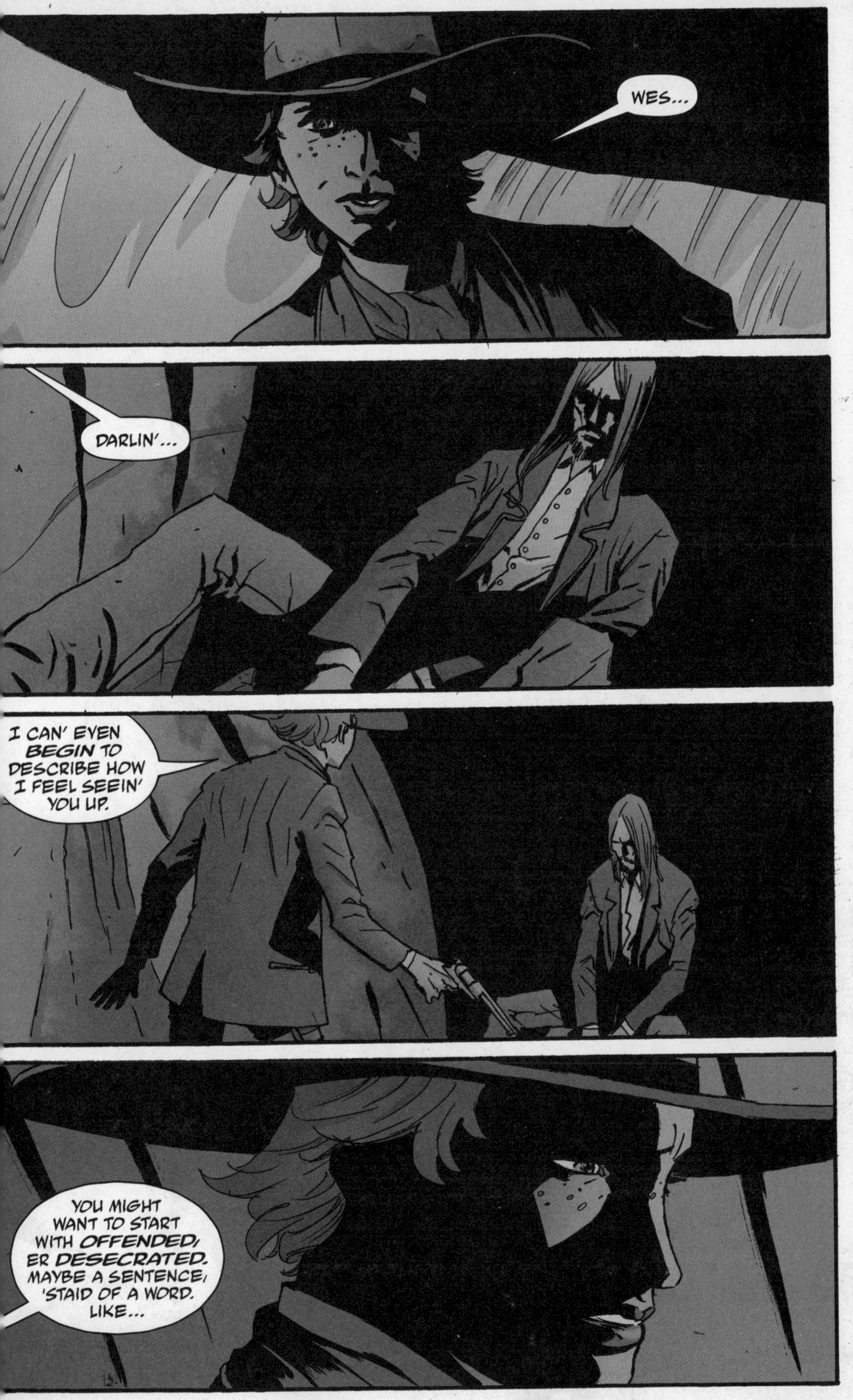
WES...
DARLIN'...
I CAN' EVEN *BEGIN* TO DESCRIBE HOW I FEEL SEEIN' YOU UP.
YOU MIGHT WANT TO START WITH *OFFENDED*, ER *DESECRATED*. MAYBE A SENTENCE, 'STAID OF A WORD. LIKE...

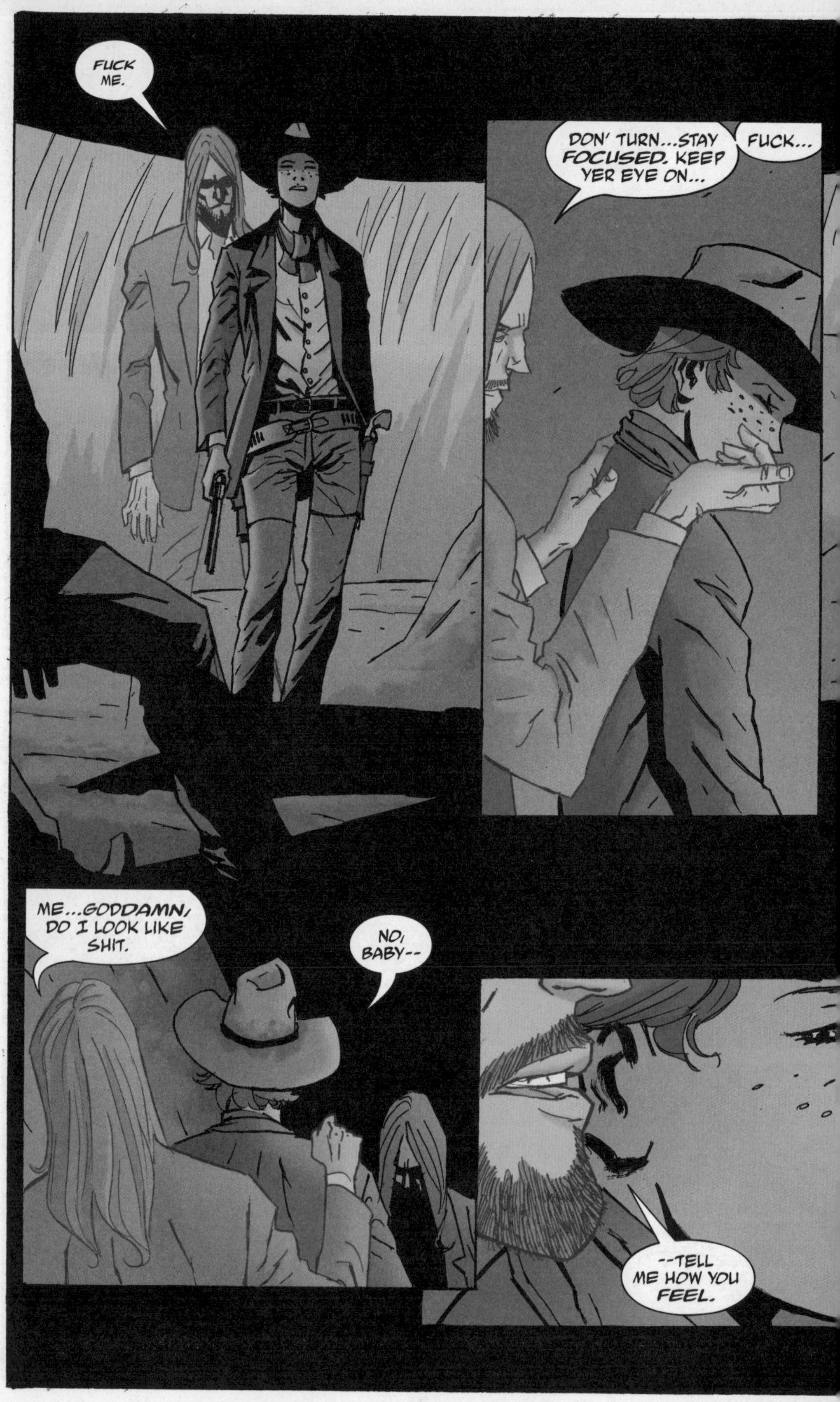
FUCK ME.
DON' TURN...STAY FOCUSED. KEEP YER EYE ON...
FUCK...
ME...GODDAMN, DO I LOOK LIKE SHIT.
NO, BABY--
--TELL ME HOW YOU FEEL.

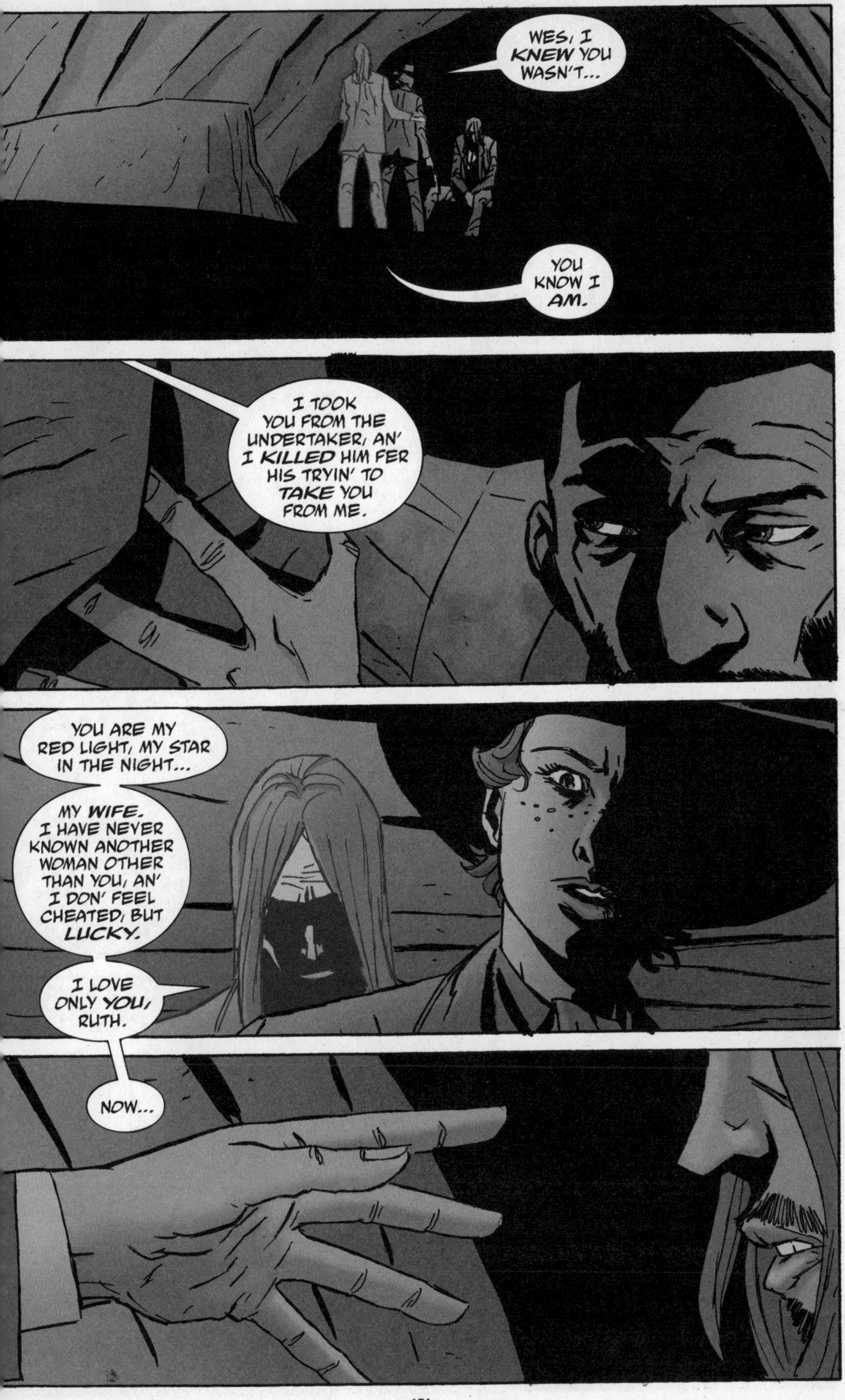
WES, I KNEW YOU WASN'T...
YOU KNOW I AM.
I TOOK YOU FROM THE UNDERTAKER, AN' I KILLED HIM FER HIS TRYIN' TO TAKE YOU FROM ME.
YOU ARE MY RED LIGHT, MY STAR IN THE NIGHT...
MY WIFE. I HAVE NEVER KNOWN ANOTHER WOMAN OTHER THAN YOU, AN' I DON' FEEL CHEATED, BUT LUCKY.
I LOVE ONLY YOU, RUTH.
NOW...

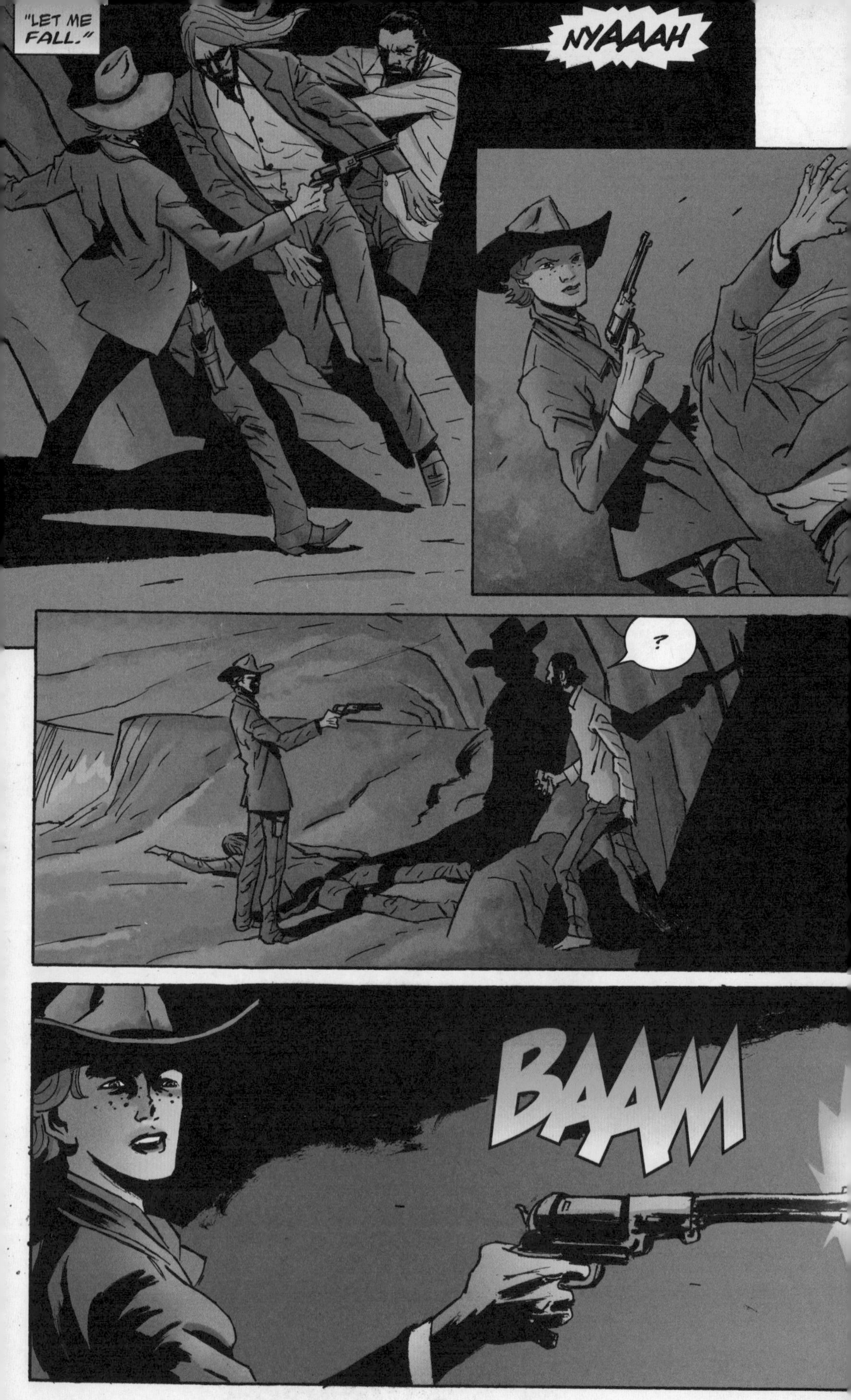
"LET ME FALL."
NYAAAH
?
BAAM

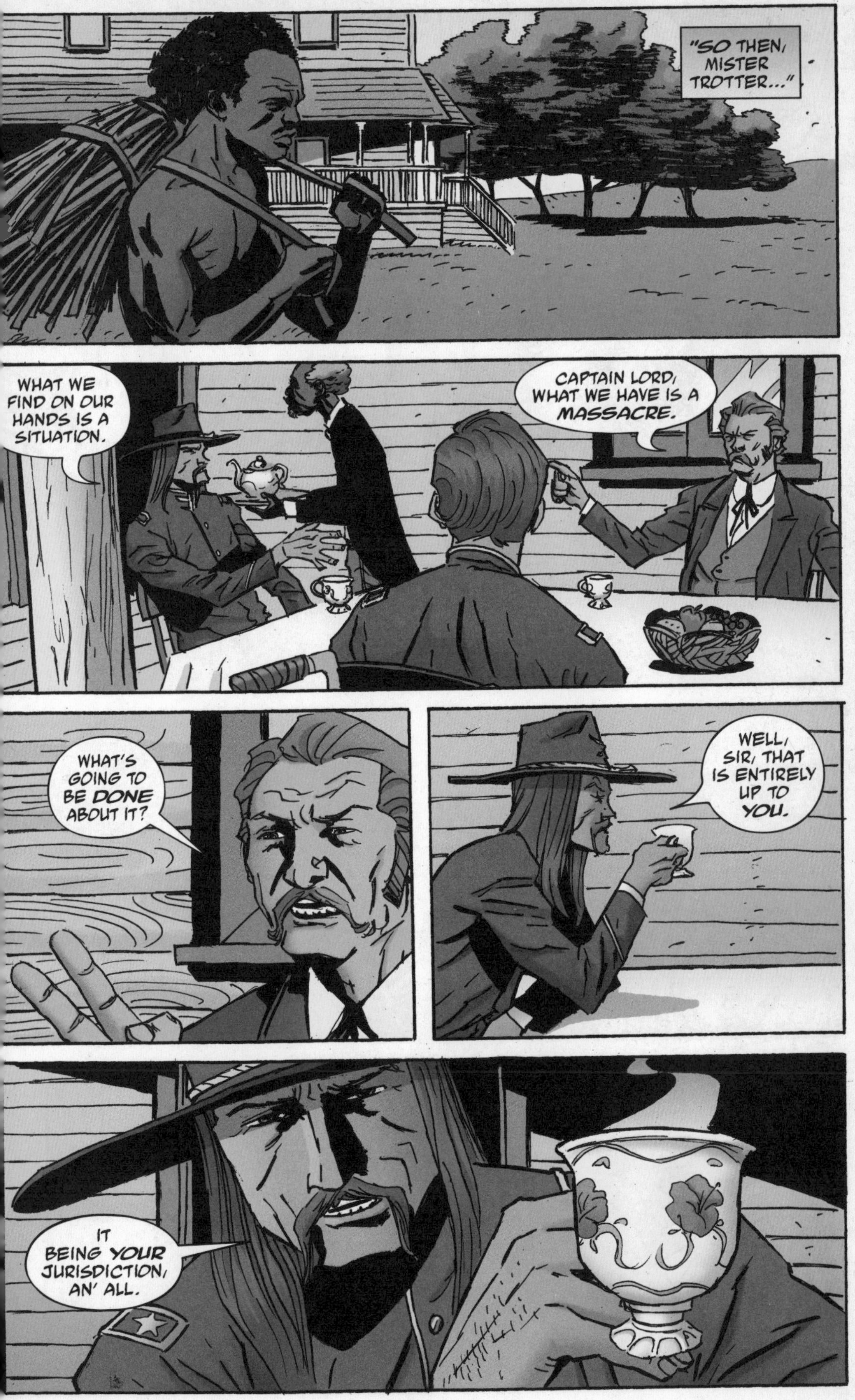
"SO THEN, MISTER TROTTER..."
WHAT WE FIND ON OUR HANDS IS A SITUATION.
CAPTAIN LORD, WHAT WE HAVE IS A MASSACRE.
WHAT'S GOING TO BE DONE ABOUT IT?
WELL, SIR, THAT IS ENTIRELY UP TO YOU.
IT BEING YOUR JURISDICTION, AN' ALL.

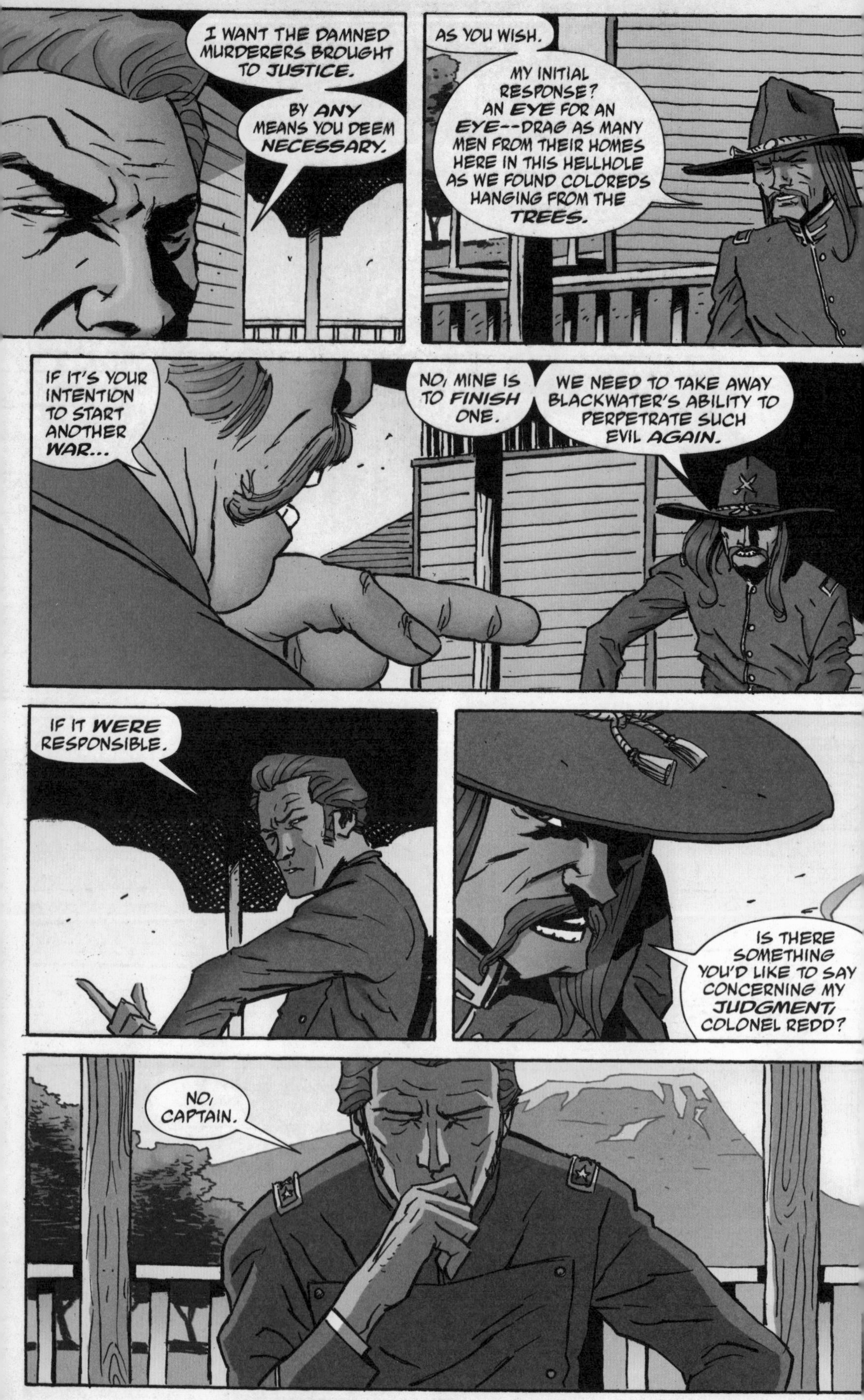

I WANT THE DAMNED MURDERERS BROUGHT TO JUSTICE.
BY ANY MEANS YOU DEEM NECESSARY.
AS YOU WISH.
MY INITIAL RESPONSE? AN EYE FOR AN EYE--DRAG AS MANY MEN FROM THEIR HOMES HERE IN THIS HELLHOLE AS WE FOUND COLOREDS HANGING FROM THE TREES.
IF IT'S YOUR INTENTION TO START ANOTHER WAR...
NO, MINE IS TO FINISH ONE.
WE NEED TO TAKE AWAY BLACKWATER'S ABILITY TO PERPETRATE SUCH EVIL AGAIN.
IF IT WERE RESPONSIBLE.
IS THERE SOMETHING YOU'D LIKE TO SAY CONCERNING MY JUDGMENT, COLONEL REDD?
NO, CAPTAIN.

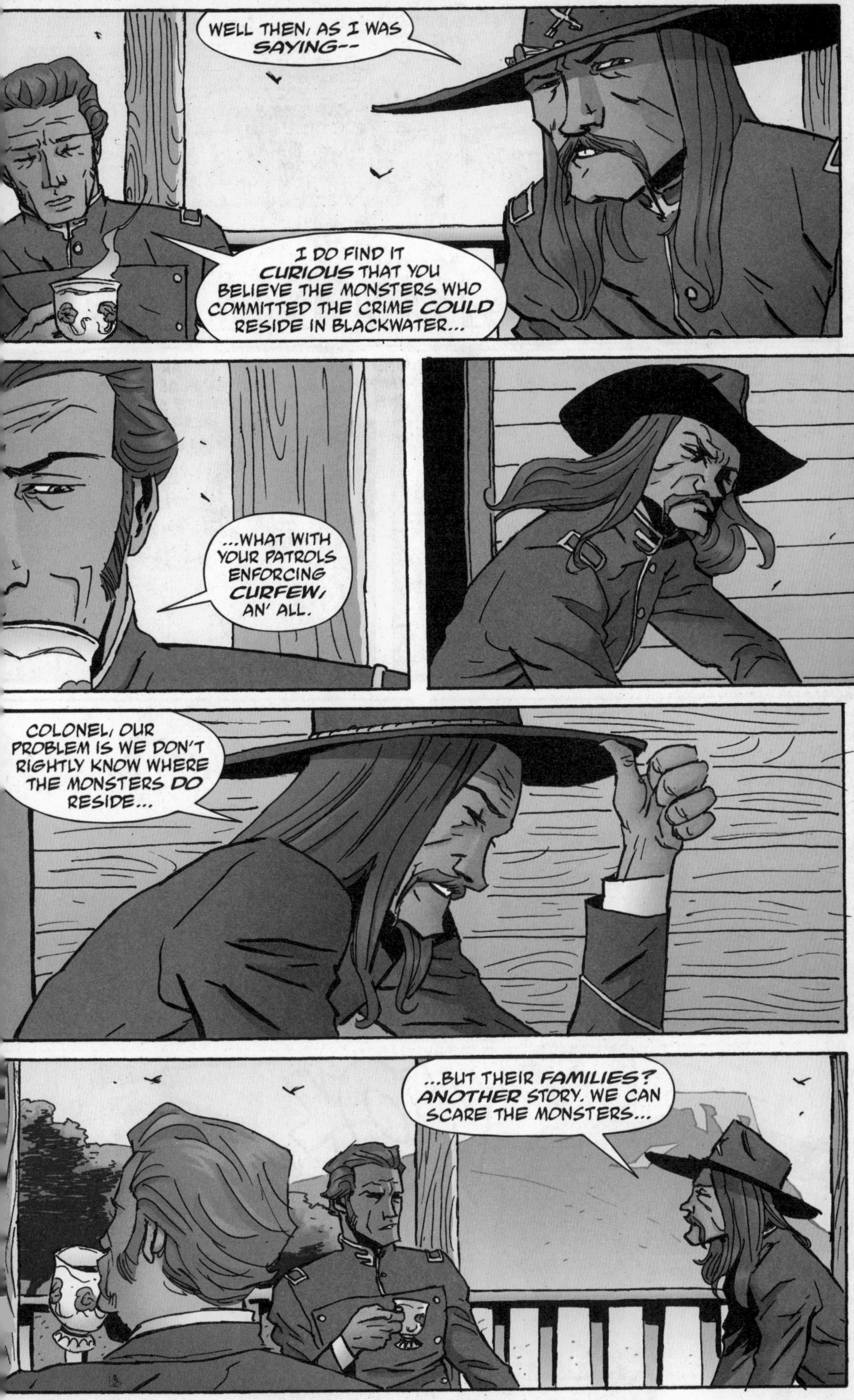
WELL THEN, AS I WAS SAYING--
I DO FIND IT CURIOUS THAT YOU BELIEVE THE MONSTERS WHO COMMITTED THE CRIME COULD RESIDE IN BLACKWATER...
...WHAT WITH YOUR PATROLS ENFORCING CURFEW, AN' ALL.
COLONEL, OUR PROBLEM IS WE DON'T RIGHTLY KNOW WHERE THE MONSTERS DO RESIDE...
...BUT THEIR FAMILIES? ANOTHER STORY. WE CAN SCARE THE MONSTERS...

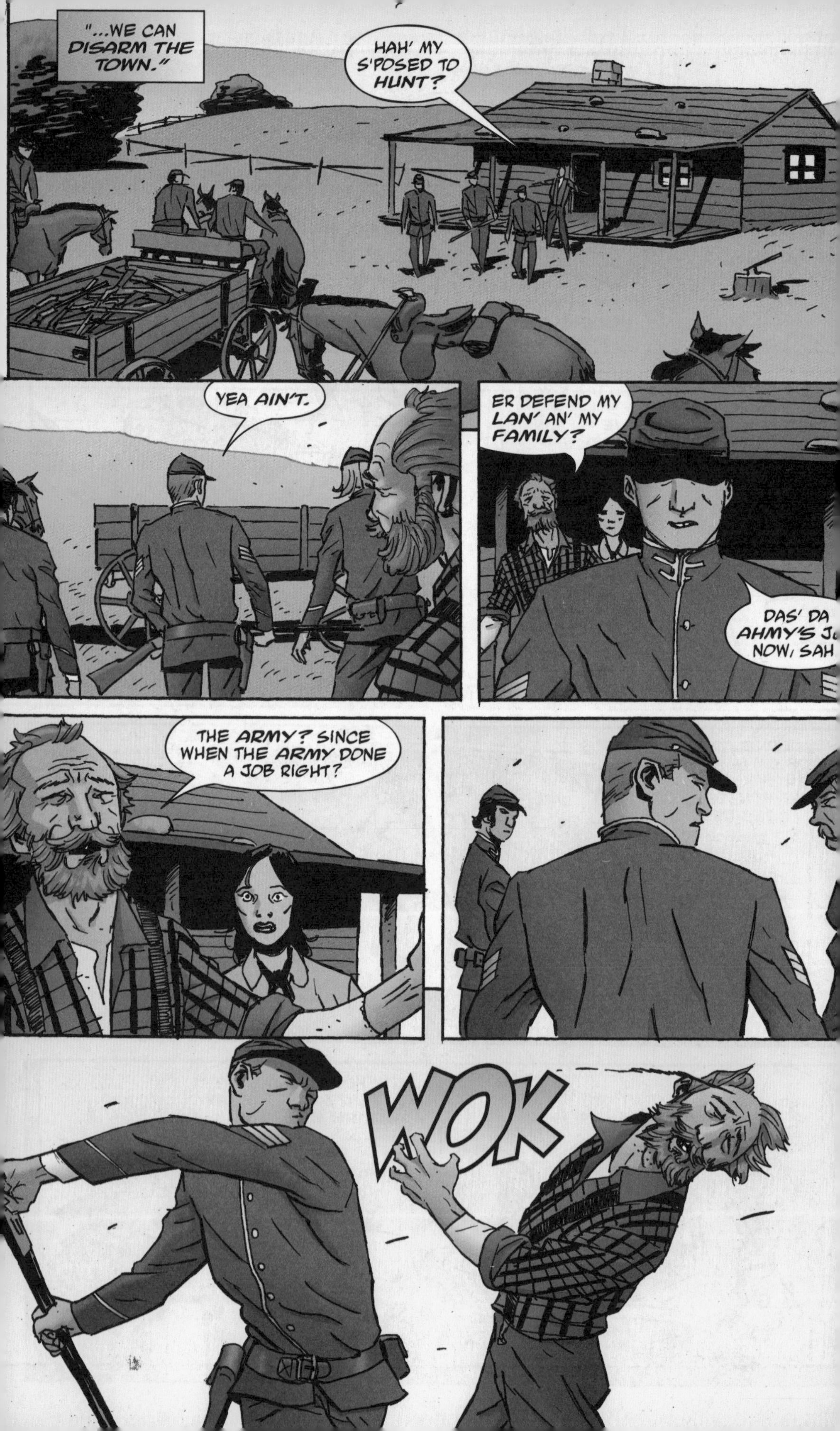
"...WE CAN DISARM THE TOWN."
HAH' MY S'POSED TO HUNT?
YEA AIN'T.
ER DEFEND MY LAN' AN' MY FAMILY?
DAS' DA AHMY'S J NOW, SAH
THE ARMY? SINCE WHEN THE ARMY DONE A JOB RIGHT?
WOK

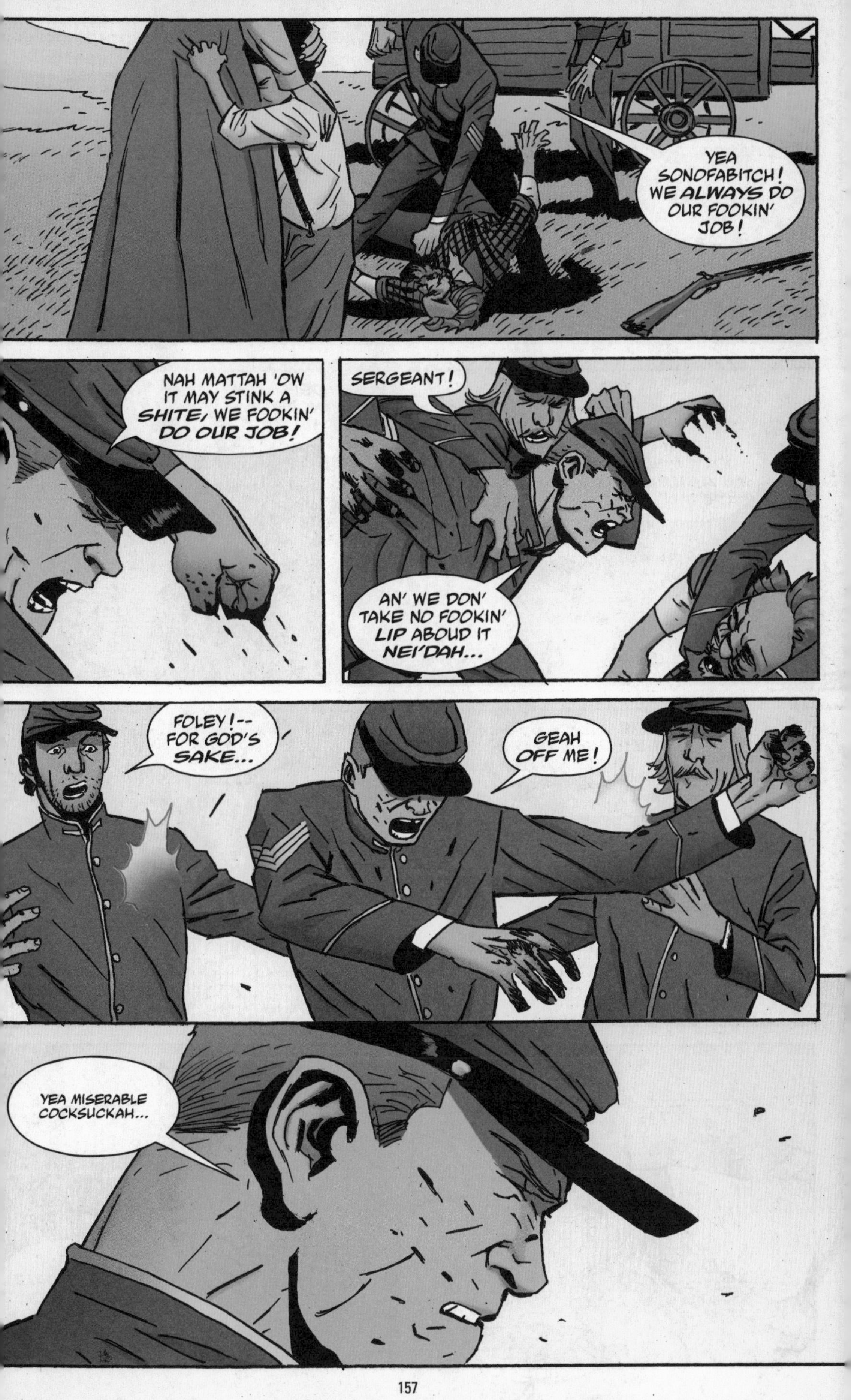
YEA SONOFABITCH! WE ALWAYS DO OUR FOOKIN' JOB!
NAH MATTAH 'OW IT MAY STINK A SHITE, WE FOOKIN' DO OUR JOB!
SERGEANT!
AN' WE DON' TAKE NO FOOKIN' LIP ABOUD IT NEI'DAH...
FOLEY!-- FOR GOD'S SAKE...
GEAH OFF ME!
YEA MISERABLE COCKSUCKAH...

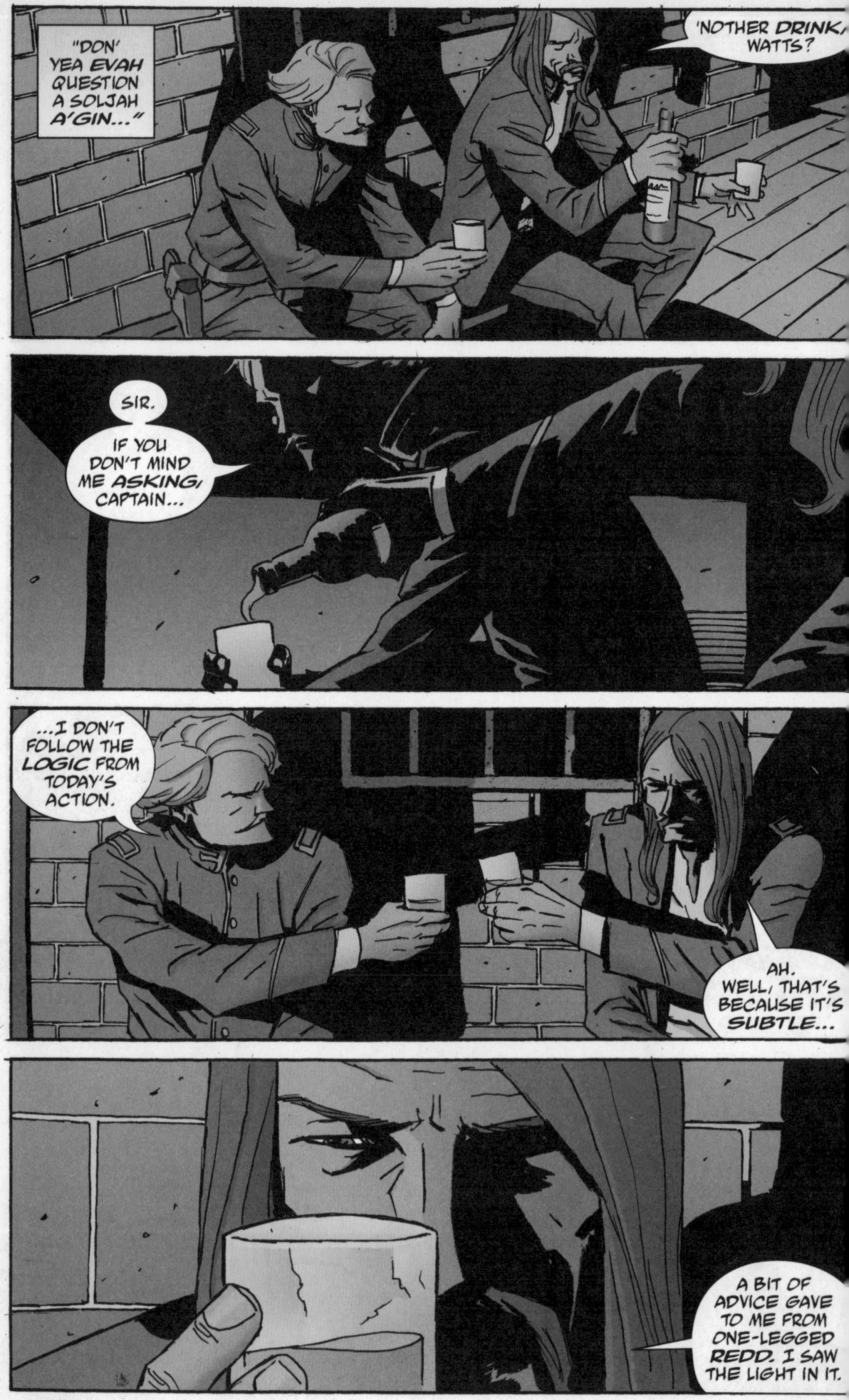
"DON' YEA EVAH QUESTION A SOLJAH A'GIN..."
'NOTHER DRINK, WATTS?
SIR.
IF YOU DON'T MIND ME ASKING, CAPTAIN...
...I DON'T FOLLOW THE LOGIC FROM TODAY'S ACTION.
AH. WELL, THAT'S BECAUSE IT'S SUBTLE...
A BIT OF ADVICE GAVE TO ME FROM ONE-LEGGED REDD. I SAW THE LIGHT IN IT.

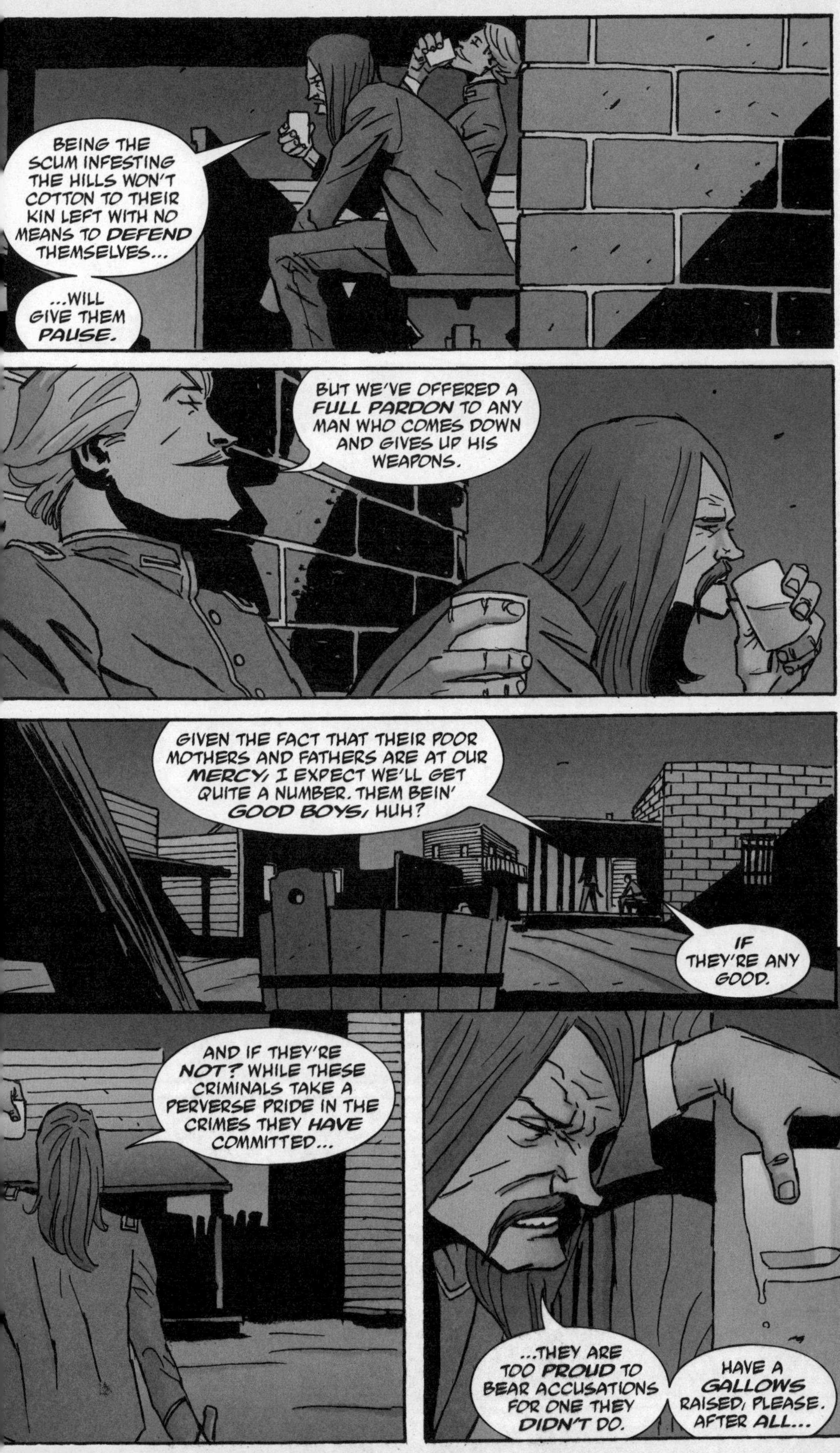

BEING THE SCUM INFESTING THE HILLS WON'T COTTON TO THEIR KIN LEFT WITH NO MEANS TO DEFEND THEMSELVES...
...WILL GIVE THEM PAUSE.
BUT WE'VE OFFERED A FULL PARDON TO ANY MAN WHO COMES DOWN AND GIVES UP HIS WEAPONS.
GIVEN THE FACT THAT THEIR POOR MOTHERS AND FATHERS ARE AT OUR MERCY, I EXPECT WE'LL GET QUITE A NUMBER. THEM BEIN' GOOD BOYS, HUH?
IF THEY'RE ANY GOOD.
AND IF THEY'RE NOT? WHILE THESE CRIMINALS TAKE A PERVERSE PRIDE IN THE CRIMES THEY HAVE COMMITTED...
...THEY ARE TOO PROUD TO BEAR ACCUSATIONS FOR ONE THEY DIDN'T DO.
HAVE A GALLOWS RAISED, PLEASE. AFTER ALL...

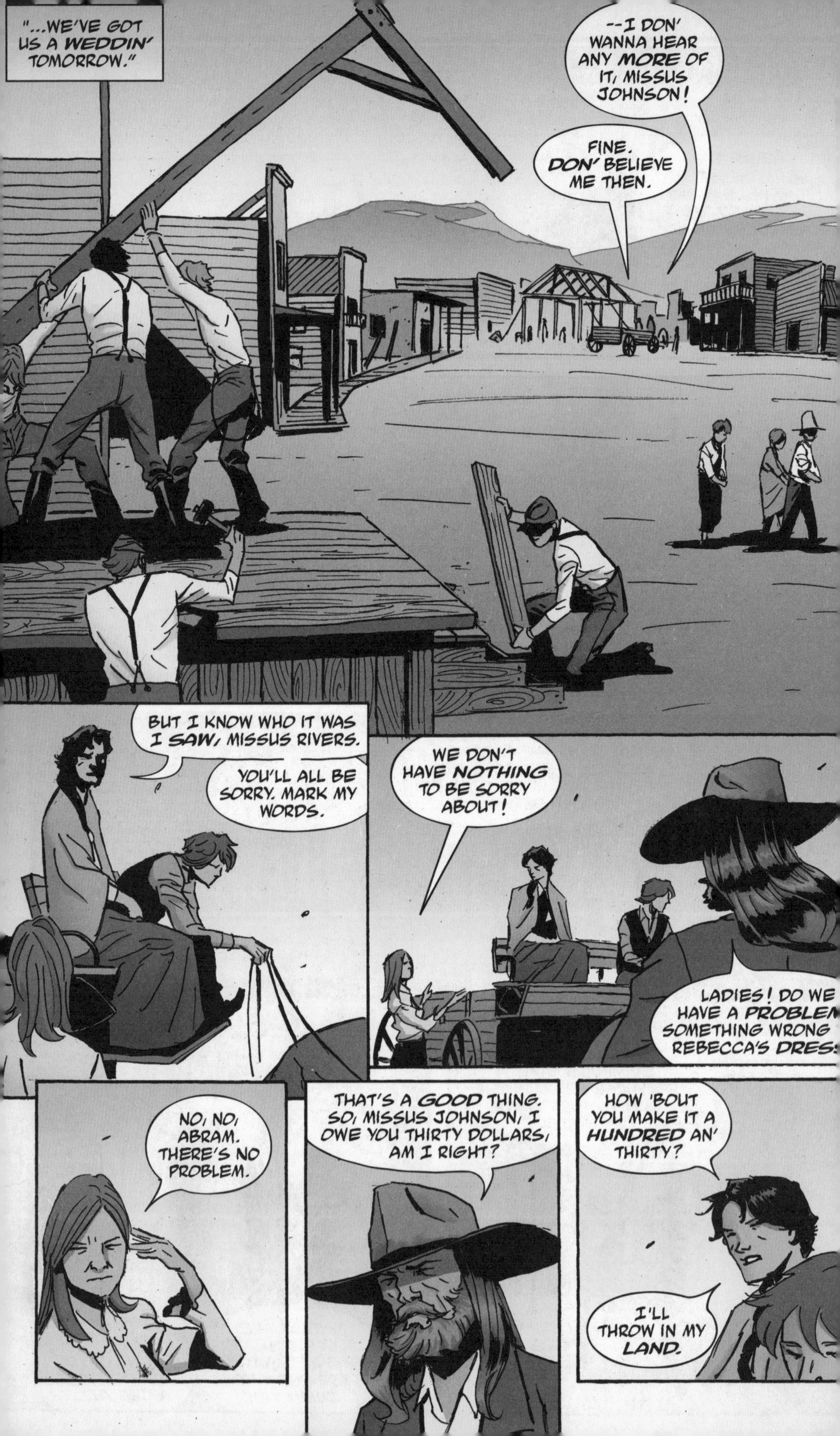
"...WE'VE GOT US A WEDDIN' TOMORROW."
--I DON' WANNA HEAR ANY MORE OF IT, MISSUS JOHNSON!
FINE. DON' BELIEVE ME THEN.
BUT I KNOW WHO IT WAS I SAW, MISSUS RIVERS.
YOU'LL ALL BE SORRY. MARK MY WORDS.
WE DON'T HAVE NOTHING TO BE SORRY ABOUT!
LADIES! DO WE HAVE A PROBLEM SOMETHING WRONG REBECCA'S DRESS
NO, NO, ABRAM. THERE'S NO PROBLEM.
THAT'S A GOOD THING. SO, MISSUS JOHNSON, I OWE YOU THIRTY DOLLARS, AM I RIGHT?
HOW 'BOUT YOU MAKE IT A HUNDRED AN' THIRTY?
I'LL THROW IN MY LAND.

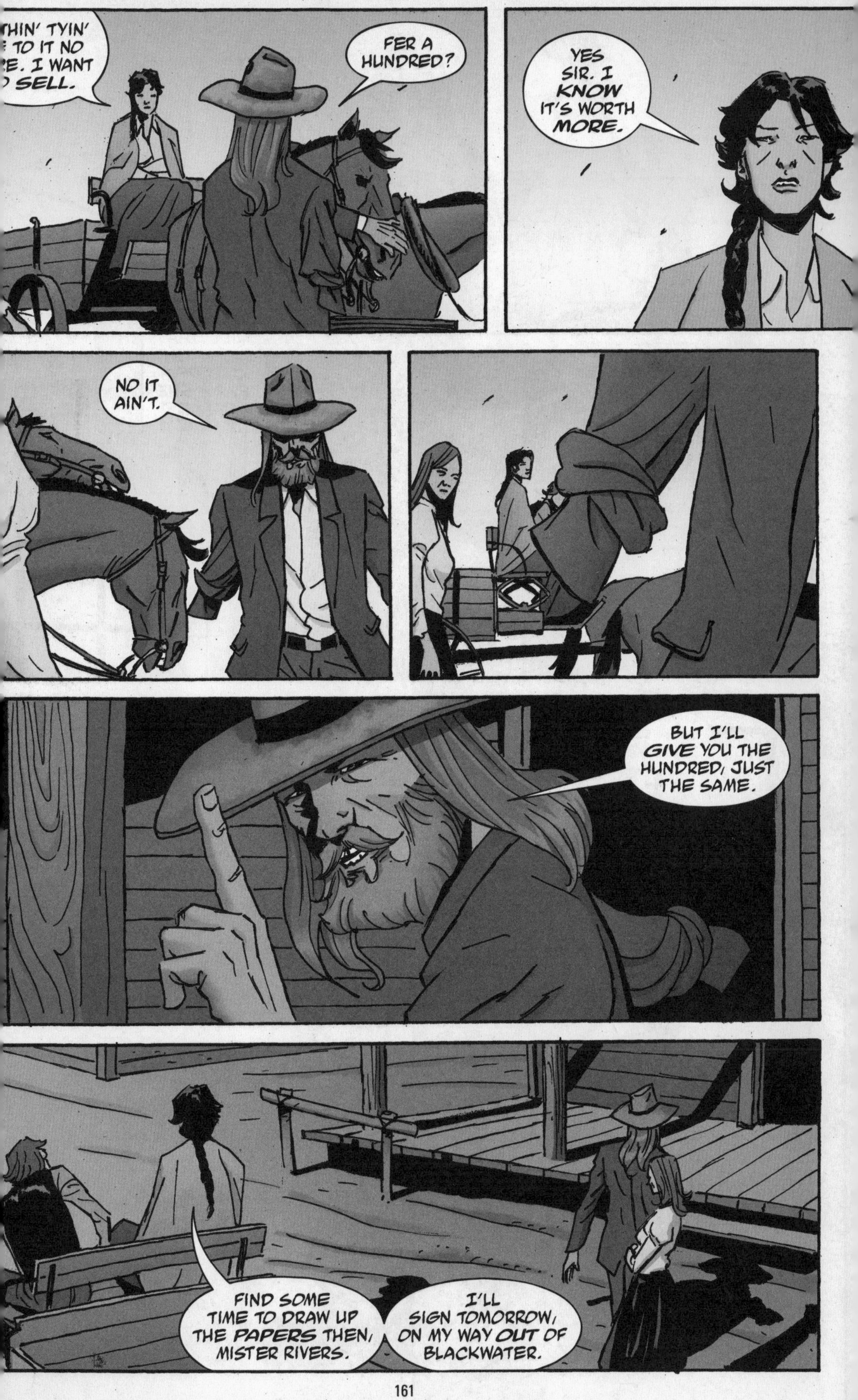

THIN' TYIN'
E TO IT NO
RE. I WANT
O SELL.
FER A HUNDRED?
YES SIR. I KNOW IT'S WORTH MORE.
NO IT AIN'T.
BUT I'LL GIVE YOU THE HUNDRED, JUST THE SAME.
FIND SOME TIME TO DRAW UP THE PAPERS THEN, MISTER RIVERS.
I'LL SIGN TOMORROW, ON MY WAY OUT OF BLACKWATER.

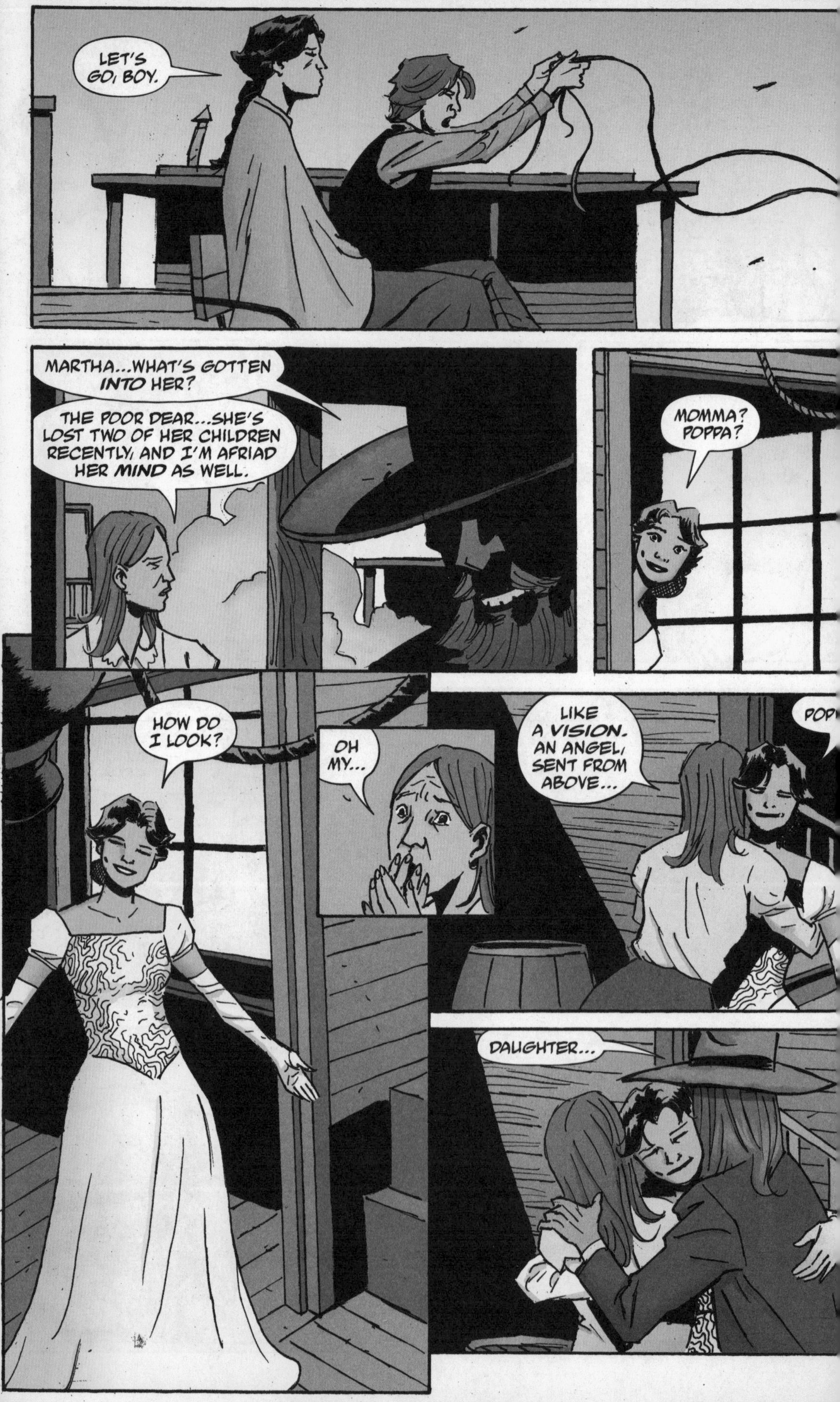

LET'S GO, BOY.
MARTHA...WHAT'S GOTTEN INTO HER?
THE POOR DEAR...SHE'S LOST TWO OF HER CHILDREN RECENTLY, AND I'M AFRIAD HER MIND AS WELL.
MOMMA? POPPA?
HOW DO I LOOK?
OH MY...
LIKE A VISION. AN ANGEL, SENT FROM ABOVE...
DAUGHTER...

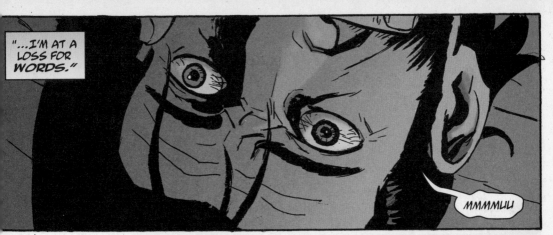

"...I'M AT A LOSS FOR WORDS."

MMMMUU

WOULDN'T TRY AN' *TALK* IF I WAS YOU, MISTER PUNCH...

AIN'T REALLY NO *POINT*.

YA *FAILED* ME, I AM SO SORRY TO SAY.

SO VERY, *VERY* SORRY.

TIME TO *ATONE*.

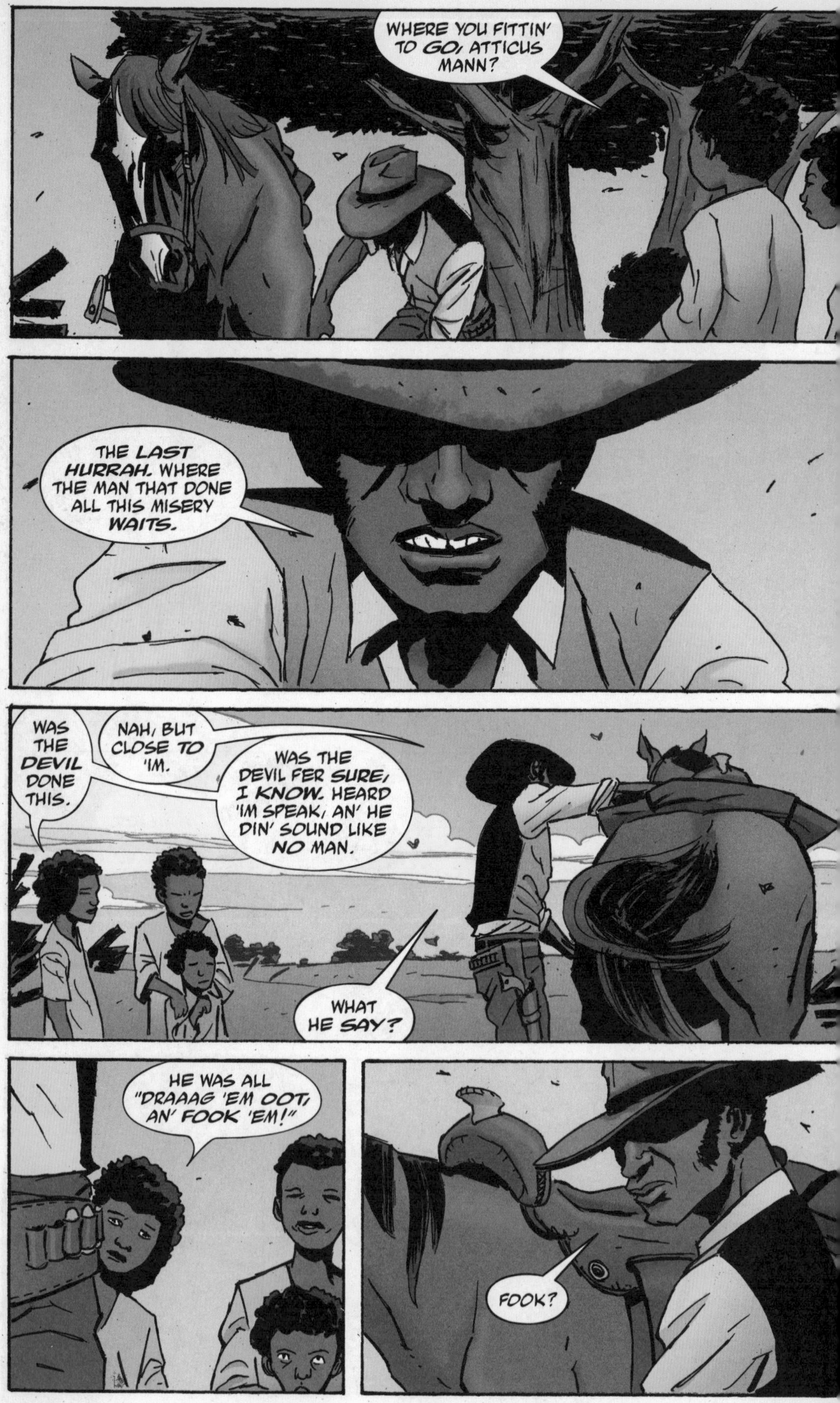
WHERE YOU FITTIN' TO GO, ATTICUS MANN?
THE LAST HURRAH. WHERE THE MAN THAT DONE ALL THIS MISERY WAITS.
WAS THE DEVIL DONE THIS.
NAH, BUT CLOSE TO 'IM.
WAS THE DEVIL FER SURE, I KNOW. HEARD 'IM SPEAK, AN' HE DIN' SOUND LIKE NO MAN.
WHAT HE SAY?
HE WAS ALL "DRAAAG 'EM OOT, AN' FOOK 'EM!"
FOOK?

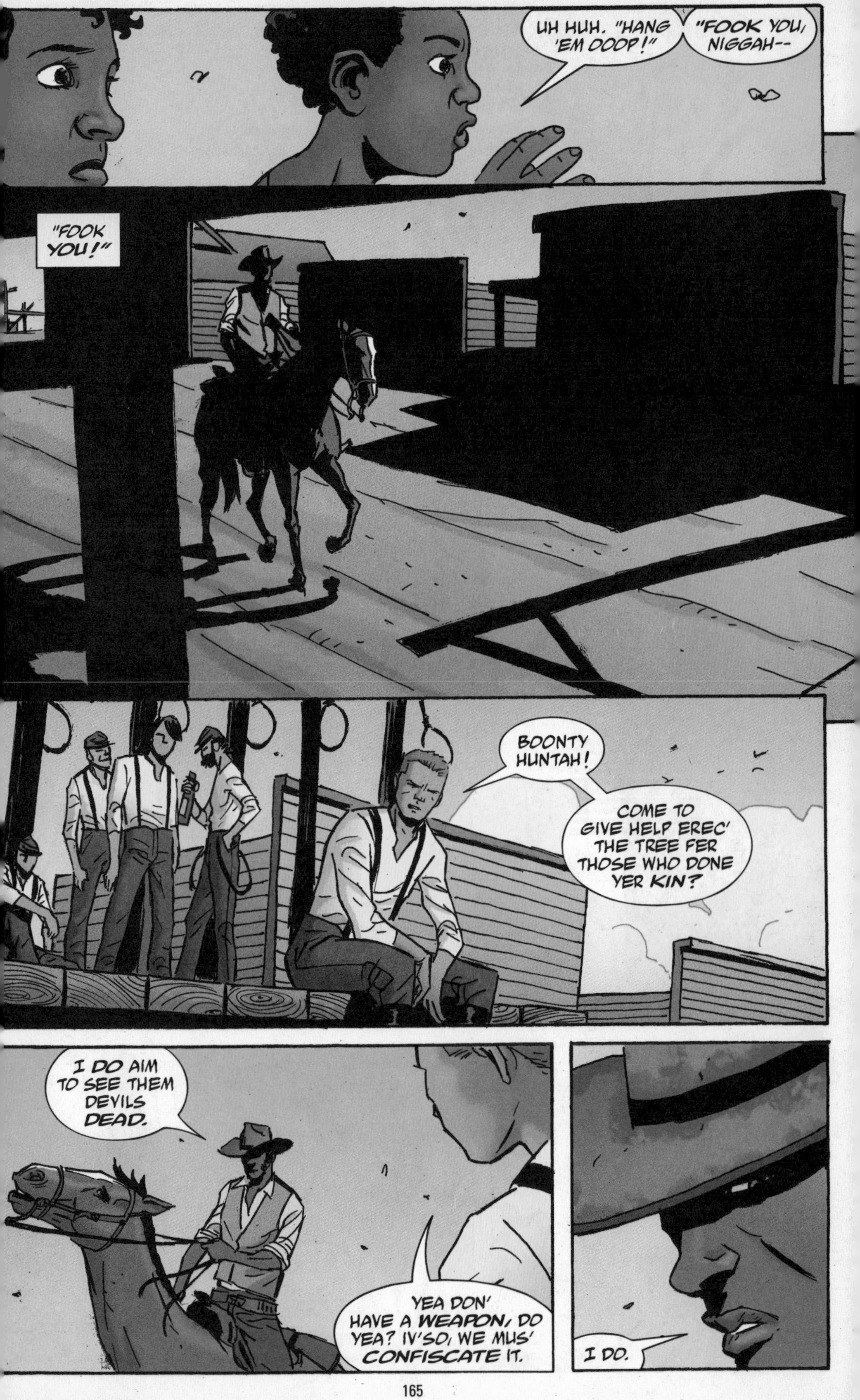
UH HUH. "HANG 'EM OOOP!"
"FOOK YOU, NIGGAH--
"FOOK YOU!"
BOONTY HUNTAH!
COME TO GIVE HELP EREC' THE TREE FER THOSE WHO DONE YER KIN?
I DO AIM TO SEE THEM DEVILS DEAD.
YEA DON' HAVE A WEAPON, DO YEA? IV'SO, WE MUS' CONFISCATE IT.
I DO.

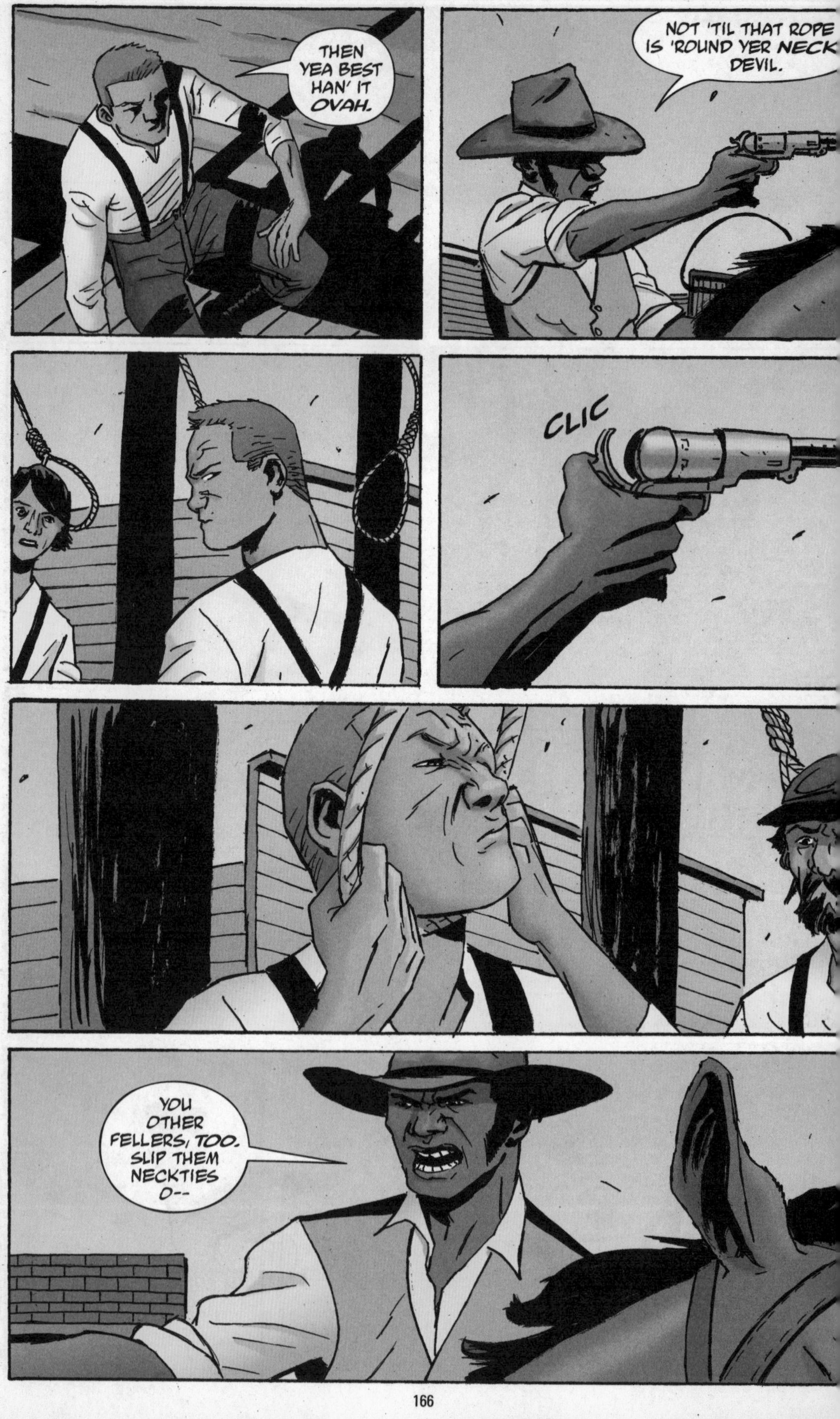
THEN YEA BEST HAN' IT OVAH.
NOT 'TIL THAT ROPE IS 'ROUND YER NECK DEVIL.
CLIC
YOU OTHER FELLERS, TOO. SLIP THEM NECKTIES O--

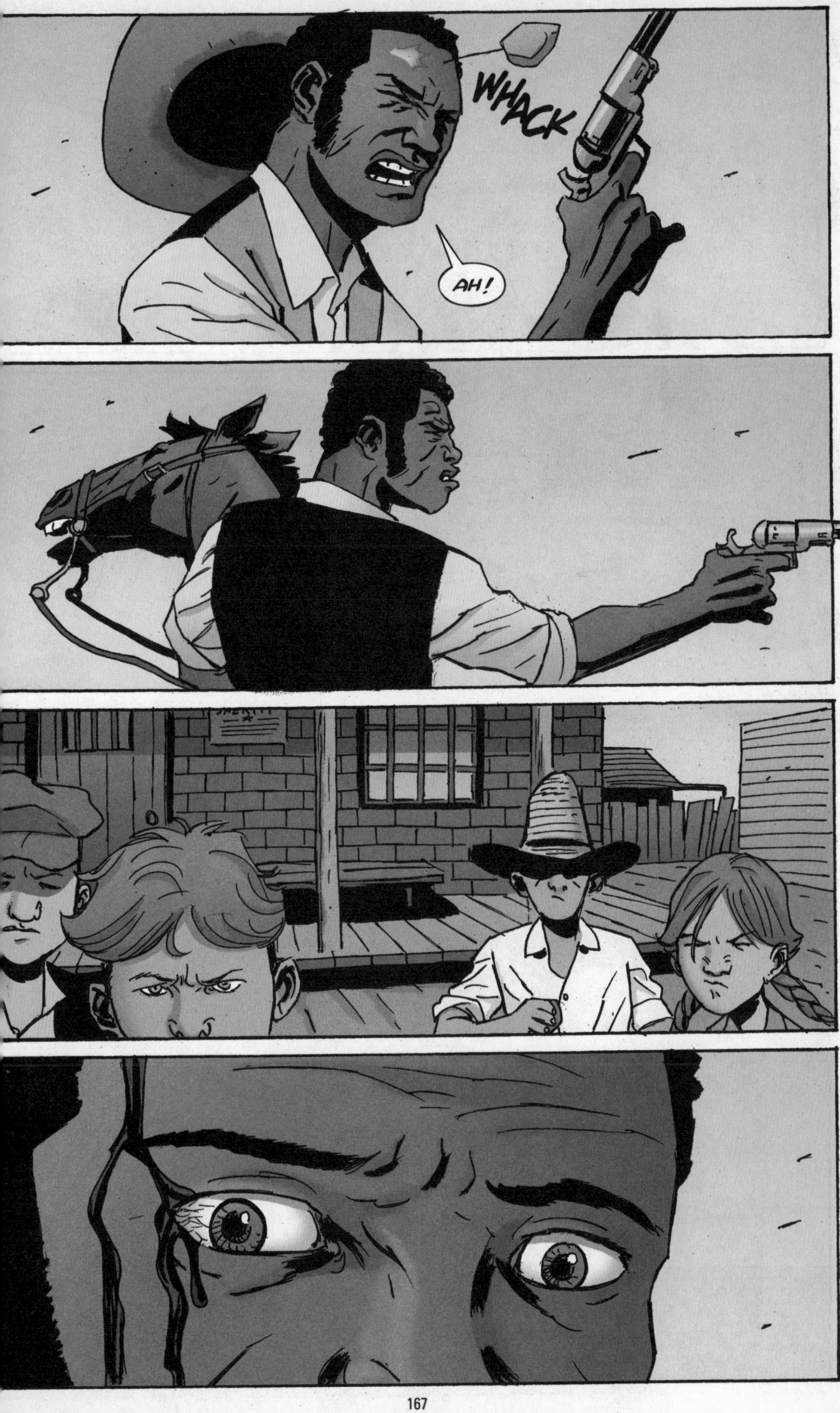
WHACK
AH!

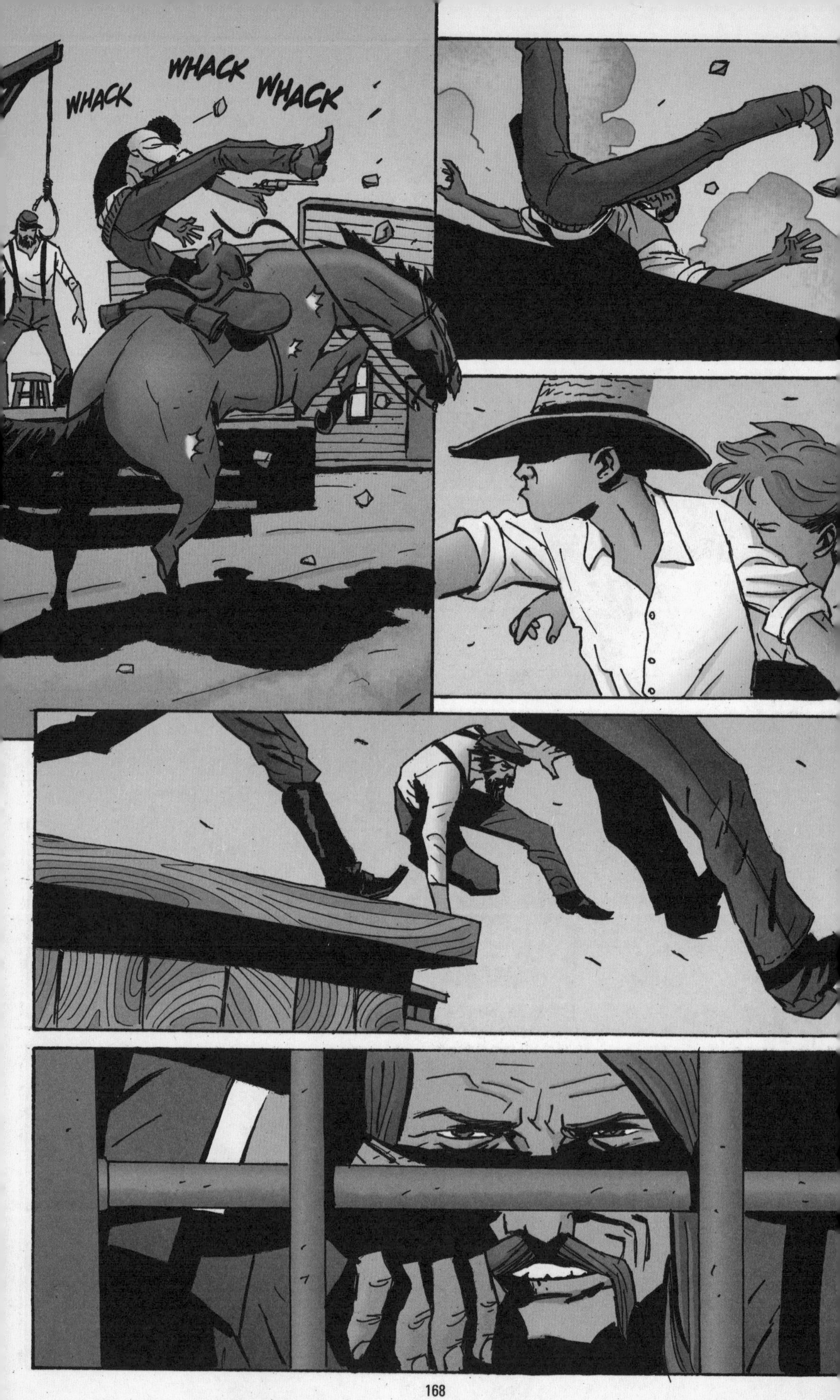
WHACK
WHACK
WHACK

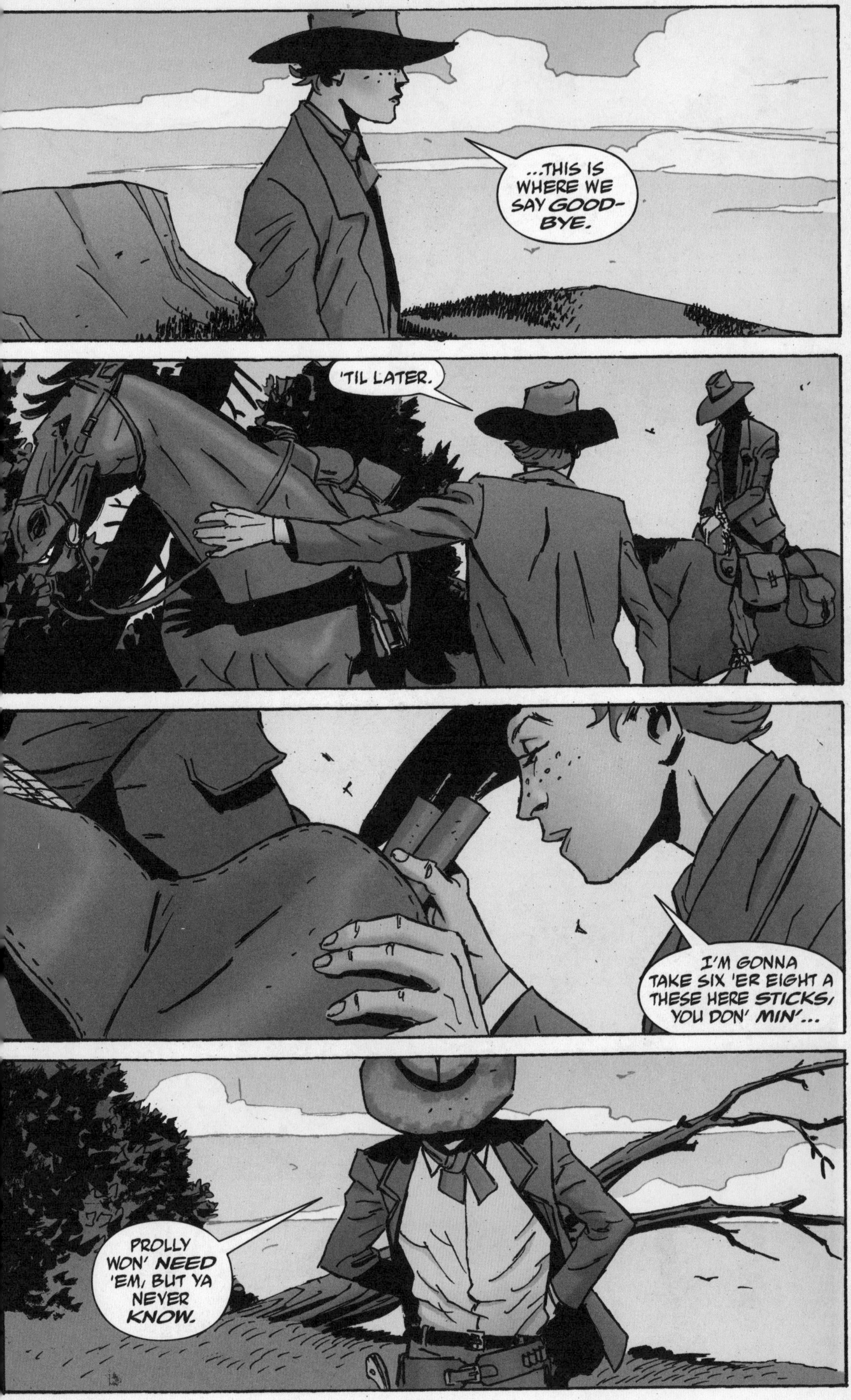
...THIS IS WHERE WE SAY GOOD-BYE.
'TIL LATER.
I'M GONNA TAKE SIX 'ER EIGHT A THESE HERE STICKS, YOU DON' MIN'...
PROLLY WON' NEED 'EM, BUT YA NEVER KNOW.

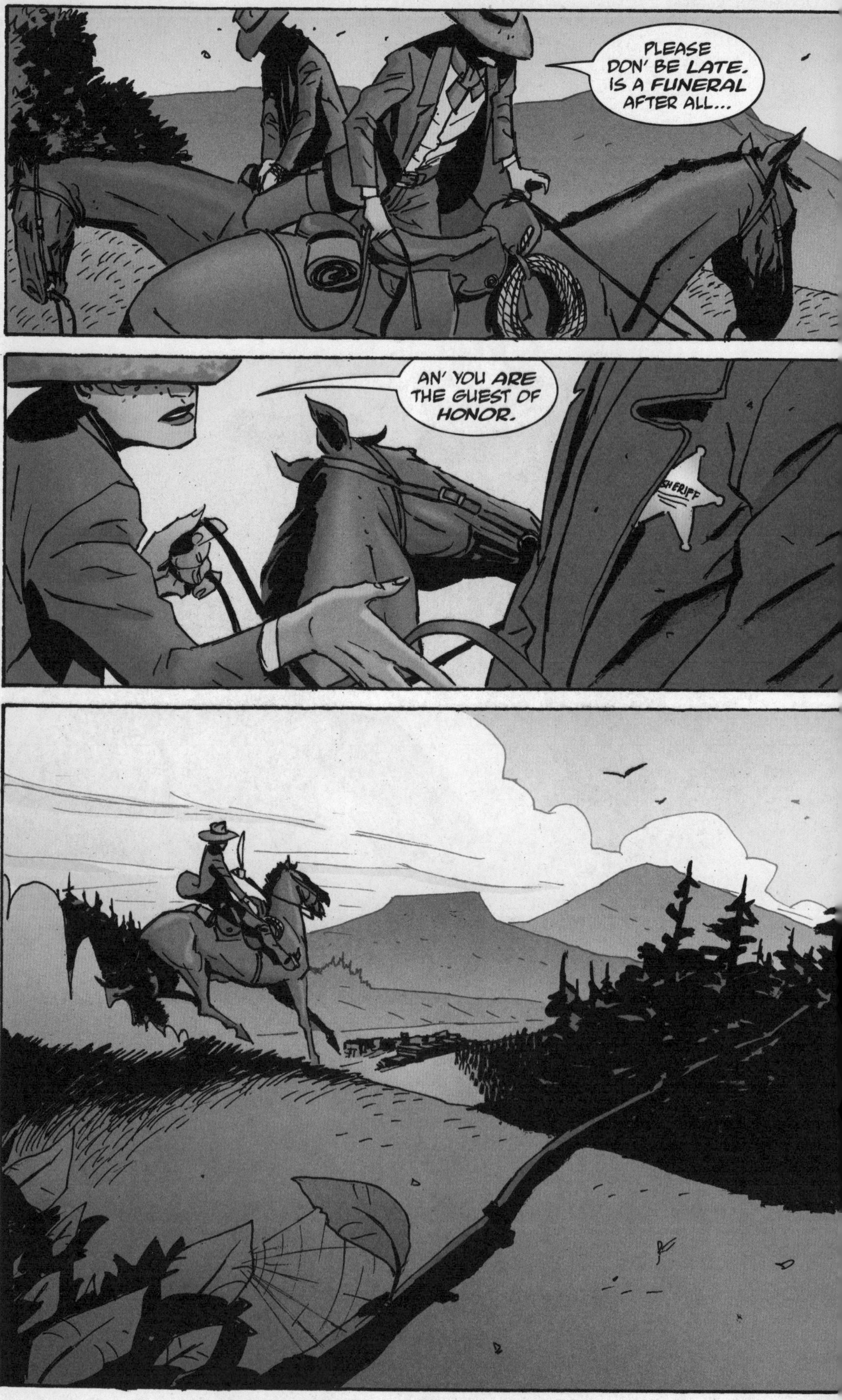
PLEASE DON' BE LATE. IS A FUNERAL AFTER ALL...
AN' YOU ARE THE GUEST OF HONOR.
SHERIFF

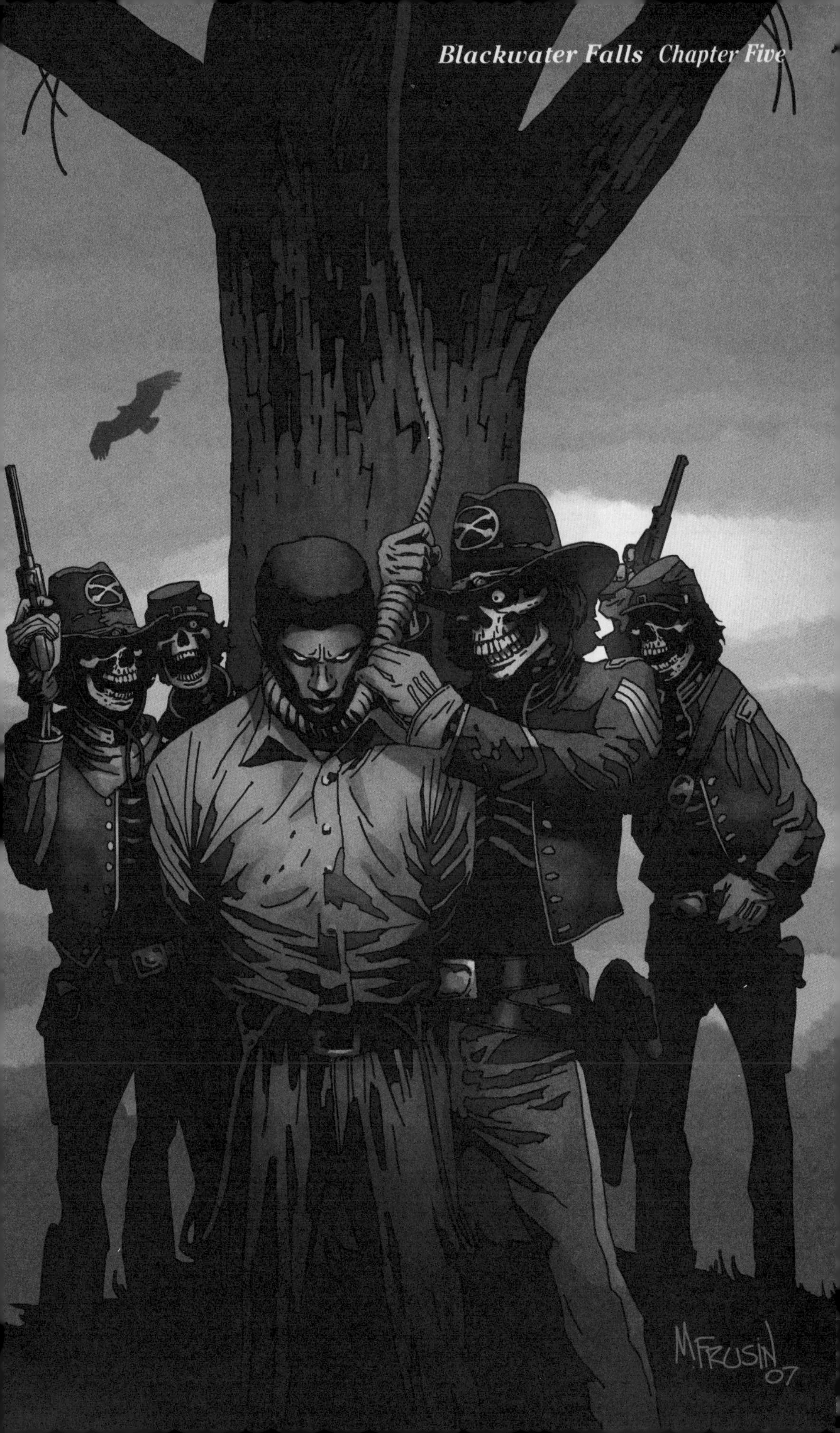
Blackwater Falls Chapter Five
M FRUSIN
07

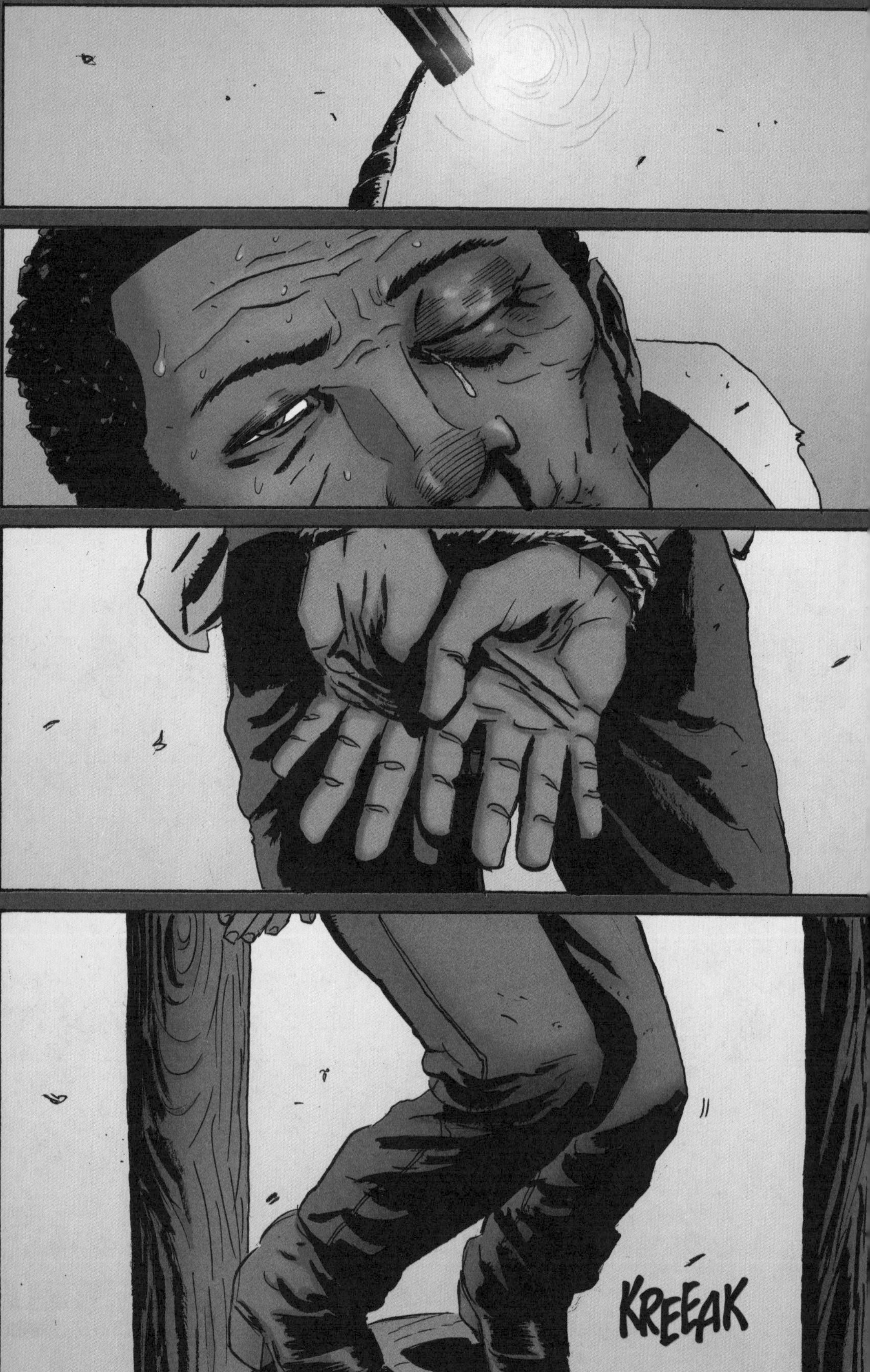
KREEAK

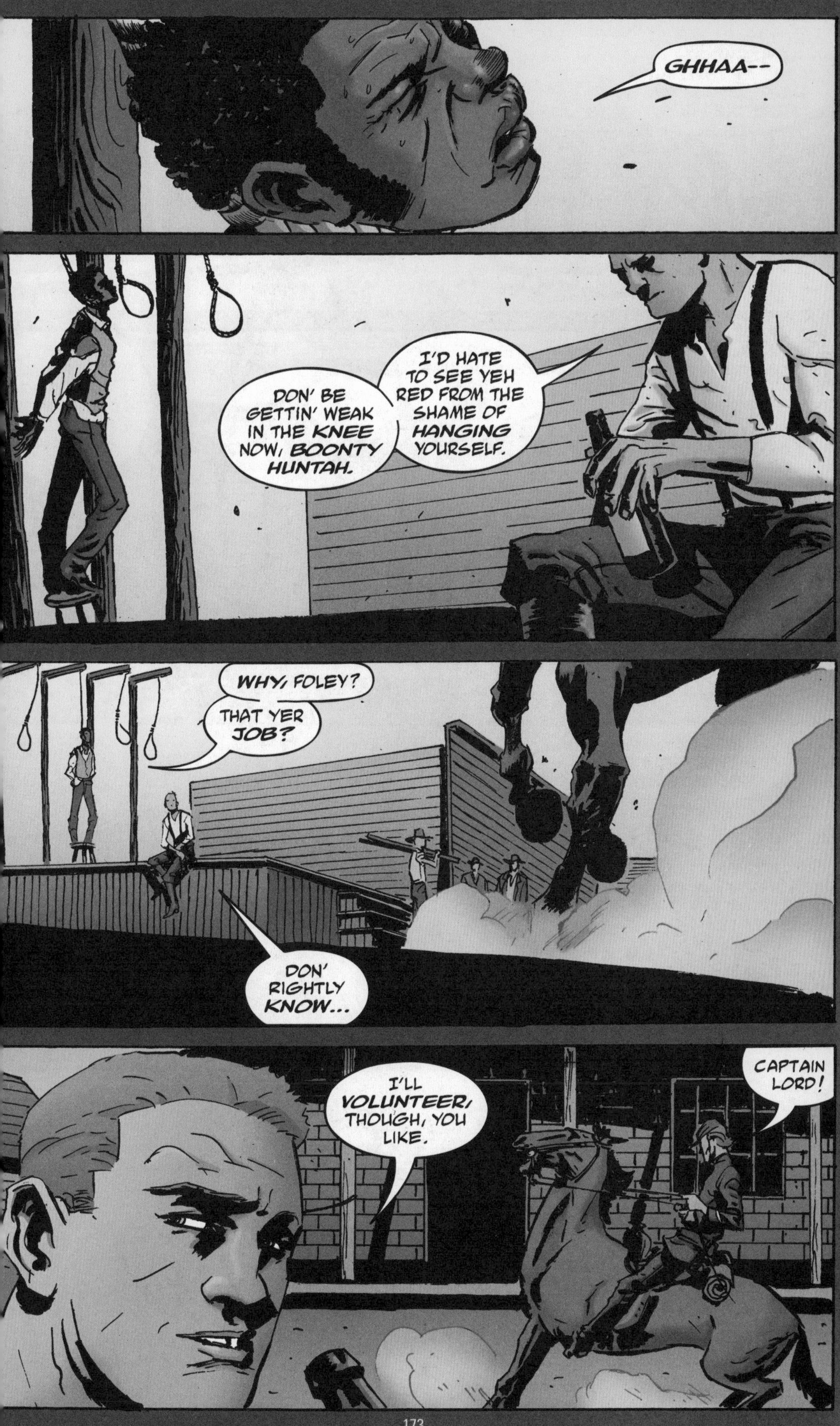
GHHAA--
DON' BE GETTIN' WEAK IN THE KNEE NOW, BOONTY HUNTAH.
I'D HATE TO SEE YEH RED FROM THE SHAME OF HANGING YOURSELF.
WHY, FOLEY?
THAT YER JOB?
DON' RIGHTLY KNOW...
I'LL VOLUNTEER, THOUGH, YOU LIKE.
CAPTAIN LORD!

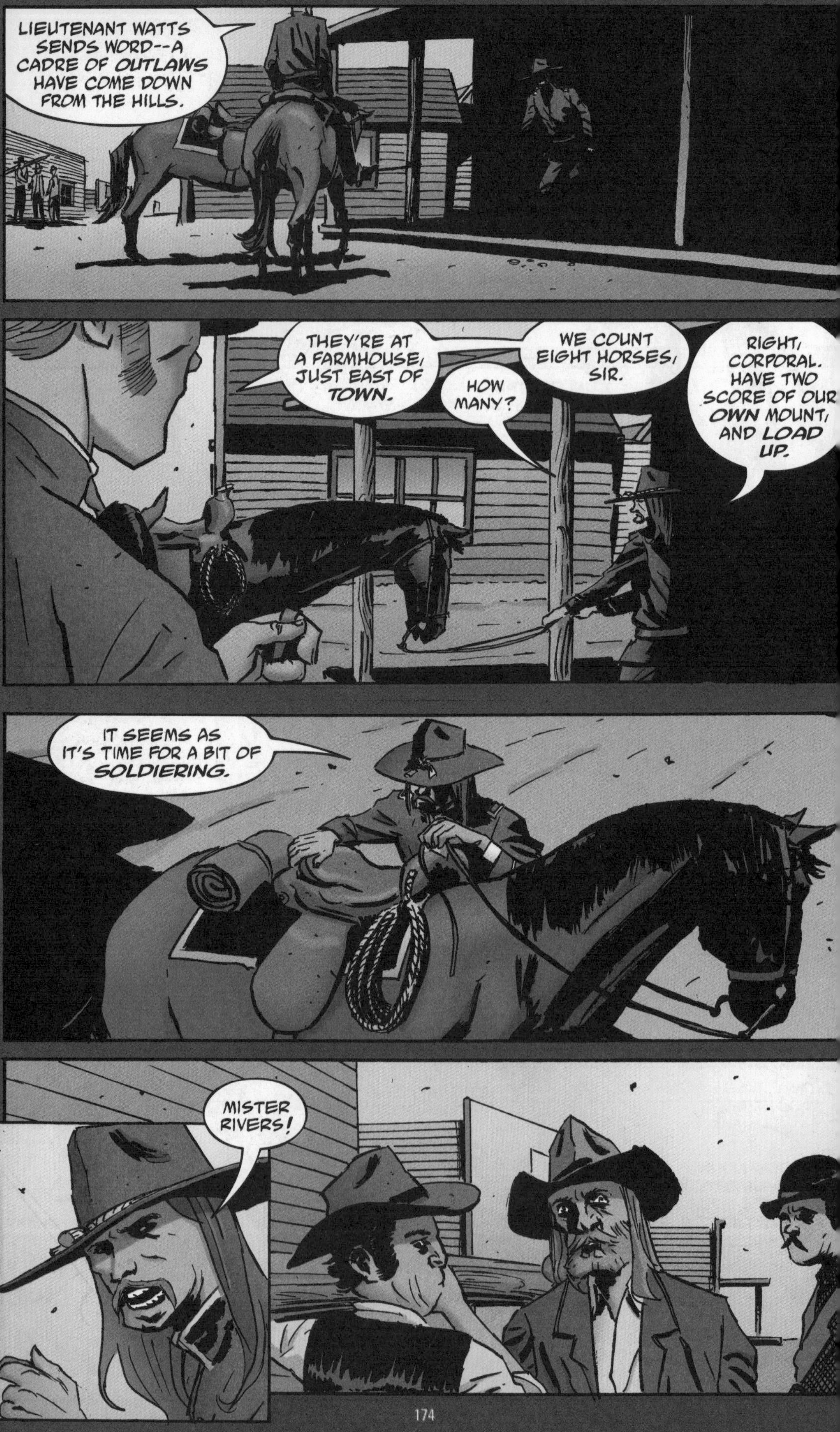
LIEUTENANT WATTS SENDS WORD--A CADRE OF OUTLAWS HAVE COME DOWN FROM THE HILLS.
THEY'RE AT A FARMHOUSE, JUST EAST OF TOWN.
HOW MANY?
WE COUNT EIGHT HORSES, SIR.
RIGHT, CORPORAL. HAVE TWO SCORE OF OUR OWN MOUNT, AND LOAD UP.
IT SEEMS AS IT'S TIME FOR A BIT OF SOLDIERING.
MISTER RIVERS!

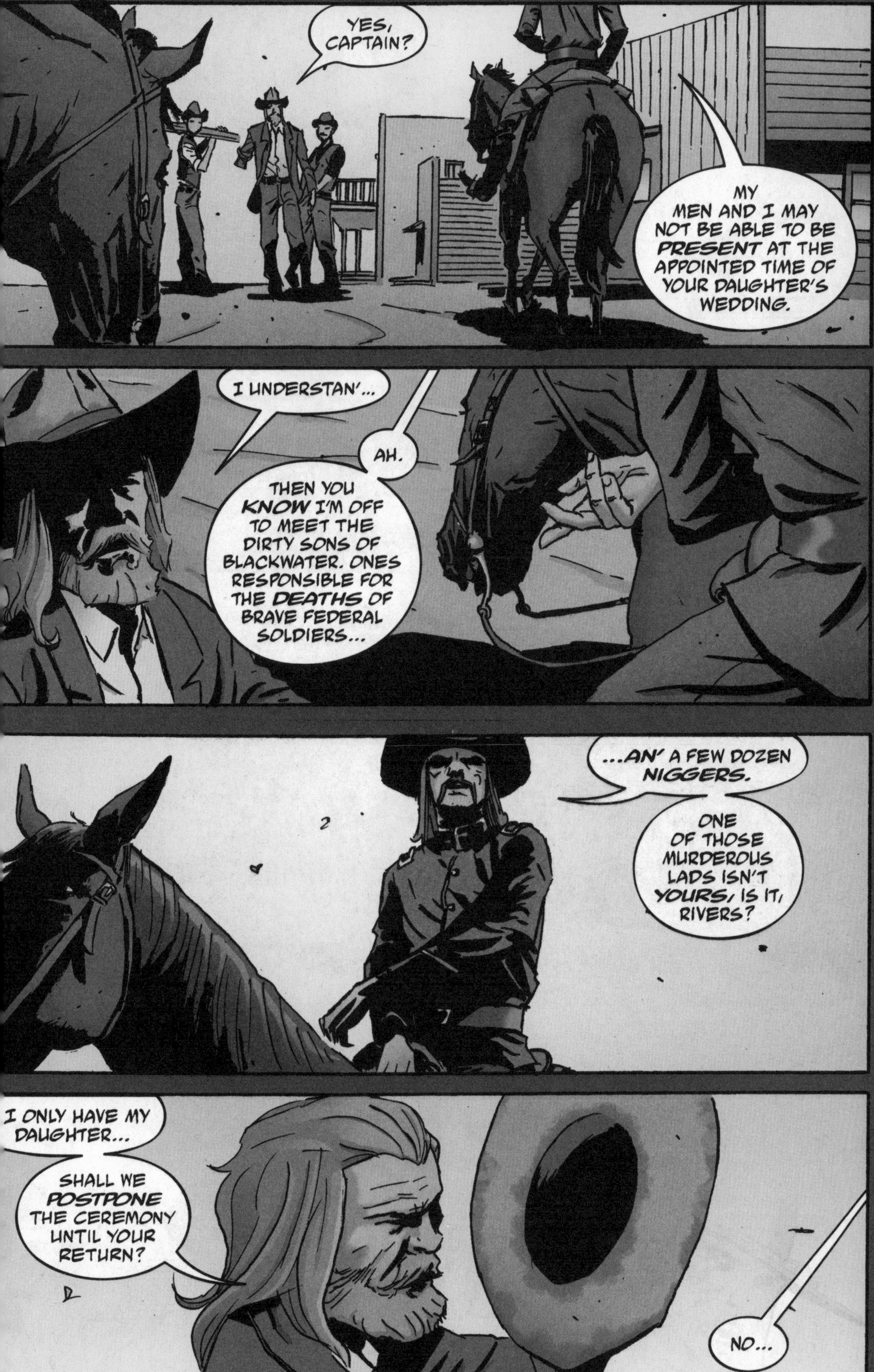
YES, CAPTAIN?
MY MEN AND I MAY NOT BE ABLE TO BE PRESENT AT THE APPOINTED TIME OF YOUR DAUGHTER'S WEDDING.
I UNDERSTAN'...
AH.
THEN YOU KNOW I'M OFF TO MEET THE DIRTY SONS OF BLACKWATER. ONES RESPONSIBLE FOR THE DEATHS OF BRAVE FEDERAL SOLDIERS...
...AN' A FEW DOZEN NIGGERS.
ONE OF THOSE MURDEROUS LADS ISN'T YOURS, IS IT, RIVERS?
I ONLY HAVE MY DAUGHTER...
SHALL WE POSTPONE THE CEREMONY UNTIL YOUR RETURN?
NO...

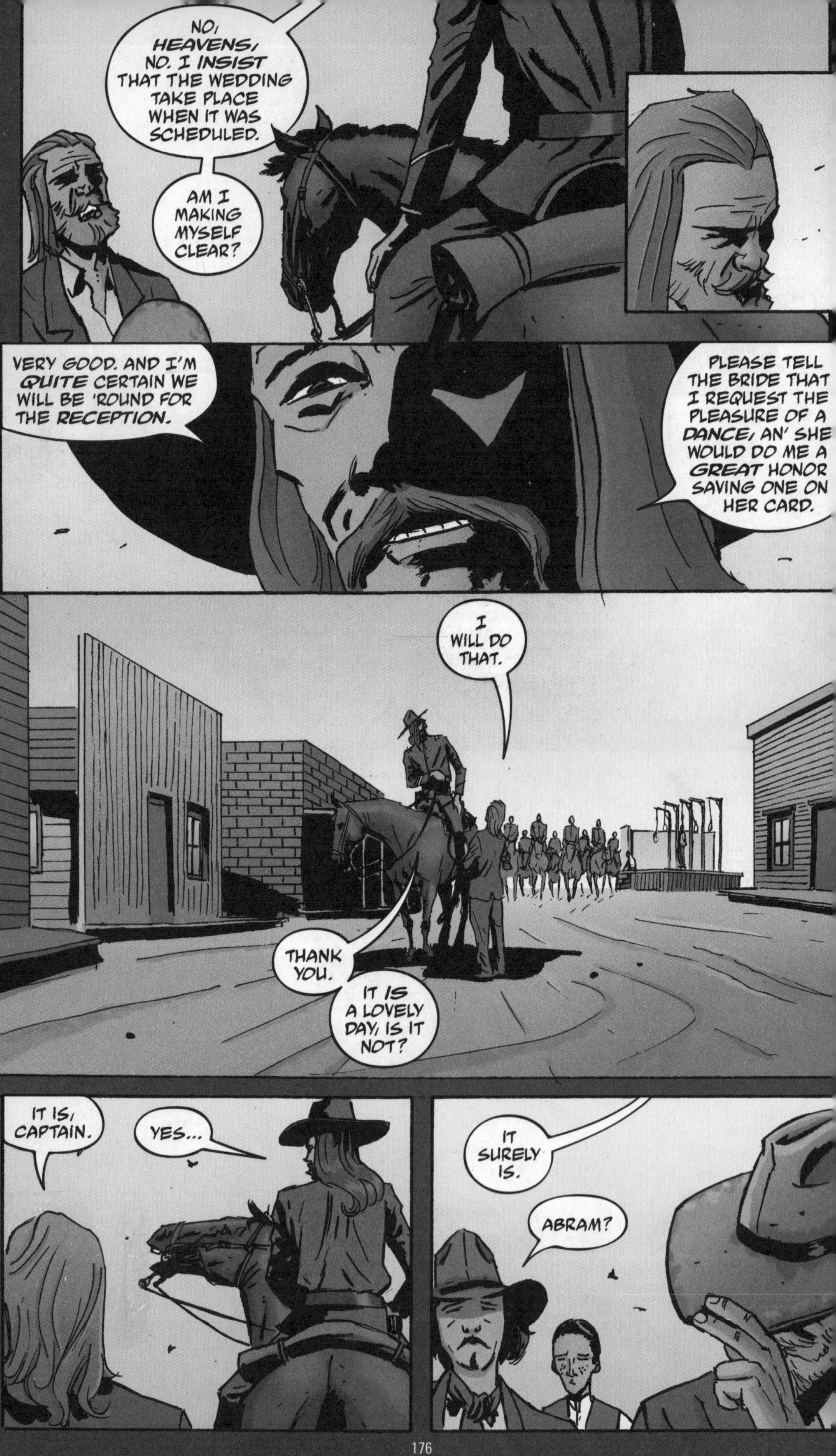
NO, HEAVENS, NO. I INSIST THAT THE WEDDING TAKE PLACE WHEN IT WAS SCHEDULED.
AM I MAKING MYSELF CLEAR?
VERY GOOD. AND I'M QUITE CERTAIN WE WILL BE 'ROUND FOR THE RECEPTION.
PLEASE TELL THE BRIDE THAT I REQUEST THE PLEASURE OF A DANCE, AN' SHE WOULD DO ME A GREAT HONOR SAVING ONE ON HER CARD.
I WILL DO THAT.
THANK YOU.
IT IS A LOVELY DAY, IS IT NOT?
IT IS, CAPTAIN.
YES...
IT SURELY IS.
ABRAM?

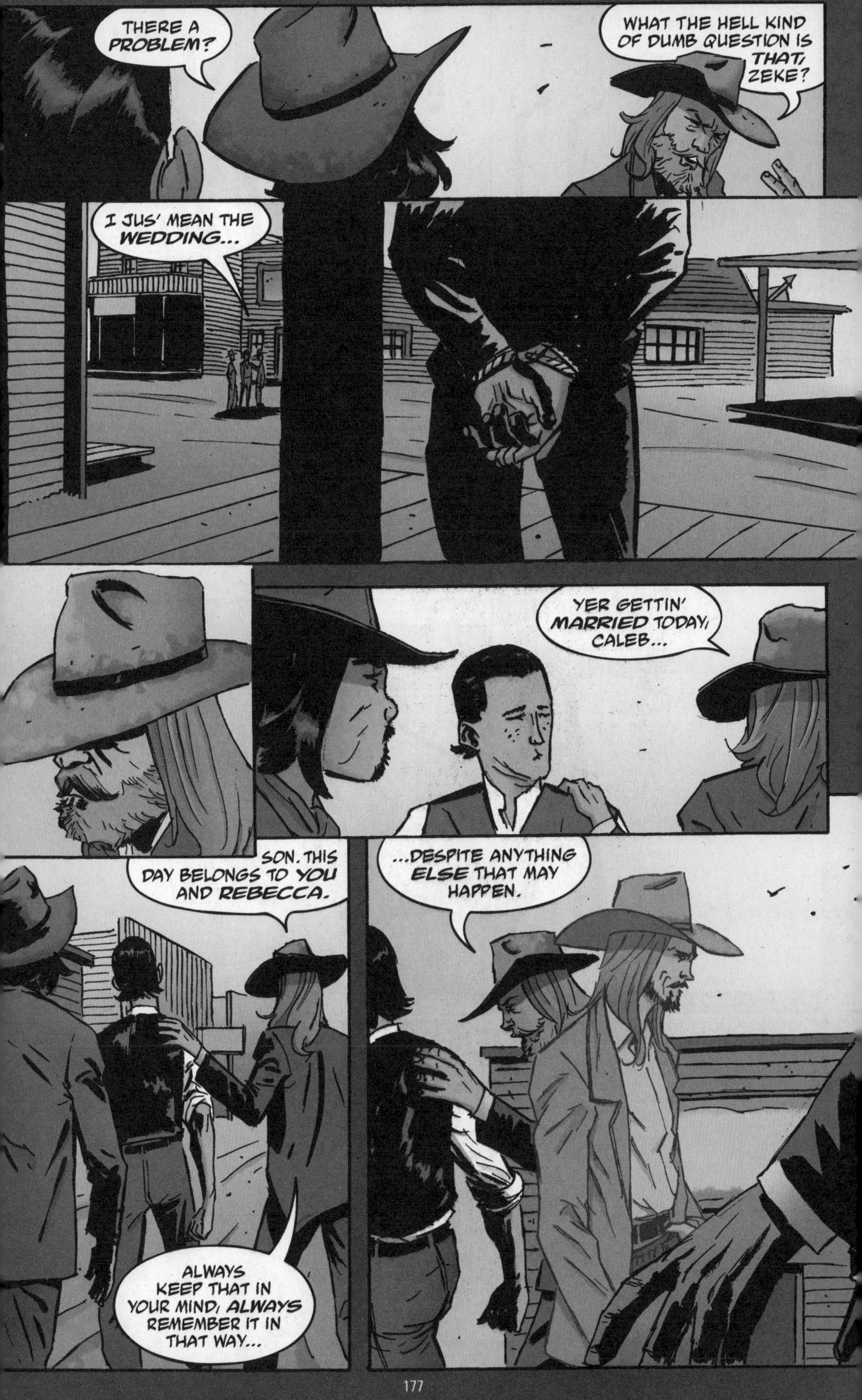
THERE A PROBLEM?
WHAT THE HELL KIND OF DUMB QUESTION IS THAT, ZEKE?
I JUS' MEAN THE WEDDING...
YER GETTIN' MARRIED TODAY, CALEB...
SON. THIS DAY BELONGS TO YOU AND REBECCA.
ALWAYS KEEP THAT IN YOUR MIND, ALWAYS REMEMBER IT IN THAT WAY...
...DESPITE ANYTHING ELSE THAT MAY HAPPEN.

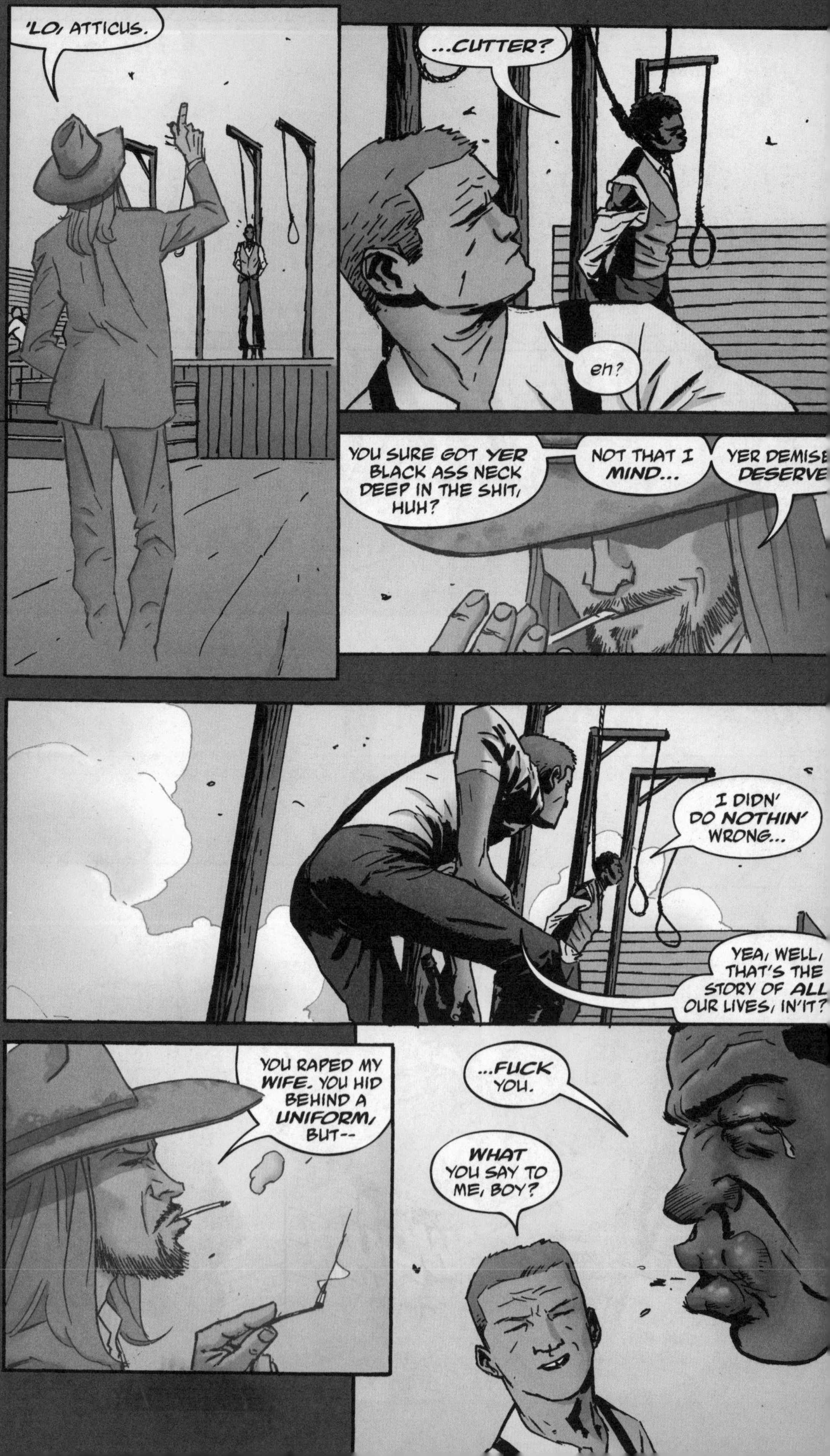
'LO, ATTICUS.
...CUTTER?
eh?
YOU SURE GOT YER BLACK ASS NECK DEEP IN THE SHIT, HUH?
NOT THAT I MIND...
YER DEMISE DESERVE
I DIDN' DO NOTHIN' WRONG...
YEA, WELL, THAT'S THE STORY OF ALL OUR LIVES, IN'IT?
YOU RAPED MY WIFE. YOU HID BEHIND A UNIFORM, BUT--
...FUCK YOU.
WHAT YOU SAY TO ME, BOY?

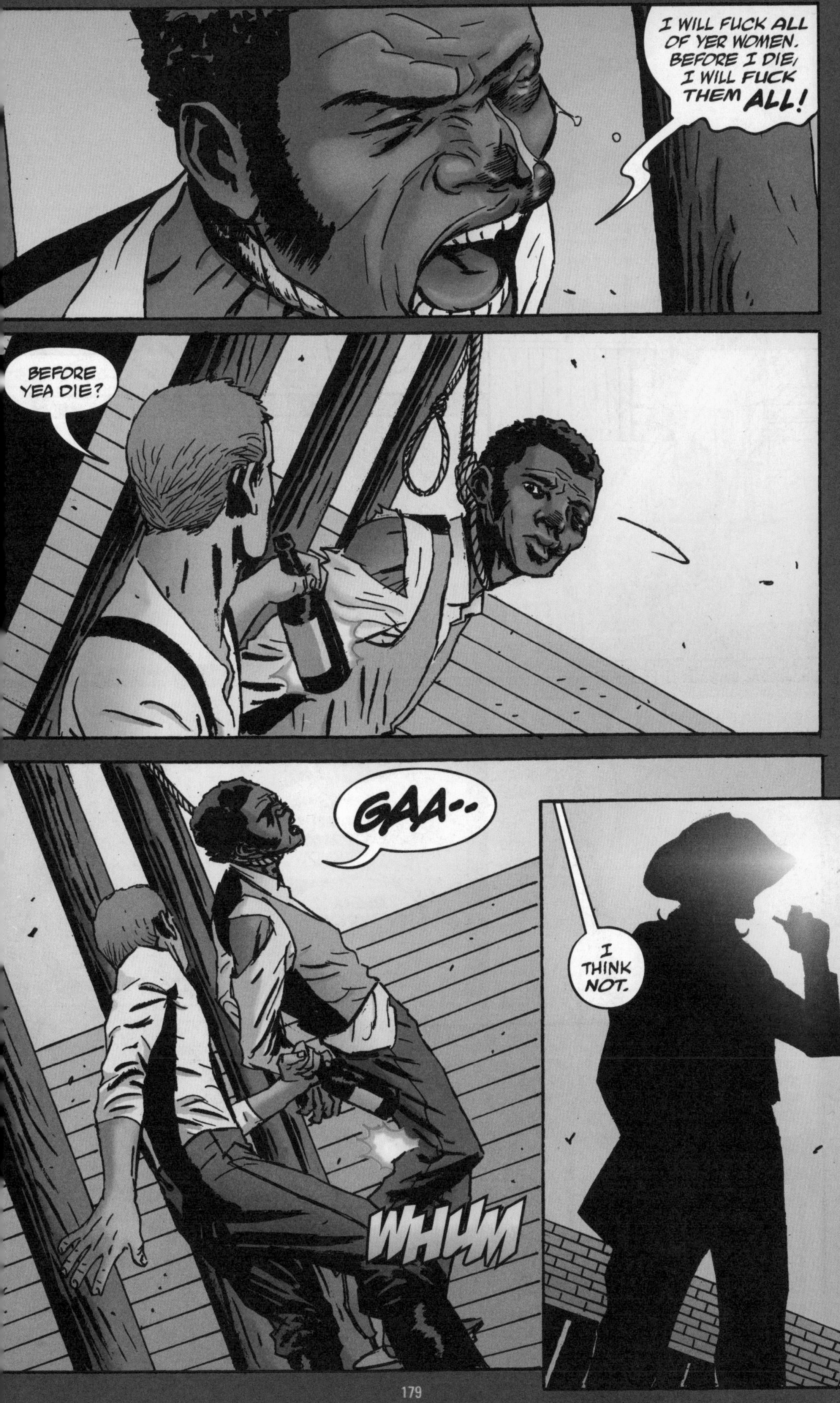

I WILL FUCK ALL OF YER WOMEN. BEFORE I DIE, I WILL FUCK THEM ALL!
BEFORE YEA DIE?
GAA--
I THINK NOT.
WHUM

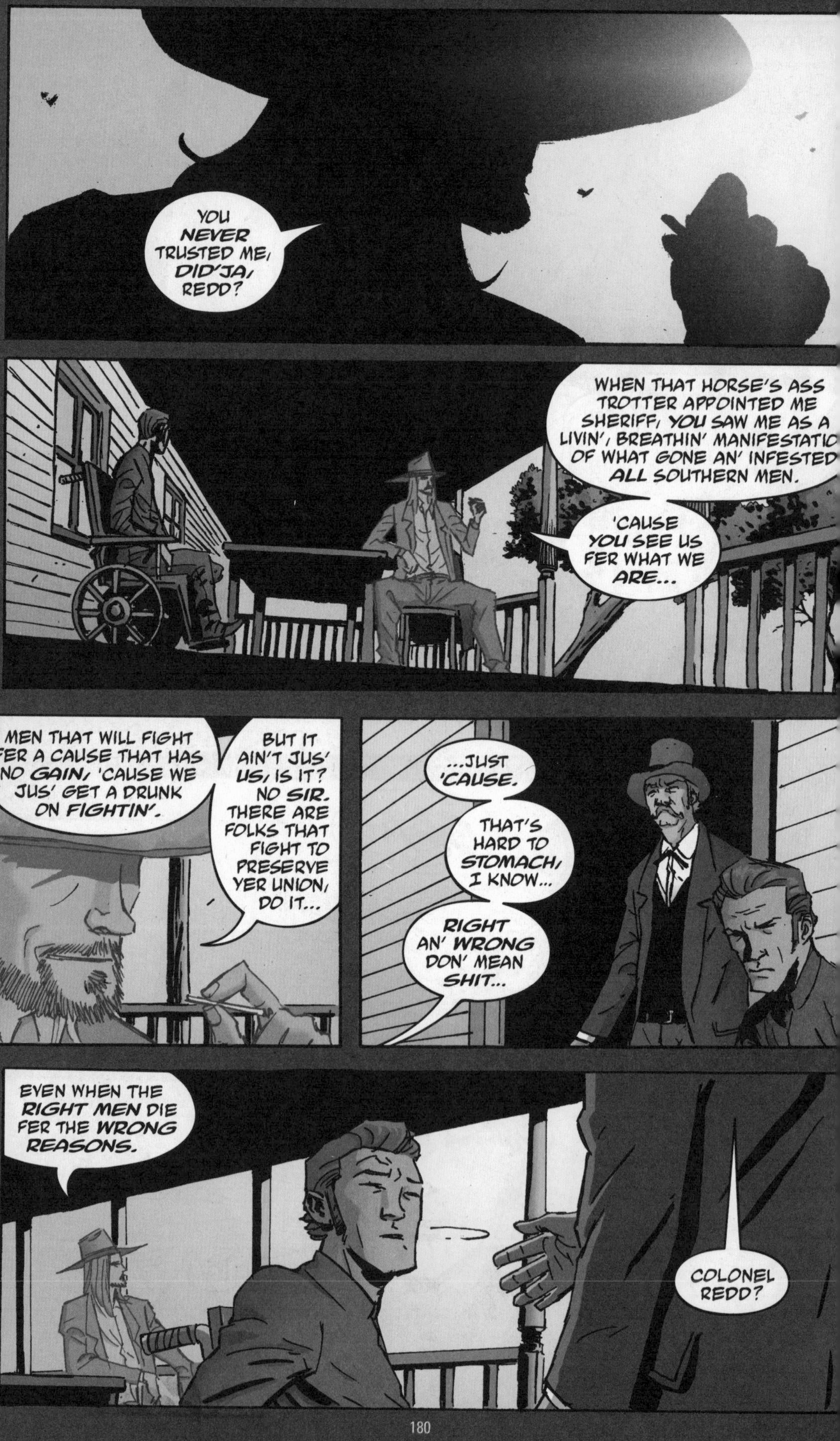
YOU NEVER TRUSTED ME, DID'JA, REDD?
WHEN THAT HORSE'S ASS TROTTER APPOINTED ME SHERIFF, YOU SAW ME AS A LIVIN', BREATHIN' MANIFESTATIO OF WHAT GONE AN' INFESTED ALL SOUTHERN MEN.
'CAUSE YOU SEE US FER WHAT WE ARE...
MEN THAT WILL FIGHT FER A CAUSE THAT HAS NO GAIN, 'CAUSE WE JUS' GET A DRUNK ON FIGHTIN'.
BUT IT AIN'T JUS' US, IS IT? NO SIR. THERE ARE FOLKS THAT FIGHT TO PRESERVE YER UNION, DO IT...
...JUST 'CAUSE.
THAT'S HARD TO STOMACH, I KNOW...
RIGHT AN' WRONG DON' MEAN SHIT...
EVEN WHEN THE RIGHT MEN DIE FER THE WRONG REASONS.
COLONEL REDD?

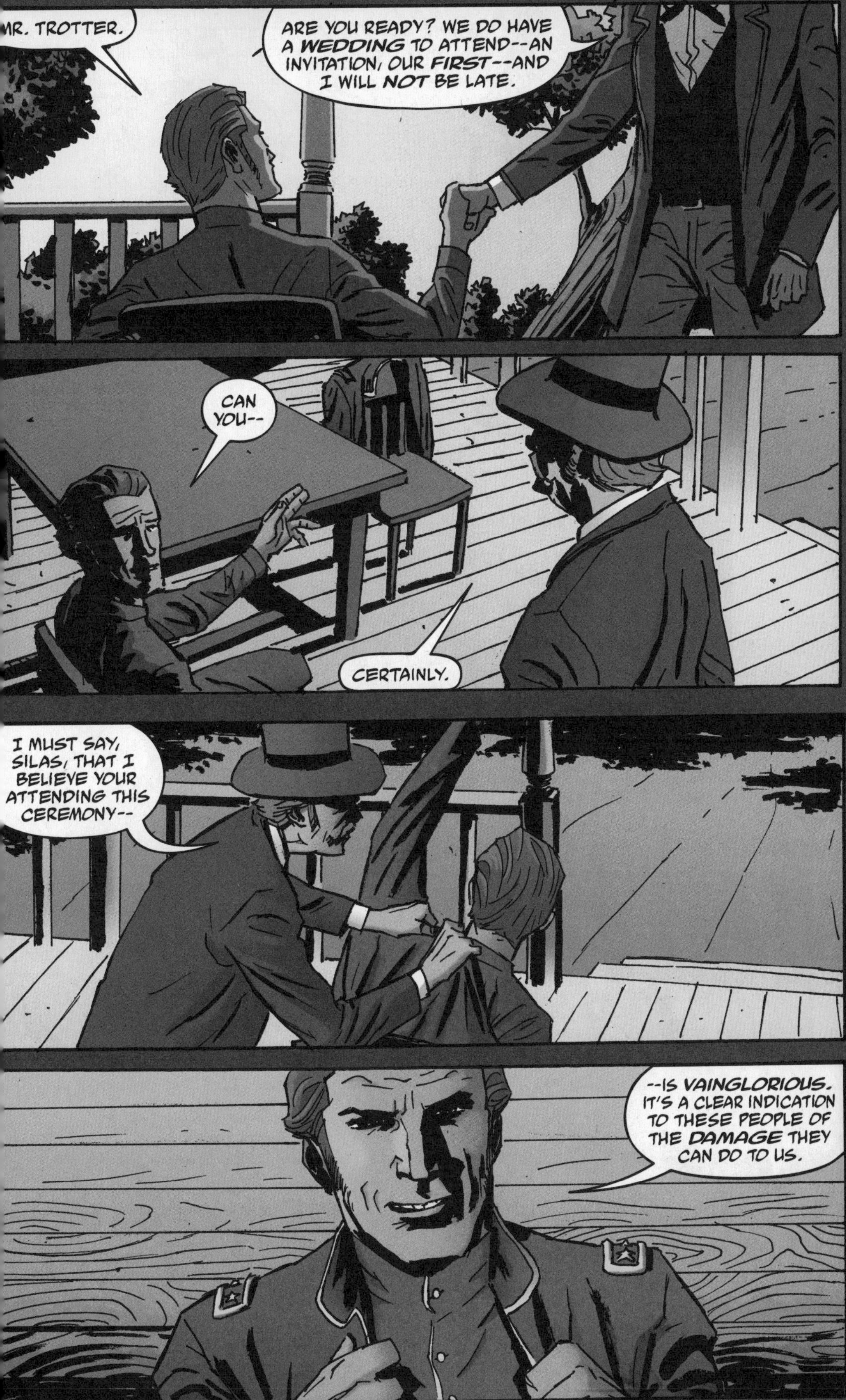
MR. TROTTER.
ARE YOU READY? WE DO HAVE A WEDDING TO ATTEND--AN INVITATION, OUR FIRST--AND I WILL NOT BE LATE.
CAN YOU--
CERTAINLY.
I MUST SAY, SILAS, THAT I BELIEVE YOUR ATTENDING THIS CEREMONY--
--IS VAINGLORIOUS. IT'S A CLEAR INDICATION TO THESE PEOPLE OF THE DAMAGE THEY CAN DO TO US.

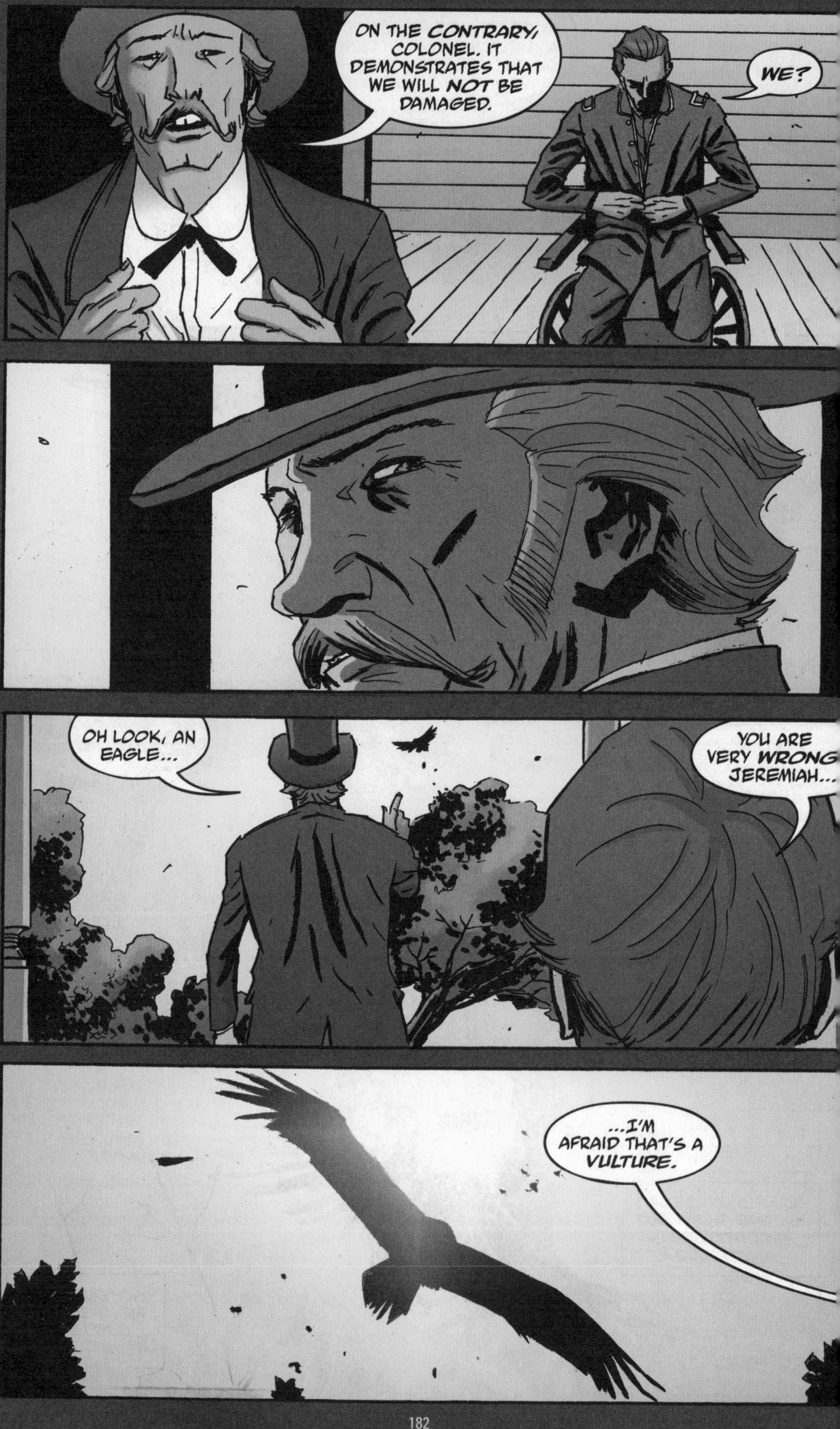
ON THE CONTRARY, COLONEL. IT DEMONSTRATES THAT WE WILL NOT BE DAMAGED.
WE?
OH LOOK, AN EAGLE...
YOU ARE VERY WRONG JEREMIAH...
...I'M AFRAID THAT'S A VULTURE.

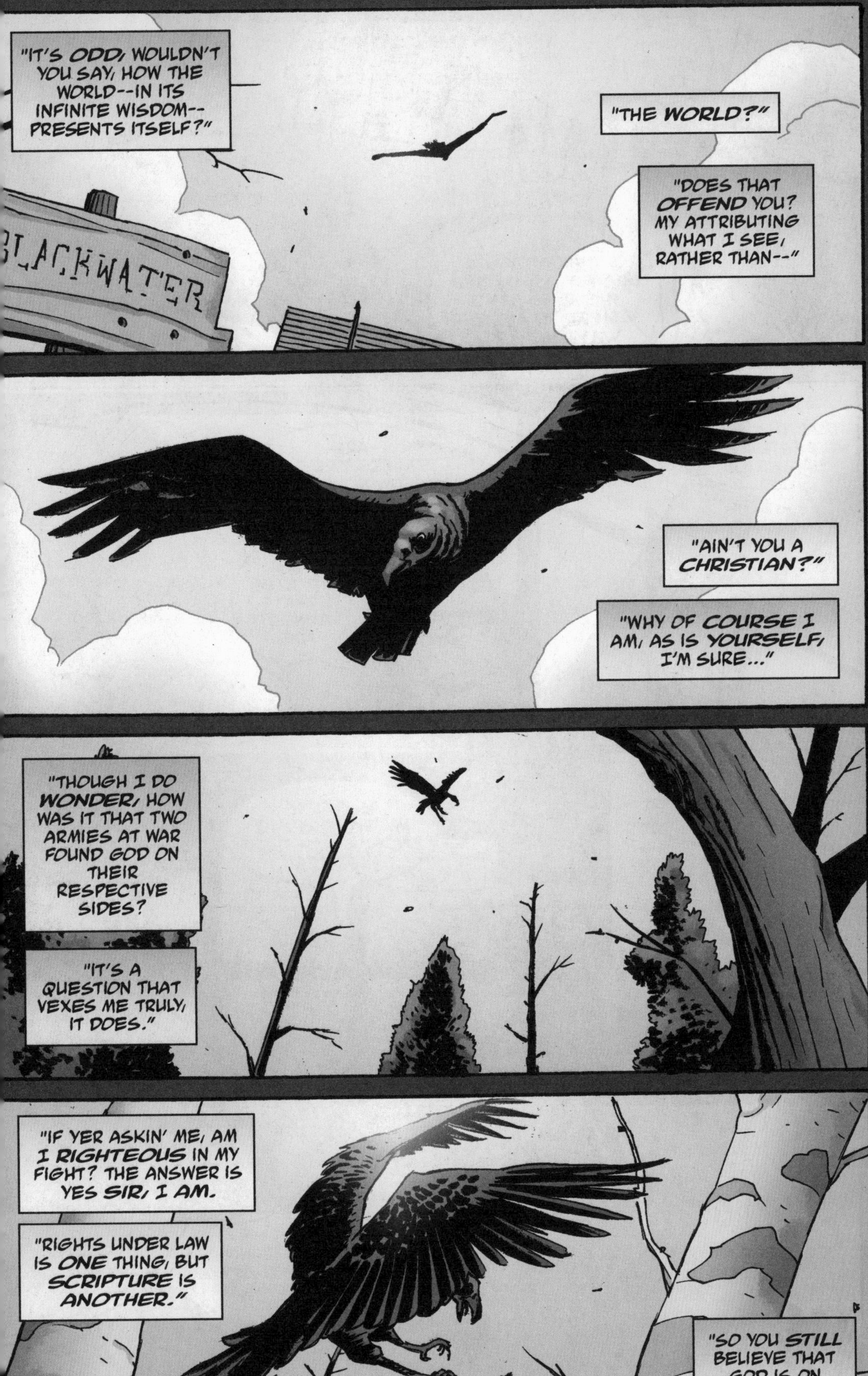
"IT'S ODD, WOULDN'T YOU SAY, HOW THE WORLD--IN ITS INFINITE WISDOM--PRESENTS ITSELF?"
BLACKWATER
"THE WORLD?"
"DOES THAT OFFEND YOU? MY ATTRIBUTING WHAT I SEE, RATHER THAN--"
"AIN'T YOU A CHRISTIAN?"
"WHY OF COURSE I AM, AS IS YOURSELF, I'M SURE..."
"THOUGH I DO WONDER, HOW WAS IT THAT TWO ARMIES AT WAR FOUND GOD ON THEIR RESPECTIVE SIDES?
"IT'S A QUESTION THAT VEXES ME TRULY, IT DOES."
"IF YER ASKIN' ME, AM I RIGHTEOUS IN MY FIGHT? THE ANSWER IS YES SIR, I AM.
"RIGHTS UNDER LAW IS ONE THING, BUT SCRIPTURE IS ANOTHER."
"SO YOU STILL BELIEVE THAT GOD IS ON YOUR SIDE?"

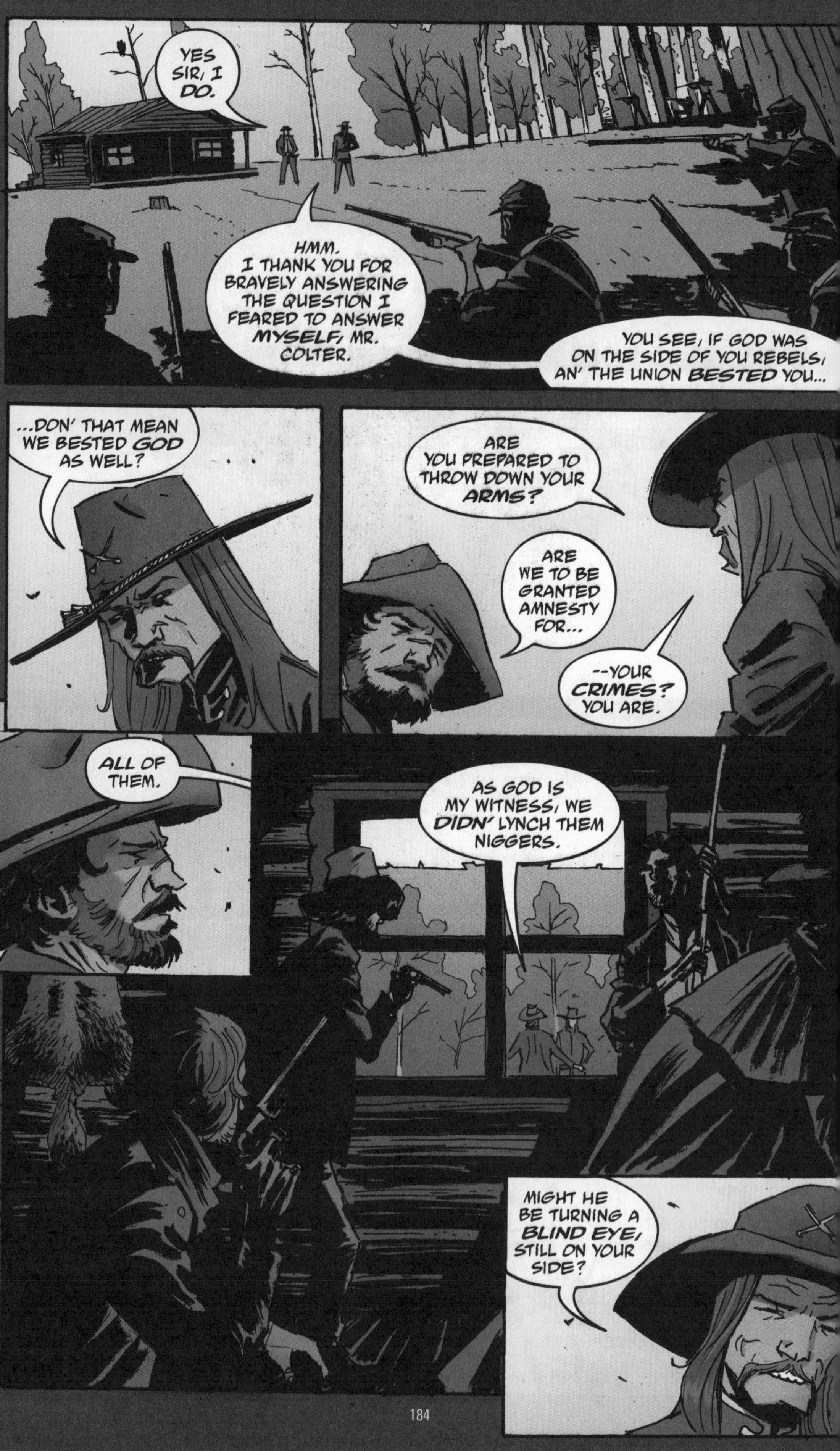
YES SIR, I DO.
HMM. I THANK YOU FOR BRAVELY ANSWERING THE QUESTION I FEARED TO ANSWER MYSELF, MR. COLTER.
YOU SEE, IF GOD WAS ON THE SIDE OF YOU REBELS, AN' THE UNION BESTED YOU...
...DON' THAT MEAN WE BESTED GOD AS WELL?
ARE YOU PREPARED TO THROW DOWN YOUR ARMS?
ARE WE TO BE GRANTED AMNESTY FOR...
--YOUR CRIMES? YOU ARE.
ALL OF THEM.
AS GOD IS MY WITNESS, WE DIDN' LYNCH THEM NIGGERS.
MIGHT HE BE TURNING A BLIND EYE, STILL ON YOUR SIDE?

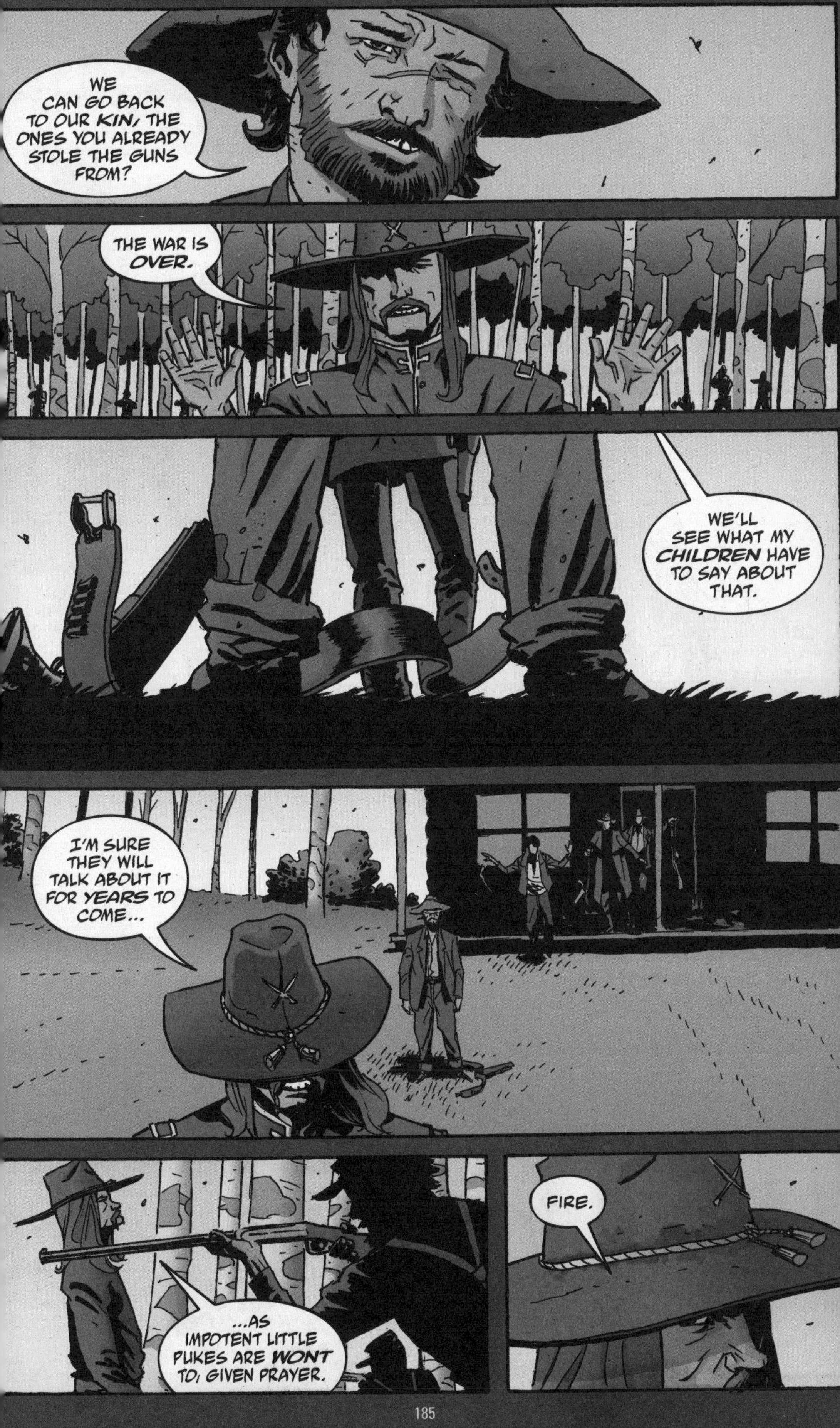
WE CAN GO BACK TO OUR KIN, THE ONES YOU ALREADY STOLE THE GUNS FROM?
THE WAR IS OVER.
WE'LL SEE WHAT MY CHILDREN HAVE TO SAY ABOUT THAT.
I'M SURE THEY WILL TALK ABOUT IT FOR YEARS TO COME...
...AS IMPOTENT LITTLE PUKES ARE WONT TO, GIVEN PRAYER.
FIRE.

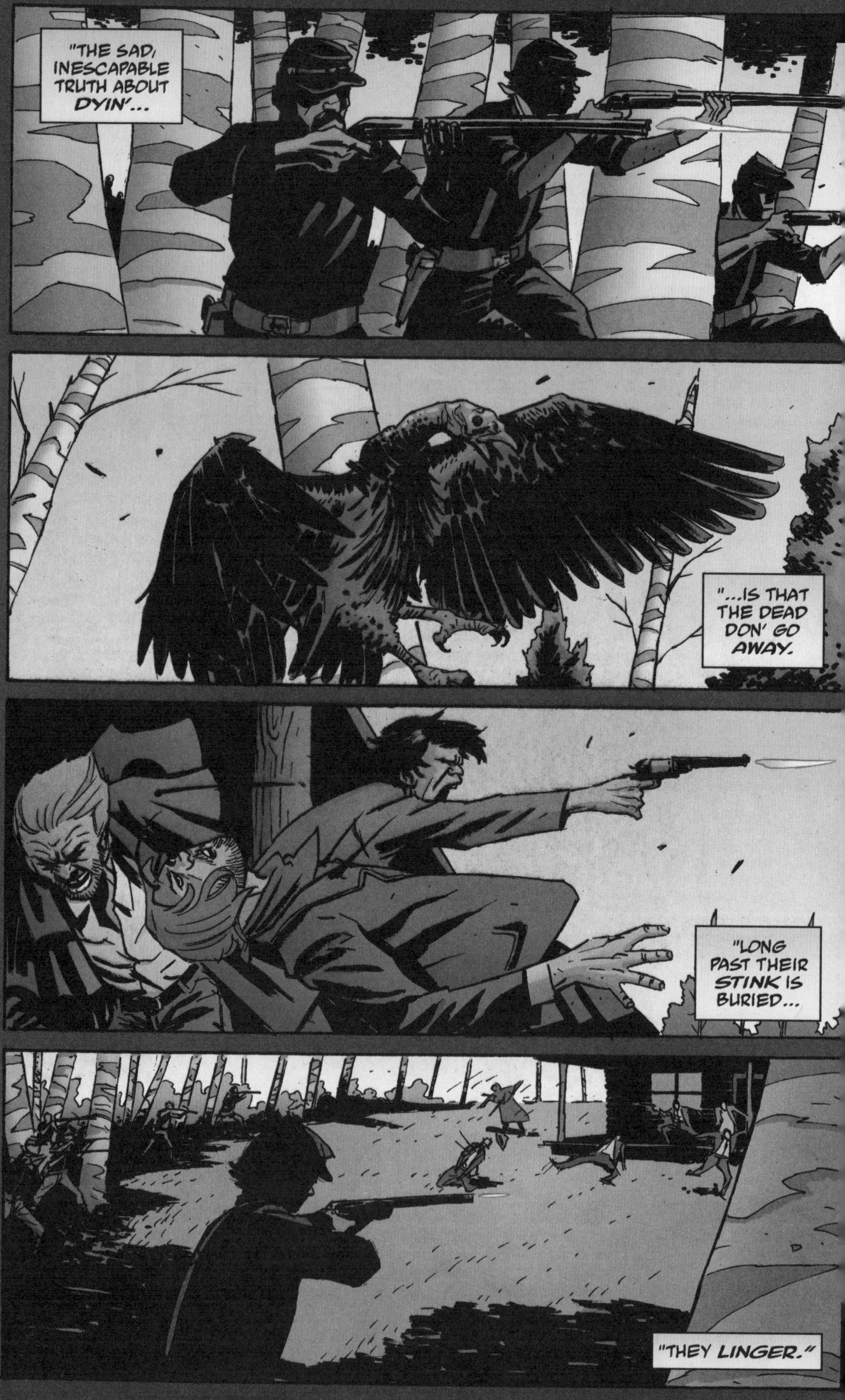
"THE SAD, INESCAPABLE TRUTH ABOUT DYIN'...
"...IS THAT THE DEAD DON' GO AWAY.
"LONG PAST THEIR STINK IS BURIED...
"THEY LINGER."

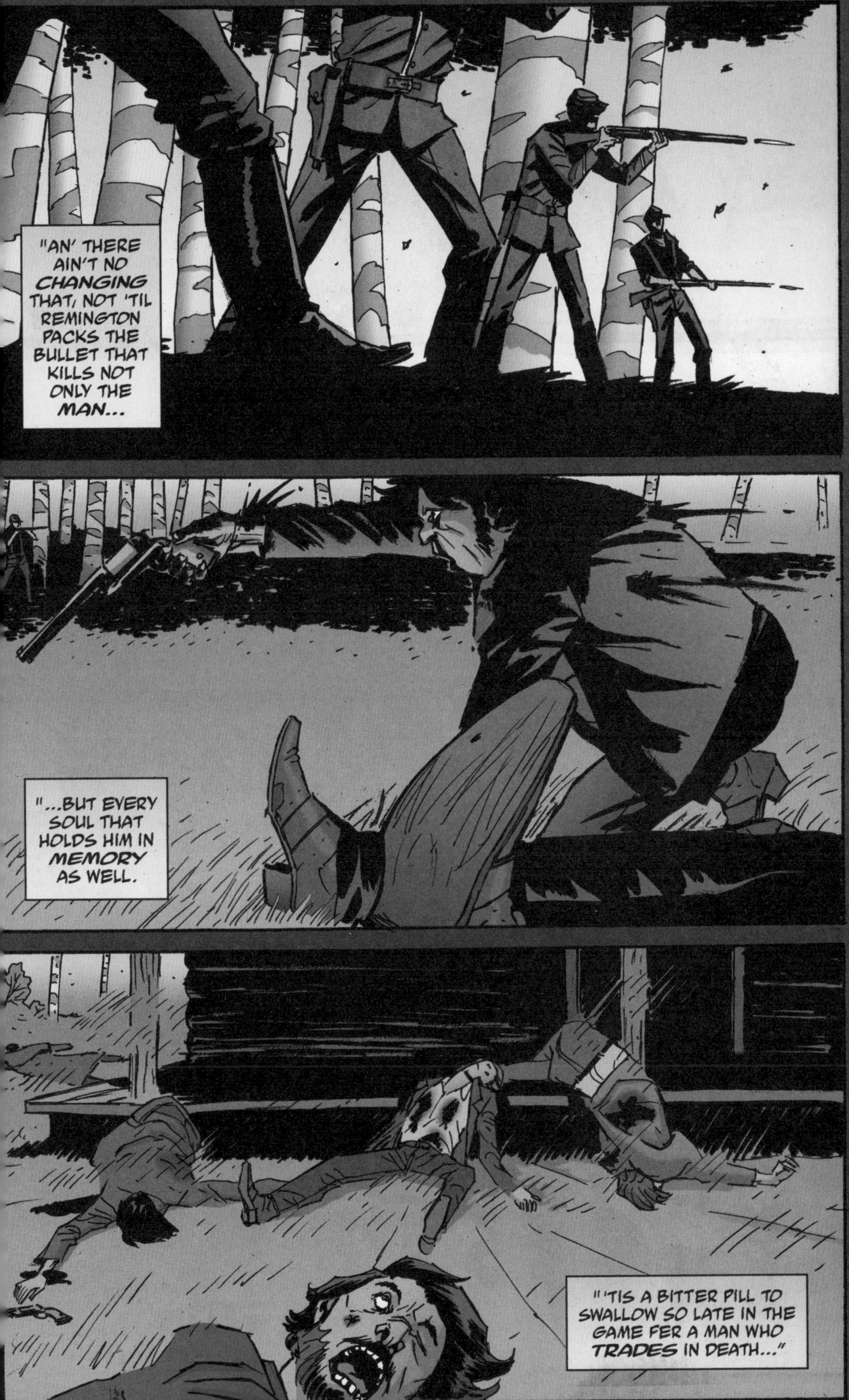
"AN' THERE AIN'T NO CHANGING THAT, NOT 'TIL REMINGTON PACKS THE BULLET THAT KILLS NOT ONLY THE MAN...
"...BUT EVERY SOUL THAT HOLDS HIM IN MEMORY AS WELL.
"'TIS A BITTER PILL TO SWALLOW SO LATE IN THE GAME FER A MAN WHO TRADES IN DEATH..."

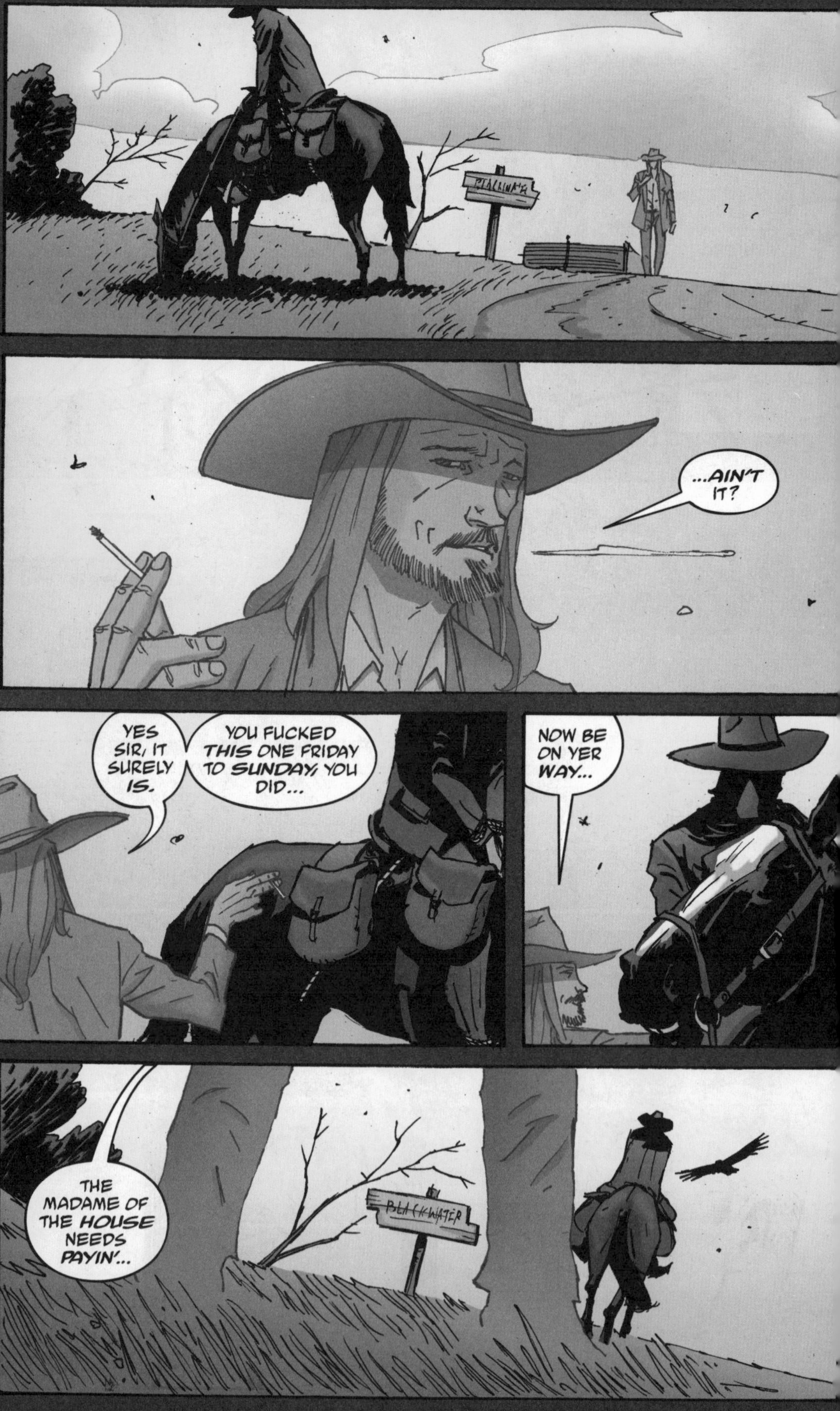
...AIN'T IT?
YES SIR, IT SURELY IS.
YOU FUCKED THIS ONE FRIDAY TO SUNDAY, YOU DID...
NOW BE ON YER WAY...
THE MADAME OF THE HOUSE NEEDS PAYIN'...
BLACKWATER

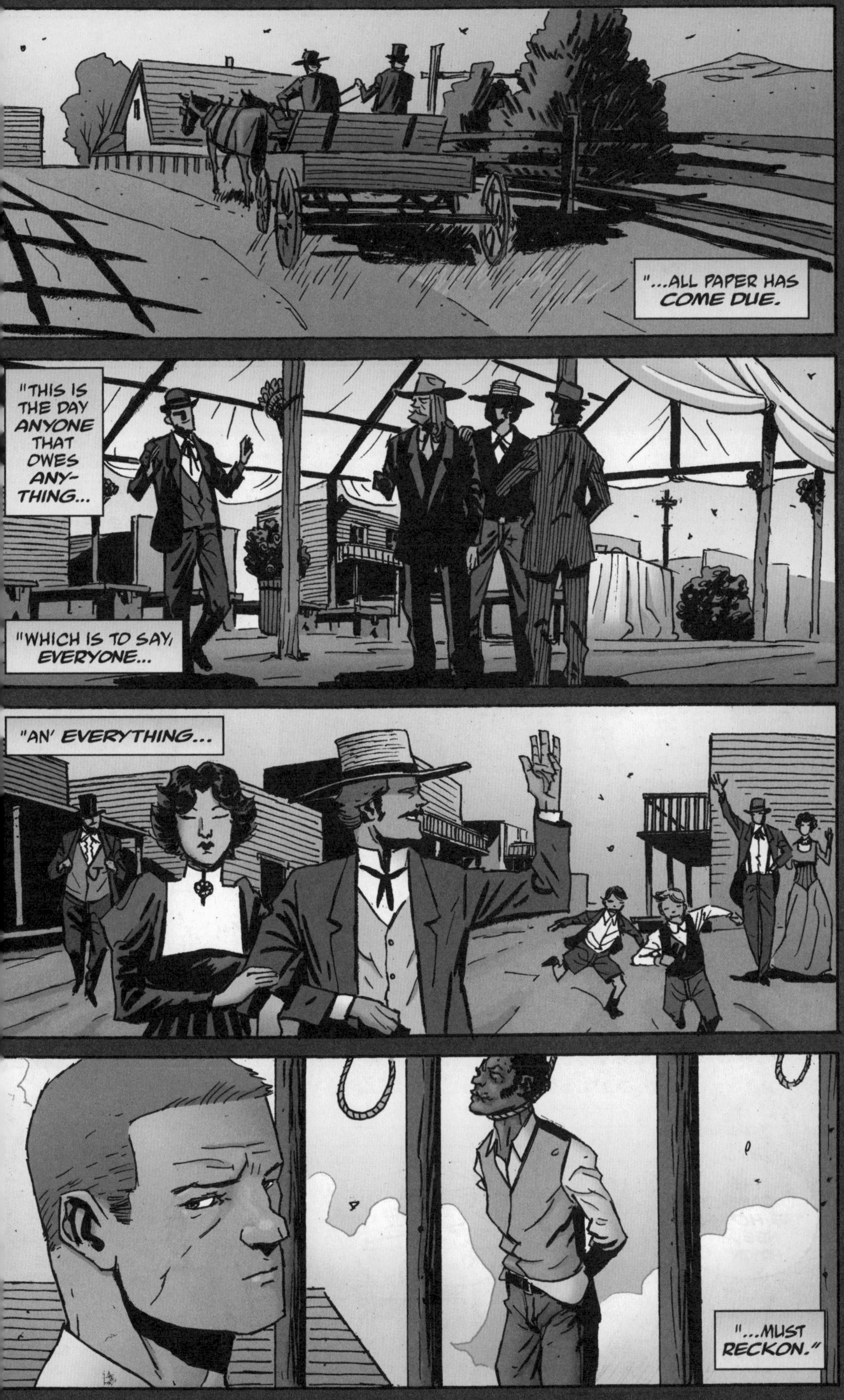
"...ALL PAPER HAS COME DUE.
"THIS IS THE DAY ANYONE THAT OWES ANY-THING...
"WHICH IS TO SAY, EVERYONE...
"AN' EVERYTHING...
"...MUST RECKON."

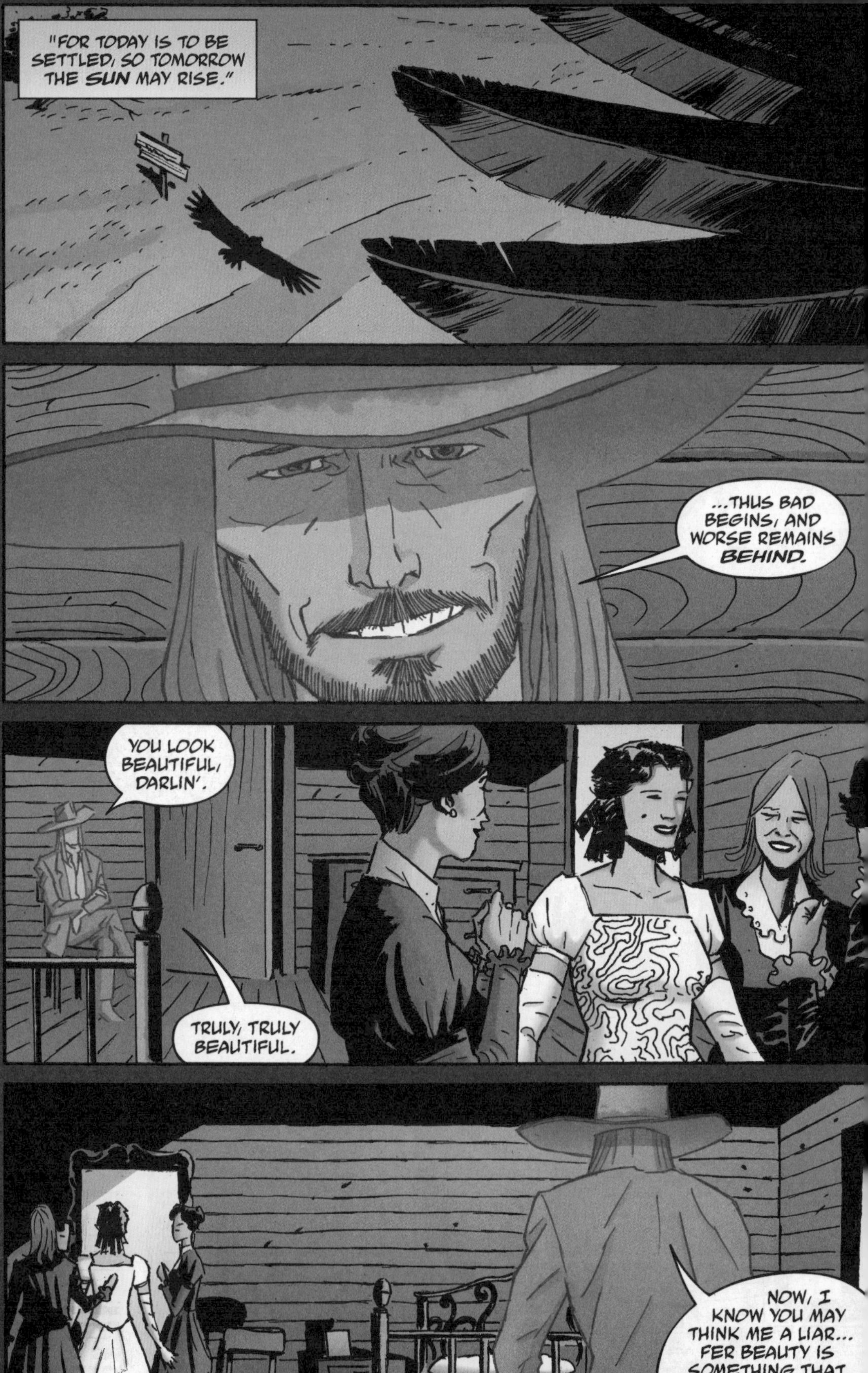
"FOR TODAY IS TO BE SETTLED, SO TOMORROW THE SUN MAY RISE."
...THUS BAD BEGINS, AND WORSE REMAINS BEHIND.
YOU LOOK BEAUTIFUL, DARLIN'.
TRULY, TRULY BEAUTIFUL.
NOW, I KNOW YOU MAY THINK ME A LIAR... FER BEAUTY IS SOMETHING THAT HAS RARELY PASSED OVER MY EYES.

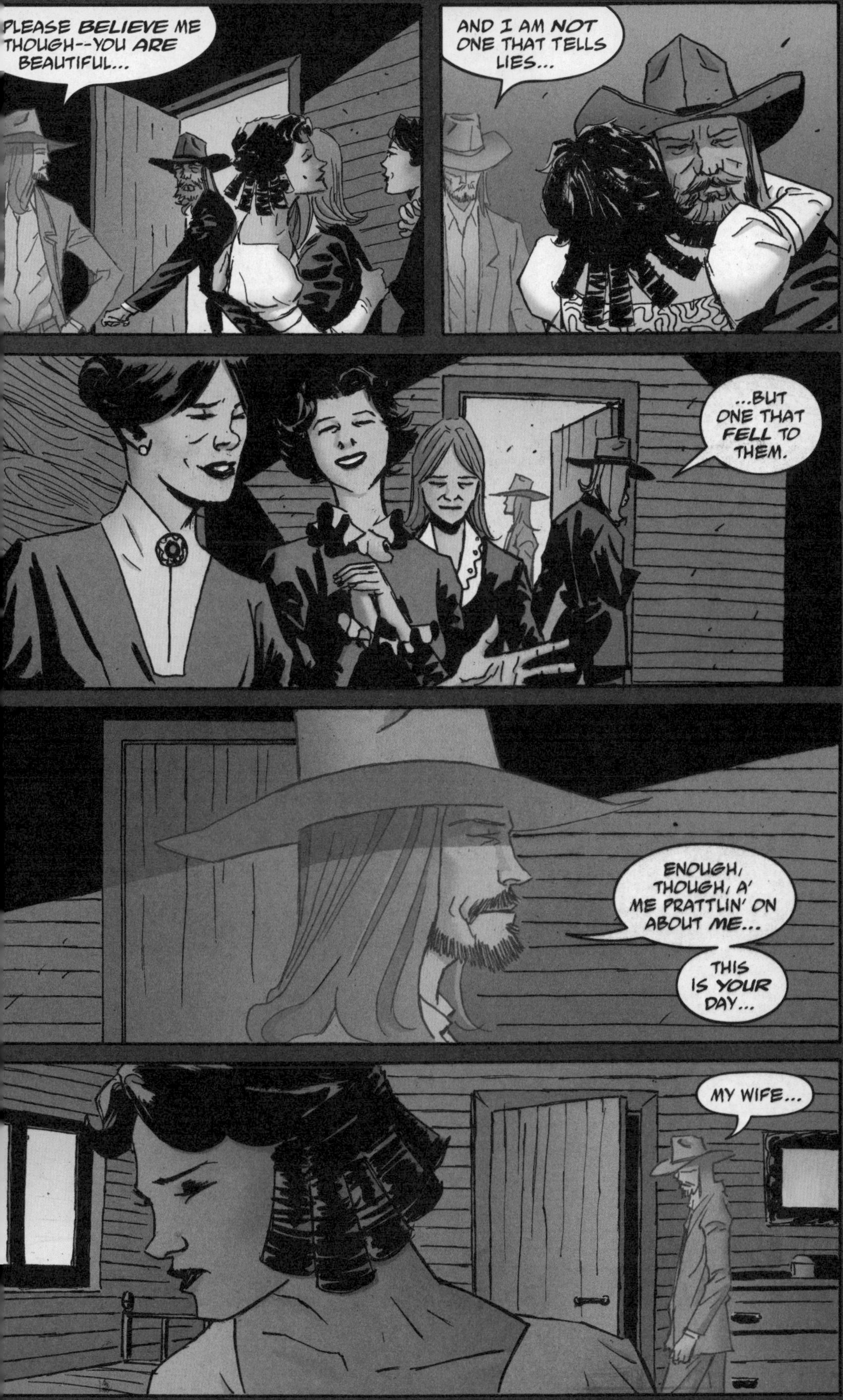
PLEASE BELIEVE ME THOUGH--YOU ARE BEAUTIFUL...
AND I AM NOT ONE THAT TELLS LIES...
...BUT ONE THAT FELL TO THEM.
ENOUGH, THOUGH, A' ME PRATTLIN' ON ABOUT ME...
THIS IS YOUR DAY...
MY WIFE...

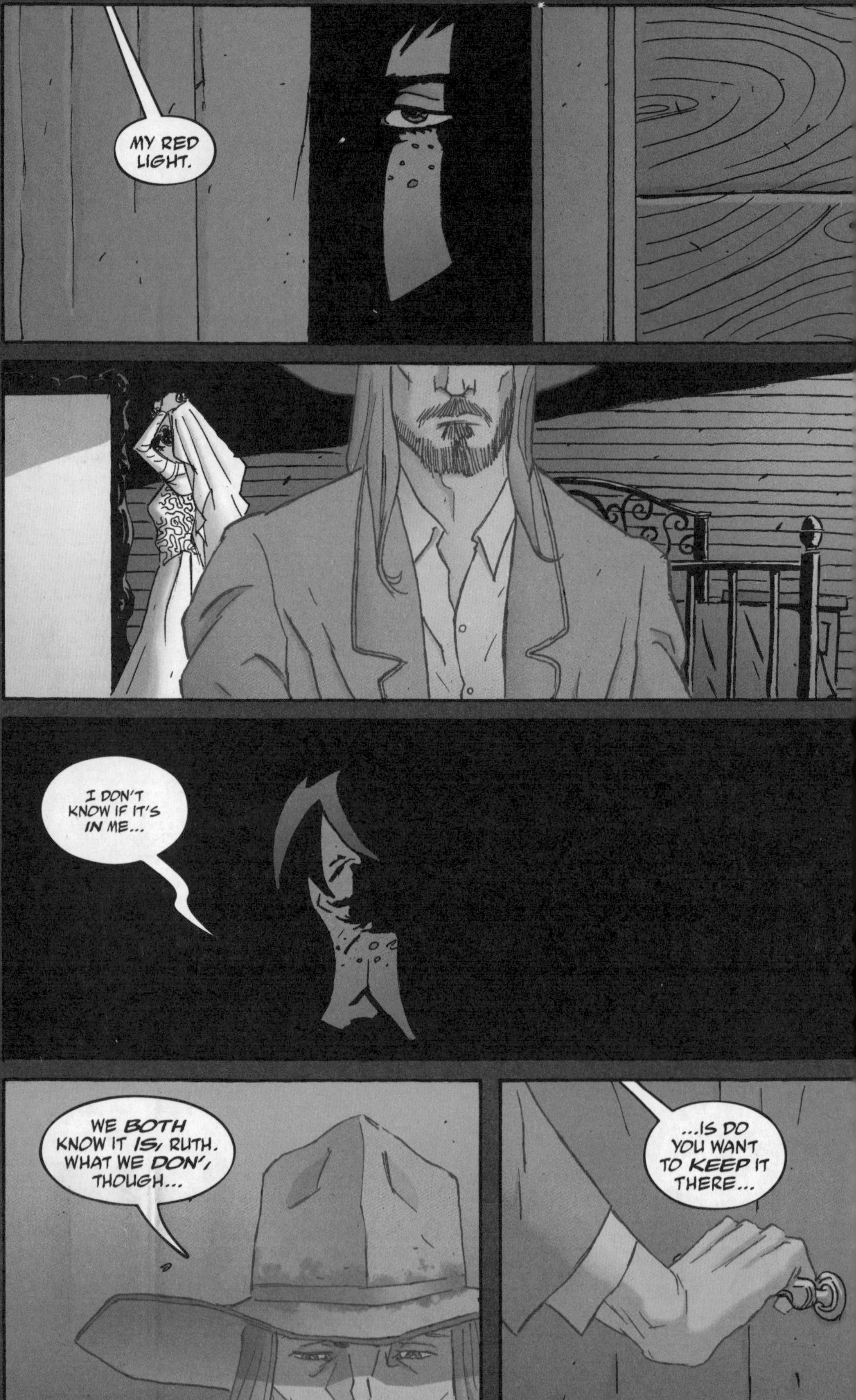
MY RED LIGHT.
I DON'T KNOW IF IT'S IN ME...
WE BOTH KNOW IT IS, RUTH. WHAT WE DON'T, THOUGH...
...IS DO YOU WANT TO KEEP IT THERE...

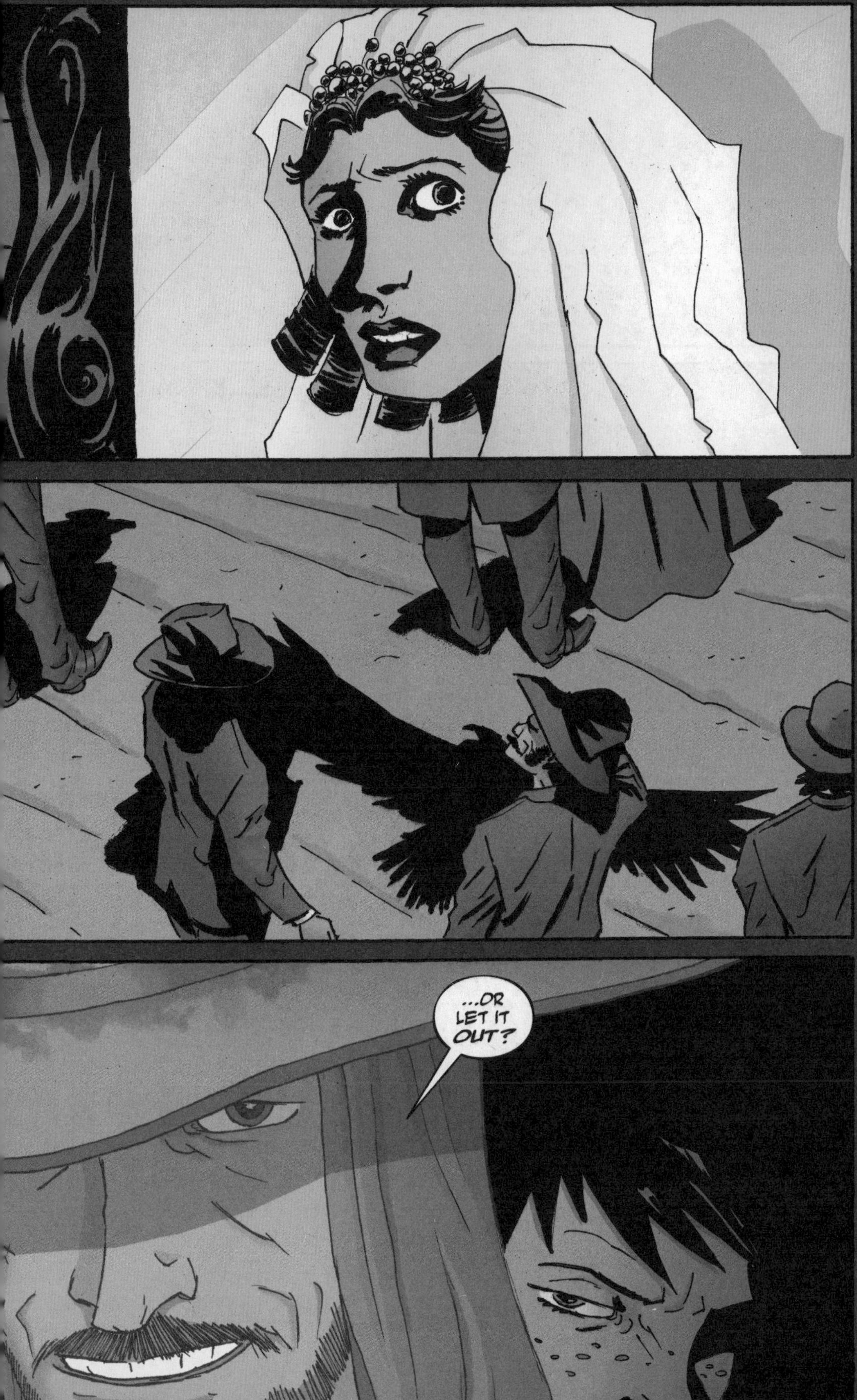
...OR LET IT OUT?

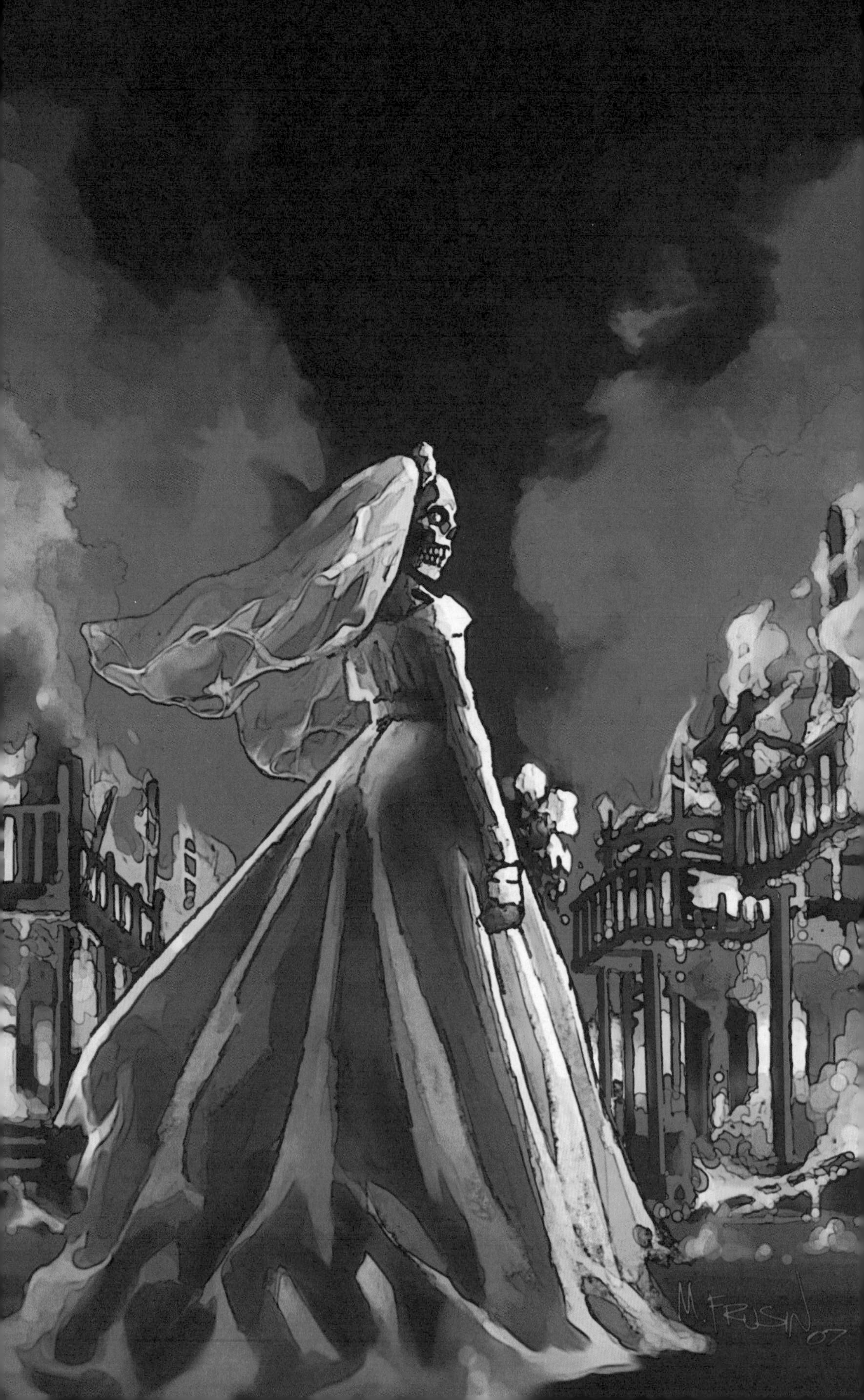
M. FRUSIN
07

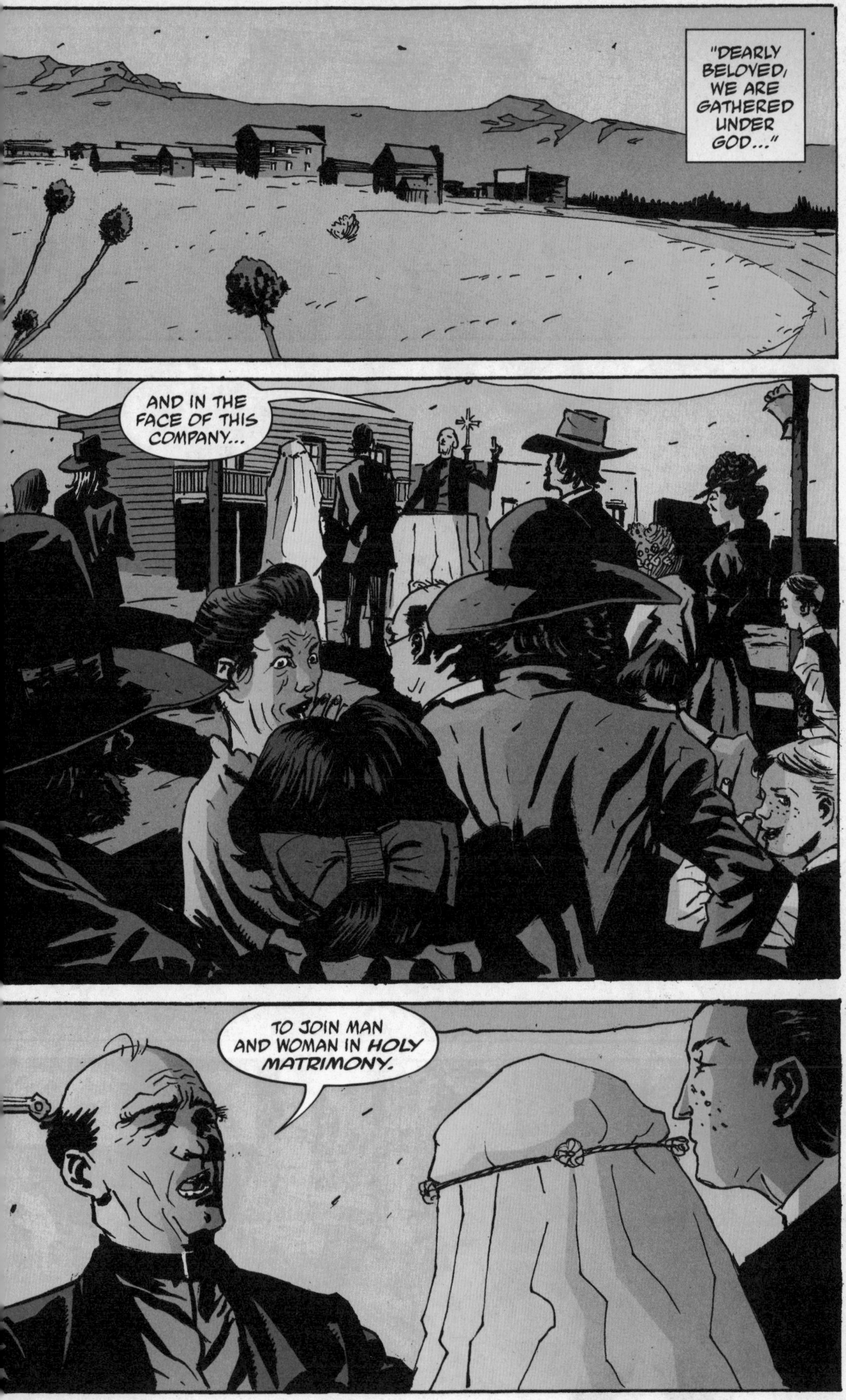
"DEARLY BELOVED, WE ARE GATHERED UNDER GOD..."
AND IN THE FACE OF THIS COMPANY...
TO JOIN MAN AND WOMAN IN *HOLY MATRIMONY.*

"IT IS A COVENANT NOT TO BE ENTERED *LIGHTLY*--BUT REVERENTLY, DISCREETLY, ADVISEDLY AND SOLEMNLY.

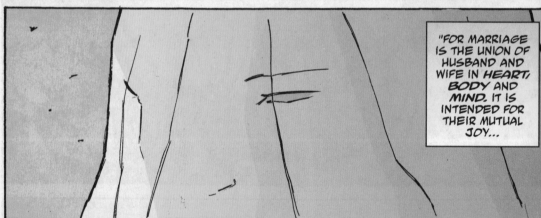

"ALSO I'D LIKE TO ADD, GIVEN *OUR* CIRCUMSTANCE, A RARE OPPORTUNITY, TO BE CELEBRATED, AND *SHARED*.

"FOR MARRIAGE IS THE UNION OF HUSBAND AND WIFE IN *HEART*, *BODY* AND *MIND*. IT IS INTENDED FOR THEIR MUTUAL JOY...

"AND FOR THE HELP AND COMFORT GIVEN, NOT *JUST* IN PROSPERITY..."

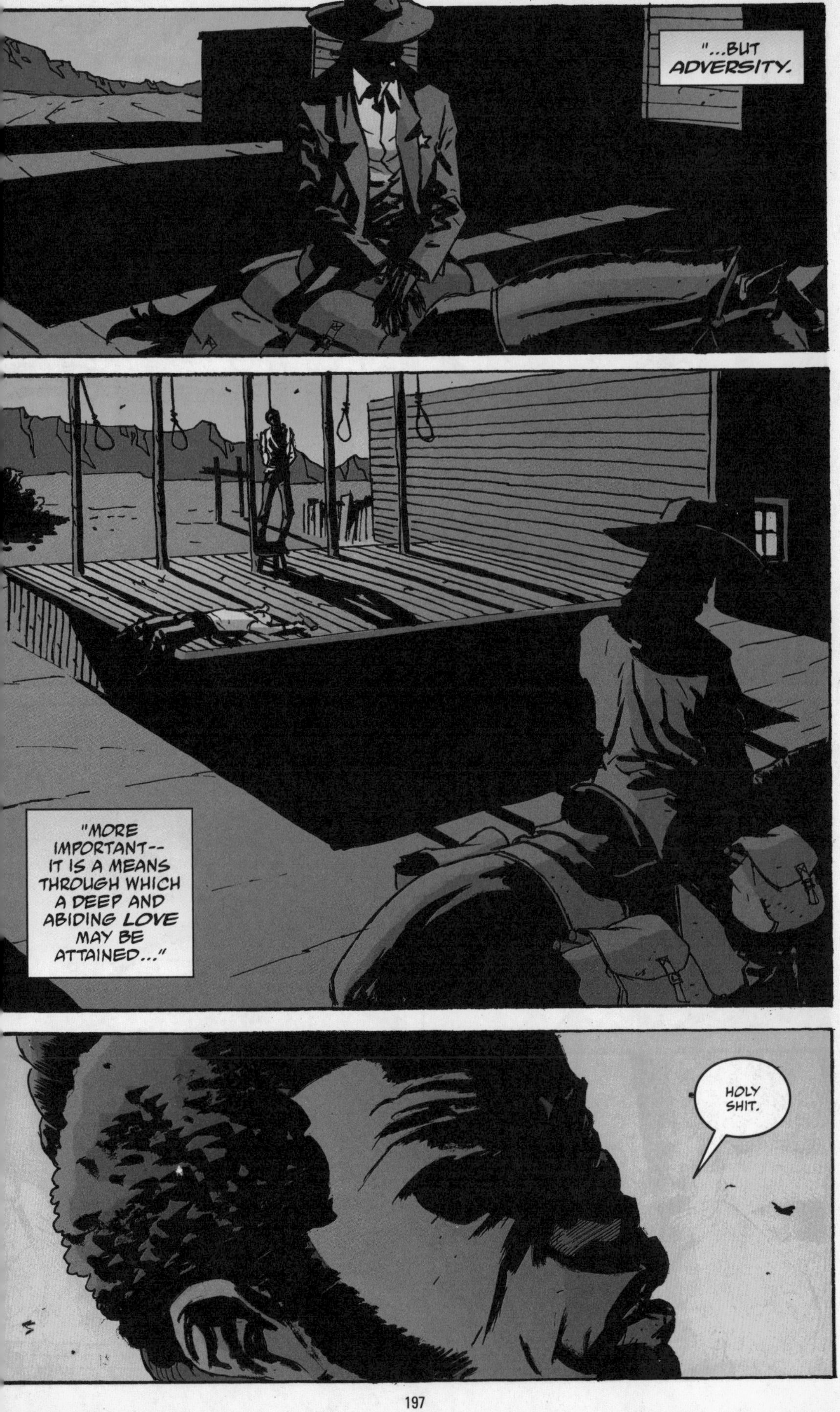
"...BUT ADVERSITY.
"MORE IMPORTANT-- IT IS A MEANS THROUGH WHICH A DEEP AND ABIDING LOVE MAY BE ATTAINED..."
HOLY SHIT.

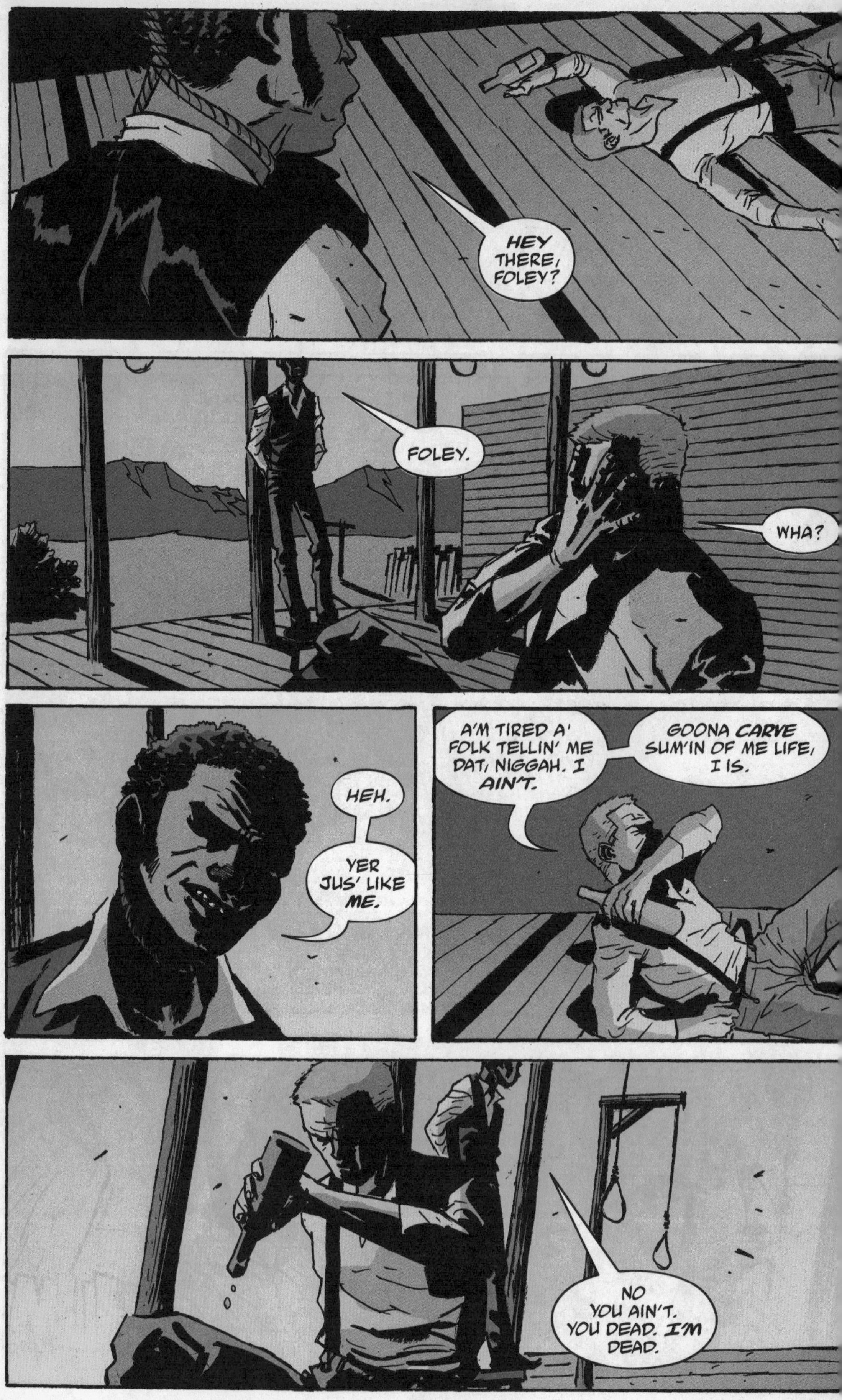

HEY THERE, FOLEY?
FOLEY.
WHA?
HEH.
YER JUS' LIKE ME.
A'M TIRED A' FOLK TELLIN' ME DAT, NIGGAH. I AIN'T.
GOONA CARVE SUM'IN OF ME LIFE, I IS.
NO YOU AIN'T. YOU DEAD. I'M DEAD.

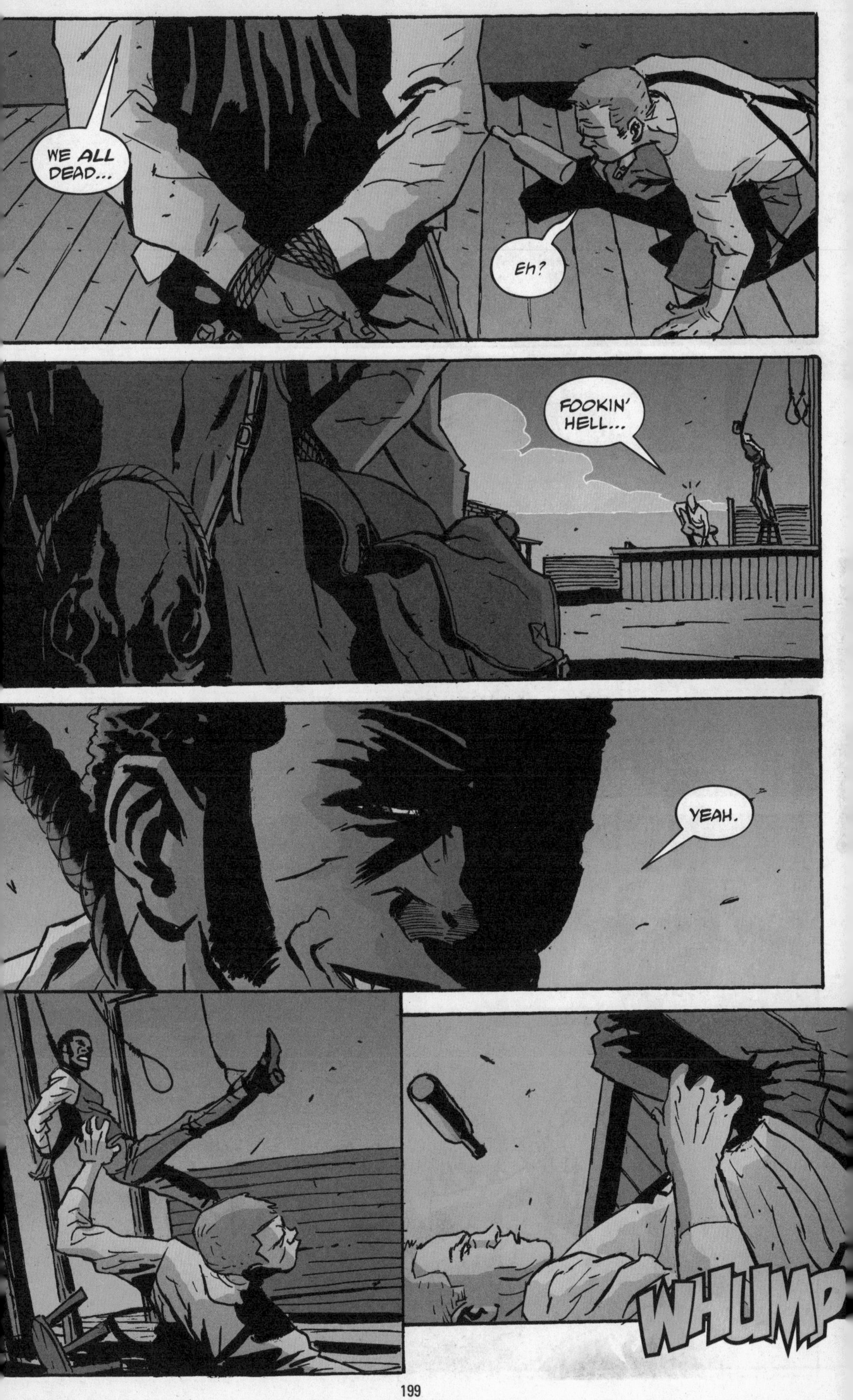
WE ALL DEAD...
Eh?
FOOKIN' HELL...
YEAH.
WHUMP

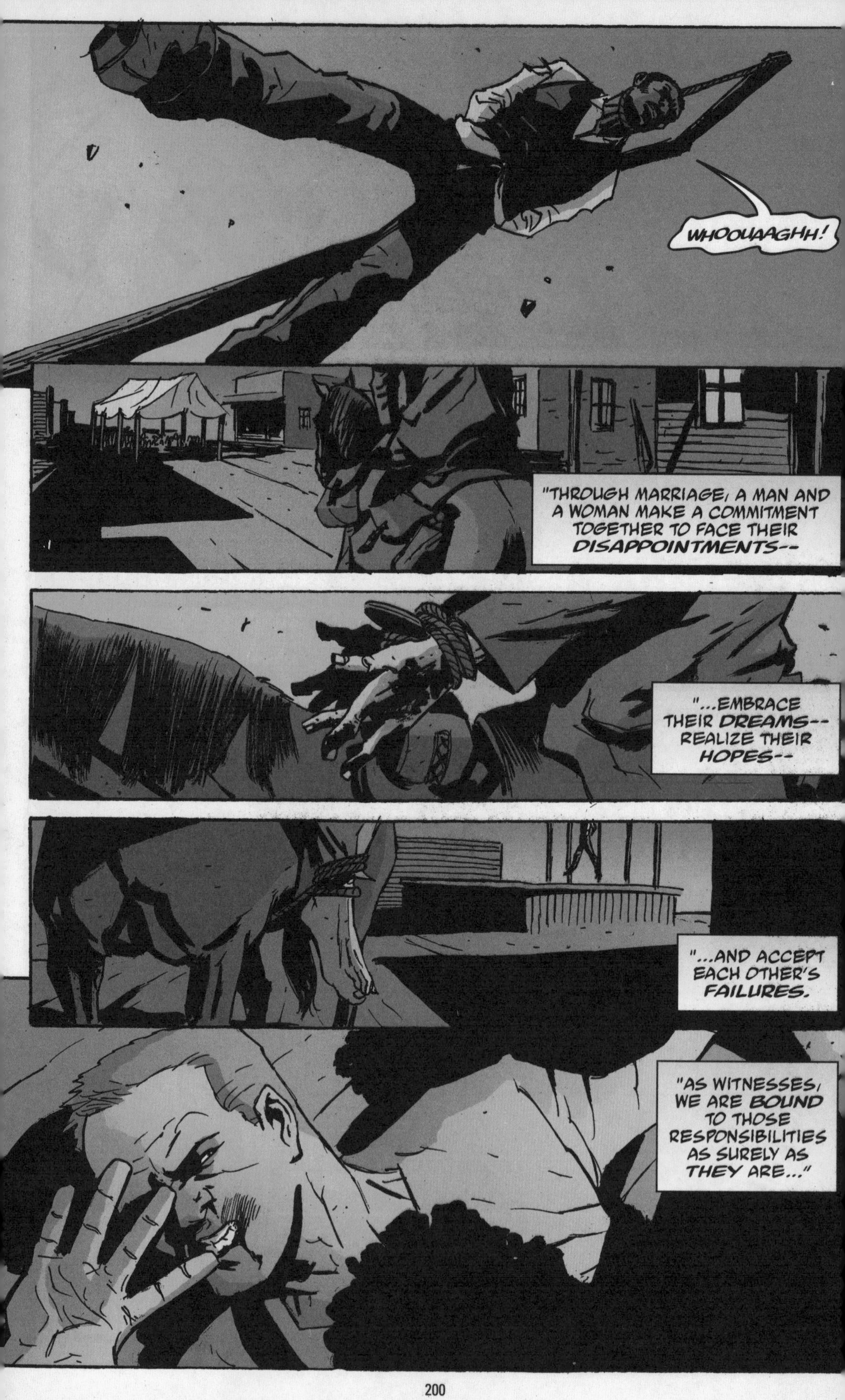

WHOOUAAGHH!
"THROUGH MARRIAGE, A MAN AND A WOMAN MAKE A COMMITMENT TOGETHER TO FACE THEIR DISAPPOINTMENTS--
"...EMBRACE THEIR DREAMS-- REALIZE THEIR HOPES--
"...AND ACCEPT EACH OTHER'S FAILURES.
"AS WITNESSES, WE ARE BOUND TO THOSE RESPONSIBILITIES AS SURELY AS THEY ARE..."

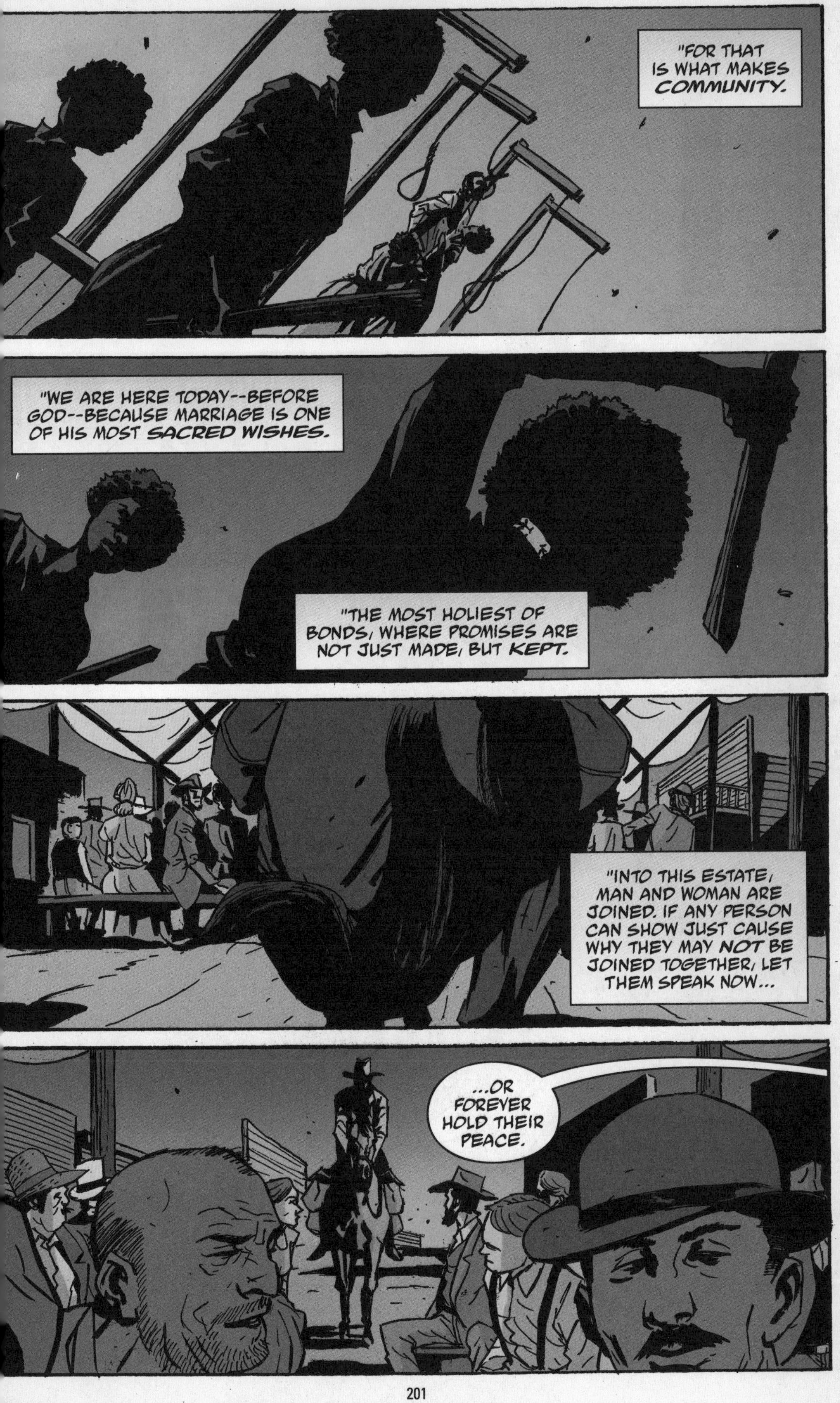
"FOR THAT IS WHAT MAKES COMMUNITY.
"WE ARE HERE TODAY--BEFORE GOD--BECAUSE MARRIAGE IS ONE OF HIS MOST SACRED WISHES.
"THE MOST HOLIEST OF BONDS, WHERE PROMISES ARE NOT JUST MADE, BUT KEPT.
"INTO THIS ESTATE, MAN AND WOMAN ARE JOINED. IF ANY PERSON CAN SHOW JUST CAUSE WHY THEY MAY NOT BE JOINED TOGETHER, LET THEM SPEAK NOW...
...OR FOREVER HOLD THEIR PEACE.

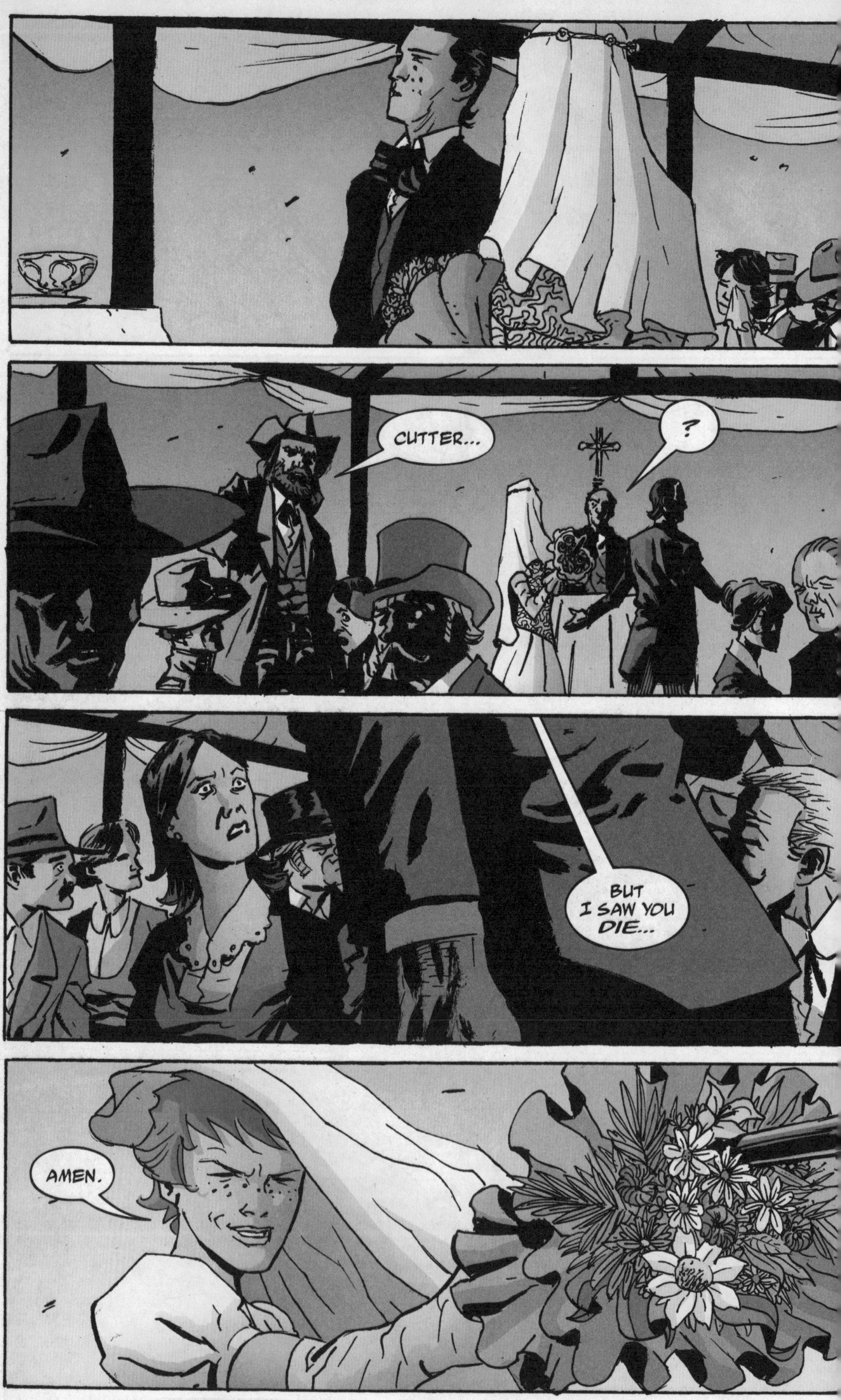

CUTTER...
?
BUT I SAW YOU DIE...
AMEN.

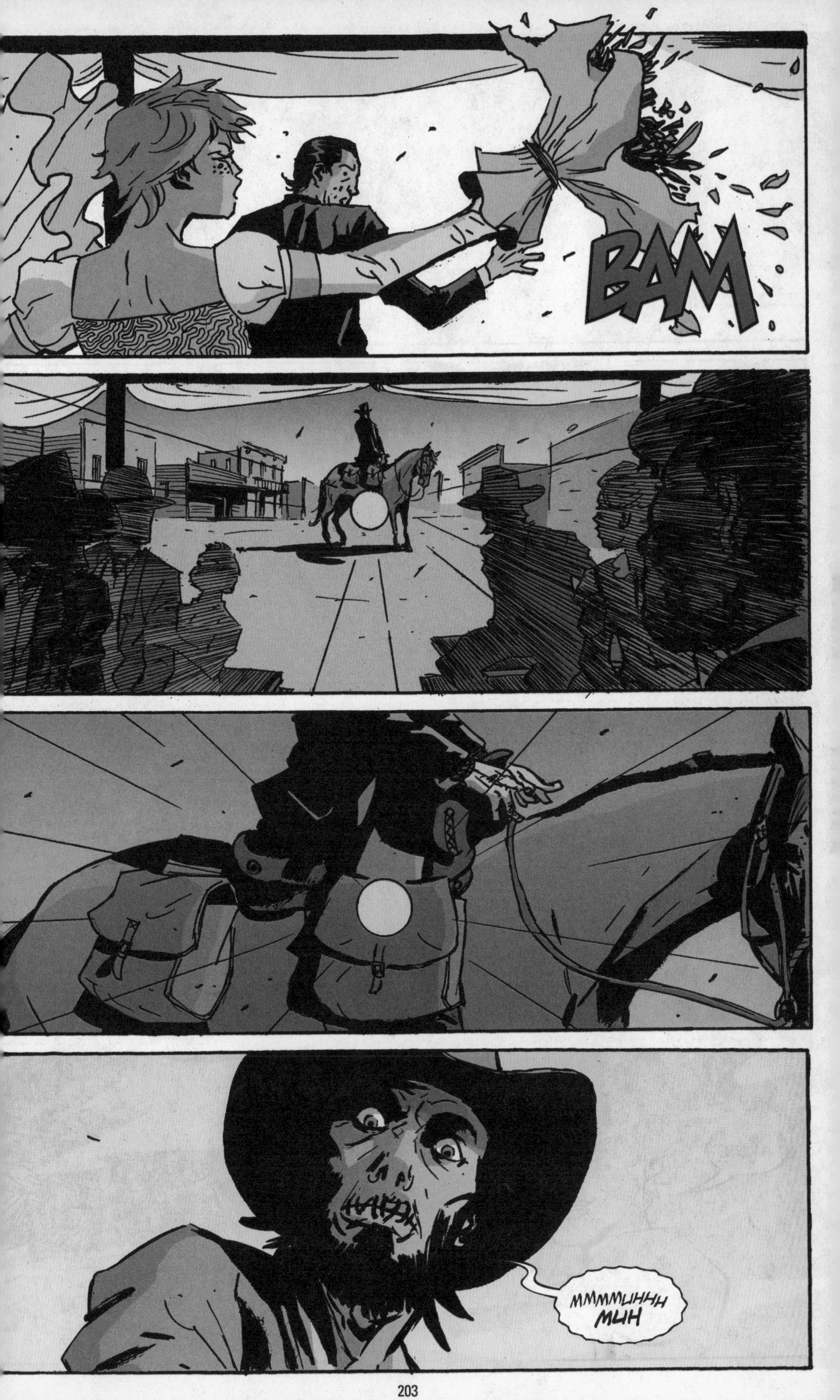
BAM
MMMMUHHH
MUH

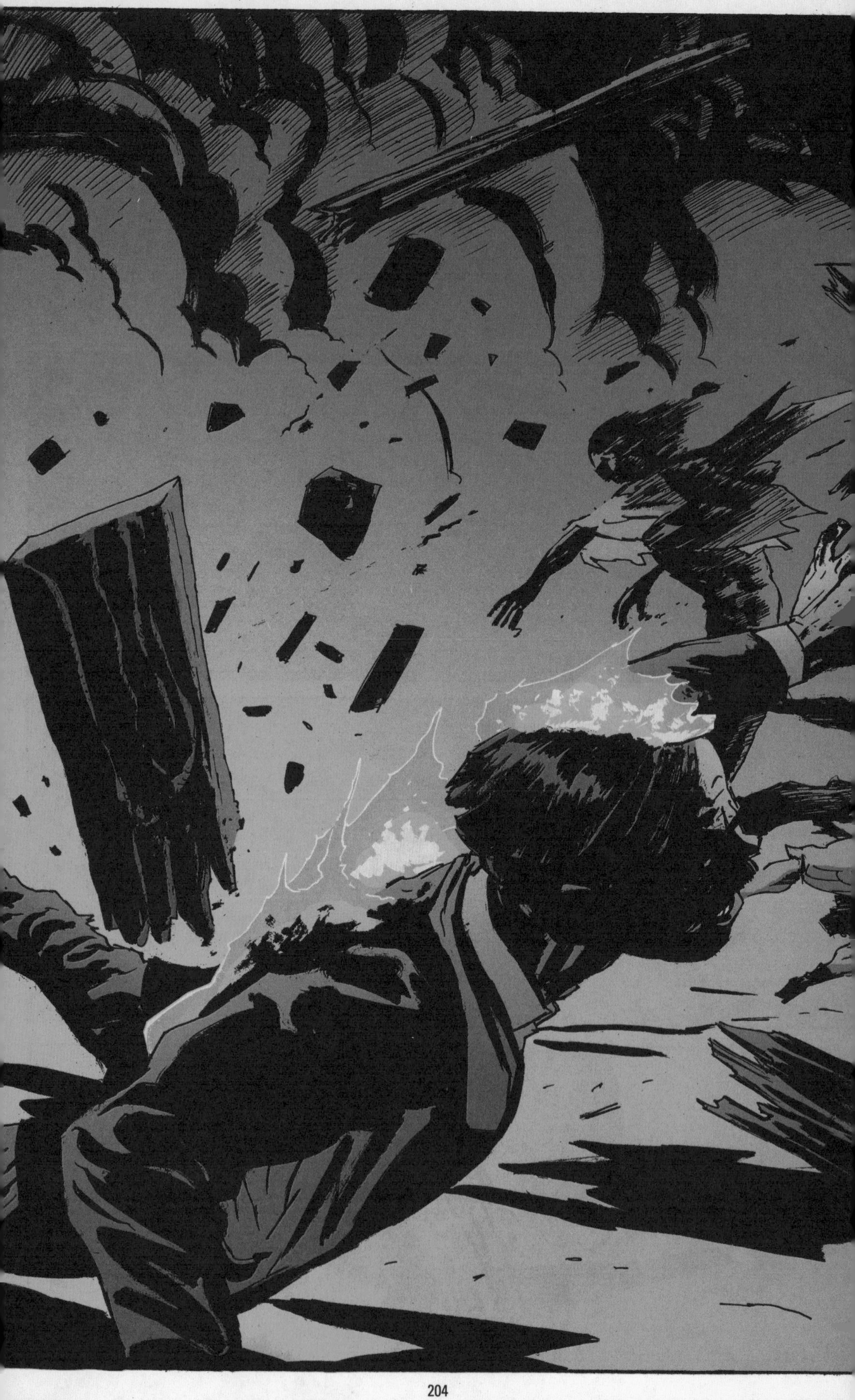

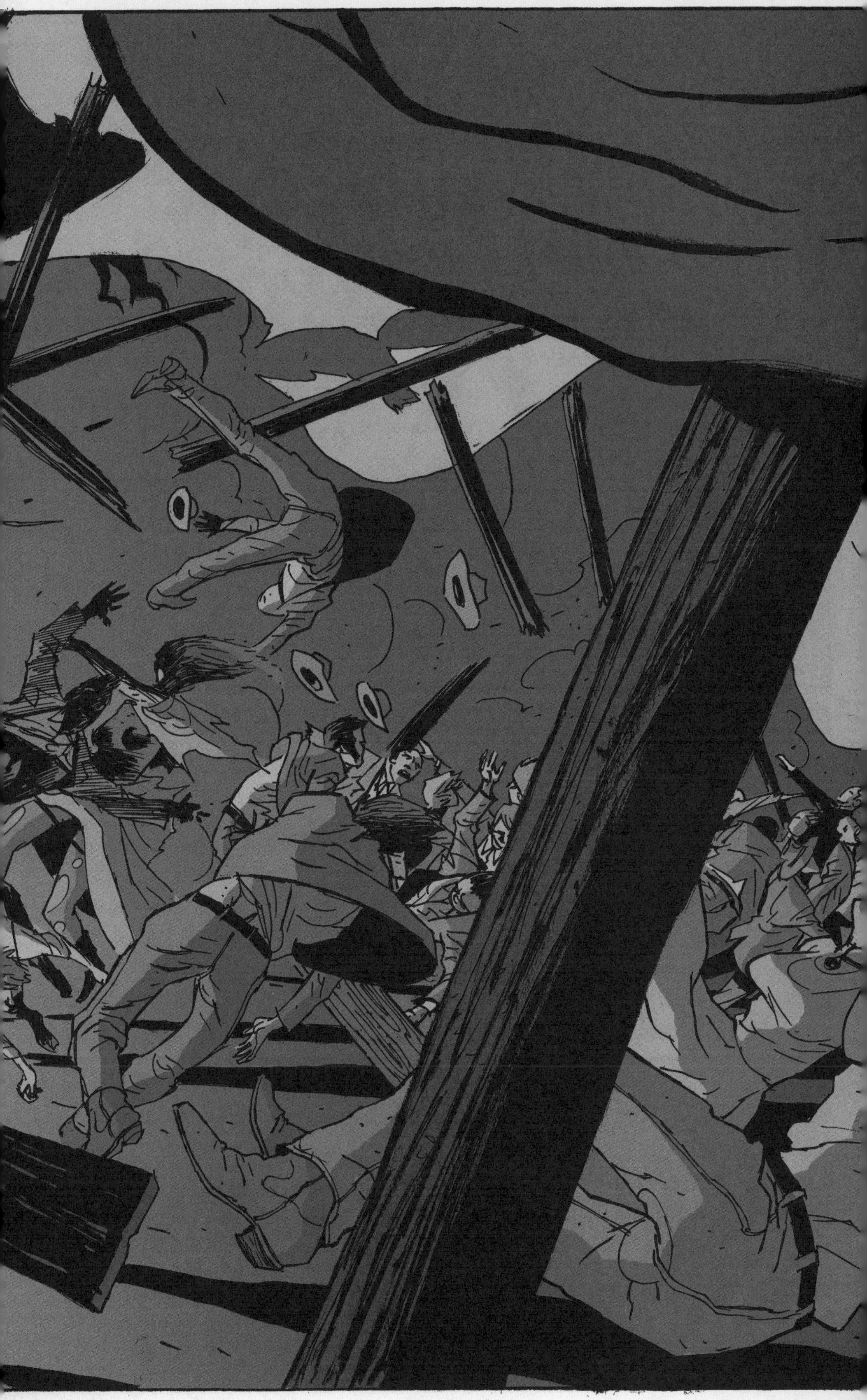

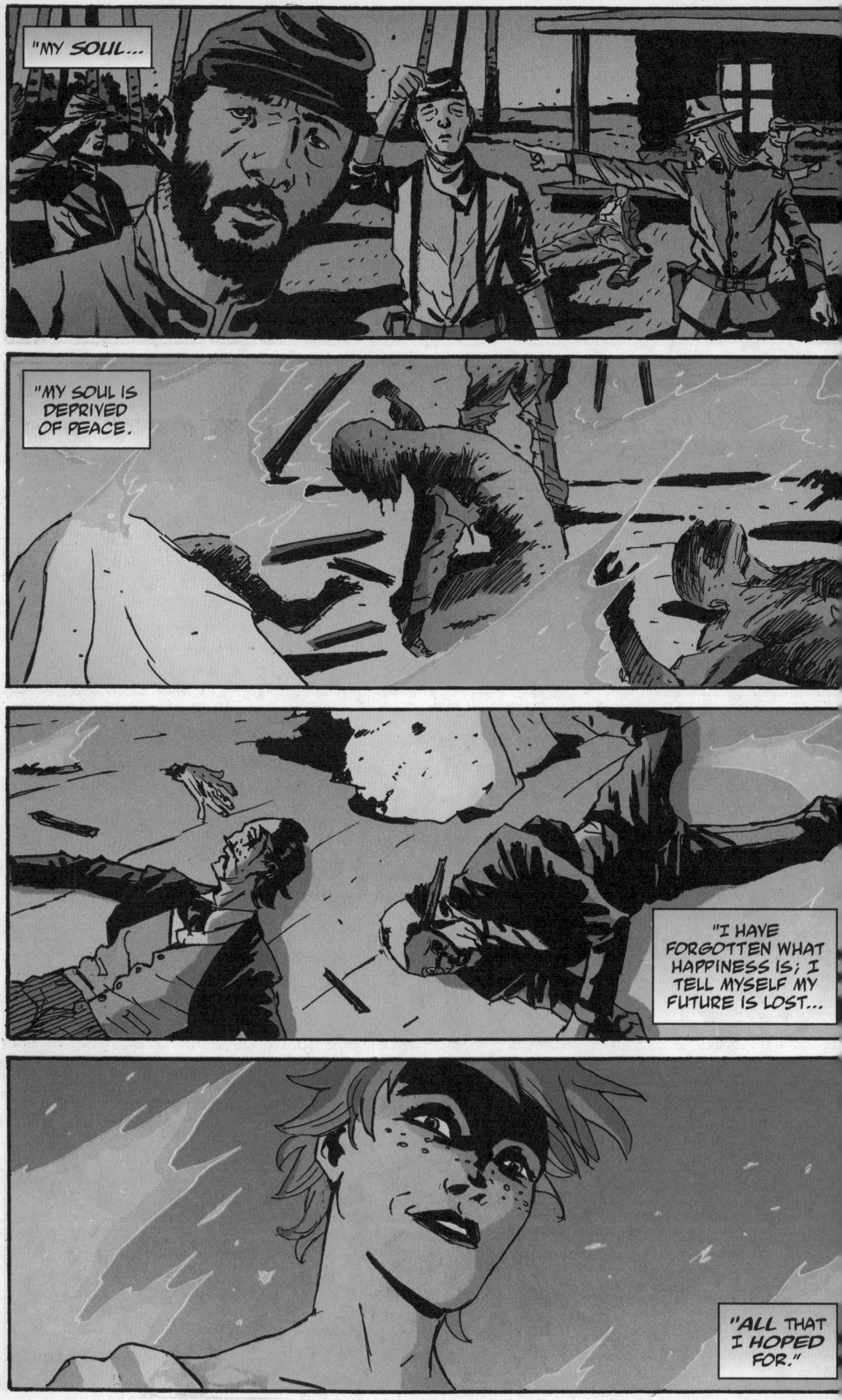
"MY SOUL...
"MY SOUL IS DEPRIVED OF PEACE.
"I HAVE FORGOTTEN WHAT HAPPINESS IS; I TELL MYSELF MY FUTURE IS LOST...
"ALL THAT I HOPED FOR."

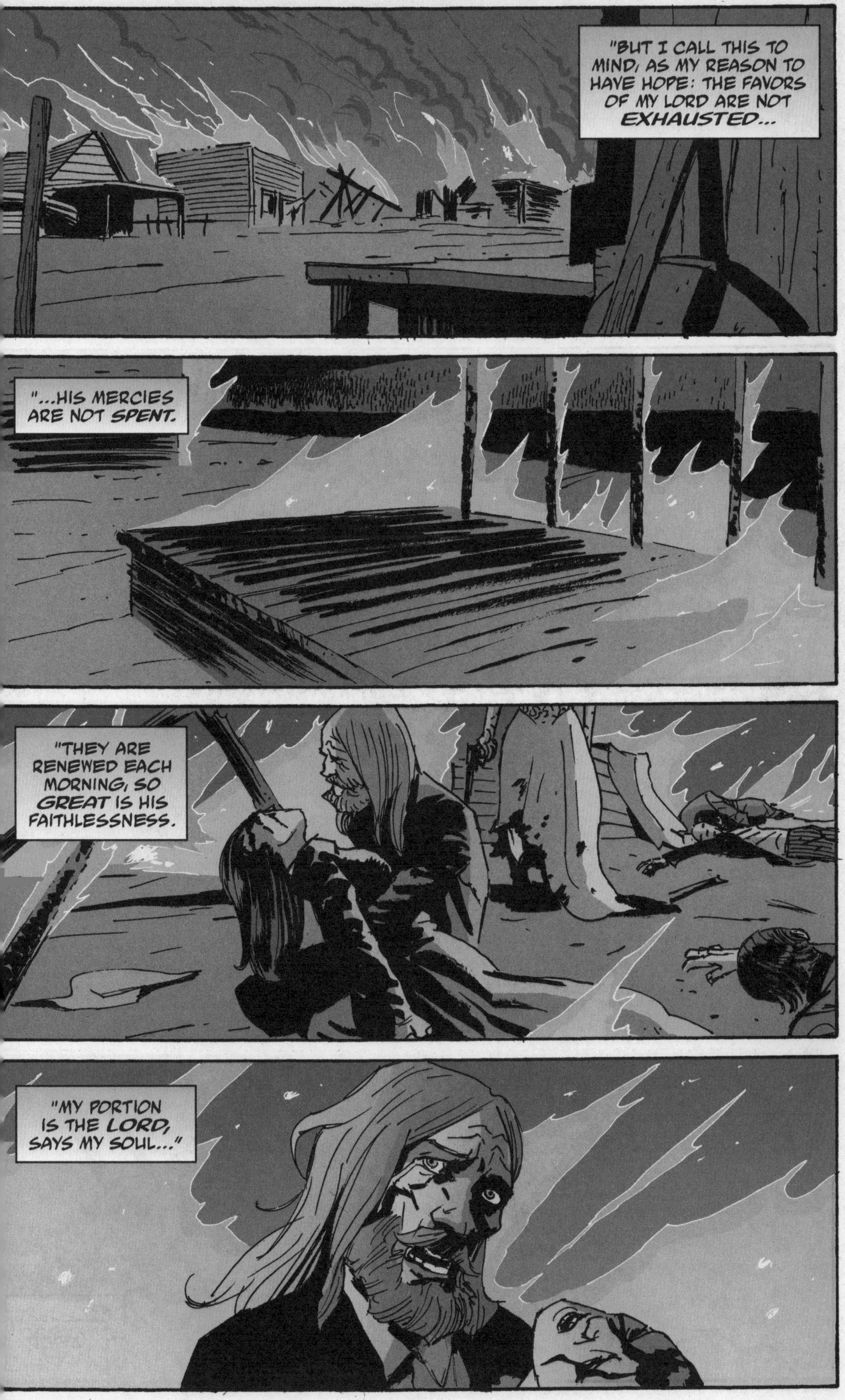
"BUT I CALL THIS TO MIND, AS MY REASON TO HAVE HOPE: THE FAVORS OF MY LORD ARE NOT EXHAUSTED...
"...HIS MERCIES ARE NOT SPENT.
"THEY ARE RENEWED EACH MORNING, SO GREAT IS HIS FAITHLESSNESS.
"MY PORTION IS THE LORD, SAYS MY SOUL..."

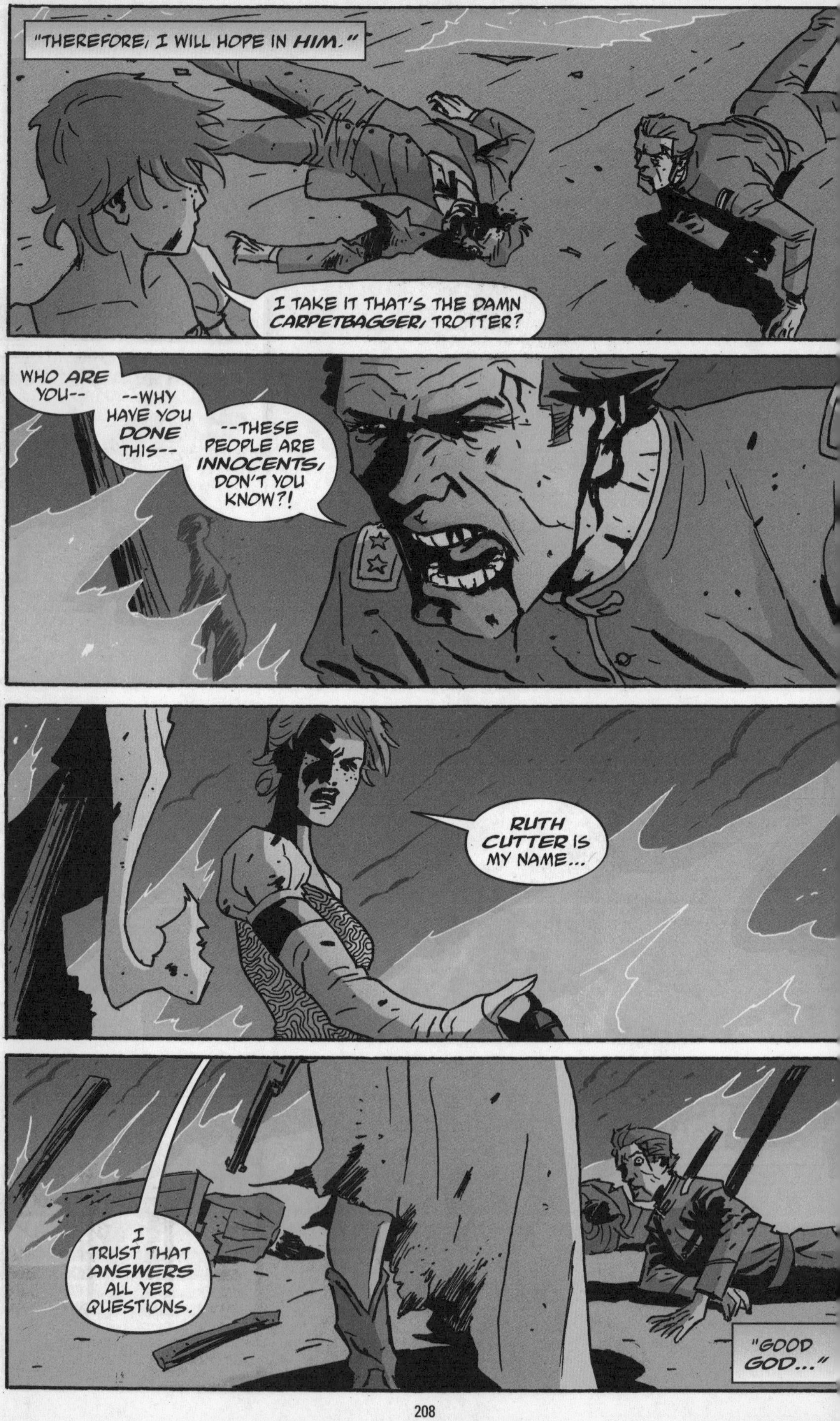
"THEREFORE, I WILL HOPE IN HIM."
I TAKE IT THAT'S THE DAMN CARPETBAGGER, TROTTER?
WHO ARE YOU--
--WHY HAVE YOU DONE THIS--
--THESE PEOPLE ARE INNOCENTS, DON'T YOU KNOW?!
RUTH CUTTER IS MY NAME...
I TRUST THAT ANSWERS ALL YER QUESTIONS.
"GOOD GOD..."

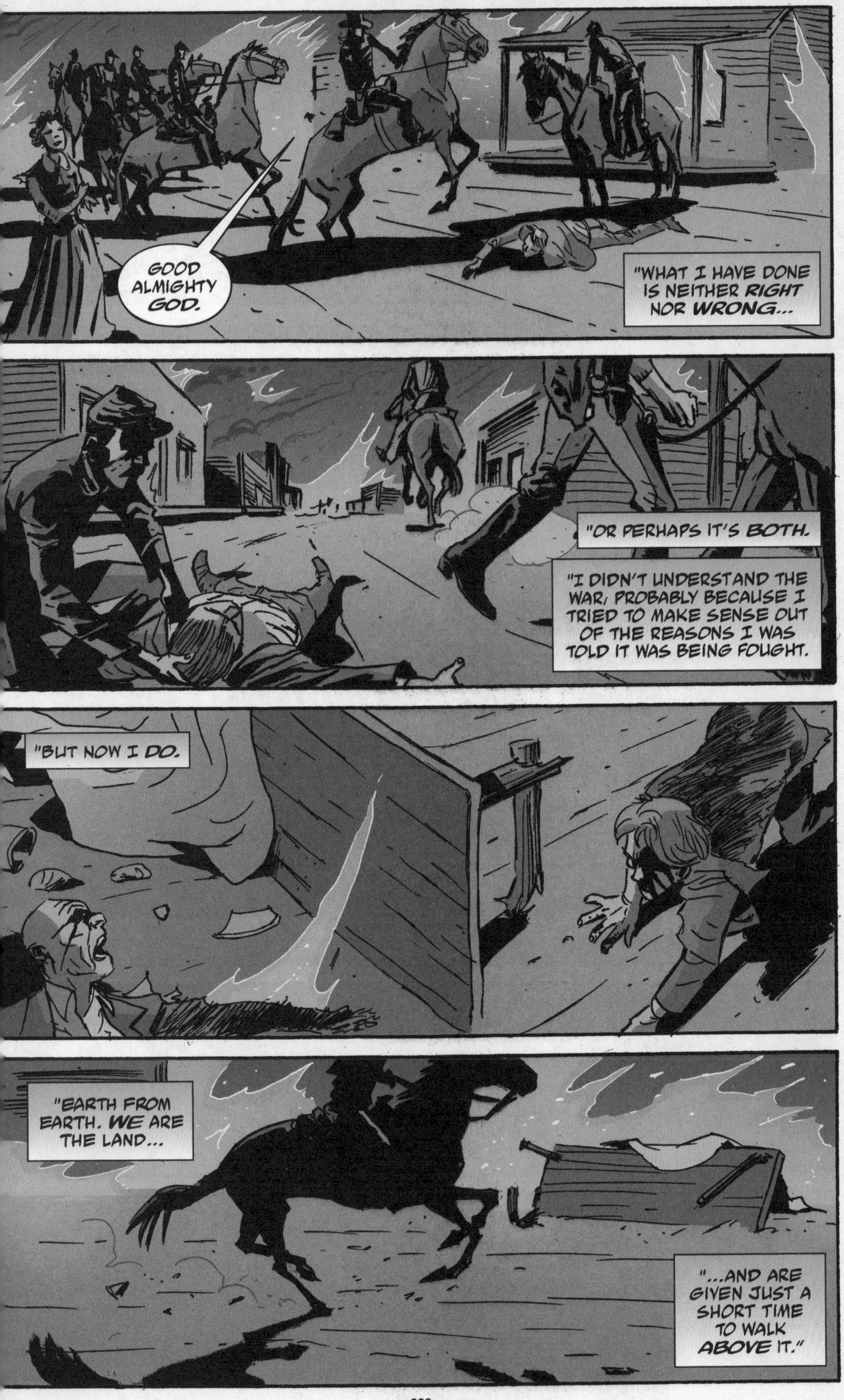
GOOD ALMIGHTY GOD.
"WHAT I HAVE DONE IS NEITHER RIGHT NOR WRONG...
"OR PERHAPS IT'S BOTH.
"I DIDN'T UNDERSTAND THE WAR, PROBABLY BECAUSE I TRIED TO MAKE SENSE OUT OF THE REASONS I WAS TOLD IT WAS BEING FOUGHT.
"BUT NOW I DO.
"EARTH FROM EARTH. WE ARE THE LAND...
"...AND ARE GIVEN JUST A SHORT TIME TO WALK ABOVE IT."

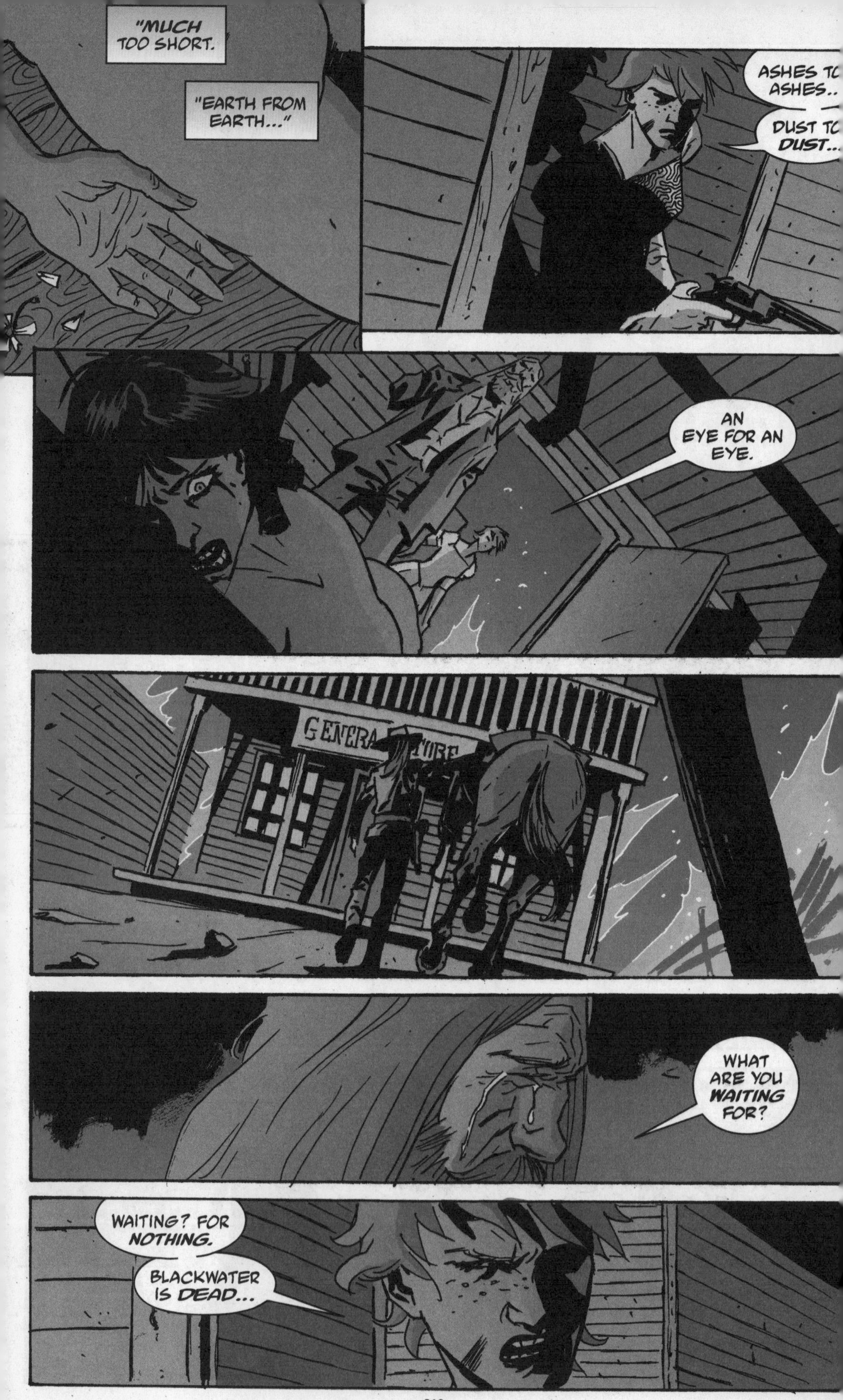
"MUCH TOO SHORT.
"EARTH FROM EARTH..."
ASHES TO ASHES...
DUST TO DUST...
AN EYE FOR AN EYE.
GENERA... ...TORE
WHAT ARE YOU WAITING FOR?
WAITING? FOR NOTHING.
BLACKWATER IS DEAD...

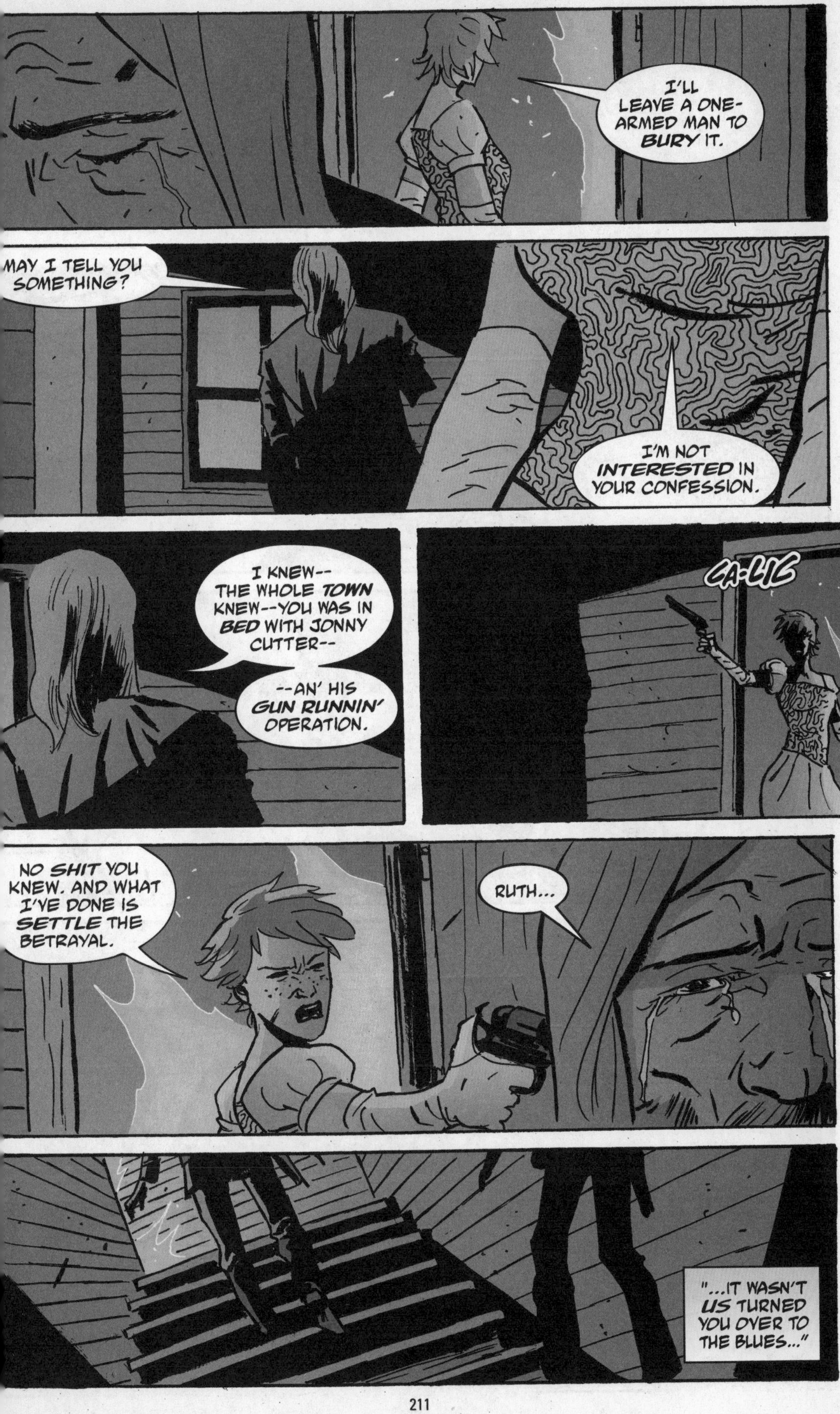
I'LL LEAVE A ONE-ARMED MAN TO BURY IT.
MAY I TELL YOU SOMETHING?
I'M NOT INTERESTED IN YOUR CONFESSION.
I KNEW-- THE WHOLE TOWN KNEW--YOU WAS IN BED WITH JONNY CUTTER--
--AN' HIS GUN RUNNIN' OPERATION.
CA-LIC
NO SHIT YOU KNEW. AND WHAT I'VE DONE IS SETTLE THE BETRAYAL.
RUTH...
"...IT WASN'T US TURNED YOU OVER TO THE BLUES..."

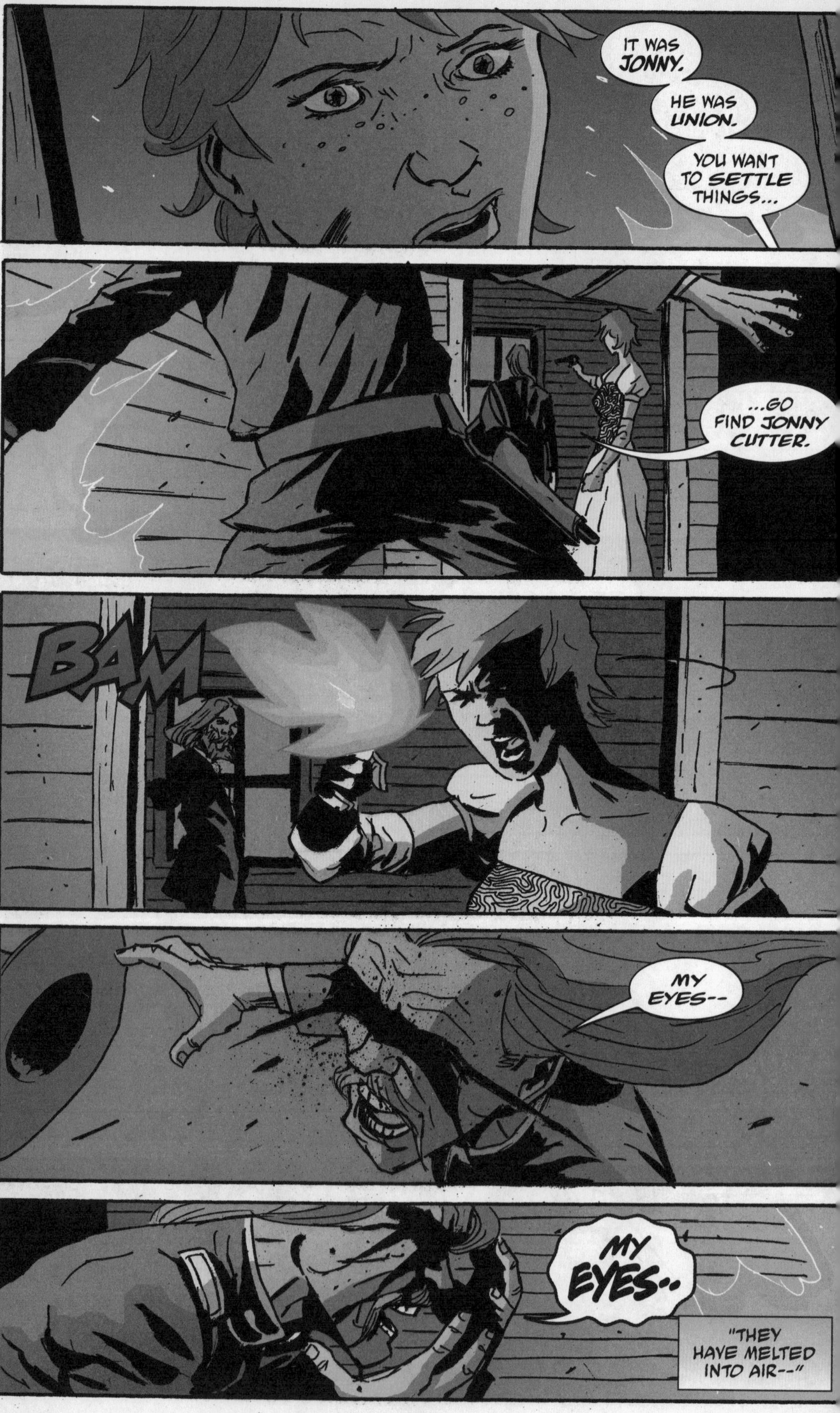
IT WAS JONNY.
HE WAS UNION.
YOU WANT TO SETTLE THINGS...
...GO FIND JONNY CUTTER.
BAM
MY EYES--
MY EYES..
"THEY HAVE MELTED INTO AIR--"

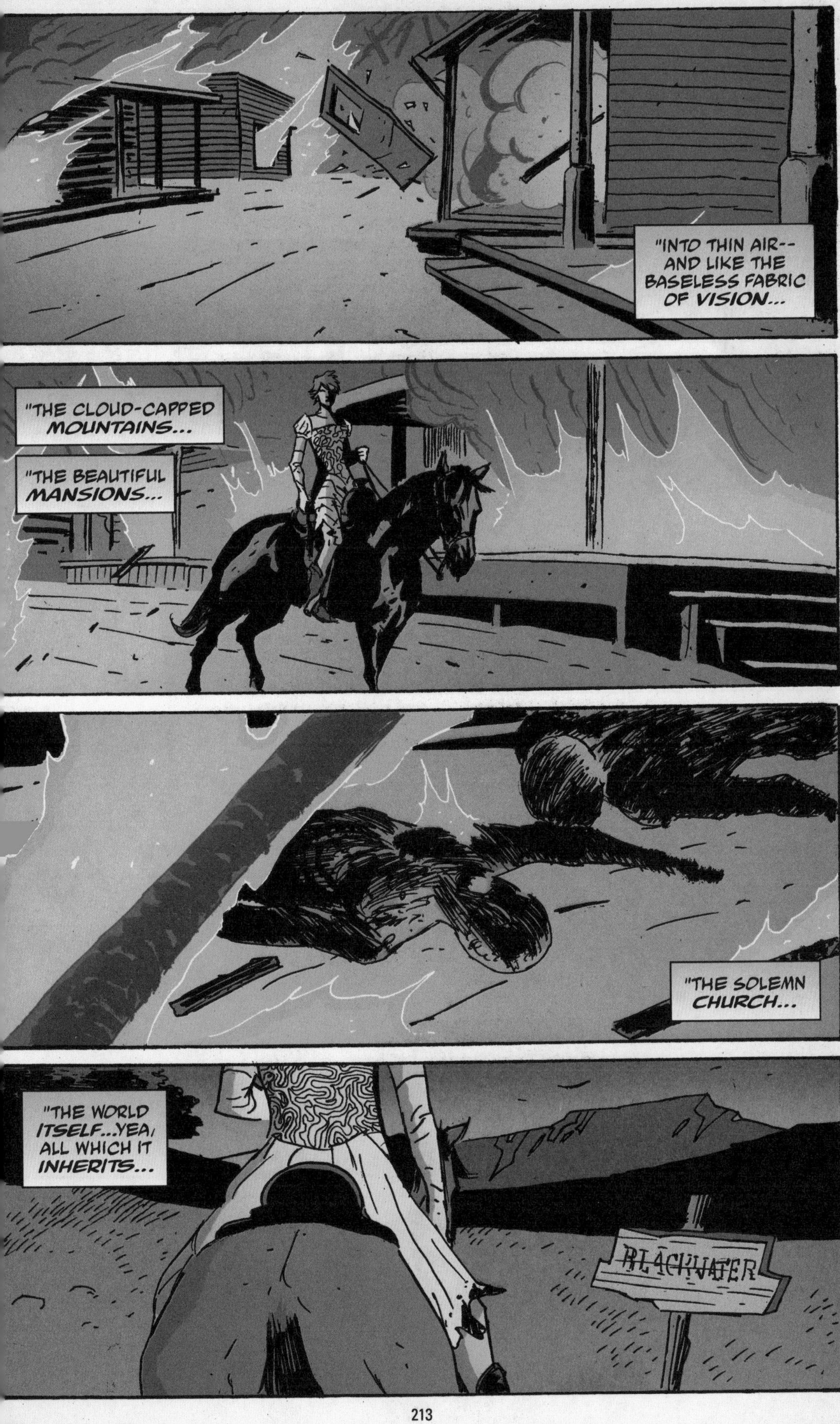
"INTO THIN AIR--
AND LIKE THE
BASELESS FABRIC
OF VISION...
"THE CLOUD-CAPPED
MOUNTAINS...
"THE BEAUTIFUL
MANSIONS...
"THE SOLEMN
CHURCH...
"THE WORLD
ITSELF...YEA,
ALL WHICH IT
INHERITS...
BLACKWATER

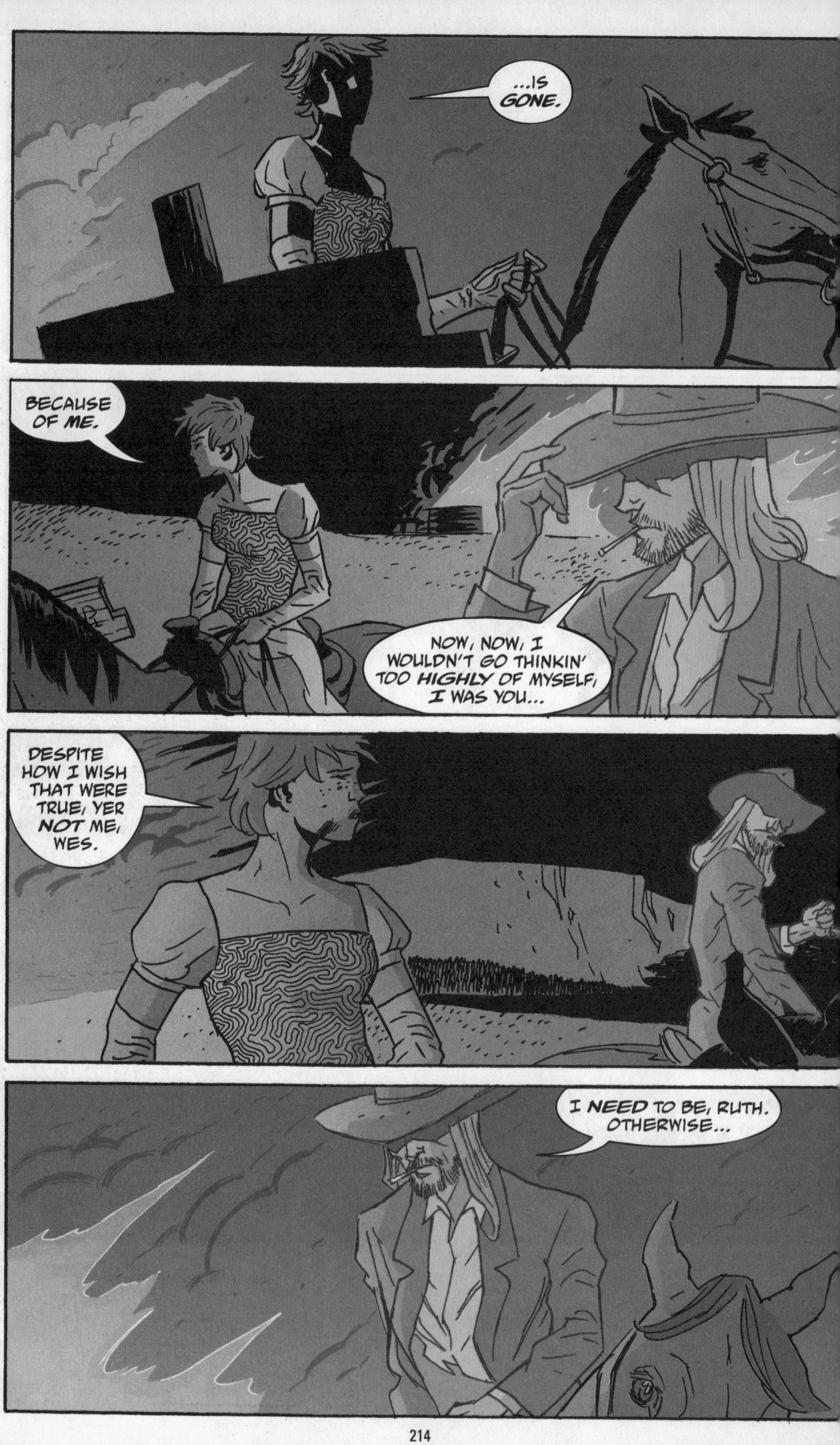
...IS GONE.
BECAUSE OF ME.
NOW, NOW, I WOULDN'T GO THINKIN' TOO HIGHLY OF MYSELF, I WAS YOU...
DESPITE HOW I WISH THAT WERE TRUE, YER NOT ME, WES.
I NEED TO BE, RUTH. OTHERWISE...

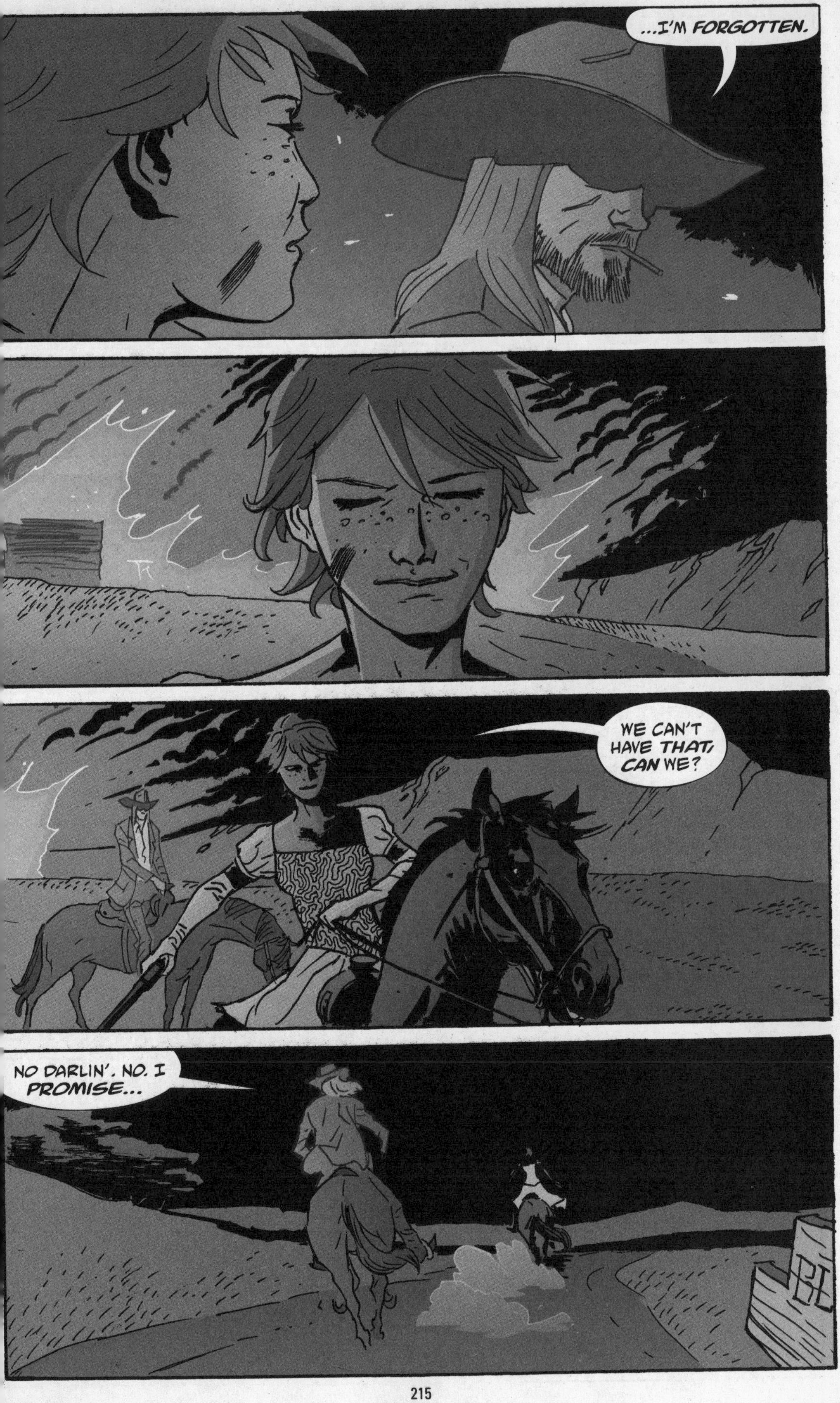
...I'M FORGOTTEN.
WE CAN'T HAVE THAT, CAN WE?
NO DARLIN'. NO. I PROMISE...

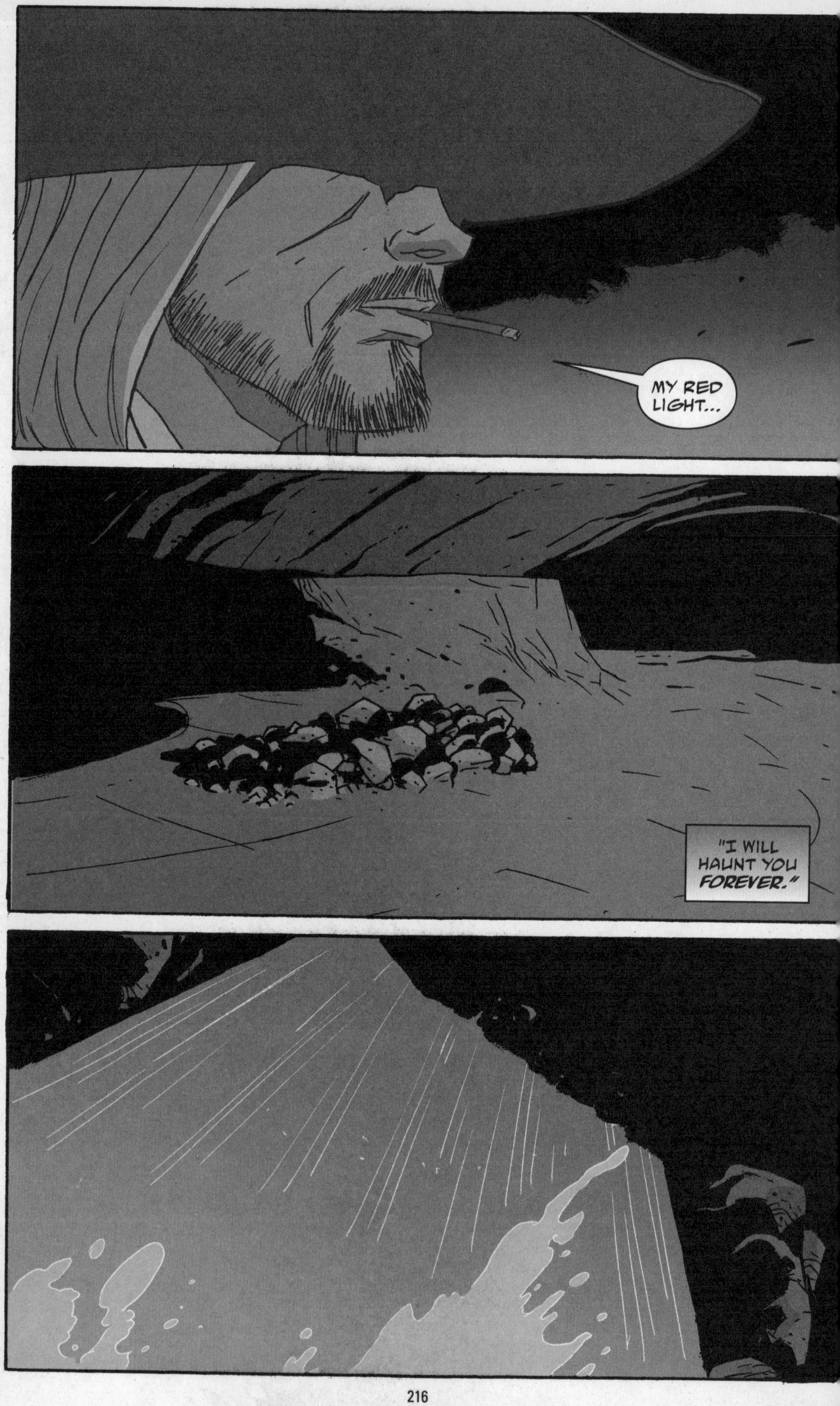
MY RED LIGHT...
"I WILL HAUNT YOU FOREVER."

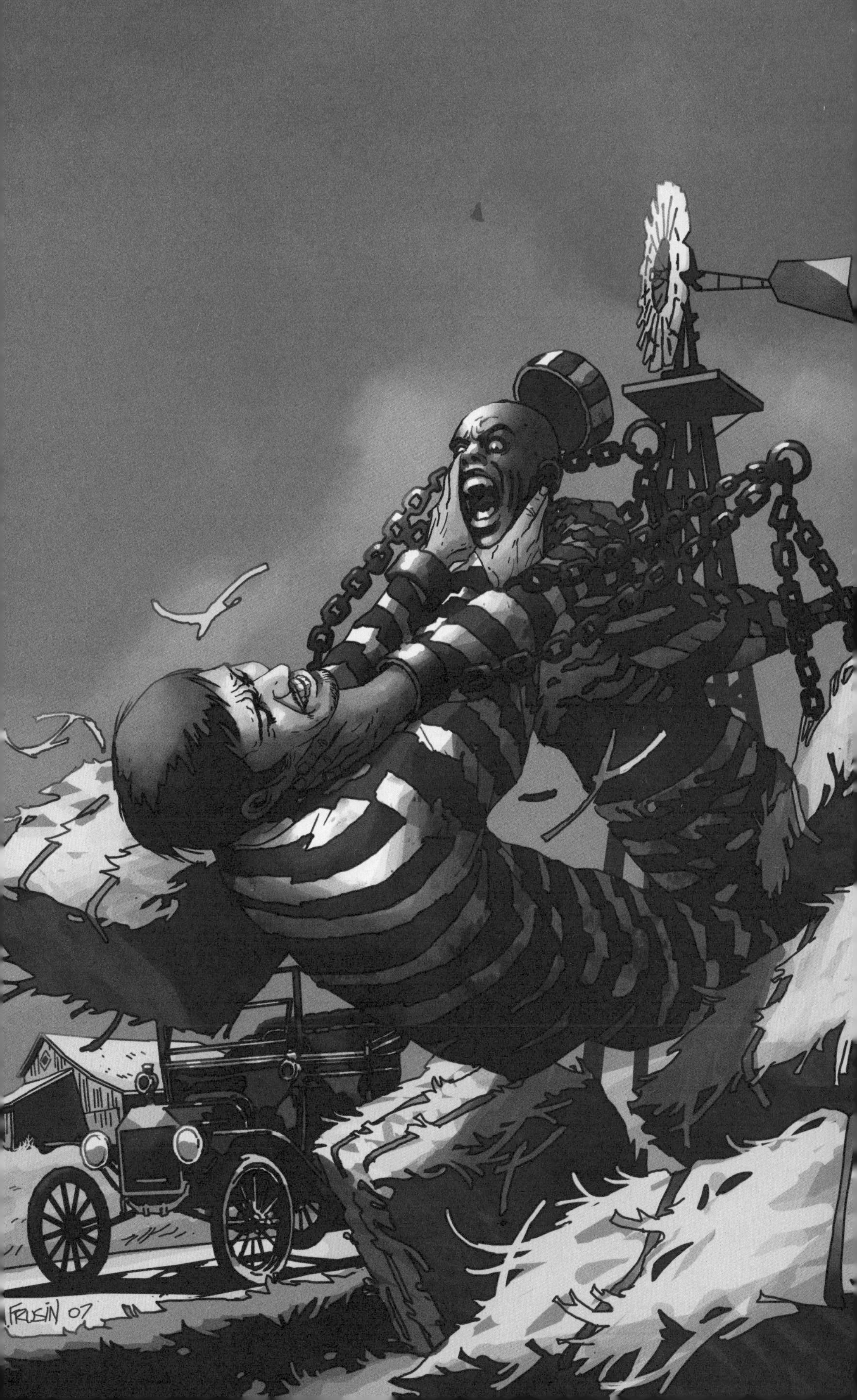
FRUSIN 07

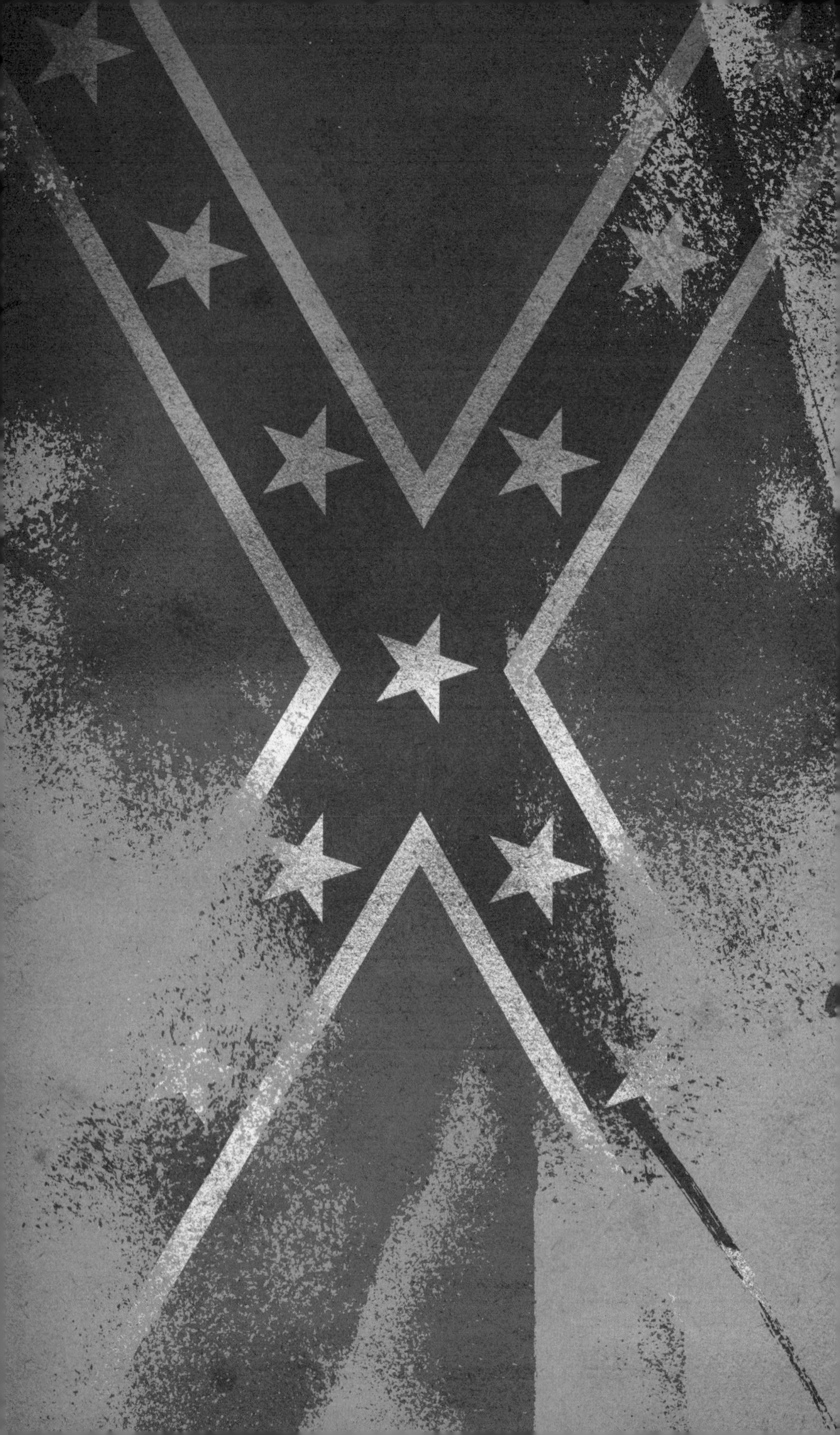

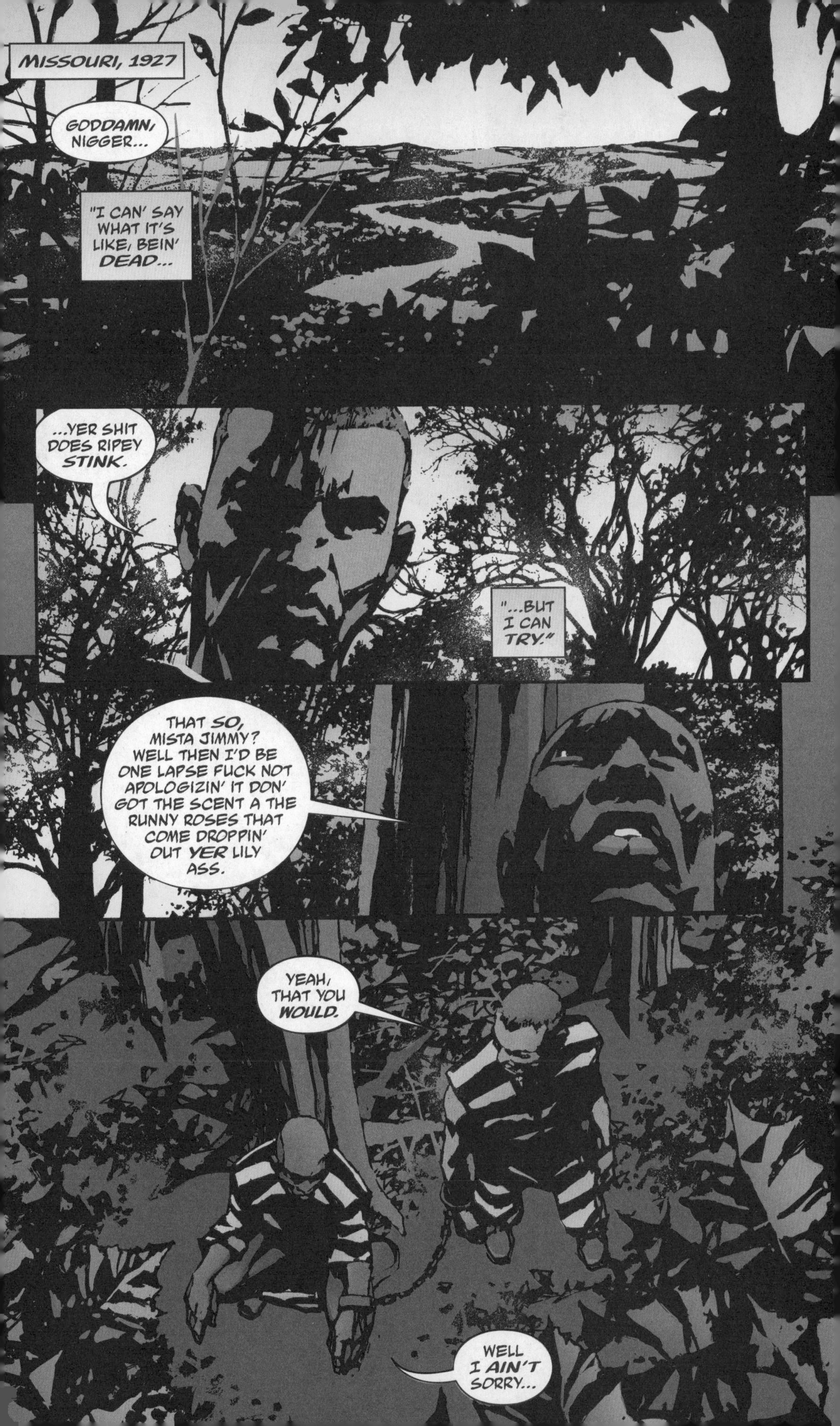
MISSOURI, 1927
GODDAMN, NIGGER...
"I CAN' SAY WHAT IT'S LIKE, BEIN' DEAD...
...YER SHIT DOES RIPEY STINK.
"...BUT I CAN TRY."
THAT SO, MISTA JIMMY? WELL THEN I'D BE ONE LAPSE FUCK NOT APOLOGIZIN' IT DON' GOT THE SCENT A THE RUNNY ROSES THAT COME DROPPIN' OUT YER LILY ASS.
YEAH, THAT YOU WOULD.
WELL I AIN'T SORRY...

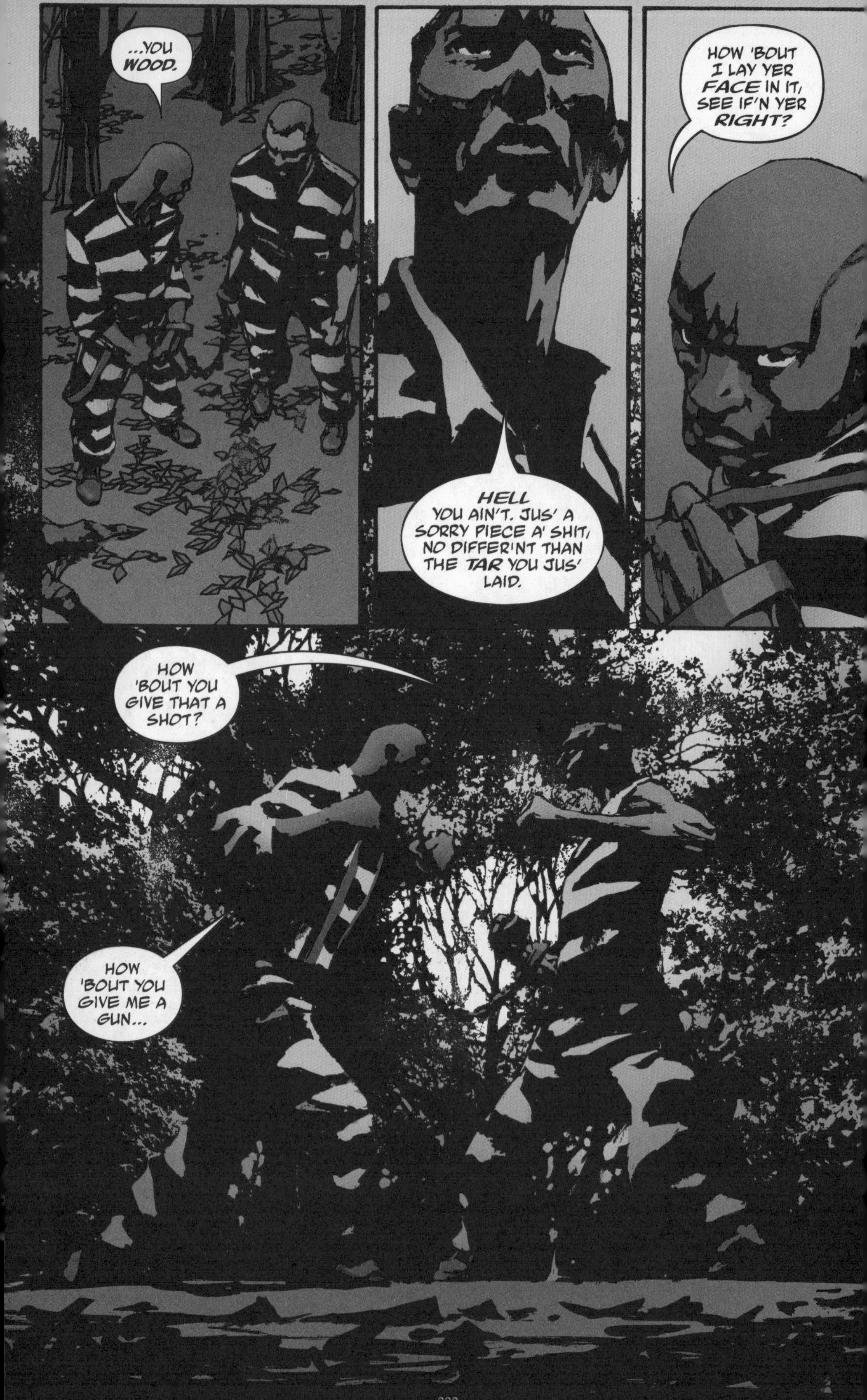
...YOU WOOD.
HELL YOU AIN'T. JUS' A SORRY PIECE A' SHIT, NO DIFFER'NT THAN THE TAR YOU JUS' LAID.
HOW 'BOUT I LAY YER FACE IN IT, SEE IF'N YER RIGHT?
HOW 'BOUT YOU GIVE THAT A SHOT?
HOW 'BOUT YOU GIVE ME A GUN...

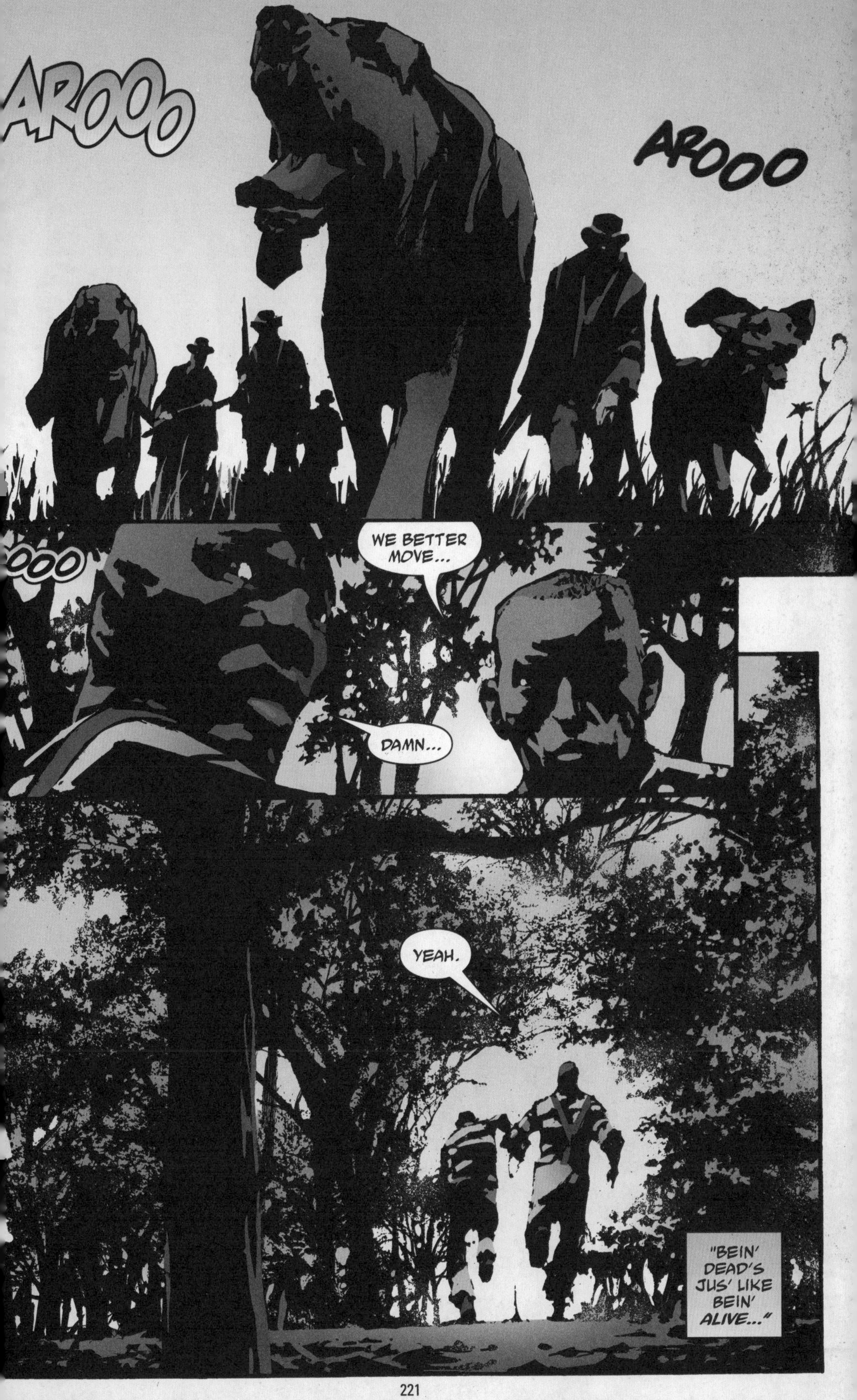
AROOO
AROOO
OOO
WE BETTER MOVE...
DAMN...
YEAH.
"BEIN' DEAD'S JUS' LIKE BEIN' ALIVE..."

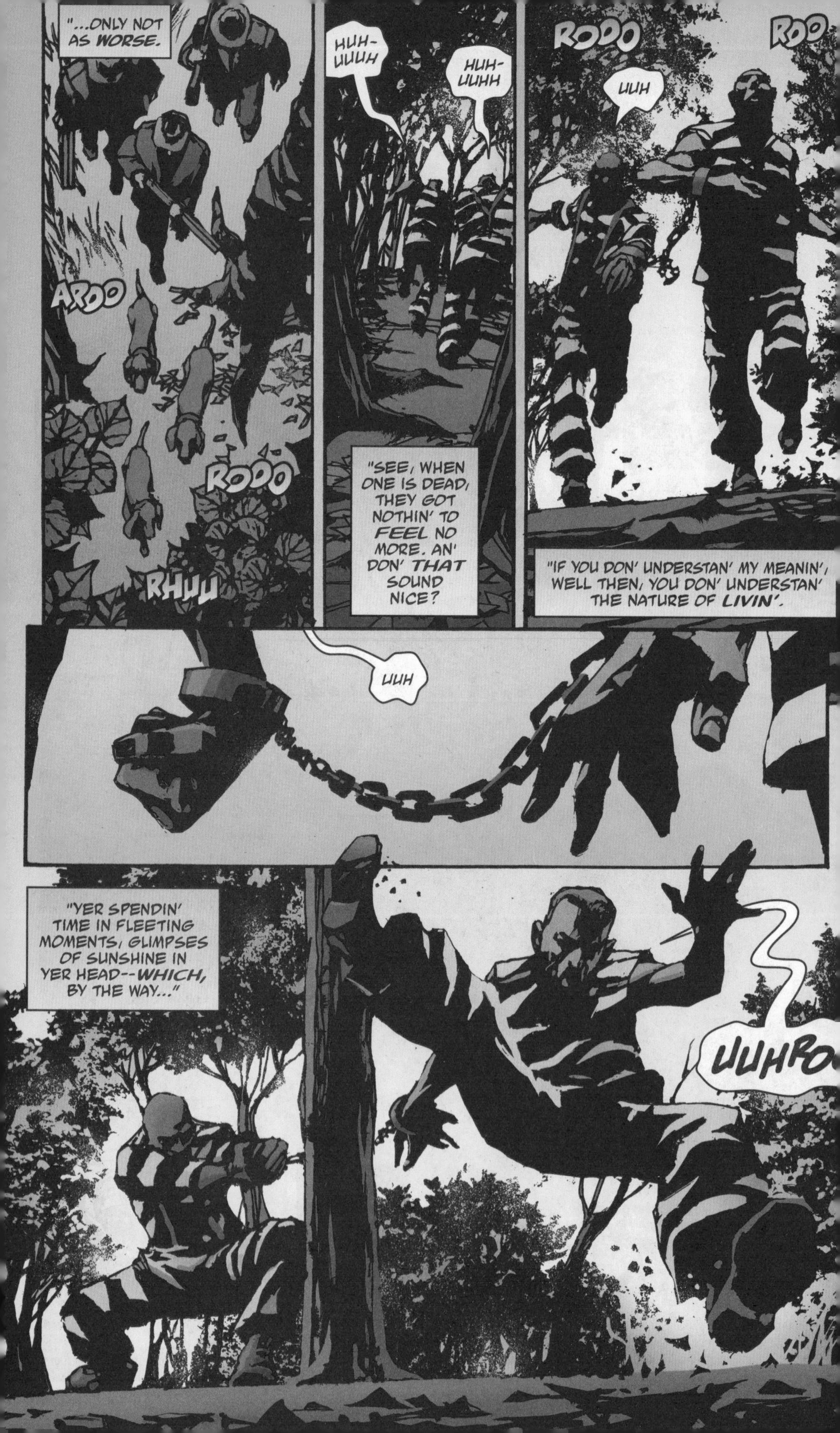

"...ONLY NOT AS WORSE.
AROO
RODO
RHUU
HUH-UUUH
HUH-UUHH
"SEE, WHEN ONE IS DEAD, THEY GOT NOTHIN' TO FEEL NO MORE. AN' DON' THAT SOUND NICE?
RODO
ROO
UUH
"IF YOU DON' UNDERSTAN' MY MEANIN', WELL THEN, YOU DON' UNDERSTAN' THE NATURE OF LIVIN'.
UUH
"YER SPENDIN' TIME IN FLEETING MOMENTS, GLIMPSES OF SUNSHINE IN YER HEAD--WHICH, BY THE WAY..."
UUHRO

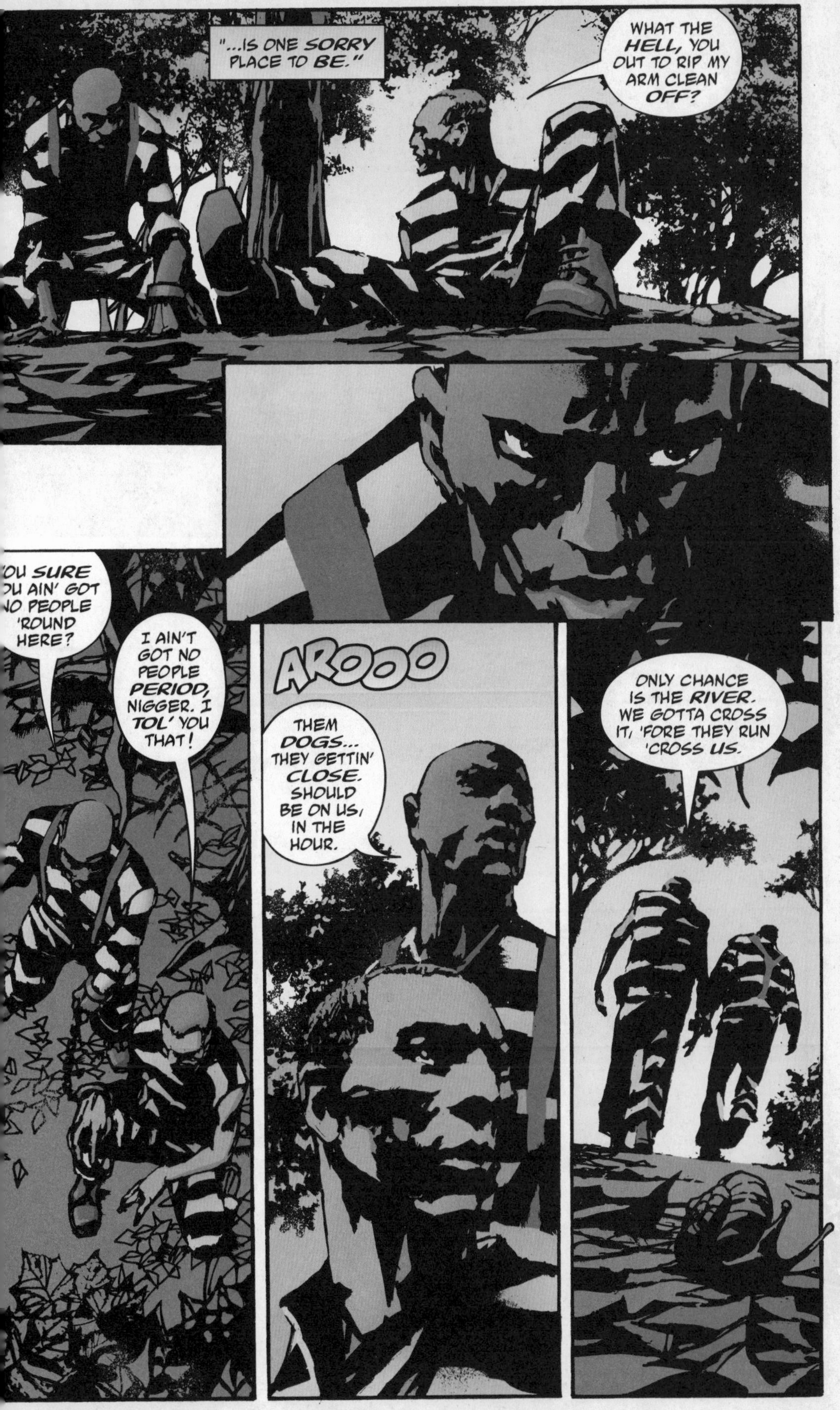
"...IS ONE SORRY PLACE TO BE."
WHAT THE HELL, YOU OUT TO RIP MY ARM CLEAN OFF?
YOU SURE YOU AIN' GOT NO PEOPLE 'ROUND HERE?
I AIN'T GOT NO PEOPLE PERIOD, NIGGER. I TOL' YOU THAT!
AROOO
THEM DOGS... THEY GETTIN' CLOSE. SHOULD BE ON US, IN THE HOUR.
ONLY CHANCE IS THE RIVER. WE GOTTA CROSS IT, 'FORE THEY RUN 'CROSS US.

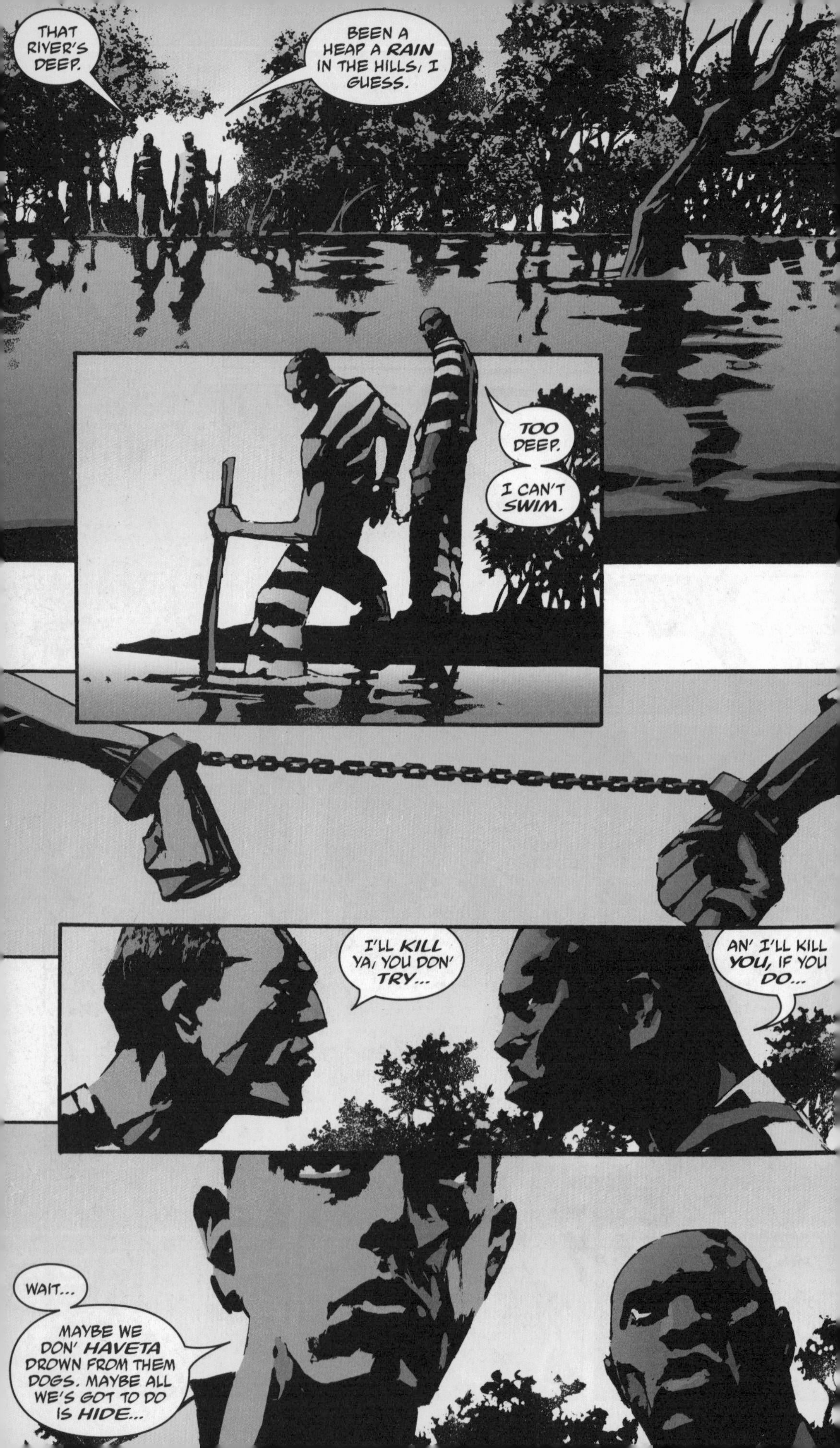
THAT RIVER'S DEEP.
BEEN A HEAP A RAIN IN THE HILLS, I GUESS.
TOO DEEP.
I CAN'T SWIM.
I'LL KILL YA, YOU DON' TRY...
AN' I'LL KILL YOU, IF YOU DO...
WAIT...
MAYBE WE DON' HAVETA DROWN FROM THEM DOGS. MAYBE ALL WE'S GOT TO DO IS HIDE...

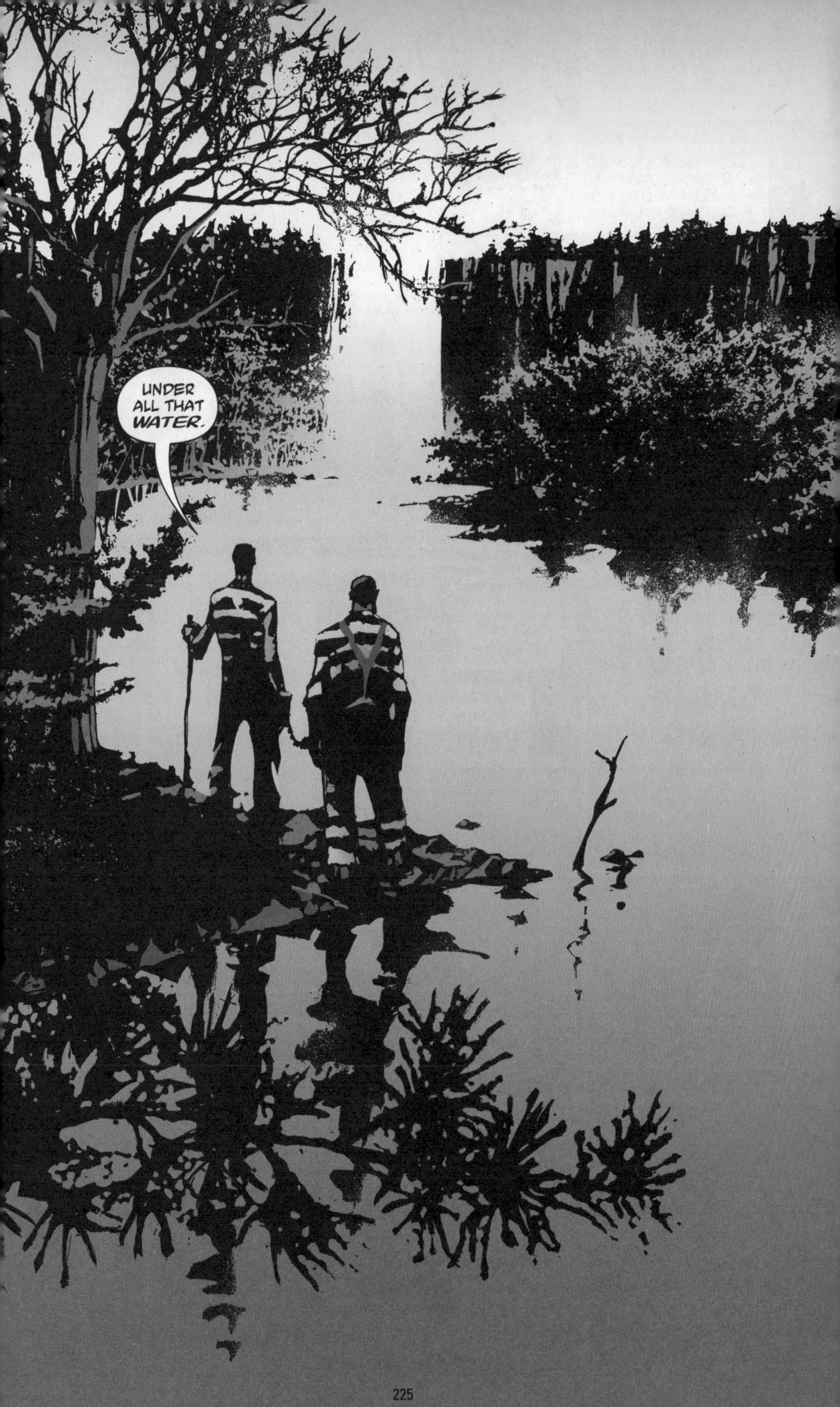
UNDER ALL THAT WATER.

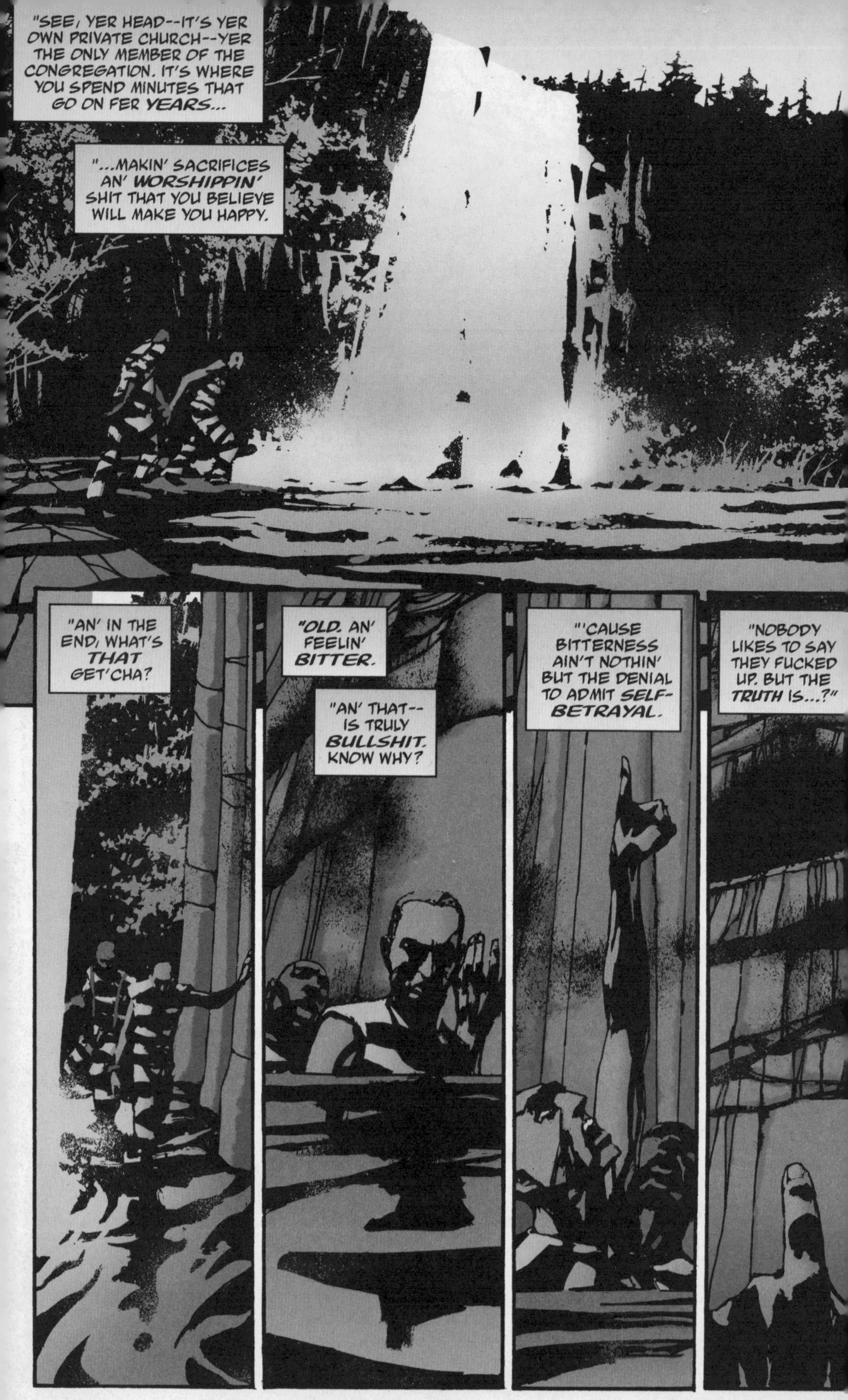
"SEE, YER HEAD--IT'S YER OWN PRIVATE CHURCH--YER THE ONLY MEMBER OF THE CONGREGATION. IT'S WHERE YOU SPEND MINUTES THAT GO ON FER YEARS...
"...MAKIN' SACRIFICES AN' WORSHIPPIN' SHIT THAT YOU BELIEVE WILL MAKE YOU HAPPY.
"AN' IN THE END, WHAT'S THAT GET'CHA?
"OLD. AN' FEELIN' BITTER.
"AN' THAT--IS TRULY BULLSHIT. KNOW WHY?
"'CAUSE BITTERNESS AIN'T NOTHIN' BUT THE DENIAL TO ADMIT SELF-BETRAYAL.
"NOBODY LIKES TO SAY THEY FUCKED UP. BUT THE TRUTH IS...?"

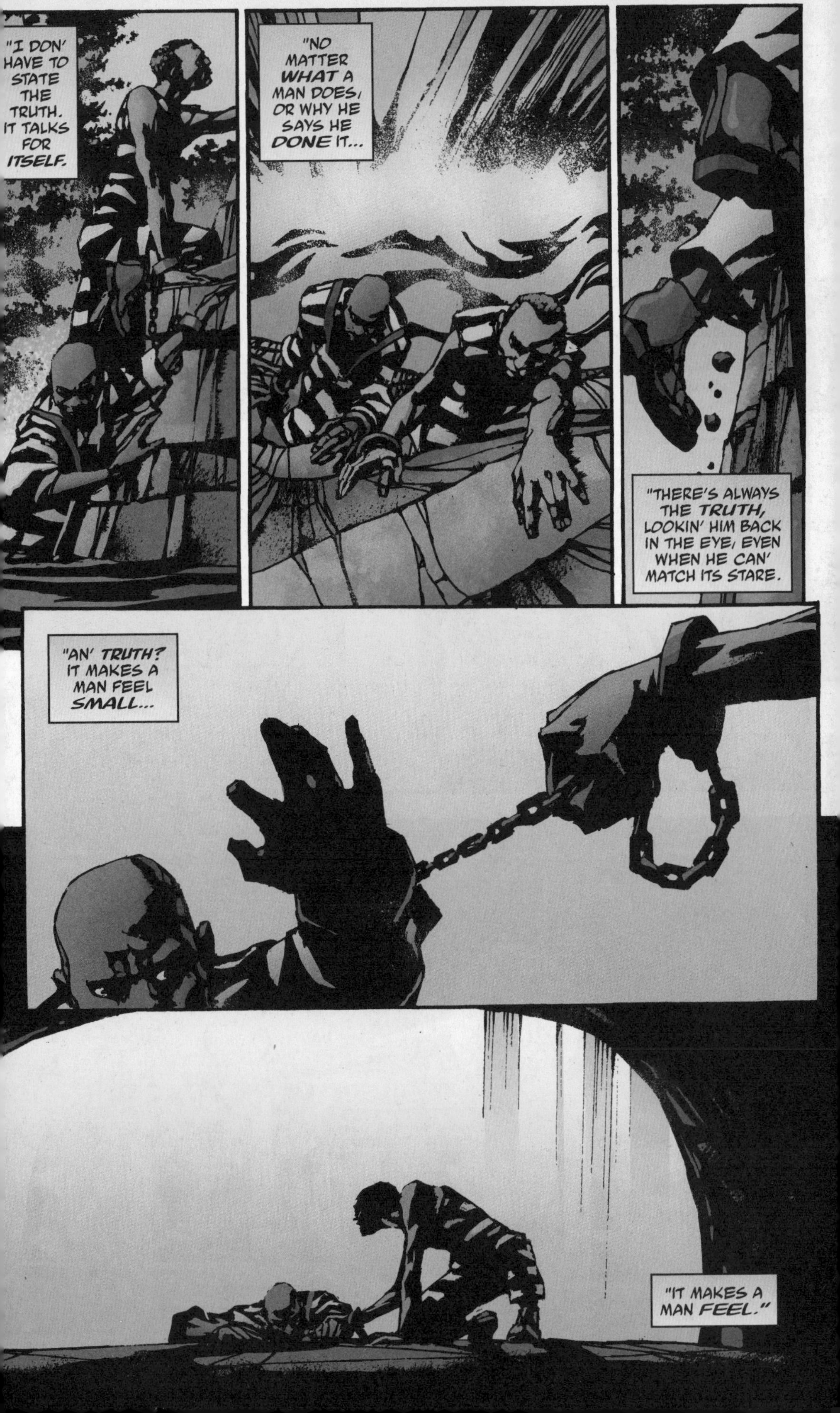
"I DON' HAVE TO STATE THE TRUTH. IT TALKS FOR ITSELF.
"NO MATTER WHAT A MAN DOES, OR WHY HE SAYS HE DONE IT...
"THERE'S ALWAYS THE TRUTH, LOOKIN' HIM BACK IN THE EYE, EVEN WHEN HE CAN' MATCH ITS STARE.
"AN' TRUTH? IT MAKES A MAN FEEL SMALL...
"IT MAKES A MAN FEEL."

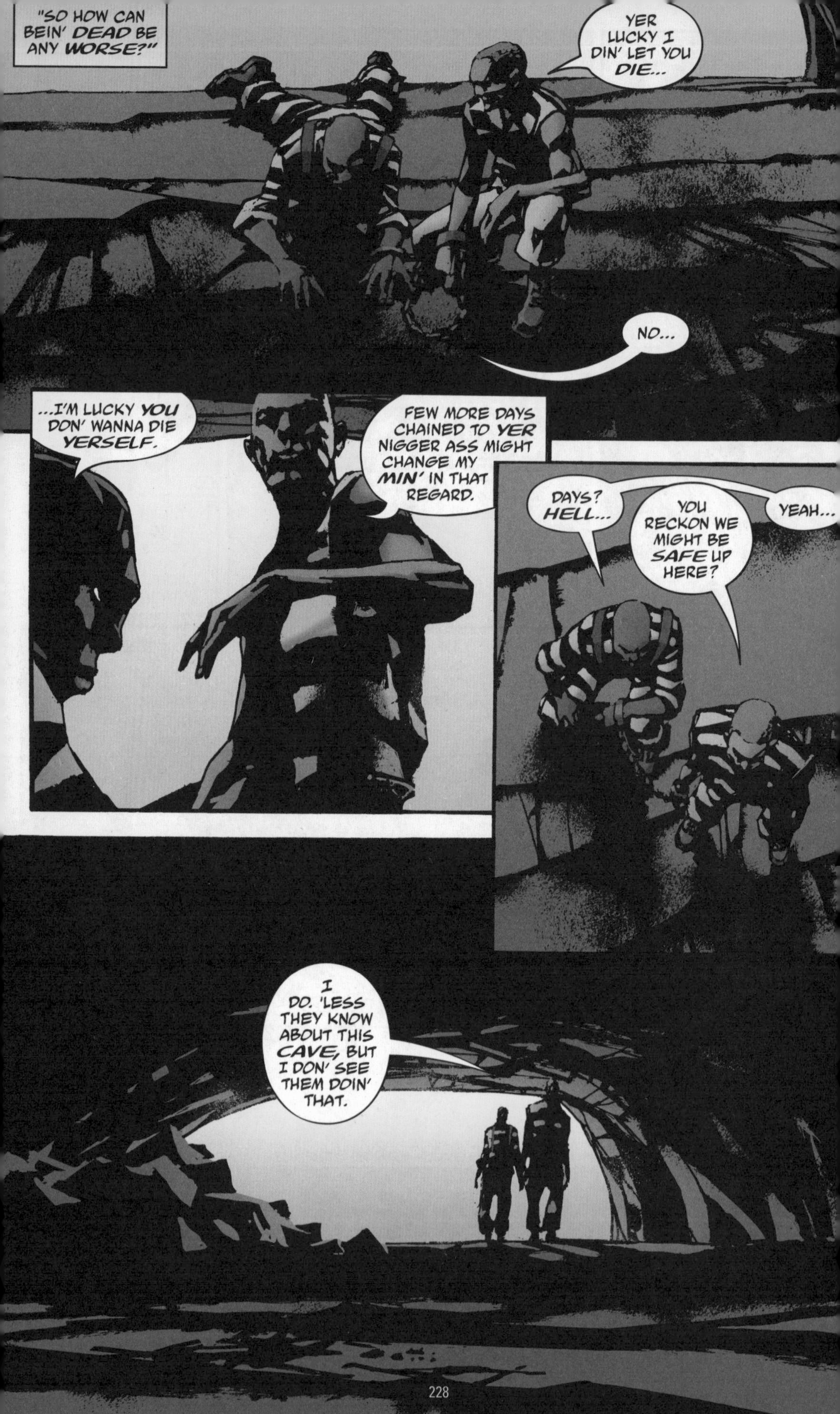
"SO HOW CAN BEIN' DEAD BE ANY WORSE?"
YER LUCKY I DIN' LET YOU DIE...
NO...
...I'M LUCKY YOU DON' WANNA DIE YERSELF.
FEW MORE DAYS CHAINED TO YER NIGGER ASS MIGHT CHANGE MY MIN' IN THAT REGARD.
DAYS? HELL...
YEAH...
YOU RECKON WE MIGHT BE SAFE UP HERE?
I DO. 'LESS THEY KNOW ABOUT THIS CAVE, BUT I DON' SEE THEM DOIN' THAT.

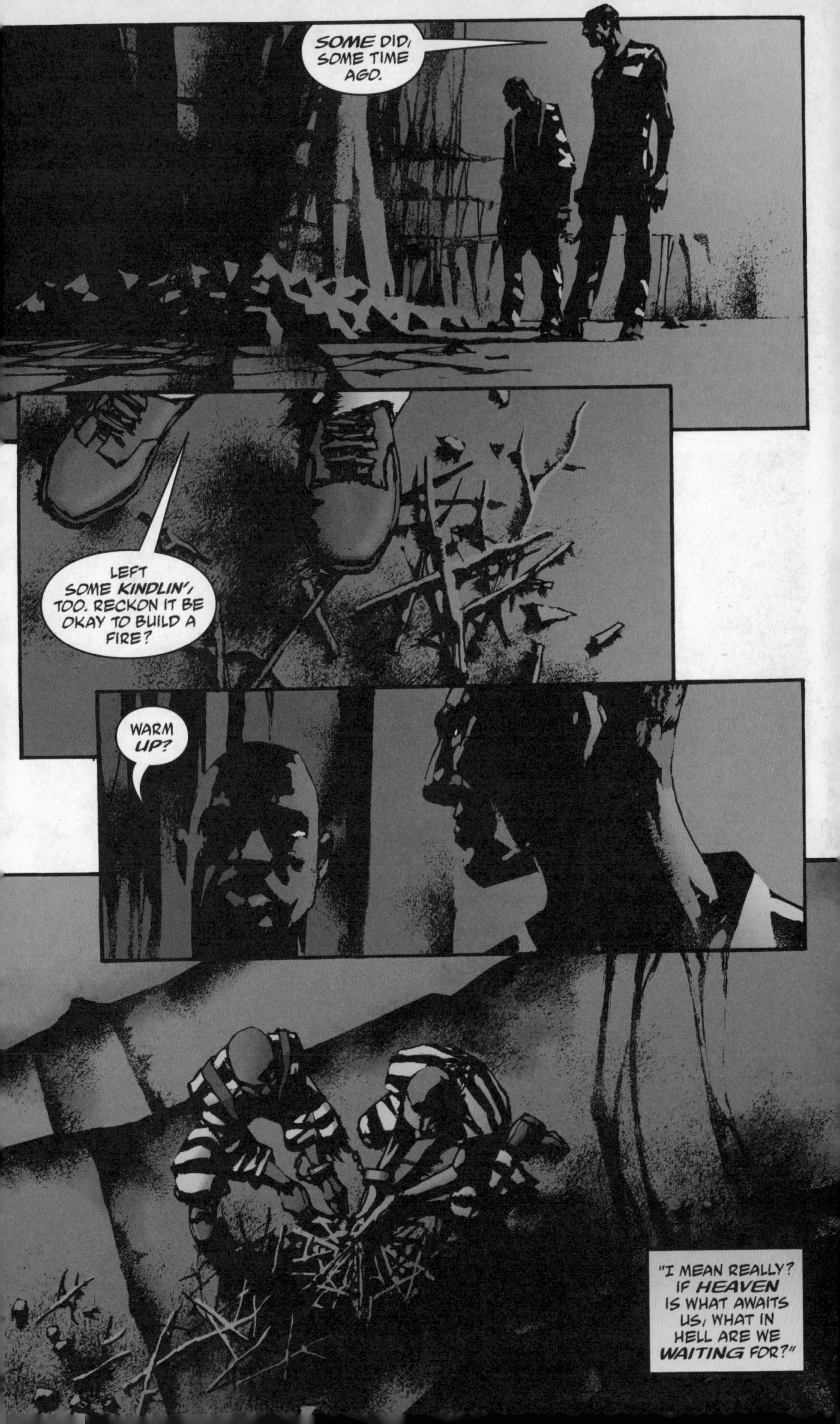
SOME DID, SOME TIME AGO.
LEFT SOME KINDLIN', TOO. RECKON IT BE OKAY TO BUILD A FIRE?
WARM UP?
"I MEAN REALLY? IF HEAVEN IS WHAT AWAITS US, WHAT IN HELL ARE WE WAITING FOR?"

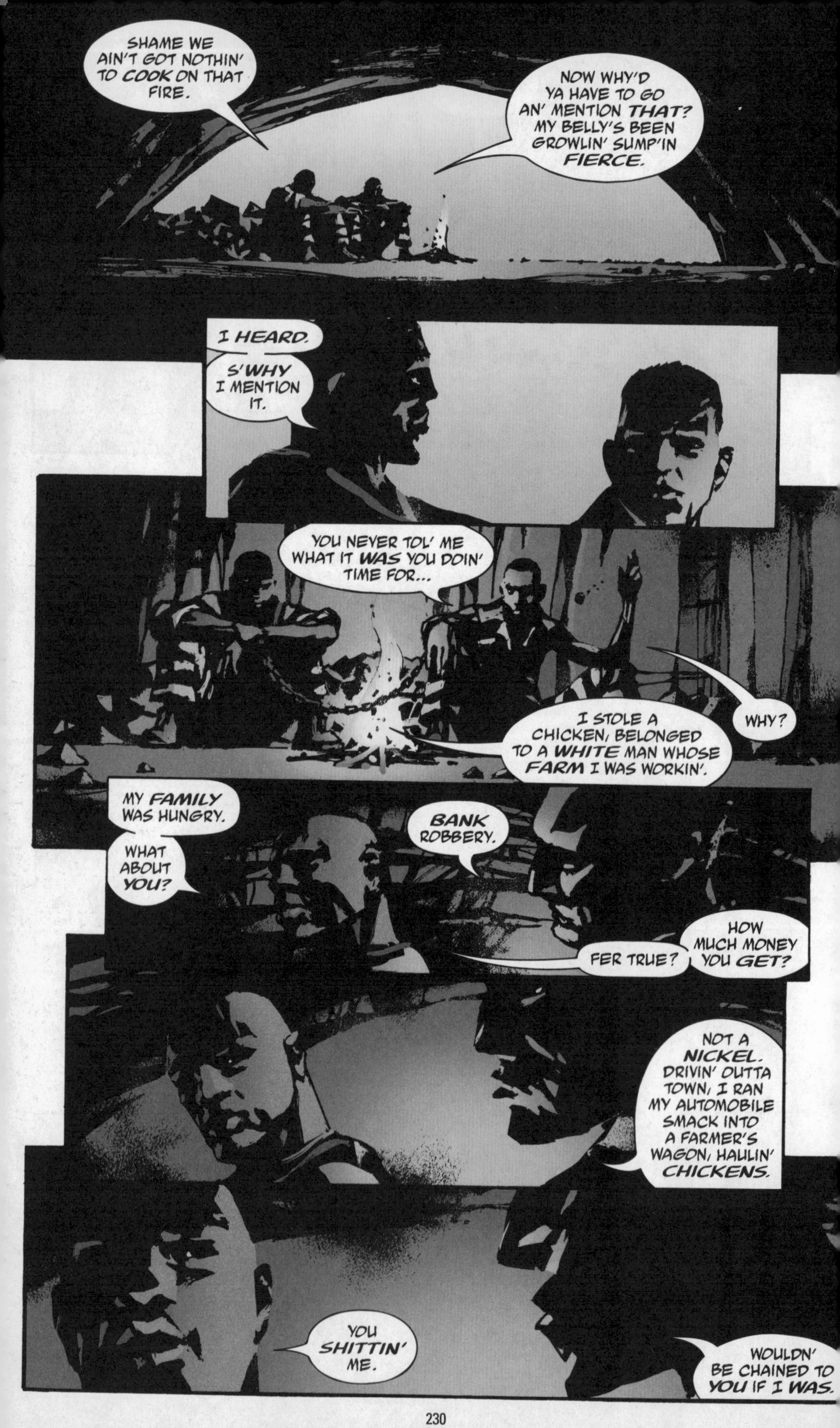
SHAME WE AIN'T GOT NOTHIN' TO COOK ON THAT FIRE.
NOW WHY'D YA HAVE TO GO AN' MENTION THAT? MY BELLY'S BEEN GROWLIN' SUMP'IN FIERCE.
I HEARD.
S'WHY I MENTION IT.
YOU NEVER TOL' ME WHAT IT WAS YOU DOIN' TIME FOR...
I STOLE A CHICKEN, BELONGED TO A WHITE MAN WHOSE FARM I WAS WORKIN'.
WHY?
MY FAMILY WAS HUNGRY.
WHAT ABOUT YOU?
BANK ROBBERY.
FER TRUE?
HOW MUCH MONEY YOU GET?
NOT A NICKEL. DRIVIN' OUTTA TOWN, I RAN MY AUTOMOBILE SMACK INTO A FARMER'S WAGON, HAULIN' CHICKENS.
YOU SHITTIN' ME.
WOULDN' BE CHAINED TO YOU IF I WAS.

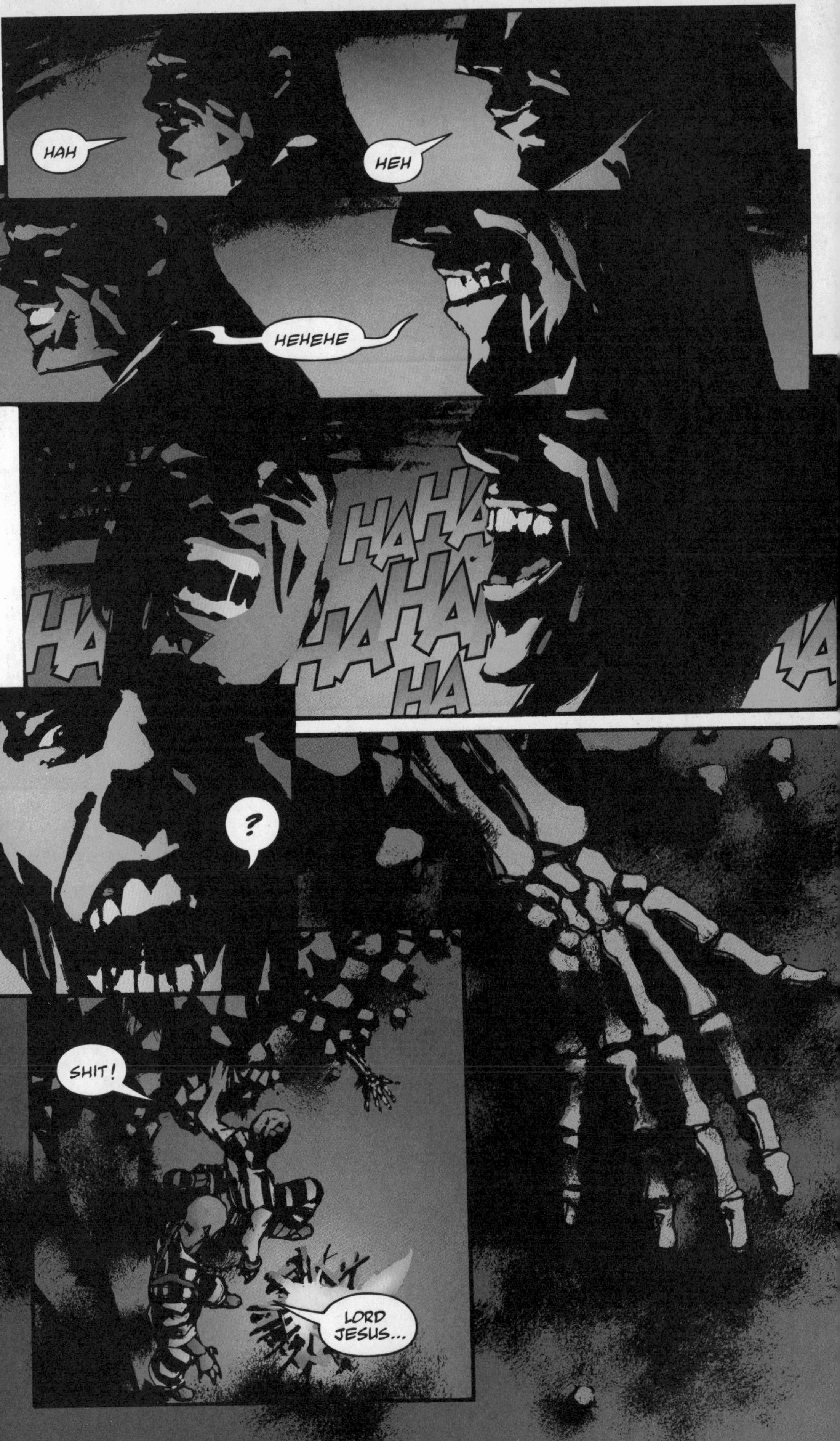
HAH
HEH
HEHEHE
HA
HAHA
HAHA
HAHA
HA
HA
?
SHIT!
LORD JESUS...

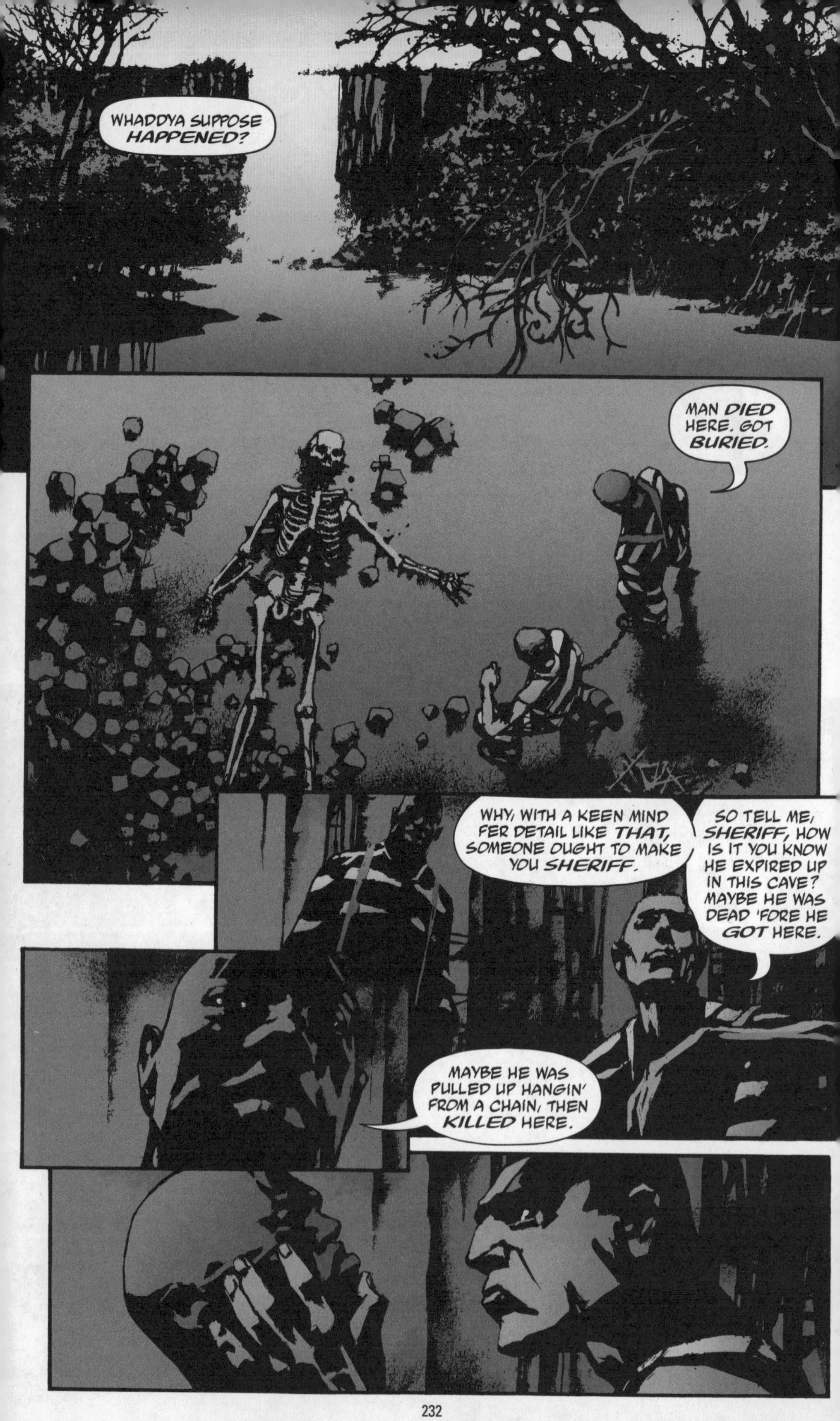
WHADDYA SUPPOSE HAPPENED?
MAN DIED HERE. GOT BURIED.
WHY, WITH A KEEN MIND FER DETAIL LIKE THAT, SOMEONE OUGHT TO MAKE YOU SHERIFF.
SO TELL ME, SHERIFF, HOW IS IT YOU KNOW HE EXPIRED UP IN THIS CAVE? MAYBE HE WAS DEAD 'FORE HE GOT HERE.
MAYBE HE WAS PULLED UP HANGIN' FROM A CHAIN, THEN KILLED HERE.

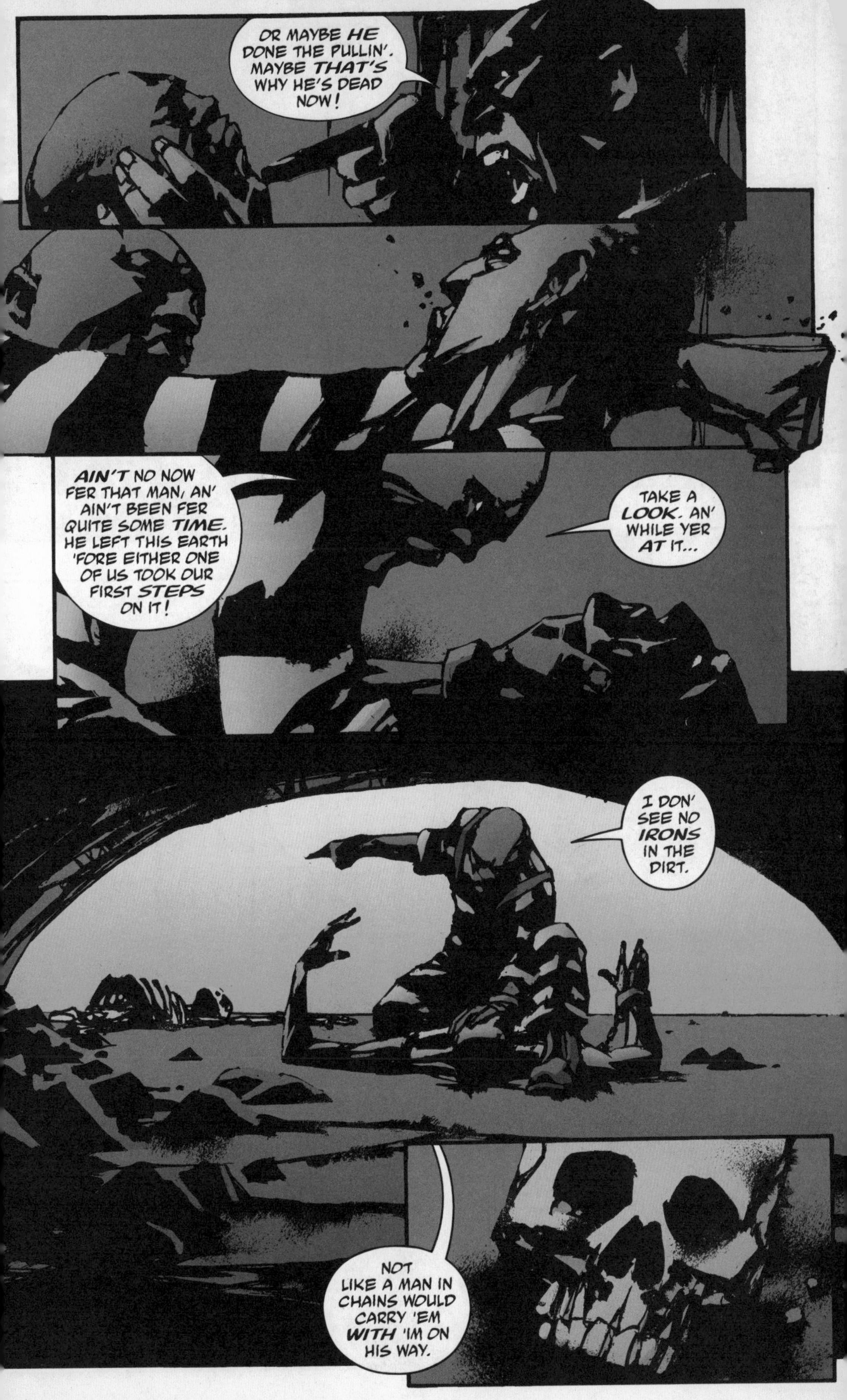
OR MAYBE HE DONE THE PULLIN'. MAYBE THAT'S WHY HE'S DEAD NOW!
AIN'T NO NOW FER THAT MAN, AN' AIN'T BEEN FER QUITE SOME TIME. HE LEFT THIS EARTH 'FORE EITHER ONE OF US TOOK OUR FIRST STEPS ON IT!
TAKE A LOOK. AN' WHILE YER AT IT...
I DON' SEE NO IRONS IN THE DIRT.
NOT LIKE A MAN IN CHAINS WOULD CARRY 'EM WITH 'IM ON HIS WAY.

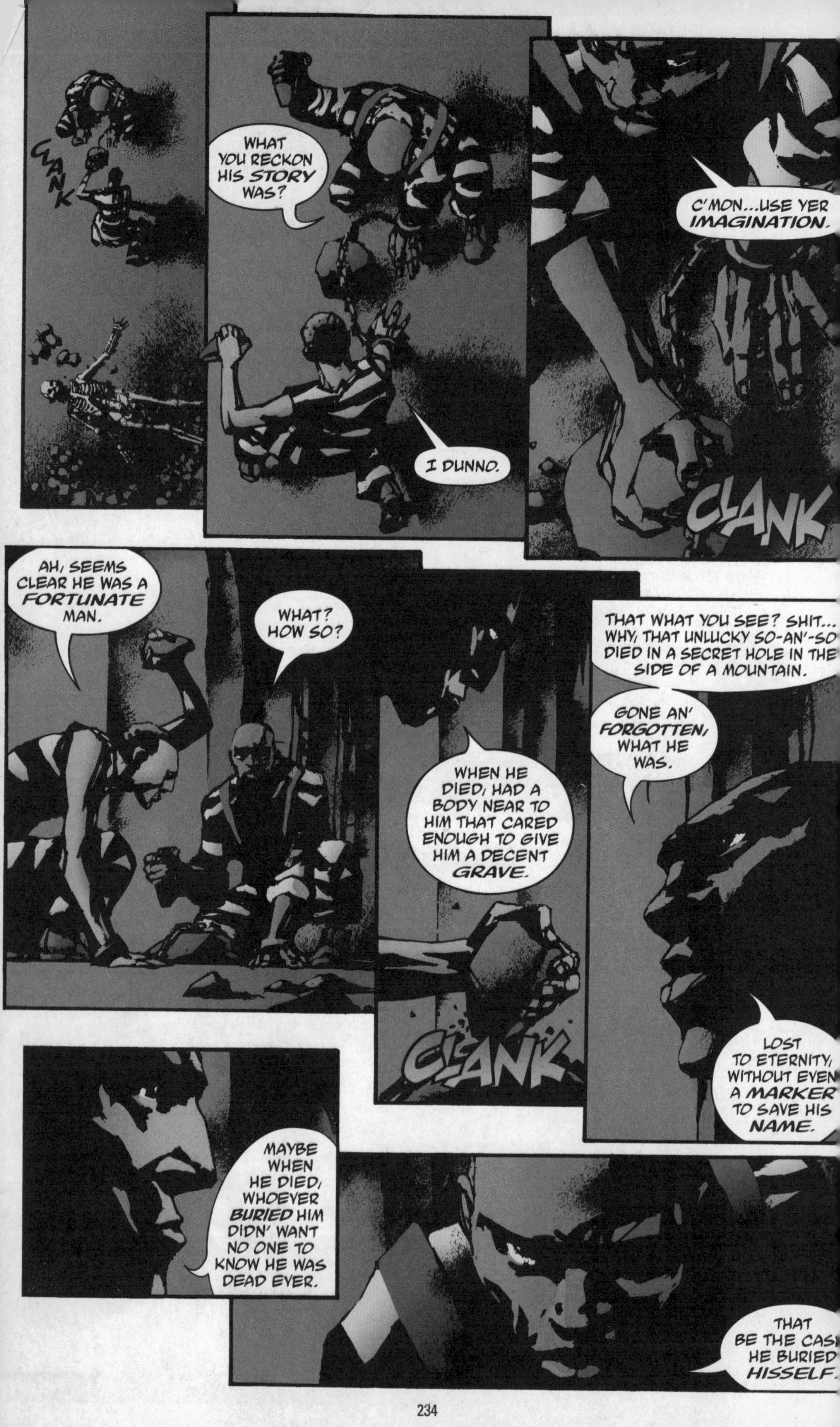
CLANK
WHAT YOU RECKON HIS STORY WAS?
I DUNNO.
C'MON...USE YER IMAGINATION.
CLANK
AH, SEEMS CLEAR HE WAS A FORTUNATE MAN.
WHAT? HOW SO?
WHEN HE DIED, HAD A BODY NEAR TO HIM THAT CARED ENOUGH TO GIVE HIM A DECENT GRAVE.
CLANK
THAT WHAT YOU SEE? SHIT... WHY, THAT UNLUCKY SO-AN'-SO DIED IN A SECRET HOLE IN THE SIDE OF A MOUNTAIN.
GONE AN' FORGOTTEN, WHAT HE WAS.
LOST TO ETERNITY, WITHOUT EVEN A MARKER TO SAVE HIS NAME.
MAYBE WHEN HE DIED, WHOEVER BURIED HIM DIDN' WANT NO ONE TO KNOW HE WAS DEAD EVER.
THAT BE THE CAS HE BURIED HISSELF.

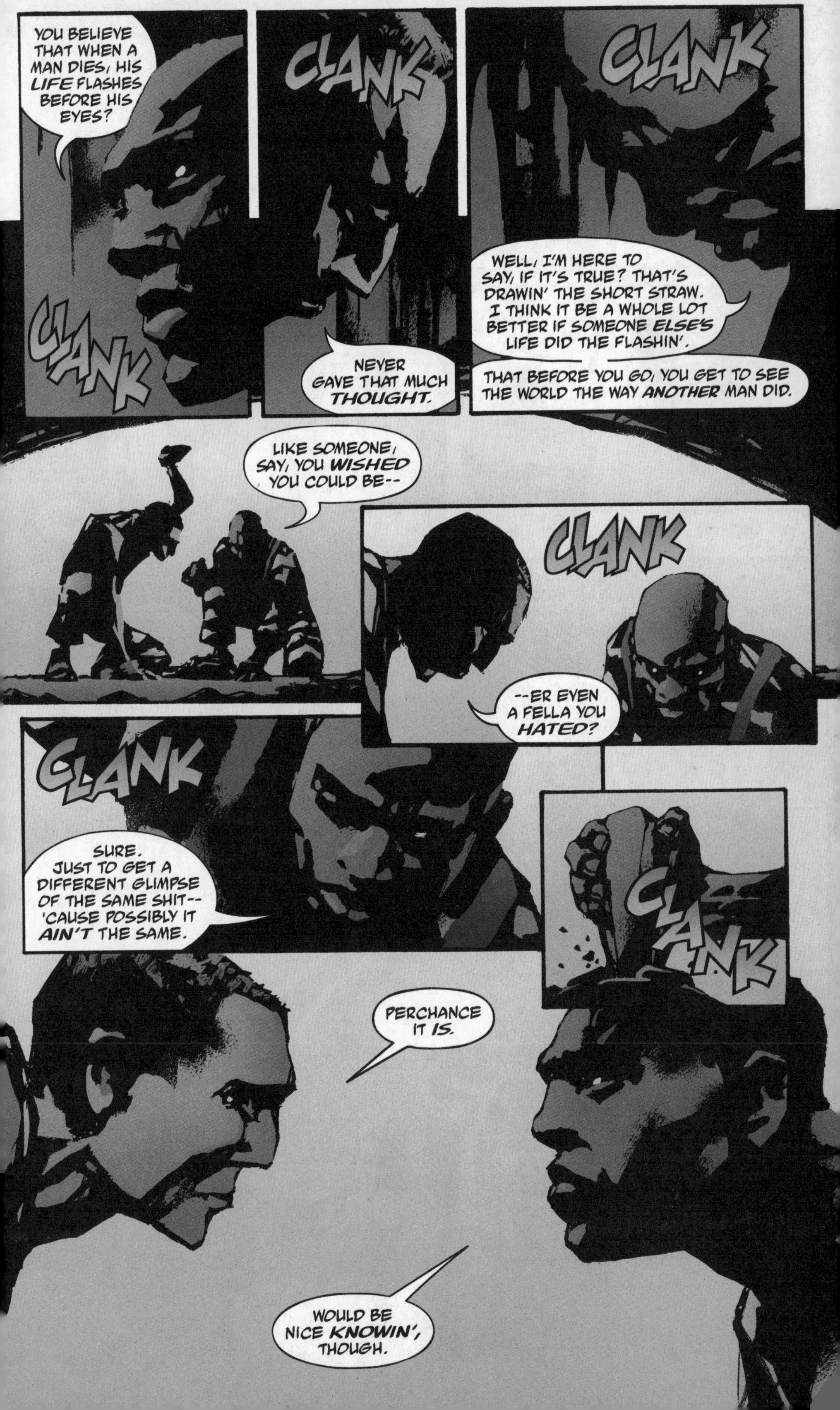
YOU BELIEVE THAT WHEN A MAN DIES, HIS *LIFE* FLASHES BEFORE HIS EYES?
CLANK
CLANK
NEVER GAVE THAT MUCH *THOUGHT*.
CLANK
WELL, I'M HERE TO SAY, IF IT'S TRUE? THAT'S DRAWIN' THE SHORT STRAW. I THINK IT BE A WHOLE LOT BETTER IF SOMEONE *ELSE'S* LIFE DID THE FLASHIN'.
THAT BEFORE YOU GO, YOU GET TO SEE THE WORLD THE WAY *ANOTHER* MAN DID.
LIKE SOMEONE, SAY, YOU *WISHED* YOU COULD BE--
CLANK
--ER EVEN A FELLA YOU *HATED*?
CLANK
SURE. JUST TO GET A DIFFERENT GLIMPSE OF THE SAME SHIT-- 'CAUSE POSSIBLY IT *AIN'T* THE SAME.
CLANK
PERCHANCE IT *IS*.
WOULD BE NICE *KNOWIN'*, THOUGH.

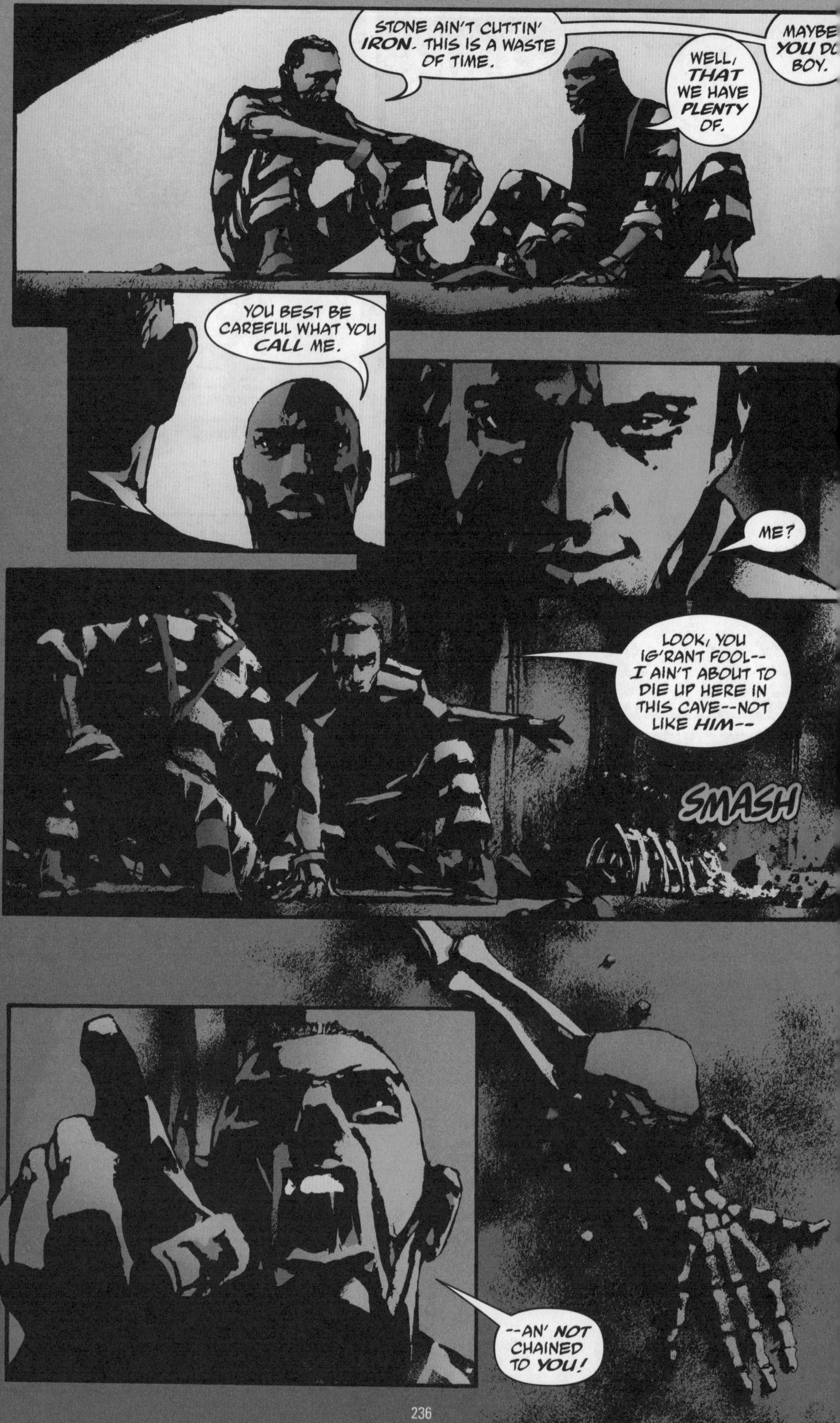

STONE AIN'T CUTTIN' IRON. THIS IS A WASTE OF TIME.
WELL, THAT WE HAVE PLENTY OF.
YOU BEST BE CAREFUL WHAT YOU CALL ME.
ME?
LOOK, YOU IG'RANT FOOL-- I AIN'T ABOUT TO DIE UP HERE IN THIS CAVE--NOT LIKE HIM--
SMASH
--AN' NOT CHAINED TO YOU!

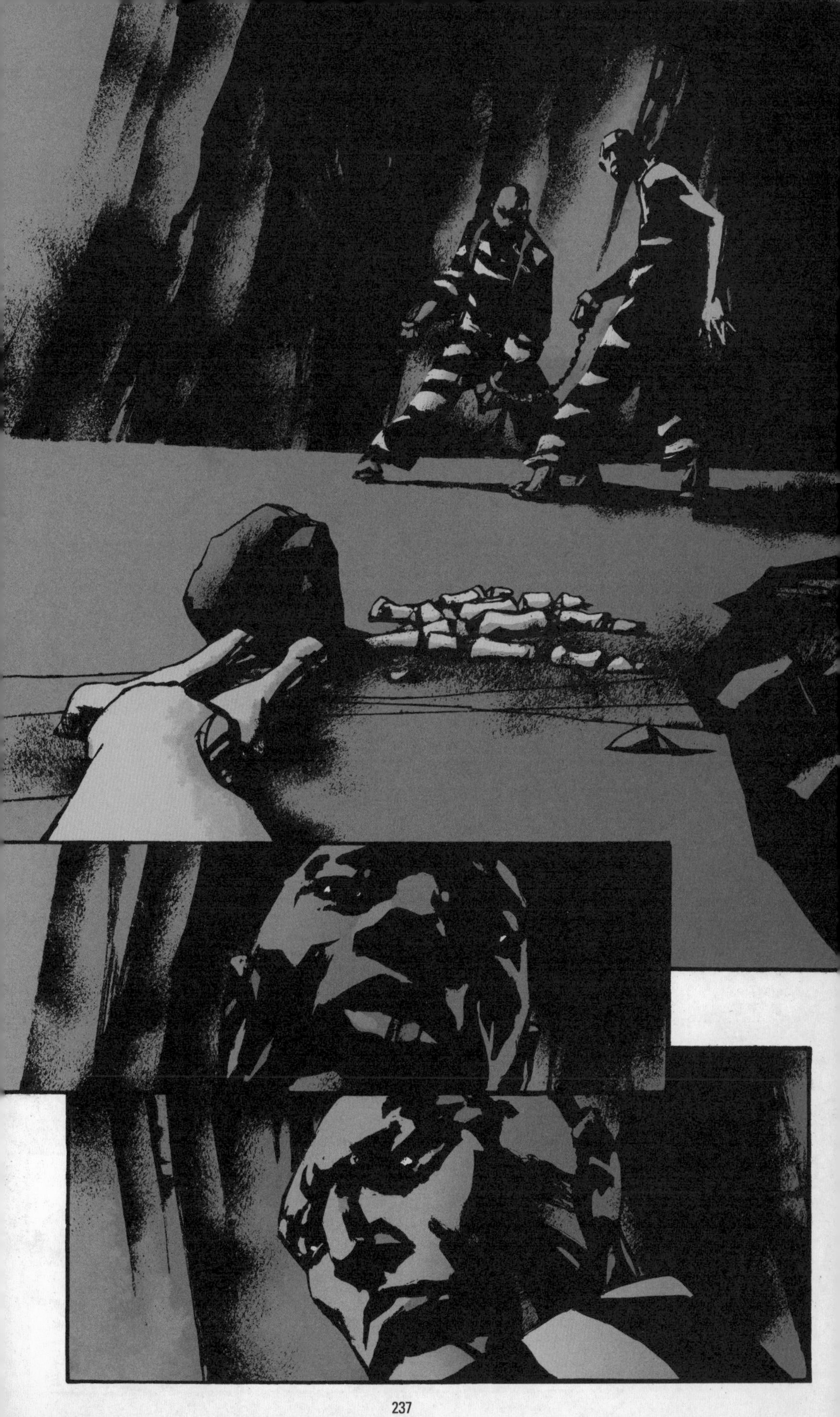

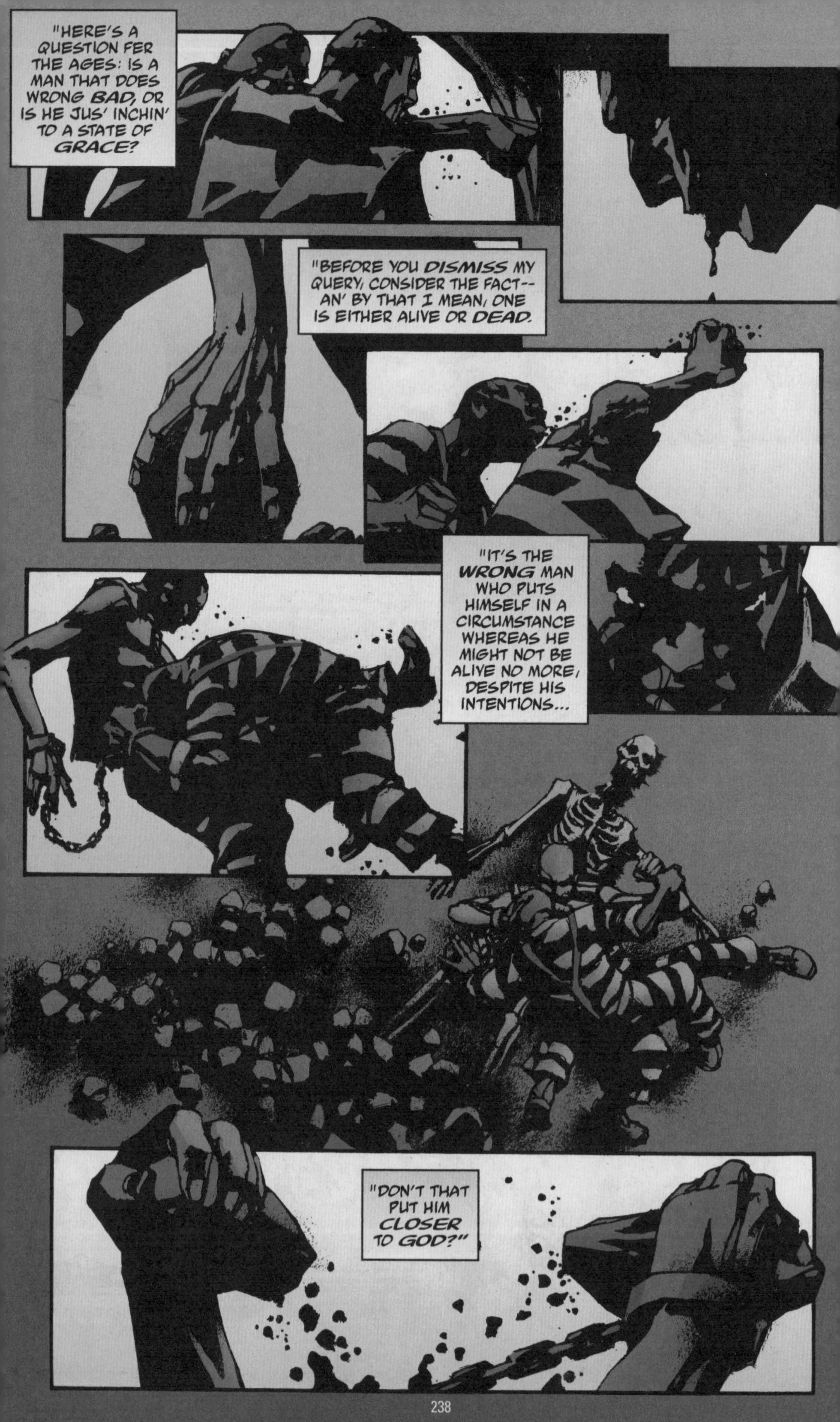
"HERE'S A QUESTION FER THE AGES: IS A MAN THAT DOES WRONG BAD, OR IS HE JUS' INCHIN' TO A STATE OF GRACE?
"BEFORE YOU DISMISS MY QUERY, CONSIDER THE FACT-- AN' BY THAT I MEAN, ONE IS EITHER ALIVE OR DEAD.
"IT'S THE WRONG MAN WHO PUTS HIMSELF IN A CIRCUMSTANCE WHEREAS HE MIGHT NOT BE ALIVE NO MORE, DESPITE HIS INTENTIONS...
"DON'T THAT PUT HIM CLOSER TO GOD?"

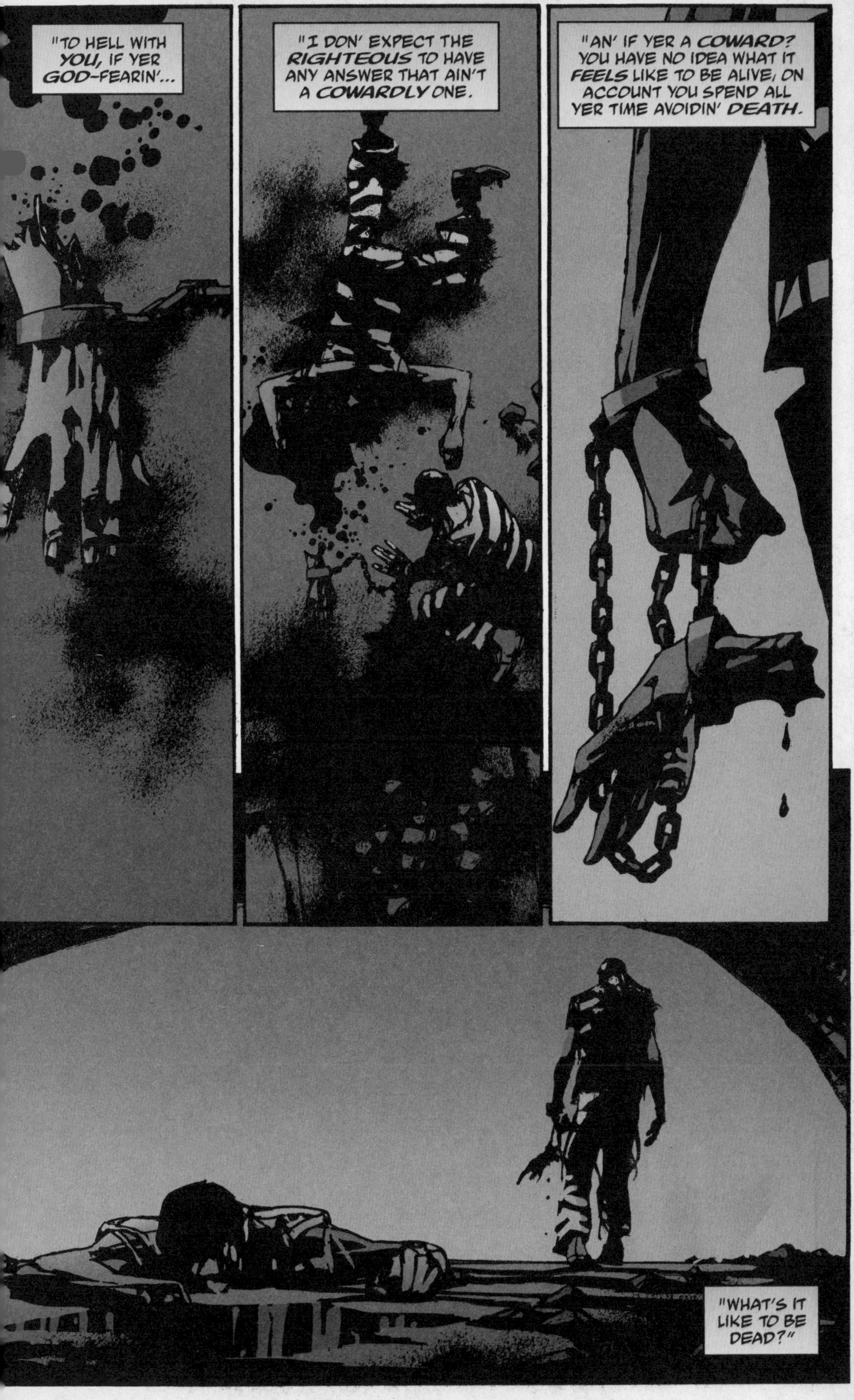
"TO HELL WITH YOU, IF YER GOD-FEARIN'...
"I DON' EXPECT THE RIGHTEOUS TO HAVE ANY ANSWER THAT AIN'T A COWARDLY ONE.
"AN' IF YER A COWARD? YOU HAVE NO IDEA WHAT IT FEELS LIKE TO BE ALIVE, ON ACCOUNT YOU SPEND ALL YER TIME AVOIDIN' DEATH.
"WHAT'S IT LIKE TO BE DEAD?"

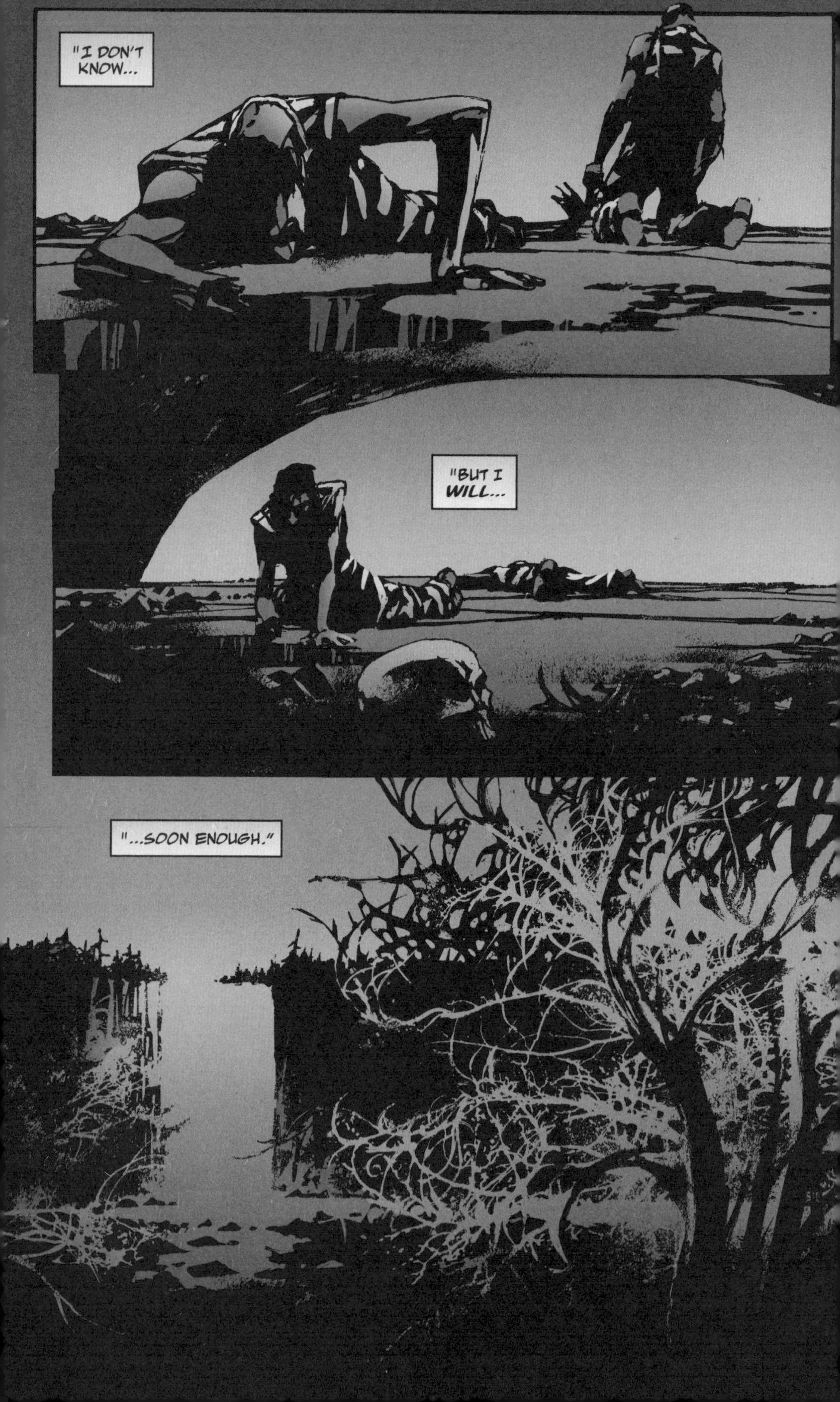
"I DON'T KNOW...
"BUT I WILL...
"...SOON ENOUGH."

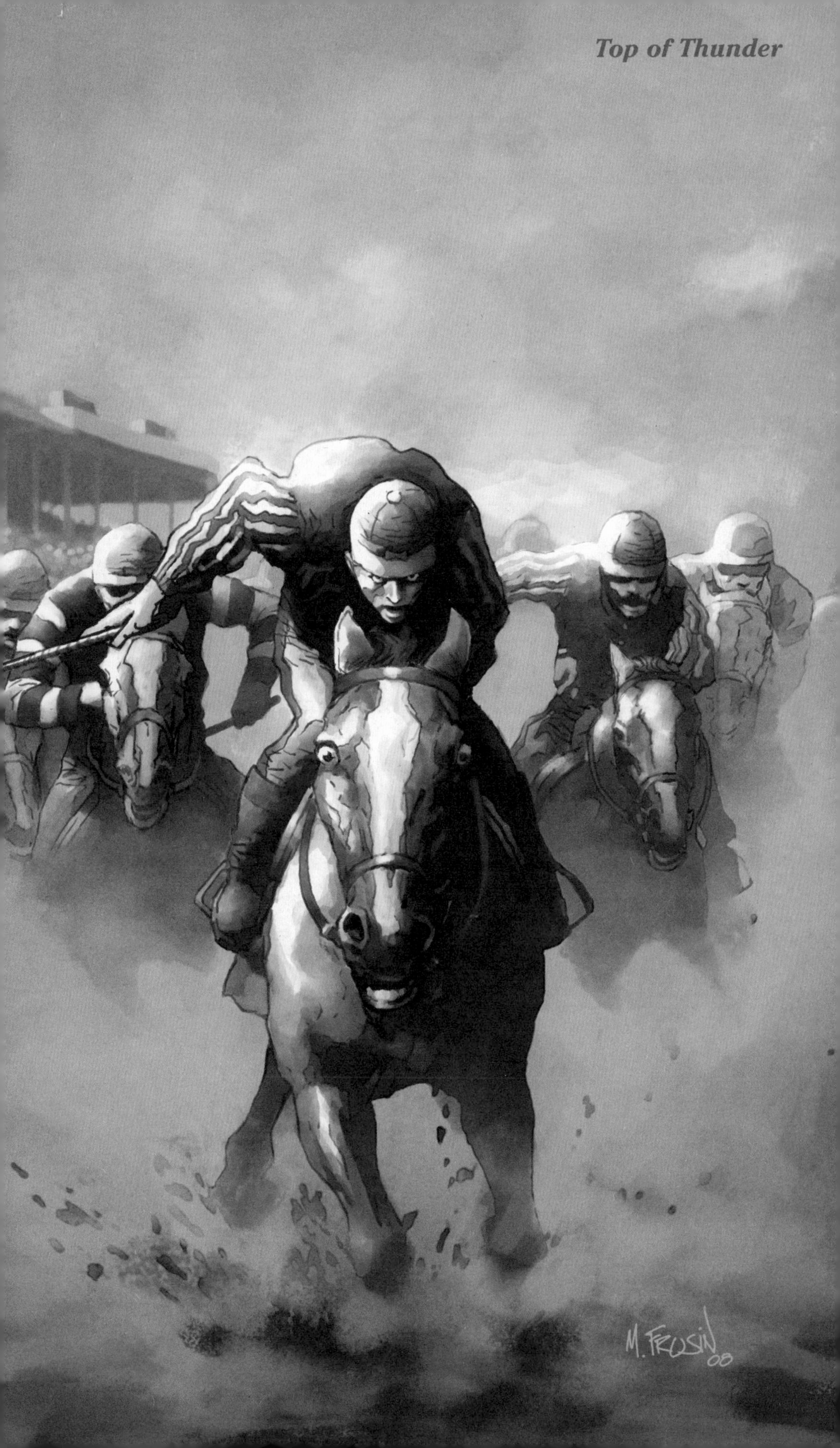
Top of Thunder
M. FROSIN 08

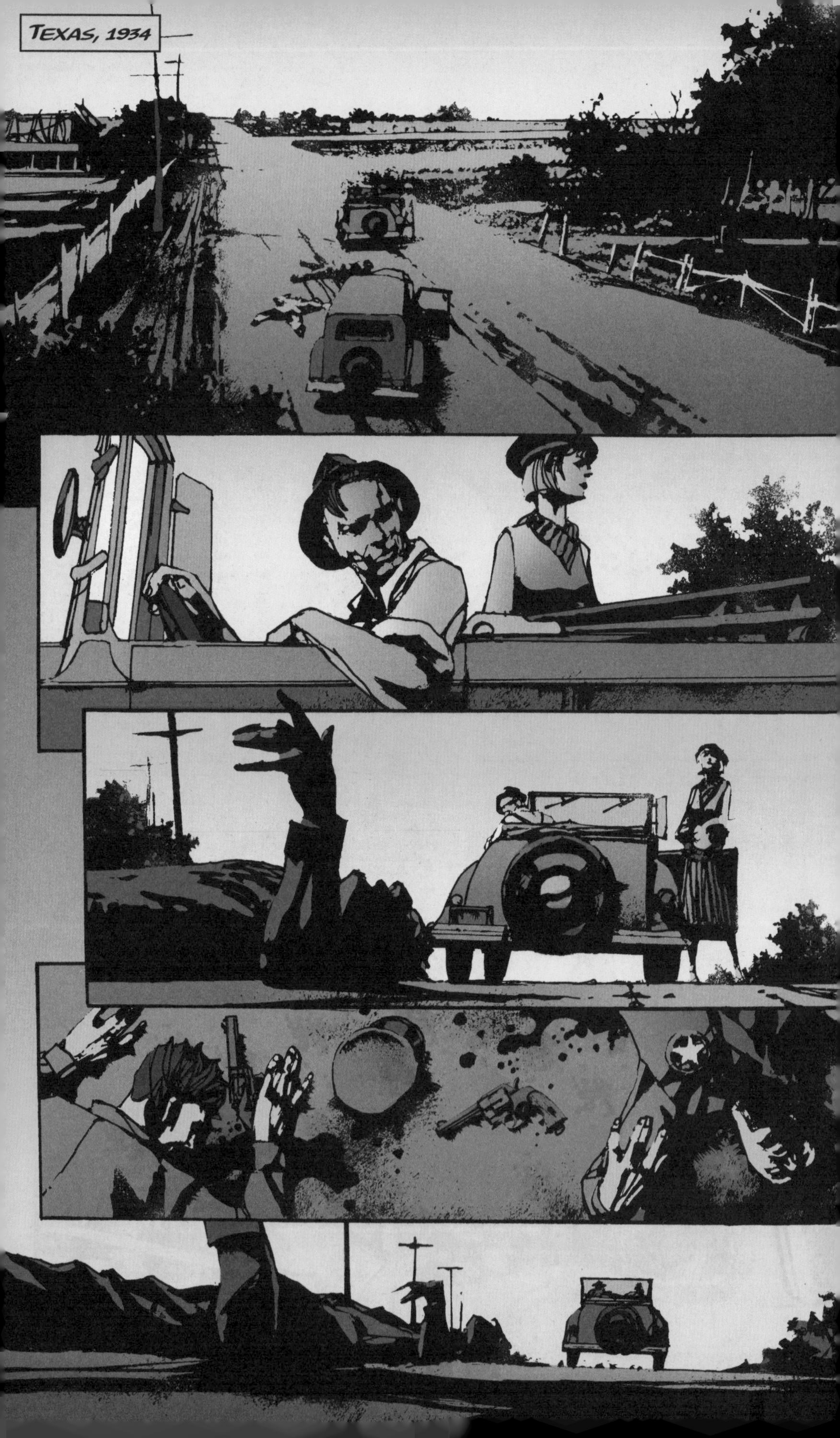
TEXAS, 1934

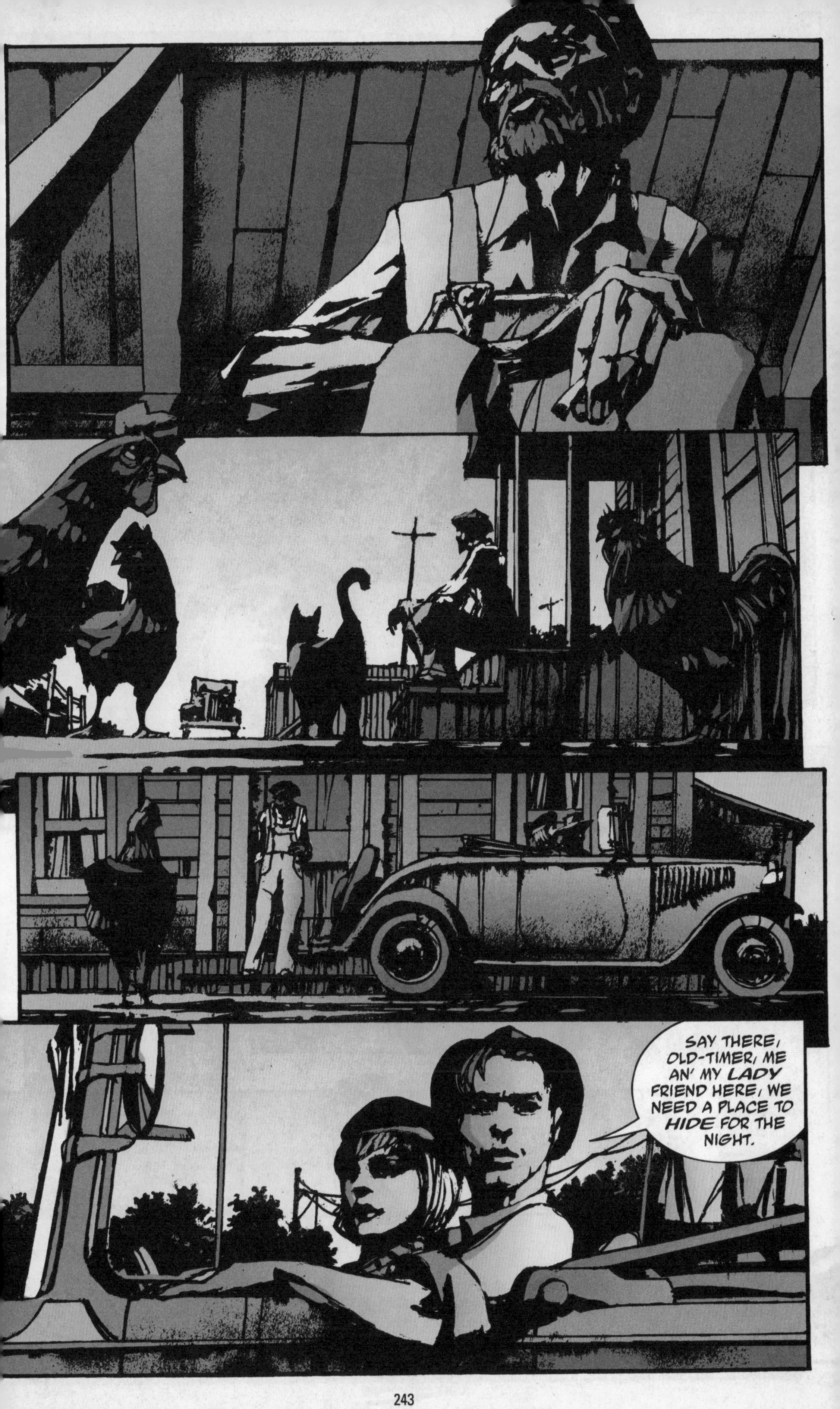
SAY THERE, OLD-TIMER, ME AN' MY LADY FRIEND HERE, WE NEED A PLACE TO HIDE FOR THE NIGHT.

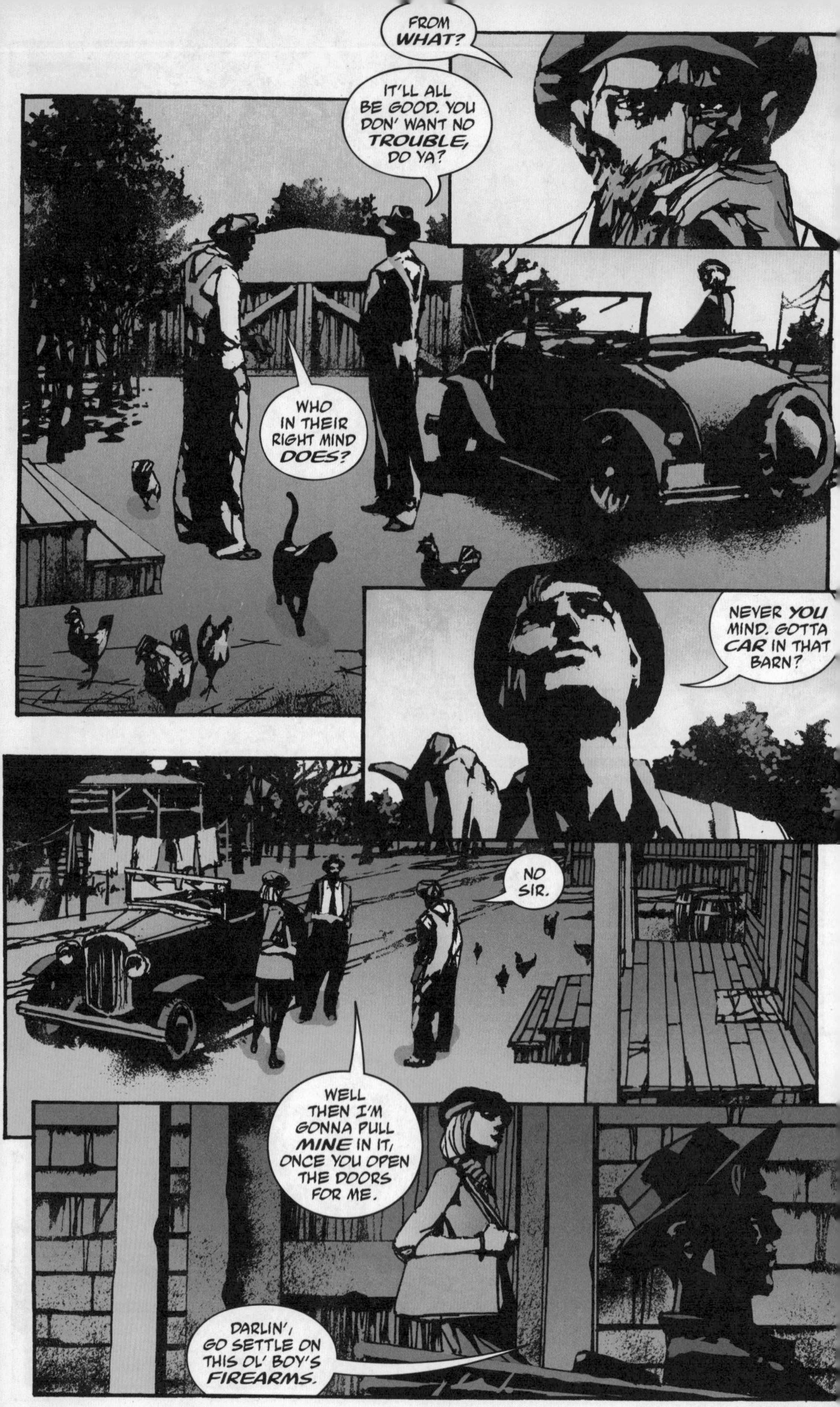
FROM WHAT?
IT'LL ALL BE GOOD. YOU DON' WANT NO TROUBLE, DO YA?
WHO IN THEIR RIGHT MIND DOES?
NEVER YOU MIND. GOTTA CAR IN THAT BARN?
NO SIR.
WELL THEN I'M GONNA PULL MINE IN IT, ONCE YOU OPEN THE DOORS FOR ME.
DARLIN', GO SETTLE ON THIS OL' BOY'S FIREARMS.

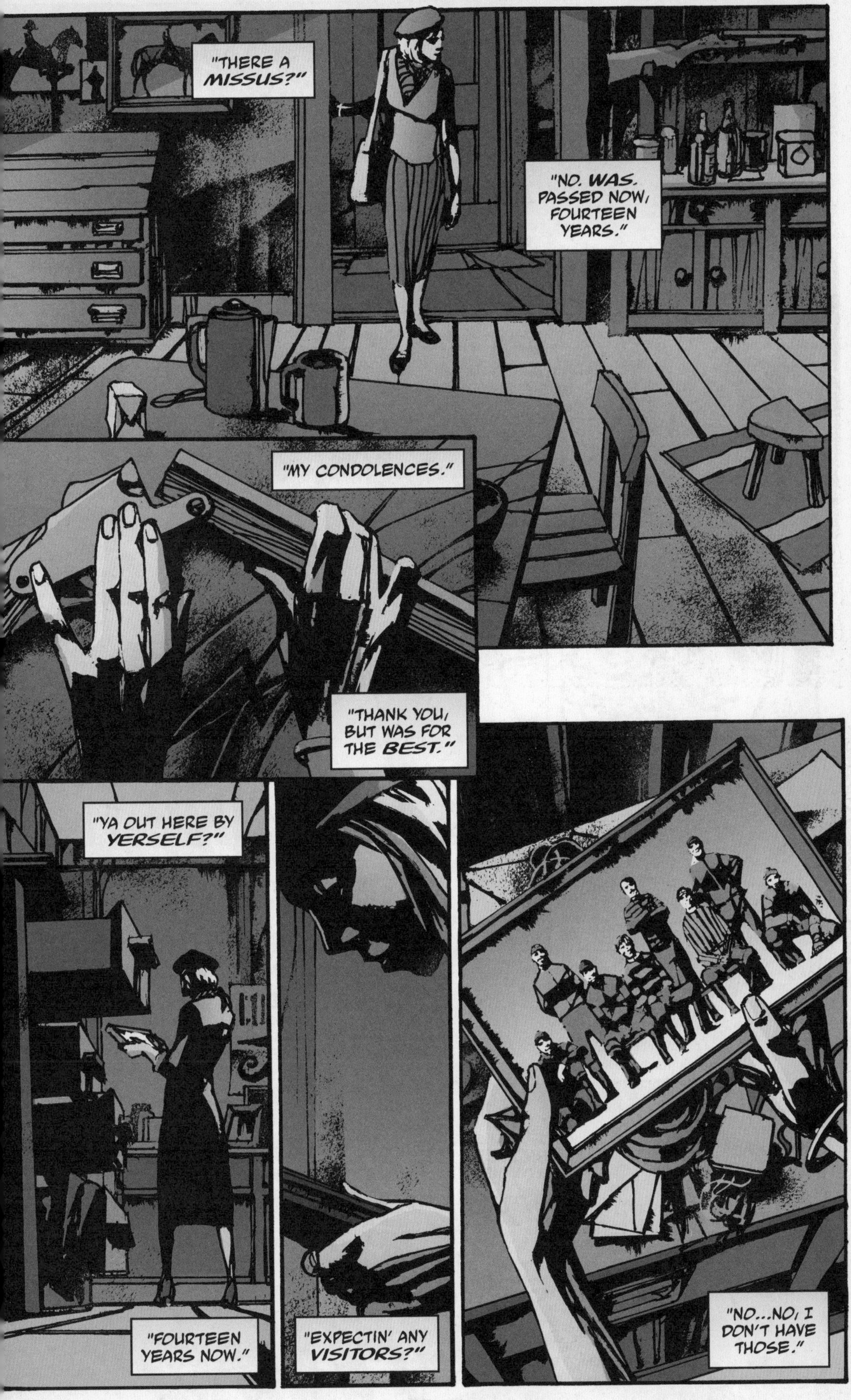
"THERE A MISSUS?"
"NO. WAS. PASSED NOW, FOURTEEN YEARS."
"MY CONDOLENCES."
"THANK YOU, BUT WAS FOR THE BEST."
"YA OUT HERE BY YERSELF?"
"FOURTEEN YEARS NOW."
"EXPECTIN' ANY VISITORS?"
"NO...NO, I DON'T HAVE THOSE."

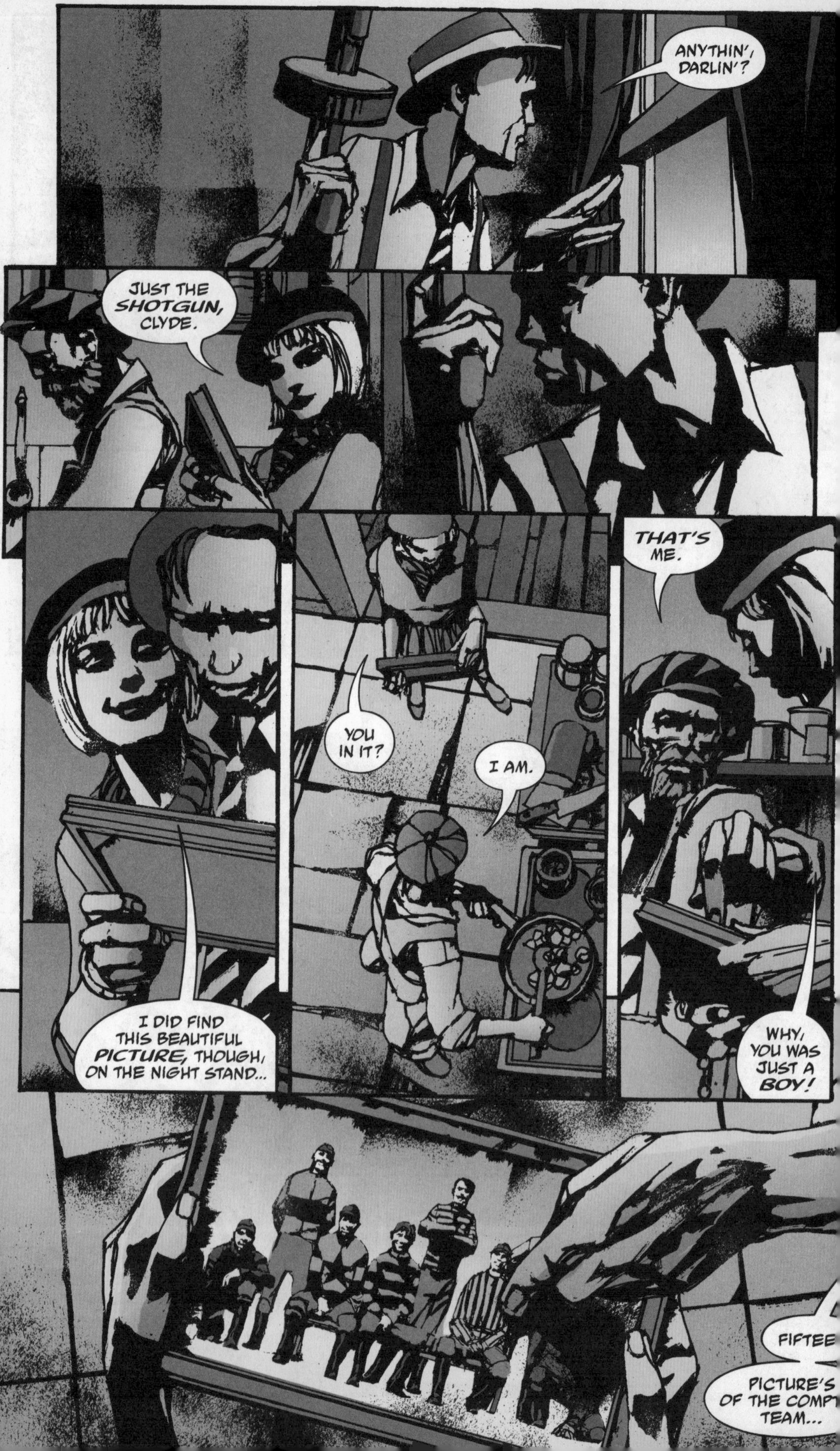
ANYTHIN', DARLIN'?
JUST THE SHOTGUN, CLYDE.
I DID FIND THIS BEAUTIFUL PICTURE, THOUGH, ON THE NIGHT STAND...
YOU IN IT?
I AM.
THAT'S ME.
WHY, YOU WAS JUST A BOY!
FIFTEE
PICTURE'S OF THE COMP TEAM...

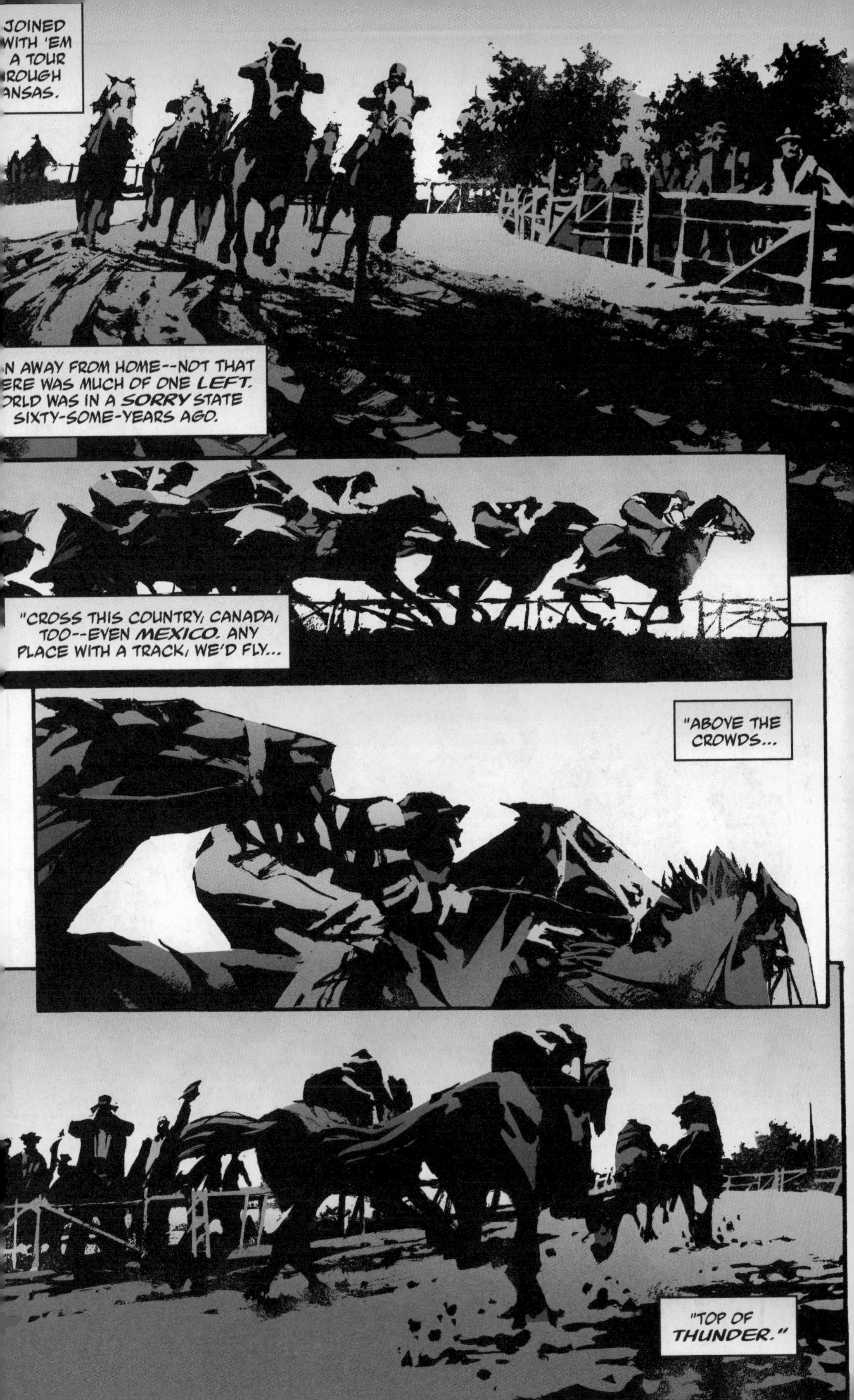
JOINED WITH 'EM A TOUR ROUGH ANSAS.
N AWAY FROM HOME--NOT THAT ERE WAS MUCH OF ONE LEFT. ORLD WAS IN A SORRY STATE SIXTY-SOME-YEARS AGO.
"CROSS THIS COUNTRY, CANADA, TOO--EVEN MEXICO. ANY PLACE WITH A TRACK, WE'D FLY...
"ABOVE THE CROWDS...
"TOP OF THUNDER."

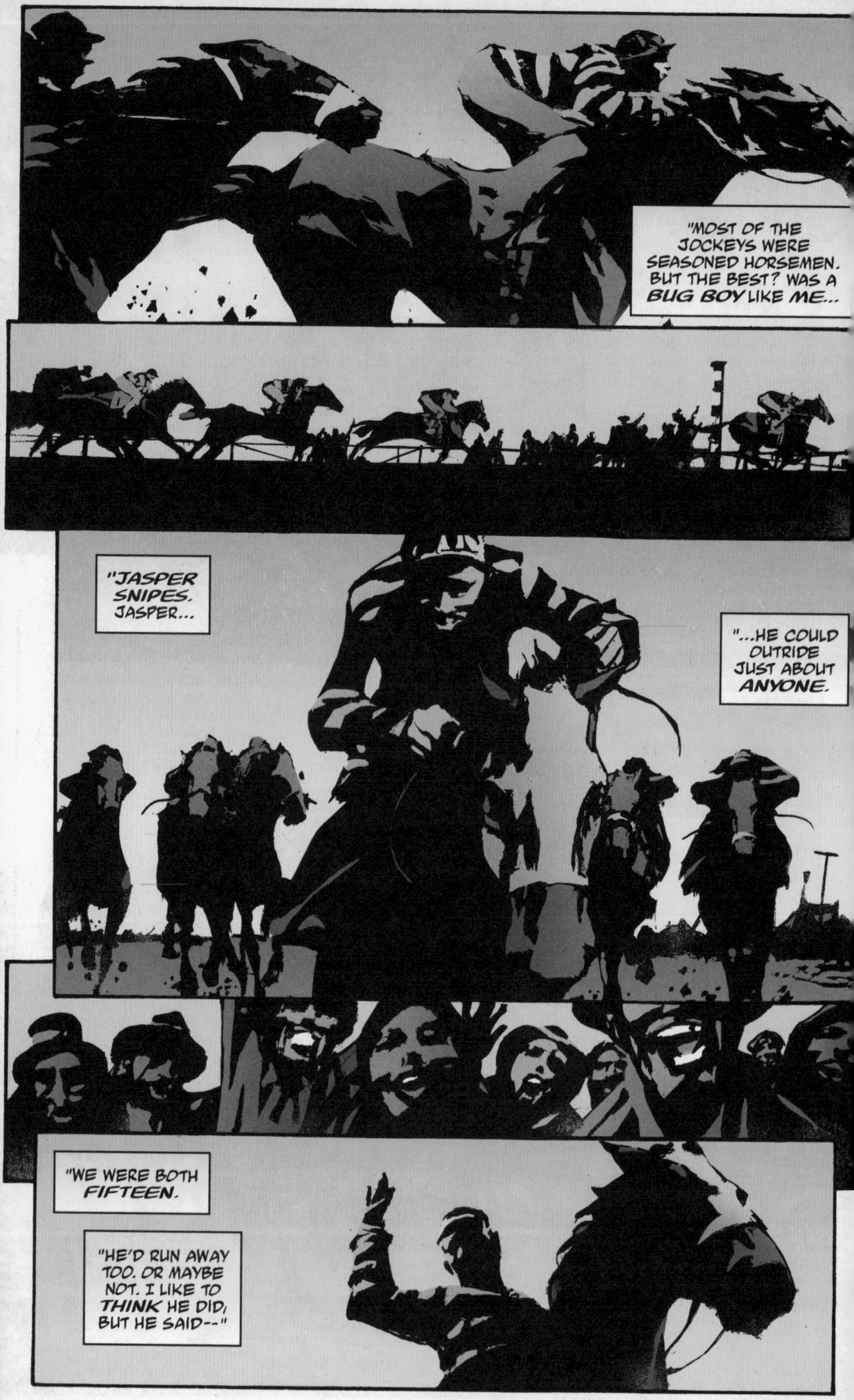
"MOST OF THE JOCKEYS WERE SEASONED HORSEMEN. BUT THE BEST? WAS A BUG BOY LIKE ME...
"JASPER SNIPES. JASPER...
"...HE COULD OUTRIDE JUST ABOUT ANYONE.
"WE WERE BOTH FIFTEEN.
"HE'D RUN AWAY TOO. OR MAYBE NOT. I LIKE TO THINK HE DID, BUT HE SAID--"

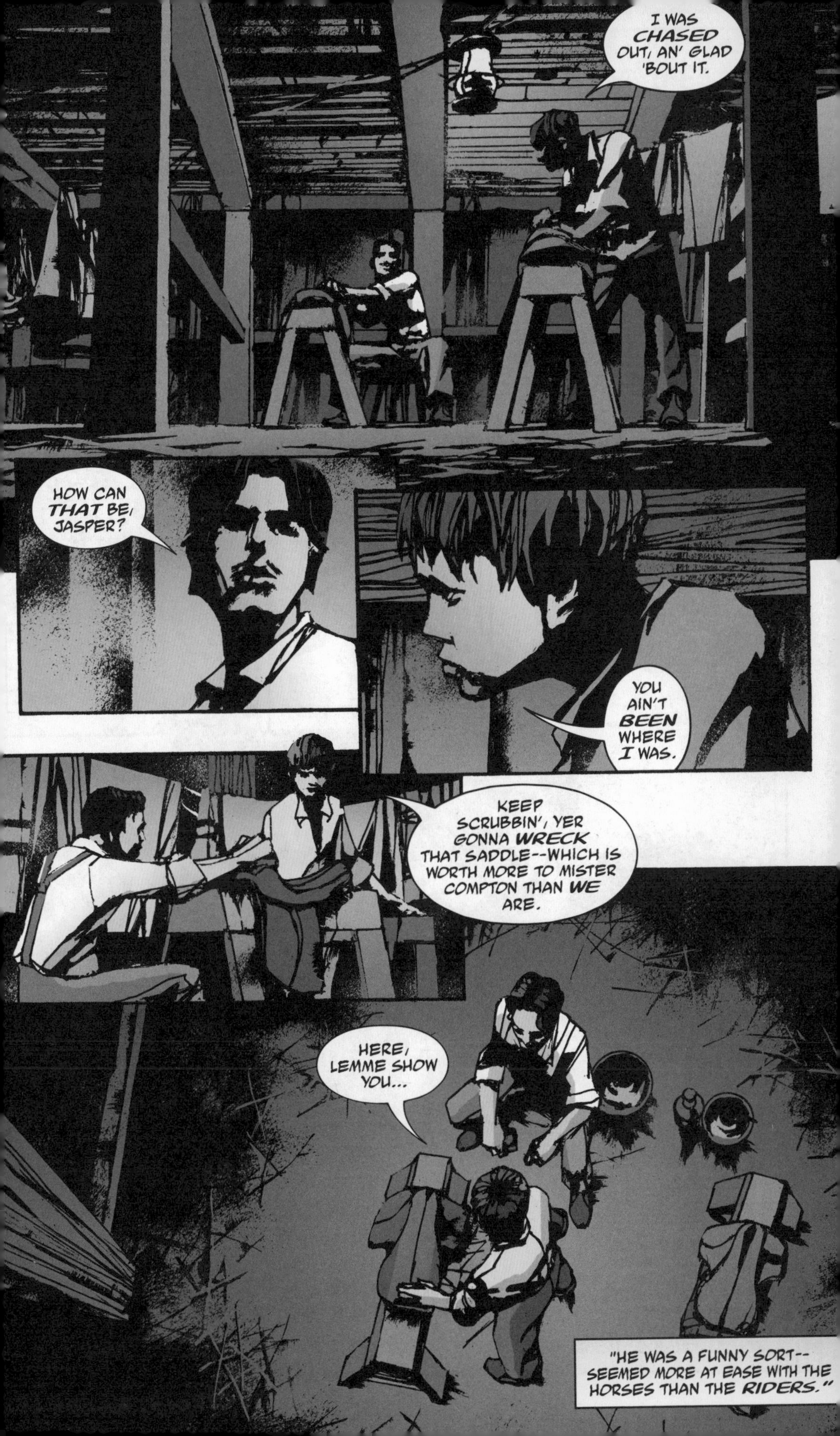
I WAS CHASED OUT, AN' GLAD 'BOUT IT.
HOW CAN THAT BE, JASPER?
YOU AIN'T BEEN WHERE I WAS.
KEEP SCRUBBIN', YER GONNA WRECK THAT SADDLE--WHICH IS WORTH MORE TO MISTER COMPTON THAN WE ARE.
HERE, LEMME SHOW YOU...
"HE WAS A FUNNY SORT--SEEMED MORE AT EASE WITH THE HORSES THAN THE RIDERS."

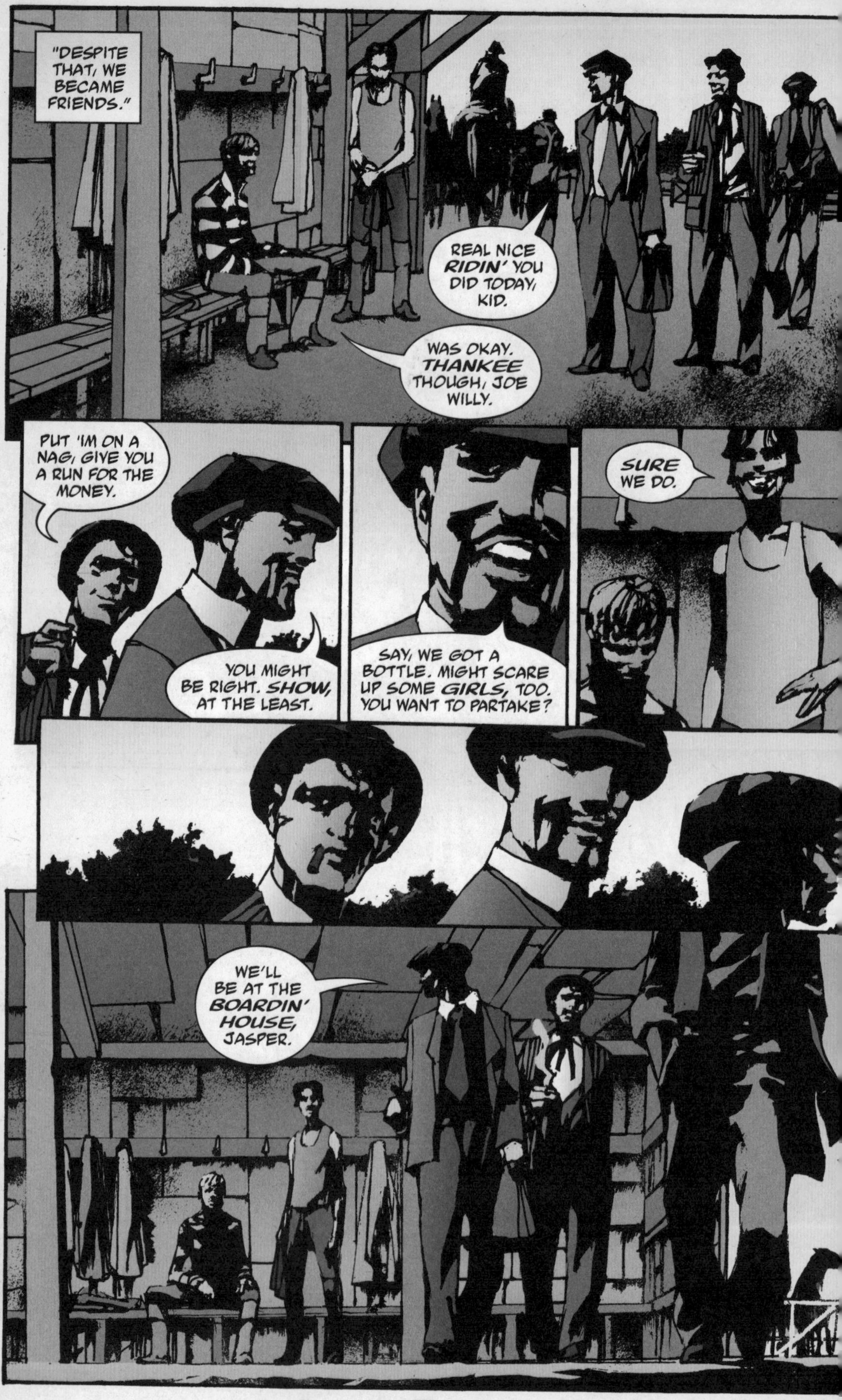
"DESPITE THAT, WE BECAME FRIENDS."
REAL NICE *RIDIN'* YOU DID TODAY, KID.
WAS OKAY. *THANKEE* THOUGH, JOE WILLY.
PUT 'IM ON A NAG, GIVE YOU A RUN FOR THE MONEY.
YOU MIGHT BE RIGHT. *SHOW,* AT THE LEAST.
SAY, WE GOT A BOTTLE. MIGHT SCARE UP SOME *GIRLS,* TOO. YOU WANT TO PARTAKE?
SURE WE DO.
WE'LL BE AT THE *BOARDIN' HOUSE,* JASPER.

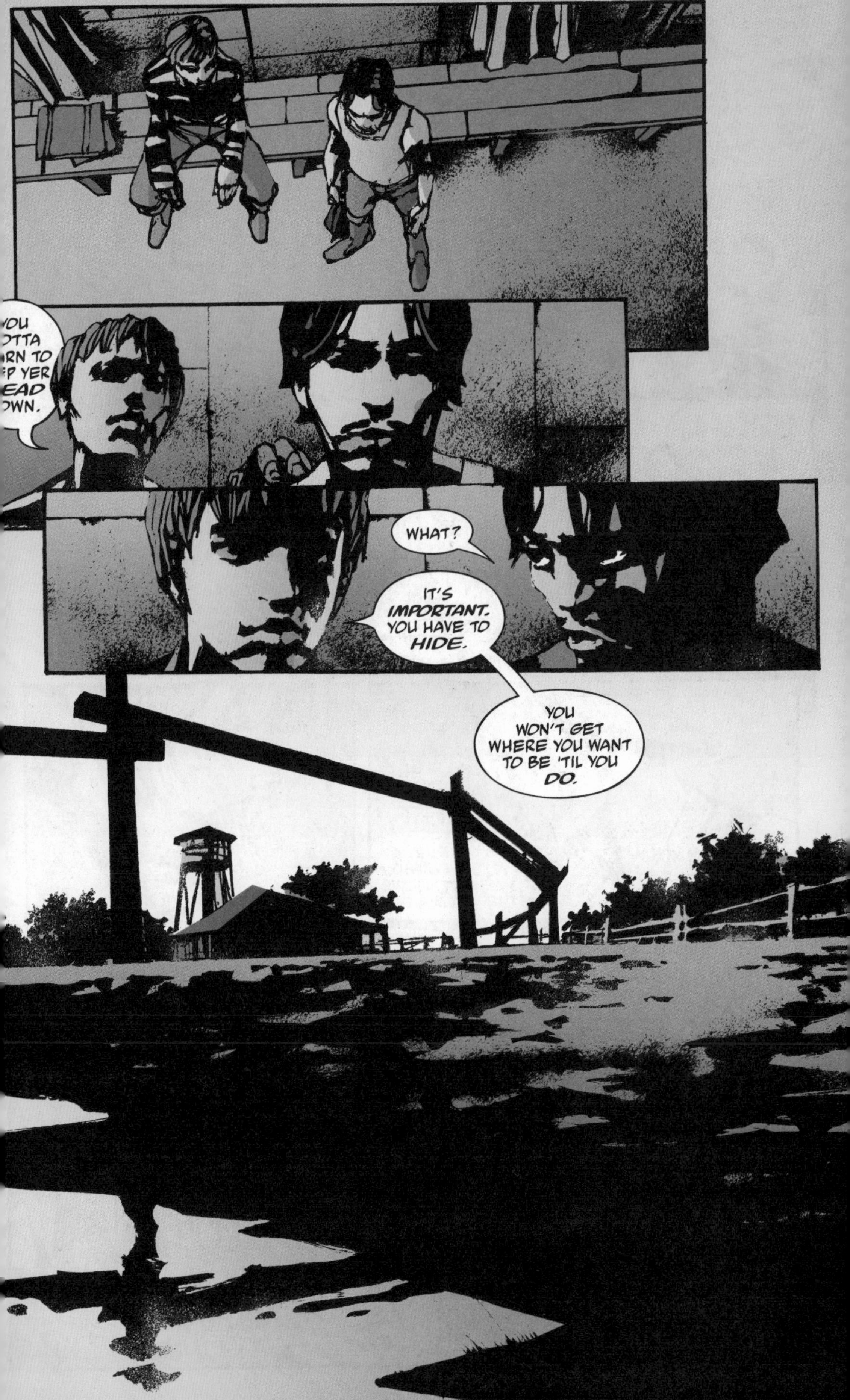
YOU OTTA RN TO EP YER EAD OWN.
WHAT?
IT'S IMPORTANT. YOU HAVE TO HIDE.
YOU WON'T GET WHERE YOU WANT TO BE 'TIL YOU DO.

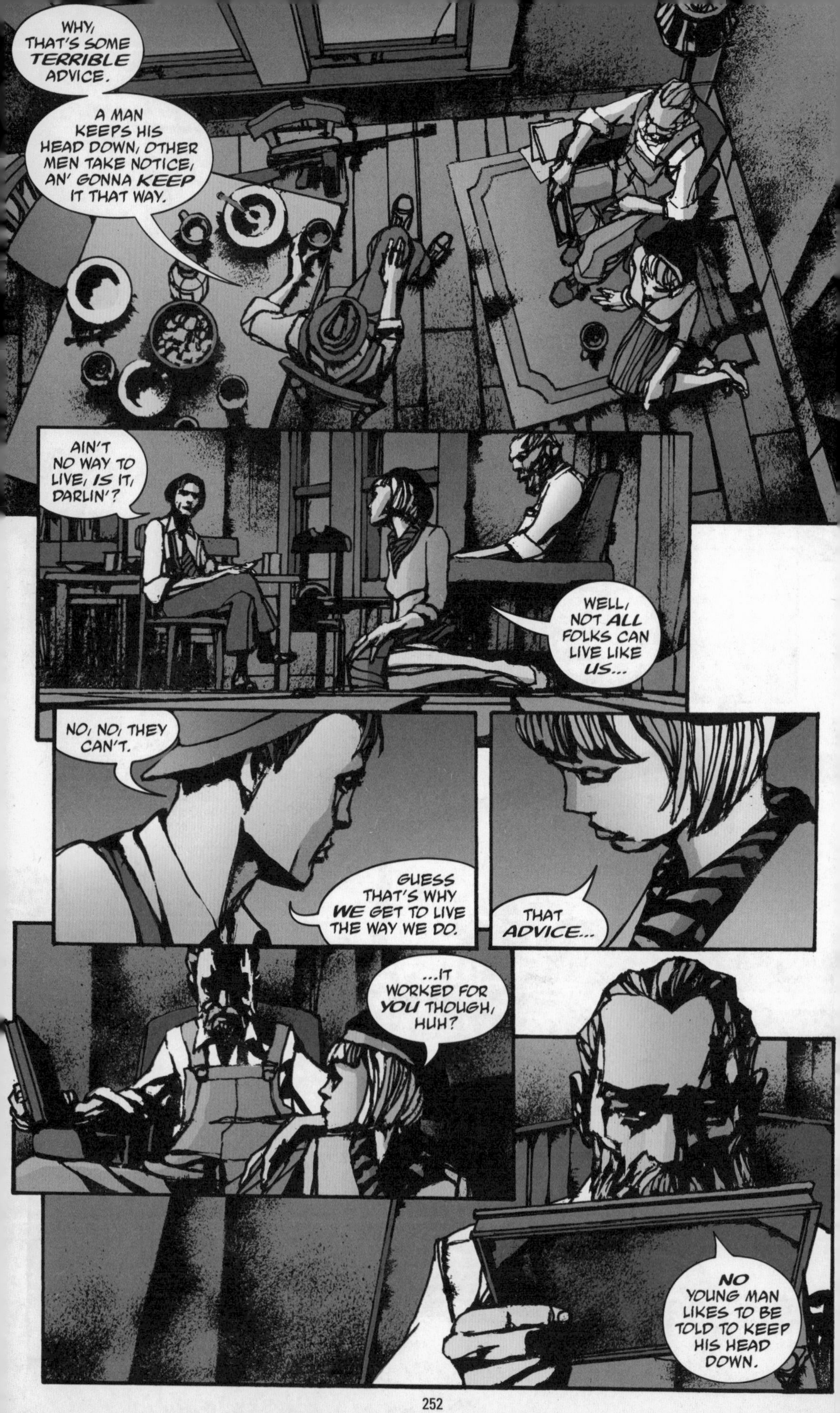
WHY, THAT'S SOME TERRIBLE ADVICE.
A MAN KEEPS HIS HEAD DOWN, OTHER MEN TAKE NOTICE, AN' GONNA KEEP IT THAT WAY.
AIN'T NO WAY TO LIVE, IS IT, DARLIN'?
WELL, NOT ALL FOLKS CAN LIVE LIKE US...
NO, NO, THEY CAN'T.
GUESS THAT'S WHY WE GET TO LIVE THE WAY WE DO.
THAT ADVICE...
...IT WORKED FOR YOU THOUGH, HUH?
NO YOUNG MAN LIKES TO BE TOLD TO KEEP HIS HEAD DOWN.

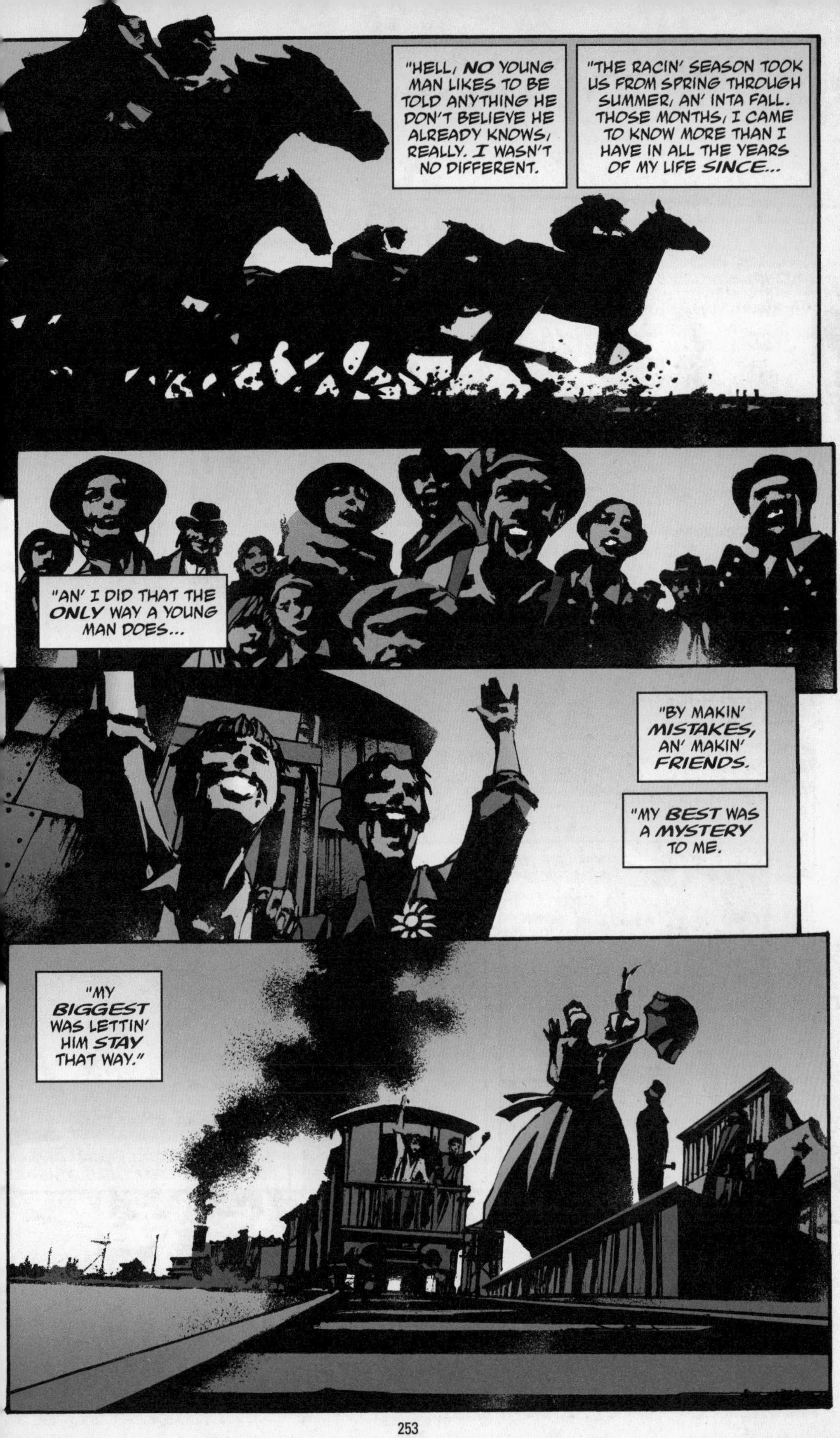
"HELL, NO YOUNG MAN LIKES TO BE TOLD ANYTHING HE DON'T BELIEVE HE ALREADY KNOWS, REALLY. I WASN'T NO DIFFERENT.
"THE RACIN' SEASON TOOK US FROM SPRING THROUGH SUMMER, AN' INTA FALL. THOSE MONTHS, I CAME TO KNOW MORE THAN I HAVE IN ALL THE YEARS OF MY LIFE SINCE...
"AN' I DID THAT THE ONLY WAY A YOUNG MAN DOES...
"BY MAKIN' MISTAKES, AN' MAKIN' FRIENDS.
"MY BEST WAS A MYSTERY TO ME.
"MY BIGGEST WAS LETTIN' HIM STAY THAT WAY."

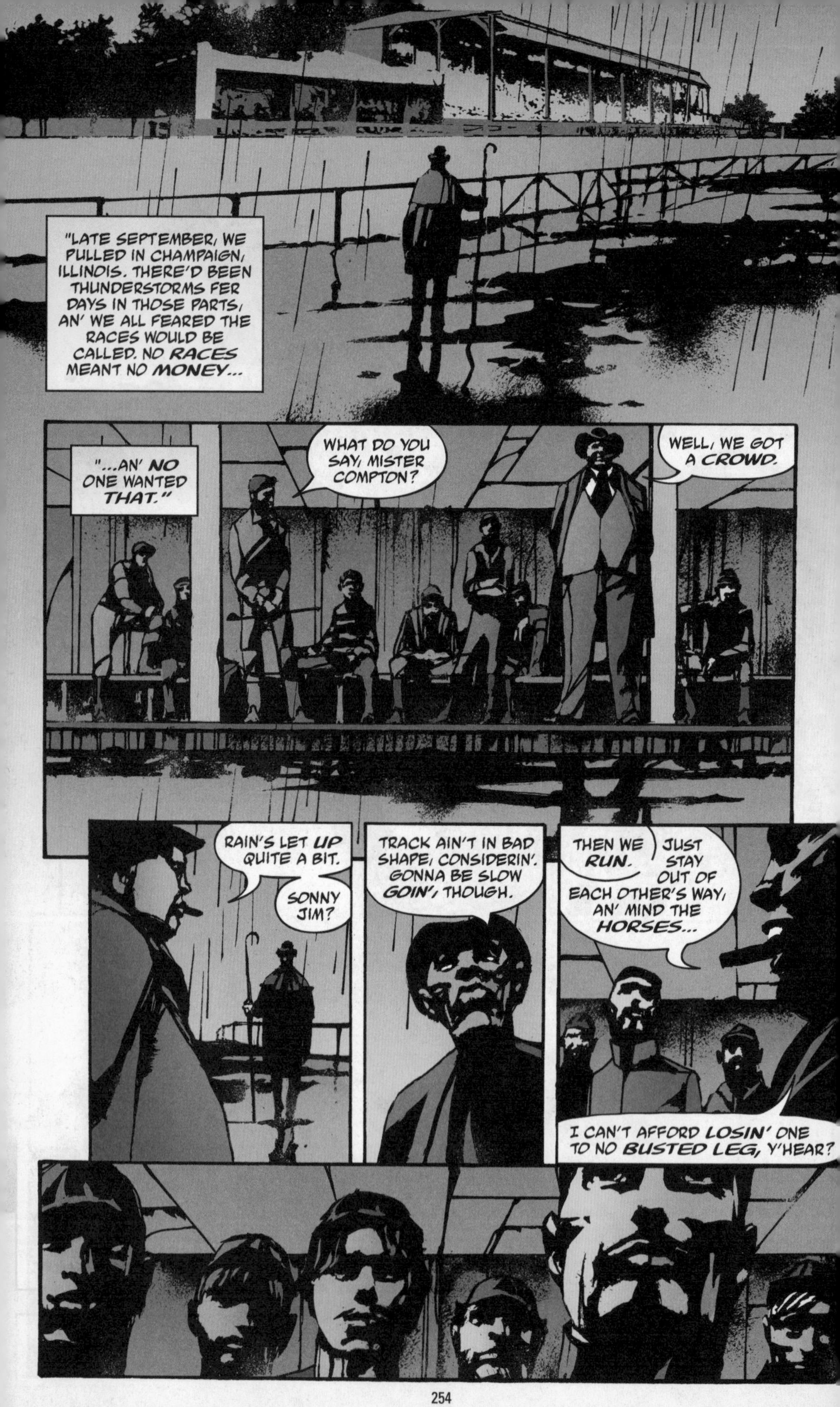
"LATE SEPTEMBER, WE PULLED IN CHAMPAIGN, ILLINOIS. THERE'D BEEN THUNDERSTORMS FER DAYS IN THOSE PARTS, AN' WE ALL FEARED THE RACES WOULD BE CALLED. NO RACES MEANT NO MONEY...
"...AN' NO ONE WANTED THAT."
WHAT DO YOU SAY, MISTER COMPTON?
WELL, WE GOT A CROWD.
RAIN'S LET UP QUITE A BIT.
SONNY JIM?
TRACK AIN'T IN BAD SHAPE, CONSIDERIN'. GONNA BE SLOW GOIN', THOUGH.
THEN WE RUN.
JUST STAY OUT OF EACH OTHER'S WAY, AN' MIND THE HORSES...
I CAN'T AFFORD LOSIN' ONE TO NO BUSTED LEG, Y'HEAR?

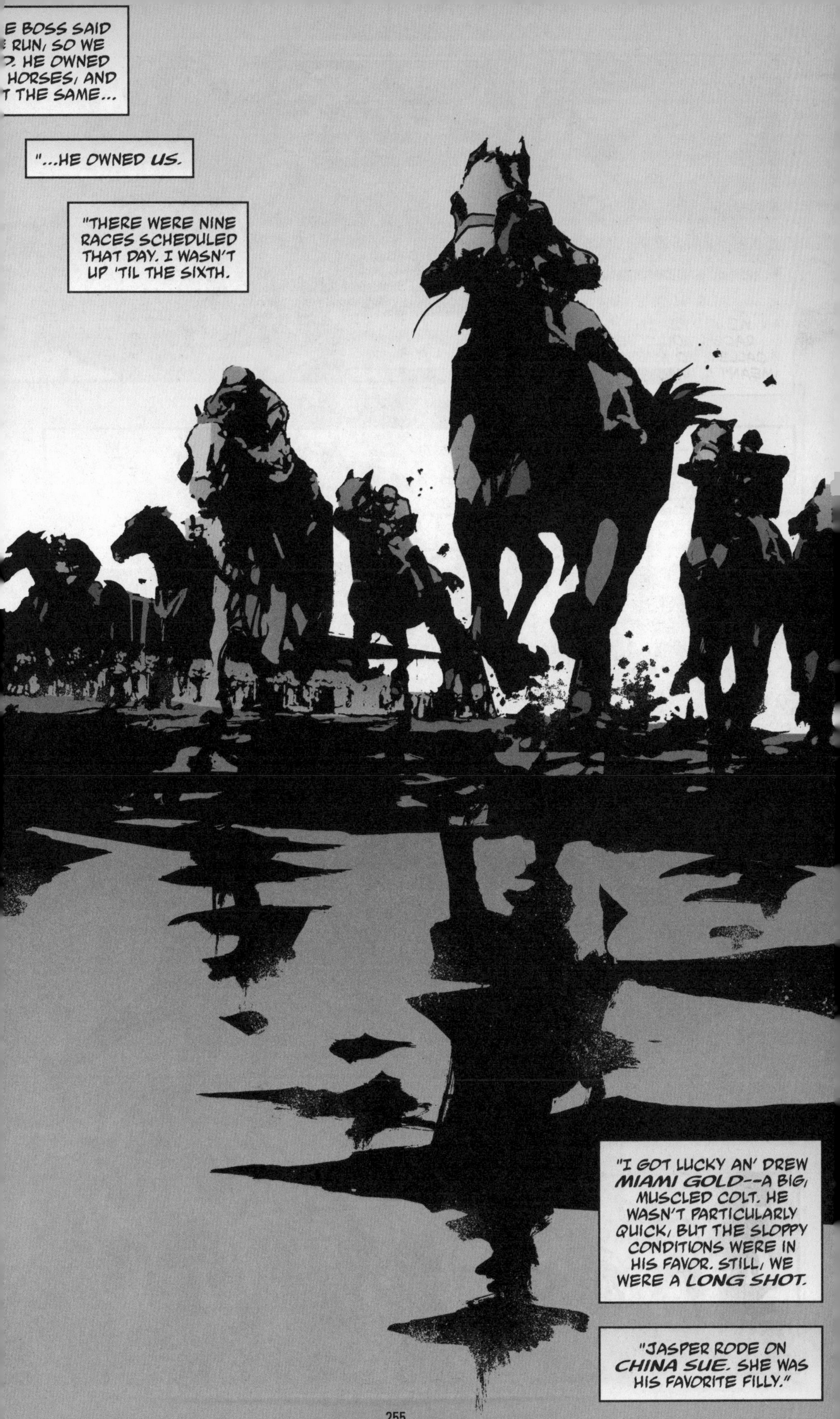

E BOSS SAID
RUN, SO WE
D. HE OWNED
HORSES, AND
T THE SAME...
"...HE OWNED US.
"THERE WERE NINE RACES SCHEDULED THAT DAY. I WASN'T UP 'TIL THE SIXTH.
"I GOT LUCKY AN' DREW MIAMI GOLD--A BIG, MUSCLED COLT. HE WASN'T PARTICULARLY QUICK, BUT THE SLOPPY CONDITIONS WERE IN HIS FAVOR. STILL, WE WERE A LONG SHOT.
"JASPER RODE ON CHINA SUE. SHE WAS HIS FAVORITE FILLY."

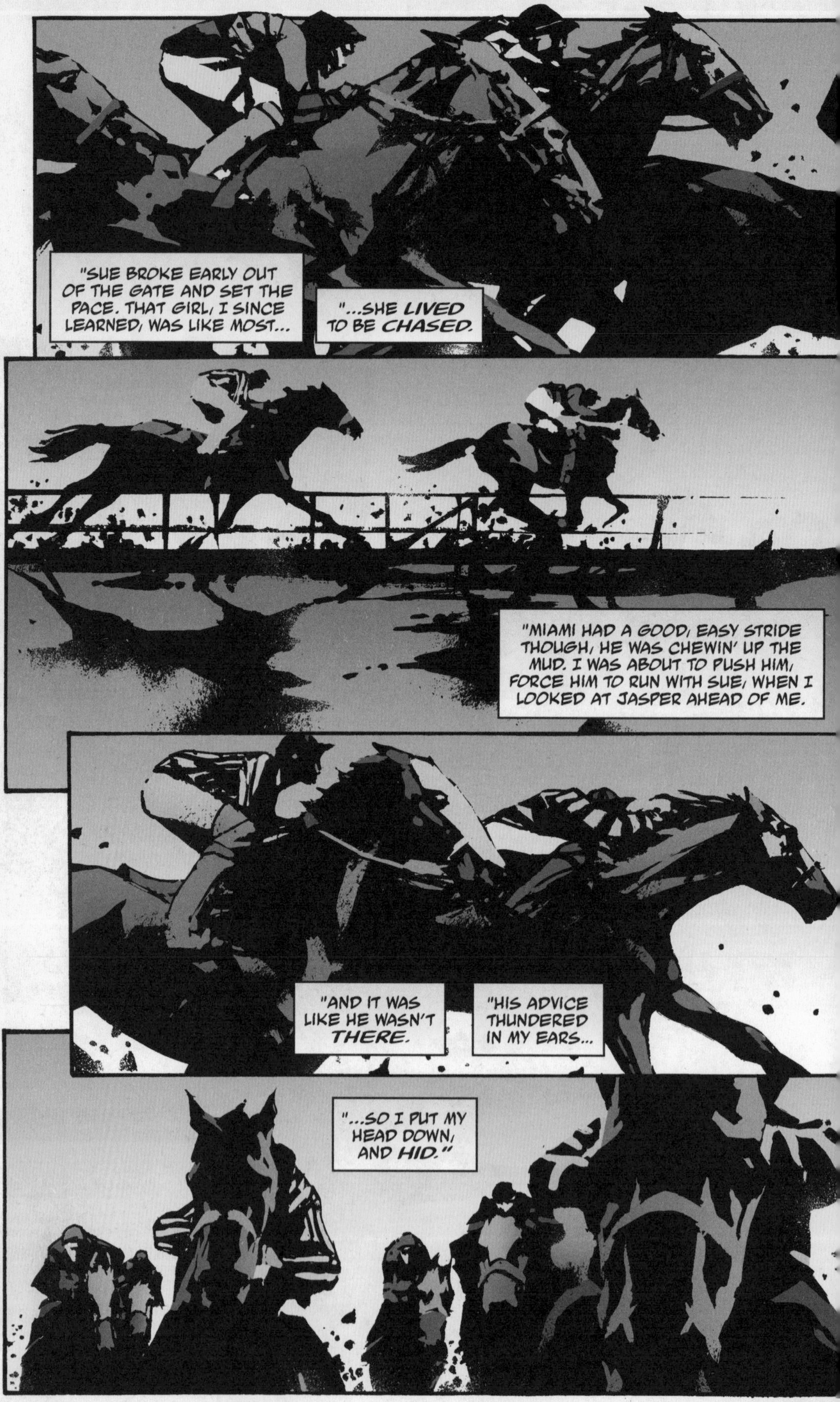
"SUE BROKE EARLY OUT OF THE GATE AND SET THE PACE. THAT GIRL, I SINCE LEARNED, WAS LIKE MOST...
"...SHE LIVED TO BE CHASED.
"MIAMI HAD A GOOD, EASY STRIDE THOUGH, HE WAS CHEWIN' UP THE MUD. I WAS ABOUT TO PUSH HIM, FORCE HIM TO RUN WITH SUE, WHEN I LOOKED AT JASPER AHEAD OF ME.
"AND IT WAS LIKE HE WASN'T THERE.
"HIS ADVICE THUNDERED IN MY EARS...
"...SO I PUT MY HEAD DOWN, AND HID."

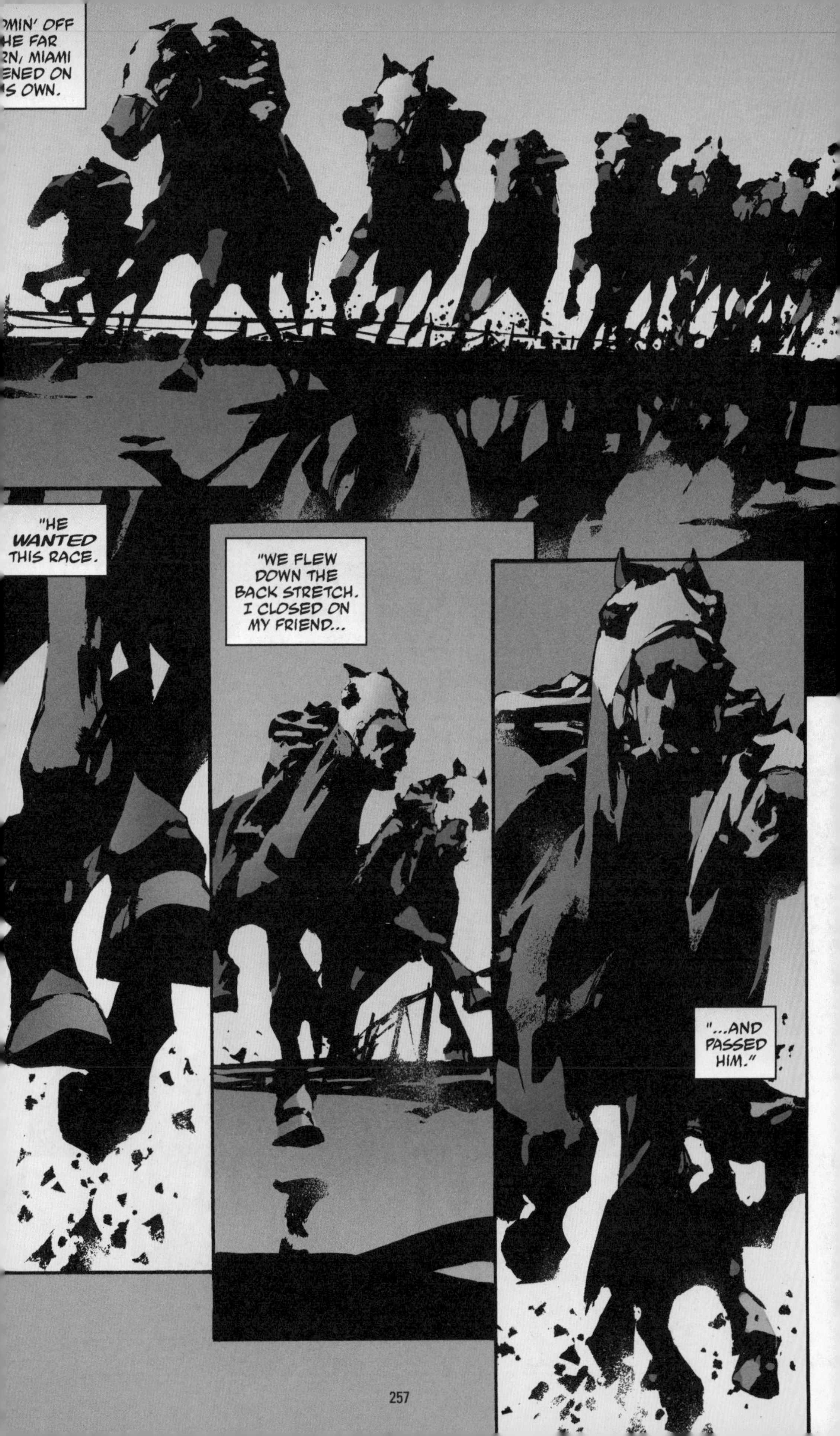

OMIN' OFF
HE FAR
RN, MIAMI
ENED ON
S OWN.
"HE *WANTED* THIS RACE.
"WE FLEW DOWN THE BACK STRETCH. I CLOSED ON MY FRIEND...
"...AND PASSED HIM."

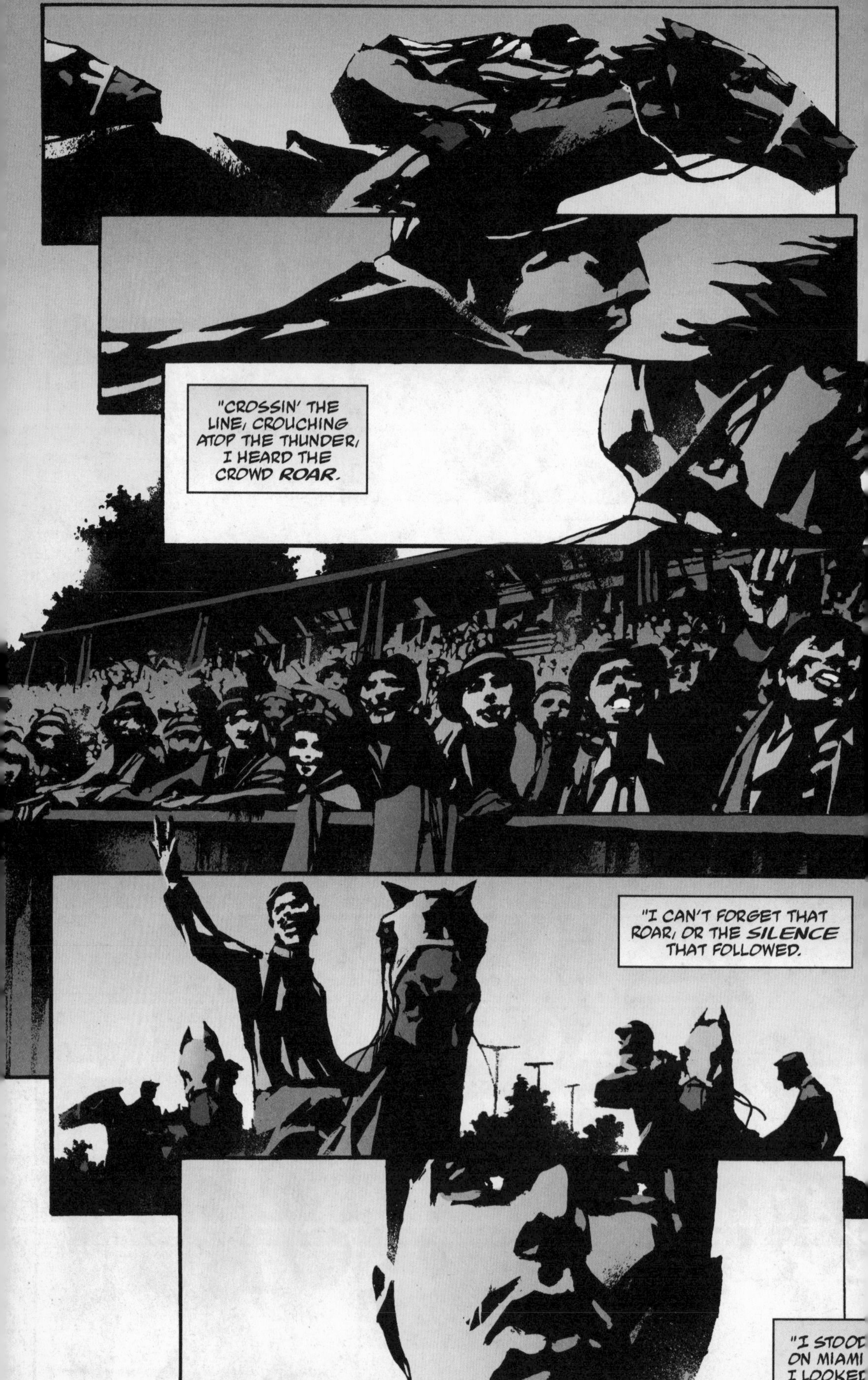
"CROSSIN' THE LINE, CROUCHING ATOP THE THUNDER, I HEARD THE CROWD ROAR.
"I CAN'T FORGET THAT ROAR, OR THE SILENCE THAT FOLLOWED.
"I STOOD ON MIAMI I LOOKED BACK..."

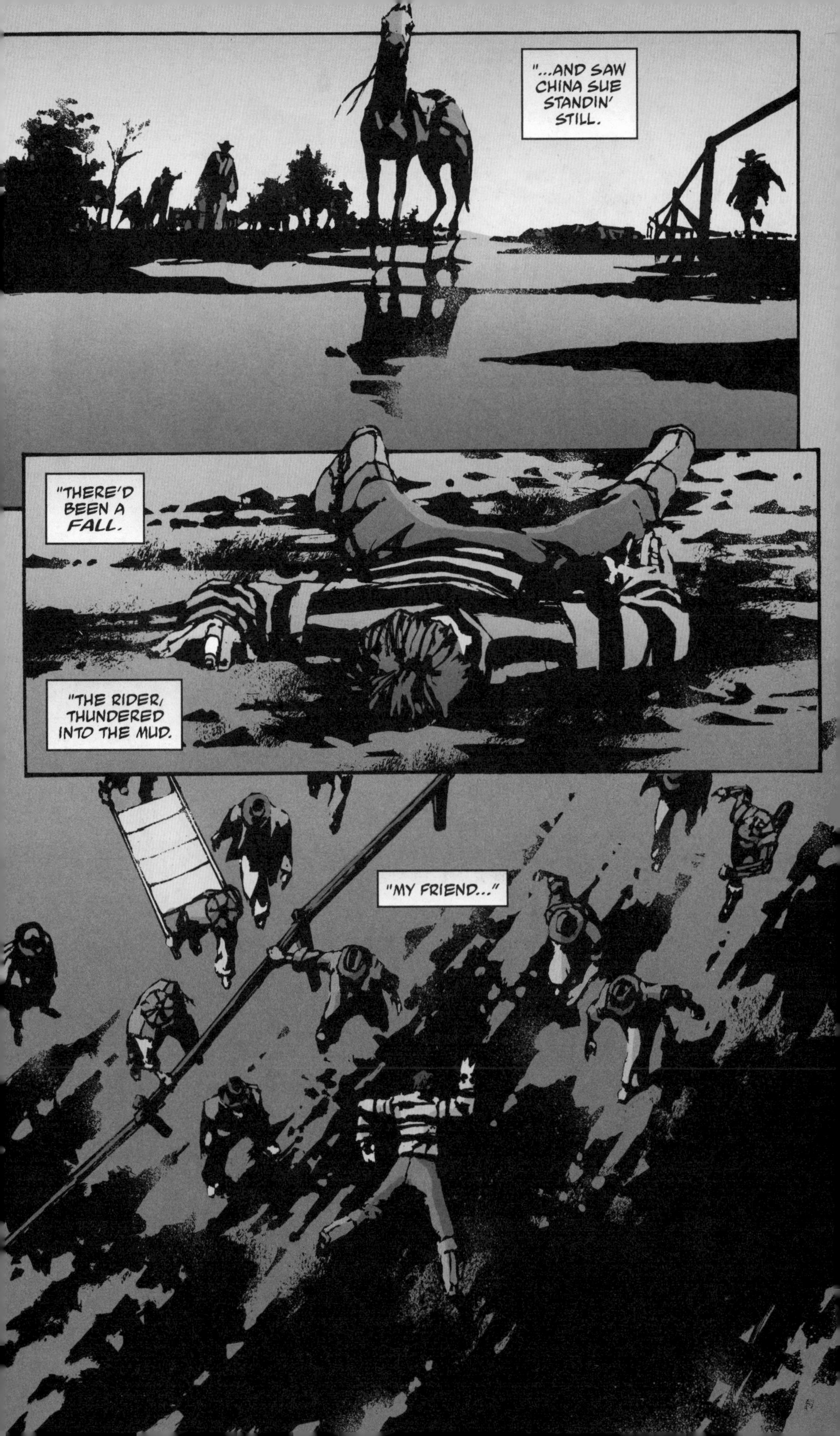
"...AND SAW CHINA SUE STANDIN' STILL.
"THERE'D BEEN A FALL.
"THE RIDER, THUNDERED INTO THE MUD.
"MY FRIEND..."

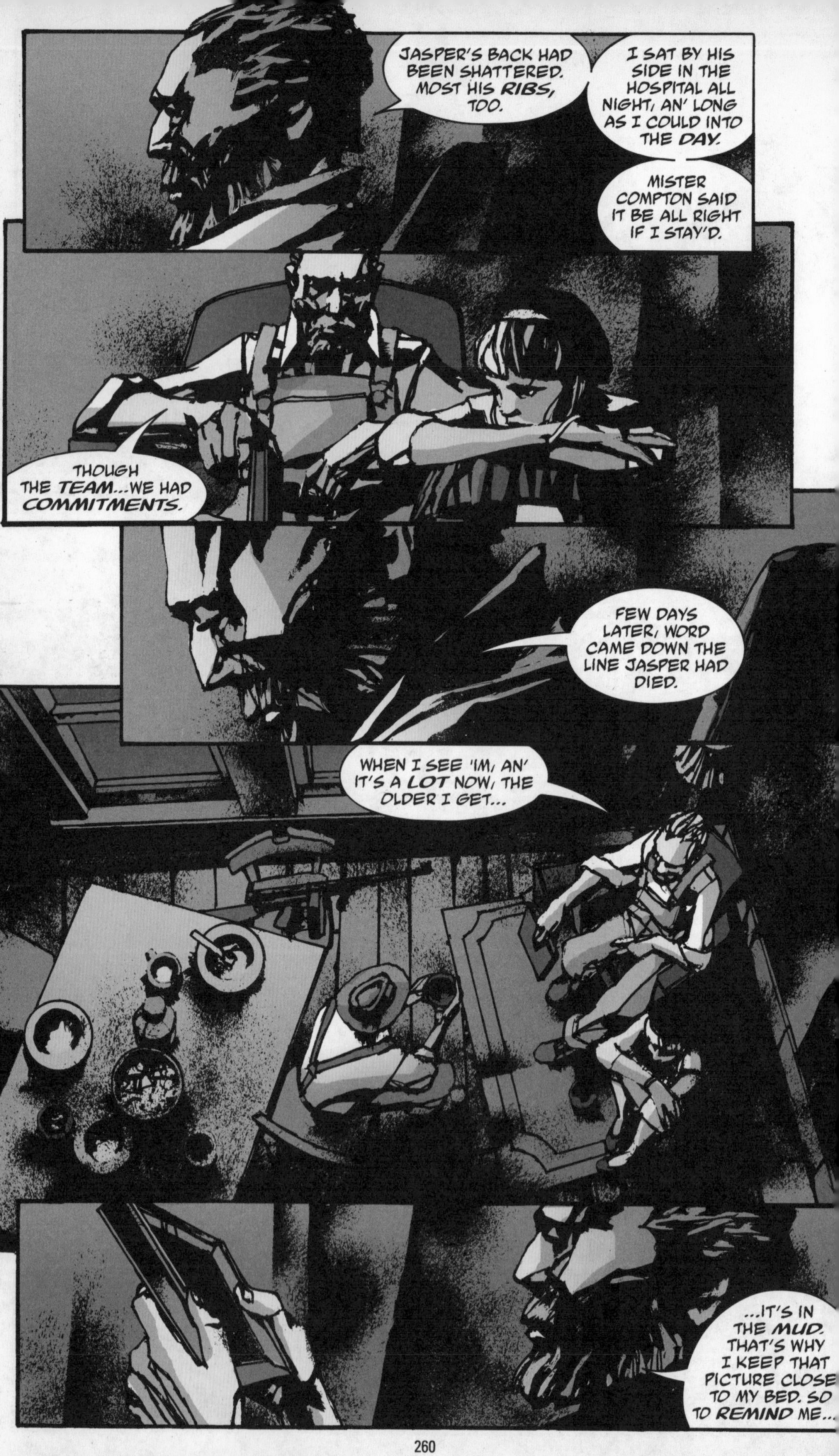

JASPER'S BACK HAD BEEN SHATTERED. MOST HIS RIBS, TOO.
I SAT BY HIS SIDE IN THE HOSPITAL ALL NIGHT, AN' LONG AS I COULD INTO THE DAY.
MISTER COMPTON SAID IT BE ALL RIGHT IF I STAY'D.
THOUGH THE TEAM...WE HAD COMMITMENTS.
FEW DAYS LATER, WORD CAME DOWN THE LINE JASPER HAD DIED.
WHEN I SEE 'IM, AN' IT'S A LOT NOW, THE OLDER I GET...
...IT'S IN THE MUD. THAT'S WHY I KEEP THAT PICTURE CLOSE TO MY BED. SO TO REMIND ME...

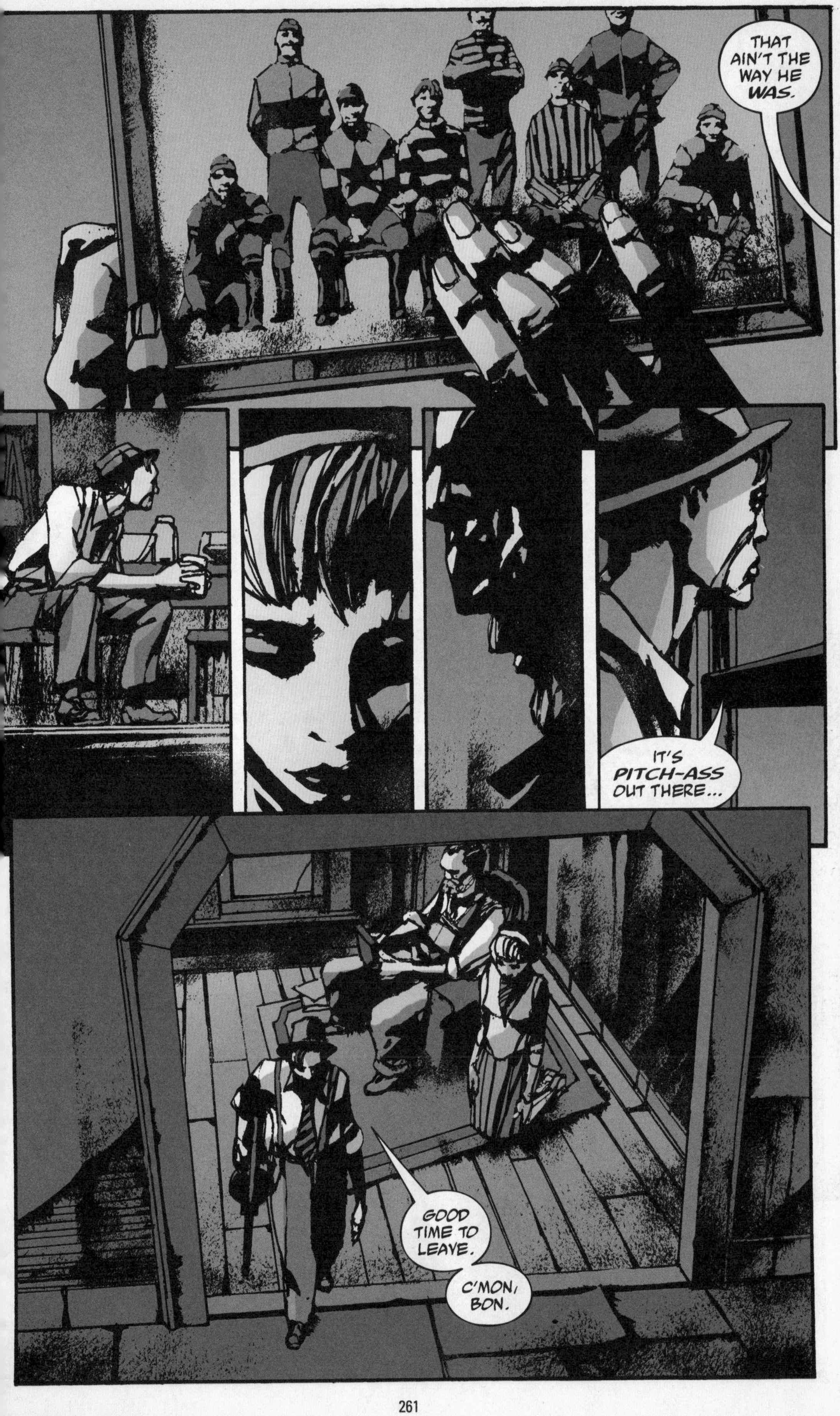
THAT AIN'T THE WAY HE WAS.
IT'S PITCH-ASS OUT THERE...
GOOD TIME TO LEAVE.
C'MON, BON.

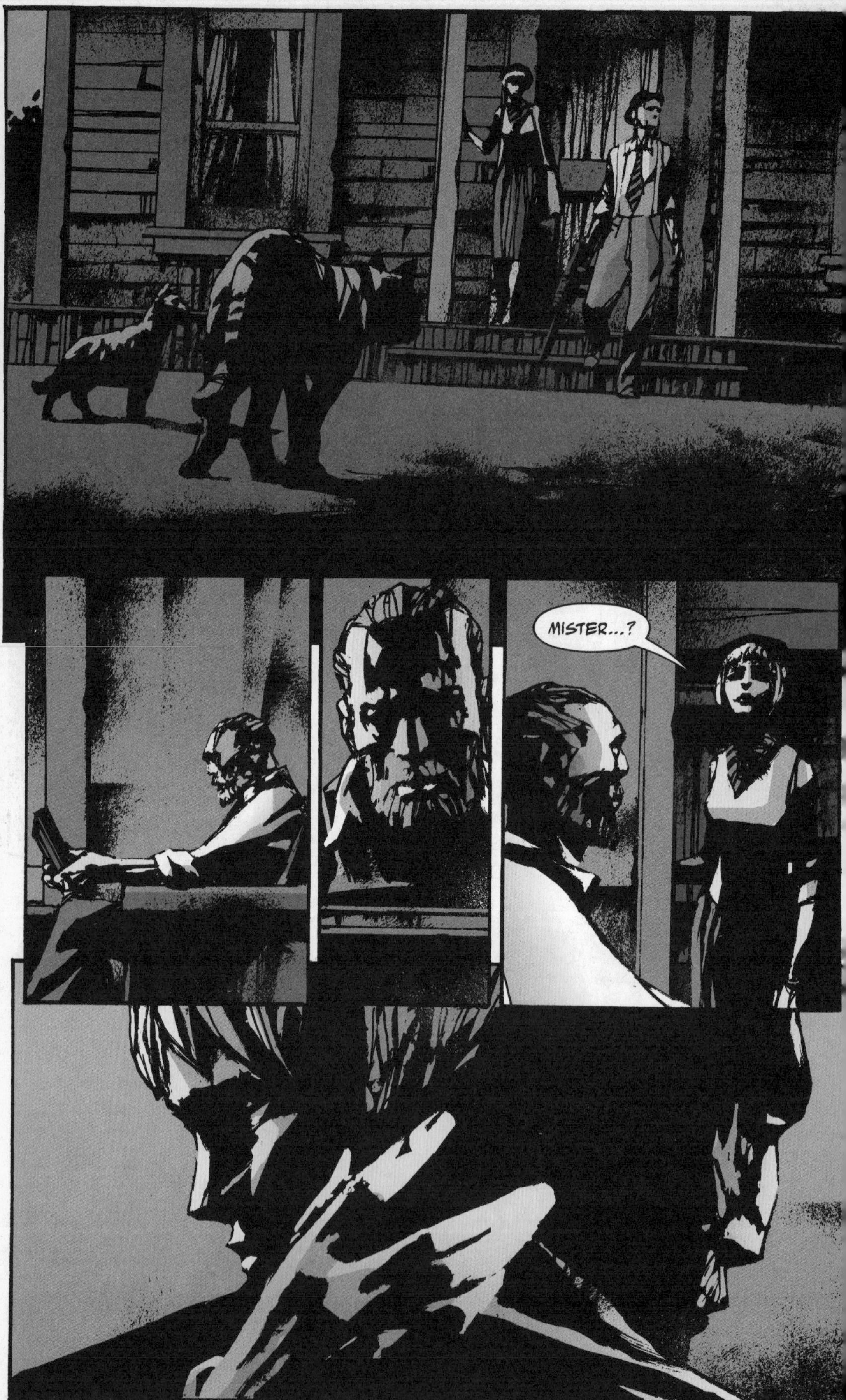
MISTER...?

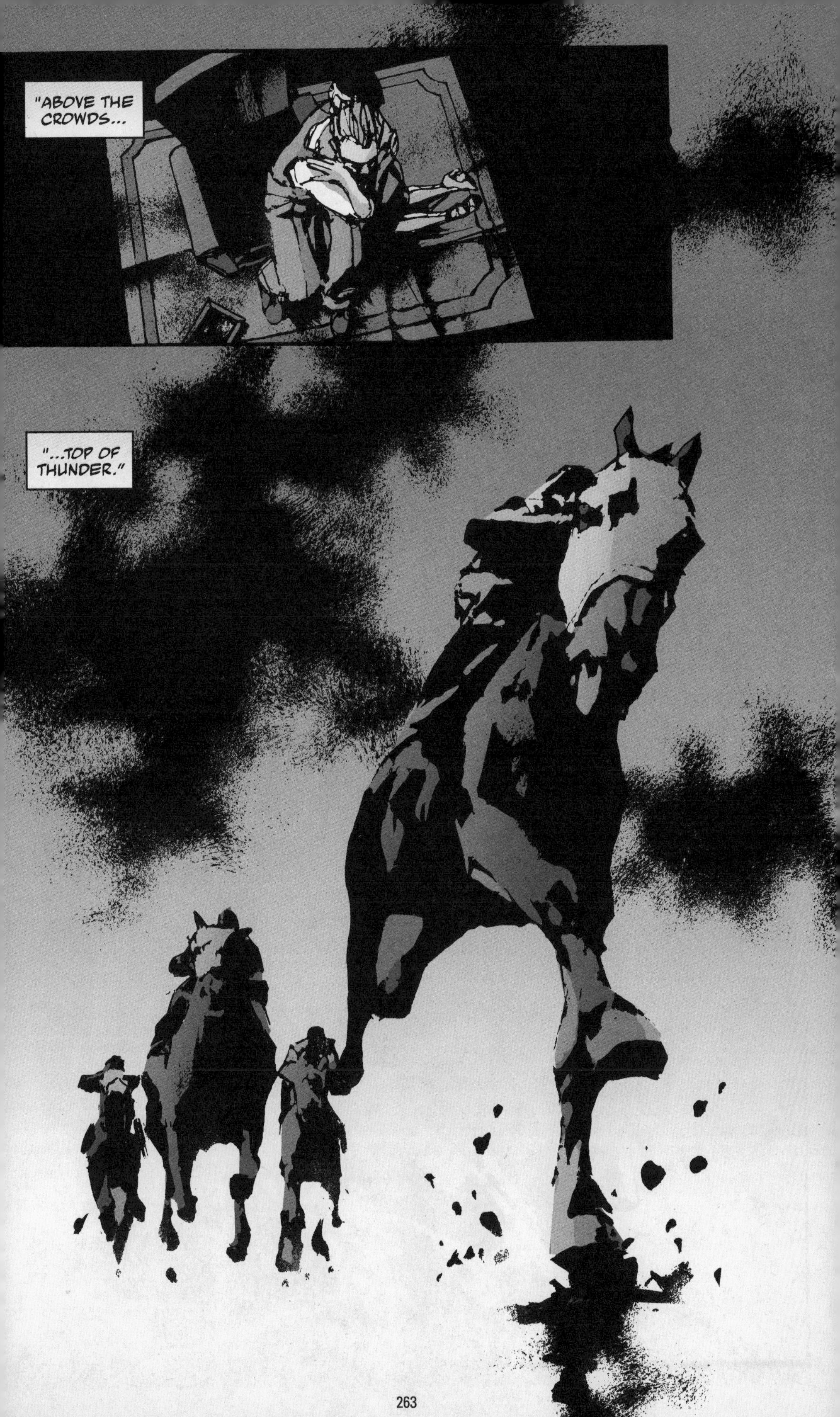
"ABOVE THE CROWDS...
"...TOP OF THUNDER."

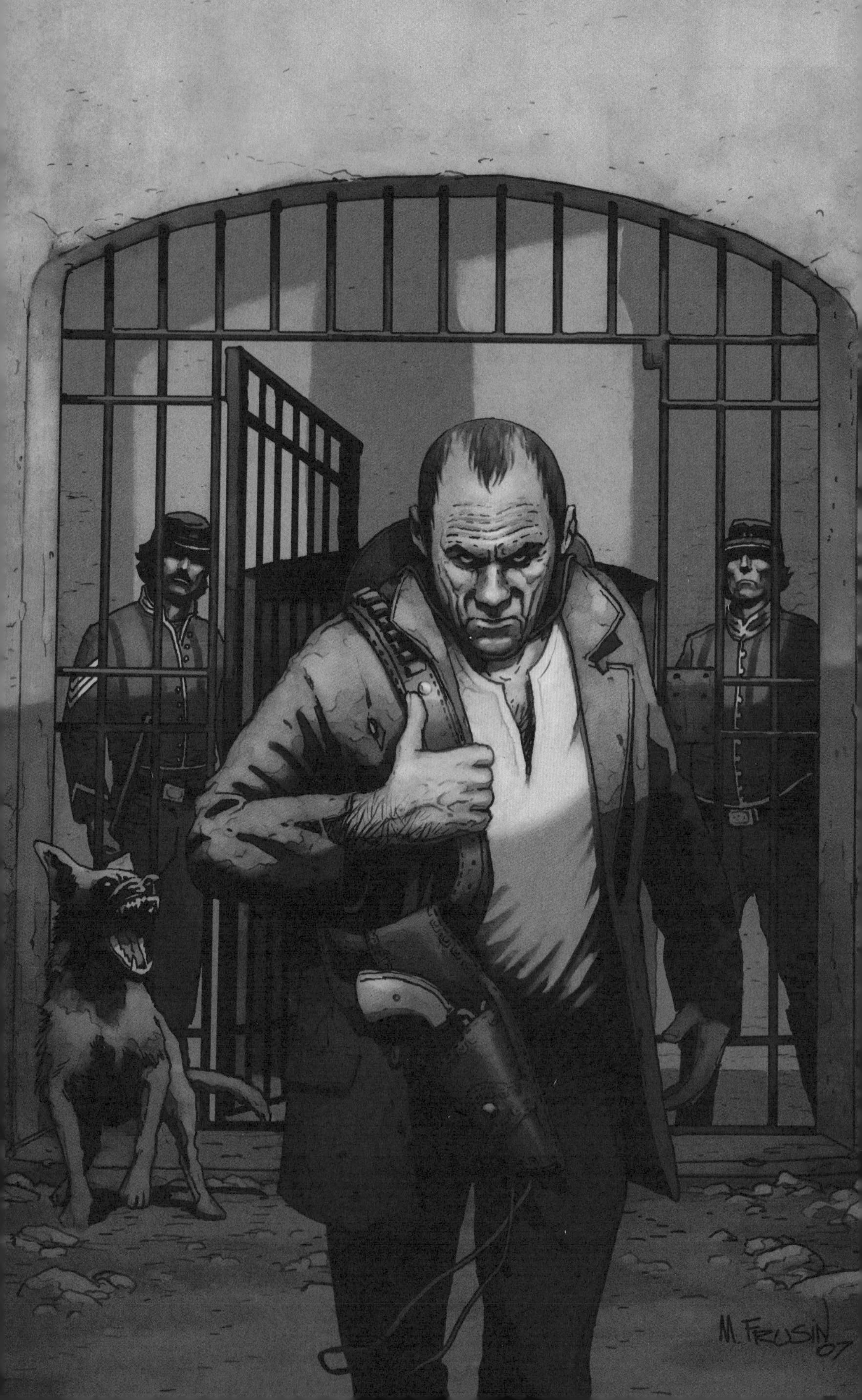
M. FRUSIN 07

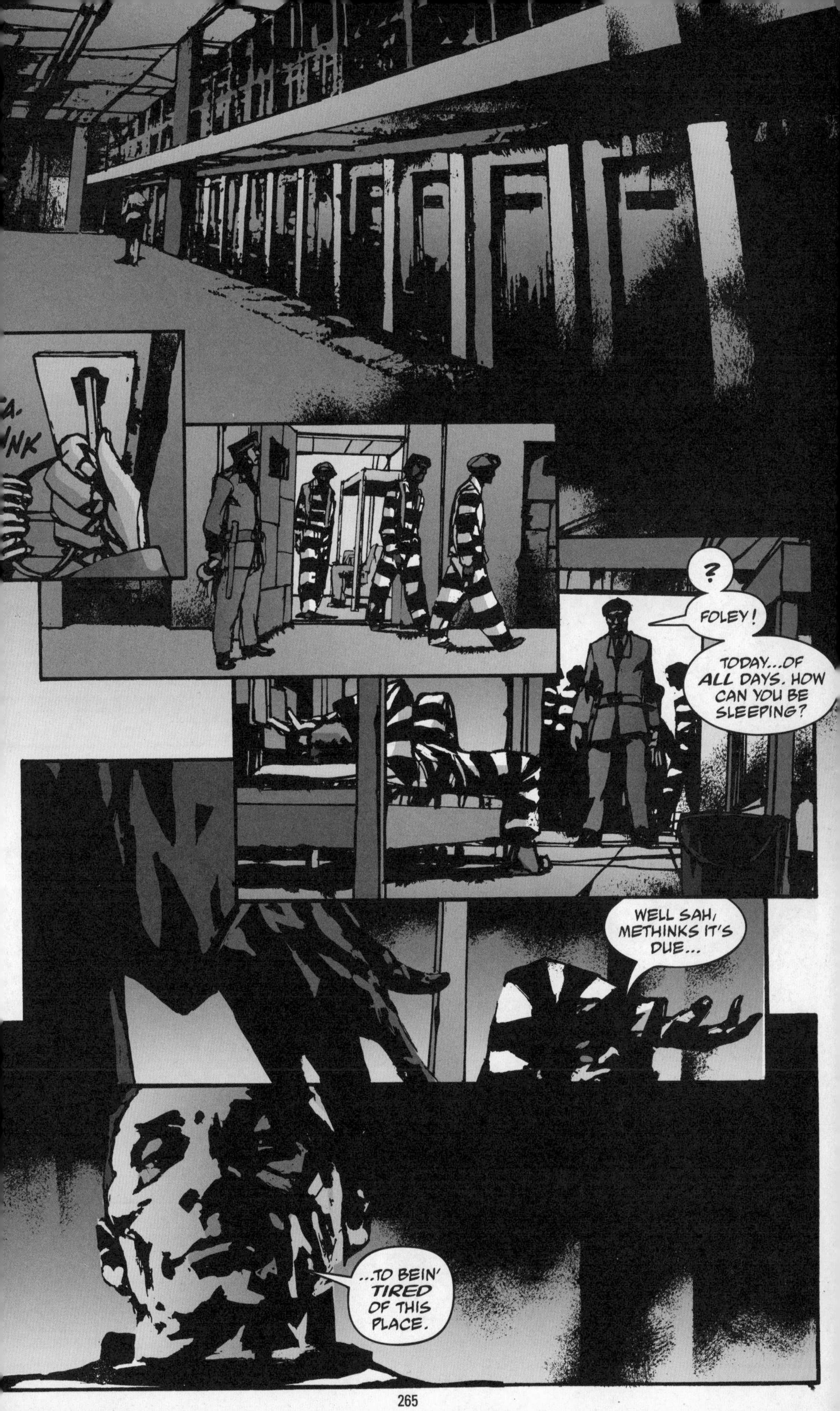
?
FOLEY!
TODAY...OF ALL DAYS. HOW CAN YOU BE SLEEPING?
WELL SAH, METHINKS IT'S DUE...
...TO BEIN' TIRED OF THIS PLACE.

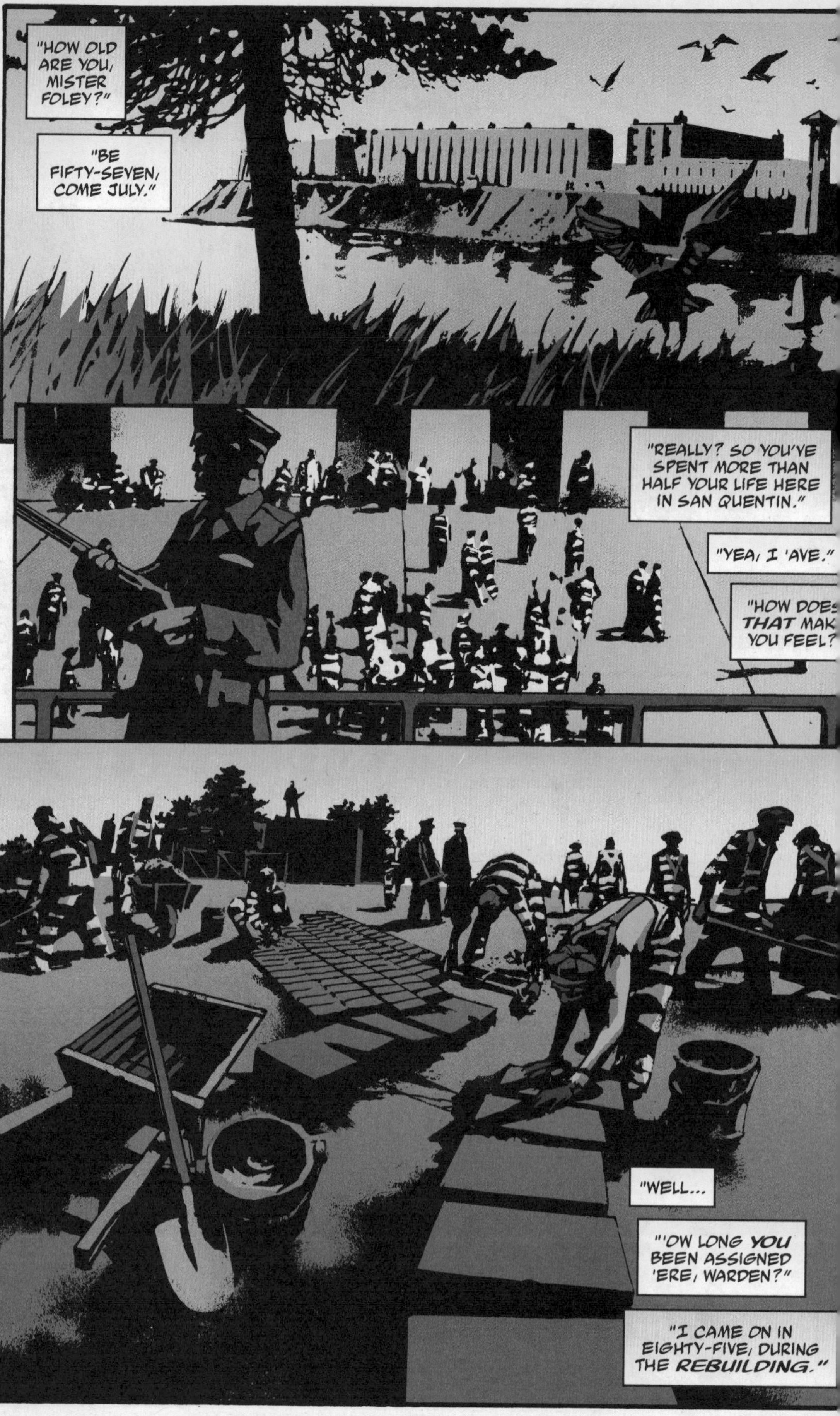
"HOW OLD ARE YOU, MISTER FOLEY?"
"BE FIFTY-SEVEN, COME JULY."
"REALLY? SO YOU'VE SPENT MORE THAN HALF YOUR LIFE HERE IN SAN QUENTIN."
"YEA, I 'AVE."
"HOW DOES THAT MAK YOU FEEL?
"WELL...
"'OW LONG YOU BEEN ASSIGNED 'ERE, WARDEN?"
"I CAME ON IN EIGHTY-FIVE, DURING THE REBUILDING."

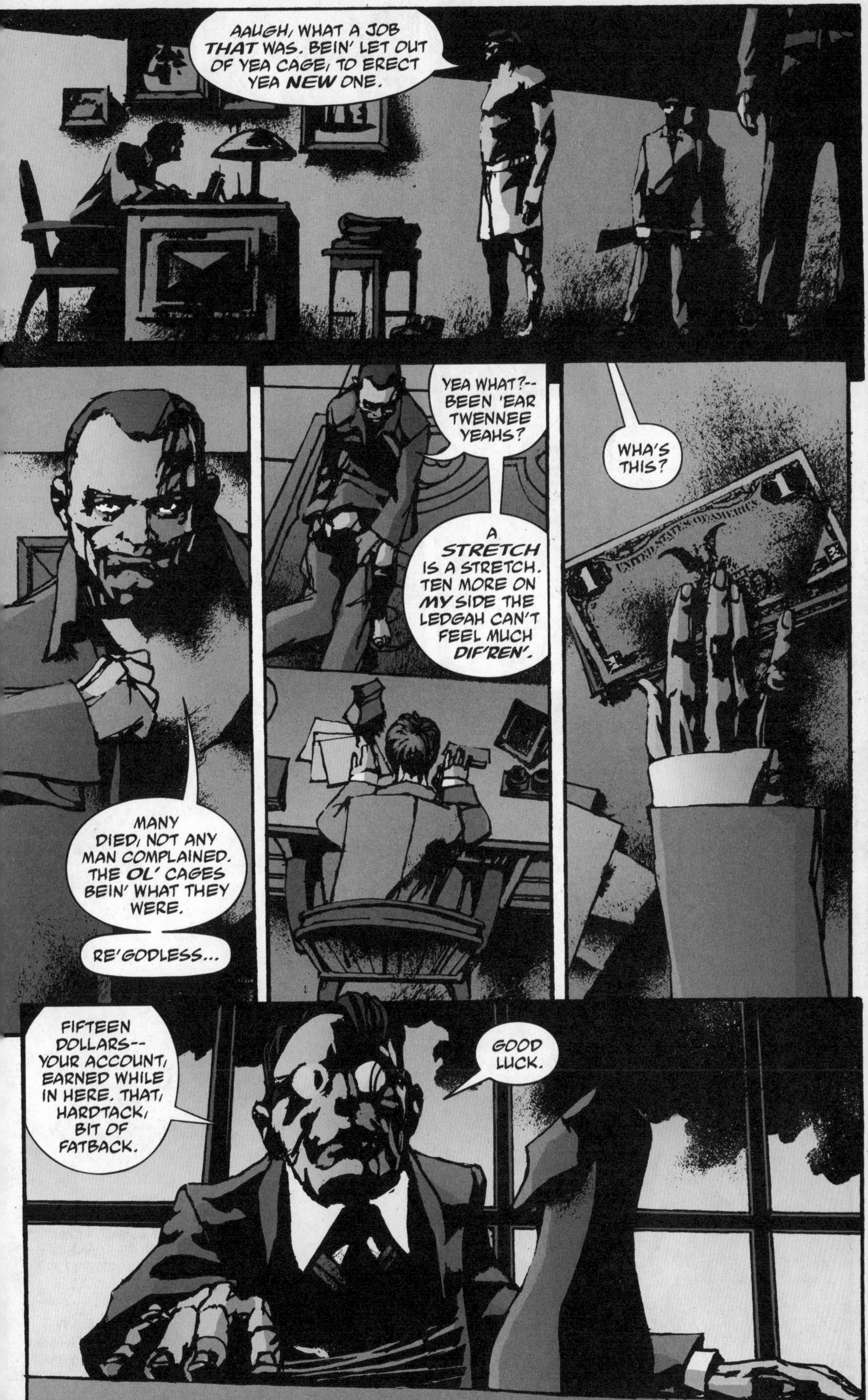
AAUGH, WHAT A JOB THAT WAS. BEIN' LET OUT OF YEA CAGE, TO ERECT YEA NEW ONE.
MANY DIED, NOT ANY MAN COMPLAINED. THE OL' CAGES BEIN' WHAT THEY WERE.
RE'GODLESS...
YEA WHAT?-- BEEN 'EAR TWENNEE YEAHS?
A STRETCH IS A STRETCH. TEN MORE ON MY SIDE THE LEDGAH CAN'T FEEL MUCH DIF'REN'.
WHA'S THIS?
FIFTEEN DOLLARS-- YOUR ACCOUNT, EARNED WHILE IN HERE. THAT, HARDTACK, BIT OF FATBACK.
GOOD LUCK.

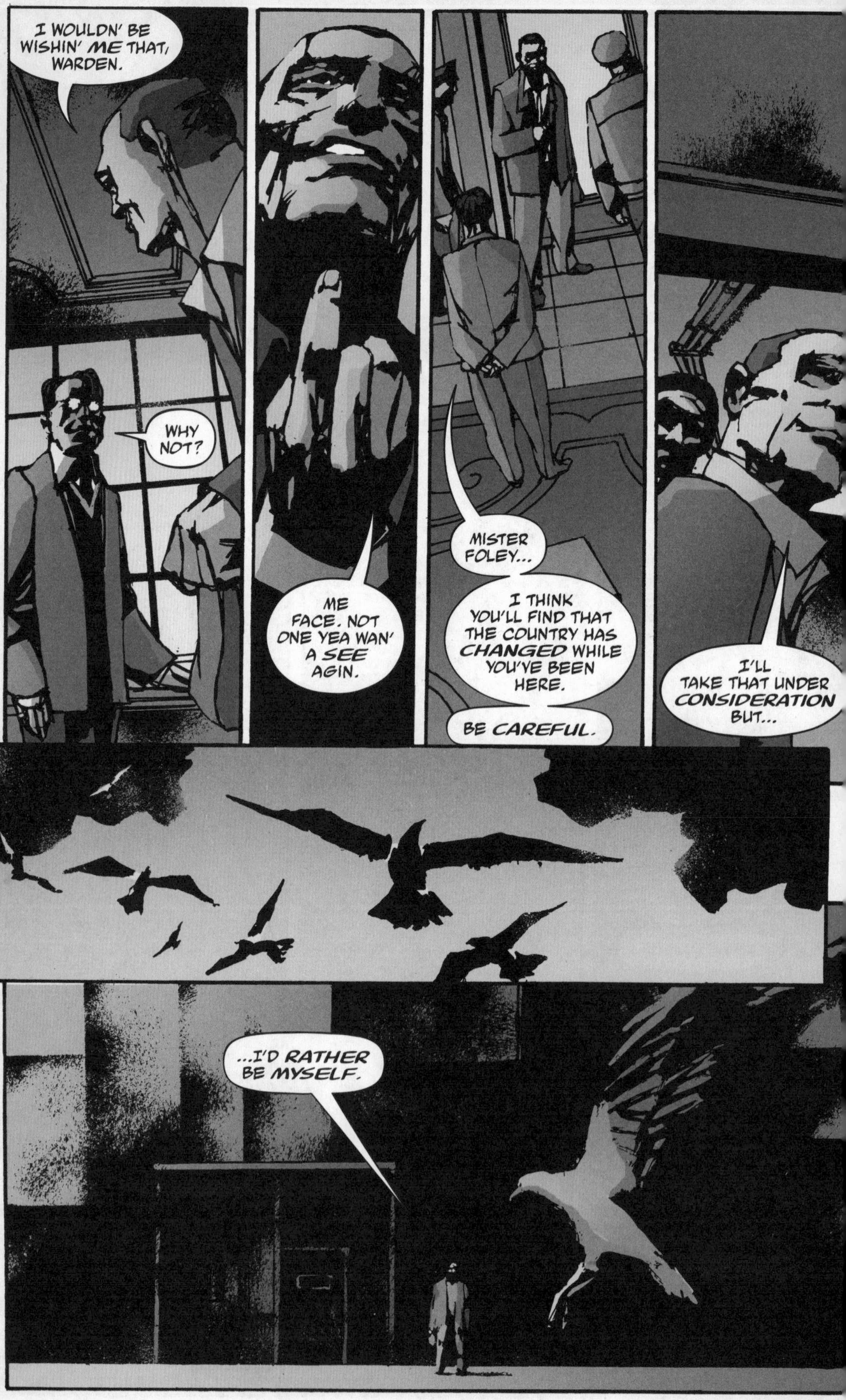
I WOULDN' BE WISHIN' ME THAT, WARDEN.
WHY NOT?
ME FACE. NOT ONE YEA WAN' A SEE AGIN.
MISTER FOLEY...
I THINK YOU'LL FIND THAT THE COUNTRY HAS CHANGED WHILE YOU'VE BEEN HERE.
BE CAREFUL.
I'LL TAKE THAT UNDER CONSIDERATION BUT...
...I'D RATHER BE MYSELF.

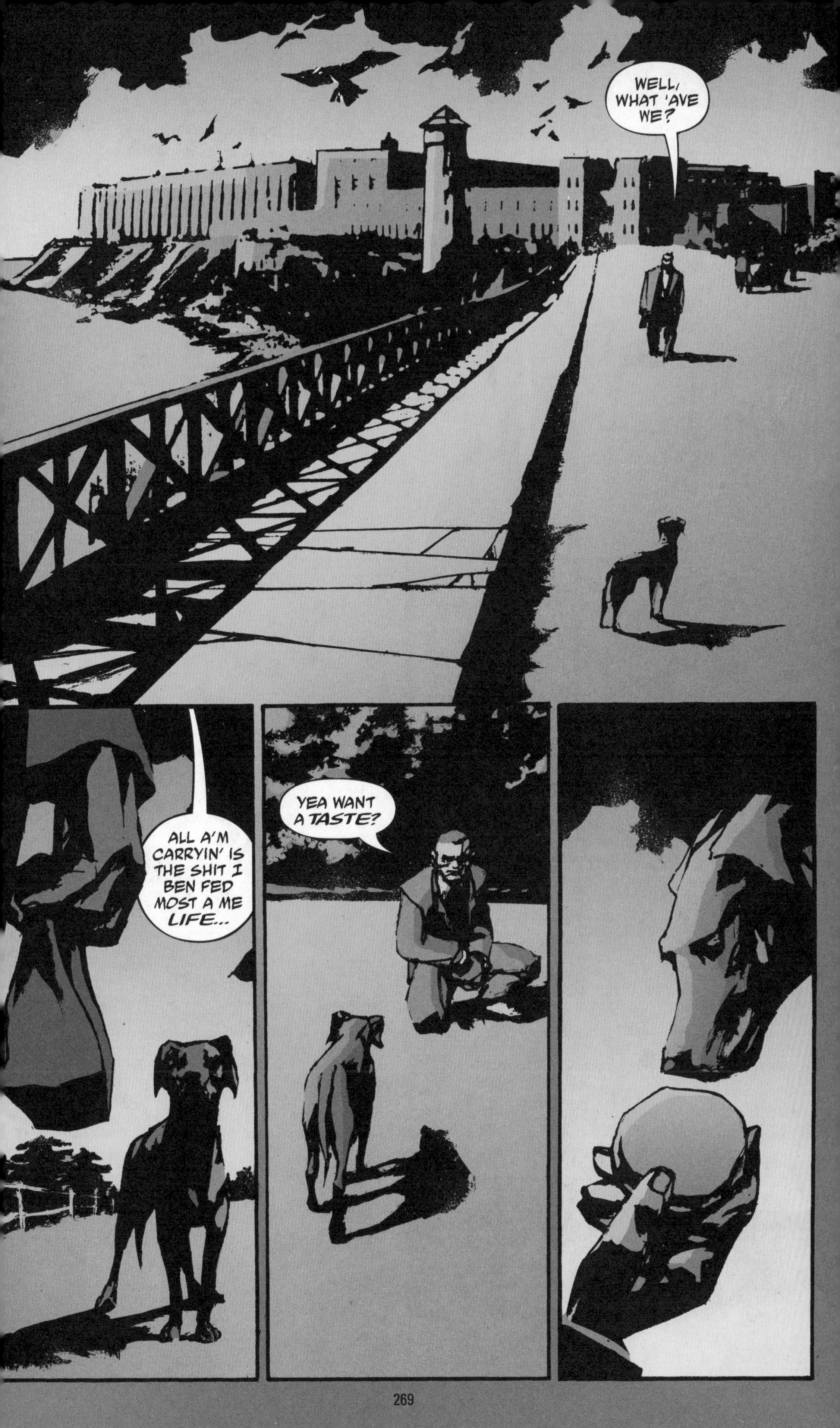
WELL, WHAT 'AVE WE?
ALL A'M CARRYIN' IS THE SHIT I BEN FED MOST A ME LIFE...
YEA WANT A TASTE?

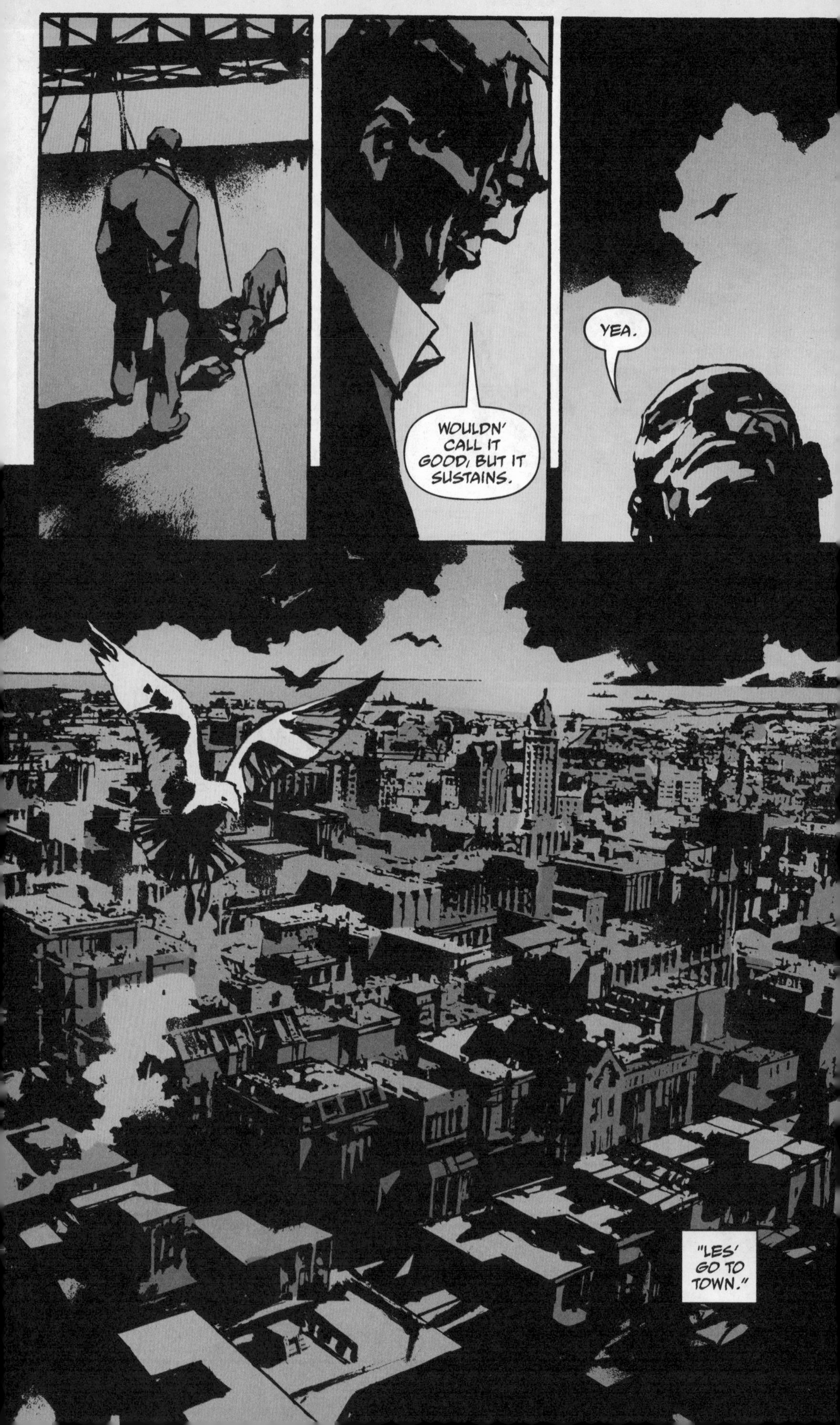
WOULDN' CALL IT GOOD, BUT IT SUSTAINS.
YEA.
"LES' GO TO TOWN."

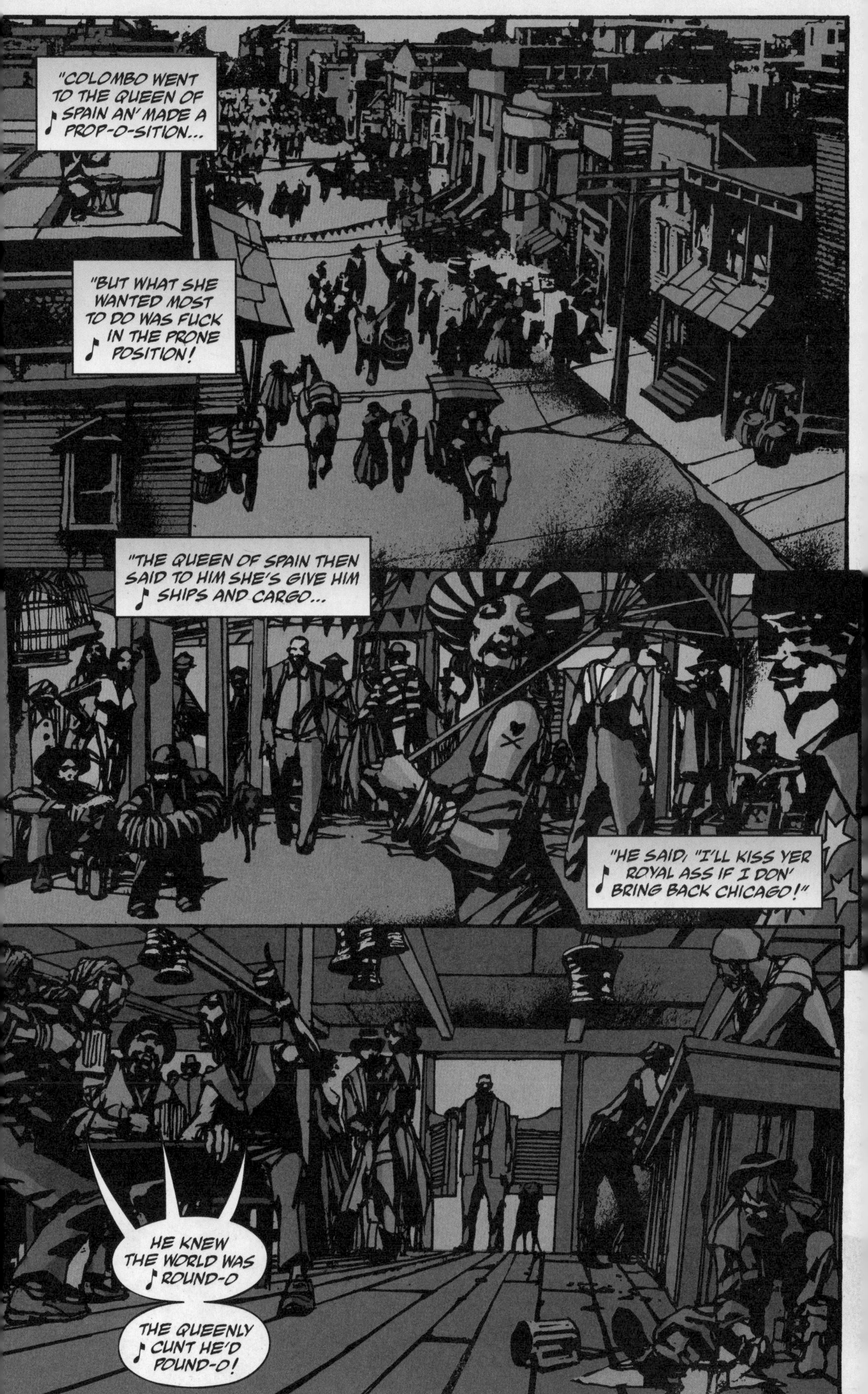
"COLOMBO WENT TO THE QUEEN OF ♪ SPAIN AN' MADE A ♪ PROP-O-SITION...
"BUT WHAT SHE WANTED MOST TO DO WAS FUCK ♪ IN THE PRONE ♪ POSITION!
"THE QUEEN OF SPAIN THEN SAID TO HIM SHE'S GIVE HIM ♪ SHIPS AND CARGO...
"HE SAID, "I'LL KISS YER ♪ ROYAL ASS IF I DON' BRING BACK CHICAGO!"
HE KNEW THE WORLD WAS ♪ ROUND-O
THE QUEENLY ♪ CUNT HE'D POUND-O!

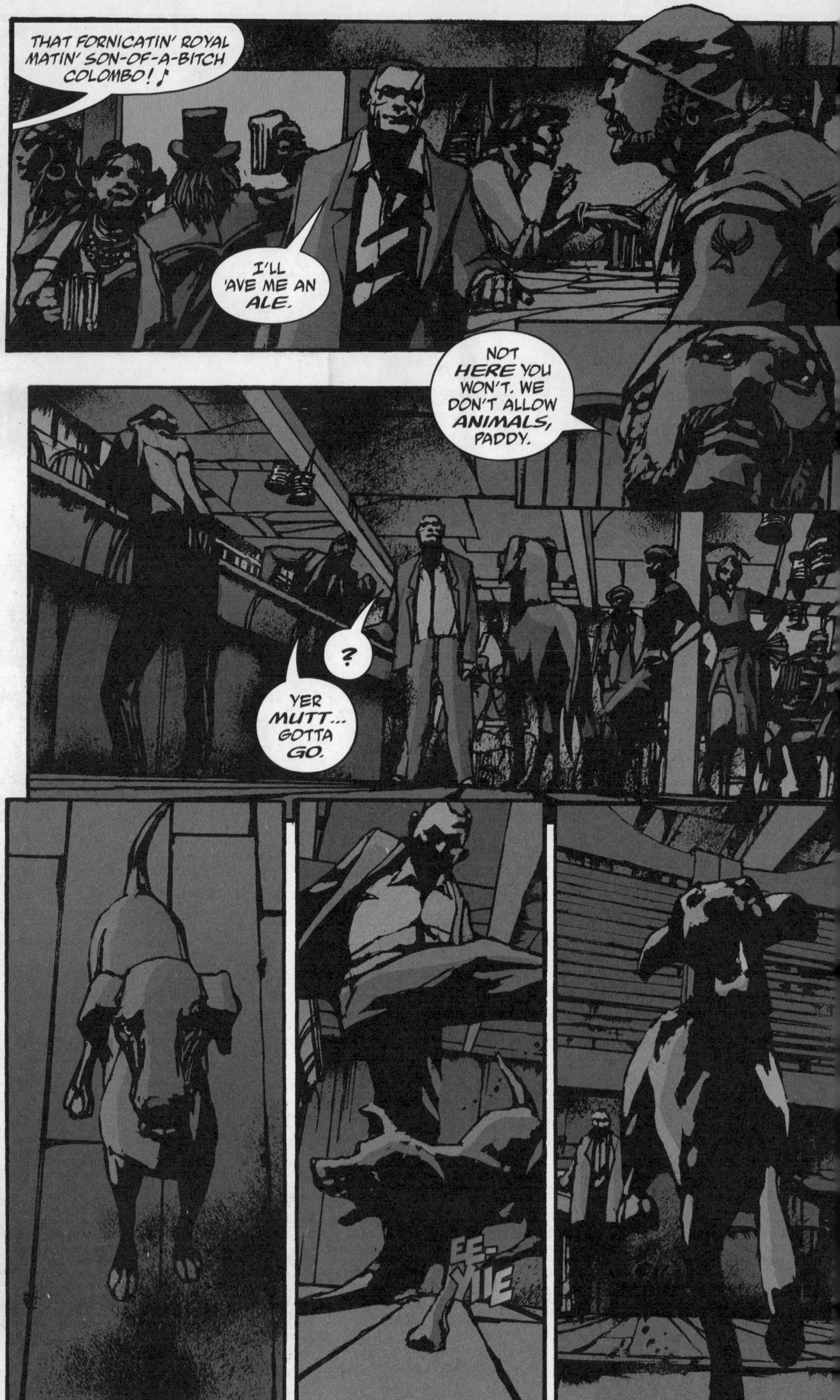
THAT FORNICATIN' ROYAL MATIN' SON-OF-A-BITCH COLOMBO! ♪
I'LL 'AVE ME AN ALE.
NOT HERE YOU WON'T. WE DON'T ALLOW ANIMALS, PADDY.
?
YER MUTT... GOTTA GO.
EE-YIIE

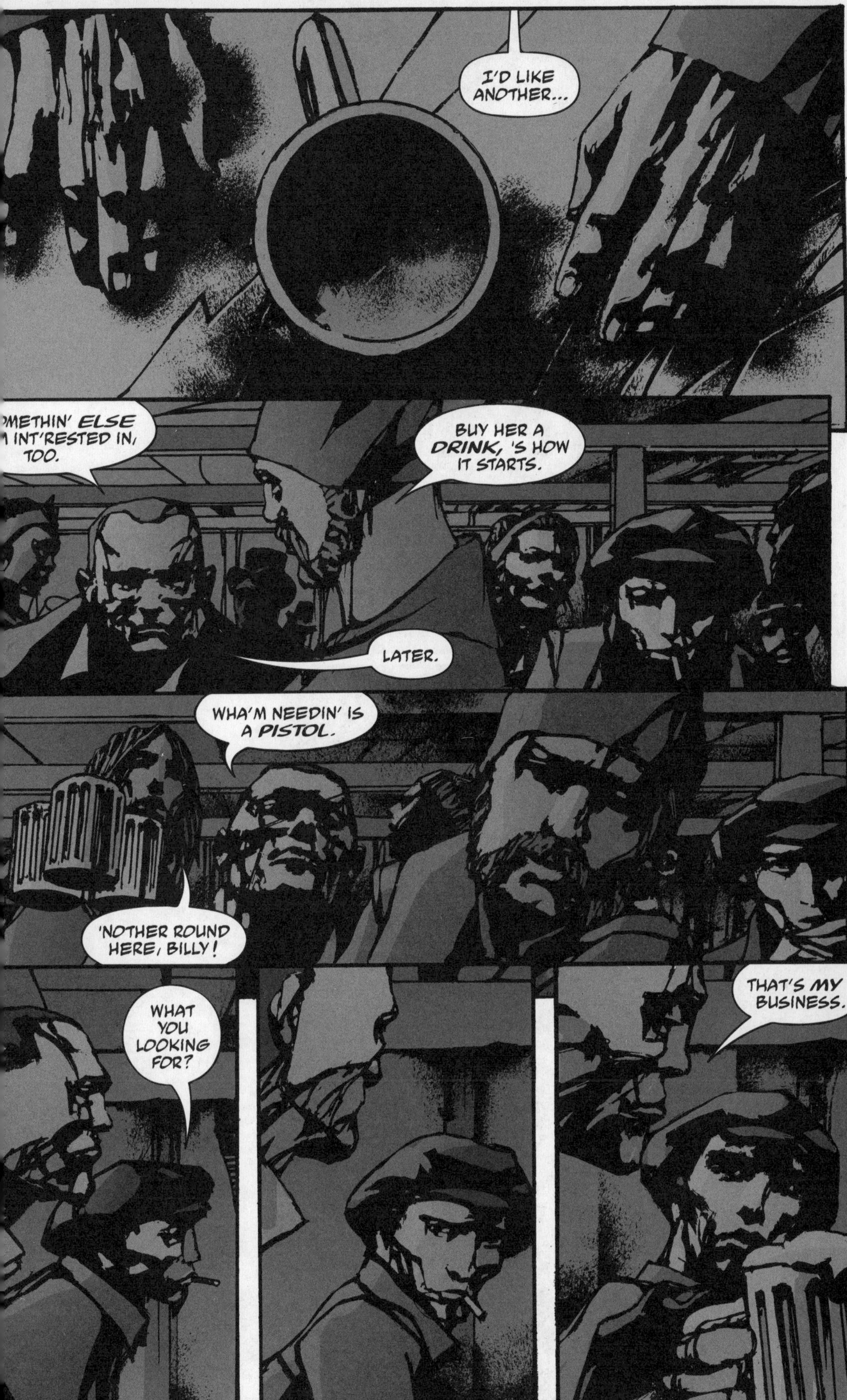
I'D LIKE ANOTHER...
METHIN' ELSE
INT'RESTED IN, TOO.
BUY HER A DRINK, 'S HOW IT STARTS.
LATER.
WHA'M NEEDIN' IS A PISTOL.
'NOTHER ROUND HERE, BILLY!
WHAT YOU LOOKING FOR?
THAT'S MY BUSINESS.

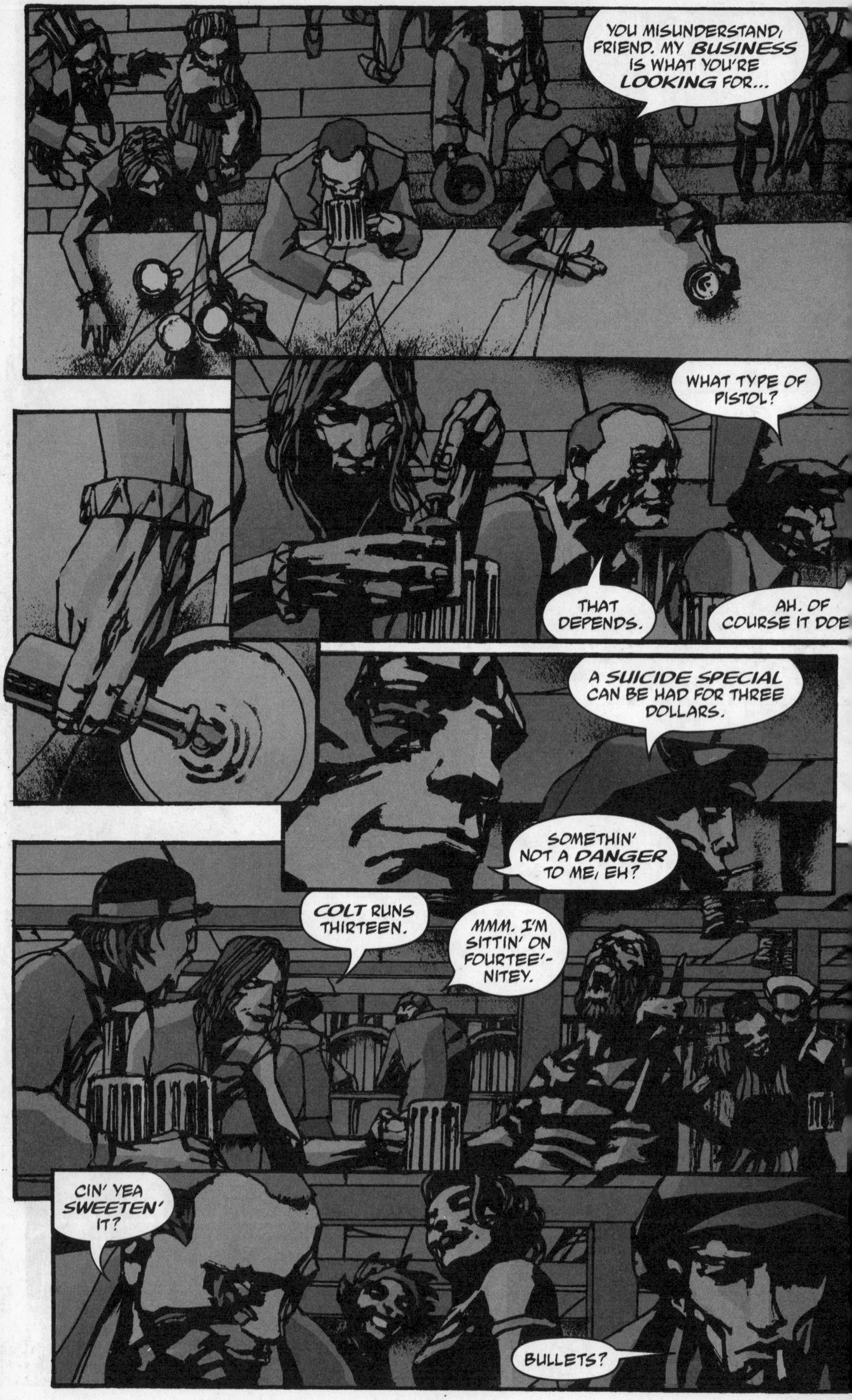
YOU MISUNDERSTAND, FRIEND. MY BUSINESS IS WHAT YOU'RE LOOKING FOR...
WHAT TYPE OF PISTOL?
THAT DEPENDS.
AH. OF COURSE IT DOE
A SUICIDE SPECIAL CAN BE HAD FOR THREE DOLLARS.
SOMETHIN' NOT A DANGER TO ME, EH?
COLT RUNS THIRTEEN.
MMM. I'M SITTIN' ON FOURTEE'-NITEY.
CIN' YEA SWEETEN' IT?
BULLETS?

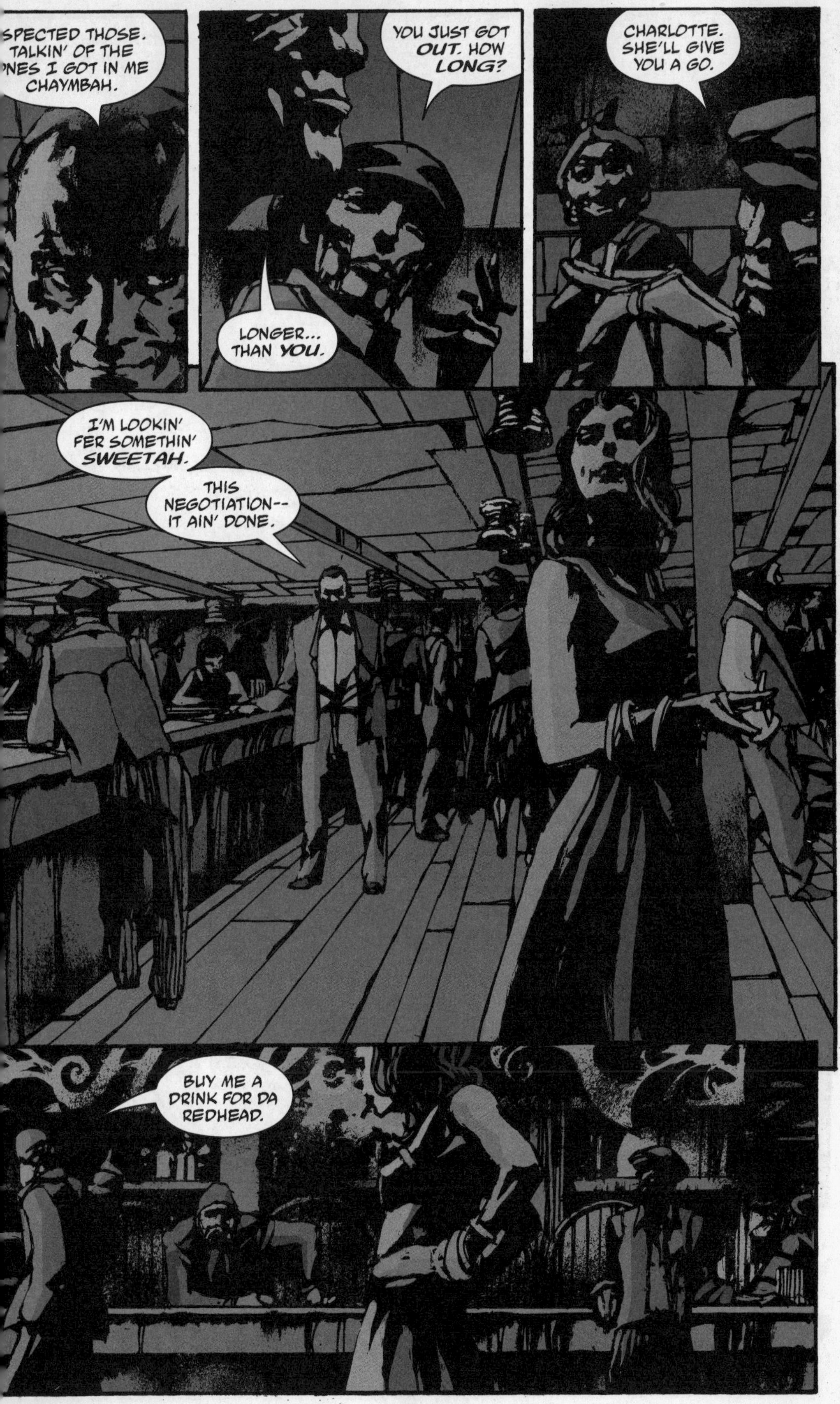
SPECTED THOSE. TALKIN' OF THE NES I GOT IN ME CHAYMBAH.
YOU JUST GOT OUT. HOW LONG?
LONGER... THAN YOU.
CHARLOTTE. SHE'LL GIVE YOU A GO.
I'M LOOKIN' FER SOMETHIN' SWEETAH.
THIS NEGOTIATION-- IT AIN' DONE.
BUY ME A DRINK FOR DA REDHEAD.

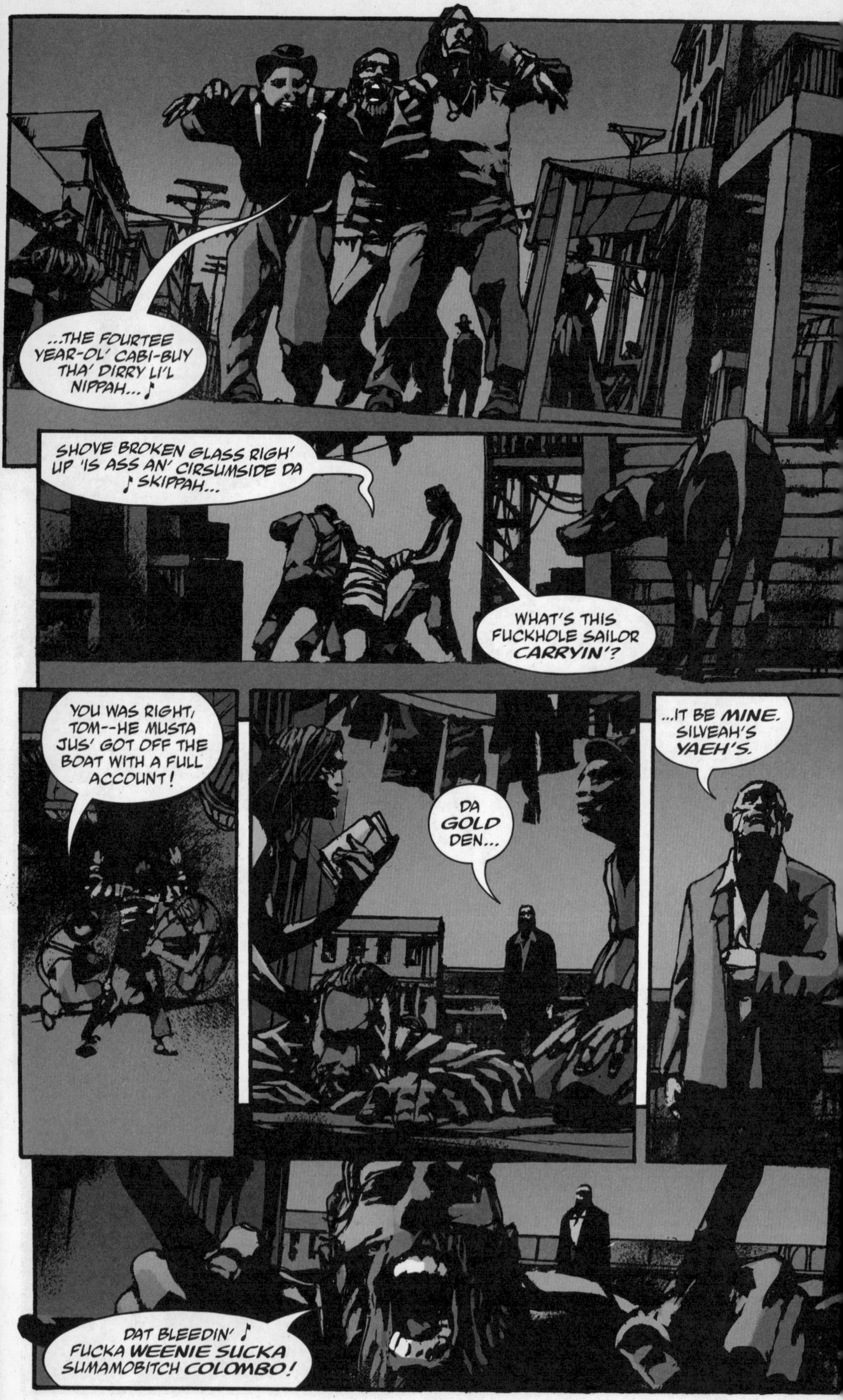

...THE FOURTEE YEAR-OL' CABI-BUY THA' DIRRY LI'L NIPPAH...♪
SHOVE BROKEN GLASS RIGH' UP 'IS ASS AN' CIRSUMSIDE DA ♪ SKIPPAH...
WHAT'S THIS FUCKHOLE SAILOR CARRYIN'?
YOU WAS RIGHT, TOM--HE MUSTA JUS' GOT OFF THE BOAT WITH A FULL ACCOUNT!
DA GOLD DEN...
...IT BE MINE. SILVEAH'S YAEH'S.
DAT BLEEDIN' ♪ FUCKA WEENIE SUCKA SUMAMOBITCH COLOMBO!

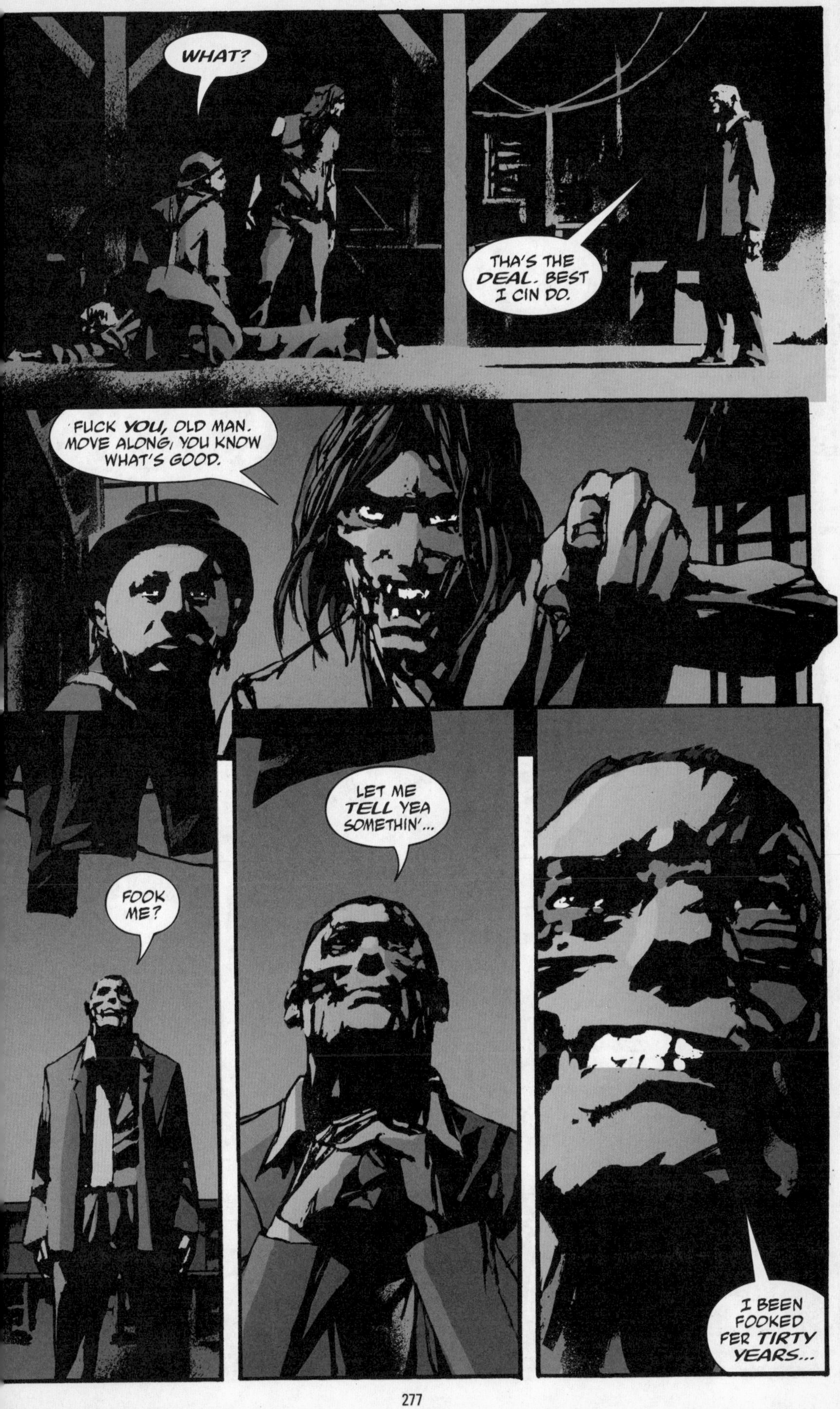
WHAT?
THA'S THE DEAL. BEST I CIN DO.
FUCK YOU, OLD MAN. MOVE ALONG, YOU KNOW WHAT'S GOOD.
FOOK ME?
LET ME TELL YEA SOMETHIN'...
I BEEN FOOKED FER TIRTY YEARS...

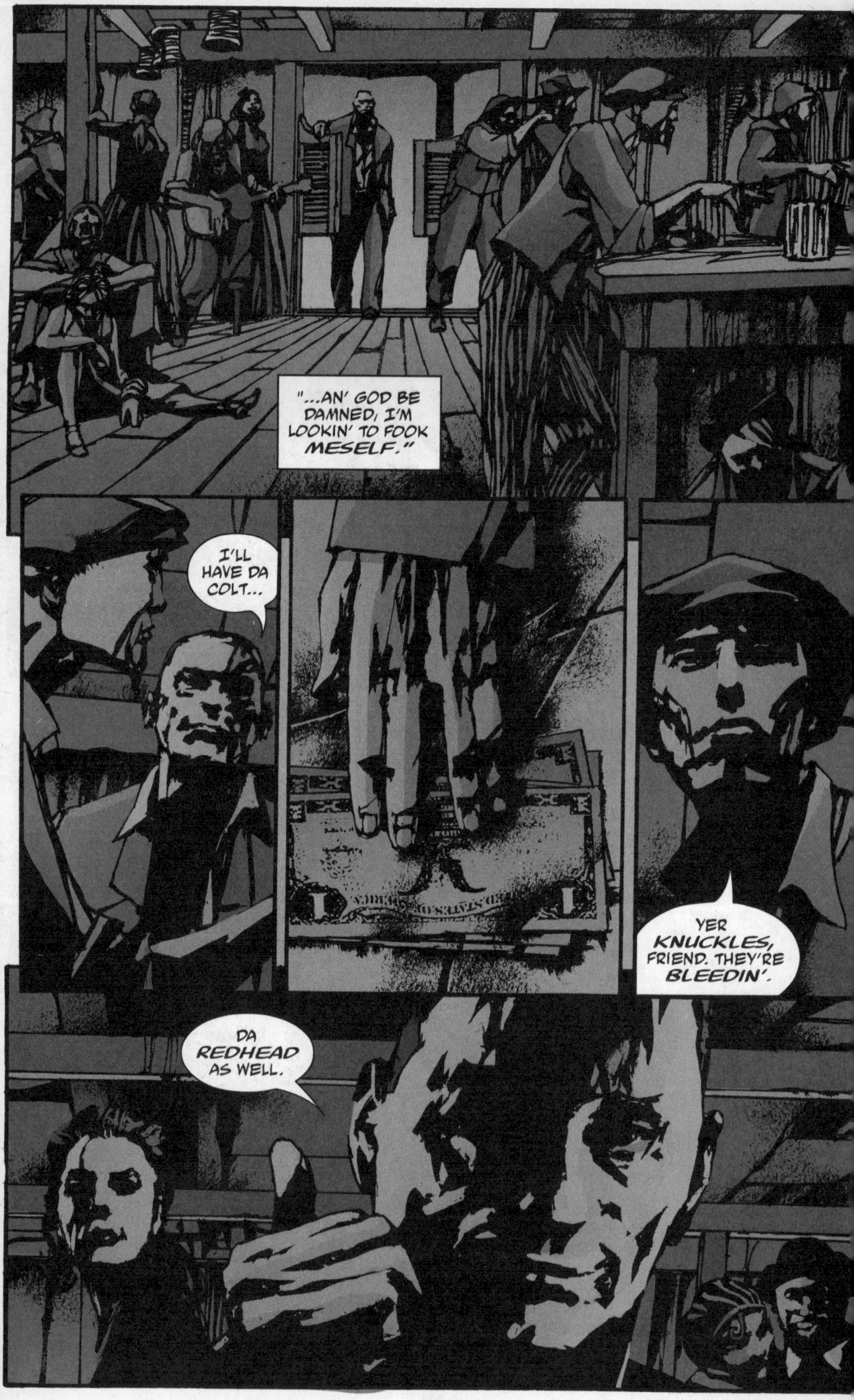
"...AN' GOD BE DAMNED, I'M LOOKIN' TO FOOK MESELF."
I'LL HAVE DA COLT...
YER KNUCKLES, FRIEND. THEY'RE BLEEDIN'.
DA REDHEAD AS WELL.

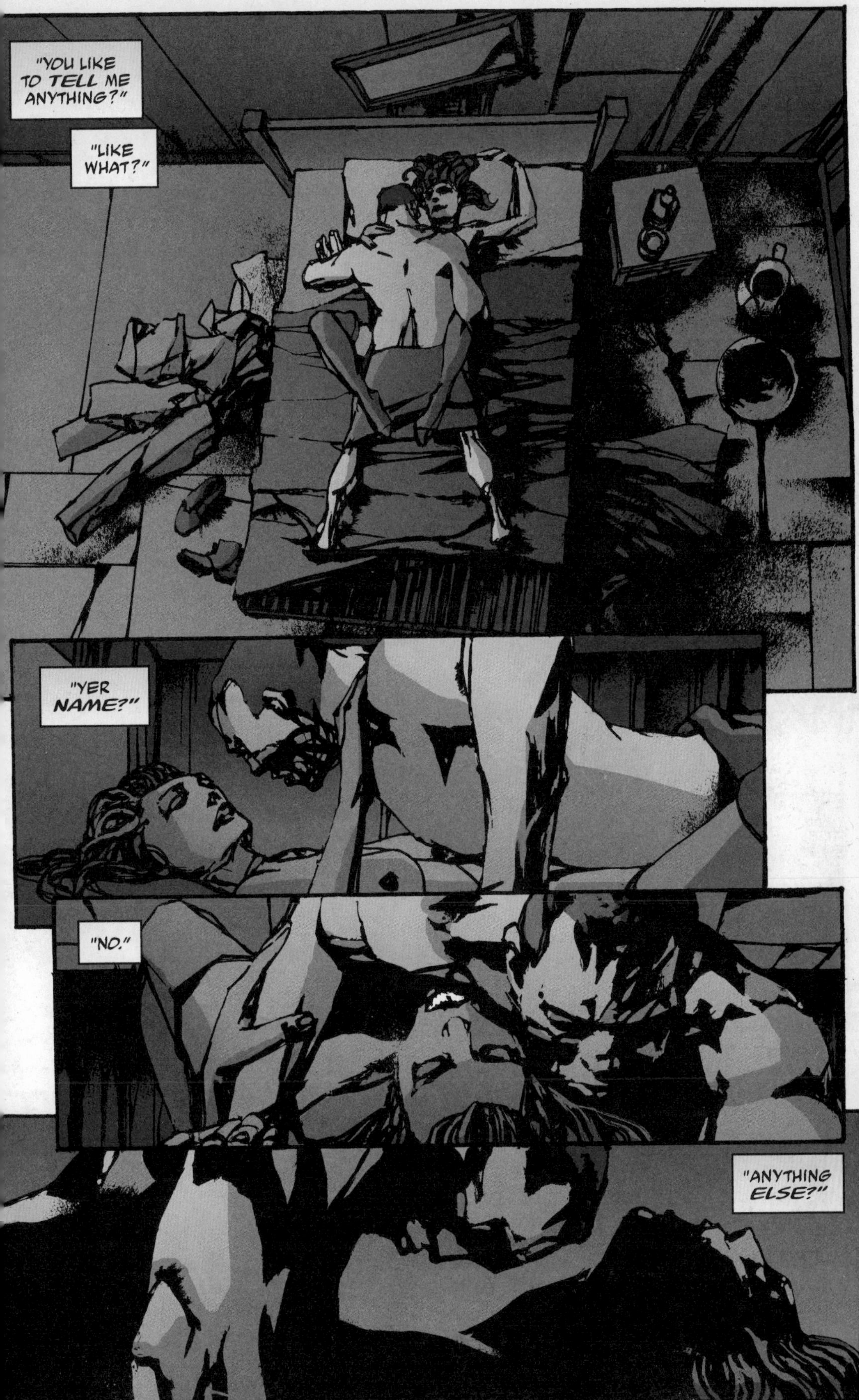
"YOU LIKE TO TELL ME ANYTHING?"
"LIKE WHAT?"
"YER NAME?"
"NO."
"ANYTHING ELSE?"

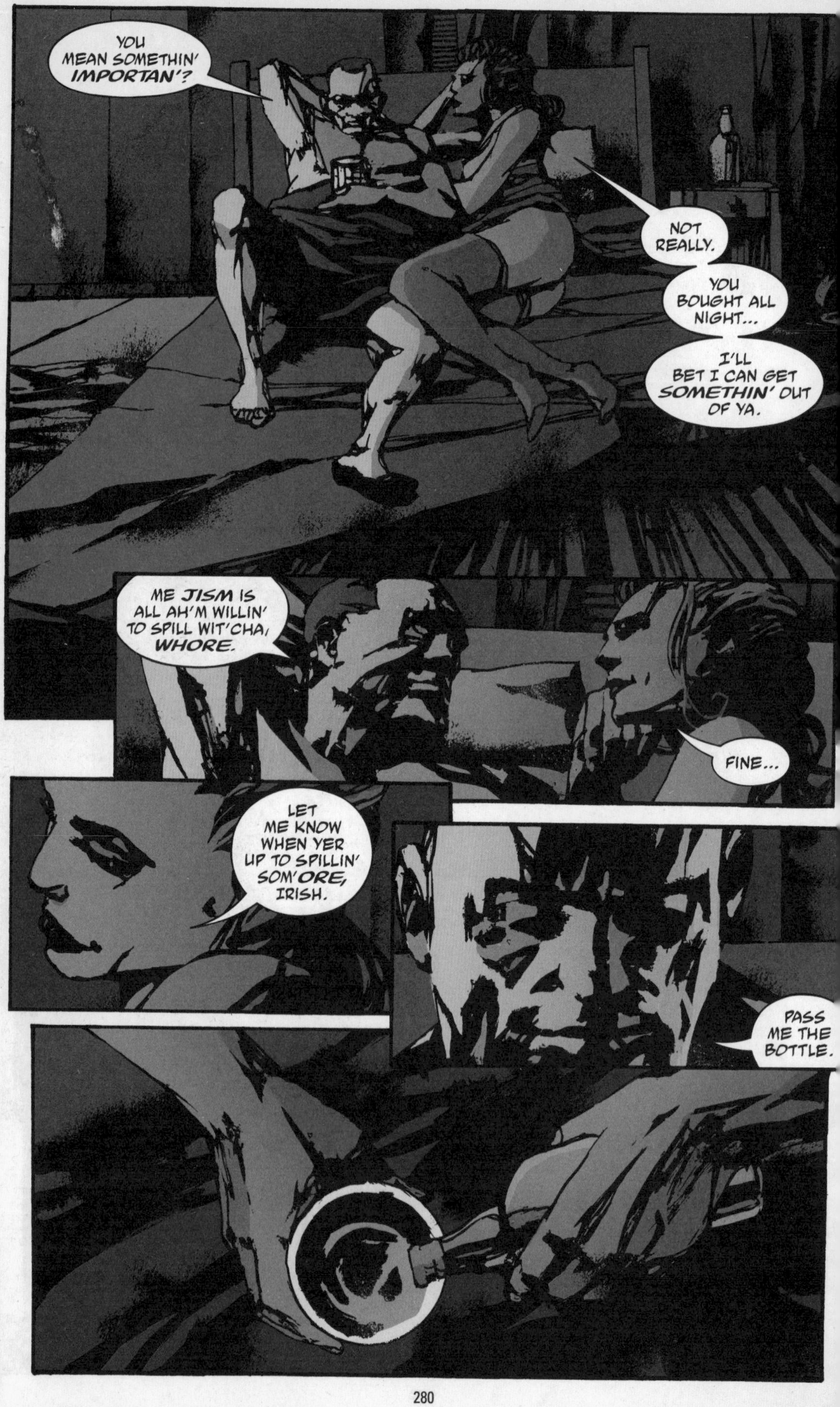
YOU MEAN SOMETHIN' IMPORTAN'?
NOT REALLY.
YOU BOUGHT ALL NIGHT...
I'LL BET I CAN GET SOMETHIN' OUT OF YA.
ME JISM IS ALL AH'M WILLIN' TO SPILL WIT'CHA, WHORE.
FINE...
LET ME KNOW WHEN YER UP TO SPILLIN' SOM'ORE, IRISH.
PASS ME THE BOTTLE.

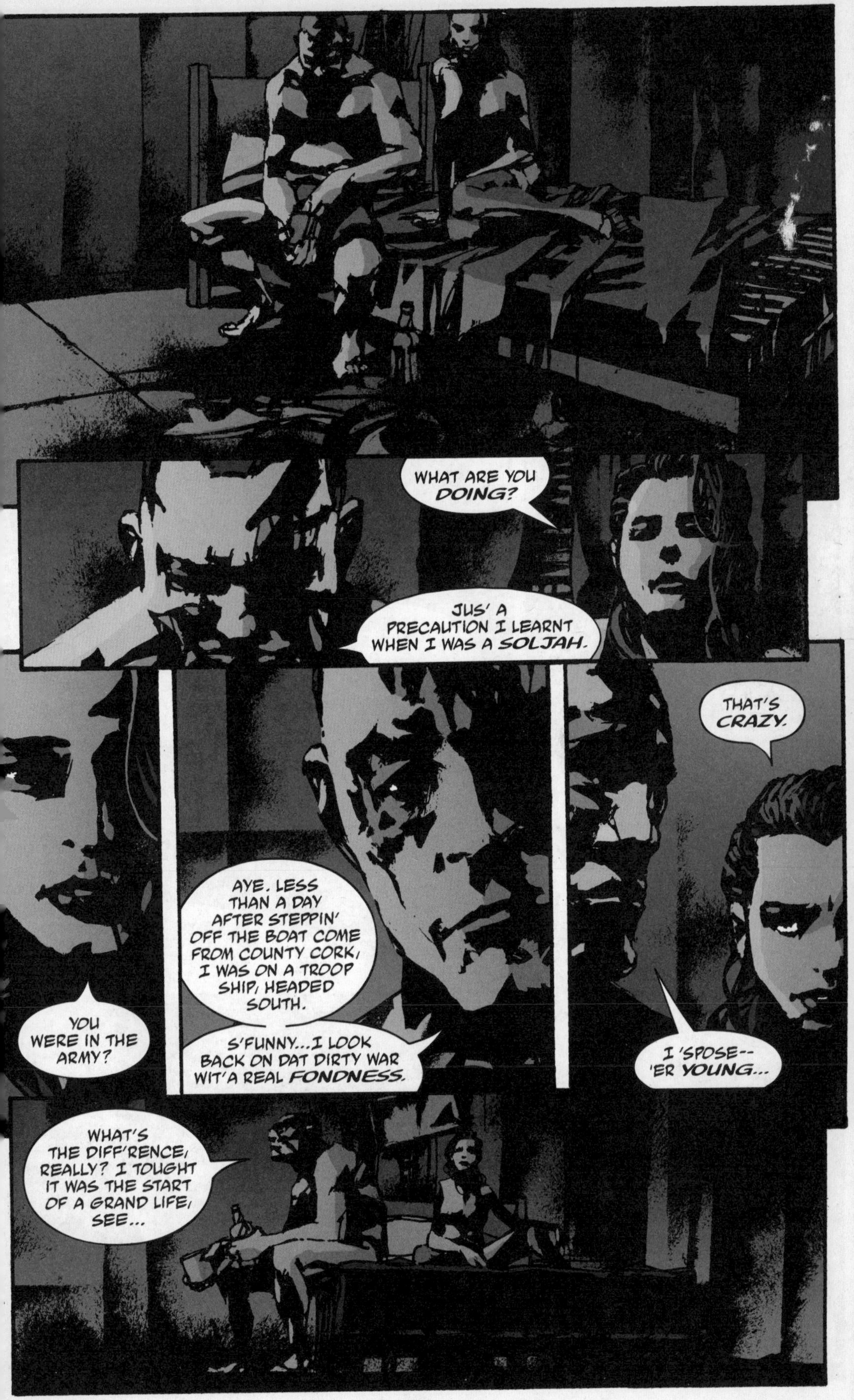
WHAT ARE YOU DOING?
JUS' A PRECAUTION I LEARNT WHEN I WAS A SOLJAH.
YOU WERE IN THE ARMY?
AYE. LESS THAN A DAY AFTER STEPPIN' OFF THE BOAT COME FROM COUNTY CORK, I WAS ON A TROOP SHIP, HEADED SOUTH.
S'FUNNY...I LOOK BACK ON DAT DIRTY WAR WIT'A REAL FONDNESS.
THAT'S CRAZY.
I 'SPOSE-- 'ER YOUNG...
WHAT'S THE DIFF'RENCE, REALLY? I TOUGHT IT WAS THE START OF A GRAND LIFE, SEE...

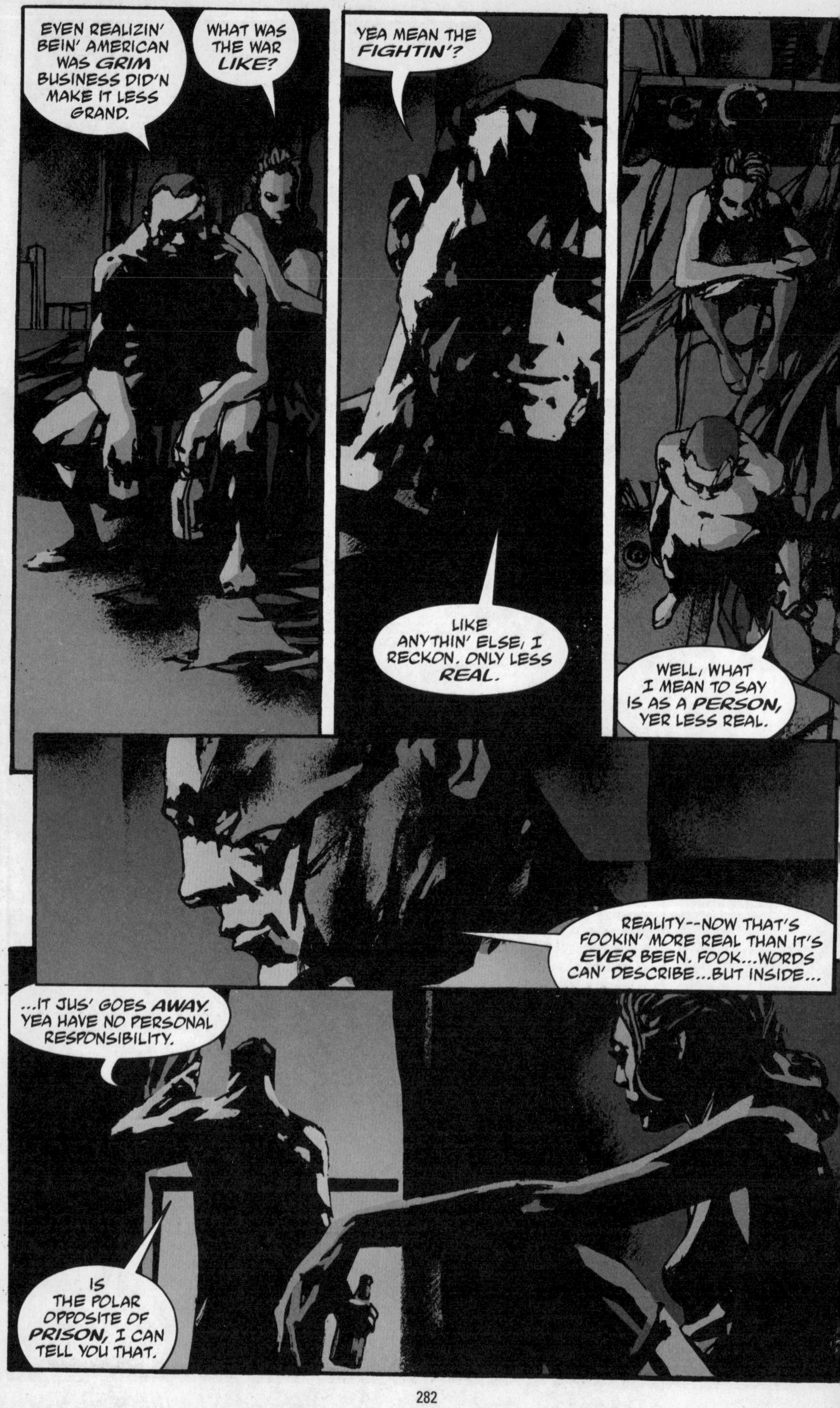
EVEN REALIZIN' BEIN' AMERICAN WAS GRIM BUSINESS DID'N MAKE IT LESS GRAND.
WHAT WAS THE WAR LIKE?
YEA MEAN THE FIGHTIN'?
LIKE ANYTHIN' ELSE, I RECKON. ONLY LESS REAL.
WELL, WHAT I MEAN TO SAY IS AS A PERSON, YER LESS REAL.
REALITY--NOW THAT'S FOOKIN' MORE REAL THAN IT'S EVER BEEN. FOOK...WORDS CAN' DESCRIBE...BUT INSIDE...
...IT JUS' GOES AWAY. YEA HAVE NO PERSONAL RESPONSIBILITY.
IS THE POLAR OPPOSITE OF PRISON, I CAN TELL YOU THAT.